Online Marketing – a customer-led approach

onlinemarketing

a customer-led approach

Richard Gay

Alan Charlesworth

Rita Esen

OXFORD
UNIVERSITY PRESS

OXFORD

UNIVERSITY PRESS

Great Clarendon Street, Oxford OX2 6DP

Oxford University Press is a department of the University of Oxford.
It furthers the University's objective of excellence in research, scholarship,
and education by publishing worldwide in

Oxford New York

Auckland Cape Town Dar es Salaam Hong Kong Karachi
Kuala Lumpur Madrid Melbourne Mexico City Nairobi
New Delhi Shanghai Taipei Toronto

With offices in

Argentina Austria Brazil Chile Czech Republic France Greece
Guatemala Hungary Italy Japan Poland Portugal Singapore
South Korea Switzerland Thailand Turkey Ukraine Vietnam

Oxford is a registered trade mark of Oxford University Press
in the UK and in certain other countries

Published in the United States
by Oxford University Press Inc., New York

British Library Cataloguing in Publication Data
Data available

Library of Congress Cataloging in Publication Data
Data available

Typeset by Graphicraft Limited, Hong Kong
Printed in Great Britain
on acid-free paper by
Ashford Colour Press Ltd, Gosport, Hants

ISBN 978-0-19-926585-5

5 7 9 10 8 6

Dedication

For Christine, Laura, Mum and my late Dad   RCG

For my Mum, Joan   AC

For Umo, Peter, Bassey and Aniekan, for all their support   RE

This textbook is intended to provide a stimulating insight into the recent developments, and their origins, in online marketing practice for final year undergraduate and postgraduate students studying marketing, business and IT-related programmes. The practical nature of the text should also provide a thought-provoking study for marketers involved in online marketing management.

Many book pages and column inches have been generated by observers following the Internet's emergence, and subsequent impact on organisations and individuals. There have been many business peaks and troughs of wild enthusiasm in the early Internet days followed by cynicism and scepticism after the 2000 dot.com crash resulting in a greater sense of realism and understanding currently in the mid-2000s. The text considers the progressive changes in online practice that have occurred during its short and turbulent history. In line with this, we deliver an enthusiastic but realistic treatise outlining the Internet's potential and its drawbacks.

The book's philosophy explores the connection between humans and technology and how beneficial relationships can prosper utilising the Internet and other media. Marketing is about satisfying customers but a changing emphasis from a transactional to a relational approach has emerged and been facilitated by database technologies. However, society has experienced an unprecedented period of technological advancement with the Internet and other digital media leading the developments and applications. This provides amazing creative potential and challenges for marketers to understand and apply the new interactive medium. Of course, the challenges have faced established firms as well as 'Internet only' players like eBay and Amazon whose brands seem to have been with us for decades. The danger for marketers and students can be a preoccupation with new technology for its own sake rather than constructing beneficial applications for organisation and stakeholder value. So the underlying focus of this book – the exploration of customer-oriented Internet applications – gives it an edge of originality compared to the more technically based texts.

The text is written in a readable and accessible style that provides subject clarity. Complex technical elements are kept to a minimum but still provide the marketer with the necessary understanding to converse with IT and Internet specialists. The text blends relevant and contemporary academic research, practitioner observations, and leading exemplars from Internet practice with web links. The text is also innovative in its content with three specific elements. First, the introduction of a 4 P's Internet Communications Model provides an analytical tool for planning online promotional activity. Second, throughout the text essential legal advice is offered to marketers via legal eagle boxes concluding with a specific legal chapter. Legal issues are often an oversight for marketers but they must not be ignored. Finally, the text also offers a diverse range of main and mini case study material to enrich the reader's learning and understanding. The authors have endeavoured to include less well known cases, where appropriate, to enhance the text and provide up-to-date and suitable illustrations.

Chapters 1, 2 and 3 provide an overview of Internet history, new marketing considerations and the strategic online planning process. Chapters 4 and 5 provide essential knowledge and skills relating to online marketing research and buyer behaviour. Chapter 6 covers search engine marketing and is the most technical in nature. We have devoted an entire chapter to the subject due to its critical role in online promotional success. Few online texts give 'search' such detailed coverage. Chapters 7 and 8 cover the role of online relationship marketing and how it can be supported by customer friendly web site design. Chapters 9, 10, 11 and 12 cover the elements of the marketing mix and how they are affected by, and applied to, the online medium. A chapter covering online legal issues concludes the text.

We hope that you get knowledge, skills and enjoyment from the book, and we genuinely welcome any feedback on any aspect of the text.

Richard Gay   r.gay@northumbria.ac.uk
Alan Charlesworth   alan.charlesworth@sunderland.ac.uk
Rita Esen   rita.esen@cyberlaw.uk.net

ACKNOWLEDGEMENTS

We wish to thank all of the book reviewers for their helpful and constructive comments on the chapters. Their suggestions were very well received and provided much food for thought. In addition, our thanks also go to our numerous 'sounding boards' in the North East of England for our ideas, they are too numerous to name them all here but colleagues from Newcastle Business School merit a special mention. First, thanks to Dr Dave Wesson for his editing and advisory skills. Second, thanks to David Bennett for his guidance in the area of logistics and supply chain management. Special thanks also go to Mike Rogers of Optimize Search Engine Marketing for his valuable contribution in Chapter 6.

Our thanks also go to the team at Oxford University Press, especially Sacha Cook for her direction and immense patience throughout, and Lindsey Davis for her efficient administrative skills.

We are grateful to the following organisations for their help in developing the book content and providing permission to reproduce copyright materials.

Guy Clack and Sudhir Joshi from Sage (UK) Limited for Figs 1.5 and 1.6. Tara Richardson and Snow Patrol for Fig 1.7 (http://www.snowpatrol.com). Sheila Allen, Press Liaison Officer for the Economic Intelligence Unit (EIU) for the 2006 E-Readiness report. Peter Dabrowa of Funky for the case material in Chapter 1 (http://www.funky.co.uk).

Dave Lomax of Bagga Menswear, Actinic Software and Jane Lee of Dexterity PR for material for the Bagga case study in Mini case 2.1. Julie Johnson of the First Consulting Group in the United States for permission to use Fig 2.3 on Stages of Internet Business development. Steven Spartinos for material and screenshot in Fig 2.4 (http://www.raceclubs.com). Jenna Jensen of BoysStuff.co.uk for the material in Mini case 2.4. Sally Osborne, Head of E-Commerce at MacDonald's Hotels and Resorts for Mini case 2.5. Gareth Deer and Patricia Ifejika at Ipsos Mori for the 2003 MORI report in Table 2.2. Damien Warburton and Jenny Catlin of Mintel for the screenshot in Fig 2.5. Mark Williams of Charles Trywhitt for the screenshot in Fig 2.7. Jo Tucker, MD at IMRG for the Internet Shopping Tips in Fig 2.9. Karl Gregory of Touch Local for the end of chapter case material.

Thanks to Friends Reunited for material in Mini case 3.2 and permission for the screenshot. Thanks also to Julie Humphreys at Crocus.co.uk for the material and screenshot in Mini case 3.4. Thanks to Darren Clark from VisualNet Centre for the screenshot in Fig 3.5. Jerry Flint of Xpower forum for the screenshot in Fig 3.6. Mike Grehan for the concept of the new Online Promotional Mix illustrated in Fig 3.7. Aoibhinn Lawlor of MultiMap for the screenshot in Fig 3.8. James Toase, Marketing Director of Direct Golf UK (DGUK) for the interview time given for the development of the end of chapter case study and screenshot.

Many thanks to David Mort of IRN Research for Tables 4.1, 4.2 and 4.3. Thanks to Andrew Webb, Picture Editor at http://www.bbc.co.uk for the screenshot in Fig 4.5. Penny Hann from Free Pint Ltd for the screenshot 4.7. Jon Puleston, Director of Media Intelligence for the screenshots 4.10 and 4.11 used in *The Times* surveys. Nicola Duarte form MyOffer.co.uk for the permission to use the screenshot in Fig 4.12. Special thanks to Jonathan Wall, Marketing Director of Dabs.com, for material for the end of chapter case study. Thanks to Roy Koerner for sharing his Marketing Research knowledge. We are indebted to Jan Storey, Principal Information Specialist at Northumbria University, for her 'search tips' in Fig 4.8.

Thanks to Alison Walden, Head of Marketing at CACI Ltd for the eTypes screenshots, Figs 5.5 and 5.6.

Special thanks go in the first instance to Mike Grehan of Smart Interactive for his fascinating and original contribution to Chapter 6, with diagrams. Secondly, many thanks to Mike Rogers, founder of Optimize.co.uk, one of the UK's leading search engine marketing organisations, for his knowledge, time and excellent support, not to mention the end of chapter case study on Kodak.

Thanks to Jody Houghton at Unilever Consumer Link for the Persil screenshot in Fig 7.2. Guy Clack and Sudhir Joshi from Sage (UK) Limited for Fig 7.3, the SalesLogix sales 'dashboard'. Jim Sterne for Fig 7.8 and his excellent writings and seminars on the World Wide Web. Ken Burke for approving Table 7.2 and for his informative and entertaining US seminars. The image used in Mini case 7.1 it reproduced by permission of Netflix, Inc., Copyright © 2006 Netflix, Inc. All rights reserved. Thanks to Brad Johnson of John Wiley & Sons, New Jersey, USA for permission to use Fig 7.8.

Gerry McGovern and Jupitermedia for permission to use Mini case 8.8. Shaun Dunn of Fresh Soap Deli for the screenshot in Fig 8.14.

Thanks to Samantha Day, Press Office Manager, easyJet for the easyGroup brand values in Fig 9.5. Envisional for Mini case 9.3 and Table 9.1. Mark Kingdon and Jupitermedia for the end of chapter case study.

Shaun Dunn of Fresh Deli Soap for screenshot 10.1. easyJet.com for the screenshot in Mini case 10.2. Haburi.com for the use of screenshot 10.3. Singlemaltwhiskies.com for the screen shot 10.4. PIPEX Communications for the use of e-mail image 10.6. ASOS.com for the screenshot 10.7. Thanks to Craig Solomon of CD-WOW for the e-mail image 10.8. Clare Waters of Albion Chemicals for her time kindly given to discuss online auctions, Mini case 10.6.

Jane Lee of Dexterity PR for her help and advice regarding online PR and her PR Tips, Fig 11.9. Thanks to News International for the screenshot in Fig 11.11. Thanks to Emma Morris of Cottages4You for the screenshot 11.12.

PetPlanet.co.uk for the screenshot, 12.4. Tiscali.co.uk for the screenshot 12.5. Comet.co.uk for the screenshot 12.7.

David Bennett for the kind offer of his Network Economy model for his unpublished Ph.D. Brian Tinham of Findlay Publications for the end of chapter case study. Ade Dougherty for his contribution to Chapter 13. TrustAssured.com for the screenshot 13.7.

CONTENTS

4 Online Marketing Research 121

5 Online Buyer Behaviour 163

12 Online Distribution and Procurement   441

13 Online Marketing Legal Issues   483

WALK THROUGH PREFACE

Learning Objectives provide the focus for the student's learning and the knowledge they should acquire by the end of the chapter.

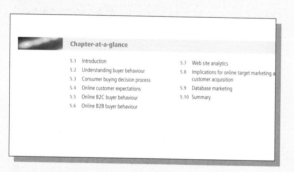

Chapter at a glance introduces the main topic areas and specific themes to be covered within each chapter.

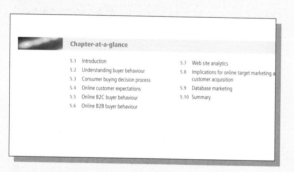

Introduction provides an overview to the chapter regarding the key issues to be explored. Each chapter subject will be set in the context of the changing marketing environment.

Bandyo-padhay, N (2002) *E-commerce, Concepts, Context and Consequences*, McGraw Hill, Maidenhead, Berkshire

Baye, MR, Gatti, R, Kattuman, P & Morgan, J (2002) *Online Pricing and The Euro Changeover: Cross Country Comparisons*, Research Papers in Management Studies, University of Cambridge, Judge Institute of Management, WP 17/2002

Bowen, D (2002) It's too early for e-business to drop its 'e', *Financial Times*, Viewpoint

Brennan, R, Baines, P & Garneau, P (2003) *Contemporary Strategic Marketing*, Palgrave Macmillan, Basingstoke Hampshire, 154

Chaston, I (2001) *E-marketing Strategy*, McGraw Hill, Maidenhead, England, 11

Experian (2001) *Enabling E-business: White paper, Experian a senior white paper, January 2001*

Mini cases provide a range of stimulating business and organisational examples that illustrate and reinforce the content under consideration. Provisions of these elements enhance the reader's learning and understanding of online marketing across a diverse range of industry sectors.

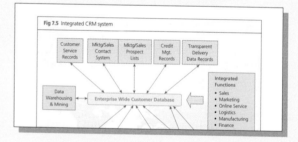

Figures and Diagrams are used to help students understand and absorb the key concepts.

Legal Eagle boxes aim to make the reader aware of relevant legislation that impact upon online marketing activities. This is particularly important to establish and underpin consumer trust. The significance of legal issues for marketers is emphasised with the inclusion of a final chapter devoted solely to legal issues.

Key terms highlighted are highlighted throughout the text and explained in the e-glossary.

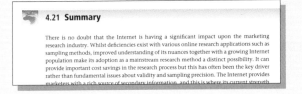

Typically, the web site owner will charge for advertising on their site usually in the form of **banner advertising**, **interstitials** (pop-ups) and **superstitials** (activated by a user-action), or permanent buttons shown on every page. The revenue generated will naturally depend upon the marketplace and the audience. Afuah and Tucci (2003) suggest two routes to online success. First, the volume-based approach where the larger the audience, the more advertisers will be willing to pay higher rates. This mimics TV advertising with higher costs for prime time slots. For example, rates are high for the Yahoo! **portal** due to the large volume of potential customers visiting. The second model derives revenue from the more precisely targeted affluent audience where the advertiser is willing to pay premium rates to reach more responsive prospects. For example, Motley Fool (www.fool.co.uk) has a highly motivated group of investment savvy visitors to its UK site and thus attracts advertising from many leading

Summary is provided to draw together the main themes and concepts within the chapter. The summary presents an opportunity for the reader to reflect and evaluate key elements.

4.21 Summary

There is no doubt that the Internet is having a significant impact upon the marketing research industry. Whilst deficiencies exist with various online research applications such as sampling methods, improved understanding of its nuances together with a growing Internet population make its adoption as a mainstream research method a distinct possibility. It can provide important cost savings in the research process but this has often been the key driver rather than fundamental issues about validity and sampling precision. The Internet provides marketers with a rich source of secondary information, and this is where its current strength

End of chapter cases offer detailed online marketing scenarios. The cases are from a variety of industry sectors and range from established brands such as Kodak to Internet players such as Dabs, BoysStuff and Funky.com. Each is designed to underpin and consolidate the reader's understanding of the chapter subject and broaden their marketing knowledge. This will be tested by case study questions.

END OF CHAPTER CASE STUDY It's Funky online for students!

During the final year at University, and after spending the summer working with one of the UK's largest ISPs, three young men, Peter Dabrowa, Gordon McNevin and Graham Bontoft put their heads together with the aim of taking advantage of what the new found Internet had to offer and in turn creating an online destination for their fellow students.

The vision

The vision was to establish a site that informed potential students of what University life was all about, and somewhere for current students to share their experiences and interact with each other, ultimately creating a community online that served the needs of the student population in the UK. A fun,

you can charge as the amount of exposure client. Once a site establishes a large a 100,000 visitors and 1 million page views pe cpm (cost per thousand) based advert at how many advertisements are being s response rates) which guarantees revenu as traffic figures stay level or increase. A standing of how Google works and its engine marketing and reciprocal links was top rankings and the critical mass to make S ive proposition for online adverti

Once Studentmax.com reached the figu visitors it was able to approach a numbe

Discussion questions provide a platform for further exploration of the chapter topic and can form the basis of library or seminar exercises.

DISCUSSION QUESTIONS

1. How can a web site be utilised to build loyalty and effective relationships?
2. Why is 'trust' so important in this process?
3. Is the concept of 'relationship marketing' a passing fad or a fundamental philosophy for business success in the digital world?
4. Have legal pressures driven permission marketing, or does it make good business sense?

References direct the reader to the academic and practitioner sources used within the text.

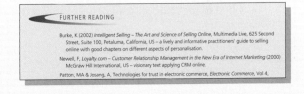

REFERENCES

Adamy, J (2000) E-Tailer price tailoring maybe wave of the future, *Chicago Tribune*, 25 September, section 4, 4

Affuah, A & Tucci, CL (2003) *Internet – Business Models and Strategies*, McGraw Hill, New York, USA, 60–62.

Ancarani & Shankar (2002) *Price Levels and Price Dispersion on the Internet: A Comparison of Pure Play Internet, Bricks and Mortar, and Bricks and Clicks Retailers*, June 2002,

Further Reading lists point the reader towards a range of interesting texts and articles.

FURTHER READING

Burke, K (2002) *Intelligent Selling – The Art and Science of Selling Online*, Multimedia Live, 625 Second Street, Suite 100, Petaluma, California, US – a lively and informative practitioners' guide to selling online with good chapters on different aspects of personalisation.

Newell, F, *Loyalty.com – Customer Relationship Management in the New Era of Internet Marketing* (2000) McGraw Hill International, US – visionary text applying CRM online.

Patton, MA & Josang, A, Technologies for trust in electronic commerce, *Electronic Commerce*, Vol 4,

Web Links lead the reader to a combination of online resources for further study and web pages that are examples of good practice.

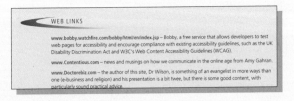

WEB LINKS

www.bobby.watchfire.com/bobby/html/en/index.jsp – Bobby, a free service that allows developers to test web pages for accessibility and encourage compliance with existing accessibility guidelines, such as the UK Disability Discrimination Act and W3C's Web Content Accessibility Guidelines (WCAG).

www.Contentious.com – news and musings on how we communicate in the online age from Amy Gahran.

www.Doctorebiz.com – the author of this site, Dr Wilson, is something of an evangelist in more ways than one (e-business and religion) and his presentation is a bit twee, but there is some good content, with particularly sound practical advice.

ONLINE RESOURCE CENTRE

online resource centre

Visit the Online Resource Centre that supports this text,
at **www.oxfordtextbooks.co.uk/orc/gay/**
to find an extensive range of teaching and learning resources, including:

For students

- Self-Marking Multiple Choice Questions
- Internet Exercises
- Annotated Weblinks
- Flashcard Glossary

For lecturers

- PowerPoint Slides
- Suggested Answers to Case and Discussion Questions
- Extra Case Material

Principles and Drivers of the New Marketing Environment

1

Learning Objectives

By the end of the chapter you will be able to:

- Understand key **Internet** developments
- Appreciate the marketing environment factors that have driven the Internet's growth
- Understand how the Internet and other **digital** media impact upon the marketing function
- Appreciate the scope and potential of the Internet
- Evaluate the relationship between the Internet and traditional marketing concepts
- Critically evaluate the Ten Cs framework

Chapter at a glance

1.1 Introduction

This chapter introduces the reader to the evolving world of **e-business** and what environmental factors have influenced its development. Various definitions relating to the digital world are introduced. The Internet's impact upon traditional marketing functions and practices is considered together with new dimensions for marketers. The chapter also considers the key benefits, and some of the drawbacks of doing business online. Numerous examples are given from a diverse range of public and private sector organisations.

Overview of the new marketscape

The telephone took four decades to reach 50 million people. The Internet has managed this within four years as digital technologies provide such efficient channels for business and consumer interactions transactions. The excitement and anticipation of what a brochure-wear site would achieve for many companies five or six years ago seems but a distant memory when we consider the transactional and multi-dimensional capabilities of most current web sites. The Internet has come a long way in a very short time as a mainstream business tool. The high profile disasters of some notable companies has at times, undermined the innovative, customer focussed, technology driven, marketing practices by organisations large and small, public and private.

> 'The Internet is a tidal wave. It will wash over nearly all industries drowning those who don't learn to swim in its waves.'
>
> Bill Gates CEO Microsoft

This is not untypical of the many quotes that emerged during the Internet frenzy of the late nineties warning organisations of their impending demise if they ignored this new interactive medium. The new industrial order created would radically change the interrelationships between buyers and sellers of products and services in ways that we could not envisage. As Bandyo-padhay (2002) observes, 'at the root of the changes in the business world is a drive towards consumer power; consumers rather than products are the focus of today's organisation'. Technology has empowered customers to take more control of their lives but it has not always led to customer-driven marketing applications. It is tempting to be evangelical about the Internet's impact but it should be tempered with the knowledge that some sectors and some businesses have remained largely unaffected by the new economy. Indeed, many consumers have resisted the online urge and organisations must be aware of any real or potential technology gap with their target market before launching new products or services.

A new entrepreneurial spirit flourished and established companies needed to reconsider their business strategies to compete with the new business models applied by new pure play operators. The Internet was creating a new corporate culture energised by the real and perceived benefits of new technology. For some marketers and academics alike, the old models and concepts such as the Marketing Mix were becoming obsolete and irrelevant for the new connected and streamlined business world, but are they redundant or capable of modification to the new order? Fig 1.1 poses some key marketing questions facing organisations operating online.

The Internet has created a new set of rules in many ways with greater transparency, cost efficiencies, more consumer power and choice, changing strategic alliances and new partnerships. Marketers have to come to terms with new technologies and new jargon. How will

---

Fig 1.1 E-marketing considerations

- How important is branding on the Internet compared to the physical world?
- What role can the Internet play in new product development?
- How easily does the Internet lend itself to the sale of non-homogeneous goods?
- What impacts have Internet technologies had on pricing levels and strategies both on and offline?
- What efficiencies have the Internet brought to the supply chain?
- Have customer delivery expectations changed?
- Has the Internet eliminated any intermediaries?
- How have the new channels affected purchase behaviour?
- How much of our promotional spend should we devote to online communications?
- What is the most important communications tool in e-marketing?
- Do traditional marketing communications methods still have a role to play in the connected world?

---

disintermediation affect an organisation? Will online auctions open up business to business (B2B) opportunities or drive prices down to uneconomic levels? Established businesses have to wrestle with the strategic headache of deciding their level of online commitment and how it compliments their traditional operation. How can they utilise the log files of customers in a more efficient, creative and legal way? Marketers must not lose sight nor understanding of the customer and what is important to him/her. Even though he/she may only appear as a customer reference number or by a tracking code from an e-coupon on the **database**, successful businesses try their utmost to stay close to the key customers by the most appropriate means, the means being acceptable to the customer. One of the most widely used definitions of marketing is offered by the Chartered Institute of Marketing with its emphasis on customer focus. It states:

> *Marketing is the management process, which identifies, anticipates and supplies customer requirements profitably.*

The thrust of this philosophy should also drive online marketing activities.

Technology can be fun and exciting for those comfortable with it. It is facilitating a new global marketplace. For many, it feeds a desire for new product innovations. It can improve standards of living by creating products and services that provide convenience and pleasure in a time-starved world. Technology is undoubtedly redesigning the marketing practices for organisations seeking to engage effectively with past, present and potential customers. The 'e' in e-marketing, e-commerce or e-business represents the applications of digital technologies across all internal and external business functions and processes. It is commonly accepted that technologists have championed the cause for substantial ICT (Information and Communications Technology) investments. The results however, have been less than satisfactory and certainly not marketing or customer oriented hence lower than expected net adoption rates resulted during the Internet's infancy. From the other side, many marketers and strategists did not have the vision or technological understanding to optimise the Internet's potential. Bowen (2002) questions organisational ability to harness the new technology:

> 'How did Cisco, Dell, Electrocomponents, General Electric manage it? Largely because people at the summit saw that the secret was in bringing technologists and non-technologists together

and making them work together and often they used the **banner** "e" as the marshalling point. The good e-business managers I have met are (or were) either technologists on the way to becoming strategists, or non-technologists with an increasing understanding of IT. On the way I stress; rarely close to achieving fluency in both.'

Combining IT and marketing competences is as desirable for modern marketing students' career development in a dynamic digital world as it is for an organisation to connect the two. Left to themselves and without an internal champion, organisations often find this difficult to achieve and turn to consultants to act as go-between amid the two functions.

New ideas were rapidly put forward at breakneck speed about how we should interact with customers and develop trust and confidence in using the new medium. Astonishing global growth forecasts were made with visions of the masses sitting at PCs conducting their daily affairs whilst the high streets and retail parks struggled in the aftermath. Businesses often constrained by their remote locations could now reach out to other parts of the domestic markets and even go global – many did, but many could not or would not. However, many consumers remain untouched by the impact of the Internet. Perhaps they have no need to use it at work or at home, or perhaps actually going out to shop remains an important social activity. It could now be accepted as just another marketing channel for consumers in an ever-increasing multi-channel marketing world. Many suggest that it will be subsumed and we will drop everything 'e'. Rather than impacting upon consumers as it matures, the Internet will have more impact upon all players in the value chain.

The Internet has impacted in the **B2B** sector in a variety of ways. For example, organisations can source new components from outside of their traditional supplier network to enhance the finished product. E-procurement has streamlined administrative processes whilst driving down costs and **e-CRM** (electronic customer relationship management) has facilitated more effective and relevant customer interactions. Not only have we witnessed more customised messages but technology has also allowed more customisation of products and services such as personal computers and holidays. This not only changes the business to consumer (B2C) relationship but also impacts upon manufacturing and supply chain partners and distributors. The end of mass media had long been forecasted in some quarters as organisations and consumers 'went direct' in significant numbers during the nineties. The modern consumer was generally more comfortable with direct communications methods such as mail and telephone. The growth of direct marketing, of course, was underpinned by new information technologies and communications. The ever-increasing power of computers for data acquisition, storage and analysis provides marketers with their lifeblood for decision-making – **information** on progressively more fragmented, niche market segments.

'To manage a business well is to manage its future: and to manage its future is to manage information.'

Alfred Sloan
General Motors 1911

This, allied to the development of new digital communications media has resulted in more effective, customised communications offers *when* good practice has been applied. However, this is another uncomfortable area where marketing meets IT with variable outcomes. For example, banner adverts were expected to be a key revenue generator but simple understanding and observation of consumer behaviour and web usage could have highlighted potential weaknesses in this advertising model initially. In the infant days of the web, visitors relied heavily on search engines to find their desired site. Their on-screen interest focussed on the search engines results and largely neglected the presence of the banner ads at the top of the screen.

1.2 E-definitions

At this point we will consider five definitions that encompass the evolving Internet driven economy:

1. e-commerce
2. e-business
3. e-marketing
4. m-commerce
5. m-marketing

E-commerce

Commerce is generally acknowledged as the interchange of merchandise on large scale between nations or individuals. Rayport and Jaworski (2001) define e-commerce as 'technology mediated exchanges between parties (individuals or organisations) as well as the electronically based intra- or interorganisational activities that facilitate such exchanges'. The emphasis in most e-commerce definitions has been on digital transactions facilitated at every stage (eg inventory, ordering and payment processing, etc) by technologies such as electronic data interchange (EDI). Standardisation of electronic data formats enables computers to speak to each other, speeds information exchanges and reduces transaction costs. Of course, not every organisation will use their site for online transactions; it may not be appropriate or part of their strategy. Some organisations may use their site to drive traffic to a physical showroom or perhaps for PR or brand building.

E-business

Turban et al (2002) suggest that the term 'e-commerce' is a rather narrow constricted definition with its emphasis on the transactional process and that it does not encompass the full range of applications and potential benefits of the Internet. Philips (2003) terms e-business as 'the application of information technologies for internal business processes as well as activities in which a company engages during commercial activity. These activities can include functional activities such as finance, marketing, human resources management and operations'. Lou Gerstner of IBM cited in Turban et al extols the potential payback from e-business saying that it is 'all about time cycle, speed, globalisation, enhanced productivity, reaching new customers and sharing knowledge across institutions for competitive advantage'. To exploit such opportunities, requires the redesign of the corporate environment and the total integration of information and communications technologies across the business functions.

E-marketing

E-marketing is described by the Institute of Direct Marketing as 'the use of Internet and related digital information and communications technologies to achieve marketing objectives'.

Mohammed et al (2001) define Internet marketing as 'the process of building and maintaining customer relationships through online activities to facilitate the exchange of ideas, products and services that satisfy the goals of both parties'. Strauss et al (2003) suggest that e-marketing covers a wide range of IT related applications with three main aims:

- transforming marketing strategies to create more customer value through more effective segmentation, targeting, differentiation and positioning strategies;
- more efficiently planning and executing the conception, distribution, promotion and pricing of goods, services and ideas;
- creating exchanges that satisfy individual consumer and organisational customers' objectives.

This appears to offer nothing startling at first glance but acknowledges that the Internet has been responsible for many organisations' refocussing their marketing strategies. It also recognises that one of the benefits of e-marketing is the increased efficiency that it can create for both parties in the exchange process. The applicability of such definitions should be taken in context as it will depend to what extent the business relies on online, offline or a multi-channel approach. Smith and Chaffey (2002) emphasise the importance of the database in e-marketing and the utilisation of a wide variety of 'e-tools' to generate a dynamic dialogue, which goes beyond a purely transactional process. Prominence is given to the role of technology in relationship building, customer retention, customisation and loyalty by means of effective two-way communications. The Internet enables more customer input to influence marketing decisions. The ideal outcomes are customer satisfaction, added value and improved company revenues. Philip Kotler (cited in Web Metrics paper, 'Winning on the Web' (2002)) sums up the changing shift in power and observes, 'Intelligent management of information and the use of technology-supported customer interactions are among the e-marketing rules for the new economy'. Marketers need to make creative and innovative use of information employing both technology and intuition to tease out trends and opportunities. However, we must not overlook the important role that the Internet can play in communicating with our different 'publics' such as employees and shareholders. As competition intensifies across sectors, it becomes more important for employees to be well informed of corporate and marketing objectives and intranets have a key role to play in effective internal marketing.

Furthermore, the Internet does have a significant non-selling function for both public sector and not-for-profit organisations especially in terms of information exchange, communications and online customer service.

M-commerce

M-commerce can be defined as 'the buying and selling of goods and services through wireless handheld devices such as mobile phones and personal digital assistants'. M-Commerce enables users to access the Internet without needing to find a place to plug in providing anytime, anywhere communications. As Philips (2003: 11) observes, 'the convergence of the two fastest growing communications technologies of all time – mobile phones and the Internet – will, they say, make possible all kinds of new services and create a vast new market'. The emerging technology underpinning m-commerce based on **Wireless Application Protocol** and **third generation (3G) bandwidth** technology has led many to believe that m-commerce with its flexibility does have greater potential than the Internet connected PC. So-called smart phones provide faster, personal and secure handheld communications content and payment abilities for a progressively mobile workforce. With the fat pipe or **broadband** slowly becoming more accessible in terms of connectivity and cost, the thirst for instant information by some is becoming a reality for individuals and a marketing challenge for organisations. Wireless Internet Access or Wi-fi enables users of handheld devices and laptops to access the Internet on the move without the need for any physical links or attachments via 'hotspots' without the need for any traditional dial up connections. Graeme Lowdon (2003) of Nomad Digital suggests that wi-fi has an advantage over many previously released technologies: 'Whereas in the past, standards have been hyped and touted, hoping that people will adopt them, this technology has occurred the other way around – it's become a de facto standard. A good comparison is something like text messaging. That was never pre-hyped, it was almost as a by-product on mobile phones. Then an awful lot of people used it and it became a mainstream technology. Wi-fi falls into this category'.

M-marketing (or mobile marketing)

Strauss et al (2003) paint an interesting scenario occurring in the next phase of e-business with a driver being notified by text message on the interstate that his 15,000-mile car service is due. The technology recognises that he is approaching the city and suggests that he may wish to exit and visit the dealership where a driver will be ready to take him on to his office. His car will be returned to him at his office. The customer just has to click and confirm and the chauffeur and service technicians will be ready and waiting. This vision of the connected customer-company relationship does not seem too far away. A Gartner research report in November 2005 claimed a 22% increase in worldwide mobile phone sales in the third quarter for that year with a further 10–15% increase expected for 2006.

Just like the distinctions made between e-commerce and e-marketing, we should recognise that similar differences apply in the mobile domain with the capability of using mobile devices for marketing functions other than buying and selling. For example, financial institutions already provide useful SMS (short messaging service) customer alerts on overdraft facilities. Other customer services can be permanently accessible. Alternatively, mobile devices could be used for instant marketing research or location based sales promotions. The mobile phone has been transformed into a multi-functional device incorporating phone, text, video and **MP3** capability as standard on new phones and provides more marketing opportunities.

1.3 The Internet and its infant development

Afuah and Tucci (2003) describe the Internet as 'technology with many properties that have the potential to transform the competitive landscape in many industries while at the same time creating whole new industries'. The growth and adoption has been unparalleled. As Harris and Dennis (2002) note, 'in 1969, the Internet was just a demonstration project linking up four university campuses in the USA, but it now boasts in excess of 300 million users across the world'. The Internet timeline (see Fig 1.2 below) charts some of the significant milestones in the Internet's development so far from both a technical and commercial perspective.

The Internet is an interactive global communications medium that changed the playing field, and language, for marketers everywhere. It has the potential to impact and influence

Fig 1.2 A timeline of Internet developments

1958	United States launched Arpanet project to lead science and military technological developments
1961	MIT research paper on Packet Switching Theory
1961–69	Ongoing research into networks and intercomputer communications
1969	Arpanet project into networks is commissioned by US Defense Dept and goes live
	US universities connect up network facilities for the first time
1973	Development of protocols to enable multi-network Internet opportunities
	First international Arpanet connections made
1976	HM Queen Elizabeth II sends an e-mail
1980	Tim Benners Lee develops rules for the World Wide Web, credited with becoming the Web Father.
	Alan Emtage develops the first search tool known as 'ARCHIE'.
1982	Standard network protocols are established: Transmission Control Protocol (TCP) and Internet Protocol (IP) commonly referred to as TCP/IP
1984	Joint Academic Network (JANET) is established linking higher education institutions
	Domain Name System (DNS) is introduced
1985	A company named Symbolics becomes the first registered dot.com business
1987	National Science Foundation (US) is the catalyst for the surge in funded work into the Internet
	Number of Internet hosts increases significantly during this period
1988–90	28 countries sign up to hook up to NSFNET reinforcing international Internet potential
1990	Senator Al Gore coins the phrase '**information superhighway**'
1991	Web Father, Tim Benners Lee with scientists from CERN release World Wide Web (www)
1992	America Online is launched and raises $23m in floatation
	The term 'surfing the net' is introduced
	World Bank goes online
1993	Awareness of the Internet increases due to attention of mainstream media
	First Internet publication, *Wired*, goes on the stands
	Mosaic introduce the first web browser with graphical interface and is the forerunner of Netscape Navigator. Its release generates Internet frenzy
	Growth in Internet service traffic measured at 341,634%
	First online shopping malls and virtual banks emerge but unfortunately so does evidence of SPAM
1995	Amazon is launched by Jeff Bezos
	Trial **dial up** systems such as AOL and CompuServe begin
	Charging is introduced for domain names
	Search technology companies such as Alta Vista, Infoseek, Excite and Metacrawler rapidly appear
1996	Yahoo! launched on stock exchange, shares up nearly 300% on first day
1997	MP3.com is founded
1998	XML is released to enable compatibility between different computer systems

Fig 1.2 (Continued)

1999	FAST Search is launched with the ability to index 200 million web pages
2000	AOL and Time Warner announce they are merging
	Monetisation or Pay-per-Click campaigns are introduced for top ten search rankings
2001	BBC rolls out 'Interactive Wimbledon' as its first incursion in interactive TV (iTV)
2002	UK online monthly consumer shopping breaks through the £1 billion barrier
	BT announces price reductions on broadband packages in an effort to boost low sign up figures
2003	Sweden overtakes the US and leads the world in e-readiness
	eBay topples Amazon as the most visited UK site
2004	CD-WOW loses court case and rights to source cheaper CDs outside EU and undermines the global concept of the Internet
2005	Iceland leads the world with broadband penetration, 26.7 inhabitants per 100 have broadband compared with 15.9 per 100 in the UK
2006	Internet usage tops 1,022,863,307 worldwide

Sources:
www.oecd.org/sti/ict/broadband
www.zakon.org/robert/internet/timeline
www.davesite.com/webstation/net-history.shtml
www.computerhistory.org/exhibits/internet_history/internet_history_90s.shtml

and organisation's competitive strategic options suggested by Michael Porter. Chaffey (2000) argued that the Internet is a critical element supporting business and marketing strategies but that it should be treated as a separate plan. Three years on and it was being recognised as a mainstream tool to be integrated alongside other and new and traditional marketing methods.

Some commentators view the Internet as 'just another channel' but consider the list of uses below (in Fig 1.3) and perhaps it offers much more. The list is not exhaustive. How many other Internet uses or application can you think of?

 ## 1.4 Internet benefits

Many practitioners and academics debate whether the Internet is just another channel or communications tool or whether it has actually transformed marketing concepts and practices forever. This will depend upon the sector that you are in, your strategic vision and application of new technologies and so on. What is undeniable is the benefits that the Internet has brought to marketers. Some have been well documented and some are evolving but it is worth considering some of the benefits and how they may apply to organisations that we are familiar with:

- The Internet can increase an organisation's geographic coverage beyond its traditional heartland.
- New customers can be reached.

Fig 1.3 Examples of Internet applications

- New distribution channels
- Providing 'real-time' business solutions – eg 'e-credit'
- Entertainment/news eg *Daily Sport* direct to your desktop (if you want it?)
- Internet trading – stocks and shares eg Charles Schwab, online bookmakers
- Electioneering eg last General Election
- Local/National democracy eg USA and voting on planning issues, shareholder voting
- E-procurement – buying groups eg Covisint in the automotive sector in US
- Strategy eg John Lewis purchasing buy.com to accelerate online effort
- Reaching new customers outside of usual market eg Teddington Cheese
- **Affiliate Marketing** – to develop 'partnerships' and receive commission
- Downloading information eg e-books
- Research, both secondary and primary (various uses)
- Recruitment eg Stepstone
- Price comparisons
- Product comparisons
- New product development eg car manufacturers and concept testing
- E-learning supporting education
- Advice/signposting, both public and private sector
- Information links
- Helpdesks eg 'Patientline'
- Special Interest Community sites
- Developing brand presence
- E-mail marketing
- Games interaction
- Music downloads
- Auction sites eg eBay and QXL
- Home shopping (24:7:365)
- Competitions

- The Internet provides a low cost, effective way of transacting with customers compared to traditional selling costs.
- A site can be open for business all day everyday providing customer convenience.
- The Internet is a fast and flexible communications tool.
- Communications can be tailored to customer needs based on account histories and other data.
- It is an interactive marketing tool enabling effective two-way dialogues between customer and organisation to help achieve acquisition and retention objectives.
- The Internet can be used as a timely sales promotion tool with the use of targeted e-coupons and specialist privileges.

- The Internet provides vital measurement of events and accountability providing marketers with ammunition to secure budget increases.
- The Internet's global reach also provides opportunities to source new suppliers and distributors to maintain competitive advantage.
- Web only models can pass cost of sale savings onto customers and offer very competitive pricing.
- The Internet provides marketers with a rich source of marketing data for decision-making purposes.
- **Online** marketing research supported with appropriate software provides real time data analysis to streamline the research process.
- The Internet can provide a test bed for products or campaigns.
- Online shoppers are growing in confidence.

1.5 Internet problems – past and present

There are also many problems associated with the Internet that marketers must understand and respond to. These are outlined below:

- customer resistance to change, especially older and disadvantaged people;
- public concerns over privacy issues, such as SPAM and chat-rooms;
- lingering security doubts over fraud and **phishing** (hackers) and **network** security and stability (worms);
- lack of trust with unknown virtual traders;
- the Internet's sensory boundaries limiting of senses like taste and touch which influence buyer decisions;
- limited web access for low-income groups and those in rural areas;
- continued high costs of broadband connections deterring high speed take up;
- social impact of the Internet such as debts generated from online gambling;
- poor levels of online customer service and fulfilment;
- technology gap between users and providers;
- complexities of cross-border trading;
- failure to provide an exciting and reliable online shopping experience.

The marketing mix

Borden's marketing mix (1964) and McCarthy's 4P's (1960) have provided generations of marketers with a framework for delivering customer value based around Product, Price, Place and Promotion. As many economies have moved from product to service based we have added another 3P's namely People, Physical and Process. For fuller discussion on these issues readers are directed to broad based marketing texts such as Kotler, Brassington & Petitt and Jobber.

Some people have sought to discredit mature models like the Marketing Mix believing they are inappropriate and outdated. Howver, they still provide a useful structure for shaping the marketing offer. We still sell products; we still set prices, distribute and promote goods. Perhaps there is something reassuring about a well-used model in a rapidly changing world and the components of the mix will be considered more fully in subsequent chapters.

1.6 Ten Cs for Internet marketers

The new tools provided by digital media, changing consumer lifestyles and the integration of technology and multi-channels increases the complexity of the business arena. We are encouraged to 'think outside of the box', to be more creative, entrepreneurial and visionary but not innovative for the sake of it. Rather than abandon the old marketers' kit bag, we can add some other tools to it to enhance market analysis and decision-making. The Ten Cs (Fig 1.4) provide a useful framework for marketers assessing for the modern digital market-scape from both an internal and external perspective.

Customer

The customer should be the central focus for any marketing driven organisation and marketing activities must be designed to achieve high levels of customer satisfaction. From satisfaction comes loyalty and from loyalty comes improved profitability through up selling, cross selling referrals and acquisitions. The customer is king but the Internet makes the customer even more powerful and demanding with tools like search engines, price comparison

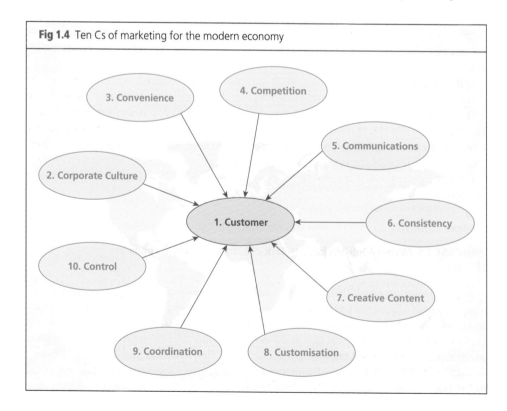

Fig 1.4 Ten Cs of marketing for the modern economy

3. Convenience

4. Competition

5. Communications

2. Corporate Culture

1. Customer

6. Consistency

10. Control

7. Creative Content

9. Coordination

8. Customisation

sites, an expectation of real time and multi-channel offerings fed by **user**-friendly technology. We must also remember that the customer is part of a wider online 'community'. Customer behaviour is more complex than ever with greater disintegration of purchasing patterns. We have a new young generation of photo-text messagers; a generation of thirty somethings using the web more at work than at home and a generation of early retirees who use the web for information and purchase by telephone. The web coupled with emerging software technologies enables more precise segmentation, targeting and analysis. This facilitates the implementation of personalised offerings but due to the power shift, it should be permission based to build trust and loyalty rather than indulge in what is referred to as interruption marketing, such as the dreaded pop-ups. The interactive nature of the Internet allows faster customer feedback, an updating of content and other web site features. However, writers like Wind et al (2002) have observed 'a new hybrid consumer' emerging who wants to 'call, click and visit' organisations, and basically wants the best of the physical and virtual world.

Web sites should be designed with the needs of different customers form the **homepage**, eg Dell, with customisation opportunities bringing tailored value to the individual or organisation. For a fuller discussion of online buyer behaviour, see chapter 5.

Corporate culture

As with any business seeking commercial success, a shared vision and commitment are priorities. An Internet based operation is no different though it has other issues to consider such as risk, appropriate IT architecture, front and back office systems and partnerships as it moves to this new channel. Initially, a visionary individual who recognises the potential of the Internet and promotes the benefits at senior level may champion the Internet cause. Alternatively, the organisation may already have an entrepreneurial culture and positive attitude towards the adoption of new technology networks such as the use of electronic data interchange (EDI). For companies and customers used to dealing 'direct' during the 1990s the culture shift online was not so dramatic.

One thing that is most apparent when we evaluate the Internet success stories is the culture of continual customer centric innovations. The exponential growth in technological improvements requires constant and expensive investment in new services and features. Without them the online operation becomes stale and fails to meet customer expectations. More committed online organisations do not just tweak their sites but opt for a complete overhaul and site redesign. However, the technology rush must be tempered with an appreciation of the potential gap between the company's rate of adoption and that of the customer (see Mini case 1.1).

MINI CASE 1.1 Michael Dell hits back at 'lack of innovation' accusations

Michael Dell (2002) responded to criticism of Dell's innovation record by saying, 'Innovation goes beyond products – it goes into process . . . We innovate in process and products and service . . . driving cost out. That's where Dell innovates. Innovation had to be focussed on customer needs. The thing that I've heard customers is if you don't have something that helps me drive cost, and which simplifies things, makes it easier to do business, then they really are not very interested in hearing about it.

Relevant innovation that matters to customers is where Dell likes to spend its R&D investments. In our industry there is a lot of technology for technology's sake. Quite frankly that is not what Dell is interested in.'

Adapted from Lacey, E ZDNet UK cited in: www.silicon.com/news/500009/1/1036257.html
5 November 2002

Online vision goes beyond providing a corporate web site but actively seeks partnerships and strategic alliances to increase traffic, brand awareness and sales. However, like successful businesses in the physical world, the leading online players in their sectors always seek to improve their online offering with customer-oriented innovations. Examples are dabs.com with Dabs. TV and dabsxchange (www.dabs.com)

In simple terms, organisations can take three digital routes:

1. **Grasp the Nettle**: The organisation may be visionary and exploit the potential of the digital tools to achieve sustainable competitive advantage. This could be as a pure play online operation; effective integration with an existing business or by streamlining processes eg ordering and distribution. First or early mover advantages can be gained.

2. **Follow the leader**: The organisation may be more cautious or less visionary preferring to see how the market reacts. Are customers demanding new channels using new devices? What online mistakes are competitors making and what can be learned from them? Alternatively, what is deemed to be good online practice and can it be implemented?

3. **Stand firm**: The organisation may resist the adoption of the Internet within its marketing function believing that it can survive and prosper without it. The culture may be encapsulated in the phrase, 'We've always done it this way!' Analysis of traditional target markets may also indicate resistance to new exchange models. This maybe the case in retailing and De Kare Silver (2000) suggest that retailers may seek to revitalise the shopping experience to consolidate or increase customer traffic. Even so there is likely to be pressure from key suppliers to progressively adopt electronic procurement and information exchange to cut costs and increase efficiency.

Convenience

The Internet and other digital media have enabled greater freedom, flexibility and convenience. The ability to shop when the customer wants signals a notable shift in power away from retailers to the consumer which marketers have to address. Changing social and economic reasons such as longer working hours, increasing divorce rates, the demise of the nuclear family and greater geographical mobility all impact upon modern living. Usually they impact in a negative way particularly with regard to time and stress therefore individuals seek out organisations, products and services to help alleviate this and which dovetail in with their lives leaving more leisure time. A prime example is the recognition that grocery shopping, for many, is essentially a mundane chore. By storing historical purchasing data of individual customers, online food retailers instantly remove this chore and allow consumers to spend more time on the more interesting aspects of shopping. The convenience does not stop there as fulfilment, a major Internet issue, is now expected to be flexible with a range of convenient delivery options including evenings and weekends.

Digital technologies also provide mobile convenience for consumers and businesses alike with Wi-fi, PDAs (personal digital assistants) and of course, the mobile phone with its expanding range of interactive tools and services. Businesses and consumers want instant access and connectivity. As Brennan et al (2003) suggest, 'e-marketers must appreciate that these "new" customers typically value their time immensely, know what they want, insist on meaningful content and refuse to be disappointed or exploited'.

From a business to business (B2B) perspective, the Internet and related technologies provide convenience with the streamlining of ordering, invoicing, fulfilment and payments processes that produce significant cost reductions, and help maintain competitiveness through improved supplier and distributor relations. Instant updating of prices, e-catalogues and other web based promotional communications creates more real time efficiencies.

Competition

Curiously, many writers on strategic Internet marketing give only limited time and space to any competitive analysis beyond Porter's revised Five Forces (2001). Online marketers should view the competition in a different light. They are certainly still a danger and a threat but as Mohammed et al (2002) observe in the new economy, that technology has made them 'fast and unpredictable'. Competition also has no physical boundaries.

The Internet has brought a greater transparency especially in terms of price, promotions, PR and new product and organisational developments. Price comparison sites such as Kelkoo do give consumers more knowledge and power but such information is also available to online competitors. This obviates the need for sales staff to carry out this laborious task. Harris and Dennis (2002) highlight the investment made by many organisations in acquiring 'competitive intelligence' for strategic planning. The Internet through its myriad of networks provides an immense information market. It should be noted that competitive intelligence could be sourced internally as well as externally as companies begin to appreciate the knowledge network of 'experts' that often exist within organisations.

Organisations may face competition from a number of angles:

1. traditional competitors moving online

2. new online only entrants in domestic markets

3. new online entrants from overseas

4. competition from newly formed online alliances and partnerships

5. competitors introducing or eliminating channels of distribution

6. revitalised traditional businesses (De Kare Silver 2000)

It is unlikely, but nevertheless possible that an organisation could face threats from all six angles. (For a fuller discussion on competitor analysis, see chapter 3).

Communications

The promotional communications mix will be discussed in more depth in chapter 11 but we will briefly consider here some of the new digital tools and dimensions.

Communications models consider the interactions and outcomes between the sender and receiver based on the one-to-many model associated with mass media. The death of mass media, the paperless office and growth in one-to-one interactions were forecasted years ago. Now the media is more fragmented than before; we use e-mails more but still print; but suffer from SPAM? The economics of the digital world makes it cheaper to mass mail electronically but have we learned from the image problems of junk 'snail' mail? However, traditional creative marketing skills like headline and copywriting have found a new home online. News, PR and online sales promotions come more quickly and more frequently via newsletters and **e-mail marketing** campaigns requiring a more succinct style in a world of sound bites and time-starved receivers. Style, tone and an attractive offer or reason to buy, or read on remain essential elements of successful communications. Receivers were formerly passive, now they actively seek out sites which appeal and deliver either by search engines,

Fig 1.5 Sage CRM e-mail marketing
Reproduced by kind permission of Sage (UK) Ltd

memorable domain names, **viral marketing** or bookmarks. With online communities, the communications dialogue is more two way than with traditional 'push' communications, and if handled carefully, can be utilised effectively to improve loyalty. CRM Software such as Sage CRM (see Fig 1.5 above) provide with marketers with customised e-mail marketing opportunities from design through to real time campaign management.

It is wiser to encourage chat-rooms within a corporate web site so quick responses can be made to adverse comments rather than leave it to unofficial external chat-rooms thus avoiding potential viral PR problems. With the Internet and mobile devices, the consumer can now select what they want to access so it has to be relevant and succinct. Technologies provide flexible interactions and enable more detailed product demonstrations. For example, video streaming allows customers to view 6–7 minute promotions online at their leisure compared to a 60-second television commercial. This is a more powerful medium especially when selling technically complex products or trying to get intricate messages across. Applying software technologies enables more appropriate communications especially with smaller niche markets more efficiently than previously possible. The changing nature of consumers has ensured that the drive of integrated marketing communications continues.

Consistency

Consistency is needed across all communications and all channels to ensure that the brand experience is unswerving, especially if the organisation is operating in both the virtual and physical worlds, such as Tesco. A firm's reputation established over many years in the high street could be tarnished by a poorly performing web operation, perhaps on the delivery side. There has been a growing number of partnerships and alliances emerging with the vendor transferring service responsibilities onto the partner. For example when you buy a PC package from a manufacturer, support for the peripherals is invariably provided by the manufacturer of the peripheral.

Brands reflect the company's personality and positioning as well as reflecting something in the customer's self image. As we rely on brands for reassurance, confidence and quality – be it premium or own label – anecdotal evidence suggests that consumers are mirroring their offline behaviour and levitating toward brands and sites they trust and enjoy, and not just purely on price, in the online environment.

Creative content

Jakob Nielsen declared that content is king in the heady **dot.com** days. It was a realisation that the notion that only price conscious bargain hunters inhabited the Internet was flawed. Undoubtedly some bargain hunters did exist but if the web was going to mature and motivate people to return time and time again, then site content had to be informative, topical, stimulating and of course relevant to the needs of the target market(s). How many times have you despaired when you read those words, 'last updated June 1999'? Content should be current except of course archives. Modernising the site should be within the capabilities of most SMEs on a daily basis if resources allow. For larger organisations with extensive product catalogues, rapidly changing prices, massive information and news platforms, updating manually is unrealistic. Organisations depend heavily upon **Content Management** systems to provide real time information from multiple sources. One of the buzz phrases in Internet marketing has been 'site stickiness' which works on the basis that the more time a customer spends online at your site, then the more likely they are to spend with you. This is important in brand building and retention but not every prospect wishes to browse languidly if they are the modern time starved consumer. Site design with creative prompts and offers may be enough to get them to the checkout earlier.

At another level, site content can also play an important role in online customer service and marketing research with knowledge management content. Well designed responses to Frequently Asked Questions (**FAQ**s) can resolve many, often minor or mundane, customer enquiries effectively and free up other resources to provide a more bespoke personal service, for example by phone. Creativity online has few limitations with so many multimedia tools to generate added value interactions but of course it must be relevant and timely for the individual consumer or the online community that it is aimed at. For a fuller discussion of online content and site development, refer to chapter 8.

Customisation

The Internet provides customised benefits to both buyers and sellers. The term 'mass customisation' is used to refer to more personalised, tailored communications as database systems redefine market niches with greater precision. Relevant customisation should help achieve the aims of the spiral of prosperity in that the more we know about the customer, the more we can tailor and time offerings to their needs rather than the tactics of interruption marketing that we often endure. Customisation also now comes from the ability of the consumer to order more bespoke products unique to them such as a PC with specific processor speeds, style of monitor, peripherals and printer. This puts demands across a range of functions but if it provides competitive advantage then it is wise to adapt systems to cope.

Coordination

Marketers have long since argued that the marketing function is *the* coordinating business function within organisations. Everything such as production and finance flows from the customer and forecasted sales. For the effective operation of an e-business the real time dissemination of information from customer to shopping cart to order and despatch requires a scalable IT infrastructure supported by organisational competence across all supporting functions.

Control

As another mode of direct marketing, the Internet has the power and ability to test events and activities. Response and measurement provide marketers with the statistical and financial accountability to further champion the electronic cause within organisations. The technologists have provided marketers with the tools to measure just about any online activity through web analytics. Many organisations are collectors of data but they do not know what to do with it or, more precisely, they have not clearly defined their online objectives and so do not know what to measure.

The Internet through e-CRM also provides real time control down to individual account level that improves profitability resulting from enhanced customer relationship handling (see Fig 1.6).

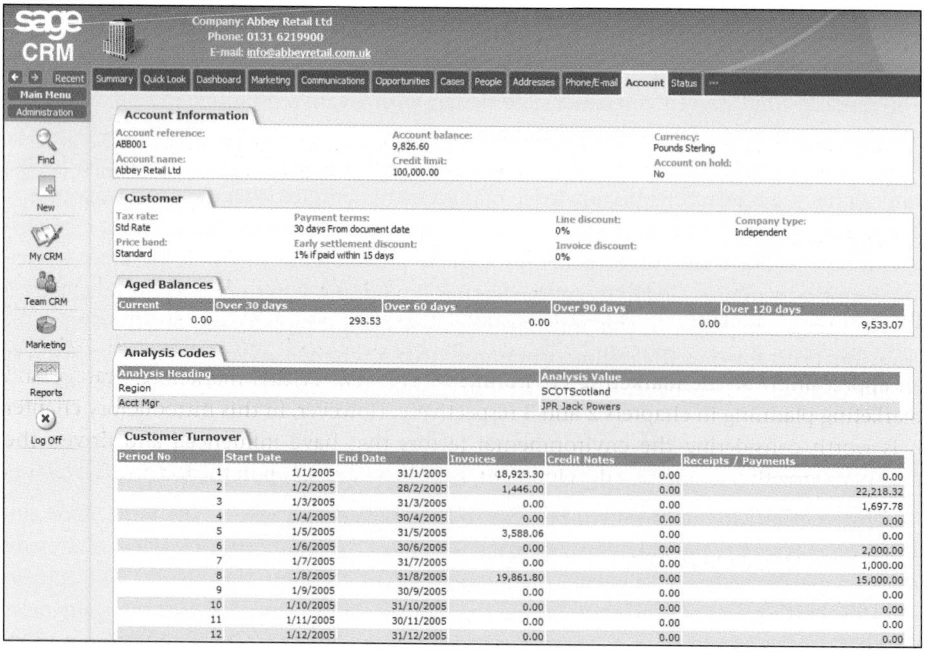

Fig 1.6 Sage CRM info portal
Reproduced by kind permission of Sage (UK) Ltd

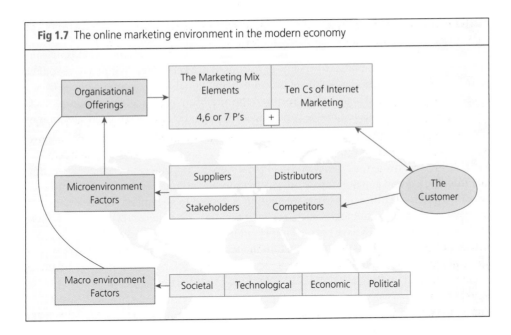

Fig 1.7 The online marketing environment in the modern economy

1.7 **The online marketing environment in the modern economy**

The organisation that fails to consider the influences of the environment around it will be in imminent danger. The organisational response to the environment will give clear indications concerning its marketing and corporate culture, aims and objectives.

> 'A company's **marketing environment** consists of the actors and forces outside marketing that affect the marketing management's ability to develop and maintain successful transactions with its target customers. The marketing environment offers both threats and opportunities' (Kotler et al, 2001).

Some argue that marketplaces change so fast that it is not worth the effort planning for the future and gut feel and instinct play a more important role. This type of entrepreneurial spirit has merit but as witnessed by the dot.com bubble burst it can be dangerous without an appreciation of the marketing environment. We shall discuss marketing strategy and marketing planning in chapters 2 and 3 respectively. However, in this introductory chapter it is worth considering the environmental factors that have influenced and driven the Internet's growth and ongoing development, as well as its sway upon the factors. The factors are grouped under:

1. Microenvironment factors

2. Macroenvironment factors

The wider macroenvironmental factors have had a more direct and significant effect on the adoption of the Internet, especially in terms of technological influences than the immediate microenvironmental factors. However, we shall consider the micro factors first.

Microenvironment factors

Jobber and Fahy (2003) state that it 'consists of the actors in the firm's immediate environment that effects its capabilities to operate in its chosen markets'. Organisations have sought to drive down costs throughout their processes. Functional areas such as Supply Chain Management (SCM) and logistics had focussed the attention on cost and developing effective business relationships to provide value and satisfaction before the commercialisation of the Internet. These issues will be discussed in greater detail in chapter 12.

i) Suppliers

The Internet has had a major impact on existing supplier arrangements as partnership relationships and more intimate vertical integration is desired to streamline supply chains and improve efficiency. Technologies such as electronic data interchange (EDI) and extensible mark-up language (XML) have enabled improved information exchanges.

The Internet has opened up the market for many companies to access potential new suppliers across national boundaries faster.

ii) Distributors

The 'Now Society' places more demands on distributors regarding their performance to meet customer expectations and to overcome the delivery problems associated with the early dot.com operators. The Internet has impacted upon traditional distribution channels removing some intermediaries (disintermediation) whilst creating new channels (reintermediation) in existing markets. In addition, the Internet comes into its own with information based 'products' with negligible distribution cost involved once the 'product' has been produced, such as, for example, an **e-book**.

iii) Stakeholders

As part of any organisation's promotional planning, communicating effectively with various stakeholders or 'publics' is critical for successful ongoing relationships. With careful use of e-mail and the corporate web site, intranets and extranets, stakeholders can be informed, influenced, persuaded and sold to in a faster and more flexible way.

iv) Competitors

Some competition issues have already been discussed earlier in this chapter within the Ten Cs framework. The reality of the Internet is that it has created more competition both within and across national boundaries.

Macroenvironmental factors

Most texts consider the wider environmental factors utilising the mnemonics STEP or PEST as the analytical frameworks for environmental scanning representing Societal, Technological, Economic and Political dimensions. Other academics have extended the model to incorporate regulatory frameworks, the natural environment and legal aspects. For the purposes of this discussion, regulatory issues will be incorporated into the Political section. The natural environment has had little effect on the Internet's development, though the web plays an important role in disseminating information and providing a forum for ecological debate.

LEGAL EAGLE BOX 1.1 Examples of mainstream legislation and regulations that impact on online marketing

The Trade Descriptions Act 1968
The Consumer Credit Act 1974
The Sale of Goods Act 1979
The Consumer Protection Act 1998
The Data Protection Act 1998
British Codes of Advertising and Sales Promotion
Distance Selling Regulations 2000

The Electronic Commerce Directive (00/31/EC)
The Directive on Privacy and Electronic Communications (2002/58/EC) I

Codes of practice or standards charters from industry bodies such as the Direct Marketing Association www.dma.org.uk and the email Marketing Association (eMMa) www.emmacharter.org

Legal issues and specific Internet legislation will be covered in depth in chapter 13. It is vitally important that online marketers are fully aware of the law wherever they trade whether it is within their own national boundaries, or inside an economic trading bloc such as the European Union or in other nation states. Time, money, litigation and public relations damage can be avoided by being familiar with the relevant legislation and applying to the organisations both in the public and private sector. In the UK, the law provides the same legal protection online as it does offline so adherence is essential. Some key pieces of legislation are outlined in Legal Eagle box 1.1.

In particular, as we relentlessly march into technologically driven **database-marketing** communications, the guardianship of customer information becomes increasingly important. We must never forget that marketers rely on customer data, which is often volunteered. If we do not use that data in a legal and ethical way, the trust of the customer is lost and the industry will struggle to gather accurate and relevant data under the auspices of the Data Protection Act 1998. Inevitably more rafts of legislation and directives from national governments and the European Union relating to direct and electronic commerce are making their way onto the statute books covering e-mail marketing, SMS marketing and the use of **cookies** and other Internet tracking devices. In addition to legislative compliance, organisations should also make their web site policy statements clear on issues like copyright, returns and any disclaimers clear to customers.

For convenience, some issues raised under the STEP analysis framework will be considered under a specific heading (eg economic factors) but they can often overlap and be considered as a joint issue (eg socio-economic factors).

i) Societal

The adoption of any technologies relies upon society's acceptance of its needs or benefits. O'Connor, Galvin and Evans (2004) suggest that customers are more sophisticated and demanding now. They observe three key developments in customers' lifestyles and attitudes.

1. **Cash rich, time poor:** Consumers generally have higher level of disposable income compared to years ago but whilst they are wealthier, they have less time to enjoy the fruits of their labours. This is particularly true of managers and senior officials with 38% working more than 50 hours per week and many in excess of 60 hours per week according to a 2002 ONS labour survey. It follows that any business activities that save time in their hectic schedules, or provide convenience will be attractive to them. But it is not just working hours that makes modern living more demanding, we seem to be developing a 24-hour culture. Social changes in terms of ever-increasing divorce rates

puts extra demands on separated parents. Of course marriage is still a popular institution and many people remarry and 'inherit' other children placing a further time premium on themselves. As we continually strive to improve our standard of living, dual income families face extra time pressures also associated with their everyday activities such as banking, shopping and paying bills. These forces of social change create needs for products and services which marketers, and of course technologists seek to satisfy. Online banking is a classic example of a service designed for the convenience of modern living. According to Forrester Research over 60 million Europeans now use online banking services and they estimate that by 2007, this will rise to 130 million. We should perhaps temper these forecasts and question whether they are purely online or whether they rely on multi-channels through branch networks and telephone support also. However, it is clear that the rise of the 24-hour culture continues to fuel the growth of such services. A 2006 Yahoo!/OMD report confirms the multi-channel interactions that are increasingly influenced by technology driven information search and gathering.

2. **Increased leisure time**: O'Connor & Galvin suggest that some other occupations have moved to 35-hour working weeks without significantly lowering their income levels which provides them with more leisure time and the resource to enjoy it. Humdrum tasks like weekly shopping trips can of course be undertaken online, freeing consumers up to live for today. In recent years, we have witnessed a significant segment emerging, the 'seniors', many of whom, in their mid-50s, have taken early retirement or faced redundancy situations, and are financially sound and have time on their hands. Forrester Research indicates 50% of Swedish seniors are online, 40% in The Netherlands and 29% in Britain. For example, they provide a significant target market for the travel industry with their newfound freedom to travel off peak all year round filling flights and hotels outside of the main holiday seasons.

3. **Increased technology ownership**: The rate of technological change has increased exponentially and the 'now' consumer society has an unquenchable thirst for new toys, gadgets and devices which amuse, entertain, inform and improve their lives. Sales of digital cameras, DVDs, Personal Digital Assistants (PDAs) and mobile telephony continue unbounded. They become essential 'must have' fashion accessories for modern living. This, coupled with the growth of wireless technology, and a younger generation growing up with it and for whom it is second nature, should ensure continued growth and adoption as evidenced below in Mini case 1.2.

In five years from January 2001 through to February 2006, we have seen adult Internet access rise from 45–63%: see Fig 1.8.

In the three months prior to interview, 63% of adults in Great Britain (29 million) had accessed the Internet in February 2006. This represents 93% of the adults who have ever accessed the Internet. (National Statistics Omnibus Survey, 31 May 2006)

Whilst statistics continue to illustrate increased usage of digital related technologies, marketers must remember that the social acceptance of the Internet is not universal. It would appear that a significant proportion of the UK's population have been termed, perhaps unfairly, as techno-laggards as they resist the use of mobile phones, digital TV and the Internet for a variety of reasons such as age, access, cost or need. Many countries are concerned about 'The **Digital Divide**' that exists between social classes and regional differences in web adoption.

MINI CASE 1.2 Children online

What Percentage of Children Use the Internet?

A comprehensive report by the London School of Economics entitled, *UK Children Go Online*, looked at the nature of Internet usage, and its associated risks, for young people in the 9–19 year-old age range. The 'milestone' study found the following:

- 74% have Internet access at home
- 98% have access somewhere
- 24% have broadband at home
- 22% of boys and 19% of girls had Internet access in their bedroom
- 24% rely on school as main source of Internet access

At home fewer than half of the PCs were located in a public place.

How do Children Use the Internet?

Many youngsters access the Internet for short, frequent periods. 40% are daily users. 19% spend up to 10 minutes online and 48% between 10 minutes and one hour.

Of the 84% of young people that access the Internet on a weekly or more frequent basis, the main activity was information search, often in connection with homework. The study highlights key online activities performed by children by popularity order.

- Obtain information on things other than school work (94%)
- Help with school work (90%)
- Send and receive e-mails (72%)
- Play games online (70%)
- Send and receive instant messages (55%)
- Download music (45%)
- Look for information on careers and further education (44%)
- Look for information and shop online (40%)
- Read the news (26%)
- Chat-rooms (21%)

Interestingly, among the 12–19 year-olds online on a daily basis, 21% owned up to having copied work from the Internet and handing it in as their own. Hopefully this trend will not continue!

Children accessed the Internet through various channels. 71% had home access primarily through a computer, 38% connected using a mobile phone not surprisingly, 17% via a digital television service and 8% through their games console.

Sources: www.children-go-online.net
www.citizensonline.org.uk
www.news.bbc.co.uk/1/hi/uk/4490879.stm

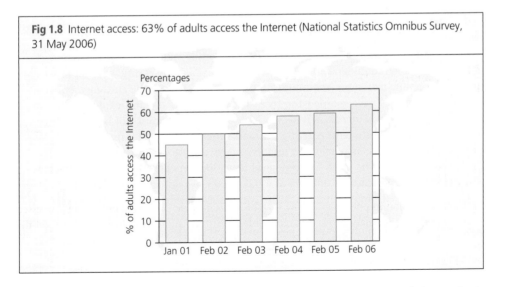

Fig 1.8 Internet access: 63% of adults access the Internet (National Statistics Omnibus Survey, 31 May 2006)

A National Statistics Omnibus Survey published in September 2003 revealed some basic reasons why some adults had not used the Internet. 40% of those adults questioned who had never used the Internet were asked why. Half of these non-users said that they did not want to use it, or had no need or no interest in the Internet, 39% had no Internet connection and 38% felt they lacked knowledge or the confidence to use it.

In addition, the survey also identified costs and security issues, which deter potential users. Government and **Internet Service Providers** have to address the cost issue. Regarding security, it is an ongoing problem with regular alerts but much of it has been fuelled by media scare stories emanating from the early dot.com days. However, security fraud remains a serious concern. Access is another important issue and will be covered in the section on political factors. Online adoption will benefit from constant security assurances as well trouble free online experiences. The Internet provides a creative challenge for online marketers to reach the non-believers. Alternatively, new and easier technologies such as interactive television (iTV) may be more attractive. If unsuccessful, they will have to encourage greater web use by those already online. Remember Ansoff, sell more to existing markets!

ii) Technological

'How technology is reshaping marketing' was the title of the *FT*'s Creative Business supplement in May 2002 and it outlined the impact that it had played in changing marketing practices such as Customer Relationship Management (CRM), **Database Marketing** applications and related privacy issues as marketers grapple with the problem of establishing and maintaining meaningful relationships with customers. CRM is a classic example of relying too heavily on technology to achieve corporate and marketing objectives without customer centric applications. Organisations are now benefiting from greater customer insight. Some, such as Tesco have used it to stunning effect through Clubcard, as its main competitors will testify, whilst others have applied it in such a club fisted way that they alienate more customers than they satisfy. In a study of the effects of e-commerce on the UK's financial services industry, Hughes and Stone (2002) observe, 'in consumer markets that pace of change will be dictated by the willingness of customers to utilise the new technology and also the adoption of easier to use technology in the form of digital television and mobile telephony. Therefore the adoption will take the form more of evolution than revolution'.

Various commentators have observed that the marketing and IT functions in many organisations have failed to integrate. In the early Internet years, the reality was that IT wizards drove most online marketing communications with little feel for the customer experience. The web visionaries have married the two functions effectively and exploited the web's potential. Marketing is increasingly technology driven but it must not be technology for technology's sake. For students entering the marketing profession, it is important to acquire as much IT knowledge as possible to understand its diverse potential across the range of marketing activities. The main technological developments have been outlined earlier in this chapter with the Internet timeline as it has rapidly developed from a military and computer science based project through to its commercialisation phase of recent years. The humble PC and networks rapidly expand their power in terms of clock speeds, data exchange, storage, analysis and mining, putting powerful devices in the hands of individuals and small businesses in a way we could not have imagined a decade ago. The Internet is here to stay, either in its PC based delivery or in its growing mobile format.

It is beyond the scope of this text to consider a wide range of technological developments including wired connections, though we should mention a few examples which have fuelled web growth and which online marketers should appreciate. Unix operating systems enabled different computers to talk to one another. The development of the concept of **Packet Switching**, and the Transaction Control Protocol/Internet Protocol (TCP/IP) standard for data packet transmission based on UNIX became the backbone of the emerging web with the support of US telecom operators, AT&T and MCI. The combination of **Hypertext mark-up language (HTML)** and **Graphical User Interface (GUI)** have transformed the web's rather dull but informative text based offerings to vibrant graphical, video, audio and text formatted communications that site visitors take for granted. Protocols associated with these and other information exchange systems such as **File Transfer Protocol (FTP)** and **Secure Socket Layer (SSL)** are essential vehicles to exchange files and other messages in a safe and convenient way. The development of **search engine** technology has been crucial for web-users to access information at speed. For online marketers, utilising expert search marketers who understand the technology behind **Google** or Overture's search engines is vital if they are to achieve top ten rankings and be highly visible.

Developments in bandwidth from narrowband (ISDN lines) to broadband (DSL) have provided a much needed impetus for the online community. Broadband provides both speed and capacity compared to traditional dial-up options with much faster **download** speeds particularly when it comes to video and audio streaming. The user experience is enhanced immeasurably and the online business has more creative tools at its disposal. Now we await the mass adoption of 3G multi-functional handheld devices supported by wireless communications. Such adoption is essential if mobile phone operators are to recoup the cost of the 3G licences.

The capabilities of these technologies can be enjoyed on many multi-functional web sites. Many leading bands utilise them to reinforce their relationship with their fan base such as Snow Patrol: see below in Fig 1.9.

Fig 1.9 Snow Patrol homepage

Apart from IT infrastructures, which provide the backbone of the Internet, rapid developments in software solutions, **server** technologies, hosting and **electronic shopping (ES)** packages present the online marketer with fast, flexible integrated customer interfaces at an ever-decreasing cost. Off the shelf solutions can provide quick and customisable sites offering secure socket layer technologies, web site traffic analysis, customer account management, fast updateable product catalogues, e-mail newsletter distribution and shopping cart integration features, for example. Technology is reshaping marketing for online sellers but they must not lose sight of customer orientation amidst the plethora of new toys and tools available.

iii) Economic

According to a D&B business report (2003), 'As economic growth falters in western economies in particular, it's no surprise that there is more pressure than ever before on the costs side of the equation'. Much attention has been given to the economic impacts of the Internet and its promise to be a key business driver in cost reduction. The unique nature of e-commerce business exchanges with global reach, have the potential to impact upon relationships between individuals, organisations, industry sectors, national and global operations. The growth of the so-called 'New Economy' and the 'Information Age' has had an immediate and lasting impact on economies, economics and prices in the short term. In the post-bubble economy, the empirical evidence is mixed on the effect of the Internet on prices as markets settle and high street retailers fight back. We should consider (1) how the Internet is changing industry structures and (2) its economic value, outputs and forecasted potential.

Much attention has been given to the economic efficiencies generated by the Internet. The term 'frictionless economy' was coined to describe how markets could work effortlessly and supposedly, in perfect competition, or as close as realistically possible. The commercialisation of the Internet has had a number of economic impacts affecting the adoption rate of web related technologies. Some are considered below but the list is but no means exhaustive:

- The Internet *should* increase competition within industry sectors leading to a position of equilibrium where demand equals supply.

- Buyers and sellers can reach markets previously inaccessible for geographic, entry barriers or other reasons creating new segments and new players in market sectors. PriceWaterhouseCoopers (PwC) in a report on European technology firms observed that the Internet was creating a more level playing field, particularly for so-called infrastructure companies (integration, middleware and security providers), when challenging their traditionally dominant American competitors.

- Promotional communications such as e-mail are significantly cheaper and often achieve higher response rates than traditional methods.

- Improved 'reach' may facilitate improved economies of scale.

- Buyers' search costs are reduced whilst choice is increased with the availability of supplier information. This may impact on traditional outlets and change consumer behaviour (see Mini case 1.3).

- **E-procurement** and online payment processing will streamline administrative and buying procedures and cut transaction costs eg Covisint (www.covisint.com) in the US automotive sector.

MINI CASE 1.3 The socio-economic impacts of online gambling

Online gambling has been one of the most significant Internet success stories with phenomenal growth though not without its downside.

PartyGaming, the online poker web site, made its debut on the London Stock Exchange on 30 June 2005 and was valued at £4.64bn with a predicted rise of over 22% per year over the next five years. Nigel Payne, Chief Executive of UK gambling operation, Sportingbet, and second largest global operation by gross profit, claims that online profits are already 10% higher than those of traditional betting shops so an industry restructuring would seem inevitable, at least in the high street. Most online gambling operations enjoy low-cost operations with their bases in low tax environments such as the Channel Islands, the Caribbean and other offshore locations. In addition, call centre staff operate from countries with poor wage rates.

Online gambling appears to have attracted new, formerly non-gambling segments such as the female market previously alienated by the stigma of entering betting shops. Remote gambling with 24-hour access provides direct entry into customer accounts, replacing cash, which explains the excitement of potential investors. However, the low cost online gambling is not without its troubles, and charities and governments are becoming increasingly concerned at the growing level of personal debt and possible exposure of children to gambling. Individual online gambling debts of £100,000 are not uncommon.

Adapted from: www.sundayherald.com/50220, 12 June 2005
www.guardian.co.uk/gambling/story/0,15248,1587888,00.html, 9 October 2005
www.e-consultancy.com/forum/102193-online-gambling.html, 11 April 2005

- The Internet has led to disintermediation and occasionally reintermediation in supply chains and distribution channels. This has often resulted in costs being driven out with the elimination of intermediaries.

- The Internet and related technologies also impact upon employment levels and practices. This can be evidenced in two ways. First, automated processes can replace human labour or a combination of the two can lead to job losses.

Media giant, Time Warner made 1,300 staff redundant from its Internet arm, AOL as online customers are increasingly more 'net savvy' and are adept at fixing their own technical problems. Since 2004, AOL claim the number of customer service calls has halved. It is also a testimony to the improved online customer service content.

Second, as location is no longer a barrier firms can relocate to areas where labour costs are significantly lower. In recent months, trade unions have expressed serious concerns at the relocation of various call centre operations from the UK to India. Similarly, many organisations have moved operations in to Eastern Europe. Finally, the Internet facilitates home or teleworking. This provides greater flexibility for employees and their families and a more productive environment. It can also be an attractive employment option that will help retain key members of staff.

Some economists viewed the Internet as the vehicle to achieve 'perfect markets' as both buyers and sellers possessed full market knowledge. The result would be a shift in the balance of power towards the customer and a reduction in the ability of suppliers to control or influence market prices. However, in reality, market distortions may still be prevalent when suppliers or controllers of resources continue to retain significant market influence as evidenced below in the case of broadband operators (see Mini case 1.4).

The economic and political impact from the introduction of the Euro was supposed to facilitate easier and cheaper cross border transactions. Baye et al (2002) provide evidence that online prices in the Eurozone have actually increased compared to prices encountered in EU countries but outside of the Eurozone. Perhaps this may be a temporary effect as traders take

MINI CASE 1.4 Broadband Internet: there is still much to do

In his speech about open competition between suppliers of Internet access, Renato Soru, Founder and CEO of Tiscali, emphasised that fair competition between the traditional operators and the new arrivals in the sector 'is not only necessary for the survival of the incumbent operators but for the entire economy. More than 50% of current growth is generated by the digital economy,' he insisted.

The round table that was held on Friday morning organised by Tiscali and the European Competitive Telecommunications Association (ECTA) allowed for a status report on broadband to be presented. The most positive aspect is the fact that there are currently 17 million Internet broadband connections in Europe, whereas one year ago there were just 8.5 million. There are however some less favourable aspects. This increase in the number of broadband connections hides a worrying aspect: the near monopoly by the incumbent operators (France Telecom and its company Wanadoo in France, Belgacom and its company Skynet in Belgium) which hinders: free competition, lower prices, faster connection speeds and technical innovation. The ADSL market is still today largely controlled by the incumbent national operators, never owning less than 60% of the market, except in the UK where British Telecom has 50% of the market. In Germany, the incumbent has 90% of the market. Many of BT's competitiors have been angered by the regulators' constant failure to force BT Wholesale to reduce its broadband prices for services to Telcos. Ironically the regulators themselves, Ofcom and Oftel, concluded that wholesale braodband was uncompetitive.

The result of this lack of competition, in the opinion of the International Télecommunications Union (ITU), is a delay in market development as compared to Canada and the USA but above all Korea, Japan and Hong Kong. In Korea for example, 21.3% of inhabitants have a broadband connection, which means about three quarters of all households! The rate of market penetration is a mere 7% in the European Union. The cherry on the cake is the fact that the connections proposed by Asian operators are considerably faster than those in Europe and connections to new clients take place on the same day. According to the ITU, this high performance is due to the number of providers that are present in the sector. In Japan for example, there are 47 operators.

To remedy the problem, the participants in the round table (representing industry, consumers and the regulatory authorities) all agreed on the need for fairer competition. They hope that the national authorities of the member states will enforce European law in this area (close to half of them are dragging their feet), and that the incumbent operators will play the competition game more honestly. Currently they employ a variety of methods to continue to profit from their positions of market dominance. The European Commission has attempted to limit these practices this year.

In the UK, there is some hope with BT having to offer greater access and equal inputs for service providers under the Enterprise Act 2005.

Adapted from:
www.europe.tiscali.co.uk/business/news/200309/broadband.html
www.btplc.com/Thegroup/Regulatoryinformation/RegulationsintheUK/RegulationintheUK.htm
www.broadband-wireless.org/pub.html

advantage of the new currency in the same way that UK traders did during decimalisation in the 1970s.

The economic 'feel-good factor' may also influence the Internet's adoption generally or in specific sectors. For example, there has been much criticism levelled at the financial services sector regarding the performance of 'managed funds' in recent years, consequently the media and industry observers like Motley Fool have encouraged would-be investors to play the markets themselves. Investing can be a risky business and requires 'information rich' sources for better investment decisions. Industry portals, specific web sites and competitively priced online share dealing services have encouraged the growth of the self-trader. However, investor sentiment has been ultra cautious since September 11 and the Iraq war. Since early 2003, there have been some signs of growing confidence both in the US and UK economies. An example of the relationship between these economic indicators and their influence on specific online services and the wider Internet marketspace is given below in Mini case 1.5.

MINI CASE 1.5   New surge in online share deals

Online share dealing has now achieved a critical mass in 2006 but it was not until 2003 that bullish investors rediscovered their share trading habit. There was a 20% jump in share deals by private investors in the second quarter of 2003, while dealing online rose by more than 40%.

The growth was the first sign of the renewed confidence from private investors for more than a year, though the total number of deals remains lower than at the height of the technology boom in 2001.

Figures from specialist research agency, ComPeer, which tracks stock market deals each quarter, show that there were almost 710,000 share trades online from April to June. This compares with just under 500,000 in the first three months of the year.

The growth includes more UK investors trading directly with shares in overseas markets such as the New York Stock Exchange or the Deutsche Borse in Frankfurt, Germany. Online broker,

E*Trade, for example, last week reported a 46% rise in its customers trading shares in the US.

Angel Knight, chief executive of the Association of Private Client Investment Managers and Stockbrokers, is cautious reading too much into one set of figures. 'Share dealing was slow in the first quarter because of string of bad corporate news and troubles in the Gulf'.

Nevertheless, the reasons for saving and investing have not gone away. With interest rates low and the FTSE 100 index at a 12-month high, private investor confidence in buying shares has been re-established and this continued in 2005 with 54% of trades transacted online. Internet brokerage services tend to be cheaper than phone deals whilst providing plenty of free research data and broadband has enabled faster access to the internet and deals without delays.

Adapted from: *Financial Mail on Sunday*, 17 August 2003, p 19.
www.compeer.co.uk/services/quarter-3-2005.cfm

In addition to the way that the Internet may shape and influence markets, we should also consider some of the economic forecasts in terms of value and cost reduction.

It has long been assumed that the US commitment to new technology would ensure that it benefits before other economies from web-related developments. Forrester estimate that US e-commerce spending will reach $96 billion this year, rising to $230 billion by 2008. 10% of all US retail sales will be online by 2008. eMarketer forecasts that online B2B global sales will top $1.4 trillion by 2003 and rise to $2.7 trillion in 2004. The potential for further online growth is evident as US companies' expend 10% of their total spend online. Surveys by Jupiter and RoperASW and AOL Time Warner both suggest that European online spending has caught up with US spending and will overtake it significantly by 2007 as broadband subscriptions increase at a faster rate in Europe. The 'always on' culture usually results in higher online spending, however there are noticeable spending differences within European countries. The level of IT investments and governmental support are important influences with Scandinavia and Northern Europe leading the way. Cited in CyberAtlas, Forrester Research forecast that online trade in the EU will surge from €77 billion to €2.2 trillion, which represents a lot of shopping carts heading for the checkout. In terms of efficiency forecasts, Goldman Sachs, cited in Chaston (2001) estimate achievable savings of 40% by e-procurement in the electronic components sector. They go on to suggest that the effect of e-commerce in the B2B sector could boost the overall outputs of the industrialised economies by some 5%. Chaston equates this to a 0.25% increase in Gross Domestic Product (GDP) per year.

It is clear that the Internet provides significant economic value and benefits to both individuals and businesses alike. In the new millennium, cost reduction has increased in importance as a critical business driver in increasingly competitive markets. All economic indicators suggest that Internet growth is now steady and encouraging rather than explosive, as buyers and sellers understand its potential after the early dot.com hype.

iv) Political

Governments across the globe have recognised the economic and social impacts of the Internet and its related technologies have had as well as exploiting its potential. The level of government commitment to e-commerce adoption will significantly influence how each nation state will be able to compete across the globe. As Jutla et al (2002) observe, 'Countries are providing a model for their citizens by becoming adopters of the network processes and technologies that enable convenient, cost effective, online business-to-government, government-to-citizen and government-to-government services.' Bandyo-padhay (2002) puts forward examples of potential e-government activities:

- Electronic polling and voting   eg to counter voter apathy
- Electronic communication by the police   eg solving cross-border crime
- Establish links with other governments   eg to support poorer countries with health
  education or famine
- The coordination of international regulations   eg to achieve consistency across borders
- The establishment of intellectual property   eg to protect the vulnerable from web
  rights   piracy
- The establishment of an efficient regulatory   eg the Internet is not owned by anyone
  framework   and so may be open to abuse

Governmental bodies have set various targets in order to achieve what is termed 'e-readiness'. E-readiness judges a variety of factors that indicate a country's ability to exploit and support Internet opportunities. It considers the level and quality of government initiatives and funding, the levels of Internet and broadband adoption, the ICT infrastructure within the country and how its business community is implementing it. In 1998, the UK government produced its White Paper, 'Competitiveness in the Knowledge Driven Economy' establishing goals and frameworks for industrial policy. The 2002 UK Online Annual Report's main goal is 'to develop the UK as a world leader for electronic business' (2003). Their e-communications team aims to have all government services online by 2005 'with key services achieving high levels of use'. In September 1999, the Office of the e-envoy was formed to drive forward online initiatives and performance. The e-envoy, currently Andrew Pinder, in tandem with the e-commerce Minister, Stephen Timms, champion the new technologies inside and outside of government both at local, regional and national level. In response to the US and Canada's setting the early e-commerce pace, the EU summit in Lisbon, 2000 set the target for Europe becoming the most competitive region in the world by 2010. So who is winning the e-readiness race?

The Scandinavian countries in particular seem to have embraced the connected world in a vigorous way with the US and other Northern European countries are not far behind. Southern European countries lag significantly behind. Is it cultural? Is it due to governmental influences? The Swedes specifically, are buying a wide range of products and services across the Internet and often utilising mobile phones to transact. It is no coincidence that Sweden has the cheapest broadband prices in Europe. Other proactive governments have initiated a whole raft of projects and polices such as:

- automating government services such as passport applications and tax assessments;
- deregulating the telecoms sectors to increase competition and drive down broadband prices to make high-speed connections readily available;

Table 1.1 Economist Intelligence Unit e-readiness rankings 2006

2006 e-readiness rank	2005 rank	Country	2006 e-readiness	2005 score
1	1	Denmark	9.00	8.74
2	2	US	8.88	8.73
3	4	Switzerland	8.81	8.62
4	3	Sweden	8.74	8.64
5	8	UK	8.64	8.54
6	8	Netherlands	8.60	8.32
7	6	Finland	8.55	8.32
8	10	Australia	8.50	8.22
9	12	Canada	8.37	8.03
10	6	Hong Kong	8.36	8.32

- providing consultancy and other support networks, especially for SMEs;
- supporting the development of leading edge IT infrastructures;
- developing e-citizen portals to improve delivery of public services whilst encouraging wider web usage;
- engaging in joint initiatives with the private sector;
- supporting IT training to overcome specific skills shortages;
- introducing legislation to curb SPAM and monitor anti-competitive practices (eg EU's antitrust case against Microsoft);
- developing training initiatives and addressing skills shortages through e-learning delivery.

The UK government has stated that its aim is to provide web access to all those who wish to use it. During 2003, it was clear that the benefits of broadband were not being enjoyed by all in the UK. Despite 75% of the country being hooked up to the 'fat pipe', the Countryside Agency (2003) estimated that in rural areas, only one in 10 villages have access. This undermined the fundamental advantages of the Internet for rural businesses and communities of reach and access to markets. Regional Development Agency, One NorthEast provided grants of £2.5 million to deliver improved broadband connections in County Durham. The government, through the Department of Trade and Industry (DTI), is backing do-it-yourself broadband schemes where technology advocates are setting up their own broadband networks. They are seen as an important element in the development of the UK's IT infrastructure and are to be coordinated through the Community Broadband UK website (www.cbuk.org). Similarly, the *Financial Times* (2003) reported moves to increase broadband access to the remotest parts of the Scottish Highlands and Islands. A unique initiative between the Development Agency, Highlands and Islands with telecoms providers, BT and Thus are extending high-speed access to the Outer Hebrides, Orkney and Shetland. The future of Internet developments will of course rest with demand as only 5% of Highlanders with access use it. In addition, estimates suggest that only 5% of SMEs utilised the government's online tax assessment service. A report from the Society of IT managers

(Socitm) and Citizens' Advice Bureaux (2003) criticised government websites. Whilst there is considerable information online, 'much of it is poorly structured and signposted'. It goes onto say that 'Government on the web falls well short of what citizens really need in terms of usefulness and **usability**'. The access issue goes beyond high-speed availability and on to the capability of individuals suffering from disabilities such as blindness, deafness and other handicaps to physically using the web. In the UK, the Web Accessibility Initiative (www.w3.org/WAI) provides guidelines and checklists to improve web access to such disadvantaged groups.

The Internet is not owned by anyone but its democracy and openness has often been abused in terms of fraud and pornography. Mounting industry and public pressure may determine how the Internet develops in years to come. Political pressure may come from industry bodies such as the Direct Marketing Association or the Advertising Standards Authority. Alternatively, consumer organisations such as the Consumers Association in the UK and multi-national groups like the 65-strong Transatlantic Consumer Dialogue (www.TACD.org) lobby governments on consumer issues such as SPAM and use of cookies. Tiered web delivery or what has become known as the 'web toll' is being considered in the US. According to Folger (2006) a notion being proposed by US telephone companies and media giants such as AT & T, Time Warner and Bell South is to fund the expansion of broadband. Supporters like Christopher Yoo, a professor at Vanderbilt University Law School, argue that consumers should be willing to pay extra for the speedy delivery of streaming video, television, movies and other high-bandwidth data. Opponents point out that this would create a two-tiered Internet, with the web sites of rich businesses having a significant advantage over smaller cash strapped online operators.

1.8 Summary

The Internet as a commercial entity has come along way in a short time, though its technical developments stretch over four decades. After the bursts of wild enthusiasm and optimism, the Internet revolution has ended to be replaced by a phase of learning and maturity as marketers begin to understand the potential benefits of the technology and how they can use it. This has also been appreciated globally by governments and other agencies that see not only the economic and competitive benefits but also the wider social impacts of the Internet. The indications are that Internet usage will continue to grow especially in the B2B sector as they focus on the cost efficiencies generated. In the B2C sector, sustained growth will rely heavily on cheaper high-speed access and of course whether the consumers wish to adopt the PC based Internet technology available or go to the easier mobile options. For marketers in the online world we need to question the relevance of traditional models and embody new ones in this rapidly changing business and social environment.

During the final year at University, and after spending the summer working with one of the UK's largest ISPs, three young men, Peter Dabrowa, Gordon McNevin and Graham Bontoft put their heads together with the aim of taking advantage of what the new found Internet had to offer and in turn creating an online destination for their fellow students.

The vision

The vision was to establish a site that informed potential students of what University life was all about, and somewhere for current students to share their experiences and interact with each other, ultimately creating a community online that served the needs of the student population in the UK. A fun, informative and interactive site was needed, a site that offered something for nothing, student discounts, competitions, fun and games . . . basically somewhere for students to 'hang out' online. A classic stock free, content rich online business model was the platform for commercial success.

Initially launched as 'TheCompleteStudent.co.uk' in 2001 with a quirky cartoon character and youthful branding, the name was seen to be too long and not the easiest to remember for their 100 visitors per day.

TheCompleteStudent.co.uk
Your Complete Student Guide To Life

After a week of printing out available domain names, one to a page of A4, and sticking them on a large wall to compare and eliminate, the new name 'Studentmax.com' was agreed and a new site design and branding was set in action.

The new name was not only a chance to create a new brand, one more attractive and memorable to the student marketplace, it was also the opportunity to restructure and re-build the entire site. A new front-end design and a back-end infrastructure were constructed, allowing a new members' area to work in parallel with several features and channels throughout the site. Essentially it was the first real step in making an interactive student community.

Once Studentmax.com was launched, students were then able to create their own user accounts, post messages on forums, send private messages to other members, add drinking games, cocktails and hangover cures, all under a unique online alias. From here the site dramatically grew in popularity, people would return on a daily basis, check their messages, see the latest updates and chat with their newfound friends. A thriving online community was established.

With all information and content-based websites such as Studentmax, the primary way to generate revenue is through advertising. In order to appear attractive to advertisers and agencies that represent them, a site needs to have a reasonably sized audience since the more users and visitors you have the more

you can charge as the amount of exposure is greater for the end client. Once a site establishes a large audience, for example 100,000 visitors and 1 million page views per month, it can expect cpm (cost per thousand) based advertising deals, (charged at how many advertisements are being shown rather than on response rates) which guarantees revenue each month as long as traffic figures stay level or increase. A fundamental understanding of how Google works and its importance in search engine marketing and reciprocal links was essential in achieving top rankings and the critical mass to make Studentmax an attractive proposition for potential online advertisers.

Once Studentmax.com reached the figure of 100,000 monthly visitors it was able to approach a number of advertising sales houses for them to take the site on board as a part of their portfolio, essentially allowing them to sell its inventory on a monthly basis on its behalf.

Once accepted by advertising sales house, Ad 2-one, one of the UK's leading digital agencies, advertisers were soon introduced to the student site and leading brands such as HSBC, Vodafone, T-Mobile, AOL and Sony were using it as a platform to reach the ever growing youth and student marketplace.

Once good revenue streams began to flow and money began to be ploughed back into the site to aid growth, the amount of users continued to increase on a daily basis and with the increase in traffic followed an increase in revenue. With low costs, covering the basics such as office space, wages and web hosting, the student site soon became a profitable online business turning over strong five figure sums every month with the majority either being saved or invested in the future of the online venture.

Investments later made included a new domain name 'Funky.co.uk', a teen site 'WickedColours.com' and the creation of a new student site in Australia 'Studentmax.com.au'.

The new Funky domain was to introduce the latest stages of development for the student site. Once again with a more memorable name and one that was more suited to the target market, a new infrastructure was built offering hotmail style e-mail accounts with 'yourname@funky.co.uk', the ability to see who was online, buddies lists, live chat and an advanced member section controlling all the new features on offer.

With the new site now established and more community focussed, Funky became a more self-sufficient site, with members driving the traffic through interacting with each other, browsing through the members' directory and chatting with new friends and those at their own college or University. The site became so popular at certain colleges that the IT departments banned access due to too many students logging on during lesson times. Certain channels continue to be updated on a daily basis, such as entertainment and competitions but as a rule the users have now become the main content writers through their own interaction.

Through years of development, TheCompleteStudent.co.uk attracting some 3,000 users per month has now grown into a

A page from the Funky.com web site

Reproduced by kind permission of Funky.com.

'Funky' brand achieving well over 500,000 users a month and 5,000,000 page views with site revenues in excess of £15,000 per month from advertising alone. The site continues to grow as the word spreads and Funky.co.uk is now a well-established and trusted brand with both advertisers and students alike. With new additional sister sites such as www.Studentdiscounts .co.uk, www.Studentstories.co.uk and www.Studentjobs.co.uk, with a fifth site (www.Studenthousing.co.uk being launched during 2006), the portfolio of student sites are bonding together with the loyal user-base being distributed over an array of sites providing a one stop shop for student needs online.

Where it will go from here only time can tell, but it has seemed to establish a winning formula through years of trial, error and change.

Questions

1. What factors related to the Internet enable start-up businesses like Funky and how would you research the market?

2. What is the key attraction(/s) to this site for the student audience?

3. How important is it to the site's success to create an online community?

4. Apart from advertising revenues, suggest other possible revenue streams for Funky and its sister operations.

5. What are the advantages and disadvantages to the Funky brand when introducing 'sister' sites?

Reproduced by kind permission of Funky.com.

DISCUSSION QUESTIONS

1. One of the objectives of the marketing philosophy has been to improve standards of living. What advantages and disadvantages does the Internet bring to society?

2. Describe the main challenges faced by marketers in the Internet age. Suggest how they may be addressed.

3. Consider an industry sector, such as travel and tourism, and discuss how the Inetrenet has impacted upon the structure of that sector.

4. How important is the role played by governments in facilitating Internet growth? Discuss.

REFERENCES

Bandyo-padhay, N (2002) *E-commerce, Concepts, Context and Consequences*, McGraw Hill, Maidenhead, Berkshire

Baye, MR, Gatti, R, Kattuman, P & Morgan, J (2002) *Online Pricing and The Euro Changeover: Cross Country Comparisons*, Research Papers in Management Studies, University of Cambridge, Judge Institute of Management, WP 17/2002

Bowen, D (2002) It's too early for e-business to drop its 'e', *Financial Times*, Viewpoint

Brennan, R, Baines, P & Garneau, P (2003) *Contemporary Strategic Marketing*, Palgrave Macmillan, Basingstoke Hampshire, 154

Chaston, I (2001) *E-marketing Strategy*, McGraw Hill, Maidenhead, England, 11

Experian (2001) *Enabling E-business*, White paper, Experian e-series white paper, January 2001

Family Expenditure Survey April 1998–March 2001, Expenditure and Food Survey (April 2001 onwards)

Financial Mail on Sunday, 17 August 2003, 19

Financial Times, 4 November 2003, Move to increase access to remotest inhabitants, 7

Frank Barrett, Travelog, *The Mail on Sunday*, 2 November 2003, 90

Folger (2006) *Coming Soon: The Web Toll*, 15 June 2006
www.popsci.com/popsci/whatsnew/46f84d972e76b010vgnvcm1000004eecbccdrcrd.html

Harris, L & Dennis, C (2002) *Marketing the e-Business*, Routledge, London
www.europe.tiscali.co.uk/business/news/200309/broadband.html

Hughes, T & Stone, M (2002) Practice Paper: The implications of e-commerce for strategy: UK case studies. *Journal of Financial Services Marketing*, Vol 6, No 4, 379–390, Henry Stewart Publications

Jobber, D and Fahy, J (2003) *Foundations of Marketing*, McGraw Hill, Maidenhead, Berkshire, 26

Jutla, D, Bodorik, P & Dhaliwal, J (2002) Supporting the e-business readiness of small and medium sized enterprise: approaches and metrics. *Internet Research: Electronic Networking Applications and Policy*, Vol 12, No 2, 2002, 144, MCB UP Ltd

Kotler, P, Armstrong, G, Saunders, J & Wong, V (2001) *Principles of Marketing*, 3rd European edition, Pearson Education Ltd, Harlow

Labour Force Survey 2002, Full time employees who worked more than 50 hours a week, Office for National Statistics

Mohammed, R et al (2001) *Internet Marketing*, McGraw Hill, New York, 4

Mohammed, R, Fisher, RJ, Jaworski, BJ & Cahill, AM (2002) *Internet Marketing*, McGraw Hill, New York

National Statistics Omnibus Survey, published September 2003.

O'Connor, J, Galvin, E & Evans, M (2004) *Electronic Marketing*, FT Prentice Hall, Harlow, England, 10

Perry Gourley, *Scotland on Sunday*, Business, 19 October 2003, 2

Philips, P, *E-Business Strategy* (2003) McGraw Hill Higher Education, Maidenhead, Berkshire, 1

Porter, M (2001) Strategy and the Internet, *Harvard Business Review*, March 2001

Rayport, RE & Jaworski, BJ (2001) *Introduction to E-commerce*, McGraw Hill Higher Education, New York, 4

Smith, PR & Chaffey, D (2002) *EMarketing Excellence*, Butterworth Heinemann, Oxford, 11

Strauss, J et al (2003) *E-Marketing*, 3rd edition, Prentice Hall, Upper Saddle River, NJ, 2

The Newcastle Journal, Business Focus, 4 May 2003, 22

Turban, E, Kind, D, Lee, J, Warkentin, M & Chung, HM (2002) *Electronic Commerce – A Management Perspective*, Pearson Education Inc, Upper Saddle River, New Jersey

Wind, Y, Mahajan, V & Gunther, RE (2002) *Convergence Marketing*, FT Prentice Hall, Upper Saddle River, NJ

www.europe.tiscali.co.uk/business/survey/200310/kids.html
www.e-envoy.gov.uk/Estrategy/ActionPlanArticle/fs/en? CONTENT_ID=400048.../G
www.silicon.com/management/govern..../0,39024677,39116684,00.html?nl=2003103

www.theregister.co.uk/content/22/32822.html
www.yahoo.client.shareholder.com/press/ReleaseDetail.cfm?ReleaseID=196082, *Yahoo! and OMD Study Reveals Online Research Plays Critical Role in Consumers Offline Purchases; Online Price Comparisons and 'Communal Shopping' Create Trust and Drive Decision Making*, 11 May 2006

FURTHER READING

For a fuller discussion of key technologies visit *E-commerce* by N Bandyo-padhay (2002), chapter 5, Communications Infrastructure for Commerce, 91–131.

Web Metrics by Jim Sterne is an in-depth insight into the measurement of e-business and the creative use of the data generated.

For those contemplating 'getting started' on the web, a very accessible and informative read is *Planning Your Internet Strategy* by Dr Ralph Wilson, 2002, John Wiley & Sons, New York.

The 2006 E-readiness Rankings, a White Paper from the *Economist* Intelligence Unit, www.eiu.com/2006eReadinessRankings

Read the *Financial Times* on a Tuesday

WEB LINKS

For UK online policy and frameworks visit **www.e-envoy.gov.uk** and **www.ukonline.gov.uk**

For up to date information on UK national, regional and local government e-business activity visit the E-government bulletins at **www.headstar.com**

For information on web trends and industry reports visit **www.nua.com**, **www.forrester.com** and **www.cyberatlas.com**

For Internet marketing information on new media, strategy, promotion and related developments visit **www.mad.co.uk**, **www.marketing-online.co.uk**, **www.silicon.com** and **www.theregister.co.uk**

For information on the history of the Internet various 'timelines' are offered, the most comprehensive is probably Hobbes' at **www.zakon.org**.

For a history of search engine marketing visit **www.iprospect.com**

Web Analytics and Web Statistics from WebTrends, the worldwide leader in web analytics **www.webtrends.com**

 Visit the Online Resource Centre which accompanies this book, for lots of interesting additional material, including self-assessment questions, internet exercises, and links for each chapter: **www.oxfordtextbooks.co.uk/orc/gay/**

Strategy and Models for the Virtual World

2

2.1 Introduction

It is widely acknowledged that the Internet has revolutionised and restructured many sectors of industry and provided a new focus for their activities. The Internet has generated opportunities and challenges for existing businesses and new entrants dealing in new direct relationships with customers. In the supply chain, new intermediaries have emerged whilst others have been replaced. New business models have emerged to show how an organisation may apply new technology to achieve competitive advantage and revenue generation. The new models must address how customer satisfaction and value will be achieved. Let us start this chapter by considering how the web has impacted upon a traditional UK operation:

MINI CASE 2.1 The Internet facilitates a change in strategic direction for Bagga Menswear

Sometimes you have to take a step back in order to move forward and this is exactly what Dave Lomax did with his designer fashion business. Bagga Menswear focuses on the top labels like Armani, Diesel and G-Star. In March 2004 he sold off his premier shop in Bexley Heath, Kent, just retaining a smaller high street presence in Chislehurst. This freed him to put his energy into building up the web business, www.baggamenswear.co.uk. In 2005 Bagga is expected to turn over £500,000 in total. This is 20% up on the pure high street sales model, and immensely more profitable due to the lower overheads of the web store (down by £130,000 pa).

Dave saw a gap in the market for a designer menswear store in Bexley Heath, where rents were low following the ravages of the recession. Thus Bagga was born in April 1994. By 1998 it had doubled in size, and continued to grow despite the Bluewater Shopping Centre opening only six miles away. 'By 2000 I was able to open a second shop in Chislehurst, and in 2002 Bagga won the accolade of FHM Small Retailer of the Year. We are respected in the industry and known for an eclectic mix of household names plus some virtually unknown brands whose profile we work hard to enhance.'

Dave decided to test out the potential of the Internet as a sales channel. In 2002 he commissioned an e-commerce site under a 'rental' agreement with the web designers that avoided upfront development costs. He explains, 'For two years the site generated a good additional income, but had limitations in design and functionality. With the proven success of the "test" site we decided to commission a totally new web store using Actinic Business. It has a host of features that are invaluable, particularly the discount pricing and coupon facilities. The order processing is easy and clear while the reports, invoicing and email facilities are very helpful in the day-to-day operation of the e-store.' Another key attraction for Dave was the scope the software had to grow with the business.

The stylish new site was launched in May 2004 following an investment of £14,000. It is maintained and updated by Dave himself. By Christmas it was the most profitable side of the business and now contributes 60% of total turnover.

Like the high street shop, the site sells around 500 lines and specialises in clothing and footwear from Armani, Diesel and G-Star. Prices go from £10 for a pair of socks to £700 for a leather jacket and orders are shipped worldwide. Online sales are up to 70 per week with an average value of £95.

Dave recognises the importance of differentiating Bagga. 'Unlike most sites selling similar products on the web, we are bona fide stockists of all products, with no end-of-line or grey market imports. We also instil confidence in our customers with our long term high street presence,' he says and adds, 'The manufacturers are still very wary of online sales, because of issues about protecting their brand. That's why I have worked hard to create a site that represents each label authentically.'

As ever, marketing is also key, and Dave has shunned the affiliate approach as too costly, but is getting impressive results with direct marketing company, PDV and its data collection service. 'You pay to pose a question that helps to qualify the leads coming through,' Dave explains. 'Entrants go into a prize draw for an Armani bag or something supplied by Bagga. In the first trial we got 5,500 leads in only two weeks for a grand. The subsequent mailing we did increased traffic by 100% for a short period, and has substantially increased the database for future mailings.'

Japan is the next target market because of their love of designer labels. Dave is researching how to market there. So far pay-per-click advertising, which works well here, is not working on the Japanese search engines, so the next step is to find the equivalent to *FHM* magazine to try traditional advertising to drive young men to the Bagga site.

Dave Lomax of Bagga Menswear (www.baggamenswear.co.uk)

Dave feels that e-commerce has certainly benefited his business by 'generating a new income stream and enhancing the turnover of our high street shop. The products we sell are in high demand but tightly distributed, and it is relatively easy to capitalise on this demand through our site. And overall life is much easier now with fewer staff and less overheads.'

www.baggamenswear.co.uk
www.actinic.co.uk

Various observers have deemed electronic commerce (EC) as *the* critical business imperative as it has evolved and matured since the mid-nineties. Internet technologies have enabled optimised business performance through streamlining and integration. The Internet provides the capability to outperform competitors whilst servicing customers more efficiently and effectively. The online transition and integration has not always been easy and has resulted in a steep learning curve for net entrepreneurs and established high street retailers alike as they strive to develop strategies for the 'The New Economy'.

The Internet has triggered a diverse range of new business models and strategic frameworks to shape the way organisations 'do business'. For some businesses, their online activities have been part of an evolving adoption of direct marketing digital technologies, whilst some retailers needed to evaluate their sustainability in light of the changing marketplace. For the new entrants, the pure players and visionaries, they have had the perceived advantage of starting with a blank sheet to develop, adopt or adapt new e-business models to satisfy the diverse segments of new online buyers of products and services.

2.2 Internet relationships

Kinder (2002) observes that online transactions and broader interactivity can entail relations between a minimum of three parties:

1. private businesses (B)
2. public administrations (PA)
3. consumers and citizens (C).

In Table 2.1, the different forms of e-commerce transactions within different business sectors are outlined.

Table 2.1 Range of e-commerce business transactions

Business Sectors	Sector Characteristics
B2B Business to business	Estimates of 70–80% of Internet business value, especially in US. Major growth area as companies seek procurement and transaction efficiencies
B2C Business to customers	Predominantly 'buy' with some bidding, commission and 'name your price' transactions. Relies on search engines and price comparison sites for Search, Assessment and Transaction (SAT) buyer decision-making process
B2PA Business to public administration	Makes electronic use of traditional public tendering Efficient downloading of tender documents, more suppliers bid results in greater competition, encouraged by both UK government and EU
PA2PA Public administration to public administration	Driven by government agenda for online business and learning (e-envoy and e-government initiatives) Importance in driving ICT initiatives forward both in public and private sectors
PA2C Public administration to customers or citizens	Providing e-commerce and e-services at local regional and national authority levels. Has potential for democracy issues, eg speed up voting on planning issues
C2C Direct exchange between consumers	Consumer initiated buys and bids with other consumers, though often through an intermediary like eBay

Adapted from Kinder (2002), European Journal of Innovation Management, Volume 5, Number 3, 2002.

We can also include the 'Not-for-profit-sector' such as charities and pressure groups that benefit significantly from the Internet for campaign publicity, membership recruitment and revenue generation.

Whatever the model or framework employed, organisations must test and evaluate what impact their chosen model may have on their relationships with their different customers or 'publics'. For example, how will online auctions in the B2B sector impact on long-standing relations with key suppliers? Business commentators have suggested there is a need to reassess or rethink the way organisations operate. Does our new model add value or differentiate our activities in a way that appeals to existing customers and potential prospects? Does our model generate significant efficiencies that we could pass on, or does it allow us to reach out into new markets when we have previously been constrained by geographic limits? It is virtually impossible to think of any sector that remains untouched by the emergence of the Internet and the implementation of new technologies. In this chapter we will explore various frameworks and strategies put forward by academics and practitioners and how online players have implemented them. The chapter will consider the success stories and failures and will pay particular attention to the retail sector and the development of e-tailing.

2.3 Dot.com flashbacks

There have been many words written on the expansionist and extravagant days of the dot.com Internet infancy. Some strategists may say that it is unwise to look back – what is done is done. Other strategists look back on history and value both the positive and negative events that have occurred and their consequences. Identifying the reasons for success and failure is vital for future planning. Within the context of this online marketing book, it is a valuable part of the strategic process to re-visit and reflect on the period from 1997–2000 before the bubble of e-optimism was burst. The period may be hard to imagine for a new generation of online e-marketers emerging from higher education institutions on a diet of Internet and multi-channel success stories. Seasoned observers and practitioners may also find this 'flashback' allows them to assess their progress to date.

The Internet revolution of the late nineties created such wild optimism and frenzy that it was likened to a Klondyke gold rush with a diverse range of prospectors seeking fame and fortune. It was envisaged that the revolution would change business practices and lead to a gender neutral, teleworking society (Verdin 2002) but it has never quite delivered what it promised, yet. The enthusiasm and opportunism of the new breed however, has been encapsulated in Proddow's (2000) testimonial to the innovators, *Heroes.com – the names and faces behind the dot.com era*. In the foreword to the text, Taylor commented on the new business leaders saying that 'they also know that in the Internet economy David can challenge Goliath, that brand dominance in the physical world can be challenged and that the physical assets of the traditional bricks can quickly become liabilities in a virtual world where speed and flexibility are vital. They are committed to the vision of the Internet economy, to open standards and to customer power. They are the driving forces behind top websites like Yahoo!, QXL and Amazon. Some may well turn out to be the Rockerfellers and Bransons of the Internet economy; others will fade into obscurity after their 15 seconds of fame. But what is beyond doubt is that they are all helping to re-write the conventional rules of doing business and defining new business models for the future.' The anticipation and excitement generated by the new breed pre-2000 who transformed business practices and office culture has been superseded by a more measured integration of online and offline channels. Whilst there were undoubtedly influential 'heroes' such as Michael Dell (Dell Computers), Jeff Bezos (Amazon) and Brent Hoberman (Lastminute.com) to commend, there have also been a few villains around whose business plans were flawed or flimsy, lifestyles excessive and the investors' slush fund of dollars and pounds too readily available. For example, it is claimed that the US online grocery retailer Webvan used up some $800m in just over two years before its collapse. Similarly, boo.com managed to burn a hole in some $130m of investors' money.

The pain of the dot.com and subsequent dot.bomb era, shook the confidence of many expectant investors and venture capitalists. Many remained jittery for three years after the crash. However, since then more durable and sustainable business models have evolved and emerged as the marketing and IT functions began working together. Perhaps the bubble burst in 2000 was a defining moment in web adolescence as it forced online exponents to re-evaluate the relevance of their objectives, tactics and performance. The unrealistic expectations of many early net entrepreneurs changed the power balance from seller to buyer as new pricing and distribution models undermined existing frameworks. Blaming dot.com failures on the extravagances and new age business cultures of the high profile casualties like Clickmango and Boo (for an eloquent case on Boo.com read Brassington & Petitt, pp 1094–5) has been easy. However from a marketer's perspective there were a number of fundamental problems with many new entrants:

- overestimating demand;
- underestimating promotional costs needed for brand building;
- over-reliance on few revenue streams;
- poor business plans with no clear strategic vision;
- target markets not adequately defined;
- basic failures to respond to enquiries eg e-mail and missing out on the benefits of interactivity and connectivity;
- poor fulfilment strategies and implementation;
- short-term objectives to meet demands of venture capitalists;
- being over-ambitious eg setting up in several countries at once;
- failing to reassure customers regarding security and trust;
- poor customer service, especially online;
- implementation of technology and web site design lacking customer focus.

The **bricks and mortar** companies who moved online had the priceless advantage of a track record to instil confidence. However, they still had to analyse how they would integrate the Internet with their existing activities. Nevertheless, most top ten league tables of popular web sites predominantly feature familiar high street names rather than dot.com firms.

Some of the failure factors raised above will be discussed in chapter 3 along with the problems of strategic Internet integration in the e-marketing planning process.

MINI CASE 2.2 The Boxman lessons

European CD retailer, Boxman.com finally collapsed in 2002 prior to launching its IPO. It was a high profile failure like the Boo.com and Clickmango crash but in a rather different context.

Boo ignored all of the business fundamentals, even by dot.com standards. Boxman did not. It had strong managers in place, good cost control and a workable business model, but it was blinded by ambition and, like so many other Internet companies, it failed to assess and manage risk. It was heavily dependent upon shareholders for financial support. The shareholders, influenced by optimistic market sentiment and high share values, actively encouraged the European expansion. However, first year profitability in a phase of rapid expansion is virtually impossible – but the marketplace was thinking short-term and sought immediate profits.

- What if demand did not grow at planned rates?
- What if competition was fiercer than anticipated?

Aiming to become Europe's number one CD retailer, Boxman tried to launch simultaneously in eight countries. That multiplied brand development and operational costs without a platform for expansion, creating unsustainable cash flow problems when market sentiment turned following the crash in Internet stock valuations. This was despite attracting one million customers across the EU.

Hindsight is a wonderful thing, but it is vital to learn the right lessons from the Boxman crash.

By comparison, other e-tailers such as ThinkNatural.com have limited their risk by initially focussing only on the UK and by selling through other channels like mail order and in shops – in ThinkNatural's case via a deal with the high street health and beauty retailer, Superdrug – as well as online.

The Boxman demise did not illustrate that online retailing was not feasible but rather that many organisations lacked the financial resources in a slowly evolving marketplace that failed to deliver its promise. The commercial expectation raced ahead of consumer commercial Internet adoption.

Adapted from: *Financial Mail on Sunday*, 15 December 2002
www.executive.lv/internet_boom
www.bathwick.com, The Bathwick Group, Internet Research Company, Founder and Chairman, John Steel.

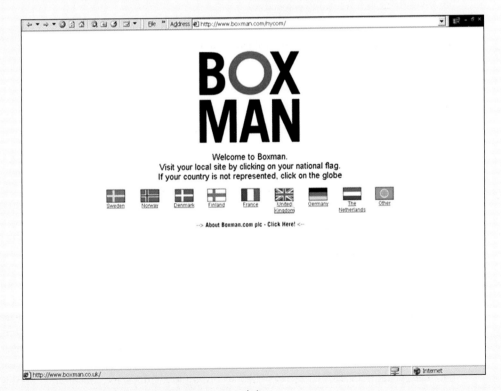

The welcome page of the original Boxman.com website

2.4 Strategy

The planning process in both marketing and corporate strategy often applies military-style terminology to reflect the strategic approaches taken by organisations. 'Attack' and 'defensive' strategies clearly rely on objective assessments of the players and environments interacting in the marketplace. When considering e-marketing, and broader e-business strategy, the planning tools applied by marketers for decades still have an important role to play in formulating an organisation's future business path. Brennan et al (2003) argue that many contemporary academics believe that few differences exist between the physical and virtual environment when it comes to the construction of marketing plans. The marketing audit, SWOT Analysis, Porter's five forces and so on continue to provide useful analytical frameworks to snapshot the internal and external environments that impact upon activities and performance. For example, the list of issues below – by no means an exhaustive one – might need serious consideration for a business setting out its 'e' or multi-channel strategy:

- The rate of net adoption by traditional customer segments
- The impact of new market entrants
- Changes in the 'supply chain' perhaps where manufacturers can go 'direct' and cut out intermediaries
- Increased competition in both domestic and transnational markets
- The impacts of existing and future technological changes to remain competitive from both an investment and training perspective

Strategic tools like Ansoff's Matrix, sometimes referred to as the Growth Vector Matrix, may also provide a helpful focus for an organisation planning its 'e-path'. Darby et al (2003) illustrate how Internet related tools could achieve various growth strategies in Fig 2.1 below.

- Market Penetration, eg by superior online customer service
- Product Development, eg new trading exchanges to existing markets
- Market Development, eg reaching new markets by online selling
- Diversification, eg customisation of industry specific products

These and many other wide-ranging issues have an effect on an organisation's trading relationships and processes, and ultimately their success or failure in the digital economy. The danger lies in the gap between the pace of technological innovations and the pace of cultural evolution amongst existing and potential web customers. Technological developments can leave all but the most IT literate consumers trailing where the technology is more product rather than customer oriented. Arnott and Bridgewater (2002) stated that 'the current failure to capitalise on the Internet's interactive potential does not relate to the inexperience of the Internet marketers but points to the fundamental difficulties in establishing fruitful interactions on the Internet . . . may relate to the reluctance on the part of the consumer to engage in this type of relationship.' By 2006, online customer confidence had improved significantly. For example, in a sample of small and medium businesses selling online, respondents reported an average 80% increase in turnover for November and December 2005, compared with the same two months in 2004. A similar rise was reported last year when comparing sales with Christmas 2003 according to e-commerce consultants, Actinic (2006).

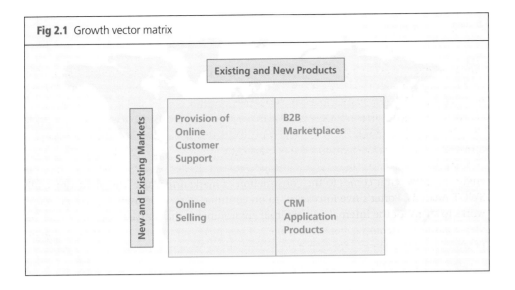

Fig 2.1 Growth vector matrix

Some Internet pioneers were more visionary in their technological applications for their own satisfaction rather than for that of the customer. Before broadband, it was no good having an award winning, full graphics, Shockwave, Macromedia Real Player site if it took an eternity to download. Some observers criticised Dell's conservative rate of innovation, but Michael Dell replied by arguing that it is no good introducing leading edge technology for the sake of it unless it provides real customer benefits. That is, after all, what marketing is supposed to deliver – customer benefits!

Any modern business model has to address technological issues such as the efficiency of the distribution channels, database applications, and a fully integrated and secure search engine receptive site. When formulating objectives, strategies and tactics it is imperative that the technology is applied with the customer in mind such as:

- Ease of site navigation
- Fast access to product information
- Ease of ordering and payment processing
- Effective distribution networks including order tracking for transparency
- Added value through speed, flexibility, interactivity and convenience

The strategies devised will depend upon each organisation's level of Internet maturity, adoption and level of integration. We will now consider two similar frameworks that are useful in identifying the key stages of Internet development.

First, Chaffey et al (2000) proposed six organisational options or levels for web presence in Fig 2.2.

At Level 0, perhaps an organisation may feel that it can survive successfully from its offline activities or it may adopt the ostrich approach to the web and hope it goes away. At Level 1, an organisation may be contemplating web involvement and safeguard an appropriate domain name by registration for the future. At Level 2 companies often just replicate their offline catalogues or brochures online, hence the term 'brochurewear'. Any customer contacts will usually be handled offline and the degree of online interaction will be negligible. Level 3 provides a basic level of Internet interaction with the use of e-mail for enquiries and

---

Fig 2.2 Levels of web presence

Level 0	No web site or presence on the web
Level 1	The web presence is minimal, with a listing of a domain name but no web site developed
Level 2	First level basic web site emerges with standard information on the company and its products
Level 3	Similar to the previous level except at this stage a basic level of site interaction exists via e-mail for enquiries and other product related details but no transactions could take place
Level 4	The site is developed to handle sales transactions
Level 5	The site is fully interactive with all stages of the buying process integrated

---

Fig 2.3 The first consulting group

Stages of Internet Business Development/Maturity

Stage 1: Publish Build Web awareness and presence with customers and employees primarily by publishing static information, eg company profile, marketing information, and news.

Stage 2: Interact Engage the community by providing relevant information and enabling the community to interact with the site and organisation (eg, online provider directory, search formulary, interact with member services).

Stage 3: Transact Deploy robust self-service capabilities and online transactions (eg, online enrolment, online referral processing, claims submission).

Stage 4: Integrate the automation of numerous transactions in an effort to automate entire business functions (eg, online medical management).

Stage 5: Transform the entire enterprise through seamlessly integrating all processes though end-to-end web-based interactions with customers and business partners.

---

orders, though the organisation is more likely to rely on other traditional forms of contact such as personal selling and telesales operators for handling transactions. At Level 4 a reasonable level of online customer service will also be developed via Frequently Asked Questions (FAQs) or other methods such as links to telephone support lines to supplement online ordering. Level 5 represents the full integration of e-business functions such as customer service, promotion, database marketing, transactions, fulfilment and invoicing online. The degree of integration with offline activities may be determined by the business activity and customer demands for flexible options via customisation, individualisation and multi-channel marketing.

Cited in Informatics-Review (2000), the US leading healthcare and pharmaceutical consultancy, the First Consulting Group (FCG) provides us with an interesting alternative in Fig 2.3. They developed a five-stage common framework for application in the sector that outlines the progressive 'Stages of Internet Business Development/Maturity'.

Each developmental stage reflects the dynamic progress of the Internet as each stage becomes more sophisticated, technologically driven and customer oriented. At Stage 1, they emphasise the need to make employees as well as customers aware of their web presence. Internal communications play an important role in generating support for 'e' developments at this stage. It is also imperative to have all customer facing staff aware of the **web content** to provide a more seamless marketing effort. Stage 2 encourages the 'engagement' of the community by providing relevant information and this can provide a point of differentiation for many web sites as they extend their content beyond the basic. At Stage 3, the deployment of 'robust' self-service capabilities online facilitates brand loyalty. Many early sites failed in this domain and fell woefully short of customers' service expectation levels.

Academically, it can be convenient to neatly fit such developments into distinct stages but in reality the transitions will be blurred. However, the models may help firms in identifying their progress and planning their next stage more effectively.

2.5 Business models for the modern economy

The term 'business model' became part of the 'new economy' language. As Carton (2002) observes, 'If there's one thing there's been no shortage of since business started moving to the Web, it's business models!' Prior to this, it was rarely heard in speeches or seminal texts of leading management gurus or other authorities, with the exception of Porter's Value Chain model, so what is a business model and how can an Internet firm 'add value'? Turban et al (2002) describes a business model as 'a method of doing business by which a company can generate revenue to sustain itself. The model spells out how the company is positioned in the value chain'. Elliot (2002) states, 'business models specify the relationships between participants in a commercial venture, the benefits and costs to each and the flows of revenue'. Elliot simplifies the business model challenge with the basic equation:

$$PROFITS = revenue - costs$$

It is best not to over-complicate issues and that is fundamentally what will determine the sustainability of the online existence. The underlying capabilities and implementation of superior marketing and technology applications allied to the changing needs of their chosen marketplace are also paramount.

Philips (2003) describes an e-business model as 'a system, how the pieces of a business fit together with an emphasis on competition and organisational dynamics.' This definition reinforces the focus on the integration of internal and external processes that enable mutually beneficial relationships between customer and organisation.

Various writers have endeavoured to categorise the main revenue generating models of the new online **marketspace**. For the purposes of this text we will consider the work of Paul Timmers (1999) who outlines the most common models that have emerged. The models illustrate the structural opportunities generated by the Internet and the level of innovation and ingenuity employed by the leading players.

1. **e-shops** – typically online retailers such as www.amazon.com and www.waterstones. co.uk in the B2C sector are seeking revenue from selling online, advertising and new markets whilst driving costs, eg procurement and inventory, down in their UK partnership.

2. **e-malls** – which provide a virtual shopping centre. Groups of e-tailers congregate here to pull in online traffic; these can be extremely beneficial for smaller companies with limited promotional budgets. The e-malls can be hosted by one player which may encourage use of its facility or product, eg Egg and its credit card or a specialist mall like

Fig 2.4 Raceclubs.com – an example of an online community (www.raceclubs.com)

www.spartium.com the US gift mall. The UK Shopping City (www.ukshops.co.uk) is populated by over 100 leading retailers and financial institutions. Many e-malls not only provide an umbrella for merchants but they may provide finance and delivery facilities.

3. **e-procurement** – changes the purchasing process for many in the B2B and public sector, often aggregating buyer power to drive down costs. Probably the most famous is the US-based automotive buying group, www.covisint.com.

4. **e-auctions** – where the age-old process of bidding for goods has gone online to widen its appeal. The eBay model has been a global success and is now one of the most recognised international brands. In the UK, leading IT reseller, DABS.com run a successful auction site www.dabsxchange.com. Online auctions occur in both the B2C sector and increasingly, the B2B sector as organisations become familiar with the online auction protocols.

5. **Virtual communities** – where groups of like-minded people and organisations congregate together to develop their knowledge, exchange information or pursue their hobbies or interests, such as www.chinatown-online.co.uk, www. yorkshiredales.net, or www.raceclubs.com (see Fig 2.4). Revenue comes from membership or subscriptions fees, and where possible advertising and sponsorship. The community of virtual racehorse owners has grown considerably over the past 12 months. Raceclubs.com launched a number of community enhancements to the game in mid-2006 to improve

its social networking elements. New enhancements will include player blogs, private chat-rooms, member profiles and distribution of content via RSS feeds.

6. **Collaboration platforms** – where providers of software tools and an information environment enable collaboration between businesses. It is difficult for one organisation to keep up to speed with the emerging technologies, hence partnerships and collaboration are essential as companies become more specialised in their area of expertise. An example is the Sun Microsystems (www.sun.com) collaborative business platform, Sun One, that provides 'dynamic, real-time collaborative services to help increase productivity, efficiency and satisfaction for employees, partners and customers. The system incorporates the sharing of e-mail, task management, instant and group messaging, content, knowledge and consultancy sharing'.

7. **Third-party marketplaces** – are where intermediaries take over the marketing role on the web and provide an interface between buyers and sellers and carry out functional roles like logistics, ordering and fulfilment and branding. For example www.commerceone.net provides e-commerce solutions such as its Supplier Relationship Management suite (SRM) for reducing supply cost and increasing efficiency across organisational spending cycles with supply partners. Elliot (2002) states that third party marketplaces enable aggregation of customer demand and allows basic web presence without the cost or time commitments.

8. **Value chain integrators** – where organisations offer services across the value chain and integrate them to form strategic alliances. Visit www.semi.org for value chain integration on the semi-conductor industry. In the UK, the Defence Diversification Agency (www.dda.org) utilises technology transfer to enhance the competitiveness of UK defence firms in global markets. The enhanced information flows produce added value for the partner institutions.

9. **Value chain service providers** – offer specialist services or specific functions within the value chain. For example, there may be a number of providers in the holiday industry, such as airlines, hotels, insurance companies and so on, who form partnerships and alliances to promote each other's activities and increase site traffic. Alternatively, e-payments processing (VISA) or logistics provision (Federal Express) provide the expertise in the value chain.

10. **Information brokerage** – the Internet is an incredible source of information and is fast and accessible. Brokering information has become big business often on a subscription or pay-per-use model such as online newspapers (www.ft.com) and market information services like Mintel (in Fig 2.5) (www.mintel.com). Other sites provide comparison tools such as www.kelkoo.com or www.moneysupermarket.com

11. **Trust and other services** – provide important digital peace of mind through the use of trust services such as those offered by Verisign (www.verisign.com), Thawte (www.thawte.com) and the former Which Web Trader scheme. Digital certificates are now becoming commonplace and verify a merchant's authenticity though the take up on Public Key Infrastructure has been slow. Client and company security is vital for confidence in the web as a transactional channel including intranet and extranets.

Timmers (1999) has categorised the business models applying two criteria, the level of functional integration and the degree of innovation needed as the models move further away from a traditional business model (see Fig 2.6).

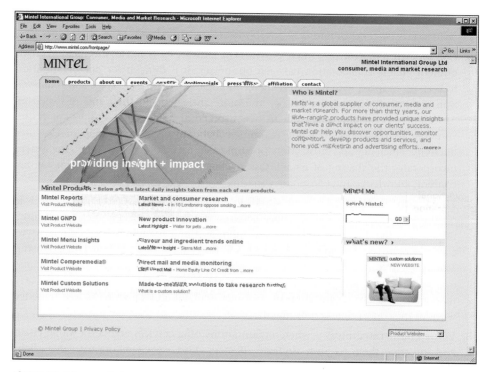

Fig 2.5 Mintel screenshot

Reproduced by Kind permission of Mintel International Group Ltd.

The principal purpose of any business model is to generate revenue. For the online business, the creation of sustainable revenue streams requires creativity and vision to develop appropriate business models. E-business models generate revenue from a number of broad streams such as sales, advertising, subscriptions and commission.

- Sales – typically through online retailing
- Advertising – eg selling advertising space for banner ads
- Subscriptions – eg in publishing media for paid content
- Commission – eg paid to affiliates for generating revenue streams to the reseller's web site

We can categorise the main revenue-based models as follows:

Advertising

Many of the early web models were heavily dependent upon additional revenue expected from advertising on their sites. However as Wilson (2002) points out, the rapid expansion in the number of commercial web sites is outstripping the demand for online advertising, with many carrying no paid adverts. Consequently, the revenue generated was less than anticipated. The backlash from the 'dot.bomb' era led to severe restrictions on online advertising budgets. However, the growth in broadband and the legal downloading of music and gaming has stimulated greater investment in online advertising.

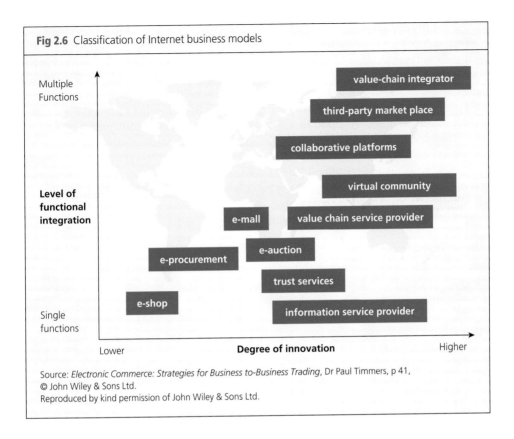

Fig 2.6 Classification of Internet business models

Source: *Electronic Commerce: Strategies for Business to-Business Trading*, Dr Paul Timmers, p 41, © John Wiley & Sons Ltd.
Reproduced by kind permission of John Wiley & Sons Ltd.

Typically, the web site owner will charge for advertising on their site usually in the form of **banner advertising**, **interstitials** (pop-ups) and **superstitials** (activated by a user-action), or permanent buttons shown on every page. The revenue generated will naturally depend upon the marketplace and the audience. Afuah and Tucci (2003) suggest two routes to online success. First, the volume-based approach where the larger the audience, the more advertisers will be willing to pay higher rates. This mimics TV advertising with higher costs for prime time slots. For example, rates are high for the Yahoo! **portal** due to the large volume of potential customers visiting. The second model derives revenue from the more precisely targeted affluent audience where the advertiser is willing to pay premium rates to reach more responsive prospects. For example, Motley Fool (www.fool.co.uk) has a highly motivated group of investment savvy visitors to its UK site and thus attracts advertising from many leading financial institutions. Online advertising has also become more targeted and relevant through **search engine marketing** with the likes of **query-based paid placements** and **content-targeted advertising**.

Sales

The sales revenue model is based on actual online sales and as more people gravitate towards the Internet, its importance as a model will grow. The B2B sector has accounted for around 80% of online transactions, largely due to the relentless drive for cost efficiencies and competitive advantage. However, the growth in consumer (B2C) online sales volume is growing and making a significant contribution to the total revenue of established organisations such as Tesco. According to Jupiter Research (www.jupiterresearch.com), there will be over 200 million Internet users in Europe by 2007. This signifies a 68% increase from 2001. Jupiter Research forecasts that the European online population will grow at a compound annual growth rate (CAGR) of 11% over the next four years, before falling to a CAGR of 9%. Both research group reports illustrate the significant and sustained anticipated growth. A PriceWaterhouseCoopers report, 'Global Entertainment and Media Outlook: 2005–2009' forecast that the growth of broadband would boost the value of the global entertainment and media industries to $1.8 trillion (£990 billion) by 2009. The legal distribution of online music, videos and games will prompt increased consumer spending. In addition, broadband has triggered a revival in online advertising.

The sales revenue model can be broken down into two main categories:

Manufacturing model

This can incorporate products and service 'manufacture'. Both take advantage of the web's ability to go direct to the customer. For example, most of the leading UK-based personal computer manufacturers, like Mesh, Evesham and Dell offer customised purchasing on the Internet. This revenue model follows the cost-plus pricing method with raw materials, components and sub-assemblies bought in and assembled to produce a final product. The product is then sold at a profit with the Internet as a channel offering value through improved efficiency, better customer service or convenience. Intangible services linked to the travel and tourism sector use the Internet as their primary sales and distribution channel. Companies like Easyjet, Ryannair, Lastminute and Ebookers are typical of the new online players but we also see the traditional players like Lufthansa and Thomas Cook growing the Internet as a sales revenue model. Licensing of products, such as software, is another model.

Subscription model

This is another traditional offline revenue model that lends itself online through the low fulfilment costs offered by the Internet. The usual process is for the subscriber to pay a charge for a specified time period, a month or a quarter, for a flat rate service for unlimited usage or for different levels of content. Metered models were used originally by Internet Service Providers (ISPs). The viability of other subscription models relating to online newspapers and digital music services has received considerable attention with tailored packages to suit customers for valued content. Media groups struggling to generate online advertising revenue and cope with cyclical spending, view subscriptions as a key way to smooth out cash flows. Whilst businesses accepted paying for market-related content, the same cannot be said of the public who enjoyed free content in the early years. Consumers are slowly accepting payment for content but providers have to balance what will be free and what is deemed important enough to attach charges to it. The *Wall Street Journal*, for example, commands ever-increasing revenues from corporate America.

Napster shook the music industry providing consumers with file sharing and downloading technologies. The response from the big music companies was a raft of lawsuits to try and close the market before it took off, as they feared loss of profits and control. Rather reluctantly they began making music available but still restricting availability to new providers like Pressplay, MusicNet and Listen.com. It was difficult to get full albums with high prices charged for new material from major artists and 'burning' usually limited to a few tracks per month. This has all changed dramatically with user-friendly distribution through the likes of the iTunes Music Store.

Referral model (or as it is more commonly known, **Affiliate marketing**)

This works thanks to the connectivity of the Internet. Revenue is generated by promoting and linking one site to another. With one click, the consumer is directed to the associate's site and income is calculated usually on the basis of sales or leads generated per month. Basic web metrics such as pay-per-click, pay-per-sales and pay-per-lead determine the revenue earned. The model provides an inexpensive low risk method of promotion, brand exposure, and traffic and income generation. The affiliate is supported by promotional material in the form of banner adverts and text links, and commission can vary between 3–20%.

This is an attractive tool for both parties and is used by an increasing band of merchants seeking more traffic and sales. For examples of affiliate schemes visit www.ukaffiliates.com. For any cost conscious business, the fundamental advantage of affiliate marketing is that no commission is paid without results being achieved, unlike other forms of promotion.

Intermediation model (sometimes referred to as the **Brokerage model**)

This is based on the impact that the Internet has on the value and supply chain and the revenues generated through the exchange of products and services. However, intermediaries are 'middlemen' and so broker buying and selling, for a fee or commission, in a range of models. The original expectation was that online businesses would do away with the need for traditional intermediaries and bypass them going straight to the end-user and eliminating a cost layer. This became known as **disintermediation**. Whilst this has occurred in a number of sectors, a new raft of intermediaries or **infomediaries** have emerged who have become vital in the flow of digital information and bring together diverse and geographically spread buyers and sellers saving the consumer time and money. This is referred to as **Reintermediation** or **Hypermediation**. Turban et al (2002) suggest two types of intermediaries exist within electronic commerce, namely matching and providing information, and value added services such as consulting. The Millennium Group (2000) suggests four broad intermediation options:

1. Online brokers eg www.selftrade.co.uk
2. Buyer aggregators eg www.letsbuyit.com
3. Exchange/auction hosts eg www.qxl.com
4. Virtual malls eg www.vassestore.com

Information content can be sold; specialist information can be supplied. In real time, no stock needs to be carried by many intermediaries and transactions are handled instantly for a fee. Intermediation has changed as a result of digital technologies. Organisations have to reassess their role in the buyer/seller relationship. They must also evaluate the required level of technological integration and performance to remain competitive.

We have outlined some of the numerous business models that have emerged since the late nineties and indeed, they have many variants. Most organisations started their online enterprise based on one primary model but for many this was unsustainable. The reality for most organisations is that one revenue stream is inadequate. They now have to implement a number of business models to survive and prosper. For example, many sites will have the sales model, the referral model and the advertising model combined. The organisations that are innovative and constantly refine and redefine their business models will be better placed to meet the challenges of the new marketspace.

2.6 Business categories in the modern economy

Bricks and mortar

This term describes a business that has a physical presence in the real world, as opposed to a virtual presence in the virtual world. Bricks and mortar businesses represent the 'old' or 'traditional' economy where reputations and brands were built over decades and shopping developed into a more sophisticated leisure pursuit. Mohammed et al (2001) state that traditional retailers have certain advantages, such as the physical proximity to their customers, face-to-face customer service, credit handling and the traditional customer shopping experience. Bricks and mortar operations have served local, regional, national and, more recently, international markets. While a substantial number of customers continue to place considerable importance on personal service, social interaction and shopping as a leisure pursuit, the physical environment still has a strong future. This view is in contrast to many observers during the dot.com era who argued that if you were not online you would disappear in three or four years. The UK food retailer, Morrisons continued its impressive expansion, prior to the Safeway takeover, without the need for any online sales unlike its major competitors, Tesco and Asda. It merely has an 'information only' web presence. Similarly, the famous Fenwick (www.fenwick.co.uk) department store has a stylish, yet minimalist site offering basic store contact details, company history and careers information. The company has invested heavily in its store interiors to provide a sophisticated experience. Many bricks and mortar operations have introduced other marketing and distribution channels as consumer and environmental factors change lifestyle and purchasing patterns.

Clicks and mortar

'Clicks and mortar' or 'bricks to clicks' are terms that describe organisations that formerly operated in the physical world and have begun establishing a presence on the Internet. There has been a solid increase in the number of companies who are putting e-commerce at the core of their business operations. They seek to exploit the opportunities provided by the new technologies in terms of reaching new markets and streamlining business processes. However, for many, costs and efficiency are often cited as the main drivers, rather than a visionary approach to the Internet's potential.

Numerous bricks and mortar companies were cautious when it came to adopting an online presence. The lack of an IT champion at board level is often cited for this indolence and complacency. First mover advantage was central to online success for a number of companies, though the downfall of others. Tesco is a prime example of the first mover advantage as they adopted a pioneering attitude to online retailing from the start. This enabled them to distance themselves from their main rivals and they have continued to innovate their site, often with key strategic partnerships.

Fig 2.7 The home page of Charles Tyrwhitt's web site Autumn 2006 (www.ctshirts.co.uk)
Reproduced by kind permission of Charles Tyrwhitt.

Well-established high street retailers and supermarket chains such as Next, Comet, Virgin, Marks and Spencer, Toys R Us and Argos all have substantial online activities making a growing contribution to total turnover. For example, gentlemen's shirt maker, Charles Tyrwhitt made their first tentative steps online in 1997. Internet sales accounted for 28% of total sales in 2003, by 2005 it rose to 36% and it is expected to reach 42% in 2006. The Internet has also enabled Charles Tyrwhitt to enter international markets more easily.

Commenting on encouraging online sales data from the Office for National Statistics on vnunet.com, Meta Group Vice President Jeffrey Mann says the online world is starting to mature. 'Most of the companies that we speak to who sell both offline and online say that their online sales represent between 5 and 10% of their total sales. A lot of the monthly variability has gone.'

Old economy retailers were wary that going online would cannibalise their offline business. However, combining channels is having a positive effect for most companies as they reach new customers, increase brand exposure and benefit from improved systems. Integration with other channels can provide a customer-oriented operation whereby the physical store, telephone and Internet operations provide multiple touch points for the same or different segments.

The traditional companies also have two distinct advantages over new web entrants. First, they already have well-established brands and marketing practices in most cases, though it is

---

MINI CASE 2.3 Teddington Cheese (www.teddingtoncheese.co.uk)

Teddington Cheese started trading on the high street in 1995 as a specialist cheese shop and quickly became known around Middlesex for its excellent range of cheeses and high levels of customer service. However, the shop was highly dependent on passing trade and serving local restaurants. This created peaks and troughs with weekend trade being very busy compared to other times of the week.

Teddington Cheese sought to reach out to new customers to boost profits and smooth out the sales fluctuations. The main objective was to create a groundbreaking cheese experience online. The web site was designed not only to give the user full details on the cheeses, for example, where they originated from, coupled with recommendations for recipes and drinks to accompany specific cheeses. More significantly it sought to have cheese accepted as a gift item.

Local customers can order online and 'call and collect' their freshly cut cheeses when the shop is normally quieter. However, business has taken off with online sales in other parts of the UK, mainland Europe and as far afield as New Zealand. Over 20% of sales are now from export.

Whilst CDs and books lend themselves to Internet distribution, as a dairy product cheese is another matter, so efficient fulfilment is vital. The company will advise customers on how well certain cheeses will travel. The company has now built up a sizeable database and customers receive a regular online newsletter, *Cheesewire* that features new cheeses and special offers amongst its features.

Integrating the Internet and its related processes with its traditional business has been hard work, requiring vision and constant innovation but the endeavour has paid off with a growing customer base, rising sales and a whole host of e-business awards.

---

vital that online brand experience at least replicates the traditional brand experience. Secondly, they have tried and trusted logistics and fulfilment processes in place. Marketers can no longer afford to view the Internet as a discrete channel. The focus in the clicks and mortar category is the traditional retailer making the technological and cultural transition online. However, it is apparent that dot.com pioneers like Amazon are making moves in the opposite direction as they move into physical warehousing to compete with traditional booksellers.

For smaller retailers, the Internet offers great potential to trade beyond traditional geographic boundaries with two revenue streams delivered by the clicks and bricks model. The case of Teddington Cheese emphasises this.

Pure players

Pure players, or 'clicks only' companies, are businesses that operate totally on the Internet with no physical or conventional attributes in the strictest sense (though physical offices and other administrative assets must exist). Some of these developed innovative new operations as infomediaries whilst others turned to new distribution models for existing products such as book selling and airline tickets. These start-up companies were the epitome of the new digital age and the frictionless economy with the adoption of new software and other IT related technologies. Many have now become household names like Amazon, Lastminute, eBay and Yahoo!. Others have become part of the e-commerce debris like Boxman, Clickmango, Boo and Dressmart. In a desperate attempt to gain first mover advantage, many over-extended themselves going into too many markets at once. Massive amounts were spent on marketing as they sought to attract customers, with Boo, for example, being rumoured to have spent £35 million on marketing alone! Quite simply, the failures spent more than they earned. Poor business plans, over-estimated demand, lack of management acumen, atrocious fulfilment records, and IT rather than customer driven approaches have been cited as some of the factors responsible for the dot.com failures. One other glaring omission was the failure to

MINI CASE 2.4 BoysStuff delivers leading Net service standards

BoysStuff Limited, the Wolverhampton based online gadget strore for 'boys' set out in 1997 with a clear mission 'to escape drudgery and boredom through toys' whilst delivering serious fun. The company sought to establish itself as the 'One Stop Shop for Big Boys Toys'. The company prides itself on its innovative and unusual gadget range at competitive prices that appeal to the core 25–34 male. After years of being on the receiving end of bad customer service, co-founder, Richard North was determined from the outset to provide new standards of online customer care unlike many other Internet based companies.

The company is market driven and customer centric. Innovation in terms of web design, product sourcing, promotional activity and customer service drive the company forward to achieve the status of the UK's leading online gadget site. Complacency has not set in and the company continues to reinforce its positioning in the minds of its target with a branding initiative with men's magazine, *FHM*, the ideal readership for BoysStuff. To complement this, a new discrete site merchandising high quality 'erotic goods' has been launched to appeal to the same segment.

Like all leading Internet players, innovation, customer interaction and evolution drive the BoysStuff business as they strive to maintain competitive advantage.

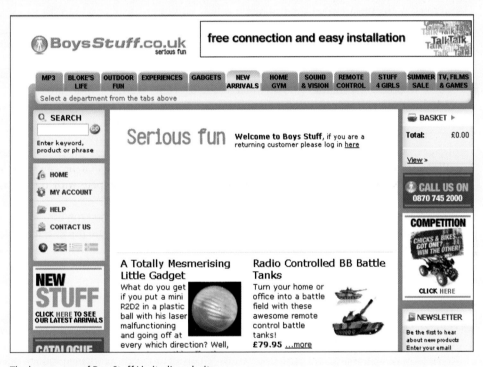

The home page of BoysStuff Limited's web site

Produced by kind permission of BoysStuff (www.boysstuff.co.uk).

realise that the majority of the public were not ready to make the cultural shift to the Internet. The soaring dot.com stock market valuations prior to the NASDAQ collapse on 13 March 2000 meant nothing until the companies starting selling goods and services in meaningful quantities. However, many survived and began to re-evaluate what they were doing, scaling down their operations or becoming involved in merger, acquisition or partnership activities. Most major Internet based players are beginning to achieve acceptable levels of return on investment (ROI). However, the Internet has also provided fertile ground for a number of niche players like Dabs.com, Firebox and Boystuff who have successfully targeted the consumer who is comfortable with the new technology.

Clicks and content

The 'clicks and content' model describes an Internet operation designed to support a business with quality content which assist repeat site visits and **stickiness** for future growth and viability. Licensing or selling content to other sites has become a significant revenue stream for content providers. Many sites buy in feature articles or columns from eminent sources. Content rich sites keep customers and prospects there for longer, increasing the chances of direct purchases or through links. Travel and tourism sites use this to good effect with contributions from travel writers. To enrich sites further they buy in destination guides and weather reports that sit alongside affiliate links with hotel, airlines, travel insurers, 'live' destination web cams and car hire companies.

Probably the most visited site in Europe is BBC Online (www.bbc.co.uk) with its extensive and diverse content, which goes way beyond the boundaries of its programmes and extends into its commercial activities, eg selling archive material and providing educational support.

Another example is the merger between AOL and Time Warner that brought together AOL's technical capabilities and married them to Time Warner's wide-ranging media content. Time Warner owns CNN, amongst other things, and so has major news content advantage over many of its rivals in addition to quality entertainment content.

2.7 Strategic options for retailers

Visionary web advisor Michael de Kare Silver in his text, *e-shock 2000* (2000) proposed 10 strategic options or responses for retailers if they are to survive in the so-called New Economy. Adopting the Internet was viewed as an essential for survival. Whilst the options were formulated in the heady days of the dot.com era, they still are worthy of serious consideration for the 21st century retailer. De Kare Silver emphasises that the options will not condemn the physical store to history but rather shows how they may adapt to the growing levels of interest in **electronic shopping**. The first eight options reflect organisations gravitating toward the new digital channel whilst options nine and 10 suggest how retailers may be creative in attempting to 'buck the trend'. The suggested integration reflects the flexible multi-channel strategies being implemented from 2003. As Rowley (2002) states, 'Integration between the e-business arm and the traditional business' can be considered in relation to functional areas such as:

- Production
- Sourcing
- Logistics
- Marketing
- Human resources
- Investment and funding sources
- Performance criteria

The integration of the online business with traditional business requires careful management of the transitional and evolutionary phases, not to mention a careful assessment of the degree of cannibalisation that may occur.

1. **Information only** – This option recognises the need for some form of web presence as more customers venture online. Many car dealerships offer information on current promotional deals in the hope that it will drive traffic into the showrooms. Similarly, many smaller retailers still just provide standard information online but request customers to contact them by phone or visit their store in person. However, as de Kare Silver pointed out in 1999, 'the absence of transaction facilities could actually turn the customer away', yet in 2005 many web sites do not offer this vital facility.

2. **Export** – This strategy seeks to protect its existing domestic retail and distribution network whilst pursuing opportunities in overseas markets. de Kare Silver provides the example of Blackwells academic publishers, with its network of UK bookstores is supplemented by its worldwide web operation allowing consumers direct purchasing and expatriates to purchase English texts. Charles Trywhitt, the bespoke shirt maker in Jermyn Street, London, referred to earlier, customises its key export markets in France, Germany and USA by language and currency. (www.ctshirts.co.uk). For small and medium sized enterprises (SME), the Internet provides a low cost entry strategy for going overseas whilst reducing many of the traditional export barriers such as operational, organisational and cultural factors.

3. **Subsume into existing business** – This option recognises the importance of an organisation's current retail activity, but seeks ways of integrating and supporting the physical store. As cited by de Kare Silver, many food retailers have utilised individual purchasing information to reduce the chore of shopping for mundane, everyday items. Customers call or e-mail their standard order to be picked up in-store at a collection point leaving them to enjoy shopping for more desirable items. However, as Benoit (2003) reports, in-store developments have moved swiftly in four years with the 'roboshop' experiment by the German retailer, Metro and some 39 partners including Proctor & Gamble, Coca Cola and Intel. The key component in the testing is 'The Personal Shopping Assistant' (PSA) which links into loyalty cards and barcodes to credit customers as they shop. The PSA also displays their 'web-shopping list' and prompts customer related offers as they approach relevant items on display. It will also direct customers to products they cannot find via an on-board search engine. The Internet and other digital technologies will play a more significant role in the food retailing experience of the future. However, for some shoppers, it is an enjoyable leisure pursuit.

4. **Treat as another channel** – For most retail operations, this has been the most typical approach as they dip their toes in the Internet water, seek to maintain market share and provide a convenient service dimension for the time-starved consumer. This is especially the case with more innovative companies who had already added a 'direct' element to their operations such as home delivery or tele-ordering. As de Kare Silver commented, 'For these companies electronic selling has not yet achieved the status of being a totally separate funded and resourced business.' However, today we see operations like www.tesco.com and www.johnlewis.com making significant contributions to their organisations' annual turnover. 2002 was a landmark for Tesco as it achieved online sales of £10 million plus per week and was ranked as the world's leading online grocery store initially. Significantly, it used its existing distribution infrastructure. In order to increase exposure and traffic many retailers such as John Lewis, B & Q, Argos and MFI also have

---

MINI CASE 2.5 Macdonald hotels and resorts

Macdonald Hotels and Resorts generates 600% increase in online revenue –

22 March 2005

Macdonald Hotels and Resorts, the UK's largest privately-owned hotel group, has increased its web revenue by 600% to just over £600k per month, since implementing a new online marketing strategy in December 2004. The company has revealed that the majority of the increase has come from customers new to Macdonald.

The overall aim is to grow the Macdonald Hotels and Resorts' brand online to ensure that this channel provides numbers of bookings on a par with those currently taken through Central Reservations' telephone system.

The new online marketing strategy has involved a complete web site re-design, Search Engine Optimisation, pay per click, cost per click, e-mail marketing, viral marketing, a retention marketing programme, online promotions and affiliate marketing. It complements Macdonald Hotels and Resorts' offline marketing promotions, including those run at the individual hotels.

Sally Osborne, Marketing Manager e-commerce, at Macdonald Hotels and Resorts, has been in charge of developing the company's online revenue generation. She comments:

'We are thrilled with the success so far of our online marketing strategy, which has resulted in a tangible increase in revenues generated from new customers. We have also seen our ranking on Hitwise climb steadily and we are now positioned favourably amongst our targeted competitors.'

Sally Osborne continues:

'We set about implementing an all-encompassing online marketing strategy last year in an effort to increase market share and these figures confirm we have opened up a previously untapped well of business for Macdonald. The success of the campaign means that we will be increasing our online budget and developing a more sophisticated campaign going forward, with the aim of achieving at least 15% of our revenue online.'

Macdonald Hotels and Resorts' newly launched affiliate marketing campaign is one of the group's primary sources of business from the web. It captures over 90 affiliates who earn a commission per booking.

Source: www.macdonaldhotels.co.uk/press/index.htm

---

a presence in online shopping malls such as www.somucheasier.co.uk For the leading hotel group, Macdonald Hotels and Resorts (www.macdonaldhotels.co.uk), the Internet has become an important channel for customer acquisition in new segments. A new online marketing strategy has generated some impressive results to compliment its traditional channels. Its new approach is outlined in Mini case 2.5.

5. **Set up as a separate business** – For retailers, especially of financial services, this strategy acknowledges the different needs of the online customer in terms of 24:7 access, convenience and site functionality. Many traditional retailers have sought to create a new online brand to meet the aspirations of the new customer. For example, the Prudential established Egg (www.egg.com) and The Halifax established Intelligent Finance (www.if.com).

The Royal Bank of Scotland diversified into a new, but related market when it introduced its car sales operation, Jamjar (www.jamjar.com) which complemented its acclaimed insurance operation, Direct Line, not to mention one of its core activities, personal loans.

Another option resulting from the dot.bomb era has been to acquire a separate business bargain by acquisition such as Great Universal Stores purchase of Jungle.com (www.jungle.com), which has now emerged as the technology store for Argos (www.argos.co.uk/jungle).

6. **'Pursue on all fronts'** – Some retailers have spread the risk by adopting a presence in every available channel. This usually applies where markets are intensely competitive.

Different customer groups are comfortable using different channels or perhaps they like the flexibility of using different channels at different times. As we demand more choice within product ranges we seem to desire increased choice in service provision. If we consider the operation of HSBC and its sibling, First Direct, traditional banking is available with the additional use of ATMs after hours. Tele-banking and secure Internet banking provides 24:7:365 services. HSBC has further extended its availability with its in store personal service and ATMs with in food retailers like Morrison's (www.morrisons.co.uk) which normally match the retailers opening hours. This also recognises that people may be comfortable with technology for routine, low risk activities such as basic transactions or depositing funds, but when it comes to more complex decisions on savings or mortgages they may prefer the reassurance of a personal advisor. Galliers and Wiggins (2002) cite the travel agent, Thomas Cook as a truly multi-channel operation offering its services across five distribution platforms: shops, phone, Internet, WAP-enabled mobile phones and **iTV** (interactive television). Many customers like using www.thomascook.com for planning holidays but still like to speak to someone for reassurance before making payment. This approach naturally requires a sizeable budget to have any significant market impact and presence.

7. **'Mixed system'** – This system recognises the growing potential of the Internet but at the same time appreciates that the 'retail shopping experience' will remain a priority leisure activity for many. On and offline operations are intertwined, especially in terms of distribution and promotions and can drive traffic both ways. Online retailing is offered alongside providing flexibility and convenience for the chameleon shopper. According to de Kare Silver, underpinning this system, is the 'flagship store' which is strategically located at major out of town retail centres such as Meadowhall, the Metro Centre or in major regional centres such as Manchester, Leeds or London adjacent to key leisure and entertainment facilities. Such locations attract high visitor numbers because of convenient transport networks and reasonable drive times.

   De Kare Silver suggests that there is a consumer expectation for a company to have a major presence at these locations. The presence provides an important shop window for the company's products and activities such as its online business whilst enhancing brand recognition. The online business can effectively reach customers beyond the immediate catchment areas who only visit the centres infrequently. An example of a mixed system is Waitrose in Mini case 2.6.

MINI CASE 2.6 Waitrose

Waitrose, the upmarket food retailer, has a strong presence in the south of England and is noted for the quality and range of its wines. Most Waitrose outlets offer a good selection from the range but at their key flagship stores at Canary Wharf and Kingston in London, the entire range can be accessed to cater for all tastes and budgets.

Waitrose is using the Internet to reach potential wine consumers in other parts of the UK. One of the main vehicles for this has been promotion through its parent company, John Lewis via its web site (www.johnlewis.com) and 'stuffers' in its monthly account statements. The association with John Lewis breeds trust and confidence in potential customers outside of Waitrose's traditional southern heartland.

Waitrose is now enhancing its online expertise with its 45% stake in the Ocado online grocery service. Ocado currently applies the Webvan model from the US to their business with a highly automated distribution centre for maximum efficiency. It concentrates on customers within the M25 so as not to cannibalise sales from Waitrose.

Adapted from: www.ocado.com/webshop
Nigel Cope, *The Independent*, 15 August 2003
www.waitrose.com

8. **'Switch fully'** – de Kare Silver questions whether any bricks and mortar organisation would be sufficiently convinced of the Internet's potential to close all of its high street retail operations in favour of going online. There are numerous examples of established bricks and mortar operations adding e-business solutions to their portfolio as customer behaviour and social trends change, such as the financial services sector, and in particular banking, PC manufacturers, clothing, food retailers, music and booksellers. Major retailers such as HMV, Virgin, Marks and Spencer, Argos and Next all see the Internet as a key strategic element, but continue to see the high street presence as essential. Dabs.com, formerly a mail order operation is purely Internet dependent now and other major players such as the Automobile Association have moved out of the high street. Other direct mail companies such as leading UK wine merchant, Laithwaites (www.laithwaites.com) also appear to have made a fairly seamless transition online. The organisational culture needed to operate a direct marketing function such as the distribution system, and customer familiarity with processes, all lend themselves to this transition. Many companies offer incentives to customers to buy online, but traditional channels remain important in terms of customer service, branding, instant access and so on. The speed of customer transfer from off to online will vary from sector to sector and from segment to segment.

9. **'Best of both'** – de Kare Silver acknowledges that previously discussed strategies incorporate elements of both traditional and electronic retailing to varying degrees eg Tesco. The best of both worlds' strategy operates both activities alongside each other. The retail strategy seeks to develop each store into a visionary and innovative leisure and buying experience which bonds retailer and consumers together more often, for longer and in a more stimulating and convenient way based on customer needs. There is no limit to the innovations such as in-store scanners, crèche facilities, superior catering, 'collect and go' schemes, financial services, in-store celebrity demonstrations, community involvement, extended product ranges and enhanced service provision generally. de Kare Silver's vision is effectively reality today, with the store developments at the likes of Tesco and the in-store trials in Germany identified later in this chapter. Each store, rather than just flagships, promote the companies' expanding range of products and services, especially those online activities that reduce costs and are emerging to make significant revenue contributions. The early commitment of Tesco to its online business has paid dividends as it is successfully integrated with its local store promotions and home delivery operations.

10. **'Revitalise and buck the trend'** – This strategy rejects the adoption of online trading. New leisure and shopping formulas are developed to attract more customers from further afield. For example, Evesham Vale Country Park offers retail and factory outlet shopping alongside a light railway and birds of prey sanctuary. The alternative for other retailers is the constant evolution of their store and development of product ranges and services, particularly when they are of significance in the local and regional community or are a special niche player. A prime example is Fenwick Limited of Newcastle who have invested heavily in the ongoing redevelopment of their store.

de Kare Silver's 10 strategic options provide a useful focus for retailers wrestling with the problem of strategic web adoption. However, as the web has evolved the distinctions between the options have blurred as retailers appreciate the critical success factors rapidly.

2.8 Partnerships and strategic alliances

For many organisations entering online markets, mergers, acquisitions and alliances have provided a relatively inexpensive shortcut in the development of a web presence and brand (eg GUS and jungle.com). Modern consumers appreciate the flexibility offered by both bricks and clicks operations to cope with modern demanding lifestyles. The Internet is a rich source of standardised product information for many but in certain sectors, particularly high-ticket value, consumers will desire the personal service element offered by a salesperson or a call centre operative thus providing the best of both worlds.

In recent times numerous complementary and diverse organisations have joined forces on the Internet to combine their specific areas of expertise. These can be technology, content, marketing, service R & D or international partnerships. In the world of auctions, the renowned auctioneer Sotheby's has joined forces with eBay. Boots the Chemist joined forces with Handbag.com, and MSN with Expedia. Most significantly, two of Britain's top e-tailers, Lastminute and Tesco have joined forces with Tesco customers being able to access a bespoke travel site designed by Lastminute. The brand awareness of the two sites will be enhanced further and will boost link popularity; as well as generating traffic and sales from affluent target markets.

The Internet has changed the way financial markets operate and has provided numerous channels from which investors can access information. In Mini case 2.7, the US based i-Deal operation is an example of how technology can facilitate online partnerships.

MINI CASE 2.7 Partnerships and technology

i-Deal – A global financial platform

In the late nineties, many financial institutions developed proprietary solutions to automate the processing of new issue offerings, says Frank LaQuinta, co-head of capital markets at i-Deal. To remain competitive, individual institutions soon realised the benefits of pooling information and systems. In November 2001, Merrill Lynch and Salomen Smith Barney, together with Microsoft and Thomson Financial, set up an independent company, i-Deal, with the objective of providing a single Internet platform to streamline and standardise the capital raising and new issue processes to support the broker-dealer relationship.

By pooling technology, intellectual assets and web services technology, they sought to create a real-time solution for investment banks, frequent users, institutional investors and multi-dealer systems that would combine all deal related records on single multi-currency, multi-product platform linking global players.

To ensure the success of i-Deal, it was vital that the original investors could operate neutrally across the financial markets.

The platform became established as an independent 'vertical service provider' for all parties involved in new issue business. This enabled each institution to rebrand the front end of their site so visitors would not be aware that it was running on the i-Deal platform.

i-Deal provides access to and generates enormous amounts of financial information linked to around 85% of Wall Street houses. It now resides on the desktops of thousands of capital market professionals and each receives a different view depending upon their role. Leading edge technology provided by the i-Deal platform means partners can concentrate on the global markets and need not be pre-occupied with keeping up with new IT and software applications.

Sources: *Financial Times*, 'Understanding Business Agility', 8 May 2003 p 15

www.i-deal.com

www.download.microsoft.com/documents/customerevidence/20633_i-Deal_MS_Services_Final.doc

2.9 **Physical and virtual worlds**

The physical and virtual world can learn from each other's best practice. Rayport and Jaworski (2002) consider the key similarities and differences between 'bricks and mortar' and Internet based operations. They observe that many business and marketing activities undertaken by organisations apply both on and offline. They selected and analysed five key elements that were deemed important to the success of an e-commerce operation and they provide a very useful structure for a 'bricks' versus 'clicks' comparison. Any online marketer must address these key issues, as they impact appreciably upon levels of customer satisfaction, experience and retention within the web's marketspace.

We shall consider five elements, namely:

1. Location and hosting
2. Marketing and presentation
3. Payment
4. Security
5. Fulfilment

Location and hosting

The location of any business is an important determinant of the level of traffic generated in terms of either the physical footfall through a store or online visitor figures. For 'bricks and mortar' operations locating in the right part of town, the right street or a particular mall will have a magnetic effect on potential customers. Rayport and Jaworski suggest the need to assess the location's image, convenience, size to cope with expected traffic flows and complementary rather than competitive businesses in the vicinity. For the virtual store, similar analogies can be drawn. In terms of traffic generation, it becomes essential to achieve top rankings in key search engines and directories such as Google and Yahoo!. A visible presence in key portals and malls, or through affiliate schemes is also important. The partnerships and associations play a key role in the development of trust, and of the online brand. This becomes important where price sensitivity is less critical and goods sold are commodities. Rayport and Jaworski also consider the virtual location represented by the domain name to be very influential as it can encapsulate the brand proposition as well as being memorable. Typical examples would be www.lastminute.com, www.boystuff.com or www.wellbeing.com (pharmacist and retailer, Boots online health advisory).

Other location and hosting comparisons can be made between bricks and clicks. Designing the store size to accommodate the expected traffic volumes is vital for both environments. If the store is too small and cannot cope, a poor customer experience results. Alternatively, if the store is too large customers could be overwhelmed by its physical size, or the complexity of the online store. Again, over optimism can lead to inefficient resource allocation. Offline stores need to consider the immediate infrastructure eg land available, road networks and factor in the local catchment area using segmentation criteria such as geo-demographic and Geographic Information Systems (GIS) profiles when securing sites for development. The forecasted traffic volumes enable the organisation to assess its staffing requirements. Technological issues play a more significant role in the online business store with the need for professional, secure hosting services capable of handling large volumes of data and transactions. This will be facilitated by bandwidth that determines the speed of data transfer and broadband, sometimes referred to as the 'fatpipe' will provide greater connectivity and increase customer expectations and experiences. The inter-computer communications infrastructure provided by web services on a global scale or LANs (Local Area Network) and WANs (Wide Area Network) over more limited distances provides the channels for Internet traffic. Organisational IT systems rely heavily on somewhat dated IT infrastructure, referred to as **legacy systems** eg Cobol, which are costly to replace. However, web service innovations in the form of Extensible Mark-Up Language (**XML**) and Microsoft's. Net framework provide a flexible, wrap-around, cost effective solution enabling disparate computer networks to talk to each other without replacing the legacy system. However some IT observers suggest these 'wrap-arounds' may hinder more significant systems innovations as buyers go for the cheaper more convenient option.

Marketing and presentation

Rayport and Jaworski discuss the importance of promotional methods to create awareness and interest in any store. Value, cost and satisfaction have been the fundamental drivers offline and have been supplemented by more measurement and targeting, as demands have been placed upon the marketing function for greater accountability. The 1990s was *the* decade of growth in direct marketing applications. This was to the detriment of mainstream advertising media as campaign costs can be measured with greater statistical accuracy. Target marketing offers greater precision and less wastage than traditional media such as TV and press. Tapp (2004) cites four social reasons for the growth in direct marketing:

- Fragmentation of society
- Proliferation of media
- Greater consumer sophistication
- Consumers want to be in control

Tapp then offers four business reasons for growth:

- Increasing competition
- Drive for cost effectiveness
- Interest in customer retention and loyalty
- Reduced Information and Communication Technology (**ICT**) costs.

Whilst all of these environmental drivers continue to influence mainstream marketing, they also have a significant impact upon online marketing functions such as streamlining procurement and transaction processes electronically, reduced customer contact costs via e-mail and the development of online loyalty schemes.

However, any discussion on marketing practice cannot underestimate the importance of *the brand* and its development. The bundled package of name, logo, design and reputation for quality provides marketers with the ability to differentiate from the competition, and in many cases achieve higher prices and margins. At the same time the consumer buys in to status, prestige, style, performance and street credibility. The brand no longer relates just to a single product or a category of products. It has been extended in recent years to encapsulate the corporate brand and all it stands for such as Virgin, Nike and Tesco as they venture way beyond their core products. The brand develops its own persona and positioning in the mind of the consumer.

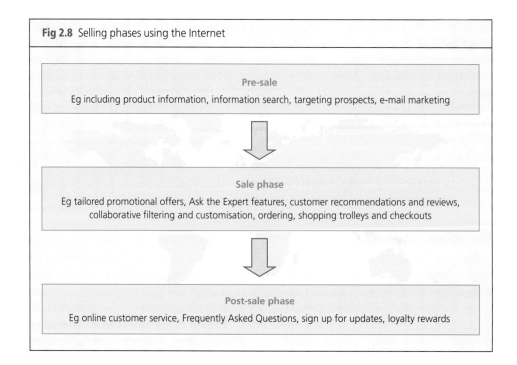

Fig 2.8 Selling phases using the Internet

Pre-sale
Eg including product information, information search, targeting prospects, e-mail marketing

Sale phase
Eg tailored promotional offers, Ask the Expert features, customer recommendations and reviews, collaborative filtering and customisation, ordering, shopping trolleys and checkouts

Post-sale phase
Eg online customer service, Frequently Asked Questions, sign up for updates, loyalty rewards

Culture often plays an influential role in marketing and it is worth pointing out three cultural features relating to shopping behaviour. First, consumers are used to a self-service shopping experience. Second, consumers are used to making payment by credit cards. Finally, consumers are becoming more receptive to shopping through direct channels such as the Internet and catalogues. These three factors are conditioning and transitional steps towards consumer web receptiveness.

For the Internet based business, marketing and presentation are essential planks for online success. Classic response models such as AIDA and the Lavidge and Steiner's Hierarchy of Response are still relevant communications tools when planning online campaigns to drive traffic through the buying process. The Internet is capable of delivering on all campaign phases as seen in Fig 2.8.

For many of the dot.com entrepreneurs, promotional communications was a costly and complicated activity. This was fuelled by the dual need of building an online brand, which consumers could trust whilst attracting sufficient prospects to make the business model viable. In the early days, Amazon used the full range of promotional methods but was particularly active with public relations and couponing in the UK broadsheet newspapers read by the early Internet adopters.

Any online organisation must present itself in an appropriate manner to all interested parties or stakeholders. It may require a number of different methods to get them to the site such as:

- Targeted e-mails with web-links
- Search engine marketing techniques
- Strategic placement of banner adverts
- Viral marketing campaigns

LEGAL EAGLE BOX 2.1 Unsolicited direct marketing mail

It is now unlawful for companies to send unsolicited direct marketing emails (Spam) or text messages (SMS) unless they have prior consent of the potential recipients. These new rules apply throughout the EU. [Note – see the Privacy and Electronic Communications Directive 2002 which has been implemented in the UK by the Privacy and Electronic Communications (EC Directive) Regulations 2003.]

The UK Privacy and Electronic Communications (EC Directive) Regulations 2003 have restricted the use of e-mails for the purpose of marketing to potential customers. Promotional e-mails will only be allowed if the recipients have given the sender prior consent to have such information sent to them.

Where such marketing information is to be sent to existing customers, it must be marketing information on similar products to those purchased by those customers. Despite the existence of a commercial relationship with such customers, they must still be given the opportunity to opt-out of receiving marketing information in the future.

E-mail permission based marketing forms an essential element in any acquisition and retention strategy. However as privacy and trust are key issues for consumers, organisations must observe good practice and current legislation as outline in the Legal Eagle Box 2.1.

Once they are there, like any storefront, the site has to be appealing with features, departments, categories and services eg FAQs, being easy to find. Jakob Nielsen (www.useit.com) has been a leading exponent of usability testing and studies to understand visitor site interactions. Site design should use the language and features relevant to the main target market. Nielsen gives a simple example with sites designed for senior citizens and he recommends larger font sizes for those with declining eyesight. A site should be user-friendly; many sites are not. Before any launch or redesign of a site, current customers and prospects should be consulted and ideally involved in usability tests prior to going live. Any usability results should be considered alongside marketing and broader corporate objectives. Factors such as aesthetics, content, convenience, product information, clarity of layout, personalisation, simplicity of checkout procedures, payment options and overall site feel all play a key role in establishing site 'stickiness'. Rayport and Jaworski make a key point which relates to the user's IT competence. The greater the level of user competence allows more design features to be incorporated otherwise use the KISS approach, Keep It Simple Stupid or more politely, Keep it Short and Simple! See chapter 8 for a more detailed discussion on web site design.

Viral marketing is a useful strategic and tactical tool in any promotional model. It is a speedy method of transmitting messages via the web. In the offline world, word of mouth recommendations provide customer assurance and a springboard for business success. In the online world, 'word of mouse' recommendations take advantage of individual and networked relationships such as chat-rooms and forums, as well as personal distribution lists. Viral marketing has proved to be a low-cost, infectious tool for online promotions using individuals to send e-mails to friends, colleagues and acquaintances without the need for company involvement. Jupiter Communications claim that 69% of people who are recommended a particular web site, pass on that recommendation to between two and six people. Internet word-of-mouth marketing has taken on a different dimension in the world of pop with the Arctic Monkeys (see Mini case 2.8 below).

The digital marketer can also use other interactive and personal applications such as mobile marketing especially in the form of text messaging or SMS (Short Message Service), and iTV (Interactive Television). For more detailed coverage of web based promotional applications, see chapter 11.

> **MINI CASE 2.8 The Arctic Monkeys harness the Internet**
>
> Teenage rock sensation, The Arctic Monkeys stormed to the top of the charts after harnessing the power of the Internet.
>
> The Sheffield based band reached number one for the second time with their latest single, 'When the Sun Goes Down' (January 2006) with the help of a fan base that increased rapidly via the Internet and new technology, not to mention high-energy sell-out gigs long before they came to the attention of any major record companies or radio audience. Their new album, *Whatever People Say I Am, That's What I'm Not*, is expected to be the fastest album since the days of The Beatles.
>
> The band argued that they had no real Internet plan. Instead, they gave away 20 CDs at each gig that led to file swapping with a generation brought up on MP3 files. It is widely reported that every gig was filled with fans singing every word, months before any of the Monkeys' songs had been officially released. They have been dubbed as the first Internet born superstars by tapping into the massive online communities visited by a younger generation.

Payment

Payment methods can be an influential factor the final stage of the buying process. Rayport & Jaworski consider its comparative influence on buying decisions and price implications. Pricing strategies and tactics will be considered in depth in chapter 10 but here we will consider the various transactional methods used by on and offline merchants. In bricks and mortar operations, cash has been the traditional method of payment, particularly for lower ticket value items. However, in Western Europe over the last 30 years we have seen the introduction *and* acceptance of various forms of credit from hire purchase agreements, extended and interest free credit, store and debit cards, gift vouchers and post-dated cheques. Rayport & Jaworski highlight two problems for the physical store, these being cash thefts from 'customers' employees and credit card fraud.

On the cost side, any retailer must factor in the processing charges levied on transactions by banks and credit card companies.

The changing attitude to cash is significant as more transactions are processed electronically including salaries (eg BACS). Talk of the cashless society has been prevalent for some time. Whilst it may be some way off, the growing acceptance of alternative payment methods will help overcome fears or resistance to the Internet.

In the online environment, most transactions take place electronically. Stores in their web infancy may still be content to accept personal cheques by post. However, the majority of online purchases are paid for by either debit (eg Switch card) or credit card (eg Visa or MasterCard) via an Internet Merchant Account (IMA) with the likes of WorldPay (see below). At this point, verification and authentication of the card is vital and relies on the accuracy of the merchant and card issuers or third parties' database, by checking issue numbers, expiry dates and occasionally personal passwords. The transaction and confirmation of order by e-mail is done instantly. Order numbers offer online tracking for despatch and delivery providing extra customer confidence and transparency. The perceived threat of widespread online credit card fraud has consumed numerous columns of newspaper space, especially in the tabloids and has been an influential in creating customer unease for online transactions. As software standards and protocols such as Secure Socket Layer (SSL) and Secure Electronic Transactions (SET) improve payment security, public confidence and trust will grow. The reality is that fraud on the web is no more serious than offline fraud. The Department of

Table 2.2 MORI Report

Which problems if any, have consumers experienced with Internet shopping?	2002	2001
1. Heard rumours or media stories about credit card fraud on the Internet	20%	28%
2. Heard rumours or media stories about credit card fraud elsewhere	11%	18%
3. Know someone who has experienced credit card fraud on the Internet	5%	6%
4. Know someone who experienced credit card fraud elsewhere	4%	6%
5. Personal experience of credit card fraud on the Internet	1%	2%
6. Personal experience of credit card fraud elsewhere	2%	3%
7. Ordered goods online but they were not delivered	3%	5%
8. Lost money to a fraudulent/fake Internet company	2%	2%

Base: All GB adults 15+, 20–25 September 2001 (2,013), 3–8 October 2002 (2,003)
Source: MORI
Reproduced by kind permission of Ipsos MORI.

Trade and Industry (2001) in its report on cross-border shopping suggests that concerns are gradually reducing year on year. Findings from a MORI below (Table 2.2) outlined the problem of rumour rather than experience for consumers a few years ago. We may question how many of these issues remain a concern for consumers and marketers alike?

The Interactive Media in Retail Group (IMRG) is an organisation that seeks to promote the benefits of online retailing for consumers and merchants alike on a global basis. In Fig 2.9 they provide guidance for safe shopping online.

Other methods of web-based payments such as e-wallets, e-cash and micro payments have not been adopted as quickly as expected. An important web service that is emerging is the multi-currency, multi-payment methods offered by financial services companies like WorldPay (www.Worldpay.com), part of The Royal Bank of Scotland. As they report, 'Forrester Research predicts that the global B2C eCommerce market will be worth $561 billion by 2006, underlining the need for retailers to focus specifically on the most productive geographies, and to do this using international currency processing and localised payment instruments.' Such systems will play an important role in the internationalisation of Internet business.

Security

Both bricks and clicks merchants increasingly rely upon technology to protect their operation, though the degree of importance differs significantly. Security is also a major concern for the consumer particularly in terms of fraud, privacy and pornography. In the physical store, security focuses on theft prevention from 'customers' and staff in the form of visible security guards, Closed Circuit Television (CCTV) cameras and security tagging of products. Such problems are rarely life threatening to an organisation but can represent an increasing cost burden. Smith and Chaffey (2002) highlight the concerns and problems for both organisations and consumers relating to e-business security as 'hackers, vandals and viruses'

Fig 2.9 IMRG'S online shopping tips

Top Ten Tips for Online Shopping

❶ All of your usual shopping rights apply online:
see www.consumer.gov.uk

❷ Know who you're dealing with: get the seller's landline phone number and postal address

❸ Be aware of terms and conditions: check payment and delivery details

❹ Keep records of what you order

❺ EU Law protects you against fraudulent use of your payment card in EU transactions: credit cards give you extra protection

❻ Only give your payment card details over a secure connection, and never by e-mail: never disclose your PIN number to anyone, and never send it over the Internet

❼ You usually have at least 7 days to cancel an order and request a refund from an EU retailer

❽ Check your payment card statement carefully: you have at least 90 days to report a suspect transaction

❾ When you buy goods online from outside the EU:

- You are an importer and may be liable to pay any Customs Duty and VAT;

- Err on the side of caution as it may be difficult to seek redress if problems arise

❿ If you have a problem, contact the seller then, if you need to, the payment company, local Trading Standards Office and any 'trustmark' organisation the seller is registered with

By kind permission of IMRG (www.imrg.org).

---

infiltrate both vulnerable personal and corporate security systems (eg invasion of chat-rooms). Governments are also concerned at the threat posed by international terrorism. They argue that many online businesses were in such a rush to get established and acquire customers that the security foundations laid were ill thought out and flimsy. The CBI study on Internet Security and Fraud (2001) suggests serious threats may come from within the organisation and from former employees. It is a constant battle for developers to keep one step ahead of these threats. As mentioned above, SSL and SET make ordering and authentication more secure. **Encryption** and decryption technology and firewalls also provide further security measures. Organisations may also employ password-controlled subscriptions to restrict site entry to desirables. Sites could be potentially closed for a sustained period by a serious attack but the chances are limited. The main downside of any breaches in security or privacy is the loss of trust and reputation, which may affect customer confidence, which can be very damaging for a web-based operation. Consequently, organisations should follow good practice in security protocols as outlined in the Legal Eagle box 2.2.

Fulfilment

This is fundamental element of the distribution process and an area which causes considerable customer frustration due to the delays and failures in processing orders and despatching goods. This process can provide competitive advantage and significant cost savings if run efficiently, and of course, with the customer in mind. Surprisingly, it is rarely given more

LEGAL EAGLE BOX 2.2 Security

The vulnerability associated with online activities puts e-marketers at risk. Appropriate security measures have to be put in place to ensure protection in today's dynamic world of interconnected networks. A security policy is essential for protecting e-assets as it provides a coherent standard for staff, users and management.

The British Standards Institute has published a Security Standard – BS 7799 / ISO 17799 /IEC 17799 – which lists 10 key controls for checking if basic security has been implemented in an organisation. These are:

- Security policy
- Security organisation
- Asset classification and control

- Personnel security
- Physical and environmental security
- Communications and operations management
- Access control
- Systems development and maintenance
- Business continuity management
- Compliance checking

Footnote: BS 7799 is a British security standard adopted by the International Standards Organisation as ISO 17799 and the International Electro-technical Commission as IEC 17799.

---

than moderate coverage in most e-marketing texts. Ensure the Internet delivers for you. As Pip Thorne, Director of TechnoPhobia asks, 'Once a customer interacts with your business via the Internet, the relationship is tested by your ability to deliver. Can your fulfilment systems cope?'

Fulfilment houses are intermediaries and carry out a number of functions traditionally associated with mail order operations. Thomas & Housden (2002) outline the following functions:

- Receipt of responses to promotions and mailings
- Despatch of ordered goods or information packs
- Receipt and storage of goods (including valuables)
- Receipt and processing of mail orders
- Banking of customer remittances
- Picking, packing and despatch of goods
- Customer service functions, often helplines
- Reporting of orders, despatches, stock, banking, and so on

Most of the fulfilment expertise has been refined through mail order and catalogue companies such as Great Universal Stores and Grattans in the UK and La Redoute in France. Fulfilment often relies on a number of partners within this part of the supply chain process.

If we return to the heady days of the dot.com era, a lot of public cynicism towards buying online was generated by the failure of many to deliver as and when promised. Many dot.coms again were setting up operations, often for the first time without the knowledge and expertise in distribution and specifically fulfilment. Hence the integration between shop checkouts, back office and delivery was not efficient. Unfortunately for many dot.coms, Amazon was the trailblazer and standard setter for fulfilment and many tried to offer the same speed of service but were not up to it. In many case they failed to deliver altogether. Others like Greenfingers.com (www.greenfingers.com) recognised the problem with high customer expectations. They subsequently lowered them and delivered more quickly than quoted, providing a pleasant surprise (eg quote five–seven days for delivery and deliver in four!).

Some of our more mature readers will remember, not so fondly, ordering goods from department stores and waiting and waiting for it to arrive, not knowing whether it was still being manufactured or at a regional depot and ready for the once a fortnight delivery to your area! Today, the Internet provides customers with the ability to see where their order is in the system. Even before buying most merchants now provide information on the number of products in stock and how many are due from their suppliers in the next three days, for example. Once an order is received, customers are given a specific order number for tracking, informed who the courier is, when it is being despatched and when it will arrive. This places new demands on all those players involved in the fulfilment process such as the manufacturer, the e-tailer and the courier to provide transparency in real-time throughout, not to mention another third party who may provide after sales support. As customer expectations rise, the distribution function has to wrestle with out-of-hours delivery issues for when the consumer is at home.

Rayport and Jaworski also highlight another critical problem with web-based fulfilment operations, which is the need to utilise their capacity as efficiently as possible. For some businesses, seasonal, weekly or even daily demand may fluctuate considerably and if the system is designed to cope with the peaks, inevitably there will be under-utilisation during quieter periods which impacts on the bottom-line. In the UK some organisations such as Sainsbury have established dedicated distribution systems for the online business. However, Tesco have utilised local deliveries from their major stores for order fulfilment from Tesco Online, which exploits their existing infrastructure.

 ## 2.10 **Summary**

The Internet has created many opportunities for a diverse range of organisations. Their diversity has spawned numerous business models that were expected to generate sufficient revenues for online profitability. However, as the Internet environment has matured it has become increasingly evident that few models would achieve this alone. Most major Internet players now recognise the need to apply a number of models simultaneously to provide several revenue streams in order to survive and prosper.

In devising their strategic options, marketers can still apply the analytical tools used in the physical world to good effect. However, they must evaluate their role, as outlined by Timmers, in the evolving 'marketspace' and assess whether they have the competences and culture of innovation needed.

It is apparent that many online businesses are now bowing to customer pressure and offering other tools such as telephone and text messaging (SMS) to complete transactions and provide customer service. In addition, some are now seeking a physical presence on the high street to complement their online operation. As many writers have identified, we are now seeing a convergence emerging between the activities of businesses with their roots in both the physical and virtual world. The result, as Forrester (2003) points out, is that the Internet is less dominant than we expected four years ago and the consumer now expects fully integrated 'multi-channels' for their convenience. Marketing departments now have to rethink the costs and benefits of this multi-channel service. It will not be cheap hence the moves towards more partnerships and alliances.

END OF CHAPTER CASE STUDY Internet portals deliver benefits to local business and communities – the Touch concept

When Vincent Isaacs set up the Guild of Excellence in 1995, little did he think that his vision of regenerating the local communities of this country, by directing shopping back to local High Streets, would result in his leading a company with the first national network of business directories and community portals on the Internet.

Some 10 years down the line and with significant investment from parent company Ambient plc, Touch (GoE) plc (www.touchlocal.com) now has an estate of 116 community portals distributed throughout the UK by postcode regions. Each of these portals has, and displays, a database of local businesses, organisations and associations and this is where the Touch network starts to differentiate itself from various other community portals that have sprung up around the country. Fig 1 below illustrates the concept of the 'e-community wheel' and its 'publics'.

The ability to provide this network of portals with a level of functionality that satisfies the needs of both businesses and residents is down to a mixture of good fortune and the Internet. The Touch metamorphosis had moved from the vision of incentivising the public to use their city centres in a traditional, physical shopping model, to a multi-function smart card approach providing discount on price from a variety of shops coupled with the ability to load the card to pay for transport such as bus tickets. Although this scheme was taken up in Nottingham and as many as 30 local authorities showed an interest in taking up

the model, Touch was an early adopter in a market that was yet to understand the benefits of smart cards. The writing of the required software, the purchase of smart card readers and the marketing of the scheme to local traders was expensive and prohibitive . . . and then along came the Internet and the community portal was borne.

Launched in Nottingham as a joint venture with Nottingham City Council, TouchNottingham, as it was to become, formed the template for the 116 postcode based community portals that is the Touch network. But it was not all plain sailing. Building a portal from scratch in a short timescale persuaded Touch that a turnkey solution for portal building must exist somewhere in the world. After intense research on the Internet, a US based solution from the DynaPortal Software Company was identified and a relationship was established whereby the DynaPortal software has been used to deploy Touch's network. And more than that, the same software has been resold to a vast variety of companies, organisations, charities and start ups as a scalable, easy to use, inexpensive and quick to deploy solution for portal building. The networks of local and regional Touch e-consultants advise on the range of e-solutions to suit different business needs and budgets.

This partnership has provided, through the Touch portal network, a cost effective way to maximise the opportunities afforded by the World Wide Web. Now organisations and companies of any size can benefit from the constantly increasing

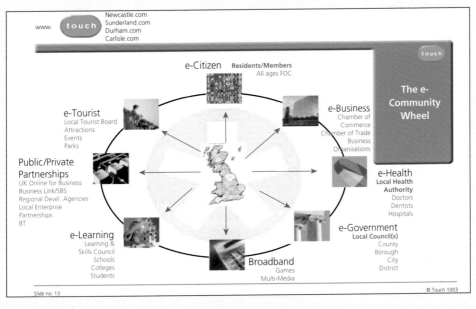

Fig 1 e-Community Wheel

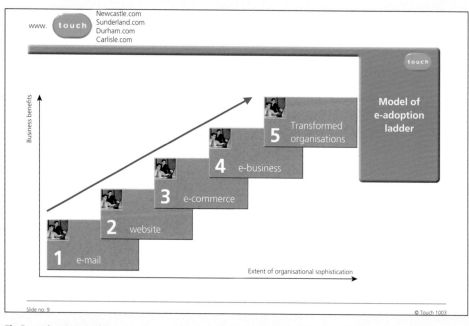

Fig 2 e-adoption model

traffic to the network and from a range of scalable solutions to suit their current position on the e-adoption ladder (see Fig 2).

No longer is a network of community portals insisting that everyone adopts *their* technology. After all, a web site built in the first generation may well have been expensive and represent a significant investment on the part of the company or organisation and a call to trash it and start again may not be welcome! However, the invitation to link that web site with the local community portal through weblink products, enhanced listings and self-publishing accounts, not to mention media products from banners and priority listings to skyscrapers, opens a range of opportunities to be part of a greater community and make that web site available to a much wider audience. This is done through the estate of local portals and the searchability of the database of businesses and organisations that the worldwide search engines are caching and spidering all the time. For many SMEs, Touch Link Listing is a cost effective promotional method that reaches a local market at £12.50 per month.

Tamer Ozmen, CEO of Touch (GoE) plc explained, 'rather than invite the various organisations and businesses in an area to join their local portal, we decided to give them exposure from the outset. We purchased a database of some 1.9 million businesses and populated the portals from Day One. After all, if you visit a website and find nothing there, why would you ever return?' Touch now boasts some 2.4 million businesses on the database.

This thinking has proved correct and the database has formed the basis on which the community portal has grown. It is now second only to Yell.com as the most used online search directory in the UK. Much of the growth can be attributed to the self-publishing function. Any community project requires that community to have a say in its development and self-publishing offers the ability to add one's material without the need for technical knowledge as 2nd generation dynamic web sites allow instantaneous adding or changing of content. The ability to self-publish gives 'ownership' to businesses and residents and they will determine the speed at which the portal grows. And hopefully eliminated the dreaded phrase 'last updated February 2003'. Again the e-consultants provide an important local advisory and moderating role.

From lowly beginnings just 10 years ago and not only surviving the Internet 'boom and bust' but coming out the other side stronger and more focussed says much for Touch and parent Ambient's resilience and confidence. Of course, like any successful operation, Touch continues to innovate and has now introduced the expansion of its offering with the launch of its unique online shopping portal, Touch Plaza (www.touchplaza.com). Touch Plaza is an e-commerce product that enables companies, however small, to grow their business online for a fraction of the price of other e-commerce packages. With 70% of businesses currently missing out on online sales, Touch Plaza provides them and larger chains alike with the ability to set up and sell online within a week.

With 4.9 million visitors a month, businesses will be provided with targeted traffic to their online shop from the day it goes live. At the same time, consumers will have access to a virtual shopping mall featuring local and high street shops and products previously unavailable anywhere online. The interactive nature of the site is enhanced with customer reviews. Tony Piedade, Touch Plaza's Commercial Director commented: 'Touch Plaza is unique in that for the first time local and niche shops can compete on a level playing field as the larger chains. For too long, many local businesses have shied away from e-commerce because of the lengthy and costly process involved in setting up to sell online. As an e-commerce application, Touch Plaza can set up merchant accounts at speed and deliver ready-to-buy online customers to the thousands of businesses who have yet to target the Internet consumer.'

Questions

1. Visit your local Touch portal (www.touchlocal.com) What are the benefits of the portal to the various publics in the 'e-community wheel'

2. What specific aspects of the Touch offering would be particularly attractive to small and medium sized enterprises (SMEs) and why?

3. How many different revenue models can be identified within a Touch portal?

4. How important is it to incorporate numerous revenue streams as part of an online strategy?

Reproduced by kind permission of Touch Local.

DISCUSSION QUESTIONS

1. What are the advantages and disadvantages of the Internet development stages models for a marketer planning his/her online strategy for the next 18 months?

2. Visit a web site of your choice. Identify how many different revenue models are present and suggest which model is likely to generate the most revenue for the organisation. Justify your response.

3. What marketing environmental factors are responsible for the emergence of 'multi-channel consumer'? Is he/she here to stay?

REFERENCES

Actinic (2006) www.actinic.co.uk/news/060103.htm

Afuah & Tucci (2003), *Internet – Business models and Strategies*, McGraw Hill

Arnott, DC & Bridgewater, S (2002) Internet, interaction and implications for marketing, *Marketing Intelligence and Planning*. 20/2 (2002) 86–95, MCB UP Ltd

Benoit, B Check out the supermarket of the future, *The Financial Times*, 16, 14 May 2003

Brassington, F & Pettit, S (2003) *Principles of Marketing*, FT Prentice Hall, Harlow, Ch 13

Brennan R, et al (2003) *Contemporary Strategic Marketing*, Palgrave Macmillan, Basingstoke, Ch 10

Carton, S (2002) *The Dot. Bomb Survival Guide*, McGraw Hill, 1

CBI Internet Security & Fraud (2001) Confederation of British Industry, www.cbi.org.uk

Chaffey et al (2000) *Internet Marketing*, Pearson Education

Consumer and Competition Policy Directorate (2002) Internet and cross-border shopping, Department of Trade and Industry, November 2002

Darby et al (2003) E-commerce marketing: fad or fiction? Management competency in mastering emerging technology. An international case analysis in the UAE., *Logistics Information Management*, Vol 16, No 2, 2003, 106, 113, MCB UP Limited

de Kare Silver, M (2000) *e-shock 2000*, Macmillan, Basingstoke, Ch 7

Elliot, S (ed), *Electronic Commerce – B2C Strategies and Models*, John Wiley & Sons, Ltd, 7–8

Financial Mail on Sunday, 15 December 2002, Lessons of the Boxman crash, 50

Financial Times, Understanding Business Agility, 8 May 2003, 15

Galliers, RD & Wiggins A (2002 – in press) Internet retailing in the United Kingdom, *Internet Retailing: An International Perspective*, Elliott, S (ed.) John Wiley & Sons, Chichester

Informatics-Review (2000) Vol 3, No 7, Stages of Internet business development

ISAC Web Advisory Group (2002) adapted from *XT3: Commercial Internet Solutions*, 18 February 2002

Kinder, A (2002) Emerging e-commerce business models: an analysis of case studies from West Lothian, Scotland, *European Journal of Innovation Management*, Vol 5, No 3, 2002, 130–151, MCB UP Ltd

Mail on Sunday, 11 August 2003

Mohammed, R et al (2001), *Internet Marketing – Building Advantage in a Networked Economy*, McGraw Hill

Philips, P (2003) *E-Business Strategy*, McGraw Hill, 133

Proddow, L (2000) *Heroes.Com – The Names and Faces behind the Dot.com Era*, Hodder & Stoughton, Foreword

Rayport JF & Jaworski BJ (2002) *Introduction to E-commerce*, McGraw Hill, New York

Rayport JF & Sviokla JJ (1994) Managing in the marketspace, *Harvard Business Review*, July, 141–150

Rowley, J (2002) Synergy and Strategy in e-business, *Marketing Intelligence & Planning*, Vol 20, No 4 (2002), 215–222, MCB UP Ltd

Smith, PR & Chaffey, D (2002) *EMarketing Excellence*, Butterworth Heinemann, 278–279

Smith, PR & Chaffey, D (2002) *EMarketing Excellence*, Butterworth Heinemann, 211

Tapp, A (2004) *Principles and Practice of Direct and Database Marketing*, 3rd edn, FT Prentice Hall, Harlow

The Millennium Group (2000), Briefing Paper 2, www.millen.co.uk/Reports.BusModels.pdf

Thomas, B & Housden, M (2002), *Direct Marketing in Practice*, Butterworth Heinemann, Oxford, 293

Timmers, P (1999), *Electronic Commerce: Strategies and Models for Business-to-Business Trading*, John Wiley & Sons, Inc

Turban et al (2002) *Electronic Commerce – A Managerial Perspective*, Prentice Hall, 6

Verdin 2002

Walters (2003), E-Stocks rise from the grave, *The Observer Business*, 4, 23 February 2003

Wilson, R (2002), *Planning Your Internet Marketing Strategy*, John Wiley & Sons, Inc, 23

www.informatics-review.com/subscribers/Vol_3/Num7/stages.html

www.vnunet.com/News/1140722

www.worldpay.co.uk/about/index.php?go=ab_article&nid=56

FURTHER READING

Afuah, A & Tucci, CL (2003) *Internet Business Models and Strategies*, 2nd edn, McGraw Hill, New York

Brynjolfsson, E & Urban, GL (2001) 'Strategies for e-Business Success', MIT Sloan Management Review, Jossey Bass, San Francisco, US

Chaffey, D, Mayer, R, Johnston & Ellis Chadwick, F (2003), *Internet Marketing*, 2nd edn, FT Prentice Hall, Harlow, Essex, England

Phillips, P (2003) *E-Business Strategy*, McGraw Hill Education, Maidenhead, Berkshire, England

Urban, GL (2004) *Digital Marketing Strategy*, Pearson Education Inc, New Jersey, US

Wilson, RF (2002) *Planning Your Internet Marketing Strategy*, John Wiley & Sons Inc, New York, US

WEB LINKS

www.1 to 1media.com – The Peppers and Rogers 1 to 1 media site. Discusses CRM and other relationship marketing issues as a key element for successful online marketing strategies.

www.wilsonweb.com – the web site of US Internet authority, Dr Ralph Wilson entitled *Web Marketing Today* that contains a rich source of e-marketing information, news and guidance.

www.marketingsherpa.com – valuable resource publishing useful news, case studies, and best practice about Internet and integrated marketing strategies.

 Visit the Online Resource Centre which accompanies this book, for lots of interesting additional material, including self-assessment questions, internet exercises, and links for each chapter: **www.oxfordtextbooks.co.uk/orc/gay/**

3 Online Marketing Planning Issues

Learning objectives

By the end of the chapter you will be able to:

- Comprehend how online marketing is integrated as part of an e-business plan
- Appreciate the impact of change on strategic options
- Evaluate the key stages, components and processes in developing an Internet marketing plan
- Appreciate the value and structure of the new 4 P's Internet promotional model
- Understand the planning process in a multi-channel environment

Chapter at a glance

3.1 Introduction

Hanson (2000) suggests that 'a full Internet marketing plan combines online market data, the strategic goals of an organisation, an honest appraisal of internal capabilities and required outside support, a detailed listing of the steps needed and an effective system of measuring and improving results.' However, like any marketing plan, it is essential that it supports the overall corporate business plan and contributes to the achievement of the company mission and objectives. Rather than focus on many well-known marketing planning tools, this chapter will address more specific aspects of Internet planning to stimulate both managerial and creative ideas.

The benefits of marketing planning are well documented by writers such as McDonald and Doyle (1998). It provides a strategic focus and framework for implementing and evaluating the chosen course of action. As Doyle suggests, business success is achievable when the strategy developed matches the organisational capabilities with the environment in which it operates. Throughout the eighties and nineties, various commentators observed that marketing plans had to be more flexible, because of the dynamic and unpredictable nature of the business environment.

The new digital marketplace has exacerbated the fluid environment. It also brings a new set of rules and conditions, which marketers have to take into consideration when constructing their marketing plans. These plans evolve from the higher-level corporate objectives and strategy. In this chapter, we will consider key issues in the development of an Internet marketing plan, including the management 'buy-in' and the context in which the plan is set. In addition to considering a separate Internet marketing plan, we will also consider matters relating to multi-channel, international and small business planning online. The chapter will introduce a new promotional planning and control framework designed for the Internet age, incorporating four key elements:

- Positioning – building brands online and using paid and organic search to drive traffic;

- Permission – opening a dialogue with potential new customers and incorporating customer relationship management (CRM);

- Partnership – including affiliate marketing, co-promotions and joint ventures;

- Performance – including the measurement of web site success and online marketing strategies using web analytics.

The relatively low cost of entry to a global audience via the web spawned scores of bizarre and ill-conceived ideas. Many 'would be' Internet entrepreneurs provided business news channels with story after story of online marketing blunders and bloated stock market prices for dot.com start-ups.

What was actually occurring was a misunderstanding and lack of communication between the technology developers and the entrepreneurs buying into the new economy. The model for many dot.com start-ups was frequently based on the simple ownership of a domain name, ie 'Fantastic, we own toiletbrush.com – what can we do with it?'

Strauss et al (2003) cite *The Napkin Model*. This was indicative of many dot.com tycoons and entrepreneurs whose plans were informal and ad hoc to say the least. The model captures the spirit of the era, suggesting that plans were formulated over lunch on napkins or the back of envelopes before sprinting off to find a willing investor. In the UK, a beer mat was also useful. SMEs were often cautious, as going online was a journey into the unknown, and they followed a more incremental approach. Short termism and 'living for the moment' typified the majority of online operations during the period. The reality is that technology allows us to build and create more effective, more (or less) complex products and services. However, none of these are of any use unless a demand for them is recognised through common sense marketing research.

It is true that there are some successful survivors from the dot.com to dot.bomb era. Take the search engine Google (www.google.com) that started as a project by two Stanford University students, Larry Page and Sergey Brin, and then progressed to a business plan of the beer mat genre. In 2004 an Initial Public Offering (IPO) raised funds close to $2.7 billion, but this success has largely been due to the shifting sands of the web landscape where search has overtaken e-mail as the 'killer application'. We should all know from the above that Google – the 'beer mat' contender – is now regarded as one of the most innovative and successful survivors of the dot.com fallout period.

3.2 Marketing plans

Brian Smith (2003) of Cranfield School of Management argues that 'it doesn't really matter what business you're in, planners outperform non-planners.'

A marketing plan in any form provides a route map for an organisation's activities. Incorporated within a document are elements that provide direction, coordination and control of the key mix elements. The plan is usually a fine balancing act between the organisation's desired position in the marketplace and its skills, capabilities and resources. The nature, formality and detail of the marketing plan, be it short, medium or long-term, will naturally vary according to the size of the organisation. Large enterprises often indulge in highly complex strategic planning processes and scenarios stretching beyond the medium-term. Small and medium-sized enterprises (SMEs) tend to plan in a more informal, flexible and entrepreneurial way. All successful and innovative organisations have a vision for the development of their business. Those with a marketing orientation have the vision to fulfil a customer need, desire or aspiration and have utilised the Internet as a technology vehicle to achieve commercial success.

3.3 Integrating the e-business

The web was designed by its inventor Tim Berners-Lee as a social creation – not a technical one. It was designed for social effect – to help people work together – not as a technical toy. It was never intended specifically to harbour and evolve as a new marketing communication or advertising medium, or as a transactional tool, but the fact remains, we have never been so connected to each other in such a way before. So the web provides marketing communications opportunities that, before its invention, we could only imagine.

Online marketing, with the four principal tools that are described later in this chapter, is not so revolutionary that it can operate without people anymore. It is not quite about my 'bot can interact with your bot' (a 'bot' being an automated programme that updates lists and content for search engines) so they can buy and sell from each other. Everything you may have learned in your academic teachings from Kotler to Belch and Belch still applies. US

Table 3.1 Evolution of online marketing planning evolution of online marketing planning

Pre-2000	Stand alone/peripheral marketing activity
2000–2003	Online marketing integrated as part of a multi-channel strategy
2003 onwards	A fundamental element in the corporate planning process

Internet authority, Larry Chase suggests that the best Internet texts are really classic direct marketing texts and that online merchants can save money and boost sales by implementing direct marketing principles and practices to the online world such as segmentation, response measurement, personalisation and database marketing.

All we know about social sciences, as applied to marketing communications, impacts one way or another online. Buyer behaviour may differ online from offline and companies may structure themselves differently, or even reinvent themselves. Maslow's Hierarchy of Needs is still just that, and corporations will still have to negotiate the minefield of politics, legislation, cultural differences and fluctuating economies of scale when they bid for cheaper toilet rolls via e-procurement systems.

Online marketing has evolved in sophistication and importance over a short period of time. In its infancy before 2000, online marketing was often viewed as a stand alone or peripheral activity as many firms went through a steep learning curve with its implementation alongside traditional activities. From 2000–2003, online marketing began to establish itself as a mainstream marketing activity as more consumers utilised different channels in the buying cycle and become more confident with the online experience. From 2003, online marketing planning has formed an essential strategic element in the corporate planning function as organisations increasingly adopt enterprise-wide IT systems that link front and back-office activities. More importantly, adoption of the Internet consumers continues to grow at healthy rates across industrialised nations.

3.4 Online marketing planning conventions

Electronic methods of procurement and trading based on dedicated telephony networks predate the World Wide Web considerably. Electronic Data Interchange (EDI) used for dedicated electronic connections between buyers and large corporations for the transfer of purchasing information have used their largest selling partners. 'Hole in the wall' automated-teller-machines (ATM) and electronic credit card processing have been fundamental in transforming the banking industry over a period of years, and electronic booking of airline tickets via centralised databases is common practice for the travel industry. So, certain industries had already embraced newer electronic forms of implementing business systems and processes before the dawning of the web.

The Internet, however, provided the first open network, and the first 'killer application' was e-mail. Even now, without a web presence, a company can still take advantage of e-mail based customer relation management (CRM) and direct e-mail marketing. Millions of companies and consumers have access to e-mail without necessarily having a web presence. Therefore, business transformation can take place without ever building a web site, but only the Internet provides peer-to-peer (or point-to-point) interactivity.

The introduction of the World Wide Web has added the extra benefit of being able to provide a graphical user interface (GUI) in the form of web pages, which can be accessed remotely by the growing millions of web surfers. To capitalise, organisation should look to develop innovative business practices. This could include better responses to customer enquiries; improving channel management; refining 24-hour customer service or incorporating full-blown e-commerce and real-time online trading. It is a fact that responsibility for the integration of Internet based business functions (including marketing) was mainly the responsibility of the IT department. During the mid-nineties, many marketing personnel were still coming to terms with the company's marketing information systems (MIS) and internal computer network (intranet), and apart from that, the Internet was for 'technology geeks' and the few 'early adopters'. The fact that the 'early adopters' were taking up the new communications medium in the millions and growing exponentially each day seemed to be taken with an anecdotal 'pinch of salt'.

However, for Internet business pioneers, establishing ownership of 'the Project' (as it is still frequently and probably incorrectly referred to) the IT and marketing departments were already in dispute. The marketing department may not have known the difference between a SMTP and HTTP and did not really care whilst the IT department may not have appreciated the difference between direct marketing, brand equity or customer relationship management. Molenaar (2002), in considering the strategic choices facing organisations in a climate of change, believes that a casual approach to the Internet is no longer viable. Organisations should take into account changing customer behaviour and the effect on their mix. Resulting from this, an organisation may have to undergo degrees of structural change. He believes that the impacts of the Internet should not be left solely to either IT or marketing people, rather that it requires a multi-disciplinary approach with IT facilitating organisational change in many ways such as procurement, communications and customer relationships. Nevertheless he emphasises the need for marketers to shape the Internet strategy and plans with markets and customers providing the focus. Obviously marketers require IT support to execute campaigns. So in developing its Internet marketing plan an organisation has to consider its technology strategy and the resources needed in terms of hardware, software and skilled personnel.

Whether from the marketing function into IT or vice versa, this new hybrid-marketer provided an early solution to the widening gap of business/technical language, interpretation and translation. Most, if not all, of the early Internet marketers had to be able to translate to contemporaries in both departments what the challenges were, and how best the theory and the practice (from a deliverables perspective) would come together. Even by 2003 the battle for 'ownership' still had not been won by either side, though a shared understanding of each functional contribution was emerging.

A 2003 study cited in Silicon.com by UK based CatchFire Systems led Marketing Director, Nigel Thomas to comment, 'Paradoxically, a successful marketing campaign can actually paralyse normal online business activity by flooding the company's web infrastructure with more visitors than it can support,' and he urged **'techies'** and marketers to 'bridge the communication chasm.'

According to their research CatchFire Systems found that 28% of marketing departments simply did not bother talking to their IT counterparts at all when they were planning a new publicity campaign, while 46% only talked to IT just before the campaign went live. The collision that often occurs between the two during the planning process can result in chaos. Even with both sides understanding the objectives, the final rollout can still cause problems as in the case of Nectar's launch (www.nectar.co.uk) in Mini case 3.1.

MINI CASE 3.1 The Nectar launch

Perhaps one of the most well documented cases was the launch of the Nectar customer loyalty card (started initially by Sainsbury, Debenhams, Barclaycard and BP in the UK).

The promotion, which was one of the largest of its kind for a loyalty scheme, used a 10.5 million conventional mailer to UK households. Under a blaze of publicity offering a reward point bonus for those who registered online, the site was inundated with more than 10,000 requests per hour bringing the service to a standstill. This is not a huge number of requests from browsers-to-servers in today's web marketing environment. In fact a million requests per hour is not difficult to handle but you do need to be prepared for it!

As with any promotional exercise, it is essential to have a fundamental understanding of the nature and numbers of your target groups. Obviously this was not the case on this occasion, as Sainsbury, on the back of this 'online marketing milestone' discovered that their own audience (shoppers) 'had taken to the Internet too quickly for them' as reported by BBC Online (2002).

This may be an extreme example of major offline brands coming online and being the subject of a severe case of 'application over inspiration' but it is not the only one where planning is called back into question. Was marketing really communicating with IT and vice versa?

Just as today's economy is a mixture of old and new, most established companies are a hybrid of the old and the new. Whilst established marketing competencies are still in play, new understandings and competencies add improved potential for growth. In just the same way consumers can now be viewed very much as hybrid. They take advantage of online shopping convenience but still visit the stores for some human interaction and the 'shopping experience'.

3.5 **Developing the online vision**

We can briefly look at two different Internet sites: Friends Reunited (Mini case 3.2) and Apple iTunes (Mini case 3.3) offering superior customer experiences and a vision for a sustainable business.

Friends Reunited is a remarkable success story based on curiosity, nostalgia and the connectivity of the Internet. The site has benefited from effective use of public relations and Friends Reunited have also been proactive in developing the site and 'sister' ventures.

The music industry has been in turmoil as the Internet and music downloads seriously threatened revenue streams and the entire industry structure. Consumers are on the move and the portability of **MP3** players provides a light, compact music source but downloading could be problematic for less capable music surfers. In Mini case 3.3, Apple has had the vision to combine the Internet as a distribution channel via its iTunes music store and iPod MP3 players with customer friendly technology.

Any marketing plan is inextricably linked to the organisation's overall corporate objectives and business mission. Brennan et al (2003) suggest that confusion can arise between strategic marketing and corporate strategy. They observed that both involve *big* decisions, but corporate strategy is concerned with the organisation's broad direction and ambitions whilst a strategic marketing involves a restricted variety of decisions, which focus upon the business unit or competitive strategy level. Some common characteristics do exist, with both

MINI CASE 3.2 Friends Reunited

As with many great business ideas, the Friends Reunited (FR) concept was a simple one that emerged out of curiosity and nostalgia back in 1999. The FR founders, Steve and Julie Pankhurst were expecting their first child, during which time Julie's thoughts turned to her old school friends and what they might be up to both at work and in their personal lives. This is something many people in their thirties and forties will do from time to time, but how can old friends be reached?

With limited Internet skills, the site originated from their back bedroom, and following a few early success stories, news spread quickly both on and offline how old friends from workplaces, schools, colleges, universities and the forces were coming together via Friends Reunited. The organisation experienced rapid growth, with membership expanding from 19,000 in February 2001 to a phenomenal 8 million by the end of 2002! Today membership stands at over 15 million.

The site has become more sophisticated and diversified through a range of history and nostalgia related sub sites such as Genes Reunited, which attracts over 3 million UK Internet users researching their family tree and an Internet dating service. In addition, they have capitalised on their members' thirst and nostalgia with the release of a 1980s compilation CD.

The phenomenal success of Friends Reunited prompted ITV to pay £120 million in December 2005 as the television company sought to develop a higher online profile as well as generate new revenue streams.

Sources: www.friendsreuntited.co.uk
Nielsen/Net Ratings press release, 24 May 2005
www.news.bbc.co.uk/1/hi/business/4502550.stm ITV buys Friends Reunited website

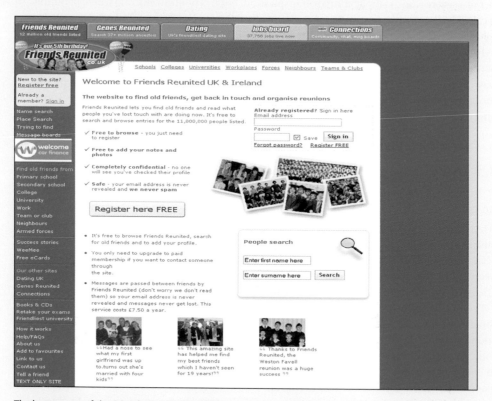

The home page of the Friends Reunited web site

Reproduced by kind permission of Friends Reunited (www.friendsreunited.co.uk)

MINI CASE 3.3 iTunes

Apple (www.apple.com) has become synonymous with innovative and user-friendly technology products during the personal computer revolution of the last few decades. Today, Apple is again at the forefront of technology with its dominance of the online music market through the iPod MP3 device and its iTunes Music Store. Unofficial download sites were undermining the traditional music industry, but now a critical mass has been achieved. And an Apple press release suggests that its iTunes Music Store has now reached 70% of the worldwide market and in excess of 300 million songs have been purchased and downloaded. The iTunes Music Store has been accepted as a key distribution channel for the major music companies, who, along with over a thousand independent music companies, now provide content for the iTunes catalogue.

The product design, both in terms of its style and ease-of-use, enables a fast, seamless downloading experience regardless of the user's technological competence with a simple connection to owners, USB port on their personal computer. The whole concept provides speed and convenience in an extremely light and portable device for a young market on the move. Further innovations provide the user with licensing arrangements to burn songs onto CDs, pre-order albums and download videos. Competitive pricing with easy and secure payment options has also helped the phenomenal success of the online music store and iPod. With the release of its 4.9 iTunes software, the phenomenon known as 'podcasting' where both professionals and amateurs alike can produce digital content for downloading suggests that Apple will continue to push for the barriers in the digital music revolution.

The iTunes Music Store ensured further global recognition when it offered a download of Sir Paul McCartney and U2's Live 8 performance of Sergeant Pepper's Lonely Hearts Club Band within a few hours of coming off stage, with all proceeds going to African charities. This made it the biggest selling download in music history.

Sources: www.apple.com
www.apple.com/uk/pr/230605_itms50m.html
www.news.bbc.co.uk/1/hi/technology/4631051.stm

iTunes drives the online music revolution

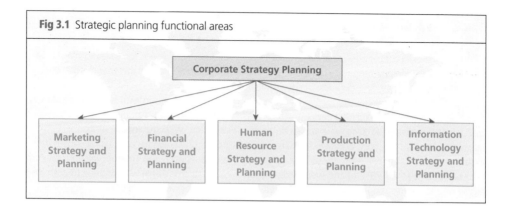

Fig 3.1 Strategic planning functional areas

corporate and marketing strategies seeking to achieve sustainable competitive advantage and value added creation for customers, shareholders and other stakeholders. Interestingly, Brennan et al commented that strategic marketing does not involve the entire organisation and it is shown in Fig 3.1 as a stand-alone function.

However, it can be argued that the nature of e-commerce is having a greater enterprise-wide impact. If an organisation is genuinely marketing-led then its functional plans should originate from customer demands for their offering which help construct the sales forecast. This in turn determines the production schedule, HR and financial resource allocations. A NatWest e-business guide (2001) reinforces the importance of making e-plans. It suggests that organisations need to consider the business in its entirety and how the Internet impacts upon business relationships with customers and suppliers as well as internal relationships. Building or sourcing products to satisfy customers or prospects may require suppliers to deliver in new ways, or new partners to be found to meet changing expectations. Adopting new back-office systems to support the distribution process requires finance, training and careful integration. Kotler (2000) quotes Steve Harrell, a strategic planning manager at General Electric in 1980, saying that 'the marketing manager is the most significant functional contributor to the strategic planning process, with leadership roles in defining the business mission; analysis of the environmental, competitive, and business situations; developing objectives, goals, strategies; and defining the product, market, distribution, and quality plans to implement the business's strategies. This involvement extends to the development of programs and operating plans that are fully linked with the strategic plan.' This may appear wide-ranging, but it nevertheless encapsulates the importance and range of marketing functional activities. Fig 3.2 reflects marketing's central role in the planning function.

It may be broken down into a *strategic* and *tactical* plan and, where appropriate, responsibilities may be assigned either an individual or divisional level. For management purposes, three stages are typically incorporated and cover issues as outlined in Fig 3.3:

1. Planning – deciding on objectives and strategies

2. Implementation – putting the plans into practice

3. Control – measuring and evaluating campaign results and taking remedial action, where appropriate.

Simkin (2002) discusses the various internal impediments that can obstruct the successful implementation of marketing plans. Typical impediments cited are cultural, operational, managerial and communications reasons. Examples of impediments are in Fig 3.4 below.

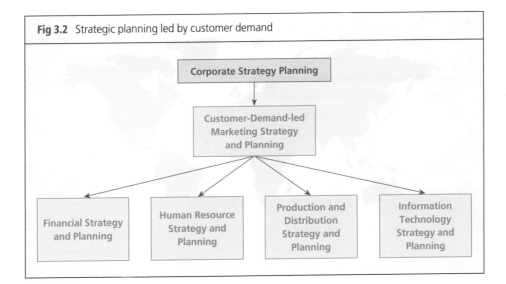

Fig 3.2 Strategic planning led by customer demand

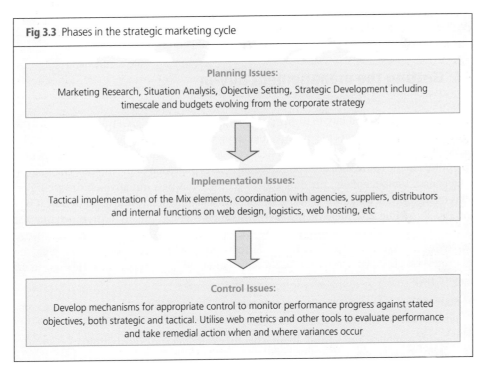

Fig 3.3 Phases in the strategic marketing cycle

Simkin comments that many business and marketing related academic programmes rarely incorporate any internal marketing elements in their syllabi, yet it is vital for the development and adoption of a marketing plan within marketing and other functional areas. Interestingly, Simkin suggests that one traditional barrier – the lack of a marketing ethos – has been removed, as it becomes recognised as a key management function. This is encouraging but just when we get non-marketing senior management to recognise marketing at board level along comes the Internet with new tools and rules to grapple with! Having said

---

Fig 3.4 Examples of impediments to marketing planning

- Lack of CEO support
- Marketing planning in isolation from corporate objectives
- Failure to understand marketing concept and function
- Poor internal communications
- Top down approach to planning
- Not Invented Here syndrome
- Poor involvement and lack of interest across functional areas
- Limited planning time available
- Perceived lip service to the planning process

---

that, we must accept that many marketers were also having difficulty coming to terms with the new medium. How many times have we read Internet articles asking, 'Is it just another promotional tool?' or 'Is it just another channel of distribution?'

3.6 Getting the management buy-in

Getting the management buy-in to any project is always a challenge. Getting them to see the value of the Internet when dot.com anxieties reigned a few years ago made a well-researched marketing plan essential for any would-be investor. It is imperative that top management is committed to the whole idea of e-commerce and shares the vision of the internal champions.

Of course, fundamentally, the only way to get the e-business initiative off the ground at all is by developing a legitimate business case with a compelling justification of how it will succeed. By getting agreement on the likely costs and benefits company-wide, much internal conflict can be avoided from the start. Senior executives may not possess the knowledge or vision to construct an online plan. Matthewson (2002) discusses ways in which the e-business case in general terms can be promoted internally to non-believers. He suggests an 8-point plan:

1. Start at the beginning – think how Internet adoption will help the organisation accomplish its aims and objectives
2. E-business applications – think about what they can offer the organisation, its customers and other stakeholders
3. Calculate the costs – eg technology, marketing and structural costs
4. Calculate the benefits – give an indication of what improvements may accrue such as new customers, better retention rates and profitability
5. Assess the impact and risk – a balanced risk assessment should be made of the advantages and disadvantages of going online
6. Think about Return on Investment (ROI) – indicate clearly with supporting evidence how the online operation will add value

7. Present your Plan – highlighting the strategy against alternatives and 'what's in it for me' for the different functional areas

8. Prove e-business will add value – summarise the key benefits of adoption and the dangers of not adopting

Whilst Matthewson's guide points to the selling of the wider e-commerce concept to management, they are still relevant for Internet marketing planning. Marketers believe that marketing must be at the centre of any organisation's activities and therefore its actions will impact upon other functional areas. Customers, products and services drive the business.

The company's core business strategy can be built around, for instance, the overall objectives of facilitating relationships before and after the transaction with prospects, customers, partners and supply chain members.

However, as is often the case, the core strategy may be made up of smaller but quite legitimate initiatives and projects that can have a tendency to conflict and overlap. It is essential to recognise all of the players and constituents early in the planning process for the purpose of coordination and prioritisation. As has already been outlined in this chapter, each initiative or project leader will want ownership and pride themselves that theirs is the most important point of focus within the overall e-business objectives. Neef (2001) in his excellent text covering the adoption of e-procurement stresses the importance of 'executive sponsorship and participation'. He suggests that business leaders' understanding of e-procurement may vary and that within an organisation, project aims and objectives may be misunderstood. His observation is just as relevant in an e-marketing context in that organisational leaders involved, either directly or indirectly, should participate in every phase of the project. Neef argues that 'if the executives themselves don't have a common understanding of the business need, and the project approach, the project from the outset is in danger of degenerating into a battle over funding and resources, languishing, running long – or worst of all – resulting in a poorly integrated technical solution that does not take into account, process and activity changes.' Zhuang and Lederer (2004) studied the impact of top management commitment, business process redesign, and IT planning and business to consumer web sites and how they contribute to organisational performance. The research found that CEO commitment and e-commerce planning combine to provide web sites with more comprehensive, user-friendly features that ultimately delivered better return on investment.

It is not only important to lobby and get support from outside of the marketing function, but it may also be necessary to educate sales and marketing staff about the benefits accruing from new technologies. For example, scepticism may be prevalent amongst sales staff about the implementation of CRM software applications to drive their day-to-day activities when previously they had a high degree of control out in the field. CRM systems also generate high volumes of market related information, and the use and benefits must be sold internally.

Other commentators have argued that Internet marketing requires a separate strategy. However, writers such as Chaffey (2003) suggest that the Internet marketing plan should now be as firmly integrated into the mix as each of the other components, whether it is viewed as just another channel to market, or business or re-engineering opportunity, the systems and processes applied will still rely on conventional marketing wisdom. It can be argued that there are no new marketing principles employed, simply a more rapid and cost efficient deployment.

In the case of companies such as Dell, Tesco, Barnes and Noble, and Cisco, business transformation was required in an effort to harness the benefits of a more dynamic online business model. However, all employ conventional offline marketing and promotional tactics as part of their overall strategy. Where business transformation is the main objective, then a greater emphasis on change management is required rather than a simple marketing strategy review meeting. Clearly, an organisation that relies heavily on technology platforms for sales and revenue must give special treatment to its online marketing activities. The nature of this focus will vary if the organisation is a pure play such as Amazon (www.amazon.com) or clicks and bricks operation such as Tesco (www.tesco.com).

The case for business automation goes as far back as the Industrial Revolution. The comparison between the Industrial Revolution and the Internet has almost become a cliché. The Internet with its unique ability to link buyers and sellers together on a global scale demands automation for efficiency. The Industrial Revolution and the invention of motorised transport may have had a huge impact on production and distribution for companies worldwide. However, with the Internet it is not just the sellers who have been empowered, it is also the buyers. Buying power has been vastly increased and the choice and variety of goods and services is huge. Information on just about every known subject abounds online, and comparison between available goods and services adds a whole new dimension to the organisation's struggle for differentiation.

When Michael de Kare-Silver (2002) declared that the trigger for writing his book, *Streamlining* was because he had seen a series of advertisements proclaiming that Oracle had saved $1 billion 'by e-enabling the business', it was a sure sign that e-scepticism was again being replaced by e-optimism. He describes the process of implementing the e-business initiative as 'enabling, automating and innovation'. Mohan Sawhney of Kellogg School of Management defines it in a similar way: 'The use of networks and associated technologies to automate, augment or redesign a business system' with the outcome of providing 'superior value propositions for customers and business partners.' (See *Winning at E-Business: The Strategic Agenda* – www.mohansawhney.com)

3.7 Online marketing plans

Online-marketing planning, in essence, will draw on everything we know about planning for conventional marketing disciplines and amalgamate the methods, benefits and expediency of IT and knowledge-network based solutions.

Online marketing is a function within the organisation's overall e-business strategy, and because terms and phrases such as 'World Wide Web' and 'Internet' are frequently used interchangeably it can lead to confusion from the very beginning. The Internet was around a long time before the World Wide Web, which is an application built on top of the Internet, ie the Internet is host to the World Wide Web. Put more simply: The Internet can exist as a communications medium without the World Wide Web, but not the other way around.

The integration of e-business into the organisation helps to pave the way for linking e-business with e-marketing strategy and identify revenue streams suggested by e-business models. Strauss et al (2003) recommend a two-tier approach:

1. Perform marketing opportunity analysis to identify target stakeholders. Specify brand differentiation variables. Select positioning strategy.

2. Design the offer, value, distribution, communication and market/partner relationship management strategies.

Many early Internet marketing plans suffered from a lack of realism and over-optimism regarding the proper opportunities offered online. For some, it was a journey into the unknown, on which they made various assumptions that were fundamentally flawed. These included over-estimating market size, the cost of acquiring new customers and building online brands, and the speed at which different consumer groups would actually adopt the Internet for buying goods and services. However, online trading experiences, coupled with available internal and external market information, now provide the basis for more accurate and relevant planning.

The nature of Internet marketing plans is not significantly different to plans formulated for an offline business or product in that they are often based upon traditional marketing principles. Chaffey et al (2003) consider the merits of utilising so called strategic process models for online planning including the ten-step model developed by Professor Malcolm McDonald (1999) that many marketing students will already be familiar with.

Six key planning elements include a situation analysis, the link from e-business to e-marketing strategy, the plan objectives, an implementation plan, the budget and a plan for evaluating success.

Situation analysis has been a primary function of marketing planning and applies to e-marketing in just the same way. It involves a review of the firm's environmental and SWOT analyses as well as the existing marketing plan and any other information that can be gathered about the company and its brands. At a macro level, the organisation will consider supplier and distributor relationships, as well as a thorough competitor analysis. A STEP analysis covering Societal, Technological, Economic and Political influences gives planners a feel for factors outside of their control which nevertheless should shape their marketing outputs. A review of the company's e-business objectives matched with strategies and performance metrics completes the analysis.

3.8 Understanding change in the digital age

Such models offer a safe framework, but Chaffey suggests that more flexible and receptive models are required for the online world. Smith and Chaffey (2002) suggest that e-marketing is essentially the principles and practice of marketing set in a new context of digital technologies. As a result, an Internet marketing plan is likely to contain a mix of traditional and new applications but the principal aim of customer satisfaction remains paramount. The Internet marketing plan differs from the traditional with the range of technologies available and their potential impacts for customers and organisations alike. Undoubtedly, consumer behaviour has changed because of the technology and organisations must understand and respond accordingly. Lucas (2002) discusses types of change and how they influence strategic plans. In the pre-Internet days, change was usually related to individual IT developments, but Lucas argues that organisations may have to restructure on an enterprise-wide scale to benefit from Internet opportunities. Any organisation should address the issue of change and how it can influence or dictate strategic choices. Lucas examines the work of Orlikowski (1996) to arrive at different models of change:

1. Planned change – this model suggest that managers or champions actually instigate change in a planned way. This requires the agent of change to sell the benefits of their vision or proposed changes internally, and to have the authority to implement them.

2. Technologically inspired change – which drives organisational restructuring either by department or across the organisation. For example, e-CRM, which is predominantly marketing-driven, requires information flows from other functional areas to be effective. Internet technologies have provided efficiency opportunities for organisations in the areas of online auctions and e-procurement and other business models as outlined earlier in chapter 2.

3. Emergent change occurs when organisations adopt the technology in new, innovative ways previously unimaginable. Such change can rarely be predicted, though it will be more prevalent in leading edge organisations where the culture is supportive and challenging.

4. Punctuated equilibrium – suggests that organisations and industries go through cycles where, following dramatic industry changes, periods of calm or punctuated equilibrium prevail. This model tends to take a medium-term perspective. Following the period of Internet boom and bust, a general caution descended upon the market whilst marketers reassessed tools like banner ads and e-mail marketing.

5. Integrated model – Lucas pulls together the threads from the previous four models suggesting that managers need to be aware of and appreciate the trends occurring during the punctuated equilibrium. However, in a market heavily influenced by technological developments, interactions between planned change and technologically inspired change is likely to occur. An e-commerce champion should sell the technological vision and seek to implement it in a planned way, which appreciates all the resource and organisational impacts. If the organisation gains knowledge, experience and confidence online, then Lucas suggests emergent change may result.

Doyle (1998) discusses the importance of adapting to a changing environment. He suggests that there are two main types of environmental change:

1. Continuous change typified by ongoing trends such as climate change and adoption of new technologies.

2. Discontinuous change when unexpected changes cause major industry and organisational reassessments of their operations. Many organisations have found the Internet to be a disruptive technology.

Doyle refers to these unforeseen changes or shocks as *strategic windows* and suggests a number of key causes which we will consider in the context of the online world:

1. New technology eg it is new technology that has facilitated the growth of low-cost air operators to the detriment of established carriers.

2. New segments eg 'Silver Surfers' have emerged as a lucrative target market for the travel industry seeking off-peak business.

3. New channels of distribution eg music downloads over the Internet or e-ticketing in the travel industry.

4. Market redefinition eg **Search Engine Optimisation** moving to Pay-Per-Click models.

5. New legislation eg European Union Privacy and Communications Directive (2003) affecting e-mail and SMS marketing.

6. Environmental shocks eg the dot.com crash of 2000.

Online marketers have to be aware of the environment in which they operate and the change evolving within it. How they react to that change depends upon the corporate philosophy, culture and resources. In crude terms, organisations typically fall into three broad categories. They may be (1) proactive in driving change; (2) reactive to follow the leader; (3) take the ostrich approach and hope that change will not affect them. Words like flexible, responsive and agile are regularly associated with Internet business models and strategies and successful online merchants reflect these organisational values. However, not every Internet business is progressive and innovative. How many fail to do the simple things effectively such as updated their site frequently or promptly responding to e-mail enquiries? Effective understanding of the environment typically relied on entrepreneurial instincts for SMEs or well structured and functioning Marketing Information Systems (MkIS) in larger organisations. The Internet offers new capabilities for environmental scanning with technologies that we take for granted like Google alerts.

Wilson (2002) observes that whilst some plans will focus purely on e-commerce (ie Pure Players), or possibly view their Internet operation as a distinct activity, the growth in multi-channel marketing invariably requires the integration of on and offline activities within a plan. From an historical perspective, marketing planning during the dot.com frenzy appeared to be split. Organisations like Amazon (www.amazon.com) had a clear vision and a longer-term view of their marketplace and put the appropriate technologies in place to sustain the online customer experience. As an alternative, the Napkin Model cited earlier offers a more ad hoc, opportunist approach.

3.9 Online marketing plans in context

The content of the marketing plan must be set in context of the organisation's Internet history, business model, vision and aspirations. Most online marketing plans fall into one of three contexts:

Brand new website

This is an organisation's first foray into the online world. If the organisation's key driver is customer satisfaction then they must really understand what the customers actually want from a web site and not *what they think* the customer might want in terms of specific features and benefits which they value. So what are the purposes, or key objectives of the new site?

- Is it to reach a wider audience, similar to the profile of existing key customers?
- Is it to provide greater flexibility to existing customers through a new channel option as part of a multi-channel marketing approach?
- Is it to sell direct to customers because of changing lifestyles?
- Is it the development of a separate online brand? eg egg (www.egg.com)
- Is it increased sales, market share or profits?
- Is it going to be purely a transactional site or a fully interactive e-commerce/e-CRM driven site?
- Is it to increase lifetime values or average order values?
- Is it all the objectives related to some aspect of business transformation to streamline the business, eg integration across the supply chain?

Whatever the nature of the objectives set, because the Internet is a form of direct marketing, they should be specific and measurable with clearly stated time frames for completion. In addition, responsibilities for the handling of the project must be assigned and for the liaison with web design and web development companies. Clearly such organisations will need briefing on the objectives, target audience, branding issues (including domain name registration), the level of interactivity, the quality and quantity of content, how enquiries and orders will be fulfilled and the available budget. All good marketers should use their eyes and ears, as so many web site ideas will evolve from the host company's online observations and experiences of leading edge and good practice. A web design agency should outline the technology and software available to provide a user-friendly experience for the consumer and measurability and tracking for the organisation. Thought must be given to the web site architecture and whether it provides an easily navigable site. It is also tempting to apply every multimedia format and application for visual appeal but tools like Flash can prove to be more of an irritant unless they are used sparingly and add value to the customer experience. It is advisable to carry out thorough usability testing with a decent sample of the target audience prior to going live.

The budgeting process for the site development and related marketing activities involves both costs and revenue forecasts. Fortunately, there has been significant cost reduction for most online marketing activities while speed and power have increased. As the Internet has for many organisations become an integral part of their marketing activity, it now commands a larger slice of the marketing budget. 15% of the overall budget is usually the bare minimum for the online element. A web site may be tailored for any budget, but the cost of design with graphics, page layouts, content management and database integration may start from around £7,500. Other site cost elements will relate to software and hardware purchases, together with site optimisation and performance costs. The online marketing costs will depend on the organisation's objectives that could be based on repeat visits, the number of cyber-registrations or brand awareness. The costs of integrated marketing communications will depend upon the methods employed. In addition to mainstream advertising, marketing planners will also have to factor in the cost of banner advertising (both the production cost and cost per page views), costs of pay-per-click and keyword purchasing. A variable element should be incorporated to the search engine budget, largely because competitor activity is an unknown and bidding wars may ensue.

Regarding revenue forecasting, Strauss et al suggest that firms use established sales forecasting methods. Generally this can be broken down into two broad forecasting category levels, macro and micro. At the macro level, planners will utilise broad industry data from a variety of recognised sources such as Mintel, Keynote and Forrester highlighting market demand and the current marketing environment impacting upon the sector. These sources will not only give data to forecast current demand but they often provide good forecasted future trends. The revenue forecasts should be time specific. For a marketing plan, others will cover a calendar year with at least quarterly and monthly sales forecasts to indicate peaks and troughs and seasonal trends. At a micro level, planners will attempt to develop accurate unit revenue forecasts both by product and the different component parts of the web site. Factors such as the product's position in its life-cycle, previous demand by product and segment, together with any market research undertaken to identify customers' current and future intentions will contribute. Different web site components may generate different revenue contributions, such as sales, site sponsorship, commission from affiliate marketing and subscriptions.

An essential element of the budgeting process is applying and understanding variance analysis that investigates the planned forecast against the actual results for a specified time

Fig 3.5 A typical web hosting solution for home and business use (www.visualnetcentre.com)
Reproduced by kind permission of VisualNetCentre.

period. The online plan should incorporate the contingency strategy that provides alternative courses of action where a significant variance has occurred.

Web hosting and other technology issues

During the course of preparing the online marketing plan, it is essential to have a grasp of some of the technical issues that are likely to impinge. The web site has to have an identity and it has to exist somewhere in **cyberspace** where it can be found. An organisation's entire web site content is located on the host's server. Rayport and Jaworski (2002) suggests that a web host 'serves as a web site's secure, high bandwidth, professionally-maintained connection to the Internet.' They highlight a number of web hosting alternatives, from *free* hosting solutions to *shared* and *dedicated server* hosting, and the main choice criteria will relate to price and the amount of web space needed. An example of a web hosting solution is given in Fig 3.5. Other web hosting consideration should be taken into account, such as:

- ease of access, speed and reliability;
- guaranteed uptime to ensure 24:7 functionality;
- relevant amount of disk space to handle the number of site pages;
- 24:7 technical support;
- e-mail capabilities to handle all enquiries including outbound auto responder messages;

- e-mail capabilities to handle multiple domain names such as .com, .co.uk, .de, .fr, .au, etc;

- availability of secure and compatible shopping cart and merchant facilities.

Purchasing and hosting the correct domain name for your service or product is crucial. During the 'wonder years' of Internet start-ups it was all about being 'cool' and choosing names such as Yahoo! or Amazon, which say little about the product or service, but lend themselves to some very interesting creative adaptations.

However, the trend now is to purchase a domain name that directly supports the brand, or relates to the content/purpose of the web site, which then, indirectly, also supports the brand.

To ensure that the site can meet unexpected demands in traffic, web managers should run system tests referred to as stress and load testing. This primarily mimics the worst-case scenario of user visits including number of pages viewed, images accessed, handling of signing-in procedures and shopping carts. This is essential to identify any weaknesses in the system that may affect its stability.

Another important consideration in an Internet marketing plan is the technology used by the receiver. Both organisations and individuals are usually protected by firewalls that may limit the type and size of file that they are capable of receiving. Fortunately, the growth in broadband reduces the problems of download file times. In addition, consumers like choice, therefore it is necessary to know which is their preferred format for receiving communications like e-mail eg HTML or plain text.

Redesign/rebranding of an existing web site

As online customer expectations rise, organisations should not become complacent. They should continually update their web site either with frequent, minor changes or a major redesign. To increase brand loyalty it is essential to improve the user experience otherwise boredom may set in and they may transfer their allegiance elsewhere. Typical improvements may include:

- Streamlining for easier and faster navigation

- Easier shopping cart and checkout procedures

- Providing advanced search facilities

- Building customer oriented new site features

Full integration with other marketing activities and channels

Simons et al (2002) suggest that there are clear synergies between electronic and traditional physical channels and that the Internet is beginning to take over some functions customarily executed through offline channels. The authors referred to unbundling of functions occurring where the Internet can offer significant cost and time savings for both the organisation and the consumer.

From a promotional and customer service perspective, full integration requires a complete change in mindset and an understanding of how each channel is valued by consumers. The organisation must recognise the contribution from each channel and how they may be evolving over time and reallocate budgets and promotional efforts accordingly.

Seth Romanov (2002) of Compaq observes, 'Designing, redesigning, and deploying web sites is part art, part science, part emotion and part commonsense.' The success of a site will predominantly be influenced by the way the customer engages with it, and if it delivers what the customer wants. Therefore, the design elements will have to incorporate creativity, functionality based on testing an experience. The design should be combined with passion and value through the brand and a coherence, which ultimately conveys a relevant experience delivering long-term loyalty. Just like the elements of the marketing mix, the component parts of any web site must strive the consistency in terms of brand image, positioning and customer service design with the relevant target market in mind.

3.10 Customer focus remains paramount

The old adage of putting yourself in the customer's shoes is sound advice for online marketing planners. Developing a marketing plan with existing strategic frameworks is often helpful because of the systematic process deployed. For example, we can carry out the situational analysis and develop objectives, strategies and implementation plans by method and eliminate each activity from our checklist. However, it is dangerous to become preoccupied with all of these elements and to lose sight of the key ingredient for business success, which should of course be the customer, or market segments whose needs shape our activities. In his speech on the marketing matrix at the 10th Annual Institute of Direct Marketing in May 2005, Professor Don Schultz (2005) castigates various marketing definitions revolving around the 4 P's and their failure to make any reference about the customer. Schultz suggests that many practitioners believe that getting the 4 P's developed as a consistent offering is sacrosanct, ahead of any customer considerations. We can understand where Professor Schultz is coming from as some marketers fail to consider the customer sufficiently. However, a deeper understanding of customer behaviour is vital in increasingly competitive and sophisticated markets, especially when customisation provides added value. Within the last few years, the term 'customer insight' has been applied by many organisations, most notably Tesco, to suggest the need for new levels of penetrative customer understanding which should populate the corporate database and feed any e-CRM activity. Insights require a meeting of the customer's key characteristics and their online/integrated behaviour such as:

- The key bases for segmentation including age, sex, income, marital status and occupation

- Detailed analysis of visitor web site usage data for extra insight into customer product or service preferences. In addition, organisations may measure campaign effectiveness and customer loyalty and value with software tools like Web trends

- Behavioural characteristics, eg those obtained through lifestyle questionnaires and other feedback to include their attitudes, interests and opinions on a range of subjects and not just the organisation's products to give clues on customer perceptions and motivations. In addition, understanding commonly used keyword search terms can give a useful insight into behavioural influences as well as optimise a web site for a search engine submission

- Purchase behaviour patterns such as the product category, how much and how often and the likelihood buying accessories, etc. Direct marketers have typically used tools like RFM Analysis (Recency, Frequency and Monetary Value) to score customers based on their responses to promotional activities such as outbound e-mail campaigns, which can be tracked and measured via source codes. Such analyses are important for targeting relevant customers with relevant offers, at the right time

- Linked to RFM is Lifetime Values (LTV)

We may wish to increase market share or brand awareness, or perhaps refine our database marketing activities as part of our objective setting, but without a fundamental appreciation of the online customer's desires and expectations then the objectives will be rendered useless. It is important to recognise that the buyer-seller relationship has changed significantly with the advent of the Internet. With the click of a mouse, a buyer may jump to a competitor's site or peruse a price comparison site, which may result in behaviour that is more fickle and less loyal than previously exhibited. The customer clearly has more information and choices at his/her disposal, not to mention a far wider range of suppliers to choose from. Any online marketing plan, therefore, must analyse the needs, expectations and aspirations of the chosen target group through an effective two-way dialogue. These expectations may manifest themselves in a number of ways. For example, certain standards of customer service may be expected online, such as the handling of e-mail enquiries, the quality of knowledge bases within web sites and order tracking systems. Customers may also value the development of an online community, which provides entertainment, relevant products and services, information and advice. The sense of community thrives on two key Internet dimensions: interactive dialogue and shared knowledge. By their nature, forums may be general or special interest groups. For example, in Fig 3.6, the X-Power forum (www.xpower-mg.com/forum) provided all of these elements for MG car enthusiasts even in the darkest days of the MG Rover demise.

From the seller's perspective, targeting has taken on greater importance, both in terms of designing a web site for specific segments, and promotional activity with relevant and timely offers. Reed Smith (2000) extols the virtue of designing your web site not for the average customer, but for the most valuable customer with high lifetime values. This indeed makes sense to attract high yield customers, and devise a site with their preferences in mind. Making their experience exclusive can be done in various ways, such as password protected, privileged promotions on special micro-sites.

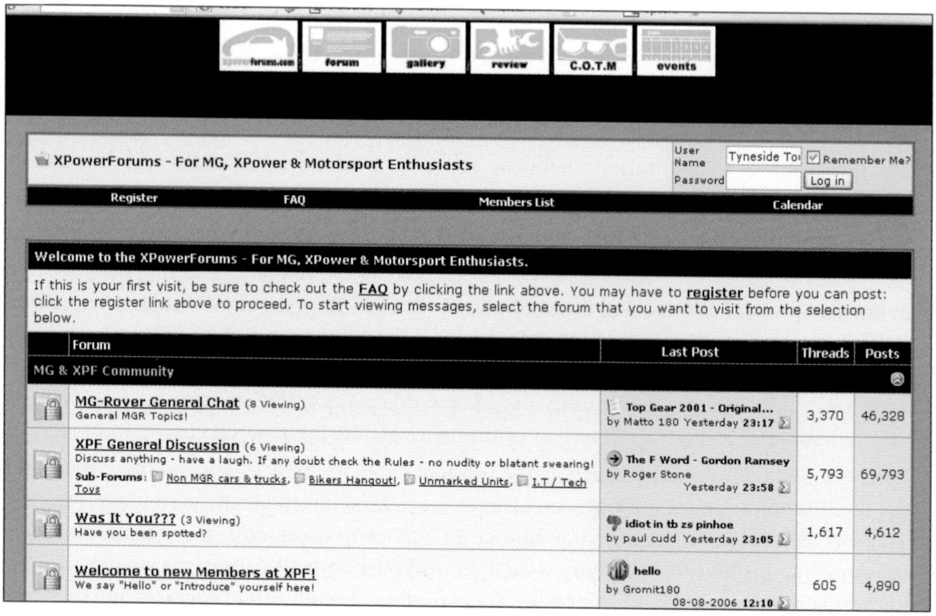

Fig 3.6a X Power forum

Reproduced by kind permission of Jerry Flint of XPF.

Fig 3.6b An image from Clearasil ForMen's web site (www.clearasilformen.co.uk)

The organisation's online marketing approach will be influenced by its primary focus, or core competencies. Molenaar (2002) suggests four orientations that will determine the marketing tactics. These are as follows:

1. Internally Focused Orientation tends to focus on its internal processes and distribution channels in the sense of a classic 'production orientation'. The organisation will rely on existing relationships with the emphasis on salesmanship and sales promotion. It is unlikely that the full potential of the Internet is realised by such organisations.

2. Target Group Orientation concentrates on meeting the needs of a precise market segment. All marketing activities, especially communications, will identify with the target group's values and will also stay close in order to identify future trends. A number of 'pure play' organisations have adopted such an approach in line with a younger, time poor and 'net savvy' audience.

    For example, the skincare company Clearasil (www.clearasilformen.co.uk/) launched a new website aimed at 16–24 year-old males. The site supports the introduction of their new product range that helps young men to fight spots whilst washing and shaving.

    For the guys who do still want to play with their toys, they can visit Firebox or BoysStuff.

3. Customer Focused Orientation moves from the needs of a target group to the needs of an individual. Molenaar suggests that this is most effective in the final stage of the offline distribution chain when sales staff in a retail environment tailor the product to customer needs. In bygone days, the shopkeeper knew his customers' individual tastes and preferences. The Internet provides organisations with the capability to capture individual transactional and lifestyle data and tailor timely and relevant offers. Molenaar suggests that the successful implementation of this orientation needs to go the extra mile and provide an effective customer bonding policy which combines three elements cited in Tracy and Wiersema, namely customer intimacy, operational excellence and product leadership.

    In Mini case 3.4 gardening and plant specialist, Crocus (www.crocus.co.uk) recognised the limited Internet capabilities and confidence of its older target audience. Their

MINI CASE 3.4 Crocus

Gardening, and in particular, buying plants, is a major leisure pursuit for many UK households, but selling them online required considerable thought and organisation by the web gardening firm, Crocus (www.crocus.co.uk).

Crocus sought to provide added value to the gardening enthusiast with a vast range of high-quality plants sourced from specialist nurseries. Whereas most garden centres typically offer around 400 different plants, Crocus now carries over 4,000 in its range, providing the same choice as professionals.

It quickly recognised that their older target market had specific needs and concerns that needed to be addressed. First, they were less comfortable online compared to younger, net-savvy users and so it was important to provide reassurance through

a user-friendly, information packed site, endorsed by leading garden celebrities, Alan Titchmarsh and Charlie Dimmock. To increase customer loyalty and reduce disappointment, Crocus also employs four two plant doctors to offer all sorts of advice on plant selection and wider gardening issues but the customer-focused operation does not stop there. Crocus' logistics operation ensures that the plants arrive in excellent condition, and even the drivers may provide further gardening advice at the point of delivery, using specially designed packaging and a next day courier service.

Sources: www.crocus.co.uk
Adapted from: *Internet Business*, April 2002, pp 36–37
www.zyra.org.uk/crocus1.htm

Help for the online gardener
Reproduced by kind permission of www.crocus.co.uk.

concerns were paramount in the design of the site and the customer service to support it.

4. Network Focused Orientation revolves around key partnerships between independent parties who combine to provide a satisfying customer experience. For example, UpMyStreet (www.upmystreet.com) is a quality source of advice for those contemplating buying a new home, or getting the best out of their existing property in a specific local area. The site contains a number of online partners with domestic household relevance such as the Halifax and co-branding with the likes of Npower and AOL. Similarly many manufacturers of personal computers combine with manufacturers of hardware and software to provide customer service expertise with peripherals.

3.11 **Multi-channel marketing**

Multi-channel marketing has increased in importance and usage in the last five years as consumers use a number of different channels to interact with an organisation at different times. Rangaswamy and Van Bruggen (2005) stress the importance of distinguishing multi-channel marketing from multiple-channel marketing. They suggest that multiple-channel marketing is when a firm uses different channels to interact with different segments. For example, Key Account Management (KAM) will utilise personal selling with high value customers whereas the low cost channels such as call centres and the Internet may be used to interact with low-value customers.

The multi-channel consumer is a new phenomenon and organisations and academics are only beginning to understand their behaviour patterns. To what extent do they seek information and buy online, or do they buy offline? Rangaswamy and Van Bruggen suggest that the multi-channel consumer is more valuable than the single channel shopper. Therefore, organisations should strive to offer a seamless and synchronised experience across its different channels. In addition, they should work out how to use each channel effectively for both acquisition and retention purposes. This could be achieved by moving consumers away from costly catalogues or retailing to flexible and interactive e-brochures. Alternatively, the retail outlet could be used, possibly with incentives to introduce people to the online channel. Going multi-channel impacts on marketing communications together with ramifications for the consistency of the brand and its message. For effective campaign management and customer service, organisations need to develop a clear strategy with supporting systems for their data integration across channels. In addition, many multi-channel organisations rely on third party supply chain partners, especially for the distribution function, and so real time two-way channel communications with those in the supply chain is essential.

3.12 **The online marketing mix**

Much has been written about the demise of the marketing mix and its relevance in the online world. It is certainly true that some new rules apply, such as permission and increased customer power, but the mix still provides a useful framework for formulating an offer to a specific target market. Stone et al (2003) define the offer as 'the total proposition made to the customer' that incorporates the product, positioning, pricing and format, which should be both personal and relevant. We will briefly look at the original 4 Ps (Product, Price, Promotion and Place) and then consider the relevance of the 3 P's of the service mix.

Product (see chapter 9)

Without a product, there is nothing to offer the marketplace. Visionaries like de Kare Silver (2000) have considered the ease or difficulty which different product categories may be sold online. We can make the distinction between physical, virtual and service products, but need to understand how to sell and distribute them effectively online. For example, it is easy to sell physical products like books, CDs and golf balls online as these are generic by nature, but it is more difficult to sell perfume for the first time online because of its sensory elements. To create interest and desire in the new perfume, offline channels may be used to send out samples direct or in-store in an integrated campaign. However, the customer can buy with confidence next time online having experienced the product. So online marketers should consider product and promotional strategies for 'new buy' and 'reorder' categories. We have also witnessed the use of customisation in the automotive and personal computer sectors to satisfy individual preferences.

Virtual products, often referred to as 'information goods' are by their nature ideal for the digital world especially in terms of fast, flexible content and high-speed, low-cost production and distribution. The web is now full of intermediaries offering knowledge-based products and services both free and on subscription including research, or white papers to enhance standing in their chosen sector of expertise. Decisions have to be made on the content offered, whether it is generated in-house or bought-in, and how it will be used for acquisition and retention via the corporate database.

Similarly, service products such as travel and insurance products, are also ideally suited to the online environment. The Internet provides wonderful convenience and an easy ability to extend its product offering. For example, Insure and Go (www.insureandgo.com) set up online as a specialist travel insurer. It has extended its range to include everything from car insurance to life insurance as well as teaming up with others to provide products such as pet insurance. Table 3.2 illustrates the core and added values of a web site.

Table 3.2 Adding product value online

Product nature	Core benefits (tangible & intangibles)	Added value
Physical (CDs, cars, food, etc)	• Style, status, satisfy thirst and hunger, entertainment, convenience, guarantees, etc	• Customer reviews and recommendations, collaborative filtering, 360-degree product viewing • Online customer service 24:7 • Customer choice
Service Banks, airlines, professional services	• Detailed service information, • 24:7 availability and delivery • Speed and convenience • Customer interactions and dialogue for increased loyalty • Self-service customer service via FAQ's/Knowledge Base = consumer empowerment. Real-time transactions, e-ticketing and account information	• Customisation, service consistency • Customer choice • Tailored responses • Digital distribution • White papers enhancing brand image
Information/Virtual News, financial data and music	• Digital distribution, 24:7, entertainment and information rich • Information is easily and cheaply replicated and disseminated online • Customisation capability • Real time delivery	• No content limit • Increasing multimedia content • Online seminars for promotion and customer acquisition

Price (see chapter 10)

An online merchant has to wrestle with his/her pricing strategies just like any offline business. A number of factors have to be taken into consideration such as:

- knowledge of the competition, eg from price comparison sites;
- whether the site combines premium products with 'clearance pages' to heavily discount discontinued product lines;
- the customer's propensity to spend and the value they place upon the product or service. For example, information products such as online newspapers were free to individuals mainly in an effort to gain customer acceptance, but now subscription models have been implemented for valuable, content-rich parts of the site.

In general, the Internet provides a more cost-effective method of distribution, enabling significant cost savings so there is an expectation of lower prices online. This is indeed the case with various online auctions and e-procurement sites such as e-bay, Commerce One and Covisint. In addition, organisations have to become more conscious of the power of price comparison web sites. For example, Uswitch (www.uswitch.com) was set up with the objective of providing consumers with the best deals on utilities such as gas, electricity and water. It is becoming increasingly important to be in the top rankings so constant monitoring is essential for utilities companies, in a similar way to search engine rankings. In addition to price comparison technology, the Internet has also introduced the instant process of dynamic pricing. This enables organisations to maximise profit and market share in line with peaks and troughs in demand.

Generally, many organisations offer slightly reduced selling prices online, but this is often offset by lower direct and indirect costs. However, when delivery charges are added, the full cost to the consumer may be more than the high street cost. In addition, you may find that in certain circumstances, an organisation's high street prices are lower than their online prices due to intense price competition eg price matching, in a particular town or city.

Place (see chapter 12)

Is the Internet just another distribution channel? For some organisations it is just another revenue stream within their multi-channel operation yet for others it is core to the business model with the potential to serve customers way beyond the normal geographic boundaries. For organisations involved in selling physical products online, the offline functions of physical distribution management, channel management and logistics are fundamental to achieving customer satisfaction with delivery as and when promised. Two key benefits for users of the Internet are speed and convenience and it is also a necessity for the distribution function. Technologies like Electronic Data Interchange (EDI) and Extensible Markup Language (XML) provide superb real-time exchange of information. Consumers may access account information or track orders, whilst parties in the supply chain benefit from greater efficiency and inventory control. Specialist logistics organisations perform a critical role within the supply chain, leaving the producer to concentrate on their core competences.

The Internet provides the opportunity for organisations to go direct to customers and eliminate intermediaries, a process referred to as disintermediation. However, planners must carefully consider the role played by intermediaries in the first instance and whether their market knowledge, expertise and customer service will be difficult to replicate online once eliminated. The benefits offered by intermediaries should be balanced against the cost reductions of going direct online. Whilst there has been some removal of intermediaries (disintermediation) in some sectors reintermediation has occurred with new facilitators emerging in the electronic marketplace. For example, in the travel industry, there has been a rationalisation of the traditional travel agent whilst new sector players such as Expedia (www.expedia.com) and Travelocity (www.travelocity.com) have surfaced to link customers together with providers of hotels, flights and associated travel products together. Consequently, market planners must assess the level of value and competitive advantage offered by intermediaries in their sector.

Promotion (see chapter 11)

Marketing communications require clear measurable objectives to be set using the appropriate media with relevant and creative messages to a clearly identified target audience. This applies to both on and offline communications plans. Online promotional activities can be highly targeted and focused whilst reaching a wide audience. The measurement via appropriate web metrics produces greater precision and control, enabling speedy evaluation for subsequent campaigns.

The Internet was previously viewed as a virtual, stand-alone channel for advertising and promotion. However, it has rapidly emerged as a key element in the promotional mix of multi-channel marketing approaches with on and offline integration. New multimedia technologies provide greater scope for innovation, creativity, timing and personalisation of communications. The scope of online promotions seems virtually unlimited only by our imagination and growing customer privacy concerns. Later in this chapter, we will introduce a new online promotional mix for the digital age developed by one of our contributors, Mike Grehan. Before we do, we should emphasise the Internet's versatility by recognising how so many traditional promotional methods have made a successful online transition.

Whilst we should acknowledge that the 'killer application', e-mail, has been used and abused, it remains a powerful tool for effective communications and relationship development and it should remain prominent in any online marketer's promotional mix, as long as current legislation is strictly adhered to. Development of an **opt-in** e-mail database list is a priceless tool. Once people have reached the site via search engines and other methods, clever web site design with interactive features such as virtual sales staff supported by customer reviews can deliver an effective selling function. In addition, the Internet (and e-mail) can be an efficient public relations weapon delivering positive messages to an organisation's 'publics' using newsletters and other frequent feeds. Sales promotion and traditional member-get-member schemes have incentivised many online campaigns in both acquisition and retention phases. The Internet Advertising Bureau (www.iabuk.net) suggests that the integration of traditional and online media at the campaign planning stage will produce better results with synergies and economies of scale. This may be easier with full service agencies, though it may require some diplomacy and bonding where several agencies from different backgrounds offer their expertise.

A web site should have the ability to lead prospects through the key stages of response models such as AIDA (Awareness, Interest, Desire and Action). Huang and Christopher (2003) utilised the work of Hisrich (2000) in their paper 'Planning an Effective Internet Retail Store' which recognises the importance of the consumer buying decision process and the five stages associated with it:

1. Need Recognition
2. Information Search

3. Information Evaluation

4. Purchase Decision

5. Post-Purchase Behaviour.

Planners should build in appropriate site features and promotional messages to enable potential purchasers to move through the various stages with increasing confidence. These elements may include product information, video clips to support such information, independent customer reviews, comparisons with competitor offerings, response to e-mail enquiries, easy and efficient shopping cart and checkout procedures, account information and order tracking, not to mention 'thank you for the order' e-mails. It is important to set the automatic or manual response levels *at least* in line with customer expectations. Loyalty programmes and other incentives should also play an integral role in any customer relationship marketing initiative targeted at different segments when applying direct marketing models like 'The Ladder of Loyalty'. The model attempts to move prospects and customers up the ladder through targeted messages and offers relevant to segment to prospects, enquirers, first time buyers, frequent purchaser and advocates.

Offline promotion is a must for online businesses. Every opportunity from mainstream advertising, from letterheads to the outside of the organisation's transport, should carry the site URL for maximum exposure. Offline competitions may be used to increase web traffic and enrich the database.

The service mix elements

Smith and Chaffey (2002) interestingly incorporate the additional service mix elements of People, Physical Evidence and Process into their online remix of the established framework. The people element revolves around customer service. The main planning issue must address the extent to which customer service may be either automated or offered via a knowledge base. The key consideration is the importance placed upon some form of personal service, eg call centre support, by the customer. Smith and Chaffey discuss the level of automation using auto-responders, on-site search engines, FAQs and so on, and how they can solve most typical customer enquiries if the buyer is comfortable using the web for such purposes. Automation frees up capacity in call centres and other customer service functions to handle individual enquiries that could be complex, personal or where the customer is seeking reassurance, especially in the case of a high value purchase. Some web sites have used virtual people or characters to provide a more personal element in the online customer service function.

Regarding Physical Evidence, customers seek reassurance from the organisation's infrastructure and the tangible components that generate confidence. The evidence can vary from the overall ambience created by the site layout to customer reviews, trust certificates and privacy policies. In planning the online operation, a two-way customer dialogue should highlight the elements that provide reassurance.

Finally, the Process focuses on the mechanisms that support transactions and relationships. Whilst they must be user-friendly, they must also integrated front and back-office systems to provide superior customer experiences and streamline functions across the supply chain. For example:

- Are response times set to handle e-mail enquiries efficiently?

- Do shopping carts link seamlessly with the checkout, stock and delivery process?

- Is effective order tracking provided from purchase and dispatch through to delivery?

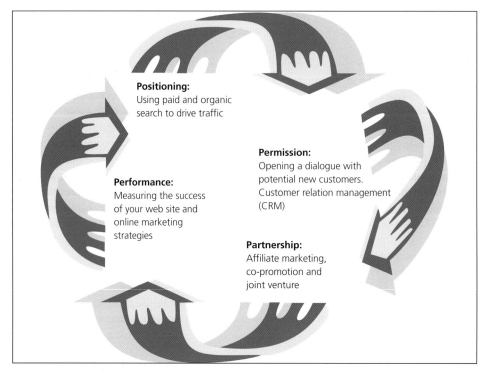

Fig 3.7 Online promotional mix
Reproduced by kind permission of Mike Grehan.

3.13 Implementation framework for online marketing promotional plans

Mike Grehan, a UK Internet and search engine marketer, has developed an effective four-stage promotional planning framework for digital marketing. Emanating from his consultancy work and exposure to online marketing in America, Grehan's model (illustrated in Fig 3.7) provides the essential elements in the online promotional mix in a practical, sequential model that employs four key tools from the electronic marketplace. Some marketers may have a jaundiced view about the introduction of another four P's model but these elements are vital for effective online control.

Positioning

Grehan's first element focuses on positioning, in particular search engine marketing and its important place within the new media mix. Branding issues and the development of the value proposition also play a key role in revenue generation and loyalty.

The techniques of search engine marketing (SEM) are fully addressed in chapter 6. Here we will give an overview of SEM applications and their growing importance as a mainstream tool. SEM is essential for driving online traffic to your site and achieving a critical mass and building the brand. Virtually anyone who has gone online will have used one of the leading search engines to source things like a holiday, an MP3 player or corporate information. Three main search engines, Google (www.google.co.uk), Yahoo! (www.yahoo.com) and MSN (www.msn.com) drive and attract the bulk of online traffic. A Nielsen NetRatings survey in January 2005 indicated the degree of loyalty that major players such as Google have built up, with 42% of Google users saying they use no other search engine. It is the case that many frequent Internet users now set up the home page of their favourite search engine as their opening default page. They have become highly visible marketplaces for promotional activity in their own right and their marketing importance cannot be underestimated. Around 80% of site visitors arrive via a search engine. Whilst the major players naturally attract the most submissions, Internet marketing planners should consider how they might reach their target market via second tier search engines rather than just relying on the elite group. There are many online **listings** of different types of search engines including general, by country or continent or by topic. Web sites such as search engines.com (www.searchengines.com) and net masters (www.netmasters.co.uk) offer comprehensive listings. Planners must research which sites are most popular for their target audience. It should also be acknowledged that search software is becoming more sophisticated and offers the consumer the opportunity to obtain search results from a number of leading search engines at the same time. This cuts out the tedious nature of search and potentially provides improved results across a range of search engines.

Until five years ago, the main form of SEM was referred to as organic search and utilised search engine optimisation techniques designed to boost search rankings. This typically includes keyword location and frequency testing in the body copy, and link popularity with reputable sites to boost the volume and quality of traffic. In any SEM campaign, keyword research is critical and requires understanding of the target audience and the common words and phrases they are likely to enter into a search box. Search terms are often colloquial and should be incorporated into the site content to cover the product range. In addition, organisations must learn the submission rules of the major search players or risk deletion. Search has become a distinct industry in itself with its own tools and applications. Marketers coming from a non-search background are likely to be baffled by the jargon and techniques but need to acquire a reasonable understanding if only to ask pertinent questions of search agencies pitching for their business. However, the commercial realities of search marketing necessitated a move towards monetisation in two forms, paid search and paid inclusion. For planning purposes, paid inclusion does not guarantee high rankings, and expenditure is likely to drop over the next few years. Paid search is predominantly performance related where the highest bidder for specified keywords achieves the highest ranking. In Google, for example, the winner will be highly visible in their sponsored links. Some bidders may, out of innocence or mischief, bid on keywords or trade descriptions related to a competitor so many search engine companies are developing policies to alleviate any trademark or local disputes. Clearly any bidding process must be factored into the budgeting and forecasting element of any online marketing plan.

Positioning is a fundamental dimension of brand strategy when an organisation develops its image and aligns its products in relation to those of its main rivals in the electronic marketplace. An organisation clearly has to consider how it can differentiate itself and formulate a unique selling proposition (USP) that appeals to their most valuable customers. The online brand should incorporate various attributes such as the domain name and added value elements such as product range, a site personality that creates trust, awareness and recognition whilst establishing clear brand values. The brand in question may be an existing brand

MINI CASE 3.5 Sony Ericsson

Sony Ericsson, the leading mobile handsets producer (www .sonyericsson.com) recognises the value of using digital marketing to build the brand experience even though they do not transact directly with consumers. The company spends up to 30% of their budget online to reach their target markets that tend to be high-end adopters of technology products. The key benefits of various handsets are relayed in a user-friendly way often through product specific micro-sites. The information rich site is also an important communications hub for Sony Ericsson's retailers and distributors.

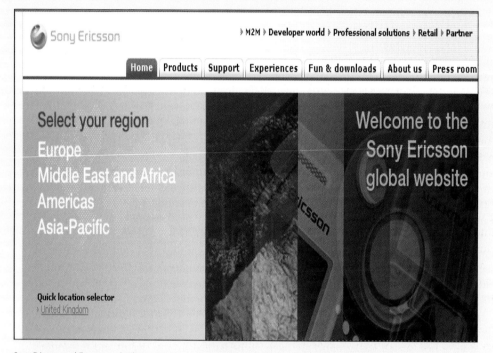

Sony Ericsson mobile communications

going online such as Tesco (www.Tesco.com) in the UK and Barnes and Noble (www .barnesandnoble.com) in the United States or the creation of a virtual brand such as eBay (www.ebay.com). The Mini case on Sony Ericsson briefly illustrates how the Internet can be applied to build the brand even though the organisation does not sell direct to the consumer.

Development of the brand personality is key. In the UK, Firebox (www.firebox.com) achieved early pure play success with their toys and gadget business largely aimed men who have not grown up. Their strap line sums up their proposition. . . . 'we don't stop playing because we get old; we get old because we stop playing'.

Planners must also pay particular attention to the issue of trust and how it can be developed through the online offering. As Lindstrom (2001) observes, 'Trust is crucial, essential to inspiring consumer ease about fundamental issues such as security and privacy.' We buy brands offline because we trust them. We trust Nike to produce the best athletic footwear and we trust Dell to produce competitively priced leading edge computers, but we are buying much more than just the product. It is about the company philosophy, its corporate image, its street credibility and the problems that it solves for the customer through the online or multi-channel experience. The brand philosophies were often enhanced through close association with the company founders such as Jeff Bezos (Amazon), Michael Dell (Dell Computers), Brent Hoberman and Martha Lane Fox (Last-Minute) and their business models. However, what made these particular organisations stand out from the crowd was their ability to differentiate their offer from the competition. Differentiation emerges through a unique product or service offering, meeting customer service expectations and connecting with them through creative marketing communications and solutions.

Permission

Successful promotional communications requires precision in target marketing through the identification of consumers who are more receptive to organisational messages. Consumer concerns over privacy, security, junk mail, Spam and the handling of personal data have risen considerably in the last five years resulting in more cynical consumers and lower direct response rates. The sheer volume of direct communications received, either via mail or e-mail, were often untargeted, badly timed or irrelevant which naturally turned off prospects and undermined customer loyalty. The term 'it is Permission Marketing' was coined by Seth Godin in his text entitled, *Permission Marketing – Turning Strangers into Friends and Friends into Customers*. This revolved around the identification of qualified prospects that had provided permission to an organisation to allow them to enter into a two-way dialogue. It also recognised that the traditional methods of marketing, which Godin referred to as 'Interruption Marketing', was quickly becoming inappropriate for marketers when consumers were increasingly frustrated over an invasion of privacy. To increase the chances of commercial success in customer loyalty through the acquisition and retention phases, the permission philosophy recognises the need to give greater control over communications to the consumer as they dictate what, when and how they receive future communications. The information required for such activity falls within the function of customer relationship management and a higher degree of personalisation with tailored messages. Apart from this being good practice, permission is now a legal requirement when organisations use e-mail or SMS, as they have to adhere to the Directive on Privacy and Electronic Communications (2002/58/EC). Whilst permission has revolutionised the thinking of many direct and Internet marketers, it needs to be even more sophisticated to understand the buyer's intentions and their strength of interest in the product or service. Many practitioners such as Roman and Hornstein (2004) are looking to go beyond permission to develop a richer two-way dialogue between buyers and sellers referred to as 'Consensual Marketing.'

Partnership

The sheer scale and risk of global business has created highly competitive markets where joint ventures, strategic alliances and other forms of partnerships have become the order of the day, particularly with regard to supply chain issues, such as the Covisint Community in the automotive sector (portal.covisint.com) originating in the United States. Daimler Chrysler Delphi, Ford Motor Company, General Motors, Johnson Controls, Lear Automotive, PSA Peugeot Citroën and Visteon are leading players in the community.

The airline industry formed partnerships such as the Star Alliance (www.star-alliance.com) involving Air Canada, Air New Zealand, ANA, Asiana Airlines, Austrian, bmi, LOT Polish Airlines, Lufthansa, Scandinavian Airlines, Singapore Airlines, Spanair, TAP, Thai Airways

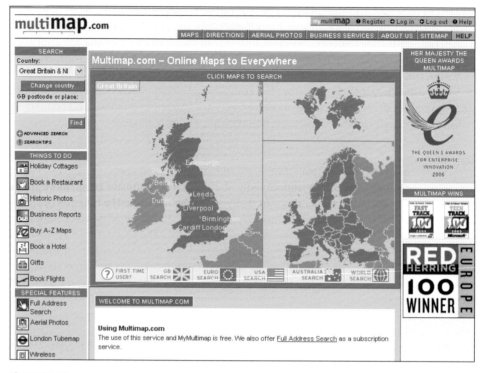

Fig 3.8 Multimap

Reproduced by kind permission of Multimap.

International, United, US Airways and VARIG. They offer joint funding, shared resources and expertise, shared databases and the commercial potential from joint promotional activities.

In the online world, similar complementary partnerships have been formed such as the online supermarket Ocado (www.ocado.com) and Waitrose (www.waitrosedeliver.com) and the joint database promotions by Tesco (www.tesco.com) and travel company Lastminute (www.lastminute.com). Co-promotions, sponsorship and joint branding can be beneficial to both the organisations involved and their target markets who may get the rewards from a better service, greater product range or loyalty programmes.

For example, Multimap (www.multimap.co.uk) has proved a great mapping tool for both business people and households for plotting journeys. The partnership element comes from accommodation providers, restaurants, gift providers and other services linked to the destination postcode as seen in Fig 3.8.

Also, following the previous section on permission, Reid Smith suggests that organisations should seek partners who are willing to provide access to their permission driven customer database, or enter into a reciprocal information sharing arrangement and who share common goals and objectives. She stresses the importance of developing a partner strategy for both B2C and B2B sectors to achieve important incremental sales for important revenue streams and loyalty. Part 3, step 4 of her text offers a thorough insight into the strategic and implementation phases of partnership development online.

Online merchants invariably look for cost-effective promotional activities. Two good examples of online partnerships are Referral marketing and Affiliate marketing.

Referral marketing typically involves selling goods and services, produced or supplied by another organisation, often a parent company. As well as carrying out transactions, the intermediary provides leads and introductions to the parent company and commission is usually paid on the basis of sales achieved. Intermediaries do not always carry inventory but merely forward on the orders to the manufacturer or distributor.

Much has been written about affiliate marketing and its ability to generate a rich source of new customers at very low cost. Basically there is no risk attached as long as the businesses you partner are legitimate. The originator of the affiliate programme will produce a branded link, which a suitable partner will place upon their web site, and again receive commission on sales generated. Amazon is undoubtedly the best-known affiliate programme in the world. These programmes work most effectively when the visitors to the two sites of similar profiles, reward schemes increase with performance, and the affiliate links are creative and prominent.

Reid Smith suggests other partnership activities to help drive traffic, build loyalty and trust such as content partnerships, certification partnerships and advertising partnerships, eg joint banner ads.

Performance

The final element of Grehan's model focuses on the Internet's unique ability to provide essential control through performance measurement of individual campaign activities. Adcock et al (1995) referred to the famous quote credited to Lord Leverhulme regarding the measurement and effectiveness of advertising, 'I know that half of what I spend on advertising is wasted, but the trouble is I don't know which half.' The authors suggest that marketing communications in general struggles to provide the precision needed for effective response analysis. However, it can be argued that mainstream direct marketing has become increasingly sophisticated in its analysis of testing prior to full campaign roll-outs. Similarly, Internet marketing has matured with a highly developed range of web metrics to provide a range of measurement and control that many would have thought impossible to achieve 10 years ago. To be convinced of this, students should read *Web Metrics – Proven Methods for Measuring Website Success* by Jim Sterne that provides extensive coverage of the range of metrics available for evaluating online performance. Sterne stresses the importance of using Web analytics on 'a needs to know' basis set against the organisation's online objectives in general and its promotional activities specifically.

In the nineties, web analytics tended to focus on measures like clickstream, number of 'hits', page downloads, number of unique visitors and the number of page visits. Such measures tend to be quantitative and do not always provide significant measurement. For example, very little can be gleaned from simply recording the number of visitors to a site. Web analytics software, such as Web Trends (www.webtrends.com) and NetGenesis (www.spss.com/netgenesis) can analyse the effect of site changes or specific campaigns with greater precision to measure Return on Investment (ROI) linked to acquisition and retention strategies. Online **conversion** rates will indicate which promotions have been successful and those that have been less than successful utilising electronic tags, known as cookies. Web analytics will identify the origins of a site visitor. They could respond to an e-mail campaign or click a banner ad. Their site behaviour could be linked to any online or offline promotional offers which might indicate their degree of loyalty or whether they are just a casual site viewer. Organisations can recognise key drop-off points that need addressing, the effectiveness of promotional micro-sites or redesign web sites on the basis of keyword/ key phrase results and so on. The sheer volume of web analytics options is bewildering, hence Sterne's advice on identifying critical measures has considerable merit.

The Performance element of this model provides the control component in the marketing strategic cycle and allows marketers to measure responses and evaluate the key components responsible for the campaign success.

The nature and tone of any written plan should be formulated with a particular reader in mind. It might be the situation that a marketing department is putting a case to the CEO and Board to reallocate more of the marketing budget online and away from offline. Alternatively, an entrepreneur may construct a plan when sourcing extra funding from a venture capitalist, and enterprise agency or a bank. The overall nature of the plan may not alter radically, but certain elements, such as operational efficiency, may have to be emphasised to the CEO or return on investment and payback to the venture capitalist.

3.14 Small and medium sized enterprises (SMEs) online

In the early years of the Internet there was a high degree of cynicism and lack of understanding by SMEs about the relevance of the Internet to their business. SMEs in general tend to be slow adopters of technology. Archer et al (2003) suggested that SMEs have been slow to adopt Internet solutions in supply chain and procurement transactions for the following reasons:

- Cost of innovation
- Lower transaction volumes
- Problems associated with integrating Information Systems internally
- Problems associated with integrating information systems with business partners.

The Internet skill levels and competences, not to mention a lack of commitment to invest in a web site other than brochurewear, meant SMEs did not capitalise effectively on Internet opportunities. However, with falling technology costs, in particular user-friendly software, coupled with local, regional and national government volume initiatives to make UK businesses 'e-ready', SMEs across a range of sectors offer much more than a basic web presence. Internet activity amongst SMEs is increasing but the potential is not being fulfilled. For example, a study of web site provision and accessibility by UK independent breweries by Fry et al (2004) notes that many web sites are accessible by online brewery directories but rarely through popular commercial search engines. In addition, the majority of sites tend to be corporate for prestige and PR purposes and seldom incorporate any marketing or selling tools. The study notes that government advice has tended to be general in nature and with more emphasis on the technical aspects of the Internet rather than commercial. The Internet is a catalyst for change for many SMEs and from a marketing perspective, their marketing, sales and customer services functions can be faster and more efficient, replicating the output of larger organisations.

Various small business guides emphasise the importance of good planning for an online business because of the need to consider stakeholder relations and resource, especially technological implications, and this is to be applauded. SMEs may use proven marketing planning tools but as suggested by Stokes (2000), successful entrepreneurs approach marketing in a more informal and unconventional way focusing on innovations rather than on a customer orientation. Stokes' 4 Is entrepreneurial marketing model suggests entrepreneurs implement frequent incremental innovations to give competitive advantage. Stokes' research found that entrepreneurs selected customer groups based on product fit and marketed to them by interactive methods such as word of mouth offline. Their feel for the marketplace comes from informal information gathering via developed networks. In practical terms, an entrepreneur may have a product or service with online potential but with the minimum of research done he/she launches a functional web site to test the market response. A typical trait of an entrepreneur is the ability to assess risk and they will have a feel for the level of investment to make and the required payback period before they terminate the venture.

3.15 International online marketing

The Internet is a global phenomenon with the ability to connect individuals and organisations across borders, and it is playing a significant role in the whole process of globalisation. It has the ability to transform small companies into international players with the removal of geographical barriers and help national players develop as global brands. It also has the ability to link international partners in all aspects of the supply chain with reductions in production and distribution times and costs. Significantly, Forrester Research found that up to 30% of site traffic can be attributed to overseas visitors and they generate up to 10% of total sales.

Marketing planners must try to understand the different landscape of the international online environment and how it impacts upon the organisation's marketing mix and related activities. It is interesting to note that many online businesses use international market entry strategies in a similar way to a traditional offline business. Fletcher et al (2004) offer a number of useful examples, eg Amazon joint ventures (eBay and NEC) and the failed multi-country strategy of Boo.com, in their excellent text, *International E-Business Marketing*. However, the level of Internet adoption and sophistication varies globally and may well influence the strategies and countries selected. What is often difficult is the ability to obtain worthwhile online marketing research data as the integrity of the data will vary across regions of the world prior to devising a market entry strategy.

Eid and Trueman (2002) suggest that the Internet 'provides a fundamentally different environment for international marketing and requires a different approach'. The strategic strap line 'Think Global, Act Local' has been well used in recent years and is still relevant for Internet purposes with national sites reflecting tastes, culture, language legal aspects and other environmental factors. From a consumer's perspective, buying from international sites may offer a wider range or more exclusive products at better prices. However there may be concerns over the identity and reliability of an international online merchant and the full cost of the purchase including local and imported taxes. In addition there may be issues over delivery times, returns and cancellation policies and any dispute resolution. From the organisation's point of view, an understanding of the buyer behaviour, culture and values of the local market are important. A more pressing matter is the legal considerations for any e-business and that is often difficult enough within its own country or trading area (UK or EU) without venturing into other areas of the world where issues such as trademark protection, intellectual property rights, legal security and contract law may be significantly different.

In the next chapter case study, we consider the research carried out by Dabs.com prior to establishing an overseas operation.

3.16 The Internet commandments

To conclude this chapter, Lindstrom and Andersen (2000) in their text, *Brand Building on the Internet*, provide a valuable customer oriented guide for online marketing planners with their 10 Internet commandments that cover the planning, implementation and control phases of the strategic planning cycle:

1. Know your mission on the Internet – have clearly defined goals for your Internet activities and know how they complement your broader marketing and corporate objectives eg Easyjet: 'Europe's Leading Low Cost Airline'.

2. Be everything for someone, *not* something for everyone – focus on satisfying the needs of your key customers/target market rather than trying to appeal to a broad audience eg Firebox (www.firebox.com) the gadget and toys web company for boys that have not grown up: 'We don't stop playing because we get old, we get old because we stop playing'.

3. Give the users something to take home – provide something of value that will enrich the customer experience and make them come back for more and encourage word of mouth marketing.

4. The company's solution must be based on a strategy – based on a clear market need or vision such as eBay.

5. Utilise the possibilities of the Internet – Tesco have utilised the Internet to foster better customer experiences and partner relationships.

6. Make sure that the company is intellectually on the net – the organisation must learn to embrace the Internet and related digital technologies. It should believe that it can enhance business performance immediately rather than something to address sometime in the future, eg Dell were innovative in going 'direct' to customers even before the Internet but new technology has revolutionised all aspects of its business, such as sales and production, to stay ahead of the competition.

7. Involve the users in the design process – customers *must* be consulted throughout the design process to ensure a user-friendly web site with content that excites them.

8. Test your solution – to ensure that the site features and links can function comfortably within expected traffic levels.

9. Give the users power and control – through a range of site features such as search facilities, account management and order tracking, privacy and permission issues and other interactive elements such as customer reviews and 'ask the expert' features.

10. We have only just begun – be prepared to change! Online marketing is evolving as a mainstream activity as organisations and consumers learn how to use its capabilities. As customer expectations rise, organisations need to regularly update and innovate to have a sustainable online business.

The authors offer a non-technological based approach that emphasises the value of providing great customer experiences that evolve from a true marketing philosophy. It can be tempting to view digital technologies as a panacea for corporate problems. They should not be viewed as quick fix solutions, but instead should be applied and implemented to provide sparkling customer benefits. The technologies provide organisations with measurement, control and analytical tools combining speed and efficiency at levels unthinkable a decade ago.

Viewing Internet marketing simply as 'a project' as opposed to an ongoing integration into the existing mix can lead to disassociation. Building a garden shed is a project. Building a web site could even be viewed as a project but integrated marketing communications is an iterative process. Crucially, it will be the combined expertise of the management team developed to create, maintain and evaluate the company's entire performance that will be key to the organisation's ongoing online success.

3.17 Summary

An organisation's web site has numerous facets that require careful planning and research if a rich customer experience is going to be delivered to the target audience. The Internet is a classic direct marketing channel and so setting measurable goals and objectives is important for the subsequent development of strategies and the timely implementation of tactics to build the online brand and achieve satisfactory return on investment. Any marketing plan will flow from the corporate objectives and then the marketing planners need to get the management 'buy in' to obtain the required resources.

The marketing environment continues to evolve and change at an ever-increasing pace and planners need to understand the nature of the change occurring within their electronic marketplace to develop an effective customer oriented experience. In the last two years, the Internet has emerged as a vital component in the integrated marketing approach of many organisations and requires collaboration across the whole range of functional areas and not just within marketing. Nevertheless, marketing planners must have a clear vision for their online brand and how it can serve the chosen target market.

END OF CHAPTER CASE STUDY   **DG UK being professional about online golf retailing**

High quality online customer experiences have guided the planning process for Direct Golf UK, www.direct-golf.co.uk (DG UK), the leading online and mail-order golf equipment retailer.

The company registered as Direct Golf UK in 1993 with two full time members of staff. It has steadily developed its retail, mail order and telesales business under the direction of founder, John Andrew. Like many of its competitors, DG UK promoted itself through established golf magazines like *Today's Golfer* and *Golf World*.

DG UK was alerted to the potential of Internet technologies in the heady pre-2000 dot.com days to reach around 3 million active golfers. According to a 2005 Mintel report, these 3 million plus golfers pay up to £1,000 per year on membership and equipment that provides a sector value totalling over £1 billion.

No other UK golf retailer had exploited the technologies thus far, and DG UK sought to gain from first mover advantage in this lucrative market. Despite the temptation to plunge into the online market, DG UK planned each step carefully for the benefit of both the customer and the business.

DG UK set about clarifying its e-business goals in line with its renowned customer led approach. The fundamental objectives were as follows:

- To achieve 10% of turnover through the online channel within 12 months
- To demonstrate the value and savings to customers
- To provide speed and security during order processing and fulfilment
- To deliver a user-friendly customer experience

Direct Golf UK Ltd.

- To provide the widest range of golf merchandise available online in the UK

- To integrate its online offering with established DG UK channels

The company had kept an open mind on the web site design and the need for specific site features. As well as looking at numerous US golf sites, DG UK also trawled a variety of non-golf online retailers for ideas and inspiration. It became apparent that online success required speed of response and creativity to help build the DG UK brand and customer loyalty. To provide a greater degree of control and flexibility, the company made a significant investment in new IT staff and infrastructure rather than relying on external agencies and web designers. DG UK bought in expertise in the shape of IT programmers, web designers and search engine optimisers to facilitate the integration of IT within the existing business. The in-house team provided the capability to design and rapidly update its web site so that it was fresh and current. The main key for driving web site traffic to DG UK's site was their ability to create precisely timed HTML-based e-mail campaigns to their expanding opt-in database.

Like many other mail order or B2B operations, the first web site was classic brochurewear replicating its tried and trusted offline catalogue. James Toase, DG UK Marketing and Media Development Manager, wryly suggested that, 'you would shake your head in disbelief at the original site when you look back but we have learnt a lot in a short space of time.' He also recognised the value of web site measurement statistics. DG UK purchased industry standard web analytics software from Web Trends (www.webtrends.com). This provided traffic site reports on an hourly, daily and monthly basis. In addition Web Trends provides detailed visitor information on pages viewed, current visitors together with navigational reports on visitor pathways such as entry and exit pages. Another important software feature for planning and analytical purposes identified key referring sites, key search engines and keyword search terms. As a result, DG UK submitted its site to the main search engines like Google and Yahoo! but also identified secondary sites such as Golf Magic (www.golfmagic.com) and golfalot (www.golfalot.com) that captured a wider target market. The in-house team constantly tweak the site to maintain a high search engine ranking for important visibility. In a price sensitive market, it was also important to have a presence in the main price comparison sites like Kelkoo to illustrate DG UK's price competitiveness.

Despite the initial limitations, DG UK had carefully researched the market and was beginning to understand more fully how the golfer's mind, or buyer behaviour manifests itself during the purchase of golf equipment. The prime purchasing conditions were recognised as being:

1. The market tendered to the price sensitive, and there was an expectation that items would be cheaper online.

2. Customers like to either try new golf clubs or rely on recommendations from trusted third parties, eg golf professionals and word-of-mouth recommendations.

3. Consumers desire trust online, and this evolves from the need for information and high levels of service.

4. A high level of PC and Internet ownership or access amongst golfers existed, with the majority in the ABC1s socio-economic grouping.

DG UK was aware that the golf retailers tended to employ keen amateur golfers in the selling and customer service functions. Generally, golf club members put great value on the opinion and advice of their club professional. DG UK saw a key opportunity to add value through the recruitment of Professional Golf Association (PGA) qualified professionals. The PGA pros provided essential equipment knowledge and recommendations online, by phone and in-store. The company provided specific skills training for each channel to ensure the highest standards of customer service. E-mail is a vital communications tool in the company's online operations. It can provide effective customer interactions, but it also has the potential for damaging relationships. This prompted special training for 'the pros', and the feedback from customers suggests they place a high value on this service.

Within the first 12 months, the online sales target of 10% of revenue was blown away completely. DG UK's turnover had been generated 60:40 mail order to retail. By early 2005, 60% of turnover came from Internet sales alone. To meet the rapid increase and demand from new customers, DG UK continually expanded its product range. Online customers constantly expect better deals plus quick delivery. To this end, DG UK actively sought special deals from golf manufacturers and distributors to remain price competitive. To facilitate their growing buying power, and continued expansion, a new head office and warehouse were opened at Milnsbridge in 2001. This gave DG UK the capability to fulfil 97% of its orders from stock with next day delivery as a customer option and strengthened its position as the leading direct golf retailer. The company was conscious to avoid the problems encountered by some of the early online retailing pioneers. The speed and convenience offered has increased customer trust and satisfaction significantly.

DG UK always seeks to improve its online provision whilst rewarding its regular customers. An essential element of this retention strategy has been the introduction of its Members Area that offers a range of benefits including a discount scheme on specially selected and exclusive offers. Other member benefits includes 'Deal of the Day' – one really red-hot deal together with reduced shipping costs. The member database has grown rapidly with 140,000 signed up members ready to receive, and take advantage of special deals highlighted in DG UK's opt-in e-mail communications. In total, they now have 350,000 golfers on their database and this continues to rise with various methods of data capture, eg in-store. With online customer expectations rising, the company is now looking to implement a CRM strategy for the first time and move on from a more time-honoured transactional approach. The core elements of the CRM approach will incorporate establishing consumers' current golfing ability and their aspirations along with some personal details that relate to the game of golf, such as age, height, dexterity, preferred brands, weaknesses in their game, etc. DG UK will then look to provide advice, equipment recommendations and special offers that are specific to their requirements. James Toase comments, 'It is my intention that we establish ourselves as the only place that our customers purchase golf equipment. We hope to increase frequency of spend and order value by knowing what our customers want/need before they do.'

Commenting on the potential of mobile applications, James sets outs DG UK's vision for the future. 'We intend to communicate with customers in the way that they prefer and taking into account both consumer convenience and cost effectiveness for the company. I see mobile technology playing a key role in our future marketing strategy and CRM, so I am currently in discussions with companies that can manage this form of communication. I hope that within the next 6 months our customers will be able to text to order and view our catalogue on their mobile phone. A mobile phone is something that almost all of us now have and it tends to be on our person wherever we are on the planet. Mobile marketing will also prove to be a great data capture tool through text to win competitions and text for a free catalogue in our various channels of advertising.'

DG UK's careful planning and integration of its online operation into its other channels evolved from a clear understanding of what its customers desire in terms of product range, price and service. The customer-focussed approach is clearly appreciated as DG UK has again won the No 1 Mail Order Golf Retailer Award voted on by the readers of the leading publication, *Today's Golfer*.

Questions

1. Suggest three key elements that were fundamental to DG UK's successful strategy. Explain why they were important.

2. What are the disadvantages of buying golf equipment online and how did DG UK try to overcome them?

3. What benefits should result in the introduction of a CRM programme for both DG UK and its customers?

DISCUSSION QUESTIONS

1. Does the Internet make it easier or more difficult for marketers to carry out an effective marketing audit?

2. How has technology, as an environmental factor, influenced internal organisational planning for online operations?

3. How important is targeting and segmentation in the development of an online operation?

4. Critically evaluate the new 4 P's Online Promotional planning model as an effective tool for Internet success.

REFERENCES

Adcock, D, Bradfield, R, Halborg, A & Ross, C (1995) *Marketing, Principles and Practice* (2nd edn), Pitman Publishing, London, Great Britain, 207

Archer, N, Wang, S & Kang C (2003) *Barriers To Canadian SME Adoption of Internet Solutions for Procurement and Supply Chain Interactions*, MeRC working paper no 5, August 2003, www.merc.mcmaster.ca/wpapers/wpapaer5(MeRC)html

de Kare Silver, M (2002) *Streamlining*, Palgrave, Basingstoke, England, 5–6

Doyle, P (1998) *Marketing Management and Strategy* (2nd edn), Prentice Hall Europe, Hemel Hempstead, England, 96–97

Eid, R & Trueman, M (2002) The Internet: New International Marketing Issues, *Management Research News*, Vol 25, No 12, 2002, 54

Fletcher, R, Bell, J & McNaughton, R (2004) *International E-Business Marketing*, Thomson Learning, London, 17

Fry, J, Tyrrall, D, Pugh, G & Wyld, J (2004) The Provision and Accessibility of Small Business Web Site: a survey of independent UK breweries, *Journal of Small Business and Enterprise Development*, Vol 11, No 3, 2004, 302–314

Hanson, W (2000) *Principles of Internet Marketing*, South Western College Publishing, Cincinnati, Ohio, United States, 400

Harrell, S (1980) in a speech at the plenary session of the American Marketing Association's Educators Meeting, Chicago, 5 August 1980, cited in Kotler (2000), *Marketing Management* (Millennium Edition), Prentice Hall Inc, Upper Saddle, New Jersey, United States, 64

Huang, AS & Christopher, D (2003) Planning an effective internet retail store, *Marketing Intelligence and Planning*, Vol 21, No 4 (2003), MCB UP Limited, 230–238

Hisrich, R (2000) *Marketing*, Barrons, New York, United States www.news.bbc.co.uk/1/hi/business/2268797.stm

Lindstrom, M (2001) *Clicks, Bricks And Brands – The Marriage of Online and Offline Businesses*, Kogan Page Limited, Australia, 71

Lindstrom, M & Andersen, TF (2000) *Brand Building on the Internet*, Kogan Page Limited, London, 304–305

Lucas Jnr, HC (2002) *Strategies for Electronic Commerce and the Internet*, Massachusetts Institute of Technology, United States, 211–218

McDonald, M (1999) *Marketing Plans: How to Prepare Them*, 4th edn, Oxford, Butterworth Heinemann

Molenaar, C (2002) *The Future of Marketing*, FT Prentice Hall, Harlow, England, 41–46

Nat West e-Business Guide (2001) *Making E-plans, Small Business Guide to E-Business and the Web*, www.natwest.com/businessedge Ebusin3/June2001

Neef, D (2001) *E-Procurement – From Strategy to Implementation*, Prentice Hall Inc, Upper Saddle River, NJ, United States, 143–144

Orikowski, W (1996) Improving organisational transformation over time: a situated change perspective, *Information Systems Research*, Vol 7, No 1, 63–92

Rangaswamy, A & Van Bruggen, GH (2005) Opportunities and Challenges in Multichannel Marketing: An Introduction to the Special Issue, *Journal of Interactive Marketing*, Vol 19, No 2, Spring 2005, 6–7

Romanov, S (2002) *Branding on the Web: A Matter of Balance,* The Association of National Advertisers (www.ana.net), United States cited in WARC, www.warc.com/fulltext/ANA/72110.htm, January 2002

Schultz, D (2005) The new marketing metrics, Speech to the 10th Annual Institute of Direct Marketing Symposium, May 2005

Silicon.com www.silicon.com/management/itdirector/0,39024673,39116970,00.htm?rolling=1

Simkin, L (2002) Tackling implementation impediments to marketing planning, *Marketing Intelligence & Planning*, MCB UP Limited, Vol 20, No 2, 121

Simons, LPA, Steinfield, C & Bouwman, H (2002) Strategic positioning of the web in a multi-channel market approach, *Internet Research: Electronic Networking Applications and Policy*, Vol 12, No 4, 2002, 339–347

Smith, B (2003) *Marketing Business*, June 2003, Chartered Institute of Marketing, 33

Smith, ER (2000) *E-Loyalty: How to Keep Customers Coming Back to Your Web Site*, Harper Collins Publishers Inc, New York, United States, 91–92

Smith, PR & Chaffey, D (2002), *E-Marketing Excellence*, Butterworth Heinemann, Jordan Hill, Oxford, 292

Stokes, D (2000) Entrepreneurial Marketing: a conceptualisation from qualitative research, *Qualitative Market Research: An International Journal*, Vol 3, No 1, 2000, MCB University Press, 47–54

Stone, M, Bond, A & Blake, E (2003) *The Definitive Guide to Direct and Interactive Marketing*, FT Prentice Hall, Harlow, Great Britain, 157

Strauss, J, El-Ansary, A & Frost, R (2003) *E-Marketing*, Pearson Education, Inc Upper Saddle River, New Jersey, US, 51

Strauss, J, El-Ansary, A & Frost, R (2003) *E-Marketing*, Pearson Education, Inc Upper Saddle River, New Jersey, US, pp 56–57

Tracy, M & Wiersema, F (1994) *Discipline of Market Leaders*, Addison Wesley

Wilson, R (2002) *Planning Your Internet Marketing Strategy*, John Wiley & Sons Ltd, New York, United States, 228–238

FURTHER READING

Fletcher, R, Bell, J & McNaughton, R (2004) *International E-Business Marketing*, Thomson Learning, London

Hanson, W (2000) *Principles of Internet Marketing*, South Western College Publishing, Cincinnati, Ohio, United States

Lucas Jnr, HC (2002) *Strategies for Electronic Commerce and the Internet*, Massachusetts Institute of Technology, USA

Ragas, MW (2001) *Lessons from the E-Front*, Prima Publishing, Roseville, CA, USA

Roman, E & Hornstein, S (2004) *Opt in Marketing – Increase Sales Exponentially with Consensual Marketing*, McGraw Hill, USA

Smith, PR & Chaffey, D (2002) *EMarketing Excellence*, Butterworth Heinemann, Oxford, 53–62

Zhuang, Y & Lederer, AL (2004) *The Impact of Top Management Commitment, Business Process Redesign, and IT Planning on the Business-to-Consumer E-Commerce Site*, Klumer Academic Publishers, Nonwell, MA, USA

WEB LINKS

Department of Trade and Industry (DTI) Best Practice Guide to E-Marketing
www.dti.gov.uk/bestpractice/assets/marketing.pdf

www.e-mori.co.uk latest e-news and market research

www.internetworldstats.com a treasure trove of internet statistics

www.marketingonline.co.uk the CIM's educational resource centre on all things digital

www.dell.co.uk provides a good example in Internet planning to meet the needs of different segments

www.cornishwebservices.co.uk a private company whose web site provides some useful advice for SME's

Visit the Online Resource Centre which accompanies this book, for lots of interesting additional material, including self-assessment questions, internet exercises, and links for each chapter: **www.oxfordtextbooks.co.uk/orc/gay/**

Online Marketing Research

4

By the end of the chapter you will be able to:

- Appreciate the potential of the Internet as a cost effective tool for marketing research activity
- Identify key sources of visible and invisible secondary data
- Understand how to collect primary data online
- Appreciate the Internet's limitations as a method of primary research
- Compare and contrast on and offline methods of data collection

Chapter at a Glance

4.1 **Introduction**

Information is often described as the lifeblood or oxygen for any marketing oriented organisation. According to Hwang and Fesenmaier (2004) 'The Internet has begun to be recognized as a legitimate social survey tool as its user horizon rapidly expands to the general public'. Its use as a method of data collection is attracting considerable academic attention, especially for primary research purposes. It has rapidly emerged as an important channel for commerce with the exchange of transactional and site data providing a rich source of customer information for creative online marketers to exploit. For many organisations, the Internet is becoming a central platform for assorted forms of information exchange. McGowan and Durkin (2002) found that that the dominant reason for Internet adoption amongst entrepreneurs was information gathering. The almost infinite number and diversity of public, private and individual web sites offer valuable marketing research information in volume and accessibility like never before. For marketing decision makers and marketing research practitioners alike, access to plentiful secondary data sources and faster, more cost effective primary research has changed the nature of business research for decision making. The Information Age is upon us bringing advantages, disadvantages and trade-offs between quality, quantity and cost, speed and accuracy.

With criticisms emerging about the quality of lifestyle and other segmentation data as personal information is often volunteered by the same ageing, affluent groups, the Internet can be used to reach new, younger lifestyle groups via online and mobile survey methods. However, some purists continue to question how representative online samples are of the population as a whole. Despite these concerns, the market for online business information in Europe is expanding progressively. An IRN Research Annual Survey in May 2006 estimated the value of the market at €3,513 million in 2005 which represents an increase of 14% over 2004. The survey suggests that most of the online services growth occurred in the legal, tax and regulatory (LTR) and scientific, technical and medical (STM) information markets.

The Internet by nature has developed its own research traits, for example software enhanced questionnaire design in online primary research. In secondary research, search engines such as Google and Yahoo! instantly generate thousands of pages for our consumption but how many do we read? Do we know that the page ranked in the top ten is significantly better than the one ranked 191st? Does that particular search engine store every possible web site available on the chosen subject? With the work of Sherman and Price (2001), entitled *The* **Invisible Web**, enlightening readers to the web's undiscovered potential, some researchers are delving beyond the information offered by the main search engines. If not there, where could we find it?

Marketing research in its various forms generates vast amounts of hard and soft data. Organisations recognise information is a vital commodity and a resource that can facilitate effective responses in rapidly changing markets. Creative and logical use of data by marketers can identify or exploit market or product opportunities. Strategists mull over numerous sources of marketing data from individual and syndicated sources, wondering about the quality and quantity. With the data explosion comes data confusion. Decision makers wrestle with a myriad of old and new information sources offered by the web. Web analytics software provides detailed measurement of customer activity in a way unimaginable less than a decade ago. The reality now is that you can test and measure every click, link and response code and probably be more confused than you were when you started. The call today is for strategists to be more discerning and selective when using data sources. Marketers need to home in on the critical factors that are more influential. For example, in selecting target markets lifestyle factors may be more important than age or sex. Information overload makes the case for data selection and retrieval on a 'need to know' basis particularly in relation to speed and costs. The need for a structured and disciplined approach to marketing research is more important than ever in the new connected information world. Information is valuable and many research agencies and organisations operating in consumer markets rely on the goodwill of the public to volunteer information. For the industry to survive and prosper it must now address the stewardship of this information in an ethical and lawful way if trust is to continue between researcher and respondent. Adherence to the Codes of Practice, conditions and guidelines of professional bodies within the research industry is fundamentally important to demonstrate good practice and build trust. Similarly, any organisation collecting, storing and analysing data and information must observe the legislation pertaining to the Data Protection Act 1998.

4.2 Research the market

Blythe (2001) highlights the distinction with *market research* being 'the process of collecting, analysing and presenting useful information about consumers' whilst *marketing research* takes a wider perspective incorporating the elements of the marketing mix and the wider marketing environment including competitor and supplier/distributive environments. *Marketing information* in its broader sense relates to data and intelligence applicable to a marketing function as represented in Fig 4.1.

The Internet has the ability to impact upon the research process at each of these four levels through speed and access to information. For example:

1. **Micro-environment** – Organisations may be able to source superior goods or services at better prices from a wider range of potential suppliers than before, due to the Internet's geographic reach. Alternatively competitor data may be accessed through www .companieshouse.gov.uk or retrieval systems such as FAME, specialising in the accounts of individual companies.

2. **Macro-environment** – The Internet provides rapid dissemination of information on social trends, economic data or political and legal issues through public and private web sites such as www.inlandrevenue.gov.uk or www.mintel.co.uk

3. **Customer Research** – The Internet can provide real-time feedback, opinions, interests and attitudes via online surveys offered by established research agencies like NOP (www.nop.com) and MORI (www.mori.com) or emerging online survey software developers. With the growing adoption of the Internet and other digital devices, there has been a developing shift by leading agencies away from traditional channels towards online methods of primary research. E-MORI, for example, targets e-mail groups on specific discussion themes and then analyses the responses. A précis of the responses is disseminated along with the next topic to be researched. Of course, secondary sources on the Internet also provide valuable customer insight, especially syndicated data such as those offered by Experian and Claritas in specific industry sectors such as financials services.

4. **The Marketing Mix** – Whilst the debate continues over the usefulness of 'The Mix' as a model for marketers in the online world, it still provides a useful focus for analysis. The

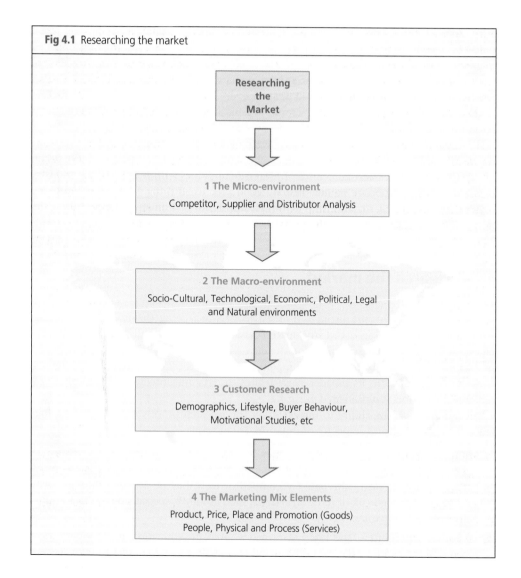

Fig 4.1 Researching the market

Internet can be used for research purposes to get feedback on a new concept such as a new design of vehicle. With regard to pricing, dynamic pricing software can be used to analyse instant customer sensitivity to price changes, up or down. Testing and analysis of different promotional offers can be carried out at greater speed and with greater tracking precision of the customer.

Baines and Chansarkar (2002) emphasise the importance of linking marketing research activity to the marketing concept, which places the customer at the centre of our activities. Nowadays, marketing decision makers draw upon a whole battery of research tools, particularly from social sciences such as psychology and sociology, to provide a greater insight into what goes on inside the mind of the treasured consumer to shape their purchasing habits.

The primary objectives of marketing research are to enhance the quality of the decision making of marketing managers. It can reduce business risk through the acquisition of relevant data and information. The Internet has revolutionised the availability of data but it still only becomes information when it is applied by the manager to a specific problem. The importance of marketing research is greater when organisations venture into uncharted territories such as revolutionary new product or service launches or market diversification where limited prior knowledge exists. Venturing into overseas markets is a typical example of this. The Internet provides almost instant access to international information through government web sites like UK Trade and Invest (www.uktradeinvest.gov.uk).

For many Internet entrepreneurs, quality information for planning was scarce, and what was available tended to be hyped up and unreliable. Consequently, organisations often relied heavily on intuition and entrepreneurial flair than a systematic approach to research in the dot.com adolescence period. This is not always a bad thing, particularly for SMEs where they have a closer relationship with their stakeholders, at least in theory. The results from marketing research are not always heeded either, as in the well-documented case with Sony and the Walkman where the research findings indicated that it would not be a success. Undeterred by this, and guided by business instinct, the Chairman, Akio Morita went ahead and launched the product, and the rest, as they say, is history.

Marketing Research usually involves a trade-off between (i) Cost (ii) Speed and (iii) Accuracy. In theory, the more you spend on research, the more accurate or representative the information generated will be.

The main determinants of research activity are as follows:

- Budget constraints
- Depth of information required
- Availability of the information
- How quickly is the information needed?
- Access to a relevant 'population'

Decision makers have to consider the likelihood of making poor decisions without marketing research and balance this against the extent to which the research adds value and the costs associated with carrying it out.

An organisation needs to make an informed guess when putting mathematical values against the decision chances. Rather than providing a specific answer, the model may give a useful indication of the costs and benefits of research.

In addition, marketers have to decide when it is sensible to draw the line under the information search as there comes a point when the chances of unearthing any more useful

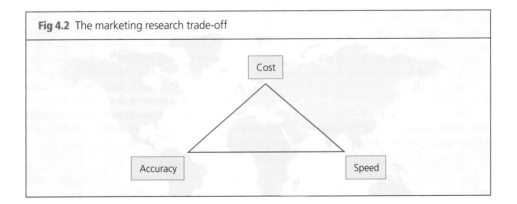

Fig 4.2 The marketing research trade-off

information are slim. At this point it is rarely worthwhile spending further time and resources when the most relevant information has probably been collected already. An obvious example is when a search engine generates six figure hits in 0.34 seconds but the likelihood of finding something relevant after the first one hundred results diminishes quickly. Gourvennay (2003) explores the concept of 'Nodal Points' emanating from William Gibson's book, *Idoru*, in terms of Internet searches. In simple terms, better results emerge when you cannot go any further with your original query (Nodal Point 1) and then you search again refining your keywords, terms or spellings until you are halted again (Nodal Point 2) and so on. It should become apparent fairly quickly what the most productive and relevant keywords are on the subject.

4.3 Overview of the European market research and information industry

European marketing research agencies, in general, are disadvantaged compared to their US counterparts when it comes to the acquisition of secondary and primary data. This is largely due to data protection and privacy laws introduced primarily by the European Union. However, it is important to understand the information differences that exist within Europe in terms of industry sophistication by country, region, market maturity and sector. Of course, the information is accessible to anyone worldwide.

In broad terms we can divide the market into two sectors:

1. (a) Business information market (mainly secondary data)
   (b) Content aggregators (content is part free but moving more to subscription)
2. Marketing research (agencies carrying out primary research for clients)

The business information market typically focuses on company information, including financial, legal issues and sector commercial news and is primarily used for competitor intelligence and credit ratings. Despite many observers commenting upon the cost benefits of information products, weak stock markets and fairly stagnant merger and acquisition activity have resulted in low levels of market value of £785 million and growth of around 2.7% in 2002. On a national level, IRN Research suggests differences in market maturity and sophistication by the number of key information players by country. The UK business information market has more established players even compared to Germany and France but market growth is more dynamic in the countries like Spain where Internet adoption is increasing. Tables 4.1, 4.2 and 4.3 highlight the major information players in the UK, Germany and France.

Consumers of online business information are moving progressively towards specialist suppliers of information who can provide integrated enterprise wide systems rather than allowing the purchase of disparate systems by individual managers. Real time information systems are the domain of larger blue chip organisations. The provision of more bespoke services will be important for both margins and growth. An IRN survey (2004) on the European Online Information Market comments, 'a repeated theme from the survey is that clients now expect their main vendors and suppliers to work closely with them, and customise products to meet the needs of their organisation and preferences of specific users rather than offer only standard packages.' Small firms do not currently consume information in such

Table 4.1 UK business information market: key players by segment

News aggregators	Company financial information	Legal, tax, regulatory	Market Research	Economic data
Factiva	D&B	LexisNexis Butterworths	Datamonitor	EIU
LexisNexis	Equifax	Thomson	Mintel	Global Insight
Thomson Business Intelligence	Experian	Wolters Kluwer	Euromonitor	Business Monitor
Ft.com	ICC	Justis	Key Note	UK Government
One Source	Bureau van Dijk	Informa	Snapdata	International agencies, e.g. ONS, OECD, IMF
Proquest	Thomson Financial	Jordan Publishing	Forrester	
Alacra	Graydon Jordans	Criminal Law Week Casetrack Emplaw	Frost & Sullivan Gartner	
Romeike	Hemscott Perfect Information RM Online Companies House	InfoLaw Linex Legal	IDC	

Reproduced by kind permission of IRN Research, May 2006.

Table 4.2 German business information market: key players by segment

News, aggregators	Company financial information	Legal, tax, regulatory	Market Research	Economic data
GBI-GENIOS	Creditreform	Verlag C. H. Beck	VNU	OECD
Factiva	Bundesanzeiger	juris	TNS Infratest	German Foreign Office
LexisNexis	Bürgel	Wolters Kluwer	IMS Health	EIU
	Bureau van Dijk	Haufe Media Group		
	Thomson Financial		Kantar Group	
			GfK	
			Euromonitor	
			Datamonitor	

Reproduced by kind permission of IRN Research, May 2006.

quantities to make them an attractive market proposition, but incentives such as trial subscriptions may entice some entrepreneurs.

According to Richard Somerville (2003), Director of Consumer New Media at the leading research group NOP (www.gfknop.co.uk), marketing research activity and budgets in the

Table 4.3 French business information market: key players by segment

News, aggregators	Company financial information	Legal, tax, regulatory	Market Research	Economic data
AFP	Coface ORT	Wolters Kluwer	Eurostaf	OECD
Pressed/EDD	BIL/D&B	LexisNexis	Dafsa	EIU
Europresse	Infogreffe	Thomson	Euromonitor	Global Insight
Delphes	Euridile	Legifrance	Datamonitor	BIPE
Factiva	Bureau van Dijk	Francis Lefebvre		INSEE
LexisNexis				

Reproduced by kind permission of IRN Research, May 2006.

early dot.com days were focussed on usability and site evaluation research. Similar to the online business information sector, 2002 single figure growth estimates for Europe are modest compared to the US. Somerville suggests the sheer geographic size of the US and quicker take up of broadband have fuelled quicker US expansion in areas such as concept and product testing. In addition, concerns in Europe have centred on the online survey samples and how representative they are. This is discussed in section 4.14 below. Somerville believes that multi-modal research has considerable potential with reduced broadband prices, plus wider adoption and advances with SMS and iTV. Further impetus was generated for online research activity in Europe when NOP World, MORI, NFO Europe and SPSS MR announced the creation of European Consortium for Online Research (ECOR) www.onlineresearch.org. These leading players in the marketing research sector appreciated the benefits of collaboration to kindle faster growth in the online research sector. At the same time ECOR has stated objectives of disseminating best practice and refining online sampling. Whilst US research market research revenues increased rapidly since 2000, concerns remain that standards were compromised as a result.

4.4 Strengths and weaknesses of online marketing research

For marketers and research organisations alike, sampling has been a key issue when using the Internet for primary research purposes. During the infant years of the Internet, online usage was biased towards high earning, affluent, IT literate groups aged 25–45. They were predominantly the target, and subsequently respondents for research agencies, and were often used time and time again due to their willingness to participate in surveys. They were not representative of the population and consequently the validity of surveys was called into question. However, as a greater percentage of the population across Europe has adopted the Internet and bought online, sampling is more representative. Below, we consider some of the strengths and weaknesses relating to different aspects of online marketing research.

Strengths

- Speed of accessing information – both primary and secondary, eg primary results can be collected and analysed in one day in some cases but usually within 3–5 days as research software applications become more efficient. This compares with weeks of analysis by traditional methods.

- Online marketing research can be extremely cost effective reaching large numbers of respondents at a fraction of the cost of existing research methods.

- The Internet is an effective tool for carrying out exploratory research to provide background information into sectors, suppliers, distributors and competitors.

- The Internet has no geographic boundaries, enabling cross-border and wider international reach, at least in theory.

- The quality and quantity of market and company information available online is evolving rapidly.

- Online surveys are more convenient, as they enable respondents to complete questionnaires in their own time and space.

- The integration across multiple platforms provides greater research and versatility linking to e-mail, interactive television (iTV), SMS, etc.

- White papers and specialist forums provide leading edge debate and insight into marketing oriented digital trends.

- As more people migrate online and become more confident with its use, they are more likely to respond and volunteer information to trusted parties.

- The increased availability of pre-screened panels will improve data integrity.

- Web metrics (see chapter 9) provide marketers with greater precision and measurement of visitor activity than could ever have been imagined 10 years ago.

- Search engines (see chapter 6) have generally become faster and efficient in generating relevant results.

- Multimedia formats, eg video streaming provide opportunities for concept testing online.

- Online research organisations (eg Jupiter and Forrester) are establishing themselves as reputable online sources of data and information.

- The Internet provides marketers with opportunity to research new suppliers at a fraction of previous search costs. This could be useful to improve product quality or drive prices down.

Weaknesses

- Serious concerns have been raised that the same sample lists are being drawn from repeatedly. Consequently, doubts are being cast upon the validity and integrity of the data generated from such samples.

- Some online sources are of dubious reliability, especially with regard to market size and usage statistics particularly in the earlier stages of Internet development.

- The uses of '**pop-up**' surveys are an irritation and reduce potential respondents willingness to volunteer information.

- Potential online respondents may be difficult to reach, as many change e-mail addresses frequently or have separate home and business e-mail addresses.

- The cost attractiveness of the Internet for research purposes may drive organisations to focus more on quantitative research rather than softer, behavioural qualitative data.

- Online surveys, like some traditional methods, are unable to record important clues from body language and eye contact.

- Self-selecting respondents can be unrepresentative of the target population and produce bias.

Table 4.4 Stages in the online marketing research process

Stage	Question
1. Defining the research required	1. What is the problem? What do we need to know?
	2. What is the underlying cause of the problem? eg social change, competition, technology?
	3. What data and information are needed to solve the problem?
	4. How should we define our objectives/terms of reference?
	5. What are going to be the key online metrics? eg 'hard or soft information'?
2. Planning the research	1. How will the data be collected? eg primary, just secondary or both? Qualitative or quantitative?
	2. Who will provide the data?
	3. Is the population reachable? Specific target web site users or a broader Internet population?
	4. Can we carry out the primary research 'in-house' or do we need an agency?
	5. What software is available for the online questionnaire and for analysing the results?
	6. Will we need to use any incentives to achieve decent online response rates?
3. Carrying out the fieldwork	1. Is the data collection going according to schedule?
	2. Are any problems emerging in the early stages? eg poor online response rates resulting from old e-mail addresses?
4. Analysing, interpreting and reporting	1. How 'valid' and reliable' is the data, especially in relation to qualitative research?
	2. What are the key findings of the research?
	3. Has the data been inputted effectively and efficiently?
	4. Are the results presented to the decision maker(s) with clarity and no bias?
5. Using the research	1. What action will be taken?
6. Feedback and evaluation	1. Log analysis and other web metrics can give vital insight to online customer behaviour to refine marketing activities.
	2. Customers, suppliers, distributors and other stakeholders can be actively encouraged to provide valuable feedback either through structured questionnaires or chat rooms.

- It can be difficult to guarantee that the person responding is the person you think they are.
- 'Opt-in' lists only give permission to question certain people and this can create sampling bias.
- Concept testing of new products is problematic online when senses like taste, touch and smell are required.
- Pure online research removes the human element where a skilled researcher may be able to tease out more information.
- Cultural and language differences may present difficulties in information gathering across national boundaries.
- Availability of a universal sampling frame

4.5 Stages in the marketing research process

It is advisable to follow a structured and disciplined approach to marketing research both on and offline. This applies just as much to SMEs as it does to larger multi-nationals. Grossnickle and Raskin (2001) emphasise the importance of the research process by suggesting that it 'is a structured approach that helps ensure all your efforts result in useful, actionable information'. Far too often, companies that are anxious to gather data skip the critical early stages of the research process, and rush to designing and fielding studies. This is a dangerous practice that frequently limits the usefulness of the eventual findings. In rapidly changing, technology markets, it can be tempting to rush the research in order to get to market ahead of the competition but it is not always the wisest move. A company may not have tested its site for usability or perhaps gone into markets naively where Internet adoption amongst its target market is relatively low and so on. A traditional staged framework for effective research is outlined below (Table 4.4) with questions relating specifically to the Internet.

4.6 Defining the research required

What is the research objective?

The development of precise objectives will help frame the research. Taken from marketing planning, SMART objectives (Specific, Measurable, Achievable, Realistic and Timely) can also be applied effectively to marketing research. Both client and research agency need to determine the scope of the research to be undertaken to handle expectations and costs. However, it is just as important if the research is being carried out in-house. It is desirable to focus on the needs of specific market segments, such as the out of season travel market for over-55s in ABC1 category, often known as 'Silver Surfers'.

Mohammed et al (2002) put forward three fundamental opportunities or problems, which will shape the terms of reference, information search and subsequent strategy. These are:

- **Anticipated changes** – Planned changes, and research may determine the success of the changes. For example, an online merchant may plan to also offer ordering by telephone.
- **Emergent changes** – Unexpected and unforeseen. For example, the adoption of new technologies has been difficult to estimate. The usage and potential of mobile phones and SMS for marketing purposes are ideal examples of emergent change.

- **Opportunity based changes** – This is when changes are initiated as a reaction to unanticipated opportunities and events. In the Internet economy this has manifested itself through surprising strategic alliances, eg eBay and Sotheby's or opportunities for diversification (eg Amazon moving from books into travel).

Understanding the source and nature of the change (ie the marketing environment) will influence the methods of data collection to be undertaken. For example, if the survey method uses for video-streaming as part of its testing and requires broadband for maximum effectiveness, preliminary research should identify broadband subscribers in their sample population.

4.7 **Gathering data**

The undertaking of any research activity requires the planning stages outlined above to be carried out. Researchers should start with low-cost sources of information, before considering the need for commissioned research. The rapid search facility created by the Internet, makes it a very attractive research tool. The process usually begins with *Secondary* or *Desk* research, which is data and information that already exists. Grossnickle and Raskin (2001) simply refer to it as 'the use of previously existing resources to meet your research goals'. McDaniel and Gates (2004) provide a similar description whilst alluding to its limitations: 'Secondary data consist of information that has already been gathered and *might* be relevant to the problem at hand'. It can be in numerical and report formats. Secondary research may be:

- **Internal** sales records, customer lists, internal surveys, annual accounts, etc.

or

- **External** such as government statistics, local regional, national and European Union. Business information companies such as Mintel, Dun & Bradstreet as well as newspaper publishers like the *Financial Times* (www.FT.com) and *Wall Street Journal* (www.wsj.com) have migrated online providing comprehensive data on countries, industry sectors and the wider marketing environment.

The task of gathering secondary data prior to the Internet era was a laborious chore toiling away in libraries and squinting at microfiche systems or wading through mammoth industry directories for hours at a time. Online data can be most useful in giving both micro and macro environment information at very low cost. The drawbacks may be that it is not totally relevant to the defined terms of reference, so the researcher must carefully select pertinent information. Information may go quickly out of date. A report published 18 months ago on the slow adoption rate of broadband would be misleading now as prices and wider access has changed significantly. Also, the sheer volume of information accessible via the web often leads to information overload. The information generated could also be contradictory, causing confusion instead of clarity.

As part of a broader research plan, secondary research can play a significant role in reinforcing or disproving some of the client's preconceptions. It can also provide credible supporting information to enrich primary results and produce a cohesive report. Secondary data is viewed as the early stages of a research project when it can actually go a long way to solving the problem itself. For instance, the author was contracted to carry out some consultancy work, part of which was to identify new potential agents and distributors in Poland and the Czech Republic. After initially searching the UK government's overseas web sites, Trade Partners UK and following other links, industry trade associations in both countries were identified. The trade associations circulated client details, interested parties responded and a short list was drawn up, followed by face-to-face meetings in both countries where contracts were entered into. Interestingly, a lot of useful data was also gathered from US government information sites for exporters (www.export.gov).

Finding information from a standing start normally relies on one of two options. The first option depends upon the knowledge and familiarity of an organisation's domain name. The choice of an appropriate domain name coupled with clear branding and promotional strategies are fundamental factors (online branding will be discussed further in chapter 9 whilst domain names will be featured in chapter six). The second option is retrieving information from a search engine, eg Google or a directory, eg Yahoo!.

4.8 Internal secondary data

Even in the pre-Internet era, analysis of internal data provided valuable background information for the development of marketing strategies and tactics. Capturing customer orders by product type, quantity, frequency of purchase, media details and basic customer profile data has been the bedrock of database marketing development in the direct marketing industry. This allows greater precision, more accountability and less wastage. McDaniel and Gates describe creating a database from a web site as 'a Marketer's Dream,' as the access to customer behaviour is much more complete online compared to the physical world. Fig 4.3 introduces some basic web measurements.

The use of cookies provides a rich source of data, but third party cookies in particular have generated considerable distrust. The free anti-cookie software, Secretmaker is one of the top 20 most downloaded software worldwide. Privacy issues have become an important ethical and legal consideration for e-marketers and clear policy statements on cookies are advisable.

Fig 4.3 Examples of web measurements

- Sales per visitor
- Cost per visitor
- Conversion rates
- Recency, frequency, monetary value (RFM)
- Length of time spent on site
- Pages visited
- Subscribers to newsletters
- Numbers of cancellations
- Responses to campaigns and incentives
- Measure impacts of site design changes

LEGAL EAGLE BOX 4.1 Cookies

Any individual or organisation that uses any device to gain access to information stored on a users terminal equipment must provide clear and comprehensive information on:

- The type of device used
- The purpose for which it was used
- The right to opt-out of its use

Information on the type of cookie should be provided in the privacy policy/statement and posted on conspicuous points of the web site as either a session or persistent cookie. A session cookie is one that is erased when the user closes the web browser. A persistent cookie is one that is stored on a user's hard drive until it expires or until the user deletes it.

Developing a functional and relevant database is fundamentally important for any organisation's information management system that drives all aspects of marketing activity including research, contact management and personalisation strategies.

4.9 External secondary data

Domestic and international marketing information can be accessed from public, non-profit and private organisations. In Fig 4.4 below we have featured some excellent sources of online business and marketing information. The list is by no means exhaustive and researchers may be using other sites.

Another useful resource for the online researcher is the **white paper**. Corporate and technical white papers disseminated by e-mail are commonplace nowadays. Whilst they may be treated with a degree of cynicism as a PR and promotional device, many genuine white papers contain leading edge best practice which can be quite illuminating and informative.

4.10 Search engines and directories

The search engines and directories that many of us utilise for everyday searches are part of the '*visible*' or '*surface*' web. Despite claims by some that search engine marketing is dead, it still remains to be the main driver of traffic to web sites. Eighty-five per cent of web site visitors arrive at a particular site via a search engine, according to Andy Beal, then VP of search marketing for Websourced, cited in the Internet information site, Iconocast (2004). Other observers offer more conservative estimates but search engines undoubtedly play a vital role in any online research activity. This may be to get a particular source of information or site, and/or to search within a site once it has been accessed. Search engines use programmed spiders or robots to crawl the Internet identifying and indexing keywords into a retrievable search database ready for a keyword search to be entered. Search engines have different indexing systems from one another, depending upon optimisation issues like keyword density, link popularity and since monetisation, pay-per-click. Typically, search engines focus on sites with numerous quality links (link popularity). They also **index** a higher proportion of commercial sites rather than public or educational sites. For organisations submitting to search engines, it is imperative that the indexing system of each key engine,

Fig 4.4 Online market research sources

External Secondary Data

1. www.statitics.gov.uk The United Kingdom government's Office for National Statistics covering a diverse range of economic and social data.
2. www.ukonline.gov.uk The United Kingdom government's online information on initiatives and support for online business development.
3. www.companieshouse.gov.uk A paid for service providing financial and other data on registered limited companies in the UK. This is very useful for competitor, supplier and distributor research.
4. www.europa.eu.int Web site operated by the European Union covering all aspects of the Commission's work, including business, industry and e-commerce.
5. www.mrs.org.uk The web site for The Marketing Research Society providing the latest research, publications and guidelines for the marketing research industry.
6. www.esomar.org An industry leading body for marketing research professionals with the latest policies, research and award winning papers.
7. www.bmra.org.uk The British Market Research Association, the industry's trade association.
8. www.aqr.org.uk The Association of Qualitative Research Practitioners, which provides leading articles on qualitative research online, a discussion forum and membership services.
9. www.cim.co.uk The Chartered Institute of Marketing provides training, consultancy and education.
10. www.dma.org.uk Provides 'best practice', legal guidelines and codes of practice with industry news and events.
11. www.theidm.com The Institute of Direct Marketing contains training, leading articles and practice on all aspects of direct marketing with a growing emphasis on Interactive Marketing. Its Knowledge Centre is a valuable resource. The Institute also provides a dedicated web site for students studying direct marketing www.think-direct.com.
12. www.imrg.org The Interactive Media in Retail Group website is rich in information articles, survey and reports on media, retaining and technology aspects of e-business.
13. www.quirks.com The US Marketing Research Review providing informative articles covering aspects of leading edge marketing research.

Market Research Publishers

1. www.mintel.co.uk The well-known UK research body loved by students and academics alike for detailed sector reports on UK consumer and retail markets. Academic institutions normally have educational subscription rates whilst price/ordering information is available for private and corporate enquirers.
2. www.keynote.co.uk Again a top publisher of UK sector reports.
3. www.datamonitor.com A publisher of international business reports, consumer sector reports and individual companies.
4. www.lexis-nexis.com Lexis Nexis produces articles from marketing, business and consumer publications with industry sector and corporate information.
5. www.euromonitor.com A provider of global sector reports with the emphasis on consumer markets.
6. www.eiu.com Provides market and country reports coupled with economic forecasts and analysis, eg European E-readiness report.
7. www.frost.com Frost and Sullivan is a well-established publisher of market reports. They are especially active in Europe, Asia and the Far East across a wide range of business sectors.
8. www.nua.com A leading resource for worldwide Internet trends and statistics.
9. www.cyberatlas.internet.com Cyber Atlas is a leading online producer and publisher of e-business information on consumers and leading players.
10. www.jupiterresearch.com Generates reports on web traffic and the leading sites.
11. www.nielsen-netratings.com Provides statistical data relating to online audience behaviour through large online panels.

Fig 4.4 (*Continued*)

Market Research Content Aggregators

1. www.marketsearch-dir.com Marketsearch provide their Market Research directory offering over 20,0000 reports from 700 suppliers Results are indexed by SIC code, date and country. With prices charged in US dollars (USD).
2. www.dialog.com A business information service offering worldwide material.
3. www.mindbranch.com Provides a pay-as-you-go facility for access to market research reports from over 250 content providers.

Market Research Agencies

1. www.bmrb.co.uk The British Market Research Bureau, a web site containing the latest research activity, MR news and publications.
2. www.nopworld.com *NOP Research* is now part of *NOP World*, a top-ten market research power uniting some of the most renowned European and US research firms. The web site gives information and summaries on the industries and sector specialisms.
3. www.sga.co.uk Provides an insight into SGA's expertise such as new product development and online research.
4. www.mori.com A leading public and market research agency. The site provides information on latest research and publications on politics, business and social research.
5. www.e-mori.co.uk e-MORI is the team within MORI, which specialises in research about – and using – electronic technologies, including the Internet, digital TV, IT, and telecommunications. e-MORI has tried and tested many new methodologies to add to our portfolio of traditional approaches such as usability studies, online surveys and moderated e-mail groups.
6. www.tnsofres.com Taylor Nelson Sofres are a global market information player with considerable sector and country information.

Examples of Country Specialisms

1. www.mrsa.co.au The Market Research Society of Australia.
2. www.01net.com A leading French web site, providing information on all aspects of e-business.

Examples of Industry Specialist Sites

Automotive

1. www.europa.eu.int/comm/enterprise/automotive/ European Commission's site providing information on regulatory frameworks and policies for the automotive industry in Europe designed at strengthening competitiveness
2. www.waitnews.com World Automotive Industry Trends provides news and statistics on worldwide development with free newsletters.
3. www.smmt.co.uk The Society of Motor Manufacturers and Traders provides market data and reports, news events and a forum for the UK automotive industry.

Legal

1. www.privacylaws.com Provides up to the minute coverage of UK and international data protection issues through its newsletter.
2. www.library.kent.ac.uk/library/lawlinks/european.htm
3. www.lawresearch.com
4. www.adinfo.com/eulaw.htm
5. www.law.nyu.edu/library/foreign_intl/european.html (New York University School of Law)

Financial

1. www.ft.com
2. www.ample.co.uk
3. www.bloomberg.com
4. www.hemscott.com

Table 4.5 55 million Europeans using Google online

Top 10 Search Channels in Europe – Jan 04	Unique Audience	Active Reach	Pages Per Person	Time Per Person
Google Search	55,641,382	47.3%	52	15:24
MSN Search	27,151,382	23.1%	12	04:08
Yahoo!! Search	12,676,097	10.8%	21	07:30
Google Image Search	10,275,673	8.7%	36	09:13
AOL Search	5,846,613	5.0%	20	09:05
Virgilio Ricerca	4,350,538	3.7%	24	07:57
T-Online Suche	3,898,809	3.3%	8	04:15
Voila Search	3,458,755	2.9%	17	08:03
Lycos Europe Search	3,117,113	2.7%	13	04:54
Microsoft Search	2,683,728	2.28%	3	01:51

Source: Nielsen//NetRatings European Index Jan 2004

the ones most used by your customers, is fully understood to increase the chances of achieving high rankings. From a researcher's perspective, it is often worthwhile checking out each search engines help tab for search tips as they may vary and affect your results. Of course you can also sign up to Google's news alerts on your chosen search query.

When researching overseas markets, marketers should also be aware of the search engine ratings, which may show that the most popular search engine in the domestic market is not necessarily the leader in other countries. This is the case in European countries like Switzerland, Sweden and Italy where more use is made of local search engines such as Virgillo in Italy. A Nielsen NetRatings report (2004) on search engine usage finds that Google is the dominant search engine across Europe and has become a way of European internet life.

These 2003 results tend to reflect the general search role played by portals. For more specific search queries, many people favour Google in the first instance with its extensive indexing and speed of generating results. Other search engines have positioned themselves in a more focussed way such as www.travelbritain.com providing travel and tourism information. BBCi at www.bbc.co.uk utilises its extensive news, business and media resources with pornography filters to provide a powerful but family friendly search facility. A new search facility in the US, Icerocket, provides greater convenience by enabling keyword searches by e-mail (www.icerocket.com/c?p=emailsearch).

A general directory, such as Yahoo!, is another valuable search tool. Rather than rely on automated technology to search the web, directories use human effort to view and index a site to predefined categories. Teams of **surf** searchers trawl submissions and manually categorise them into a range of subject categories, eg Sport, Travel, Finance, etc. In addition to the general directory, there are also more specialised subject specific directories which maybe academic, eg Social Sciences or Professional, or Accountancy. Also Value Added Search Services like Northern Light www.northernlight.com offer extensive information resources and partner links with their business library, portal and customised search facility.

Fig 4.5 Information at the Beeb (www.bbc.co.uk)

4.11 The 'invisible' or 'deep' web

Harris and Dennis (2002) suggest, however, 'The exponential growth of the web is making the task of search engines increasingly difficult because of the sheer volume of new sites and information being placed on the web'. Apart from sheer volume of existing and rapidly expanding sites and pages, search engines normally only gather pages of text and do not recognise graphics and picture content. As a result millions of web pages will never appear in the results of the leading search engines. A similar problem arises with directories because of the human element and the time taken categorising sites. They simply cannot view and record even a fraction of submitted sites. Estimates vary regarding how many sites are indexed by search engines and directories. Back in 2001, Google had approximately 1 billion pages indexed but that equated to around 25% of all information accessible via the web only. This is due to technical aspects of web page design, the way search 'bots' crawl the web indexing flat pages, how access may be restricted to 'unseen' searchable databases. Search engines also operate **spider** policies where only a limited number of pages from each site will be indexed. Most web sites contain hundreds of pages and sub-categories but the search engines may have decided to index only the first 30 or 50 pages leaving other site pages hidden. Add to this the fact that many databases will not talk to one another, then market researchers are potentially missing out on a rich source of hidden information. So intuition and insight remain are valuable traits rather than relying solely on the machine.

The term 'invisible web', often linked to Sherman and Price (2001), relates to information that is unavailable by ordinary searches. They define the invisible web as 'Text pages, files or other often high quality authoritative information available via the World Wide Web that general purpose search engines cannot, due to technical limitations, or will not, due to deliberate choice, add to their indices of Web pages. Sometimes also referred to as the "Deep Web" or dark matter'. Bergman (2001) states that 'Traditional search engines can not "see" or retrieve content in the deep Web – those pages do not exist until they are created dynamically as the result of a specific search.' Access to the home page of databases is possible but the individual data records within cannot be reach by normal queries. Furthermore, many web sites may require a personal password or **login**, particularly membership or subscription sites, to all or part of a site which a search engine spider cannot know. There has been a game of cat and mouse with many database owners seeking to prevent spiders from indexing their data sets whilst software developers are seeking new spider technologies to access these databases.

There is a growing consensus that small is beautiful. As the web matures, a large number of portals, each of which specialises in a topical area, will be preferred to broad-spectrum search portals. The invisible resources alluded to by Sherman and Price, such as directories, gateways and databases, are invariably more subject-specific and targeted than those generated by all-purpose search engines. They highlight the reporting differences of the two. For example, Yahoo! would give a broad account of what is happening in the money markets compared to the detail offered by Bloomberg's or the *Financial Times*. Targeted directories such as www.ribafind.org of the Royal Institute of British Architects provide industry specific resources and links.

Academic directories or gateways and pathfinders such as OMNI, Bubl, and Virtual Library, etc would be your usual access to information on the deep web for research purposes. Summaries of UK Higher Education gateways are also listed on the central CTI Web site at www.cti.ac.uk/links/t&l/info.html. Another useful UK academic gateway is the Blacknet education resource www.blacknet.co.uk/education/refdirectories.htm.

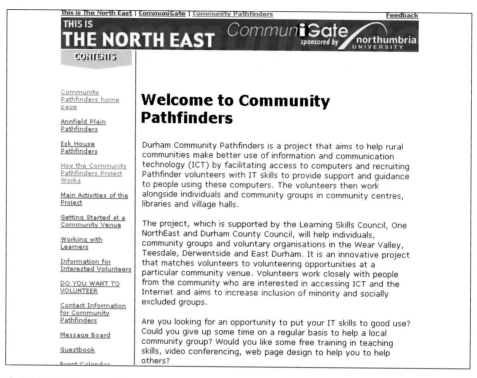

Fig 4.6 Pathfinder screenshot

Reproduced by kind permission of Durham County Council.

Pathfinders are primarily directories containing links to superior specialist information. The content is provided by leading institutes, trade bodies or individual experts in their field and supplied by credible information providers, eg www.teacherpathfinder.org a US educational Internet village for teachers, parents and pupils. In the North East of England, the Communigate project aims to help rural communities make better use of information and communication technology (ICT) by facilitating access to computers and recruiting Pathfinder volunteers with IT skills to provide support and guidance to people using these computers. An example of the Durham Community Pathfinders portal is illustrated in Fig. 4.6. (www.communigate.co.uk/ne/pathfinder)

Other examples of gateways and pathfinders include:

- www.lii.org The Librarians 'index to the Internet' provides a directory of 10,000+ Internet resources for information specialists and the public alike.
- www.nypl.org The New York Public Library web site is a fine example of a database and index resource.
- www.ipl.org/div/pf/ The internet pathfinder titled The Internet Public Library and hosted by the School of Information at the University of Michigan provides subject specific category links with a US bias.
- www.drugscope.org.uk Drugscope is a UK drug information and portal resource for accessing specific drug-related online information.

Topic or focused crawlers are important weapons for researchers on the invisible web. They are more sophisticated than general search engine crawlers and are able to find more detailed 'deep' pages as they follow specific links or themes on a single subject and analyse their value. Sherman and Price suggest that as the topic crawlers concentrate on single subjects rather than the visible web, they can review and index their findings more frequently. This should generate more relevant, current and detailed search results. As software becomes increasingly more sophisticated 'intelligent crawlers' are emerging that learn web structures to produce better topic specific results.

4.12 Newsgroups

Newsgroups, or bulleting boards, have emerged as useful communication forums for industry or subject professionals and those indulging in their hobby. Whilst some newsgroups exercise a degree of control over the messages, forums generally enable open discussions or provide help and advice such as Freepint (www.web.freepint.com). Most browsers facilitate threaded discussions that can be followed and replied to. This can be very useful for secondary research purposes.

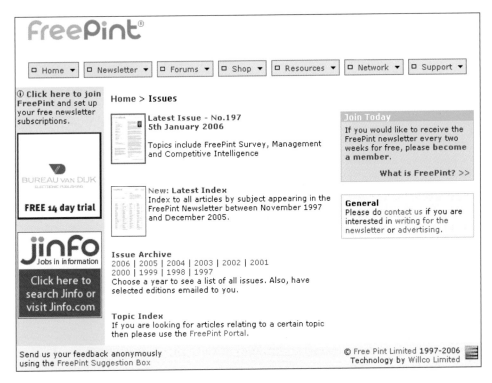

Fig 4.7 Freepint.com

Reproduced by kind permission of Free Pint Ltd.

4.13 Secondary search tips

The previous sections highlighted rich and diverse sources of secondary information available for online researchers. Of course, as we have all experienced, time and effort can be wasted surfing the web for quality information. Here are a few pointers for better results:

- Use search engines that generate credible results from subject authorities and other reputable sources.
- Cross reference with other sources to check the accuracy and relevance of the data where possible.
- Follow each search engine's search tips to get the best results.
- Check to see how current the web site and its pages are from the last update.
- Bookmark the best sites and develop your own researcher's toolkit for your own regular use.
- Search subject specific Internet pathfinders to delve into the invisible web.
- Once you have identified sources, sign up for regular newsletters and web alerts for information.

And to refine your search results further we are indebted to Jan Storey, Principal Information Specialist at Northumbria University for the following advice:

Fig 4.8 Jan Storey's Internet search tips

10 Internet Search Tips

1. Keywords! Keywords! Keywords!
Think carefully before you start to type in the search box. Try writing your information needs as a question – the keywords should be more obvious. 'What is the **market size** for **trainers** in the **UK**?'

2. Extend your Keywords
Try the following so you don't miss important results
- plurals
- alternative/similar words eg size/data
- different spellings, eg color/colour
- narrower terms eg fitness trainers
- broader terms eg footwear
- remove the hyphen from hyphenated words
- use of words in different countries eg soccer/football

3. Key People
Make a list and search the web sites of
- key writers/researchers
- companies
- brands
- organisations (spelt organizations too!)
- trade and professional associations
- government bodies

Fig 4.8 *(Continued)*

4. Refine your keywords

As you continue with your research seek out new and relevant keywords and search again

5. Advanced Search Techniques

Click on 'Advanced Search' or 'Search tips' or even 'Help' to find more relevant results.

Try

- phrase searching eg 'market size'
- truncation eg retail* for retailing, retailer, retailers boolean logic operators *and* (or +), *or* and *not* (or –)
- proximity searching so that the words appear *near* each other eg Sport N5 Footwear (within 5 words of each other)
- field indexes – your keyword must be in the title or contents lists field
- searching by country eg .uk, .fr
- domain search eg .gov .ac .edu .org
- limiting by date
- limiting by file type eg html, pdf

6. Try out different Search Engines

Search engines rank results in different ways – experiment with

Google	www.google.co.uk/
Google Scholar	www.scholar.google.com/
Yahoo!	www.yahoo.com/
Lycos	www.lycos.com/
Ask !	www.uk.ask.com/

7. Use Meta Search Engines

These will combine the results of various search engines and some will sort the results into relevant folders for you.

Dogpile	www.dogpile.com
Jux2	www.jux2.com/
Ixquick	www.ixquick.com/
Kartoo	www.kartoo.com/
ez2find	www.ez2find.com/

8. Look up Classified Directories and Subject Gateways

Try out these directories that have been compiled by humans.

Yahoo!	www.uk.search.yahoo.com/dir
Bubl	www.bubl.ac.uk/link/
Intute	www.intute.ac.uk/
Pinakes	www.hw.ac.uk/libWWW/irn/pinakes/pinakes.html

9. Evaluate Your Results

How credible is the data you have found? Do check for:

Authority

Currency

Objectivity

Accuracy

Completeness

Fig 4.8 *(Continued)*

---

10. Ask an Expert

Visit your local Library and make an appointment with an expert.

Boolean Logic Operators Definition

Several definitions below:

'boolean' refers to a system of logical thought developed in the 19th century by the English mathematician, George Boole.

Boolean Logic Operators are used to combine search terms to construct more complex searches in a database. Using the boolean operators AND, OR, and NOT can help expand or narrow a search.

The logical operators (AND, OR, NOT) are used to construct complex searches in online databases to produce more precise results.

Jan Storey

Principal Information Specialist

Northumbria University

August 2006

4.14 Primary research

A considerable amount of academic research has sought to compare and contrast traditional survey methods, especially mail, with new online survey methods (Ranchhod & Zhou, 2001; McDonald & Adam, 2003).

Hollerson (2003) defines primary data as 'information that is collected first hand, generated by original research tailor-made to answer specific research questions.' Crouch and Housden (1996) also refer to it as 'made-to-measure' research process that is customised to answer explicit information needs. The Internet provides marketers with a diverse range of platforms for research purposes, including mixed mode where on and offline methods are used to reach different segments. The platforms include e-mail and web-based surveys, chat rooms, online panels and bulletin board focus groups. With the high rate of mobile phone adoption, SMS provides another valuable platform to reach specific markets such as students and under 25s generally. In Mini case 4.1, Peter Wills from online survey specialists, Snap Surveys (www.snapsurveys.com) provides an interesting overview on developments in web surveys practices.

Many of the strengths and weaknesses of online surveys were discussed earlier in the chapter but speed and reduced costs have been key attractions to marketers. In this section we will consider some of the new survey applications together with other primary research methods. Speed is particularly important in competitive markets when rapid, accurate decision making can undermine market rivals. Invariably, primary research required the expertise of a marketing research agency to fulfil the agreed terms of reference, or brief, with a client. This remains the case with online research applications still in their infancy. Organisations will benefit from the hard lessons and experience gained by research agencies, as well as their independence. It may be tempting to try and manage customer feedback through your own forums but without sound advice, it could develop into a PR disaster. However, the development of specialist user-friendly research software is enabling organisations to design and manage their own survey projects more easily.

MINI CASE 4.1 Expert insight

When Internet surveys first appeared, the market research industry poured scorn on them, claiming all sorts of problems with sampling. With hindsight, much of this criticism was born out of a fear of new technologies.

Today, with over 600 million Internet users worldwide, online surveys are not only a force in their own right, they are rapidly replacing telephone surveys. Increasingly, web survey software packages are incorporating many of the features previously deemed to be the remit of CATI packages, including quota control, rotation of questions, text substitution, etc.

Internet surveys are often supported by versions of the survey for other modes, such as paper, phone or PDA, and as a software supplier, we have found it necessary to ensure that the same functionality exists across all platforms. This can be a struggle for developers, but fortunately, today's modern PDA does now enable this integration.

The design of web surveys is at the forefront of everybody's mind when selecting appropriate software, but surprisingly few packages provide full data cleaning and analytical features. It is assumed that everybody is an expert in Excel or Access and can quickly produce the necessary tables and charts. It is important to consider software packages that provide full integration from design and publication, to data collection and analysis.

Since web surveys can be quick and easy to set up, it is also assumed that the cost of a web survey is always lower than other methods, such as paper or phone. Typically this is true, but with the flexibility of design options for web surveys, and the ability to alter the questionnaire right up to the last minute, design costs can often get out of hand. Designing for paper is reassuringly restrictive – you are limited by paper size, perhaps the number of pages, and very often you are working in a single colour – a scenario quite unheard of for web surveys.

The one question that we are always asked – 'Do you get a higher response rate with online surveys?' Unfortunately the short answer is 'no'. It is true that you get a faster response but simply taking a questionnaire and putting it online will not automatically improve response rates. The traditional techniques of reminders still apply to increase response, and fortunately, this technique is easy to generate with modern software packages, and is very inexpensive.

In short, online surveys are now mainstream in all areas of research, and software developers are working hard to add every new features from a demanding audience. The future for online surveys is certainly bright.

Peter Wills
CEO
Snap Surveys
www.snapsurveys.com
2005

Primary research involves one of two approaches:

1. Quantitative Research
2. Qualitative Research

1. Quantitative Research produces hard statistical data when measuring aspects of consumer behaviour, their attitudes and key characteristics. Powerful statistical packages like SPSS can generate tables and graphs, produce averages and means together with complex multivariate analysis from large scale structured surveys. Web metrics seemingly can produce any amount of data for marketers to analyse. Quantitative data is deemed to be more scientific, rigorous, and reliable whilst producing more representative samples of the population under investigation. A fundamental method of quantitative data capture online is similar to offline in terms in that they are usually linked to accounts and ordering departments. Online subscriptions, payments and product registrations provide the first formal opportunity for gathering vital customer data.

2. Qualitative Data is more concerned with producing customer insights into *why* they behaved the way they did, they way they *feel* now and what they might do in future interactions with an organisation. Qualitative research enables marketers to get under the skin of the respondent to understand their attitudes, interests and opinions that shape their lifestyle and online behaviour. As the Internet can be quite impersonal, qualitative research is a vital tool in determining the likes and dislikes of web users through methods such as usability studies. This has become increasingly important, as personalisation is

---

Fig 4.9 Common online primary research activities

- Advertising research (including content analysis and media exposure)
- New product testing
- All aspects of web site evaluation in terms of design, layout and usability incorporating techniques such as eye tracking technology
- Customer satisfaction surveys
- Partner and reseller satisfaction surveys
- Online omnibus surveys eg NOP's e-Omnibus
- Online focus groups
- Link with other digital (Mobile/PDA Surveys) and traditional offline methods
- Testing any aspect of your online provision

---

a critical element in Customer Relationship Management (CRM) programmes. Whereas quantitative research can be implemented on a large scale, qualitative methods are carried out on much smaller samples that may not be representative. They can be applied in a variety of ways, such as product concept testing, focus groups, online chat rooms to e-mail feedback forms but the results and observations rely more heavily on interpretation, or the skills of a moderator rather than statistical rigour.

Hague & Morgan (2004) suggest that quantitative and qualitative research are often complementary with quantitative research at the front end and qualitative research exploring deep values.

Pop-up surveys have become a popular tool for online data and opinion capture, though not always with consumers.

Typically, three research approaches can be implemented:

1. Observational research
2. Survey Research
3. Testing (or Experimental) Research

Practitioners in their field will argue the merits of the different practices, especially those involved in surveying and testing. The application of each will depend upon expertise, access to respondents, budgets and time to market.

Observational Research is a form of qualitative research that looks for clues in human behaviour by observing appropriate populations in action or in specific test conditions relevant to the research problem. Armstrong & Kotler (2004) state that it 'involves gathering primary data by observing relevant people, actions and situations.' Observations may generate valuable

---

MINI CASE 4.2 Masterfoods put pop-up collection ads on relevant sites

This year (2004) Masterfoods embarked on a puppy research programme for its pet foods. Its agency Media.com asked ValueClick for a cost per lead means of generating participants for research.

A pop-up data collection ad was put up on specialist pet information advice sites. They provided the perfect environment for high completion rates with users able to put their details directly into the creative. Users were incentivised with an £8 voucher offer and ValueClick generated the booked amount of leads in the campaign period between February and March 2004.

Adapted from: The Online Direct Marketing Guide, Interactive Advertising Bureau UK (2004). www.iabuk.net

customer insights, which other approaches fail to master as we note what customers do and how they behave. Traditionally, observational research would monitor behaviour such as shoppers' movements around stores or their reaction to new products. Mystery shoppers are a well-known research method used to test employee performance especially in a retail situation.

For e-marketers, observing the ways customers use and navigate a site has become a crucial area of observational research. The term 'usability', largely associated with Jakob Nielsen (www.useit.com), focuses on web design for successful customer interactions. Typically, *usability testing* is carried out in laboratory environments with 10–12 representative users involved. A multitude of usability testing agencies have emerged providing test services. This can be done by observation, using trained interviewers to elicit deeper understanding. Some agencies actively encourage participants to talk through their experiences in real time and record their views for later scrutiny. For researchers and strategists alike, decisions have to be made *when* usability testing should be undertaken to get the most benefit from it. Ideally, this should be done at the start of any project before going 'live'. It may also take place when a site is being redesigned with new navigation or service features under consideration. Alternatively, usability studies may be employed when competitor research takes place and users are asked to assess the client's site against that of a key rival. For valid results, it is important to involve participants with the right demographic and web experience. If your target market is predominantly new 'silver surfers' with limited web savvy, then this group should be involved in the research rather than employed 45–50 age groups who use the web frequently at work and play. The former are the ones using your site, navigating their way around it, trying to find products and services, and you need to know their likes, dislikes, expectations and abilities.

Eye Tracking Technology can also be used for online research purposes. This employs Pupil Centre Corneal Reflection (PCCR) monitoring instruments to track eye movements and specific participant interests. Dreze & Hussherr (2003) used such technologies to research the effectiveness of banner advertising using the French portal Voila (www.voila.fr). Size, location and brand were influential factors in banner ad effectiveness. However, the eye tracking technology also identified very different eye movements between expert and novice web users, suggesting that different levels of design and content expectations exist. Eye tracking technology could indicate where page hot spots exist and where special offers could be placed, for example, observing experts could highlight how they shortcut their way around sites whilst the novice could be infuriated because of their inability to carry out what many consider to be fairly simple tasks.

Online Observation can also take an impersonal dimension. Strauss & Frost cite stateside research companies who will observe chat rooms and postings on USENET and provide reports and analysis of the entries.

4.15 Online survey methods

Baines and Chansarkar (2002) suggest four main survey methods for obtaining consumer information online:

- E-mail questionnaires
- Web questionnaires
- Public chat and discussion groups
- Online focus groups

Fig 4.10 Excerpt from Times Newspapers e-mail surveys

Each week, *The Times* and *The Sunday Times* publish three very popular glossy magazines. Not only do our readers enjoy the award winning photography and variety of stories covered by these magazines, our advertisers too love to use these glossy pages to showcase their products. We have recently been experimenting with new advertising formats within the magazines and would like to understand more about how you view these innovations and how this affects your experience of the magazines.

To complete the September questionnaire please follow the link below:
www.yass.newsint.co.uk/04294077-180963-190264/http%3A%2F%2Fwww.media-intelligence.com%2Ftimessurvey

If you have any views as to how you think we could further improve the survey, please do not hesitate to get in touch.

E-mail questionnaires

E-mail questionnaires were more commonly used in the early Internet days due to speed, cost and access. Access was a particular factor when targeting people in the B2B sector, as many had e-mail but without complete web provision. However, these tended to be text based, visually uninteresting with no graphics often resulting in poor completion rates. Strauss et al (2003) identified fundamental problems with this mode where respondents did not have the technical capability to answer in 'reply and edit' mode or when they did answer they were slipshod, making data processing and analysis difficult.

Firms may now survey by e-mail with questionnaires implanted, by **attachment** or by directed links, either using in-house or external e-mail lists. See *The Times* example below (Fig 4.10). E-mail surveys like these now incorporate multi-media elements and encourage greater interaction and response rates. Broadband adoption makes this a more effective research tool and overcomes survey download problems.

On the downside, e-mail surveys lack anonymity, which may introduce bias and reduce response rates.

Web based questionnaires

Web based questionnaires offer immense data collection potential in terms of speed, cost, data processing and survey completion. They also offer versatility in terms of multi-media rich formats and flexibility in terms of survey design.

Web software development costs have fallen considerably, making the survey process easier and commercially more attractive. Web software is usually fully integrated from questionnaire design through to data collection, analysis and graphic presentation of results. With the likes of Snap Surveys (www.snapsurveys.com), SurveyGold (www.surveygold.com) and WebSurveyor (www.websurveyor.com) the research process can be self-managed or hosted by the developer. Of course, this depends upon the existing in-house expertise in questionnaire design and statistical analysis. However, bias may occur so the research may benefit from the input of independent parties. Different question modes such as single response, multiple choice and open ended are simply incorporated, providing web, e-mail and PDA interviews as well as offline options like telephone interviews. A fundamental factor in the evolution of online surveys has been the growing acceptance over many years of self-administered questionnaires (SAQs). Members of the public will have completed an SAQ at one time or another, which makes online completion less difficult. Offline SAQs have suffered from respondent completion errors, which well-designed online SAQs should eliminate.

Web surveys can be:

1. *Open* – access

2. *Closed* – password protected

3. *Hidden* – as pop-up surveys either embedded in a main survey or stand-alone pop-up.

Couper (2000) is widely quoted when making the distinctions between different types of web-based surveys:

1. Non-probability based surveys

2. Probability based surveys

Non-probability surveys are not statistically sound, as they do not employ any recognised selection techniques. Couper cites three categories of non-probability surveys. The first are *entertainment surveys*, where generalised surveys are posted on web sites and anyone can respond. These tend to be polls with voting on burning issues like the greatest rock'n'roll album ever, the most beautiful volleyball player at the Olympics or Alan Shearer's greatest goal. From a marketer's perspective they add an element of interaction and fun into a site, which may increase traffic and have some news value rather than research merit. The second type is *self-select* surveys where high traffic sites post surveys and promote involvement. Feedback can be useful to a point especially if a precise target market is reached but any findings generated may contain sample bias and affect the validity, particularly where multiple submissions are possible. The third category is made up of *volunteer panels* where users have registered their personal details and opted–in to participate in future research. Data collection like this enriches the database and information can be overlaid to improve customer profiling. Research organisations like the British Market Research Bureau (www.bmrb.co.uk) and NOP (www.nop.co.uk) offer a range of such panels.

Couper (2000) points to numerous types of probability-based methods. The first is referred to as an *intercept survey* where every *nth* visitor to the site may be invited to participate in the survey. This method is potentially attractive for satisfaction and site evaluation surveys. However, self-selection and non-response raises questions over the validity of this method. Those responding may be extremely brand loyal and provide favourable answers whilst those having an indifferent Internet experience may choose not to complete Consequently, bias will occur unless the characteristics of respondents and non-respondents are known. *List-based samples* are the second probability method referred to by Couper with invitations to participate sent by e-mail where specific populations exist. Examples of this could be where membership, internal distribution or University lists of students exist. Alternatively, researchers may seek to build their own contact lists to overcome the sampling problem. However, Hwang & Fesenmaier (2004) argue that since survey costs are so low, it is likely that researchers will use the entire list. Another probability method is the *mixed mode survey* where the web survey is seen as one of a number of ways of reaching the desired audience(s) in sufficient numbers. Respondents are given the choice whether to complete online, download a paper version or perhaps by telephone. The final type put forward by Couper is the *Pre–recruited Panel* of either (1) *Internet users* or (2) *full population*. Internet users can be recruited by probability using random number generated telephone surveys or interviewer

LEGAL EAGLE BOX 4.2 Online chat rooms

Although the Internet enables easy group discussions, it also allows researchers to engage in covert observations. A researcher can record the online discussions of a group without having to disclose his/her identity.

With online chat rooms, the key issues are privacy and confidentiality of personal information relating to members of the group.

Invasion of privacy can easily occur in such a group where the participants lose control of their personal information that is disclosed to others in the group.

Where confidential information is disclosed, it must be used confidentially and ensured that it is not disseminated to members of the group without that data subject's consent.

quota selections against pre-determined characteristics. In order to obtain representative samples, the full population can be approached even though web access may not be universal. In such a case, IT equipment may be provided to overcome any technical problems like browser compatibility. There are a number of issues to consider such as cost, population coverage and possible respondent effect to unfamiliar equipment.

Public chat and discussion groups

Chat rooms and bulletin boards are another rich source of gathering qualitative data on net issues. Participants are invited to offer opinions on posted topics and specific subject threads can be developed. Researchers can merely observe the discussions or participate if they wish to clarify or stimulate debate. However, as Baines and Chansarkar (2002) suggest the stimulation has to be carefully handled without pressing respondents on key issues otherwise feelings can be aroused and reactions sometimes excessive. The major drawbacks of employing this method is the time and subsequent costs involved in rummaging around the boards to find a few pearls of wisdom as no automated systems exist to capture and analyse this soft data.

Online focus groups

The use of focus groups for collecting amorphous qualitative data has been a hot topic for the industry as the tool has drifted in and out of favour. For the last decade, focus groups have definitely been in vogue with diverse applications in public and private sector organisations, not to mention political parties. The emergence of online focus groups has fuelled the debate further as some observers have suggested that they can supplant face-to-face methods. Traditional researchers hotly dispute this. It is more likely that online focus groups will complement traditional methods, especially when they lend themselves to specific situations, for example, when the target population is geographically spread.

Respondents are typically recruited via the Internet, though occasionally by phone, and selected on the basis of pre-determined characteristics. Most observers (Herbert, 2001, McDaniel & Gates, 2004) recommend a maximum of six respondents per group, primarily because of the limitations of moderating responses. Herbert recommends two synchronized moderators 'behind the scenes' to facilitate and stimulate responses, and recognises that the traditional skills of the moderator are valuable and transferable online. However, the moderator should possess fast and accurate keyboard skills and be competent with the software platform. Online focus groups typically last around two hours enabling moderators and clients to gather rich data. Respondents are identified individually but use an alias to retain anonymity. Their responses are usually colour coded which allows both the moderator and other respondents to follow each input more easily.

There are arguments for and against online focus groups. Significant cost and time-savings accrue, with easier recruitment of participants and reduced travel costs associated with moderators reaching dispersed audiences. In addition, the Internet provides the opportunity to bring time-starved professionals together, eg medical professionals, who otherwise would not have the time to participate. Online focus groups are different to offline in that we cannot monitor the expressions and body language of participants that often give clues to the strengths of opinion held. However, the fact that participants have to type in their responses may result in more detailed responses generated. They can also express themselves with the use of emoticons or 'smileys', which are symbols that convey the way they are feeling, eg ☺ ☺ ☹ For research, or to lighten up e-mails, various sites like www.smileycentral.com offer free smiley downloads.

In traditional groups, the moderator always strives to stimulate and capture representative views of those present, but group dynamics often produce dominant players who may stifle open debate. The freedom and anonymity offered by an online group may also produce more honest and open answers. With the client present, the moderator can ask pertinent questions and develop key areas of interest with skilful probing, though on the downside this may impact on the independence of the research.

Online focus groups as a method has always had the advantage of generating automatic transcripts but new software developments have enabled more effective management of the process. Reminders and confirmations to pre-screened individuals encourage participation rates. Security and sensitivity is very important for participant confidence so secure logins and the passing of sensitive data is carefully controlled. New technology also enables the use of multimedia formats providing greater research flexibility. Nevertheless, despite these advances, the jury is still out regarding online replacing traditional focus groups. Instead, they provide another useful tool in the researcher's armoury.

4.16 Sampling issues

Crouch and Housden (1996) state that, 'a sample is a limited number taken from a large group for testing and analysis, on the assumption that the sample can be representative of the whole group.' Sampling is currently the main area of weakness for online marketing research organisations, as no universal sampling frame exists and Internet research is restricted to markets covered totally by the web. It is a similar situation to the eighties when the telephone became an important research tool as UK telephone ownership exceeded 80% of the population.

McDonald and Adam (2003) suggest survey errors occur primarily due to:

- Coverage error – where the sample frame is not representative of the whole population. Is the sample frame made up of only highly active Internet users?

- Sampling error – where survey results lack accuracy often due to the size of the sample.

- Non-response error – when selected respondents do not participate in the survey and the impact their absence results have on the overall results, eg due to changing e-mail addresses.

- Measurement error – where question and other survey design and mode issues may produce bias.

Strauss et al (2003) note that marketers are unable to call upon a controlled probability sample, as no global list of Internet users exists unless they utilise in-house e-mail lists. With multiple e-mail addresses and regular switching of ISP accounts, even such lists are problematic. These factors have caused an increase in non-response error.

McDaniel and Gates categorise Internet samples as follows:

- Screened Internet samples from self-select samples
- Recruited panels
- Opt-in list rentals
- Opt-in panels
- Random web intercepts, eg via pop-up surveys.

Online sampling frames have tended to be unrepresentative of the population as a whole, reflecting the more affluent demographic characteristics of mainstream Internet users resulting in coverage error. This is gradually becoming less of a problem with wider Internet adoption though recruited panels often suffer from high churn rates once the novelty of participation has worn off. Whilst pop-ups have produced encouraging response rates, again there is an element of self-selection to contend with, not too mention the growing adoption of pop-up blockers. Hwang and Fesenmaier (2003) conclude that factors in non-response error have led to many sampling frames to include both voluntary and non-voluntary participants who may maintain significant differences in opinion causing possible sample bias. When researchers implement systematic sampling with such frames, the validity of the results is doubtful.

4.17 Questionnaire design

Designing questionnaires for online usage should adopt the same principles employed offline, with some fine distinction allowing for multi-media innovation such as sound, video and graphic images with HTML links. Software developments facilitate a higher level of sophistication and provide a distinct advantage over paper-based questionnaires including greater analysis. Design must also consider online respondent behaviour. Modem speed, screen resolutions and browsers used, eg IE6/IE7 all impact upon the research success.

Grossnickle and Raskin (2001) provide six key guidelines for questionnaire design and flow:

1. Kick off the survey with easy questions that will arouse interest

2. Cluster questions on the same topic

3. Questions on a topic should flow from general to specific

4. When addressing a topic, ask behavioural questions first, and then move to attitudinal questions

5. Place 'easy' questions, such as demographics, near the end of the survey

6. If you must ask about them, place sensitive topics at the end of the survey

In the main, online surveys are self-administered questionnaires (SAQs) and therefore it is advisable to go for simplicity and clarity in question design, as no interviewer is present to guide the respondent through the content. This also influences survey length, which is an important factor affecting questionnaire completion rates. The Internet is about customer speed and convenience and these two factors should influence questionnaire design. Nielsen (2004) suggests that people already suffer what from he refers to as 'survey bloat' resulting from information thirsty marketers. He stresses the importance of limiting the number of questions and only asking on a 'need to know' basis.

Surveys may be single or multiple pages. People do not like scrolling down pages so when extra pages are needed they should be sectioned according to topic. However, the load-up time from page to page must be efficient to reduce drop out. Respondents should be advised about the survey length from the outset in terms of the time it will take or the number of pages they have to complete. If they do not know what the questionnaire parameters are they could lose interest halfway through and fail to complete. Once they are in a multi-page survey, respondents should be informed about their progress. This is usually shown at the bottom of a page by a statement such as 'Page 3 out of 4' or the use of a progression bar illustrating that they have 'completed 75% of the questionnaire'. Non-completion of specific questions in a SAQ can be overcome when the respondent has to complete specific boxes before moving onto the next question or section. A negative aspect of this is that the question could be personal or sensitive and the respondent may not want to answer and decide to **opt-out** of the research altogether at this point. However, McDonald and Adam (2003) found that there is a lower level of item-missing data regarding sensitive demographic issues in online surveys compared to postal surveys.

Various tools can be used in survey construction depending upon the type of question. Check boxes allow more than one response in multiple-choice questions. Radio buttons are used when only one response is allowed to a question. Where space and length is at a premium, drop down or selection menus are useful in capturing ordinal data such as strengths of opinion or recent usage. However, they should be used carefully as they can cause visual clutter and confuse or irritate the respondent. Likert scales have always been a popular method for rating customer attitudes. Radio buttons have been used for this in the past, but the Times Online Panel (Fig 4.11) have recently introduced 'slider buttons' for respondents to indicate their opinion which encourages greater interaction.

Boosting response rates – incentives and other tools

There is a growing public expectation to be rewarded for providing valuable customer insights and participating in traditional surveys. Rewards vary from free products to gift vouchers and clearly they help develop some tenuous goodwill towards the research industry. Many data collection and research agencies have viewed incentives as an essential tool to boost online panel response rates. However, they increase bias and do not universally appeal to all. In Fig 4.12 below we can see the incentivised offer of entry into a free prize draw in return for registering for the consumer panel.

Some survey companies suggest that incentives have significantly improved click through, participation and completion rates of surveys and there is no reason to doubt their claims, but the validity of the responses could be called into question. Traditionally, incentives have been issued following completion of an offline survey without the prior knowledge of the interviewee. However, most online incentives are promoted prior to the commencement of a survey. This raises the possibility that those respondents may be more interested in receiving

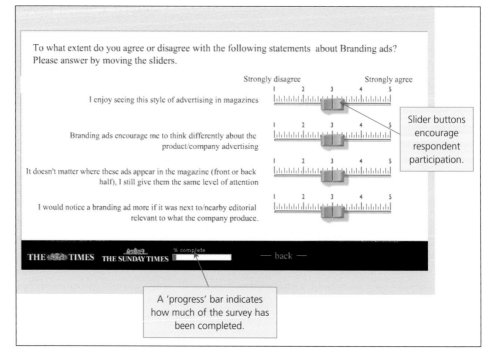

Fig 4.11 Example of Times survey
Reproduced by kind permission of Media Intelligence.

Fig 4.12 My offers consumer panel
www.myoffers.co.uk is one of the data collection sites run by Interactive Prospect Targeting
Reproduced by kind permission of MyOffers.

MINI CASE 4.3 South Bank surveys users' views on mobile marketing

The South Bank Centre is eyeing the potential of mobile marketing for its portfolio of venues, including the Hayward Gallery and the Royal Festival Hall. The group has commissioned its agency, De-construct, to devise an online questionnaire that visitors to all web sites will be encouraged to fill in, in return for £20 vouchers to spend at the Royal Festival Hall.

The aim of the research is to gauge customers' receptiveness to mobile marketing communications, including special offers and promotions from the different venues.

Dan Douglas, business development director at De-construct said that because the South Bank Centre has such a diverse offering of events it's hard to aim blanket communications at customers. He added that mobile marketing will help it to 'build

more personal, permission-based relationships with our audience, self-selecting the type of events, information and offers they want to be contacted about at different times.'

The research will also look at the revenue potential of mobile services such as premium content, as well as personalised and location-based services.

The online survey will run throughout April. Douglas said that depending on how comprehensive the results are, it could be followed by focus groups.

Adapted from: www.de-construct.com
www.rfh.org.uk
New Media Age 15 April 2004, 10

the free product or gift vouchers than providing genuine responses. Incentivisation may also generate multiple survey submissions from the same individual.

Researchers may turn to more recognised and acceptable ways of improving response rates. Solomon (2001) cited in Gunn (2002) states that various methods could be applied to boost web based survey response rates. These include advance notification by e-mail of the survey purpose, personalised e-mail covering letters, and e-mail followed ups to remind non-respondents as well as better, simpler questionnaire design. In Mini case 4.3, theatre incentives are offered to increase response rates.

4.18 Testing (or experimental) research

Testing, sometimes referred to, as experimentation, is the third primary research method, and a tool that enjoys much support from elements of the direct marketing industry where testing of A/B splits and control packs have boosted campaign response rates. Similarly, testing has traditionally been used in various aspects of new product development. However, it should not be confused with the technical testing that must be carried out such as browser, platform and connectivity testing. Usability testing in lab environments has already been referred to under observation research.

Tapp (2005) define testing as 'the small-scale measurement of individual campaign elements in order to maximise returns on rolled-out full marketing campaigns'. Wyner (2000) argues that the Internet offers unparalleled opportunities for market testing. It provides marketers with the ability to experiment and alter almost any aspect of online content and product or service configurations at speed to optimise marketing performance. Testing tends to be carried out by larger companies using direct marketing agencies that understand the benefits of testing and may have slightly longer planning cycles. Smaller companies tend to rely on small surveys and intuition. There are so many variables that can be tested in any online offering. Firms may use single variable tests with other variables remaining constant or alter them using A/B splits. Examples of online testing opportunities are given in Fig 4.13.

Fig 4.13 Possible opportunities for online testing

- Headline tests for web sites and e-mails.
- Impact of different 'FREE' offers, eg free downloads versus a free camera.
- The use of bulleted benefits versus editorial style block text.
- Testing registration forms to see how many potential customers 'drop out' because it is too complex or personal.
- Testing where special offers work best on a page (top, centre, bottom right, etc).
- Who responds to different offers?
- Varying the tone of site copy from formal to informal, informative and serious to irreverent and brief.
- The impact of different types of third party content.
- The use of different images. Real people versus cartoon characters.
- Trying different keywords in search engine optimisation.
- The effect of providing offline touch points such as telephone support for older segments.
- Use of different external lists.
- Page layouts – cluttered or minimalist.
- Use of different colours, size of logos, size and placement of banner ads.
- Different checkout procedures to reduce shopping cart abandonment.
- Effects of price changes.

 ## 4.19 **Multi-modal research**

We have so far discussed the benefits and some of the limitations of online primary research methods. The limitations have led to research organisations combining other major research modes, eg telephone, mail, face-to-face, etc together with web-based surveys to boost response rates and the quality of results. Various observers (Dillman et al, 2000, McCalla 2002 and Gray, 2003) have all indicated that that multi-modal approaches have generally improved response rates, or at least maintained them. This is significant, as most online surveys, other than niche or specialist markets, have tended to report lower response rates than traditional methods. The response rates can be influenced by:

1. allowing respondent mode choice or
2. user different modes to recontact non-respondents.

Gray suggests the need to consider the impact of mixed mode surveys on coverage, sampling, measurement and non-response errors. Gray also outlines other mixed mode issues such as:

- **Mode effects** – eg where scales/lists are used in surveys, visual formats such as self completion generate higher scores at the start of the scale whilst aural formats produce higher scores at the end.
- **Design issues** – eg where survey design and application may vary between modes such as in-depth questions and prompting face-to-face compared to self-completion.
- **Response rates** – eg significantly higher non-response rates to e-mail surveys compared to postal.

- **Cost implications** – eg combining different modes is likely to increase costs compared to using one cost effective method such as online.

Multi-modal survey applications are increasing in popularity as the shortcomings of single mode surveys are recognised. Software technology developments are enabling researchers to apply mixed modes more effectively. For example, Macer (2004) reviewed survey software that allowed two modes, Computer Assisted Telephone Interviewing (CATI) and Computer Assisted Web Interviewing (CAWI) to be developed and run simultaneously. Features such as consolidated scripting offer the opportunity to produce one script that can be produced seamlessly in the two modes with results entered into a common database.

4.20 Ethics and privacy – the effect of database marketing

Marketers rely on information and data from clients for decision-making purposes. This relies on goodwill and trust. To build trust, the marketing research industry needs to operate within ethical and legal frameworks, especially when Internet research is in its infancy. The direct marketing industry in its broadest sense has always had to operate with a veiled threat of restrictive legislation hanging over it due to the negative image of practices like junk mail and Spam. The industry had managed to stave off legal strait jackets through self-regulation instigated by trade associations and other professional bodies. The Market Research Society (www.mrs.org.uk) has issued new binding ethical guidelines for their members. These guidelines cover such areas as:

- Methods of accessing respondents via the web
- Disclosure of e-mail addresses
- Client identification
- Seeking consent for surveying children.

However, civil liberties groups have campaigned on privacy issues and brought pressure upon governments to introduce restrictive legislation. Marketers and researchers were extremely concerned with the implications of the Privacy and Electronic Communications Directive (2003), which made the sending of unsolicited e-mail illegal without prior consent of the recipient. Following strong industry lobbying, it was accepted that legitimate research fell outside the legal definition of direct marketing. Consequently, market research, which incorporated promotional material linked to the research activity, could be deemed illegal and should not happen. Adherence to this Directive and the Data Protection Act 1998 are essential for legal and consumer protection. Of course, this is not just about privacy but customers desiring greater control.

LEGAL EAGLE BOX 4.3 Database marketing

An organisation's database will normally contain personal data and, therefore, needs to be used, stored, shared, cleaned and destroyed in line with data protection rules. Marketers should only process personal data in databases for the purpose for which the data was collected.

Data subjects have a legal right to object to the processing of their personal data for marketing purposes. To give effect to this right, marketers should have a way of identifying and recording objections to the use of personal data from their databases for marketing campaigns.

Before using databases for marketing, they should be screened against the telephone, fax, and mail preference service lists.

The Mobile Marketing Association (MMA) has also developed its own privacy guidelines for the collection and usage of information as it seeks to encourage good practice in mobile commerce. The MMA makes the point that privacy is all the more important in the wireless world as mobile devices are carried everywhere and tend to be very personal.

4.21 Summary

There is no doubt that the Internet is having a significant impact upon the marketing research industry. Whilst deficiencies exist with various online research applications such as sampling methods, improved understanding of its nuances together with a growing Internet population make its adoption as a mainstream research method a distinct possibility. It can provide important cost savings in the research process but this has often been the key driver rather than fundamental issues about validity and sampling precision. The Internet provides marketers with a rich source of secondary information, and this is where its current strength lies. However, marketers need to be more discerning about what they need to know to make business-critical decisions. For us as individuals, the web is becoming the first port of call for product or service searches. However, as we adopt more mobile and digital devices, the integration of different research modes will be essential.

END OF CHAPTER CASE STUDY **Secondary research for overseas expansion: the launch of Dabs France**

There have always been significant barriers to entry into overseas markets, particularly for small and medium sized enterprises such as access to market information, logistics and intermediary issues and financing arrangements. Selling online in an international market also requires research and understanding of market competitiveness, cultural, political and legal factors, as well as site design and content issues. In this case we consider how the Internet has made internationalisation through secondary research easier for one UK organisation.

Dabs.com is the UK's leading internet retailer of IT and technology products, offering over 34,000 lines from the world's leading manufactures to over 850,000 online customers across Britain. This pioneering operation is serviced from state of the art premises in Bolton and processes in excess of 5,000 orders every day. The company has received numerous business awards for its customer centric adoption of new technology in all of its business functions including finalist in *The Sunday Times* Business Awards for 2003, business of the Year in the North West regional final of the National Business awards as well its founder, David Atherton receiving 'Entrepreneur of the Year' award. Buoyed by its rapid success, Dabs' entrepreneurial approach sought opportunities further afield and sought to dip its toes overseas.

In 2003, dabs.com announced the acquisition of French company SOS Developers, an established specialist reseller of developer software with offices in both Nice and Paris. This thoroughly researched move represented the first step in developing the Dabs' pan-European business model with an organisation having a similar technological and entrepreneurial culture.

Dabs identified France as the optimal starting point for European expansion due to similarities between the French and British technology markets. Marketing Director Jonathan Wall explains, 'Although France was initially slower on taking up e-commerce, the uptake over the last 12 months has been very encouraging. The composition of the overall French IT marketplace has much in common with that of the UK, and France is currently a close 3rd in market size to that of the UK. These synergies, together with very positive indicators such as the rapid take up of broadband in France over the last year, means we're confident we can replicate our successful model of logistical excellence and low-cost, high return marketing in France'.

Rather than indulge in costly and time consuming primary research when speed of market entry was important, Dabs used a variety of secondary sources to evaluate the potential of the French market. Forrester Research found that for many commercial sites, 30% of traffic came from overseas and 10% of total sales. In the UK, like many online merchants, Dabs regularly uses the likes of Hitwise (www.hitwise.co.uk) and Nielsen Net Ratings (www.nielsen-netratings.co.uk) for audience measurement and top performing sites by category. Their French equivalents provided a good basis for traffic comparisons with the UK. Dabs also subscribe to online merchant comparison sites such as Dealtime (www.dealtime.net.uk) and Kelkoo (www.kelkoo.co.uk) and compared prices and product range with their sites in France. They also evaluated key measures for sponsored links such as cost-per-click against UK prices as cost control is critical to the Dabs model. Other comparisons were drawn from analysis of site traffic comparing Google in the UK and France in terms of how busy they were. Offline secondary research was carried out trawling the key French IT and computer magazines to identify key competitors, their ranges and prices. In addition, Dabs.com found that 'the PC press in France is very strong with a range of highly circulated titles reminiscent of the UK news-stand and as such, there's a big PC hobbyist sector with very strong demand for PC components, which currently account for around 40% of our total UK online business'.

The overall trawl of secondary data that sought as many exact matches to UK data sources suggested that commercial conditions were favourable for Dabs first overseas venture. 20 April 2004 was a significant day in the history of dabs.com (www.dabs.com), with the launch of Dabs France (www.dabs.com/fr).

The new site almost doubled the number of potential consumers for Dabs' products, with minimal set-up costs but Jonathan Wall commented, 'Costs have been kept to an absolute minimum because of the way we have structured our UK business model and the technologies used to power it'. Prior to the launch, dabs.com restructured their existing UK site to support dual-language and currency, to help them prepare for further overseas expansion.

'We see the launch of Dabs.France (www.dabs.fr/fr/) as a key point in our development,' said Wall. We do have ambitions to expand further into Europe, but our plans are for safe, measured and profitable growth, so putting a timeframe on our future expansion isn't possible. We are focussing on making Dabs.France a success, and only when we have achieved this will turn our attentions to the next stage.' By 2006, overseas business accounted for one-tenth of Dabs business and it now employs around 40 staff in France.

Dabs had become such a significant player in the IT and computer peripheral market that it attracted the attention of some big companies and has subsequently been bought by British Telecom for an undisclosed sum in April 2006. Marketing Director, Jonathan Wall said the company is looking at other opportunities in Europe and Scandinavia, especially Spain, Sweden and the Benelux countries where broadband is well established. It will be interesting to see how the Dabs overseas plans evolve under the stewardship of BT.

Questions

1. What are the key benefits offered by online secondary research compared to traditional secondary research?

2. What market similarities between the UK and France were identified by Dabs during its secondary research?

3. How can online research assist SMEs when considering exporting or internationalisation?

4. How could Dabs have enriched its data with online primary research methods?

Adapted from: Dabs.com Press release, 9 April 2003
www.theregister.co.uk/2003/01/23/dabs_com_buys_french_reseller, 23 January 2003
www.news.bbc.co.uk/1/hi/business/4956100.stm, BT buys online retailer Dabs.com, 28 April 2006

The original home page of Dabs.com French operation (www.dabs.com/fr)

DISCUSSION QUESTIONS

1. What were the problems with the early online sampling population?
2. Should marketers collect online information on 'a need to know' basis?
3. What are the advantages and disadvantages of online focus groups?
4. How can online marketing research assist small and medium sized enterprises?

REFERENCES

Armstrong, G & Kotler, P (2004) *Marketing – An Introduction*, (7th edn), Pearson Education, New Jersey, 117

Baines, P & Chansarkar, B (2002) *Introducing Marketing Research*, John Wiley & Sons, Chichester, England, 3, 271, 236

Bergman, MK (2001) The deep web: surfacing hidden value, *Journal of Electronic Publishing*, University of Michigan, July 2001

Blythe, J (2001) *Essentials of Marketing*, Pearson Education Limited, Harlow, England, 78

Crouch, S & Housden, M (1996) *Marketing Research for Managers* (2nd edn), Butterworth Heinemann, Oxford, England, 75, 115

Dillman, D, Phelps, G, Tortora, RD, Swift, K, Kohrell, J & Berck, J (2001) *Response Rate and Measurement Differences in Mixed Mode Surveys Using Mail, Telephone, Interactive Voice Response and the Internet.* www.survey.sesrc.wsu.edu.dillman/papers/ Mixed%20Mode%20ppr%20with%20Gallup_%20POQ.pdf

Dreze, X & Hussherr, XD (2003) Internet advertising: is anybody watching? *Journal of Interactive Marketing*, Vol 17, No 4, Autumn 2003, Wiley Interscience (www.interscience.wiley.com)

Gourvennay, Y (2003) *The Internet as a Source for Marketing Intelligence*, www.visionarymarketing.com/articles/internetsearch2003.html

Gray, S (2003) *Is It Safe To Combine Methodologies in Survey Research?* www.mori.com/pubinfo/scg/combine-methodolgies.shtml

Grossnickle, J & Raskin, O (2001) *The Handbook of Online Marketing Research*, McGraw Hill, New York, United States, 3, 18

Gunn, H (2002) Web-based surveys: changing the survey process, *First Monday*, Vol 7, No 12 (December 2002) www.firstmonday.org/issues/issue7_12/gunn/index.html

Hague, P, Hague, N & Morgan, C (2004) *Market Research in Practice: A Guide to the Basics*, London & Sterling, Kogan Page

Herbert, M *Online: An Introduction*, www.aqr.org.uk?inbrief/document.shtml?doc=michaelherbert.05-01-2001.online

Hollerson, S (2003) *Marketing Management – A Relationship Approach*, Pearson Education Limited, Harlow, England, 736 www.iconocast.com/Real7_Estate30_04/MortgageNews9A.htm www.irn-research.com/pressrelease23June04.htm

Hwang, YH & Fesenmaier, DR Coverage error in self selected Internet based samples: a case study in Northern Indiana, *Journal of Travel Research*, Vol 42, February 2004, 297

IRN Research May 2006, *Stronger Sales Growth in the European Online Information Market in 2005 and Profit Margins Continue to Climb for the Leading Players* www.irn-research.com/pressrelease24May06.htm

IRN Research, *The European Online Information Market*, May 2006

Macer, T (2004) *CAWI and CATI*, www.macer.com/quirks/09.html

McCalla, RA (2002) Getting results from online surveys – reflections on a personal journey, *Electronic Journal of Business Research Methods*, Vol 1, No 1, 57 www.ejbrm.com

McDaniel, C & Gates, R (2004) *Marketing Research Essentials*, John Wiley & Sons, New Jersey, United States, 42, 47

McDonald, H & Adam, S (2003) A comparison of online and postal data collection methods in marketing research, *Marketing Intelligence and Planning*, Vol 21, No 2 (2003), 93

McDonald, H & Adam, S (2003) A comparison of online and postal data collection methods in marketing research, *Marketing Intelligence and Planning*, Vol 21, Nos 2, 4 (2003), 85–95 MCB University Press

McGowan, P & Durkin, MG Toward an understanding of Internet adoption at the marketing/ entrepreneurship interface. *Journal of Marketing Management*, 2002, 18, 361–377

Mohammed, RA, Fisher, RJ, Jaworski, BJ & Cahill, AM (2002) *Internet Marketing: Building Advantage in a Networked Economy*, McGraw Hill International, New York

Nielsen, J (2004) Keep online surveys short, *Alertbox*, 2 Feb, 2004, www.useit.com/alertboz/20040202.html

Nielsen//NetRatings European Index Jan 2004, *55 Million Europeans Using Google Online*

Ranchhod, A & Zhoui, F (2001) Comparing respondents of e-mail and mail surveys: understanding the implications of technology. *Marketing Intelligence and Planning*, Vol 19, No 4 (2001), 254–262, MCB University Press

Somerville, R *Online Research in Europe – An Overview*, www.bmra.org.uk/mrbusiness/content_frame.asp?ezine=104&article=736

Solomon, DJ (2001) Conducting web-base surveys, *Practical assessment, Research & Evaluation*, Vol 7, No 19 at www.erice.net/pare/getyn.asp?v=7&n=19

Tapp, A (2005) *Principles of Direct and Database Marketing* (3rd edn), FT Prentice Hall, Harlow, England, 427

Wyner, GA (2000) Testing on the Internet, *Marketing Research: A Magazine of Management & Applications*, Fall 2000 Bell & Howell Information & Learning Company, American Marketing Association

FURTHER READING

Grossnickle, J & Raskin, O (2001) *The Handbook of Online Marketing Research*, McGraw Hill, New York, United States

McDaniel, C & Gates, R (2004) *Marketing Research Essentials*, John Wiley & Sons, New Jersey, United States

Sherman, C & Price, G (2001) *The Invisible Web: Uncovering Information Sources Search Engines can't See*, Information Today, Inc., Medford, New Jersey, United States

WEB LINKS

www.researchbuzz.com/ a US oriented research newsletter.

www.profusion.com/ a top site providing links to invisible search engines and databases. The Invisible Web catalogue contains over 20,000 databases and searchable sources often overlooked by search engines. The site contains a very useful search tool.

www.aip.completeplanet.com Offers over 70,000+ searchable databases and specialty search engines.

www.hero.ac.uk/sites/hero/uk/reference_and_subject_resources/resources/internet_search_ facilities473.cfm – a useful source of information with well referenced links to key sites, databases and directories.

www.brightplanet.com/technology/deepweb.asp good discussion paper on the 'deep web'.

www.searcheurope.com/

www.searchenginelinks.co.uk International links.

www.ex.ac.uk/library/internet/search.html

www.hummingbird-one.co.uk/linkmaster.html A useful site to access the best of the web, including guidance on the invisible web plus a few miscellaneous direct links in subject order.

www.virtualsurveys.com The web site of Virtual Surveys Ltd run by leading Online Marketing Researcher, Pete Comley. The site contains quality articles and published papers covering key aspects of online research.

 Visit the Online Resource Centre which accompanies this book, for lots of interesting additional material, including self-assessment questions, internet exercises, and links for each chapter: **www.oxfordtextbooks.co.uk/orc/gay/**

Online Buyer Behaviour

5

Learning objectives

By the end of the chapter you will be able to:

- Understand buyer behaviour
- Appreciate the extra dimensions of online buyer behaviour
- Evaluate the various buying process models and how they operate online
- Understand online customer expectations and how they impact on the marketing function
- Appreciate how data on the visitors to a web site can be analysed to produce information that can be used by marketers
- Recognise the need for online target marketing for acquisition and retention
- Appreciate the key elements and applications of database marketing

Chapter-at-a-glance

5.1 Introduction

Understanding your customer and utilising that knowledge effectively via creative and logical marketing plans are fundamental for marketing success. A Yahoo! Inc. and OMD study in the US, *The Long and Winding Road: The Route to the Cash Register* (2006) of consumer buyer behaviour suggests that the Internet's biggest impact is in the decision making process at the research stage. Its impact as a trusted source for information gathering has grown regardless of whether the consumer is buying goods or services online or in the high street. The study cites three key determinants in the online information search as trusted sites, choice of brands to compare and competitive prices.

This chapter considers the fundamental buyer behaviour influences such as demographic, lifestyle and cultural factors, together with decision-making process models, how relevant they are to the Internet and how they might differ. Subsequent sections look at what the online customer might expect from the online business and the online behaviour of both B2C and B2B customers. The chapter goes on to look at buying process models and how off and online elements can be intermixed by the shopper. Consideration is then given to the buying cycle and the existence of a pure online buying cycle. The chapter also reflects on how e-marketers can collect relevant data that enables them to develop information for analysis of customer behaviour using web metrics. Consideration is also given to how e-marketers can collect relevant data that enables them to develop information for analysis of customer behaviour using web metrics. We conclude with sections on how customers can be targeted online and how the use of databases can aid the e-marketer.

5.2 Understanding buyer behaviour

Cotte et al (2006) advocate that the unique characteristics of the Internet offer new ways for consumers to interact with one another, organisations and the wider e-marketplace. It facilitates a two-way dialogue for different target customers that exhibit different types of behaviour for different benefits. Brennan et al (2003) suggest that 'effective strategic market-ing requires business planners to be almost obsessive about understanding the needs of their customers.' Marketing decisions should, therefore, be based upon an awareness of the pro-cesses and the influences that shape both consumer and organisational purchasing habits. This may involve gathering knowledge of general needs, motives, attitudes and other stimuli that mould behaviour, or specific variables such as time, that may determine the purchase of a particular product category or brand. Understanding buying behaviour is essential for the development of effective marketing mix decisions. Adcock et al (2001) observe that this has become a fundamental element of many academic marketing programmes and draws heavily from the social sciences such as psychology, sociology and economics.

Many writers on buyer behaviour refer to Maslow's Hierarchy of Needs model (1970) as a key tool for categorising different levels of consumer desires and needs with the belief that basic, lower levels needs would be met prior to satisfying or indulging in higher level needs. The nature of buyer behaviour will vary from buying basic products, such as bread, milk and mobile phone cards, to higher involvement products such as selecting a holiday or buying a car. Solomon et al (2006) describe this as a continuum of effort with habitual decision-making at one end (typified by everyday mundane purchases) and extended problem solving at the other (typified by important and involved decisions such as longer term financial services products). Solomon suggests that many purchase decisions fall between the two extremes with some work and thought going into the purchase. He refers to this as limited problem solving. Naturally, the *effort* put into the purchase by the customer varies and this has implications for web site design such as the detail of product information, third party supporting information, product images, guarantees, promotions and other elements to develop trust and credibility, especially at the far end of the continuum. Hollensen (2003) suggest that personality and lifestyle are not connected to the purchase of low involvement, routine purchases as they are not strongly linked with their beliefs, self esteem and identity but this changes significantly with high involvement purchases when the product takes on greater importance for the individual. Consequently, customer expectations rise and the quality of the online offering must meet the required level to achieve customer satisfaction in both initial and repeat purchases.

In making a purchase decision, the consumer is faced with a range of stimuli that they may or may not respond to depending upon their choice criteria. The range of stimuli and buyer characteristics are illustrated in the model of buyer behaviour in Fig 5.1.

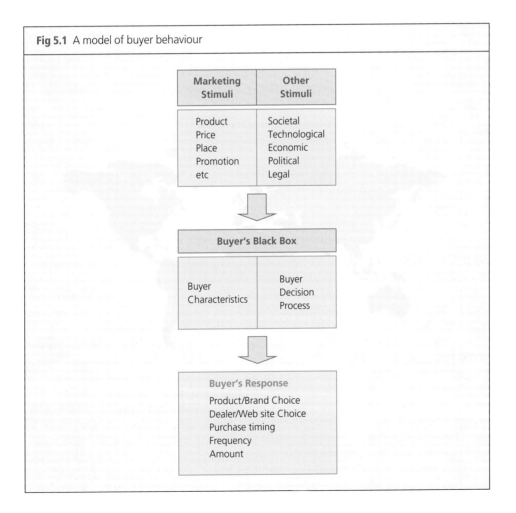

Fig 5.1 A model of buyer behaviour

At the first level, the mix elements and marketing environment factors such as social influences can inspire and induce personal buying decisions often in an impulsive way rather than on sound rational and economic grounds. For younger consumers, it is often peer pressure that stimulates the initial product interest. Urban (2004) argues that organisations need to do much more than expose consumers to information but that the message itself must appeal to the consumer in a marketplace where they are overloaded with communications messages. The level of involvement in the purchasing process may affect whether a consumer has to be targeted online, eg by e-mail or whether they energetically search online for information, reviews or visit specific web sites to compare products. Culture is another behavioural element that must be understood by the online marketer. Burgman et al (2006) recognised cultural differences in web site design and usage in a three-country study looking at banking and education web sites. The study, based on Hofstede's dimensions of culture (1980, 2001) observed significant content differences such as use of language (explicit or implicit), metaphors, hyper links, and levels of masculinity in a number of web sites which influence how consumers programme and process communications. Singh and Pereira (2005) in their valuable text on the subject *The Culturally Customised Web Site* made use of Hofstede's work, along with that of Hall (1976) to develop their 'cultural values framework for web design'. The framework consists of five elements:

1. Individualism-Collectivism – reflects whether the individual is more important than the group

2. Power distance – reflects the society's recognition level of power, authority and hierarchy.

3. Uncertainty Avoidance – reflects the relative value place upon security and structure as opposed to vagueness and risk in the society

4. Masculinity-Femininity – reflects the masculine nature of a society eg ambition, power and progression against the feminine disposition of caring for others, social well-being and support

5. High-Low Context – reflects the way in which cultures interact on a daily basis. Latin American, African and many Pacific Rim countries are typical of 'high context' cultures where social harmony is important and communications rely more on gestures and symbols than words. Low context cultures are typified by advanced western societies and communications are more formalized, explicit and make greater use of words.

The framework has implications for Internet marketing across international boundaries and may require adapting sites for specific markets. Web sites may have to be adapted to satisfy different sub-cultures, for example in Malaysia, Malay, Chinese and Indian sub-cultures co-exist successfully. Readers are directed to Singh and Pereira's text that gives a fascinating insight into the cultural debate on customisation in the global marketplace.

Secondly, the buying decision process (see Fig 5.2) outlines the key stages that a consumer may go through. This can depend upon factors such as the availability of time, product alternatives and information. The nature of the Internet has had a positive impact on all three elements for the benefit of consumers but not every stage will be activated. This will depend on the product or service, its importance and its complexity. Also at this stage, the buyer's choice is further influenced first by their demographic and lifestyle characteristics such as their socio-economic grouping, occupation, income, marital status and their attitudes, interest and opinions. At the final level, customer perceptions, experiences, attitudes and beliefs are processed and respond to a particular brand or product category offered by a particular online merchant at a time, quantity, payment method to suit the customer. Physiological, psychological and perception factors can sway the decision process online also. This can include how we learn and process information and include short and long-term memory processes. Urban comments on how web site features such as shopping carts or recently viewed items or pages can aid the online consumer's memory. Brennan et al suggest that our consumption patterns are also influenced by the way we view the world and for the online world this has revolved around issues like trust, security and privacy. Einwiller (2003) argues that vendor trust and reputation are critical in reducing the consumer's perceived risk regarding shopping online.

5.3 Consumer buying decision process

A commonly accepted process model of consumer buying decisions is the five-stage model in Fig 5.2. In this section we will consider the stages and their implications for buyers and sellers in the online marketplace.

1. Recognition that a problem exists – all purchases are made to solve a 'problem' or to meet a need or a want.
2. A search for information on solutions to that problem.
3. An evaluation of the alternatives identified in the search.
4. The purchase decision.
5. Evaluation of the process (buying and consumption).

Let us now consider the elements of the 'online buying cycle' in more detail.

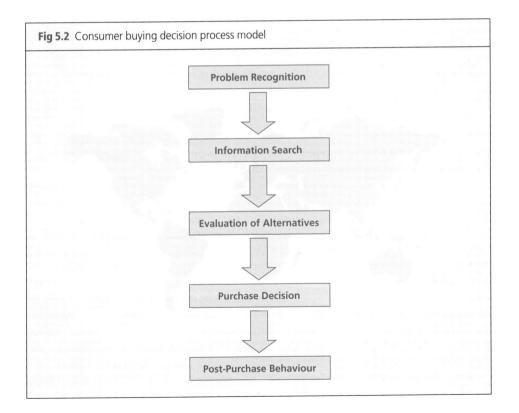

Fig 5.2 Consumer buying decision process model

Problem Recognition

Information Search

Evaluation of Alternatives

Purchase Decision

Post-Purchase Behaviour

Problem recognition

Jayawardhena et al (2003) suggest that the stimulus that triggers need recognition may come from a number of diverse sources that could initially be either on or offline, especially as many organisations use both channels for communications. Huang and Christopher (2003) believe that a web site should prompt a customer's interest in the online store and that the capture of customer information is paramount to develop the interest or ongoing relationship.

Can a customer go online being unaware that they have a problem, and come away having not only recognised the fact, but having sought information, evaluated the findings of that search and taken action to solve it? Serendipity is an important aspect of casual browsing.

For most users, the web is a tool to use in seeking information that may help to solve a problem. The web can be used by the marketer primarily as a promotional tool. For example, online advertising or e-mail direct marketing can stimulate consumer interest. The advantage of the web is that it lets the customer use the same site to make a purchase that other media cannot.

This leaves us with two scenarios where the user could be made aware of a problem online.

1. The 'problem' is a generic, ongoing one for which people are always receptive to a solution. For example, people who are trying to lose weight will always be amenable to an advert promoting a food product that is low calorie and low fat, but also tasty. Typing keywords into a search engine can generate relevant results that illustrate the problem.

2. The second is one that other media can address, but not as efficiently or effectively as the Internet. This is because users choose to be on the web, and they select the web sites they visit. This is self-segmentation at its best. With the correct use of target marketing, (see section 5.8 below) web site visitors can actually be made aware of a problem they might have, but have not yet realised it. This could be through on-page banner advertising or more effectively through product promotion within the textual content of the web page – the hypertext links within the text being a marketing aid not available in other media.

An example might be something that is health and fitness related. The customer might regularly participate in a certain type of sport or exercise. In pursuing their interest, the user goes online to increase their knowledge of their hobby. Whilst on a site specific to the sport they might see an advert, or more likely read within a textual context, that repetition of the sport can cause a specific strain on their body. The advert (textual or otherwise) makes the sports person aware of a 'new' problem and sets them on the 'cycle' that may result in a purchase of a piece of equipment that solves the problem.

Information search

Information and communications technologies have revolutionised this element of the buying cycle for both consumers and organisations. Never before has the customer had so much product or service information at their dipsosal. Indeed, some users would argue that there is an information overload, and the wealth of data makes the issue more confusing rather than clearer. The important message for e-marketers is that web sites and emails (the two elements of the Internet) should be developed properly (see chapter 8). Understanding customer search behaviour is essential so that information can be provided in the most convenient and user friendly way. Behavioural research will identify what are the key information triggers that lead to a purchase such incentives, detailed product information, discussion groups or independent customer reviews and this must feed into the web site design. Huang

& Christopher (2003) suggest that basic design attributes such as FAQs, site index, product index and product search function must be incorporated to meet fundamental customer expectations though online customer service best practice is pushing the creative boundaries for the benefit of the consumer. At this stage, some offline support may also be beneficial such as call back services for customer service representatives, especially with high involvement products. One key tool in the information search element that cannot be ignored is the search engine (see chapter 6). Numerous studies and reports suggest consumers utilise search engines between 50–80% of the time when seeking product or service information. Therefore, it is imperative to select the best search engines to submit to based on customer research and traffic, and then optimise web pages to get the best chance of high rankings.

In the Internet age, information about products is available from a myriad of online sources. Some of these sources may be independent, but most will belong to competitors. If their web site or email communication is *better*, and that means more user-focussed, customers will use that source of information. They may buy your competitor's product even if the actual product is inferior to yours. It should be recognised that the Internet is now an integral part of the marketing mix but at the same time provides choice, convenience and other benefits to the consumer. A growing influence is the online communities who share knowledge and experiences of products, services and the organisations that provide them, in a sense this is classic word of mouth marketing but disseminated faster and more widely. Some online communities may have influential members who are opinion leaders and their views may sway the community in a positive or negative way towards a product or its supplier. Organisations should consider the role they may play either directly or indirectly in that community.

Each stage of buying can be facilitated through on or offline channels, or in combination. For example, a customer can choose online, then make the purchase and collect the goods offline. As the use of the web as a buying aid increases, the term 'choose' becomes a little vague. 'Research' is perhaps a better description of what customers do when making a buying decision. Shim et al (2001) describe such research as an 'information search' and the process by which consumers gather information about goods or services before a purchase is made. It is this information gathering element of the buying process that is most enhanced by the use of the Internet. Shapiro and Varian (1999) make the point that access to the Internet gives consumers new power because of the relative ease of information gathering. Alba et al (1997) state that a key difference between online and offline shopping is the ability of online consumers to obtain more information about their potential purchases. Bakos (1997) adds that not only is the information search quicker and easier when conducted online, it is also cheaper. Much is made of this but it may be irrelevant to those who value the theatre of shopping offline. Consequently, the importance of these advantages may vary from customer to customer depending upon their motivations and other influences. However, online buyer behaviour is influenced by search, then comparison, and finally evaluation prior to a purchase.

This concept of increased opportunity for information searching brings into play another practice – that of researching a product in a variety of locations and/or media. Furthermore, the purchase is not necessarily made from the vendor who provides the most significant information on the product but factors such as branding and efficient delivery may be influential. This makes the customer purchase behaviour options more extensive. Table 5.1 shows a matrix of some of the options available to the buying public.

For the web-enabled customer, things have never been better. As comprehensive as the list in Table 5.1 is, it does not include the following:

Table 5.1 The purchase behaviour matrix

Research	Purchase	Fulfillment	Purchased from
online	online	home delivery	same vendor that provided the original information
online	online	home delivery	different vendor to that which provided the original information
online	online	customer collects	same vendor that provided the original information
online	online	customer collects	different vendor to that which provided the original information
online	online	online	same vendor that provided the original information
online	online	online	different vendor to that which provided the original information
offline	online	home delivery	same vendor that provided the original information
offline	online	home delivery	different vendor to that which provided the original information
offline	online	customer collects	same vendor that provided the original information
offline	online	customer collects	different vendor to that which provided the original information
offline	online	online	same vendor that provided the original information
offline	online	online	different vendor to that which provided the original information
online	offline	home delivery	same vendor that provided the original information
online	offline	home delivery	different vendor to that which provided the original information
online	offline	customer collects	same vendor that provided the original information
online	offline	customer collects	different vendor to that which provided the original information
online	offline	online	same vendor that provided the original information
online	offline	online	different vendor to that which provided the original information
literature	online	home delivery	same vendor that provided the original information
literature	online	home delivery	different vendor to that which provided the original information
literature	online	customer collects	same vendor that provided the original information
literature	online	customer collects	different vendor to that which provided the original information
literature	online	online	same vendor that provided the original information
literature	online	online	different vendor to that which provided the original information
literature	online	online	different vendor to that which provided the original information
offline	offline	online	same vendor that provided the original Information
offline	offline	online	different vendor to that which provided the original information
literature	offline	online	same vendor that provided the original Information
literature	offline	online	different vendor to that which provided the original information

Key:
Online – using the world wide web
Offline – using traditional 'bricks and mortar' outlets
Literature – any printed material including brochures and catalogues
Home delivery – product is delivered to, or service is performed at, the buyer's home or premises
Customer collects – buyer collects goods from, or attends for service at, vendor's premises
Online fulfillment – product or service is delivered using Internet technology

- Bricks and mortar shopping that does not include any use of the Internet.
- The use of the telephone to enquire about product attributes, price or availability and ordering. The phone calls could be to an individual outlet or a call centre.
- The use of web sites such as Kelkoo (www.kelkoo.com), a shopping search engine that help customers to track the cheapest source of a product.
- The customer researching in a combination of visits to outlets, web sites and printed literature that might be spread over a significant period of time.
- The use of an in-store kiosk (where connection to the Internet or a store intranet is available) or in-store computer to search for products without physically walking around the whole shop. According to a joint study in the US by Fry Inc, comScore Networks Inc and the E-Tailing Group Inc (2005) – described by them as the 'first evolution of the multi-channel consumer study' – 36% of customers have used instore computers. Searching for gifts was the most popular use.
- That web surfers might have no real intention to purchase, off- or online. Perhaps one of the more overlooked elements of online behavior is the use of the Internet for window-shopping (Leonard 2005). This could lead to a deferred purchase.

Kuo et al (2004) introduce an additional stage to this process that is not included above. That is, before the customer searches for the information, they must first search for the web sites that will provide the information. Mini case 5.1 illustrates influential purchase decision resources used by consumers.

Evaluation of alternatives

It could be argued that the evaluation takes place in the mind of the potential customer. Evaluation involves the bringing together and analysis of the information gathered in the search stage. Offline, this might involve laying out various pieces of paper and physically matching or comparing figures or data on the various sheets, or writing up your own tables in a 'pros and cons' fashion. Online, technology can help complete this task. For example some web sites allow you to 'save' info on products and then show them on one page. One

---

MINI-CASE 5.1 Web sites influence buying decisions

Internet marketing company DoubleClick's (www.doubleclick.com) third annual Touchpoints study, published in July 2005, examined the different media channels relied on by consumers when making purchase decisions. Consumers were questioned on their buying decision influences in 10 categories: travel, automotive, telecommunications, banks and credit cards, mortgage and investment, movies, consumer electronics, home products, personal and home care, and prescription drugs. The findings showed the importance consumers' attribute to web sites, email, and search engines with regard to their impact on awareness, information gathering and purchase decision, even when compared to traditional media such as TV and print ads. When asked which touch points most influenced their purchase decision, respondents cited web sites as more important than TV advertisements in seven out of 10 product/service categories. Web marketing programmes collectively (web ads plus opt-in email programmes) also outranked TV ads in three categories (Travel, Banking and Credit Cards, and Investments and Mortgages). The category that web sites were the most dominant in was travel, where 46% of respondents were most influenced by web sites, compared to 3% influenced by television ads. In eight out of the ten categories, respondents cited the official web site of the manufacturer or service provider as one of their top four choices as a resource for learning more about a product in which they were interested.

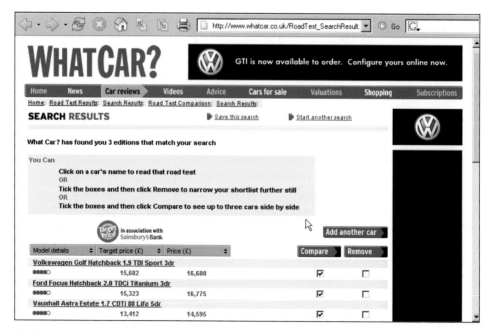

Fig 5.3 A search results page from WhatCar

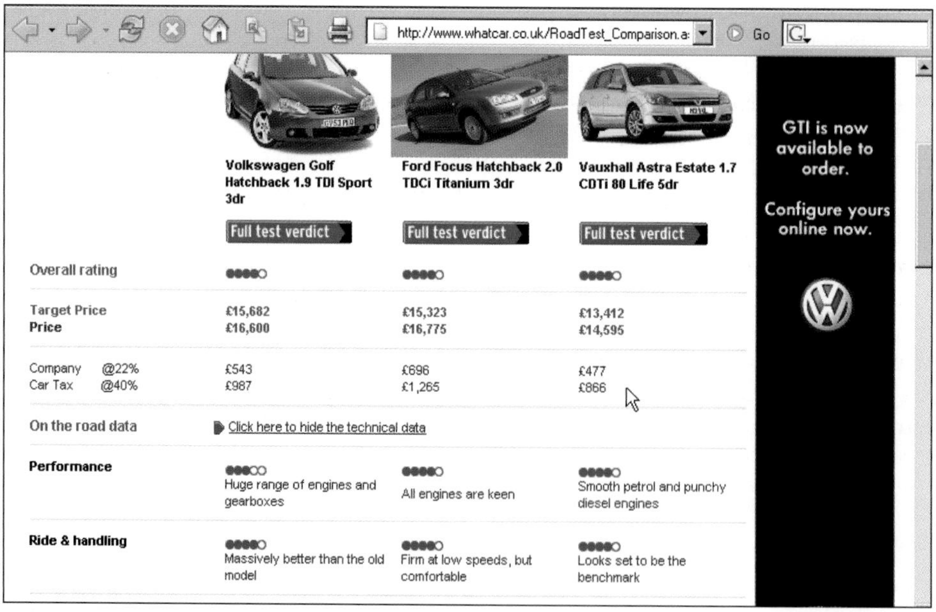

Fig 5.4 A car comparison page showing test verdicts of cars selected from the search results page shown in Fig 5.3 (above)

Car comparison pages from What Car (www.whatcar.co.uk)

such is the online version of What Car? magazine (www.whatcar.co.uk). The site allows you to choose three cars from their reviews section and show them on the same page to make comparison easy.

Figs 5.3 and 5.4 show car comparison pages from What Car? (www.whatcar.co.uk). The first shows the models being selected, the second 'test verdicts' of the three cars side by side.

Purchase decision

This most definitely can be completed online. In its most accurate definition, this is what e-commerce is. Customers can make a purchase online; a donation to a charitable cause; subscribe to a newsletter; join a club; download a PDF map for directions, or any other of numerous actions. In practical terms, the actual operating mode of the order processing function must be trouble free and easy for the consumer, especially if they have limited IT competence. In particular, functionality though the shopping cart, check-out and payment procedures is critical to ensure that the consumer completes the transaction otherwise all of the marketing efforts up to this point may be in vain if the customer leaves the site in frustration.

The purchase occurs on two levels. The first is the product and the other mix elements that combine to provide the total offer with branding being a critical deciding factor in consumer perceptions. In addition, careful targeting and timing of promotional offers can be very effective, especially with impulsive consumers. Second is the decision to purchase from a particular online vendor. The choice of vendor can be just as complex as the product decision itself and involve many influences. George (2002) considers the influences on the intent to make Internet purchases and focuses on privacy, trustworthiness and experience as key issues and any vendor must work hard on these elements to establish its credibility and reputation in the online marketplace. Online security, management of personal data and efficient distribution processes all play a role in building customer confidence and satisfaction. Brand familiarity is another influence and many online vendors have become household names in a relatively short time period, such as Easyjet, Amazon and eBay. Clicks and bricks organisations are aided by an existing offline reputation such as Tesco (www.Tesco.com). The consumer's choice of vendor will depend upon their own values, attitudes and motivations. For example, many consumers are using price/product comparison sites such as Kelkoo and Pricerunner. One consumer may seek the cheapest price and have little concern about the vendor's background. Another consumer may be seeking a competitive price but based on customer ratings and guaranteed delivery promises, may be happy to pay a higher price for the convenience and peace of mind. Huang and Christopher (2003) suggest that an easy return policy or money back guarantee can also be persuasive at this stage.

Post-purchase evaluation

This can begin as soon as the transaction is completed with customers expecting to receive e-mail confirmation of the order within seconds and a customer reference for order tracking purposes. Jaywardhena et al (2003) contend that the emergence of virtual communities demonstrates amongst online consumers the need to share post purchase reassurance. The speed and diffusion of customer feedback across the Internet needs careful management as satisfaction helps build longer-term relationships. It can be very important when third parties are also involved in some aspect of the transaction or delivery. For example, visitors to Amazon have the opportunity to buy direct from Amazon or try to obtain a cheaper price with vendors in the Amazon marketplace. If a consumer has a poor experience with one of the marketplace vendors, then the Amazon brand could also be damaged. Amazon are keen to survey customers in the post purchase period about their experience with the vendor which could determine whether that vendor stays or leaves the marketplace.

In answer to the question 'Does a *purely* online buying cycle' exist?' then, yes it can. It might not be common, but it is one that the e-marketer should be aware of and be prepared to take advantage of. In the 'sports person' scenario presented earlier the customer could have gone from not being aware of a problem through to a purchase in a matter of minutes. If the product does what it is supposed to do it will be very easy to develop a relationship with that customer, with all the sales potential that goes with that.

5.4 Online customer expectations

A significant development brought to business by the Internet is to give impetus to the marketer's objectives shifting from 'helping the seller to sell', to 'helping the buyer to buy'. Customers now expect to be facilitated in their research for the product or service that most suitably meets their wants and needs. The web is significant in this as it is a 'pull' media, meaning that the user, those to whom any marketing message is directed, requests the information rather than having it forced – or 'pushed' – upon them, as in TV or billboard advertising. For the marketer this means the customer chooses *which* marketing messages they see.

So what are the customer expectations in the online environment? What do marketers have to put into place to satisfy, or even exceed, these expectations? The online marketer must focus in the first instance on identifying these needs.

Whilst the Internet makes price search and comparison much easier, some customer segments are driven online by cheaper prices. For many dot.com companies, the preoccupation with price was a significant element in their downfall. Selling at a profit is a business fundamental but many dot.com entrepreneurs found it difficult to develop a business model that maintained keen prices whilst coping with the investment cost of developing a new online brand.

Whilst the attraction of lower prices may be true for certain products, for many customers, a key attraction of the Internet is the 24:7 convenience that it provides. Academics and writers have come to appreciate this. Kotler (2000) and Skyrme (2001) ranked convenience as the number one benefit to customers of e-commerce. Alreck and Settle (2002) found that Internet shopping was viewed as saving more time than traditional modes of shopping; Bhatnger et al (2000) found that customer's perceived convenience of shopping on the Internet had a positive impact on their purchase behaviour, and Constantinides (2004) rated convenience a major influence on online consumer behaviour. For industry practitioners, however, empirical evidence was making this point long before formal research was conducted.

'Cost' is not limited simply to the buying price to be paid by the purchaser. It can include the cost of his/her time through search costs as well as the convenience provided and the time saved to engage in other aspects of their work, hobbies or family life, for example, consider the benefits of weekly online grocery purchases. Athiyaman (2002) makes the point that the Internet minimises a customer's transaction costs, such as time spent travelling to a store to purchase a product.

As other elements of this text make clear, online sales are only one aspect of how the contemporary marketer can use the Internet. A customer using the web to search for best prices available offline, for example, is not the same as one seeking a product for sale on a web site at the cheapest possible price. In all of the marketer's online objectives the goal must be to satisfy the needs of the customer. Smith and Chaffey (2002) state that 'online customers have raised expectations. They expect higher standards in terms of service, convenience, speed of delivery, competitive prices and choice.'

This reinforces the earlier statement that buyers now expect to be helped to buy – that the organization (or its representatives) should present all of the relevant information necessary for the buyer to make that decision. They are no longer willing to simply accept a limited amount of information – the sales pitch – and the Internet has helped raise customer expectations. Interestingly, Yahoo! chief scientist, Jan Pederson, has stated that 'We [at Yahoo!] think of shopping as basically an application of search'.

5.5 Online B2C buyer behaviour

In the previous section we introduced the notion of e-marketing practitioners experiencing empirical evidence of events some time before formal, academic, research was regarding, and confirming, that evidence. Studies into online consumer buyer behaviour follow a similar pattern. There are three significant reasons for this:

1. The Internet developed quickly, in particular the technology;

2. Partially as a result of (1), the way that the Internet is used has changed – not only the way in which the Internet is utilised by marketers, but the way in which web surfers use it;

3. The actual users have changed. The technically adept, relatively young, early adopters of the mid-nineties have been joined by the wide age range mainstream majority.

Parasuraman and Zinkhan (2002) make the point that there is a considerable knowledge gap between the practice of online marketing and the availability of sound, research-based insights and principles for guiding that practice. This suggests that they feel practitioners need to be 'guided' by research. Whilst research can improve practice, most 'academic' theories are developed from observation of practice. For example, traders around the world knew the value of having the right product in the right place at the right price with the right promotion centuries before McCarthy published his '4P's' of marketing in 1960. Practitioner research can also be just as valid as that conducted in academia. For example, research presented in Jakob Nielsen's Alertbox in March 2005 (www.useit.com) suggests that users with a lower literacy level have online behavior that is radically different than that of higher literacy users. Though much academic research has been conducted into the use of the Internet by the disabled, for example, Hooper & Stobart (2003), it is practitioner Nielsen's results that are original in this particular field.

Buyer behaviour

An important part of the marketing process is to understand why a customer makes a purchase. Without such an understanding, businesses will find it impossible to fully meet the customer's needs and wants.

Businesses now spend considerable sums in an attempt to address such issues as:

- Who buys?
- What do they buy?
- How do they buy?
- When do they buy?
- How often do they buy?
- Where do they buy?
- Why do they buy?

The answers to these questions might depend on:

- Psychological factors, such as the customer's perceptions of the product or business, their motives for the purchase, the benefits sought from the purchase, their personality and their learning;
- Social factors, such as the customer's social classes, culture and family role.

If the marketer can appreciate these issues better than the competition, it is a potentially significant source of competitive advantage.

The benefits sought by customers are of particular interest for many web-retailers. When using the web to make a purchase, is the buyer demonstrating the benefits sought (a) of the product; or (b) the method of purchase? Is the convenience of using the technology offered overriding the benefit they seek from the purchase? For the buyer, is there a trade-off situation between the convenience offered by online delivery and the product quality? Are they seeking information, a shopping experience, advice, entertainment or just browsing? Such questions become even more relevant when the purchaser is buying for someone else, particularly as a gift. How many of us have received gifts that are unsuitable, but were easily purchased? Is online shopping more of a benefit to the buyer than that offered by the actual product? The answer probably lies somewhere between, but the online marketer should know where their product range lies.

Types of online behaviour

When considering the ways in which consumers behave once they are online (as opposed to *why* they are online), there are two key aspects of online behaviour that can be monitored to help assess that customer's behaviour:

- Explicit behaviour is based on data provided by the user. This would include such things as a user profile if membership or registration details were required to access the site or make a purchase. Also included would be any recorded actions on the site, like signing up for an e-newsletter or placing an order.
- Implied behaviour is based on data derived from the observation of a user's actions as they interact with the site.

For example, a grandmother goes to Amazon.com and purchases a book on extreme sports for her grandson. Her *explicit* behaviour (the purchase of a book) might suggest she is an active individual and Amazon might target her for emails promoting snowboarding and parachute base-jumping. Grandma, of course, has no interest in these activities. Tracking her *implied* behaviour might have revealed that during the same visit Grandma also searched for, but did not purchase, books on pony care for her teenage granddaughter and Disney DVDs for her great grandson.

MINI CASE 5.2 Customer profiles are worth their weight in gold to advertisers

The Google Toolbar has been available since the turn of the century. Installation of the advanced version entails the user accepting an 'End User License Agreement' that says that the toolbar will send information about every URL the user visits back to Google.

Although Google use this for the relatively benign purpose of retrieving that site's page rank and other information (for use in their search criteria), Google has the ability to track each and every web page the user visits. Google is upfront about letting the user know that the information is being gathered and how it is used. Other search tool bars and spyware applications might not be quite so ethical.

Topographic association

The concept of topographical association takes implied behaviour a stage further, working on the premise that one individual's implied behaviour will be matched by others. This can work within narrow fields. Amazon uses the concept well in their book sales. A search on a book title will return a page that not only describes the book in question, but also includes a list of similar or associated books designated as 'customers who bought this item also bought'. To encourage sales there is also feature that takes the most relevant of the '. . . also bought' list and packages it with the sought book as a 'perfect partner', offering the two at a discounted rate if they are purchased together.

The problem with the topographic concept arises when the concept is extended beyond a limited subject area. Few people have *totally* shared interests, so their implied behaviour is unlikely to run parallel. In a worst-case scenario, customers could actually be alienated by promotions based on flawed topographical association. Imagine, for example, a football supporter who purchases several similar *general* football items to other online users, and is then presented with an advert to buy the replica shirt of a team that is a rival to his own.

How and when?

This segment of the chapter started by commenting on *why* people might choose the web to do their shopping. Although the subject is covered in other chapters of this book, another aspect of consumer behaviour is that of *how* and perhaps *when* the user accesses the web.

For example, let's consider the 'at-work audience', those people who access the web on their employer's computer and Internet connection (this could be with or without the employer's permission).

Users' behaviour presents a number of benefits and challenges to the e-marketer. On the plus side, the at-work user is far more likely to access the Internet via a broadband connection, meaning a much faster **download time** and facility to view rich media applications. On the down side, people at work are usually more time constrained and efficiency-focused than at-home consumers, which usually means poorer click-through rates.

For the online marketer that is targeting the at-work consumer, it is important to choose content and tactics that appeal to a broadband, goal-oriented user. The 'home-user' on the other hand, might, for example:

- use a slower connection – so during its development, the site's download times should be of paramount importance;

LEGAL EAGLE BOX 5.1 Computer and network usage policy

Organisations should put in place a policy that applies to all computers, computer communication facilities, word processing equipment, workstations, network systems and any hardware or software used by its staff.

As the Internet is an unsupervised environment, all organisations have a responsibility to ensure, as far as possible, that their staff use the Internet appropriately. It is, however, the ultimate responsibility of individual users to ensure that their use of the Internet does not contravene legal rules and the firm's policies.

Computer and network users should respect copyright and licences to online information. Copyrighted work should not be copied except as specified by the copyright owner and copied material must be properly attributed. Users of a company's computer and network systems should not alter any software/

computer data or intentionally enable others to do the same unless authorised to do so.

Employees should not intentionally develop programs that disrupt other computer users. The use of any unauthorised or destructive program that interferes with other systems users should attract disciplinary actions. Users of computer and network systems should not abuse such resources. In this regard the following should be prohibited:

- The use of computer and network systems for playing games;
- The use of systems for unauthorised monitoring of electronic communications;
- The use of systems for political campaigns or advertising.

- have fewer time constraints – so longer, more expansive, product descriptions might be used;
- if a cost-per-minute dial-up is used, users frequently go 'offline' to read page content – this means dynamic pages developed 'on-the-fly' might not be available when the user reconnects.

Cotte et al consider web usage behaviour and their effective use of time. Where the consumer has time constraints, site features can offer a personalised experience based on the consumer's past transactions and stated preferences. The stored information provides customised pages that save time for repeat purchases whilst suggesting relevant product offers.

5.6 Online B2B buyer behaviour

Business to business (B2B) marketing (also known as organisational or industrial marketing) buying behaviour differs from consumer buying behaviour. The key issue is that the ultimate buying decision lies not with the individual but with a group of individuals, a so-called 'decision making unit' (DMU). The DMU can be made up from any combination of the following actors within the organisation:

- Those who initiate the purchase procedure
- Those who actually use the product
- Those who have the authority to select the product
- Those who influence the buying decision
- Those who have the authority to make the purchase

The power base will differ from organisation to organisation and industry to industry. The e-marketer must take this into account when developing their online strategy. To target one group (or individual) when developing a web presence is to take the chance of alienating others eg complex technical content might appeal to *influencers* but put off *users*. A neutral web site that attempts to appeal to all might well attract none. Dell's homepage segments the market by providing a gateway to small, medium and large/global business solutions as well as public sector solutions such as healthcare and education.

In the offline world, far more businesses trade with other businesses than with consumers. This is also the case online. Although B2C web sites might get the attention of the popular media, and the general public, it is in business-to-business trading that the vast majority of online commerce takes place.

The use of electronic communications to facilitate business-to-business (B2B) transactions did not begin with the Internet. For many years before the Internet became commercially viable many large, mostly manufacturing, companies used electronic data interchange (EDI) technology in procurement and distribution. However, this technology was not cheap, with the mainframe computers that facilitated the EDI systems of the fifties to the eighties being affordable to only the biggest corporations.

What the Internet – and associated technologies – did was help bring electronic exchange into the price range of all businesses. The Internet required only a PC and a dial-up connection. The availability of this new, more accessible technology accelerated the adoption of more sophisticated supply chain management structures that had been the subject of much research and development in the years prior to its introduction. In turn these sophisticated structures have helped develop closer working relationships between suppliers and purchasers and so affect B2B buyer behaviour.

The Internet, however, presented businesses with more than a method of direct electronic communication – the World Wide Web. Businesses, large and small, that had historically purchased supplies from local companies, catalogues, or visiting sales representatives now had a world of new suppliers at their fingertips. Repeat purchases could be automated. Orders raised, innovations browsed, better quality prices or products sought and all at any time of the day, 365 days a year (a major benefit to the **SME** often committed to the core function of their business during 'office' hours). As with other aspects of the Internet, business buyers soon saw, and embraced, the advantages offered by the new technology. When a Nielsen/NetRatings report (2002) asked business decision makers which advertising media influenced them most in making a purchase or obtaining services for their business? 47% of respondents cited the Internet. This figure rose to 65% when the question posed was 'Where do you prefer to find out about new products?' More recently, a poll from the UK Association of Online Publishers (2005) revealed that 24% of business decision makers agreed that B2B web sites are the most useful source of information and that 39% said that search engines were the most useful source for finding information relating to their work. The report also revealed that decision makers actively respond to advertising on B2B web sites, with 83% saying they have taken action as a result of seeing advertising on a B2B web site, and that 75% use B2B web sites to keep up to date with news in their sector. The report also depicted B2B manager's attitudes to the Internet with 64% finding B2B web sites a trustworthy source of information and 63% believing that B2B web sites provide a modern environment for a company to advertise, and more than 50% using these sites to research and inform business decisions.

If those procuring goods and services for businesses have embraced the Internet, then the B2B marketer must also embrace the medium. For many businesses the Internet could well become the most important element of their marketing effort.

Perhaps the most significant issue with regard to buyer behaviour of the B2B web user is that they consider the web to be a tool of their trade. As such they compare it to other tools that they use in the course of their business. These will normally be efficient, capable and cost effective. If a supplier's web site does not match these criteria, the business buyer will soon look towards competitor's sites. This has a direct parallel with prior comments (in the previous section of this chapter) about benefits sought by B2C buyers. All other things being acceptable – price, quality, lead times, etc – commercial buyers could well choose their suppliers based on the quality of the seller's web site.

The off and online buying cycle

Table 5.3 suggests, customers can (and do) use both off and online sources to seek, evaluate and purchase products. Today's marketer must develop their marketing efforts in order to make best advantage of the off- and online buying process that customers go through. This on and offline buying cycle may soon be so integrated that marketers will refer to it as the buying cycle.

Getting off the cycle

Marketers should be aware that there are no guarantees that the customer who sets off on the online buying cycle will necessarily be there at the end. Cutler and Sterne (2000) make the point that customers can be lost throughout the cycle. They suggest that the organisation can lose customers:

• at the acquisition (information search) stage, when users abandon the web site – before they even become a customer;

• at the conversion (evaluation of the alternatives/action) stage – they choose the product of a competitor. This is often referred to as 'attrition'.

However, further examination of the online buying cycle suggests that customers could get off the cycle at the recognition and action stages.

If we consider the earlier 'sports person' example, the potential customer might be introduced to the concept of a new problem but poor copy or design fail to take the customer to the next stage of the cycle. It is also possible for the same sports person to be introduced to a problem, have the information presented, stimulate interest, evaluate alternatives and decide to make a purchase, only for the check-out procedure on the web site to be flawed and they abandon the online purchase. Worst still, they might then buy the product elsewhere (off or online) meaning that our sports web site has done all of the hard work (the first three stages) but has not profited from it.

5.7 Web site analytics

Marketers must be aware of how technology can help collect data that facilitates the analysis of online behaviour. Offline, such data is referred to as metrics, from metric – 'of or related to measurement' (Collins English Dictionary). Online metrics are dubbed 'e-metrics' or 'web metrics. Here we consider only the use of the data gathered, not how it is gathered. Suffice to say that software is widely available to 'do-it-yourself' or good **application service providers (ASP)** will offer the data as part of their overall service. There is a caveat to this statement however. In the 1990s most new e-metrics software originated from the techno-

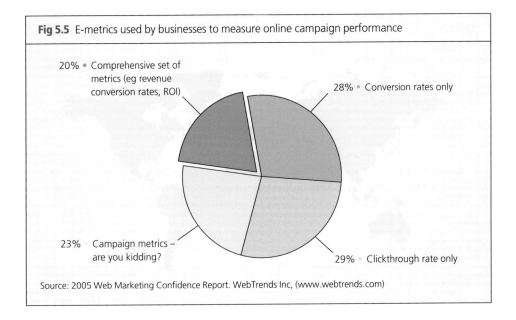

Fig 5.5 E-metrics used by businesses to measure online campaign performance

20% • Comprehensive set of metrics (eg revenue conversion rates, ROI)

28% • Conversion rates only

23% Campaign metrics – are you kidding?

29% • Clickthrough rate only

Source: 2005 Web Marketing Confidence Report. WebTrends Inc, (www.webtrends.com)

logists, not market analysts. As a result, much of this software gave users what technology could deliver, not what the marketer needed to know or what they could actually use effectively. This situation has now been addressed with technology development responding to market demand rather than trying to dictate it. Offline, the use of metrics is common, being used to assess a company's strategy and performance for competitive assessment in relation to benchmarks (Wisner and Fawcett, 1991). The area of web metrics and strategic Internet marketing is, however, a developing field that has not been extensively researched (Weischedel et al 2005) and experts in this science are few. It is only recently that organisations have come to appreciate the value of e-metrics and their analysis beyond rudimentary goal setting and profit targets. Given that any organisation that invests in a TV advertising campaign for example, would always demand data to judge the return on investment (ROI) for that campaign, this is a strange state of affairs. A common reason for this is that organisations rarely define the objectives of their web presence (see also chapter 8). It is not uncommon to hear of an e-commerce web site objective to be something like 'having a thousand **unique visitors** per week' – and the site's publishers being delighted when that figure is exceeded. That a very small percentage of those visitors might actually buy anything is often ignored. Research conducted by worldwide market leader for web analytics, WebTrends Inc, (www.webtrends.com) in 2005 revealed that analysis of web site metrics was still far from the norm for most businesses, with some 23% of respondents collecting no data at all.

Definition of terms used

Table 5.2 provides a list of the most common and/or popular definitions of e-metric terms. To date there is no industry standard, however, any organization that is undertaking any e-metrics (or web metrics) exercise should determine their definitions of the terms to be used with both staff and outside contractors/consultants.

Table 5.2 Terms used in e-metrics

Cache	A temporary storage space for electronic files. Caches can be in the hard drive of a user's PC or the servers of service providers
Clickstream	The route a visitor takes through a web site
Clickpath	See clickstream
Conversion	When a site visitor completes whatever the objective of the web site is (eg orders a product or subscribes to a newsletter)
Conversion rate	The ratio of site visitors to conversions
Cookies	Files containing information created by web sites that are stored on the user's hard drive. Web servers use cookies to keep track of patterns and preferences. When a visitor goes back to the site that put out the cookie, the web server recognizes that visitor
Cost per order	Total marketing expenses divided by total value of orders
Cost per visit	Total marketing expenses divided by number of visits
Depth of visit	How far (deep) the visitor goes into the site, measured by number of pages
Distinct visitors	Individual visitors when assessed over a period of time eg a site might have 100 distinct visitors per day, none of whom have visited that site previously that day. 100 (non-distinct) visitors might be 50 visitors who have been on the site twice in the same period of time
Firewall	A combination of hardware and software that prevents access to a network
Hit	The downloading of any file on a web site. A web site is made up of a series of 'document files' including images and bodies of text. Hits were the earliest form of metric, and are now probably the most useless. Eg one web page might include 50 images, therefore downloading that one page would record 50 hits – unless you know how many files each page consists of a 'hit count' is merely a number
Host server	See 'server'
Impression	The downloading of a specific file. Usually used to describe the downloading of an advertisement banner eg an ad impression
ISP	Internet Service Provider – an organisation that provides access to the Internet, normally for commercial gain
Length of visit	The visit measured in time
Log files	See web logs
Order acquisition ratio	Cost per order divided by cost per visit
Page views	How many times a web page is downloaded
Proxy server	A server that sits between a client application, such as a web browser, and a real server. It intercepts all requests to the real server to see if it can fulfill the requests itself. See also 'server'
Referring site	A web site that sends a visitor to another site eg search engine
Repeat order rate	Existing customer orders divided by total orders
Repeat visitors	A visitor who has been to the site on a previous occasion
RFM	Recency, frequency and monetary value. How long is it since a customer made a purchase (or visited a site), how often do they make a purchase (or visit a site), how much do they spend?
Server	A computer, or a software package, that provides a specific kind of service to software running on other computers. The term can refer to a particular piece of software, such as a www server, or to the machine on which the software is running

Table 5.2 (Continued)

Single access	When a visitor accesses only one page – normally the 'front' or 'home' page
Spyware	Software that covertly gathers user information through the user's Internet connection without their knowledge (also known as adware)
Stickiness	The ability of a web site to retain the attention/presence of a visitor
Traffic	Term to describe the body of visitors to a web site
Unique user session	A visitor's time and activity on a web site in one distinct session
User	See 'visitor' – a user can make a visit to a web site. Also used as a generic term to describe a web surfer
Visit	The time that a visitor spends on a web site in one session – sometimes called the visitor session
Visit duration	The visit measured in time
Visit tenure	Time elapsed since first visit to a specific web site
Visitor	A unique or individual visitor to a web site. See also 'distinct visitors'
Visitor session	See 'visit'
Web log	Software applications that record all activity on a web site, also known as log files

The types of e-metrics gathered will depend on the objectives of the web site. Those objectives might include:

- Increasing revenue to the organisation through direct sales
- Providing after-sales service that enhances offline efforts
- Generating sales leads that can be followed up using traditional offline methods
- Brand development complementing offline branding
- Reducing corporate costs by replacing traditional modes of communication with Internet based technologies.

Table 5.3 summarises some of the different e-metrics that might be considered for different online objectives.

Potential problems with e-metrics

We have already considered how data can be gathered on web site visitors, the analysis of that data and how it can aid the marketer. There is, however, a flaw in that practice – how the data is sourced. There are two main origins for that data, **web logs** and cookies – and both have inherent inaccuracies. Potential problems with web logs stem from how the Internet works. Figure 5.6 illustrates how, from an e-metric perspective, the Internet functions.

In the real world step 3 is where the request goes initially to the servers (so-called 'proxy' servers) of the Internet Service Provider (ISP) before being forwarded to the **host server**. A similar process takes place if the user is behind the firewall of a corporate network. At a university, for example, the initial request goes to the proxy servers of the university's IT department before being forwarded into the outside world. This additional step is also included in the return of the original request. When the host server sends out the requested

Table 5.3 E-metrics used to assess online objectives

Site objective	Potential e-metrics

Increase sales	Sales – value per visitor
	        – per visit (of same user)
	        – made online
	        – by telephone contact
	        – by order and collect offline
	Average order size
	Items per sale
	Conversion rate (sales/visitors)
	Sales trends (eg time/day/geographic)
	Exit point (front page = bad, after completing order at checkout = good, mid way through checkout procedure = bad)
	Point of entry (referral from search engine/link from another site)
	Click stream (cross selling opportunities)

Provide after-sales service	Visits to FAQ page Page downloads (eg instruction manuals) Length of visit (long = bad, an indication that the information sought is hard or impossible to find) Newsletter opt-ins
Generate sales leads	Conversion rate – all methods of communication including: • e-mail contacts • online forms completed • telephone contact Page downloads (eg product details, maps to local stores) Time spent on site (long = good, prospect reviewing product/company information) Depth of visit (how many pages accessed) E-mail list opt-ins Discount vouchers download Newsletter sign-ups
Develop brand	Number of visits/visitors Time spent on site Depth of visit (how many pages accessed) E-mail list opt-ins
Maximise readership (to sell on-site advertising)	Number of visits/visitors Time spent on site (long = good, user finds content interesting/useful) Depth of visit (how many pages accessed) Subscriptions Newsletter sign-ups
Reduce corporate costs	Downloads (PLC accounts, corporate information, recruitment information, press releases)

Analysis of these metrics will provide information on which the marketer can act both tactically and strategically.

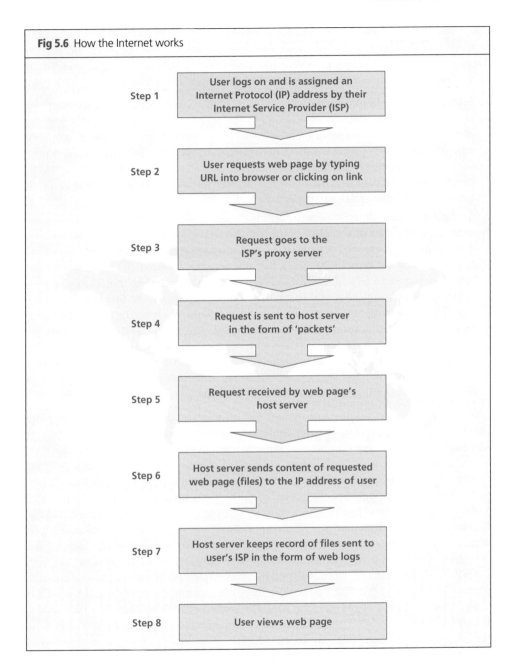

Fig 5.6 How the Internet works

Step 1 — User logs on and is assigned an Internet Protocol (IP) address by their Internet Service Provider (ISP)

Step 2 — User requests web page by typing URL into browser or clicking on link

Step 3 — Request goes to the ISP's proxy server

Step 4 — Request is sent to host server in the form of 'packets'

Step 5 — Request received by web page's host server

Step 6 — Host server sends content of requested web page (files) to the IP address of user

Step 7 — Host server keeps record of files sent to user's ISP in the form of web logs

Step 8 — User views web page

web page to the user, it goes via the proxy servers of the ISP or network firewall. Effectively this is how ISPs and company IT departments block unwanted, or prohibited, web sites – AOL blocking sex industry sites being accessed by children for example – as the request is blocked at that point and not forwarded to the user. Significantly, as the user's request passes through the proxy server, the request is given the Internet Protocol (IP) number of that server, over-riding the IP address of the user's computer. As far as the host computer is concerned, the request is coming from the proxy server, not the user's PC – think of the proxy as a kind of 'middleman' in the proceedings. To handle their customers' traffic, ISPs like AOL will have multiple proxy servers that are designed to balance the traffic load. This is an automated procedure. It is also random. This affects web logs in two ways:

1. An ISP might have 10 proxy servers handling the requests originating from a specific town or city. Suppose, for example, an AOL user in the city requests 10 pages from the web site of a hotel in Dallas. The user does not request all the pages at one time, but in sequence (one at a time as they read the content of the web site). Each time the user requests a page the request is handled by a different proxy server, each allocating a different IP number to the request. This means that the web log of the web site will actually show that 10 different users have requested the 10 pages.

2. As the requested web site passes through each proxy server on its way to the user, the server saves that data in a 'cache'. In the scenario above, let us assume that all of the first user's requests were routed through the same proxy server, so the web logs of the Dallas hotel's web site are accurate, showing that one user has accessed 10 pages. Around the same time suppose a second AOL user in the city requests a web page from the same hotel in Dallas and that request goes through the same proxy server as the first user. When the second request arrives at the AOL server, that server looks into its cache to see if the file(s) exist. As the web site is already in its cache in the location, the server thinks, 'Why bother sending the request all the way to Dallas when the stored file(s) can be used instead?' The request never reaches the web site's host server, yet a second user has viewed the web site. The web logs of the hotel web site will show only one visitor to the web site, yet two different people in the same city have read its content.

Cookies are electronic calling cards that are left on the hard drive of the user's computer when they visit a web site. Essentially, a cookie facilitates the recording of data about the user and their visit(s) to the web site that issued that cookie. They provide a number of useful marketing applications. For example, when a registered member of Amazon.co.uk types into their browser the URL of Amazon, the opening page gives them a personal greeting – something to the effect of 'Welcome back, Alan'. That happens because the web site server sees that it has left a cookie on the member's computer during a previous visit and so reacts to the data on it – in this particular case that data includes the user's personal Amazon log-in details, and therein lies the potential problem. Staying with Amazon as an example, the organisation uses some very sophisticated software applications to 'personalise' the web pages it shows to members. The adverts on it, for example, will be tailored to complement previous purchases. This is fine if it is the member who is using the computer, but what if it is their spouse who has logged on? They would be greeted with 'Hello Alan', and then shown ads relevant to their spouse's previous purchasers. Amazon recognises the computer, not the person. Or what if the member uses a friend's PC, or an Internet Café, to surf Amazon's pages? They would still be visiting the site, still looking for products to buy, but Amazon does not know it is the member, unless of course, they actually **login** to the membership element of the site using their unique password. If the Amazon member were to look for a book from their work PC, then that evening make the purchase from home, the Amazon web logs will show that one customer looked but did not purchase, and another customer bought something. In itself you may not think this is a great problem. But Amazon has millions of 'buyers' and even greater millions of 'visitors' who may or may not be customers. Someone at Amazon has the responsibility of making strategic marketing decisions based partly on these types of metrics.

LEGAL EAGLE BOX 5.2 The use of cookies

The Privacy and Electronic Communications (EC Directive) Regulations 2003 recognise that although electronic communications hold immense benefits, they also bring about risks. One of the areas that these new provisions regulate is the use of cookies.

Under these Regulations cookies and similar devices cannot be used unless the subscriber or user of the terminal equipment has been given 'clear and comprehensive' information about the reasons for storing or accessing information collected by the cookies. The equipment user should be given an opportunity to refuse the storage of, or access to information collected by cookies. The mechanism by which the user exercises this right should be prominent, intelligible and readily available to all users.

Another significant problem with cookies is that it is becoming more and more common for users to delete them from their PCs. A 2005 Jupiter Research (www.jupiterresearch.com) study showed that 10% of users said they deleted their cookies each day, 17% did so each week, and 12% did it monthly. The Firefox **browser** (www.firefox.com), which quickly gained popularity after its launch at the end of 2004, has the capability to erase cookies with a click of the mouse. The issue for the e-marketer is that if returning users cannot be identified as returners (by cookies on their PCs), and then every visitor to a web site is deemed to be a new visitor.

Other problems that might arise for the e-metrics analyst in the form of:

* Random spiders. A spider is an automated programme designed to seek information on web sites. Search engines use spiders (sometimes called 'bots', an abbreviation of 'robots') to gather the data that is used in their algorithms in order to rank the web sites in the engine's search results. When spiders visit a web site they show up on the log files as a 'normal' visitor. Fortunately, most log file analysis tools now recognise search engine spiders (they actually identify themselves as such), but this is not the case of all spiders. Any competent programmer would be able to create, and send out, a spider. No one actually knows how many spiders are out on the web, thousands would be a conservative estimate. If any of these spiders visit a web site, then there would be an artificial inflation of visitor numbers. An example of random spiders used for nefarious means is that of the 'e-mail harvester'. This kind of spider visits web sites and records any e-mail addresses found on those sites. These e-mail addresses are then used for spam mailings. However, privacy software projects like Spybot (www.spybot.com) provide a potential solution to **spyware** problems.

* Frames. A popular design option in the early days of web design, frames are not so common now. They have advantages in their use, but also several detractions, one of which is that as each page is made up of multiple files. These frames will also increase the number of page loads recorded compared to the pages actually seen by the user. Typically this ratio would be around three to one.

* Dynamic or Flash sites. Next time you visit such a site (eg www.franzferdinand.co.uk) keep one eye on the URL in the browser bar as you navigate around the site. It may well remain the same. Effectively, the technology used to develop the pages makes the log file record only one page – the front page – as being visited. Fortunately not all Flash and dynamic sites are programmed in this manner.

* Sharing security certificates. When a user makes the decision to purchase a product online they will click on a link to confirm that decision (eg 'buy now' or 'go to checkout'). On all

legitimate e-commerce sites, this will take the user to a 'secure' part of the web site. This part of the site is designated as having a secure socket layer (SSL) making it 'secure' for credit card payments to be transmitted safely. Such processes are often hosted on a different secure server and are recorded on a different log file. Consequently, analysts must be aware of this to monitor user activity in a vital part of their web site visit – the purchase.

5.8 Implications for online target marketing and customer acquisition

Any analysis, or even consideration, of the purchasing influences of the online customer can only benefit the e-marketer if the results of that analysis are used in any online marketing strategies. The key elements of those strategies should focus on a selected segment(s) in any marketing efforts.

Target marketing

The concept of target marketing involves the delivery of a marketing message to the segment most likely to purchase the product. An important aspect of the target customer selection is consideration of their buying behaviour. This is commonplace in the offline world of marketing. If a customer joins a supermarket loyalty scheme, then the supermarket's marketers combine the information volunteered by the shopper (post code, age, marital status, car owner, etc) with their shopping habits. From this a profile of the customer can be developed and subsequent marketing initiatives can be targeted at them. If that supermarket were to combine its data with that of a third party – a credit card company for example – then that targeting will become far more accurate.

In recent years, customer profiling has been fundamental in driving effective direct marketing campaigns, particularly with use of geo-demographic systems like ACORN and MOSAIC in traditional offline markets. Geo-demographic information systems providers such as Experian, Claritas and CACI have extended their services to provide industry standard classifications of online consumer behaviour incorporating data from leading Internet research company, Forrester. CACI (www.caci.co.uk/etypes) for example, has developed its 'e-types' classification on how consumers in different segments behave, which sites they visit, for how long and what they buy on the Internet. As consumers, we have tended to use multi-channels more frequently in recent years and such systems now provide data on how we migrate from one channel to another for different purposes in the buying process. Such knowledge enables better promotional planning and timely targeting of product which helps in enhancing the customer relationship.

E-types offers seven groups with 23 e-types sub-categories based on life-stage and recent Internet usage levels along outlining online behaviour. The main seven groups have trendy titles and are as follows:

- Wired 4 Life
- Surfing Suits
- Generation E
- Dot Com Dabblers

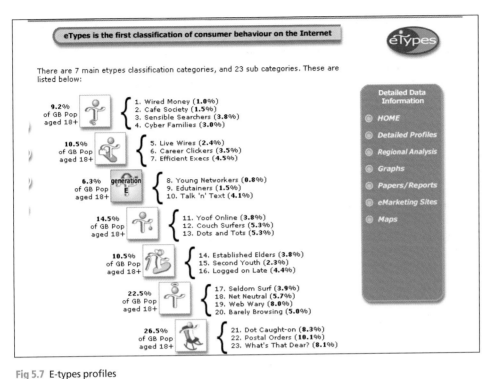

Fig 5.7 E-types profiles

- Silver Surfers
- Virtual Virgins
- Wireless Wonders

Fig 5.7 shows the e-types profiles and the percentage of the UK population accounted for in each group.

Fig 5.8 summarises the key characteristics of each group as a starting point for target marketing.

Understanding the needs and wants of different groups is important for targeting purposes through product offers and other aspects of the mix. It can also highlight potential online opportunities. For example, the 'Silver Surfers' is a group that attracts more and more attention from online marketers. 'Silver surfers' were typically slower to adopt the Internet and were often least comfortable with new technology and therefore under-represented amongst online populations. However, they possess key characteristics that suggest they are a lucrative segment worthy of development. Fundamentally, the 55+ age group can expect to live for another 25 years, they generally have double the disposable income available compared to those half their age, and significantly, they have the free time in which to spend it.

Online there is a similar situation in that surfers can use one portal to research and/or buy a number of items. Someone using MSN as their homepage and a registered MSN member, might search for flight schedules to New York from Newcastle. They might compare the best prices and times for those flights. Hotel accommodation in Manhattan for certain dates in May might be next. There might follow a quick check on the weather for late spring before

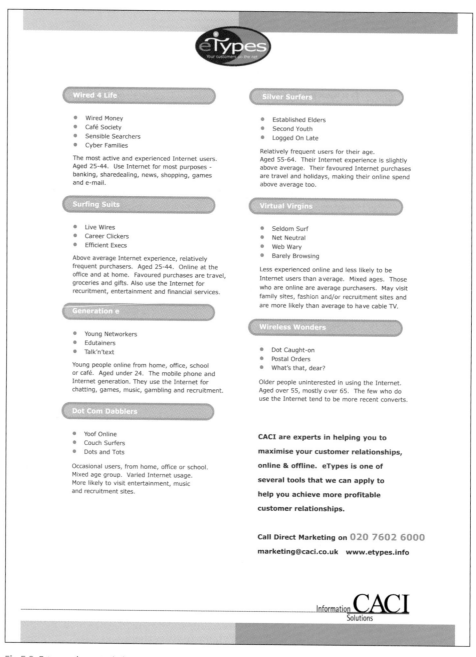

Fig 5.8 E-types characteristics
Source: CACI Limited
©2006 CACI Limited, London. All rights reserved

going over to the National Baseball League's fixture list, followed by a visit to the New York Yankees web site.

By tracking the user's progress through the MSN online presence, MSN marketers can target the user for specific ads, for which they will earn income from third parties. By forming

MINI CASE 5.3 Off and online collusion

In the summer of 2003 behaviour-based marketing research consultants, AC Nielsen affiliated with Yahoo! to develop Consumers Direct, a joint effort designed to appeal to the massive advertising budgets of the consumer packaged goods (CPG) companies. Consumers Direct compiles offline demographic and purchasing habit data from Nielsen's 'Homescan' participants who are also Yahoo! users. Advertiser messages are matched with online users who demonstrate interests and habits similar to their online counterparts. The result is an ultra-targeted advert delivery to web surfers. However, marketers should be sensitive to the use of targeted ads and ensure that they are not deemed to be an invasion of privacy.

an alliance with an offline entity that collected customer data, an online service provider could make that targeting even more specific as illustrated in Mini case 5.3.

This issue has another dimension. Many web site publishers sell advertising space on their site. Rather than handling all advertising arrangements, payments, etc, the publisher will use an intermediary between the publisher and advertiser. Perhaps the most well known of these agents is DoubleClick (www.doubleclick.com). Adverts from the DoubleClick network are not hosted on the publisher's servers. To the user they appear as part of the web site. In reality however, the publisher has actually left a space on their web site and an HTML 'request' for DoubleClick to serve an advert into that space. This means that DoubleClick can issue its own cookies, and so can keep a record of every site a user visits that features that agency's adverts. Hence they can match the profile of the user with adverts published on a web site.

Behavioural targeting vs contextual targeting

Like other aspects of e-marketing (online metrics and advertising, for example) players in the target marketing industry are adapting, adopting or simply making up the rules as they go along. This has created a somewhat confusing state of affairs within that discipline. The industry currently has various system vendors using a variety of technologies that are all promoted (and sold) as 'behavioural targeting' tools. These vendors use a number of criteria for determining the 'behaviour' of users. For some vendors, user's **clickstream** is preferred, whilst for others **IP address** and personal information or frequency of online activity are favoured. In an evolving industry, this is not unreasonable as different products might actually lend themselves to those different criteria. There is a significant issue however, in that what some describe as 'behavioural' targeting' is not that. Although both are described as behavioural, online target marketing is currently being divided into two camps, behavioural and contextual.

Contextual targeting is the less complex of the two, though that is not to say that it does not offer anything to the e-marketer. In simplest terms, adverts are placed where the adverts are in *context* with the content of the host web site or page. Hotel ads on a tourist information portal is a rudimentary example – and when used in the *right* context this can be very effective. It is not, however, 'behavioural' as the same adverts are presented for all users. The behaviour – prior or post – of the user plays no part in the selection of the adverts posted.

Behavioural targeting goes several stages further. Offline, behavioural segmentation might be based on such elements as:

• Benefits sought – eg, convenience or status

• Purchase occasion – a gift perhaps

- Usage frequency – occasional or frequent
- Usage status – non-user, user, lapsed user

So it is with online behavioural targeting. More information about the user is required before they can be truly targeted either individually or as part of a segment. The data cannot be collected ad hoc, it must gathered in a formal, structured manner and it must then be stored in such a way that it is easily extracted and analysed. This practice is more accurately called database marketing and is covered in detail at the end of this chapter.

Geographic targeting

Geographic segmentation is one area of advertising that traditional media holds an advantage over the Internet. Billboards for a local store can be placed in that store's locale. Radio ads can be placed with stations that serve only specific areas. Local newspapers deliver a marketing message only to those people in their catchment area. Although web sites can be delivered to users in different regions of the world (by controlling servers) in the main, published web sites can be accessed by people in all parts of the globe. It can be a waste of resources to place an ad for a local company on a web page that can be viewed by people outside the geographical area in which the company trades unless it covers the target audience better than other media.

The issue can be partially addressed by advertising on geographical portal-type sites but the application is limited to certain products. Tourist web sites are a good example. Anyone seeking information on a certain city or region will invariably find a local tourist web site. It makes sense that an ad for a specific restaurant might be included on the 'eating out' section of that web site. However, it may be accessed worldwide and can assist potential tourists seeking information at the planning stage of their trip.

Technology can also help the geographic target marketer, though there is still the necessity for the user to identify their 'region of interest' rather than the advertiser being able to identify where the user either is, or where they are interested in. An example of this is the alliance between Google (www.google.com) and Multimap (www.multimap.com). In this application, users who search on Multimap for a specific city will find that the page on which the requested map appears will also include ads for local hotels, restaurants and places to visit. This applies technology already used in Google searches where the results page features 'sponsored' ads as well as generic results. If this initiative proves to be successful, the future could see more specific targeting by individual shops, pubs or take-a-ways on streets sought on Multimap, for example.

5.9 Database marketing

Database marketing is a form of direct marketing using databases (lists) of customers in combination with other databases (products, suppliers, distributors) to generate personalised communications which drive targeted marketing efforts at both strategic and tactical levels. Tapp's (2005) marketing database definition describes it as 'a list of customers' and prospects' records that enables strategic analysis, and individual selections for communication and customer service support. The data is organized around the customer.' Compared to other forms of marketing, branding for example, the analysis of outcomes of database marketing

LEGAL EAGLE BOX 5.3 Database marketing legalities

Data subjects have a legal right to object to the processing of their personal data for marketing purposes. To give effect to this right marketers should have a way of identifying and recording the individual data subjects who have shown their objection to the use of their personal information for marketing campaigns. Such objectors' personal data should not be deleted from the system but simply suppressed. The suppression of the names, addresses and telephone numbers of objectors will enable future 'bought-in' lists to be checked and screened against those that have already objected to receiving marketing material.

Before using its database to market goods or services, organisations should screen it against the telephone, fax and mail preference services lists. In order to screen their databases against these different preference services lists, organisations will have to build certain facilities into their systems design.

Action Points

1. Identify marketing information that needs opt-in and that which needs opt-out.

2. Suppress personal data of objectors.

3. Screen your database against the preference service lists.

4. Develop systems that will enable suppression and screening of personal data.

efforts is relatively straightforward, for this reason it can be described as 'marketing with measurable results'. Database marketing has a close association to both e-mail marketing (see chapter 11) and CRM (see chapter 7).

Database marketing involves the gathering, storage, and 'mining' of data that can be used to provide information on customers that might be useful in future marketing efforts. Technology has provided the marketer with the means to collect and store large quantities of data on all their customers. Every company, no matter how decentralised, now has the ability to consolidate customer information and to gain a much better picture of who its customers are, what products and services they buy, and how they like to be served (Seybold 1998).

As with all aspects of business practice, database marketing must bring a return on the investment made – which may be substantial if the practice is to be successful. Kotler (2003) suggests four examples of when database marketing is unlikely to be worthwhile:

1. Where the product is a once in a lifetime purchase;

2. Where customers show little loyalty to a brand;

3. Where the unit sale is very small;

4. Where the cost of gathering information is too high.

In mainstream direct marketing, key measures such as Recency, Frequency and Monetary Value (RFM) or Frequency, Recency, Amount and Category (FRAC) provide essential data capture elements as part of the e-CRM and data warehousing functions for marketing purposes. The danger for any database marketer is to design a support system that contains too many fields and holds too much customer data. A balance must be struck between having too much and too little consumer data.

Kalakota and Robinson (1999) give an indication of just how expensive database marketing can be in their description of the components of a genuine data warehousing process. Those components are:

• Transactional applications – to ensure data is stored in appropriate format

• Data extraction and transformation tools – to read data for business critical applications eg MySQL

- Data scrubbing tools – to detect or remove raw data that may be inaccurate, out of date, incomplete or inappropriately formatted. It also includes de-duplication of data.

- Data movement tools – to move data from immediate to the **data warehouse** mainly referred to as ETL (extract, transform and load) but now more sector specific tools are available.

- Data repository tools – to maintain **metadata** (data about data).

- Data access tools – to retrieve, view, manipulate, analyse and present data.

- Data delivery – to communicate and deliver, store and retrieve data safely for the end-user access.

The complexity of these operations means that only the largest companies can handle data warehousing in-house, with the majority outsourcing to specialists.

For some, a database is merely a list of names and contact details. In marketing terms this is insufficient. Fig 5.9 shows some of the individual's details a marketer might store on a database.

As well as the generic marketing data shown in Fig 5.9, the e-marketer might gather data specific to the individual's online habits, for example:

- How often does the user access the web – every day, once a week?

- How long do they spend online in a single session – 10 minutes, an hour?

- When do they go online – weekdays, weekends?

- At what time(s) of the day do they go online – morning, evening?

- What type of access do they have – dial-up, broadband?

- Where do they access the web – home, work, library?

Fig 5.9 The type of information held on a marketing database for a B2C campaign

Age	Usually collated in age groups – eg 18–21, 22–25, 26–30. Grouping will vary depending on the product or service being marketed.
Income	Usually collated in scales – eg less than £10k pa, £11–15k, £16–20k, £21–25k.
Birthday	For personalised messages, or reminders to purchase for family member.
Family unit	A single woman living on her own will have different purchasing needs and habits to one of the same age who lives with her partner and has two children.
Location	Wide or narrow geographical focus – ie post code valuable to local company, town, region, country for global traders.
Interests	Those with specific non-work related interests may purchase associated products – eg Wimbledon tickets for tennis fans.
Hobbies	Active participants in particular hobbies can be targeted for related products – eg anglers for fishing rods.
Purchasing Habits	What are shopping habits? – eg frequency, value, location.

Other data might be specific to the product or service being offered by the marketing organisation, eg type of car owned /driven; eating preferences eg vegetarian.

A B2B database might include such things as:

- Volume of previous purchases
- Frequency of previous purchases
- Profitability of customer
- Credit/debit history
- Customer's share of organisation's business
- Buying practices and patterns

As well as these generic variables, the B2B customer can also be profiled in a similar way to B2C customers. The 'personalised' elements will be relevant to the organisation's use of the technology available. In small businesses this may refer to the owner, in larger organisations the profile might be that of the head buyer. The organisational elements – company size, industry sector, organisational type, geographic location, etc – will be the same as those required for traditional marketing efforts. There may, however, be elements of the offline profile, both organisational and personal, that are made redundant when Internet techno- logy is used in the buying process. For example, demographics of those in a position to make buying decisions might be important to the 'physical' salesperson, but online the age or sex of the purchaser may be irrelevant.

Interactive data gathering

Marketers can use the interactive potential of the Internet to gather, and respond to, data. Like other e-marketing applications these are online applications of 'traditional' offline practice. Offline, for example, a potential customer might visit a trade exhibition and see a demonstration of a product. The salesperson would endeavour to get the contact details of the prospective customer. A week or so later the salesperson would contact the prospect in any effort to take the buying cycle to the next stage.

Online, the business or manufacturer might offer a free service, eg to design and customise their new car. If the design service is high quality and entertaining, the prospect may be will- ing to register for other information feeds on new releases, product modifications and local dealer promotions. To use the interactive design tool, the prospect would enter features of importance to him/her such as engine size, fuel type, saloon or estate, colour – all of which could be used by the database marketer to target the user in a timely fashion for products or further services in the future. The registration page plays a vital role in capturing data such as vehicles currently owned, forecasted date to change the vehicle and demographic and postcode data for locating the nearest dealership to start the relationship, perhaps with a test drive.

5.10 **Summary**

As with offline marketing, it is often impossible to address many aspects of online marketing in isolation, this chapter is no exception. The chapter started by considering traditional buyer behaviour and decision-making models and how online tools are used by consumers when buying online. Information search, trust and price were cited as key purchasing influences. Online customer expectations were considered, with an emphasis given to how the concept of the web 'helping the buyer to buy' affects the customer expectation. The section recognises that low price is not the over-riding expectation of the web user, but that having their needs, whatever they might be, met. The different types of online buyer behaviour were covered for both B2C and B2B customers. Significant attention was given to buying process models, with an extensive purchase behaviour matrix illustrating how the contemporary marketer must use a combination of off and online methods to successfully meet customer needs. Whilst the offline buying cycle is an accepted model, the chapter presents the theory that a purely online buying cycle exists. Web analytics has also grown in importance as a tool for measuring all forms of site activity and other data gathering. This provides valuable clues to individual online behavioural patterns that help construct online marketing strategy and tactics. The preceding content is brought together in the last two sections which look at target marketing and database marketing – effectively how the return on the investment used in the study buyer behaviour can be made by first acquiring, then keeping, customers. Note that we have to consider increasing activity across channels.

The Internet has come a long way in a short time. Buyer behaviour has changed during this time with greater confidence and spending emerging, and expectations rising. By addressing the changing customers' demands and aspirations, organisations have a chance to prosper in the competitive digital world.

END OF CHAPTER CASE STUDY Behavioral targeting boosts airline's Internet ad results

A just completed study of an integrated advertising campaign last fall from American Airlines has determined that online ads delivered through a database-driven behavioral targeting system achieved higher results than any other ad format used. The campaign, produced by TM Advertising of Dallas, included TV, print, radio, out-of-home messaging and online placements on 14 web sites. The behavioral targeting portion of the effort took place on WSJ.com, the web site of the *Wall Street Journal*.

WSJ Online

The Wall Street Journal Online has been offering behavioral targeting on its web site for about a year and a half, said its vice president of advertising, Randy Kilgore. The objective of the overall campaign across all media was 'to remind business travellers that what American Airlines has to offer is still very desirable and relevant to them, while airlines like JetBlue are trying to make people believe that the only thing that matters is price', said Rob Britton, managing director for brand development and advertising at American Airlines. The specific goal was to increase brand awareness and reach the maximum number of audience members likely to have a live interest in making business travel plans in the near future.

The other parts of the campaign were placed and conducted in the normal manner. But working with WSJ.com and Revenue

Science, TM Advertising created a behavioural targeting execution of online ads.

Revenue Science

Revenue Science, with offices in New York and Seattle, offers the software and services required to turn a publication's web site into an enclosed database management system that recognises and directly interacts with specific individuals. One of the ways it does this is to track and record where visitors go and what they read within the web site. In this case, the system was watching for readers who frequented WSJ.com travel columns and features, such as 'Middle Seat', 'Desktop Traveler' or 'Takeoff and Landings'. These readers were tagged as 'travel seekers' and segmented as a group within the Revenue Science database.

In effect, the database-targeting system invisibly creates a virtual audience of a different composition, or a different demographic, than the web publication's larger, overall audience. Once they are identified, these segmented audience members can be 'followed' around the site and served American Airlines ads, no matter what section of WSJ.com they are reading.

Assumptions

The more time the readers spend in the travel features, the more business trips Revenue Science assumed that they were interested in taking. If someone spends time looking at a travel article on one occasion, Revenue Science made an educated guess that that person travelled once a year on business. 'That one flight-a-year site visitor was the airline's target,' Britton said.

Pinpointing the individual members of that target audience was the key to the test. 'Then we could determine what degree of lift we could obtain in terms of audience composition,' said James Hering, senior vice president and director of interactive marketing at TM Advertising, America's agency of record.

Individuals in the travel-seeker group were served ads based on their behaviour on WSJ.com. A control group, which had no demonstrated travel interest, was exposed to ads placed in the normal manner across the various sections of the site. The study compared these two groups. All visitors saw rich media, large format ads, which featured testimonials from customers. They talked about the amenities offered by American Airlines that low-cost airlines lack, such as the ability to upgrade to First Class; that AA flies often to many places around the world; and the benefits of a frequent-flyer programme, Mr Hering said.

Dramatic results

The results of the behavioural targeting were dramatic, according to American Airlines and TM Advertising. For instance, compared with the general run of web ads, the behavioral-targeted ads were seen by 115% more business travellers who take one trip a year, the marketer and the agency said. The lift among those who take five or more trips a year was 145%. 'Composition counts,' said Omar Tawakoi, senior vice president of marketing at Revenue Science. 'It tells the marketer we delivered the right people.' And, the targeted business consumers remembered the message better than others did, he said. That group did 3% better than the average in aided brand awareness, according to TM Advertising.

Dynamic Logic

When they were asked about specific messages that plugged American Airlines' 3,900 flights a day, there was a 26% lift in message association. Online survey firm Dynamic Logic provided the brand awareness results, which showed these to the best-performing ads in the campaign. Behavioural targeting was cheaper, too, according to the agency. Using a cost-per-target metric, Revenue Science determined that it was 25% cheaper to advertise to the group that flew once a year, and 45% cheaper to reach the segment that flew five times a year. That is even though run-of-site ads are priced at a slightly cheaper cost per thousand, Mr Hering said.

Confusing terms

Database marketing, of the kind described in this case, has been called different names by different companies, as it has emerged in recent years, leading to much confusion. These include 'behavioural targeting', 'addressable advertising', 'online database marketing', and 'targeted marketing'.

It is also often confused with customer relationship marketing (CRM), which is a different kind of database-driven technique, largely focussed on the management of relationships and marketing interactions with existing customers. Behavioural targeting, on the other hand, is a strategy employed to identify potential customers within a larger online or cable system audience and execute one-to-one advertising programs designed to ultimately turn those individuals into customers.

Source: Advertising Age (www.adage.com). Copyright 2004, Crain Communications Inc.

Questions

1. Why do you think this campaign was so successful?

2. The paragraph titled 'Revenue Science' describes how the pages that users visit identified them as being in the target market for AA. Choose another major newspaper's online offering and identify the visited pages on it that might help target potential customers for:

    – Ford Motors

    – Hilton Hotels

    – Toshiba note book computers

    – The World Wild Life Fund

    – Or any other organisation you might wish to add, eg your employer

DISCUSSION QUESTIONS

1. Section 5.7 of this chapter looks at e-metrics and considers the use of technology in collecting information on web users. Discuss the ethical issues that surround the issue of covert collection of data.

2. The text raises the issue that the convenience of using the technology offered by online shopping might over-ride the benefit they seek from the purchase on buyer behaviour. Discuss this assertion.

3. Many companies trading in B2C markets are using database marketing in order to develop relationships with the consumers. Discuss what sorts of products might benefit from this kind of strategy, and which products would not.

REFERENCES

Adcock, D, Halborg, A & Ross, C (2001) *Marketing Principles and Practice* (4th edn), FT Prentice Hall, Harlow, UK, 75

Alba, JW, Lynch, J, Weitz, B, Janiszewski, C, Lutz, R, Sawyer, A, Wood, S (1997) Interactive home shopping: consumer, retailer, and manufacturer incentives to participate in electronic marketplaces, *Journal of Marketing*, Vol 61, July, 38–53

Alreck, P, Settle, R (2002) The hurried consumer: time-saving perceptions of Internet and catalogue shopping, *Journal of Database Marketing*, Vol 10, No 1, 25–35

Athiyaman, A (2002) Internet users' intention to purchase air travel online: an empirical investigation, *Marketing Intelligence and Planning*. Vol 20, No 4, 2002, 234–242

Bakos, JY (1997) Reducing buyer search costs: implications for electronic marketplaces, *Management Science*, Vol 43, December, 1676–92

Bhatnagar, A, Misra, S, Rao, HR (2000) On risk, convenience and Internet shopping behavior, *Communications of the ACM*, Vol 43, No 11, 98–105

Brennan, R, Baines, P & Garneau, P (2003) *Contemporary Strategic Marketing*, Palgrave MacMillan, Basingstoke, England, 19

Burgmann, I, Kitchen, PJ & Williams, R (2006) Does culture matter on the web?, *Marketing Intelligence and Planning*, Vol 24, No 1, 2006, 62–76

Constantinides, E (2004) Influencing the online consumer's behavior: the Web experience. *Internet Research: Electronic Networking Applications and Policy*, Vol 14, No 2, 2004

Cotte, J, Chowdury, TG, Ratneshar, S & Ricci, LM (2006) Pleasure of Utility? Time Planning Style and Web Usage Behaviours, *Journal of Interactive Marketing*, Vol 20, No 1, Winter 2006, 46

Cutler, M & Sterne, J (2000) *E-metrics. Business Metrics for the New Economy*, White paper, Netgenesis Corporation

Einwiller, S (2003) When reputation engenders trust: an empirical investigation in business-to consumer electronic commerce, *Electronic Markets*, Vol 13, No 3, 196–209

George, JF (2002) Influences on the intent to make Internet purchases, *Internet Research: Electronic Networking Applications and Policy*, Vol 12, No 2, 165–180

Hall, ET (1976) *Beyond Culture*, Anchor Press/Doubleday, Garden City, New York

Hofstede, G (1980) *Culture's Consequences*, Sage, Beverley Hills, CA

Hofstede, G (2001) *Culture's Consequences* (2nd edn), Sage, Thousand Oaks, CA

Hollensen, S (2003) *Marketing Management*, FT Prentice Hall, Harlow, UK, 117

Hooper, P & Stobart, S (2003) Using third party services to reduce the development costs and improve the effectiveness of charity web site, *International Journal of Nonprofit and Voluntary Sector Marketing*, November 2003, Vol 8, no 4, 328–336(9). Henry Stewart Publications, ISSN: 1465-4520

Huang, AS & Christopher, D (2003) Planning an effective Internet retail store, *Marketing Intelligence and Planning*, Vol 21, No 4, 230–238

Kalakota, R & Robinson, M (1999) *E-Business: Roadmap for Success*, Addison Wesley

Kotler, P (2000) *Marketing Management*, Prentice Hall

Kotler, P (2003) *Marketing Management*, Prentice Hall

Kuo, H, Hwang, S & Wang, E (2004) Evaluation research of information and supporting interface in electronic commerce web sites. *Industrial Management & Data Systems*. Vol 104, No 9, 2004, 712–721

Jaywardhena, C, Wright, LT & Masterson, R (2003) An Investigation of online consumer purchasing, *Qualitative Market Research: An International Journal*, Vol 6, No 1, 58–65

Leonard, K (2005) *Taking Their Time: It's Not Shopping Cart Abandonment, It's Comparison Shopping*, Internetretailer.com

Maslow, AH (1970) *Motivation and Personality*, New York, Harper Row

Nielsen/Netratings (2002) cited in An elephant in the room: the online at work audience, *The Wall Street Journal* and Emarketer.com

Parasuraman, A, Zinkhan, GM (2002) Marketing to and serving customers through the Internet: an overview and research agenda, *Journal of the Academy of Marketing Science*, Vol 30, No 4, 286–95

Seybold, PB (1998) *Customers.com*, Random House

Shapiro, C, Varian, H (1999) *Information Rules*, Harvard Business School Press

Shim, S, Eastlick, MA, Lotz, SL, Warrington, P (2001) An online prepurchase intentions model: the role of intention to search, *Journal of Retailing*, Vol 77, No 3, 397–416

Singh, N & Pereira, A (2005) *The Culturally Customized Web Site,* Elsevier Butterworth Heinemann, Burlington, MA, US, 53–70

Skyrme, DJ (2001) *Capitalizing on Knowledge from E-commerce to K-business*, Butterworth-Heinemann

Smith, PR & Chaffey, D (2002) *EMarketing Excellence*, Butterworth Heinemann

Solomon, MR, Marshall, GW & Stuart, EW (2006) *Marketing – real people, real choices* (4th edn), Pearson Prentice Hall, 137

Strong, EK (1925) *The Psychology of Selling*, McGraw-Hill

Tapp, A (2005) *Principles of Direct and Database Marketing* (3rd Edn), FT Prentice Hall, Pearson Education, Harlow, Great Britain, 25

UK Association of Online Publishers (2005) *The Role of B2B Websites.* Available on www.ukaop.org.uk

Urban, G (2004) *Digital Marketing Strategy*. Pearson Education, Upper Saddle River, New Jersey, US 25–26

Weischedel, B, Matear, S, Deans, K (2005) A qualitative approach to investigating online strategic decision making, *Qualitative Market Research: An International Journal*. Vol 8, No 1, 2005, 61–76

Wisner, JD, Fawcett, SE (1991) Linking firm strategy to operating decisions through performance measurement, *Production & Inventory Management Journal*, Vol 32, No 3, 5–11

Worzala, EM, McCarthy, AM (2002) E-commerce and retail property in the UK and USA, *Journal of Property Investment & Finance*, Vol 20, No 2, 142–58

Yahoo! and OMD (2006) *The Long and Winding Road: The Route to the Cash Register*, www.yahoo.client.shareholder.com/ReleaseDetail.cfm?ReleaseID=196082

FURTHER READING

Eisenberg, B & Novo, J (2002) *The Marketer's Common Sense Guide to E-Metrics*, Future Now Inc. New York – an excellent guide that includes a 'Conversion Rate Marketing Calculator' workbook.

Seybold, P (1998) *Customers.com*, Random House – an excellent text on how e-technology can be used to meet customer needs. The section on how American Airlines adopted the web is a case study of how it should be done.

Singh, N & Pereira, A (2005) *The Culturally Customized Web Site,* Elsevier Butterworth Heinemann, Burlington, MA, US.

Sterne, J (2001) *World Wide Web Marketing*, Wiley – readers should take particular note of anything Jim Sterne says; he is a leading practitioner with blue chip clients.

Sterne, J (2002) *Web Metrics – proven methods for measuring web site success*, Wiley – see above.

WEB LINKS

E-consultancy.com **www.e-consultancy.com** – Research, information, training and events on best practice online marketing and e-commerce.

Larry Chase's Search Engine for Marketers **www.searchengineformarketers.com** – this site offers reviews and links to the top sites in 40 marketing categories.

Marketingexperiments.com **www.marketingexperiments.com** – offers free copies of their extensive research results.

Marketingprofs.com – excellent e-marketing content, though terminology used and models/theories quoted mean the articles are mainly for readers with a background in marketing.

 Visit the Online Resource Centre which accompanies this book, for lots of interesting additional material, including self-assessment questions, internet exercises, and links for each chapter: **www.oxfordtextbooks.co.uk/orc/gay/**

Search Engine Marketing

6

Learning objectives

By the end of the chapter you will be able to:

- Appreciate the importance of search engine marketing and optimisation for online success
- Understand how search engines have developed over the last decade
- Critically evaluate the new revenue models impacting on online marketers
- Understand how search engines work and how they differ from each other
- Critically evaluate why marketing managers need to have an appreciation of search engine optimisation techniques
- Understand key techniques in optimisation and ranking of web pages

Chapter at a glance

MINI CASE 6.1 **Search engines beat all other media for driving visitors to web sites with 77% of internet users employing search engines to find web sites**

Results from a survey indicate that the majority (77%) of Internet users employ search engines more frequently than any other online media – surpassing banner ads, web links, e-mail links, and other forms of offline media as the leading vehicle for discovering web sites. In addition, the survey found that 84% of Internet users who are online four or more hours each day reported they use search engines frequently to discover web sites. In fact 81% of long-term web users reported recurrent search engine use to find web sites. Just 46% of that same group claimed to use web links often when locating sites.

'Time and experience online drive Internet users to utilize search engines to locate Web sites, and with 91% of Web users going online daily, search engines are rapidly becoming key drivers of traffic to marketers' Web sites,' said Dr. Amanda Watlington, Director of Research at iProspect. 'The results demonstrate that Internet users, especially frequent users, recognize the value and efficacy of search engines, opting to utilize them instead of other forms of media.'

Source: www.iprospect.com/media/press2002_09_16.htm

6.1 Introduction

This chapter is devoted entirely to search engine marketing, as it is a critical success factor in online marketing. Every marketer should have a fundamental understanding of how search engines work and the techniques employed to boost site traffic and build brands. It is also important when briefing web designers and search engine optimisers. The importance of search engine marketing was highlighted in the iProspects press release of 2002 in Mini case 6.1.

Rayport and Jaworski (2002) observe that search engines and directory listings are the most popular method used for information retrieval by Internet surfers. Search engine marketing encompasses a variety of technical and marketing applications that must combine effectively to increase site traffic. Numerous studies point to search engines as the primary tool for anyone seeking information online. Other promotional techniques lag behind in terms of effectiveness to drive potential customers to a specific web site. Haig (2001), for example, estimates '80 to 85% of web users use search engines as a tool of first resort'. However, stories abound amongst the search engine optimisation (SEO) community about marketing managers allocating large slices of their budgets to web design only to be mystified as few visitors call in on their way around cyberspace. Failure to get top 20 rankings with the major search engines is the fundamental reason.

Most traffic on the web starts with search ie surfers use a search engine to start their cyberjourney (the terms surfer and searcher are used interchangeably throughout this chapter). Marketers should understand the importance from an online marketing perspective of having their web site indexed with the major search engines. In 2006, search marketing remains to be one of the hottest topics in the entire mix. It is still relatively new; it is providing the highest return on investment (ROI) and lowest cost per acquisition (CPA) than any other form of advertising and promotion. Figs 6.1 and 6.2 from Pipar Jaffrey illustrate the cost effectiveness of search techniques and the growth of search engine marketing.

E-consultancy predicts that search engine spending in the UK will reach £598 million in the UK alone. This is likely to expand further as local and mobile search tools are adopted.

For visionaries in the online marketing industry, it was clear that search engines would provide the most obvious method of finding information on the web. This is how a cottage

Fig 6.1 Search provides the lowest CPA

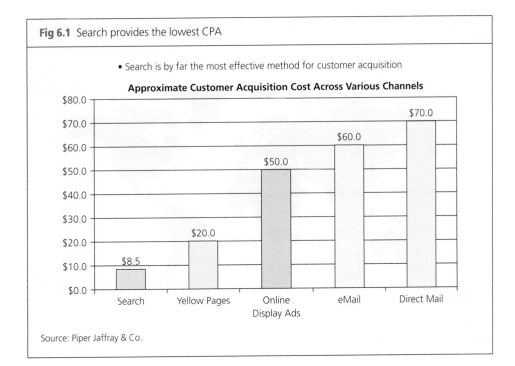

- Search is by far the most effective method for customer acquisition

Approximate Customer Acquisition Cost Across Various Channels

Source: Piper Jaffray & Co.

Fig 6.2 International 'Search' projections

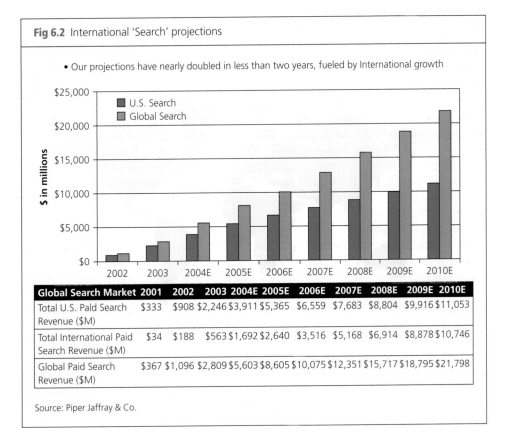

- Our projections have nearly doubled in less than two years, fueled by International growth

Global Search Market	2001	2002	2003	2004E	2005E	2006E	2007E	2008E	2009E	2010E
Total U.S. Paid Search Revenue ($M)	$333	$908	$2,246	$3,911	$5,365	$6,559	$7,683	$8,804	$9,916	$11,053
Total International Paid Search Revenue ($M)	$34	$188	$563	$1,692	$2,640	$3,516	$5,168	$6,914	$8,878	$10,746
Global Paid Search Revenue ($M)		$367	$1,096	$2,809	$5,603	$8,605	$10,075	$12,351	$15,717	$18,795	$21,798

Source: Piper Jaffray & Co.

industry of 'search engine optimisers' (**SEOs**) as they were originally known, started to emerge.

6.2 **Search engine definition and forms**

Webber (2000) defines a search engine as a 'searchable catalogue, database or directory of websites', of a reasonably large size. Mohammed et al (2002) suggest that there are three basic forms of marketing relating to search engines.

* The simple submission, typified by 'free to subscribe', where a site is indexed under certain keywords

* The paid advertisement indexed by keywords, often resulting in a top ranking

* Banner ad displays tied to keywords

This chapter will outline some of the influences affecting the selection of one of these methods.

As the number of web pages continues to grow, the more people rely on search engines to help them filter out irrelevant information and provide them with authoritative, reputable and relevant results to their queries. Millions of searches take place at the major search engines by people all around the globe looking for answers to their information queries. If a company's web pages are always ranked in the top 20 to 30 results at the larger web search engines such as Google, Yahoo!, MSN or Ask Jeeves then there is the potential for hundreds, thousands or sometimes millions of qualified, targeted traffic streaming through from search engines. It is a marketing professional's dream.

However, the dream of millions of people hitting an organisation's web pages, interested in their products or services, is often thwarted by the technological twist between search engines and web site developers. And even more so by the surfers (end users) at search engines who have no idea how to formulate a query and little idea of what they really want or expect. They rely very heavily on search engines providing the solution to their problem, whatever it is, and the search engine knowing who and where to send them.

To illustrate this point, imagine the following scenario. A major financial institution wants to be found at the top of the search results to attract people looking for low interest loans. Their web site is full of pages telling potential customers that they lend money. They lend money at the lowest rates ever and the searcher is typing in queries at Google (for instance) that refer to borrow money or loan money. This appears to be a perfect match. However, the search engine index only understands a match between the words in the searcher's query and the words on the web pages it has indexed.

In the past, if the searcher did not use the word 'lend' in the query and the financial institution did not have pages with text referring to 'borrow' or 'loan' then a true match would not have emerged. This can still arise today with some search engines but others (such as Google) have become more sophisticated in the way they look at search queries and 'decide' what sites to list. That said, it is still important to consider the actual words used in the content of pages to ensure they have the best possible chance that a search engine will match them with a search query. Furthermore, if the financial institution's web pages have not been successfully crawled by the search engines, ie they have not been indexed due to some technical barrier preventing the search engines from downloading the data, then there is no chance of ever being found in what are known as the 'organic results' (the listings down the left hand side of the page following a search) whatever the searcher's query is.

6.3 A brief history of search engines

It is generally accepted that the history of search engines, as we know them now, started with university student projects, which then evolved into major commercial organisations. Search engines and directories have attempted to provide a more methodical and logical method for retrieving information from the billions of pages that exist on the World Wide Web.

Around 1990, prior to Tim Berners-Lee's introduction of HTTP, the programming code used to produce web pages and the communication **protocol** for the World Wide Web, Alan Emtage, a student at McGill University in Montreal, Canada, wrote a program called Archie. The program was one of the earliest attempts to provide a method of identifying and retrieving files on the Internet. Gopher, Telnet, Veronica and even Jughead followed this. There is a wealth of information about these early programs and their strange names available on the web. For anyone who really wants to study the history of search on the Internet visit Wes Sonnereich's (1997) site, 'A History of Search Engines'. This brief look at the history of search engines really begins with the World Wide Web Wanderer, the first real robot on the web. Developed to capture URLs (web page addresses) to measure the growth of the web, it resulted in Wandex, the first web database.

Robot technology, or search engine spiders, as we know them now, became the focus of many university projects. Spiders are computer robots (software programs), which automatically perform repetitive tasks at speeds that would be impossible for humans to achieve. When referring to **crawler** based search engines, the terms 'spider', 'crawler' and 'bot' are generally used interchangeably.

By 1994 American universities were alive with search and information retrieval projects on the web. Student Brian Pinkerton developed the web's first full text retrieval search engine called WebCrawler which started as his own single user application and rapidly became the web's first commercial search engine. During 1994, Excite, another crawler-based search service was launched, quickly followed by Lycos and also the web's first human powered directory Yahoo!.

In the mid-nineties, as technology rapidly developed, came the launch of Infoseek, Alta Vista, HotBot, Ask Jeeves and more recently Google. Many of the early search services have developed into the major commercial portals used by hundreds of millions of surfers worldwide to find information on the web. With such huge audiences to tap into, it was not long before online marketers realised what a rich source of targeted traffic the major search engines and directories provided.

It seems that searchers have high expectations from search engines, and when they are used purely for research, searchers ask very vague questions about topics they do not understand much about, anticipating a concise answer. Similarly, when carrying out commercial searches for products or services, in the same manner as the problems outlined above, surfers may frequently get the name of the brand wrong by typing something such as 'Harley Davison' and fully expect the search engine to know that they meant Harley Davidson. In fact, searchers often expect a computer to supply the information they want – not the information they actually asked for. This is not a phenomenon unique to search engines.

Reference librarians have been dealing with these problems for many years. However, the difference is that, the librarian gets to share a few minutes listening to someone and in return asking questions to get feedback. They are then usually more able to direct a person to the source that will best satisfy their information needs.

This is the type of dialogue that is never undertaken with a search engine. Search engines usually only have one to three words to attempt to ascertain the nature and intent of a query. What is more, they also have the rapidly increasing size of their index. By August 2005, Yahoo! posted that they had access to over 20 billion documents. So one to three words are submitted, and out of that huge database of web sites the search engine has to provide the top 20 to 30 results which most satisfy an individual's information needs. It is worth remembering that this represents only a fraction of the entire web, probably under 10%.

A search engine is the fundamental traffic builder online, so marketers must have a basic appreciation of how they work to enable them to brief web designers and search engine optimisers. The methods applied are often technically complex, but an effective marriage between marketing and technology will substantially enhance the chances of online success. Understanding what search engines like Google and portal platforms like Yahoo! and MSN like and dislike, is critical to achieve a high rank and visibility for any organisation's site.

As marketers, we are applying a classic type of buyer behaviour analysis in reverse to understand the intermediary's information need. The search engines themselves have become more sophisticated as they adopt different criteria when indexing sites, for two primary reasons.

1. They need to be able to tackle what is known as 'the abundance problem'. A search for digital cameras can bring back as many as 80 million web pages. The search engine has to decide which are the most important (or authoritative) of those pages to rank in the top 20 to 30 listings.
2. The search engines are increasingly recognising the sharp practices of some optimisers who try to fake their 'importance' to get higher rankings (more commonly known as search engine spam). Some of these practices are referred to later in this chapter.

Furthermore, the search engine marketing community is changing as the 'free to submit' model is being replaced with 'paid placement' and '**paid inclusion**' models from companies such as Yahoo! Search Services (formerly Overture), Google AdWords and Miva (a company formed from the joining of Espotting and FindWhat in the US). It is far more likely that if a company seeks a top ranking or just a guarantee to be in the search engine index, they will have to pay for it.

The search engine's job is to promote and drive a prospect to a site; once that occurs, conversion to sales will depend on many other marketing, design and relationship factors.

It is commonly accepted that surfers rarely ever go beyond the second page of results following a query. If they cannot find the answer they are looking for on the first page (and less frequently the second) the surfer either attempts another search or simply moves to another search engine.

Having established that a company needs to be in the indices of all the major search engines to attract traffic, it is also preferable to be in the top 20 to 30 results to increase their chance of being found by a potential new customer. Getting into the index itself is not too difficult, as there are many workarounds to technical issues. However, getting a top 20 to 30 rank is far more difficult. By understanding more about how search engines actually work it becomes easier to rationalise the process of getting into the index and set realistic expectations in relation to getting that all-important top ranking position.

6.4 Revenue models for search engine positioning

Three fundamental problems existed with early search engines. These were:

1. Consumers suffered from poor quality and outdated machine-generated sales results;

2. Listings were poorly or randomly ordered;

3. The business model was deeply flawed with poor revenue generation potential (eg 'free to subscribe').

In June 1998, GoTo launched its **Pay per Click (PPC)** model which is sometimes referred to as 'the first monetisation of search' in America. A few years later GoTo rebranded as Overture and changed again to Yahoo! Search Marketing after it was acquired by the portal. The fundamental principle of Yahoo!'s PPC service was to provide organisations with a way to obtain top ranking search results by bidding on keyword phrases. Further revenue generation models emerged as advertisers and search traffic partners such as Internet service providers and portals joined forces. This form of performance-based marketing allows organisations to carefully target sites and customers at a price to suit their advertising budget. Other major search engine players like Google with its AdWords service and Miva have quickly followed suit and the 'pay for performance' advertiser network model is now an accepted part of online marketing. At the time of writing, MSN was testing its own pay-per-click service scheduled for launch in 2006.

The adoption of the model has gathered pace with the players like Google and BTLooksmart leading the way. (For an insight into the BTLooksmart service visit www.bidsmart .looksmart.co.uk). However, Tom Loosemore (2002), head of applications for broadband and new platforms at BBCi, believed that due to commercial influences caused by the new revenue models, search engine results were becoming less relevant. He cites search partnership agreements, and differentiation between 'paid for' and 'pure searches' as two key factors that contribute to consumers not getting 'the best of web' searches. These claims are disputed, not surprisingly, by Martin Child (2002) of Overture and Sebastien Bishop (2002) of Miva who both stressed the importance of their strong editorial teams who evaluate web page submissions to them, thus ensuring relevant, quality search results.

This can present problems for a high profile portal such as Yahoo! as it has to satisfy different audiences and objectives. Yahoo!'s Director of Products and Services, James Bilefield (2002) observes, 'The search function is where Yahoo! began, so we have been very careful how we alter it. The listings are still heavily featured, but you must strike a balance between the commercial needs of partnerships and editorial judgements in the best interest of our customers.' Many industry observers link the rise in popularity of paid-for listings with the temporary demise of banner advertising a few years ago, as they seek an alternative revenue stream to achieve their desired return on investment.

Partnerships in paid search result distribution networks

When you look at Yahoo! Search's strategic partners as well as Google's in Fig 6.3, and the traffic they generate, it is not surprising that they lead the field in both the UK and US in 'pay for performance' advertising. However, with MSN getting ready to launch their own PPC service, it will be interesting to see how the marketplace divides as competition intensifies.

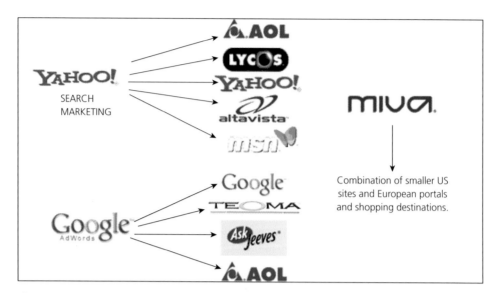

Fig 6.3 Strategic partners in search engine marketing

Pay Per Click (PPC); Pay For Consideration; Pay For Inclusion

PPC, PFC and PFI are now common terms in search engine marketing. And yet a couple of years ago they did not exist at all in the industry vocabulary. Although banner advertising was utilised at search engines, it is surprising that we now see paid for adverts (as sponsored listings actually are) occurring at the top right next to the primary results following a query. Marketers can no longer optimise pages for search engines without considering their budget. Now, 'if you want to play – you've got to pay' and this has serious cost implications for the online marketer.

The marketer needs to consider:

1. How does Pay-Per-Click work?

2. Who do you pay?

3. What do you get for your money?

MINI CASE 6.2 You cannot be serious!

If someone from a search engine dropped me a note a few years ago saying: 'Guaranteed number one position for your key-word/phrase for as little as $0.15 per click thru', I'd have dismissed it immediately thinking: 'Who'd be daft enough to pay a search engine even fifteen cents for a rank when you can do it for nothing.' If I received a note from a search engine back then saying: 'Give us $39 for your first URL and $25 for the rest up to 500 and we guarantee to crawl your pages every 48 hours – but sorry can't guarantee a rank.' I'd have said, 'Get outta here.' And

what about if I had received a note from those nice people at Yahoo! saying: 'Give us $299 and we'll come around and have a look at your site within the next seven days. If it's any good we'll put it in the index, but if not, you won't get in and I'm afraid we won't give you your money back.' I'd have been checking the date to see if it was April 1st.

Mike Grehan, Search Engine Marketer, 2002

Organisations must set their **paid search** budget carefully and be disciplined and adhere to it or they can overspend and get little in return. It is important to know exactly how the model for each of these new revenue streams at search engines and directories actually work.

Pay Per Click (PPC Model)

Although founded in 1997, it was 1998 when a new type of search engine called GoTo (now Yahoo! Search Marketing), began generating revenue in the search engine world. With their newly-patented technology, they developed a method of allowing web-masters to select their most popular keywords or phrases and then bid for them in an auction style.

An account is set up and a deposit made, then each time a surfer keys in that specific keyword/phrase, the company appears at the top of the listing. This assumes that the company has bid enough for the top spot. When the surfer actually clicks on their link and lands on their site, that amount of money is then deducted from their initial deposit. It could be as little as $0.15, or it could be $20.00. Whatever the amount, that is how much the company pays for that one visit. However, if a competitor decides to raise the bid and offers $0.10 more, the initial company gets relegated and they appear at the top of the results. The company are advised that they have been 'out bid' and they can decide whether to increase their own bid by increasing the amount of money they have on deposit. The danger is that companies may get involved in a type of bidding war with someone before they realise that their ROI may not be increasing to cover it.

Bidding wars are becoming far more common as many advertisers rely heavily on automated bid management tools to manage their campaigns automatically where they try and keep their paid for listings exactly where they want them to be. If two competitors bid on the same keyword and both use a bid management tool to keep them in the top spot, it is not uncommon for both to pay very close to their maximum bids with each click-through. This is because Yahoo! Search Marketing guarantees that an advertiser will pay no more than a penny above the bid of the advertiser listed below them. This is one of the real selling features of their service (along with the fact that an advertiser only pays when a surfer clicks on their ad). Therefore, keyword bids only determine the rank order of PPC ads – bids are treated as maximum bid. So, in many cases the cost per click (CPC) that is actually paid by an advertiser is less than their maximum bid – but that depends on the level of competition. If Advertiser 1 bids $0.20 on a keyword and the next highest bidder, Advertiser 2, bids $0.10 on the same keyword. Advertiser 1 will only pay $0.11 for every click-through he receives. Similarly Advertiser 2 will only pay 1 cent more than the advertiser below him. But if both advertisers use bid management tools, each specify they want position 1 and each set their maximum bids to $0.20, within a very short space of time the actual CPC of the top ad will rise to $0.20.

Bidding levels and the management of bids are very important factors with the PPC model. In the early days of PPC advertising those organisations with greater financial muscle were often in a much stronger position. However, more astute and sophisticated advertisers can compete with much larger organisations by adopting different tactics in their campaign. For example, a top position does not necessarily deliver the greatest ROI and so running a campaign with thousands more keywords and targeting lower positions can boost return by a significant margin. Clearly, the clicks have to be quality and must be converted to improve the return on investment (ROI). The economics of PPC are illustrated in Mini case 6.3.

Yahoo! Search Marketing, Google and the other PPC engines say that it is highly targeted traffic that companies are paying for. However, organisations cannot fully rely on the quality of the traffic to their site – particularly if they are bidding on one or two-word (very broad)

As a small business, if you are bidding at $0.50 for position #1 for the keyword 'widgets,' and you're selling widgets for $20 each with a wholesale cost of $10 (leaving a profit margin of $10), and the PPC delivers 200 visitors to your site in a given period, that's $100.00 spent to get 200 visitors. If your site's conversion rate (CR) is 2% (which would be good), that's 4 cus-tomers for $100.00. Your CPS would be $25.00 per customer, $15 per sale OVER your profit margin. With a PM of $10, and four sales netting $40, you're swiftly going in the hole with every sale attributable to this PPC advertising.

Source: Steve Harrison (2002)
Mastering the PPC's

keyword phrases. Organisations should ensure that they discourage surfers who have no interest in their products or services from clicking through. If they bid for the phrase 'vacations Turkey', then they will get visitors who want to go to Turkey and are not looking for 'Christmas Turkey'. Once the prospect has clicked through to the site, the job of the PPC engine is finished and it is up to the site design, content and promotional offers to make the conversion.

Pay for consideration

Originally introduced by Looksmart and then rapidly followed by Yahoo!, this was the standard model for directories. Basically, *pay for consideration* at a directory means: an organisation submits its URL, pays a fee and within a specified period of time, their site is viewed and a decision made whether to put it in the index. However, if they decide not to include the site in their index, the organisation does not get its money back. Yahoo! charges for the Express Inclusion service and for a profit-making organisation, this is the only way to get into the directory part of the Yahoo! index. It is important to note that only directories provide 'pay for consideration' models, as 'human editors' have the final say.

Yahoo! still charges $299 PA for the Express Inclusion service. For a profit-making organisation the key benefit is that it is the only way to get into the directory part of the Yahoo! index. It may not be a King's ransom, but whether you are a large or small company, you would rather not be throwing your search budget into a black hole. It is important to note that only directories provide 'pay for consideration' models as 'human editors' have the final say. Linkage is very important in ranking ie the number and the quality of the links that point to your site. A Yahoo! link, for instance, is a good 'authoritative' link.

Pay for inclusion

In 2000, Inktomi (now operating as part of Overture, a Yahoo! company) became the first of the crawler-based services to develop its own revenue stream via 'paid for' services. This revenue model only applies to crawler-based engines. **Pay for inclusion** means that an organisation submits their own specified URL's, pays a fee to the search engine and they guarantee that they will be included in their index, based on their terms and conditions.

At the time of writing, Yahoo! Search Marketing is the only organisation that continues to offer this type of service. Within 72 hours of payment of a fee, their Spider (YahooSlurp) will visit the site and index the pages that have been submitted guaranteeing inclusion. However this does not ensure a high ranking – and so search engine optimisation of the site is still required. If the pages are not optimised for Yahoo! and its partner sites (at the time of writing these include Alta Vista and AllTheWeb), an organisation could find that it is paying for a place which is lower in the rankings and has less chance of being viewed. The fees paid are non-refundable.

So what is the real benefit of these types of pay for inclusion services? The main benefit is the refresh rate. At one time, search engine optimisation was a painfully slow process. How well a site ranked with a search engine depended on how well its pages were optimised, but to find out how well optimised the pages were, companies had to wait for an index update. With many of the early major search engines, this could be anything between four to eight weeks, even 12 weeks was not unknown. So, if optimisation was weak and the site only appeared somewhere in the top 50 at first attempt, they would have to re-optimise the pages and then wait for another refresh/update.

At the moment, Yahoo! Search Marketing offers a 48-hour refresh rate. What this means is that if pages are weak on the first attempt, the designers only have to wait 48 hours to see if the re-optimisation works. Of course, there is also much more control over time sensitive pages, ie those promoting events, etc, or those which involve having a sale or promotion. Sometimes it may take longer to get pages out of the index than it does to get them in. Deactivating certain pages for various reasons can sometimes take between two and three refreshes before they actually disappear from the index. The good thing is, if you do want to reactivate your pages they are back in after the next refresh.

Another method of paid inclusion is known as a '**trusted feed**' and is aimed more particularly at larger e-commerce/shopping cart type sites with a large inventory, ie many products to sell which are changing on a regular basis. This is a more technical approach which requires the expertise of an XML programmer to prepare a database feed of all items which are then uploaded directly to the search engine (in this instance, Yahoo!). Once again, with trusted feed there are no guarantees of ranking or preferential treatment. The model is slightly different to PPC as it works on a fixed cost-per-click (CPC) basis. Pricing is based on tiers, eg it is more expensive per click for a visitor in adult categories such as online gambling than it is for, say, and a B2B site. Fig 6.4 illustrates the main methods for index inclusion.

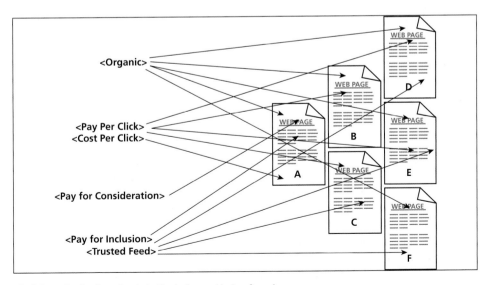

Fig 6.4 Methods of getting into the index and being found

Jupiter Research's semi-annual Search Engine Marketing (SEM) Executive Survey 2005 observes that as SEM becomes increasingly complex and advertisers' return on investment decreases, marketers must cultivate sophistication to remain successful. In the US, for instance, currently only one quarter of search marketers use sophisticated SEM tactics. Jupiter also reports that paid search will continue to grow faster than any other sector of online advertising, increasing in the US from $2.6 billion in 2004 to $5.5 billion in 2009.

A sharp increase in the average cost per click is the primary driver of this market, with incremental growth in the number of searches also driving spending. With the majority of marketers using unsophisticated bid strategies, improved measurement and increased efficiency will be necessary to maintain an effective return on investment.

6.5 How search engines work

There is a pervasive myth about search engines that when you issue a query at the search box (type in some keywords to search on), the search engine then goes out onto the web and looks for matching pages to return. However, this is not the case at all. Search engines continually crawl the web downloading millions of pages everyday to place in their own proprietary or custom databases. When a query is issued at the search engine interface, the search engine returns pages that have been indexed in its own database.

This is one of the main reasons that you get different results for the same query at different search engines. The term search engine is used generically to refer to any search service on the web, however search engines fall into two distinct categories (plus variants):

1. Crawler-based search engines

2. Human powered directories

For example, Yahoo! started as a human powered directory, not a search engine. By 2004, after working with partners such as Inktomi, Alta Vista and Google, Yahoo! launched its own crawler-based search engine to compete directly with Google. Google is a crawler-based search engine that relies wholly on technology, not human beings, to build its database. In this section we explain the difference between the two types and how they can be used effectively in your online marketing efforts.

The quest to drive highly targeted traffic to commercial web sites has become a major focus for professional online marketers. As previously mentioned, the term 'search engine' is used generically for all search services on the web. It is also interesting to note that, when we use the term with regard to true search engines (the crawlers), we talk about them as though they were all the same thing. However, even though they all use Spiders/robots to build their indexes, they all collect different information in different ways. The **algorithm** (the computer program which sorts and ranks search results) that each of the major search engines uses for ranking purposes is unique to each specific service.

Whilst the home page is important to a search engine spider, content and relevancy is critical. If the content on a site page has a much greater relevancy factor for a specific search term than a competitor's home page, the content-rich site page is the one that the search engine will return in a keyword search. It should be noted that not everyone would enter a site through the page deemed to be the 'front door', ie 'The Home Page'. Internal pages of a web site can be more potent in attracting traffic to a site than a home page, as they often have specific or more relevant content, whereas a home page is normally very general. However,

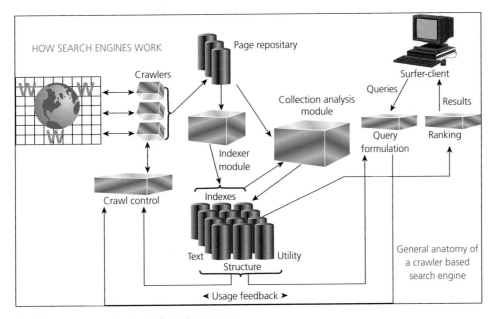

Fig 6.5 How crawler-based search engines operates
© Mike Grehan (2002)

some search engines will not crawl so deeply into a big site with many pages, so it is important to make the most relevant site pages available to search engines. Marketers need to think of the spider as a librarian gathering indexing information for the library filing system with so much information to catalogue some things may get overlooked, particularly if they are not 'flagged up' to be noticed.

On a less complicated level, search engines could simply be described as suites of computer programmes interacting and communicating with each other. Search engines in their development and research use different, or various terms for the particular components, but here we will use basic terms. These explanations and descriptions will be easier to grasp than those in more technical and scientific papers. Essentially, the anatomy of a crawler-based search engine can be broken down into the following components:

- The Crawler
- The Indexer
- The Query Handler

Search engines view the World Wide Web as a graph and use linear algebra to programme the depth or breadth of a crawl. They keep their methods for crawling and ranking web pages very much as trade secrets. Each search engine has its own unique system. Although the algorithms they use may differ from one search engine to another, there are many practical similarities in the way they build their indices.

The Crawler

Although crawling is a rapid process, conceptually a crawler is doing just the same thing as a surfer.

Browsers such as Internet Explorer or Firefox, sends HTTP requests, the most common protocol on the web, to retrieve web pages to download and show them on your computer monitor. The crawler does something similar, but downloads the data to a client (a computer program creating a repository/database interacting with other components).

- The crawler retrieves the URL
- The crawler connects to the remote server where the page is being hosted
- The crawler issues a request to retrieve the page and its textual content
- The crawler scans the links the page contains to place in a queue for further crawling.

As a crawler works on 'autopilot' and predominantly only downloads textual data, it is able to jump from one page to the next via the links it has scanned at very rapid speeds. Most of the major search engines can now download tens of millions of pages every day. Simply put, crawlers are unmanned software programs operated by the search engines that traverse the web, recording information to add to their index. Basically, they collect text and follow links. Given the schematic shown above, this may seem fairly simplistic, but in essence, this is all a crawler is doing. If you check the log files (analysis of web site activity) of a site you will frequently see names like YahooSlurp or Googlebot, respectively the names of spiders for Yahoo! and Google.

So what happens when Googlebot, for instance, visits a site?

1. The text from the <title> tag is extracted. The <title> tags on their web pages are probably the most important pieces of information an organisation can feed to a search engine spider.
2. Next the actual text from the page is stripped out of the HTML code and a note of where it appeared on the page is recorded.
3. For those search engines that use the information in <meta> tags, the keywords and description are extracted.

Note: There was a period in which only a few of the major search engines used the information contained in description and keyword <meta> tags – because they were frequently being used by spammers to try and artificially inflate their rankings. At present, they do not have the high importance that they once had (and which many people still assume) but the major search engines sometimes consider them more favourably. It is important to ensure that description and keyword meta tags are created individually for every page in your site and that they accurately reflect the content of the page on which they are placed. Creating site-wide meta tags will usually work against a site.

4. The spider then pulls out the hyperlinks and puts them into two categories: those that belong to the site (internal links) and those that do not, such as links to external sites that the pages point to.
5. External links are placed in 'crawl control' where they wait in the queue for future crawling.
6. Each page from a site that is downloaded is placed in the page repository and given an ID number.

All of this information is then returned and stored in the search engine's database. The search engine now knows what the title and the keywords are, how many internal links there are in a site (assuming a way has been provided for them to follow) and how many external links there are pointing to other sites.

The search engine also knows how many web pages from other sites in their database point back to the original. **Link analysis** is one of the most important factors taken into account when it comes to ranking pages following a query. So links are very important. It also makes sense to identify sites offering complementary services that are also likely to be of interest to your site user. Reciprocal linking arrangements can often build traffic and increase possible revenue generation. For example, a discount golf equipment outlet could link with an established tour operator specialising in golf holidays. Easyjet provides links to hotel, car hire and holiday and insurance sites. However, reciprocal arrangements need to be entered into with caution since many search engines (in particular Google) will downgrade the value of such links if there is no connection (such as through a common relevant theme) between the two pages. Also, search engines such as Google can easily identify link exchanges between whole networks of sites – so, if you are developing numerous websites (mirror sites, doorway sites) and inter-linking them simply because you have heard Google likes links and will boost your rankings – the chances are you will be doing more harm than good. At best, the rankings will suffer but you might end up being banned from Google's index altogether – and no site can afford that to happen.

It is here at the indexer and link analysis module that the process of analysing the individual page contents occurs. All of the words on each individual page are indexed and given a document ID number.

The link analysis module then looks at the surrounding connectivity of the page, ie which pages link to you and which pages do you link to. In Mini case 6.4, Andrei Broder emphasises the importance of link quality.

This information is very important to search engines and works on a similar principle as citation analysis – when one author gives credit to the work of another author in academic

Table 6.1 A simple example of how a document index is created

Doc. 1	Doc. 2	Term.	Doc.
Imagine all the people living life in peace.	Yesterday all my troubles seemed so far away.	imagine	1
		all	1
		the	1
		people	1
		living	1
		life	1
		in	1
		peace	1
		yesterday	2
		all	2
		my	2
		troubles	2
		seemed	2
		so	2
		far	2
		away	2

© Mike Grehan (2002)

Andrei Broder, Chief Scientist, Alta Vista about *web linkage* data:

'You know, what's very interesting about the web is the hyper-link environment which carries a lot of information. It tells you:

"I think this page is good" – because most people usually list good resources. Very few people would say: "Those are the worst pages I've ever seen" and put links to them on their pages.'

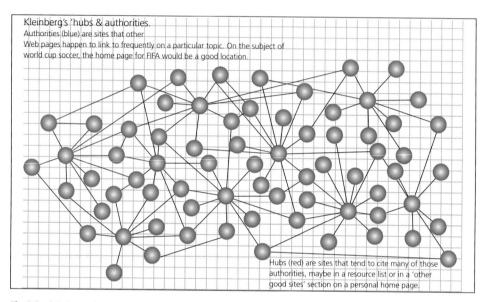

Kleinberg's 'hubs & authorities.
Authorities (blue) are sites that other
Web pages happen to link to frequently on a particular topic. On the subject of
world cup soccer, the home page for FIFA would be a good location.

Hubs (red) are sites that tend to cite many of those
authorities, maybe in a resource list or in a 'other
good sites' section on a personal home page.

Fig 6.6 Kleinbergs' hubs and authorities model
© Mike Grehan (2002)

papers, for instance. What this means is, if many pages point back to an organisation's site, then it is likely that their page may be an authority on a given subject.

Search engines refer to this process as 'hubs' and 'authorities' where 'hubs' are sites that point to many others and authorities are the pages they point to. The process is based on an algorithm developed by Professor Jon Kleinberg (www.cs.cornell.edu/home/kleinber)

Running a keyword (or key phrase) search at a search engine, it is just like running a query into a database. Based on the keyword or phrase that is input, the retrieval programme (algorithm) returns up to as many as millions of pages containing those keywords or phrases.

Examples of factors that may determine ranking:

- **Link popularity**

- Keyword weight (how many times the keyword appears on a page and where)

- How old the domain is

- How long it has been in the database?

- How fresh the content is on a web site

However, the weightings that search engines give to each of these factors has changed over time as their algorithms become more sophisticated. It is still the case that points are added or subtracted depending on the number of times a keyword phrase is repeated on pages within a site. However, search engines determine the relevancy between a search query and the keywords contained within a phrase in a more sophisticated way than simply considering keyword weight.

In fact, Google claim to consider more than 100 factors in its algorithm to determine rankings. These days Google's ranking algorithm may give more weight to the age of web sites and the pages within them, as they seek to present fresh and up-to-date (and often more relevant) content to searchers. Nowadays Google records the frequency with which (1) page content is updated; (2) new pages are added; (3) how many new links point to your web site, etc. If positive changes happen in a consistent, steady way over time, Google will reward the pages with higher rankings. If Google detects sudden spikes in these metrics, such as when the number of sites linking to a site dramatically increases, then it may assume that somebody is embarking on an aggressive link building campaign and may downgrade the rankings accordingly.

All of these and other factors that are programmed into the algorithm determine in which order of preference the results will be returned. It is very important to remember that search engines, from time-to-time, will change their ranking algorithm and therefore what scores a top 10 result today may not do so tomorrow. This is why it is so important to monitor for changes. It is also important to ensure that organisations do not rely on one single factor to help give a boost to rankings. If organisations simply rely on exchanging links to their site (perhaps because it has worked in the past) but do not continue to keep the content updated their rankings could fall rapidly. This frequently happens after Google makes a major change to its algorithm. As long as organisations grow their site in a way that is genuinely of benefit to human (as opposed to search engine spider) visitors, long-term growth in search engine traffic will be sustainable.

The query interface is where the whole thing has to come together. The average length of a query at a search engine interface is two to three words. From these three words (some of which may be 'stop' words: explained further into this chapter) the search engine has to decide from the billions of pages it has in its database which ones to return. This is where organisations have to think about the construction and optimisation of web pages.

In order for a web page to be returned in the top 20, it needs to have pages that are tightly targeted around the three words that the surfer issues on any given subject, and organisations need to have the 'link popularity' to go with it if they are to be successful. However, success is not merely about increasing the **number** of links to a site: it is, more importantly, about the quality of links received. For example, Google and other search engines look at the theme surrounding a page that links to a page on another web site. It looks at words contained within the text of that link too. If they match in some way then Google will consider the link more favourably which, in turn, will give an added boost to the rankings. Search engines know that many links are bought and influenced by distribution partners (see Fig 6.7) so it will also treat such links in a less favourable way, even if such links appear on pages that have some relevancy.

How directories work

Directories work entirely differently to the way crawler-based search engines work, even though the generic term 'search engine' is often applied to both. Directories are created as

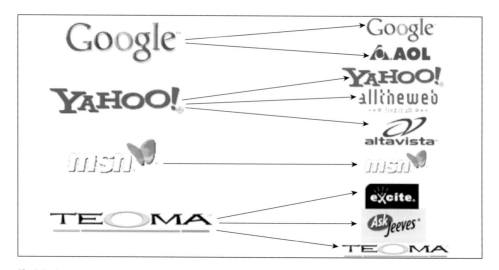

Fig 6.7 The major crawler based search engines and distribution partners

portal or destination sites, which employ people in the role of analysts or editors to review submissions.

Although very much a crawler-based service now, probably the best known of all directories is Yahoo! The company started life as a pure directory and over the years has gradually moved directly into competition with Google as a crawler-based search engine. However, they still maintain the directory area of their site. There are many more directories scattered around the web. Many of them are much smaller than Yahoo! and many tend to be far more specialised, ie company listings for vertically integrated markets that drive more tightly targeted traffic to an organisation's web site.

When beginning a link building campaign, organisations should prioritise and submit to the major directories like Yahoo! Business.com and Open Directory (DMOZ). Although a major directory like Yahoo! may be able to provide a type of 'detour' traffic from the human-edited database, directories, by virtue of the fact that they are human-powered, can never have the amount of information that a crawler-based search engine would hold in its database. At Google, you get quantity and their best attempt at quality, ie relevant results. At Yahoo! Directory you get quality, ie hand picked entries, and their best attempt at quantity. However, both crawler based search engines and human powered directories have a lot to offer each other when trying to provide the best 'user experience'. This is the reason that Yahoo! maintains its own directory and Google has partnered with Open Directory (DMOZ) to create their own directory portion or the ability to 'browse the web by category' as they phrase it. That said, as Google's spidering and indexing technology has improved, its reliance on the Open Directory has diminished dramatically. It is all about quality and relevancy to Google and so a directory powered by thousands of volunteers (as the Open Directory is), many of whom can take months to update entries, does not add value to the searchers experience in Google's eyes.

When discussing crawler-based search engines, the words 'connectivity', 'topology' and 'algorithm' are inextricably linked, but with directory services like Yahoo! and DMOZ the words 'ontology', 'taxonomy' and 'hierarchy' are those that are used most frequently. So, what do they mean? How are they applied to web search? The word ontology is most frequently used within the field of artificial intelligence. The World Wide Web Consortium (2004) state that an ontology as 'the terms used to describe and represent an area of knowledge'. Ontologies are used by people, databases, and applications that need to share domain information (a domain is just a specific subject area or area of knowledge, like medicine, tool manufacturing, real estate, automobile repair, financial management, etc). Ontologies include computer-usable definitions of basic concepts in the domain and the relationships among them (note that here and throughout the text, definition is not used in the technical sense understood by logicians). They encode knowledge in a domain and also knowledge that spans domains. In this way, they make that knowledge reusable. So what does this have to do with Yahoo!? Ontologies are often equated with taxonomic hierarchies of classes that is exactly what Yahoo! and the other major online directories are.

What do we mean by 'taxonomic' or 'taxonomy'? The word is borrowed from biology, where taxonomy is concerned with the classification of organisms into groups based on similarities of structure and origin and so forth. In essence, taxonomy is the science or practise of classification. As for hierarchy, you simply need to view the category structure at one of the major directories to see 'a system of persons or things arranged in a graded order'. To say that the Yahoo! directory is 'kind of like a worldwide yellow pages' makes it easier to understand as a concept, but it is also a bit like saying a computer word processing package like Microsoft Word, for instance, is 'a bit like a typewriter'.

Being listed in a directory in the correct category can be extremely beneficial in an organisations long term online marketing plans, as, usually, once they have their listing they are likely to be there for a very long time, unlike the crawler-based search engines where they can be in the top 20 one week and out of sight the following week.

Submitting to search engines

Initially, it was possible to go directly to a search engine web interface and simply cut and paste the URLs of all of a web site's pages into it, and then, at some point, the spider would come around and index their pages. However, this proved to be a huge problem, as search engine spammers started submitting thousands and thousands of duplicate pages in an effort to fake their way to the top.

At the time of writing search engines now rely almost totally on finding web pages via links from other web pages in their index. In order to guarantee that a site gets crawled, an organisation needs to ensure that there are links from pages that have already been indexed. However, there are many online services and many software packages that still claim to get a site into hundreds or even thousands of search engines and directories but as stated earlier in this chapter, over 90% of all traffic on the web comes from four major search engines. These are the search engines where an organisation will need to concentrate its efforts to maximise traffic to its site.

6.6 Search engine optimisation

Search engine optimisation (SEO) is the technical process of engineering (or re-engineering) web pages and gaining quality links from other web sites in an effort to acquire top positioning (or ranking as it is mainly known) on the web's major search engines and directories. Optimisation can generate quick results as highlighted in Mini case 6.5.

The Best Western Hotel marketing group significantly improved its web site visibility after working with search engine marketing specialists Spannerworks. Best Western's e-business manager, Jo Burman, commented that, 'From no visibility and low traffic volumes, we have enjoyed more than one million visitors from the major search engines in the last year (June 2004– June 2005)'.

Adapted from: Search Strategy, Direct Response, September 2005, 39–42

Until recently, it was also one of the cheapest methods of online promotion, as getting indexed with the major search engines and directories was completely free. This is still largely the case, although getting high rankings has become far more difficult. It is for this reason that many online marketers have adopted 'pay per click', 'pay for inclusion', or even 'pay for consideration' services that have been introduced by most of the major services.

This means they guarantee that within a specified period of time, an organisation's web pages will be included in their index. Even so, with these guaranteed paid-for models, they do not guarantee that any priority will be given in the index, ie if web pages are not optimised for search engines and directories, then an organisation could actually be paying to sit virtually undetectable with a very lowly ranking.

As an Internet marketing student, it is important to have basic background knowledge of the rapid growth of search engines and the development of information retrieval technology on the web. A basic operational knowledge of HTML is also required for a better understanding of web site optimisation techniques.

Meta tags and other important HTML tags

Meta tags are hidden bits of code on a web page that are not visible to the human eye, but are recognised by search engine crawlers. Many people think that meta tags are the 'magic bullet' that will get their pages to the top at search engines. In fact, this is not the case. Before we look at meta tags in more depth, we should, first of all, note what really is the most important tag in the HTML code on a web page – the <title> tag.

<title>

The title tag is the one that shows up in the blue bar at the very top of a browser in the left hand corner. Go to any correctly optimised web site and you'll see an intelligent title there. A title tag, even when intelligently thought out, composed and correctly weighted holds only the most basic information. So, why is it so important? It is a fact that all search engines pay more attention to what is in the page title.

An organisation may also want a title that appeals to a human, so it is not advisable to incorporate a string of repeated words that may not only get penalised by a search engine; it can also put off a potential visitor because it is senseless or boring. In the section 'How Search Engines Work' above, it was explained how a spider first of all pulls the text out of the title tag for indexing. When a keyword search is run through a search engine ie a search engine visitor types the word 'salmon' for instance, the first place the search engine looks is for all pages with that word in the title tag.

If a site is full of beautifully researched pages about the history of salmon fishing in Scotland, or even smoked salmon recipes, but empty title tags exist (or worse, title tags which

Fig 6.8 Meta tags
<meta name='description' content='Scottish smoked salmon and fresh salmon delivered directly to you in 24 hrs'>   <meta name='keywords' content='Scottish salmon smoked salmon fresh salmon salmon delivery'>

have nothing to do with the subject matter on the page) then the pages will sit well below the pages that do have an intelligent title tag. As search engines use the title of the web page as the link they display when they return their search results, the page really needs something that would compel a surfer to want to click through.

<meta>

Meta tags are bits of hidden text holding keywords and descriptions in the HTML code of a web pages, which are not visible to the human eye, but can be detected by search engines. These tags are placed in what is known as the <head> of the HTML document. When used carefully, certain meta tags can add some enhancement to an overall ranking with the search engines that do support them.

Search Engine Optimisers need to include the tags that give a description of their page/site and a number of relevant key words to go with it. In Fig 6.8, we give an example of what meta tags actually look like:

Repeating a single word more than a few times in a keyword meta tag is more likely to work against your ranking efforts these days. However, repeating a word such as 'salmon' a few times in a keyword meta tag is fine, provided it is used alongside other words that form a phrase that has relevancy to the content of the page. If a page, or web site does not sell Scottish salmon the phrase should be removed from the meta tags on pages where there is no mention of Scottish salmon. However, since it is likely that those searching for Scottish salmon are the target market, pages should be added, or even a new site section that compare the benefits of the offering compared to Scottish salmon. Search engine rankings will usually rise by doing so.

These are basic examples of how the **meta** keyword and description tags are constructed. Note that the meta description tag is written as close to a plain English sentence as possible because search engines that do support meta tags may use that information and place it under title tag that appears whenever a search engine delivers its results arising from a keyword search. Organisations will want the tag to provide them with extra ranking points, but at the same time they need to make sure the wording used in the tag is as appealing as possible to a potential customer in order for them to click on the listing and not one of their competitors.

Unlike most search engines Google usually shows a 'snippet' of text beneath a page title in its listings. Google attempts to show a 'snippet' of text that is most relevant to the search query. For other search engines, if a description meta tag is omitted, a search engine spider may retrieve the first hundred or so characters from the top of a page and use that instead. So if, at the top of a page, there is a copyright notice, caveat or a row of text links to the other pages on a site, then this may be what a search engine displays in its listings.

Organisations need to be careful not to repeat key words too many times or they will certainly be penalised by search engines for attempting to spam them. However, as they are not visible on the actual pages of the site, they provide a good opportunity to place the misspellings of keywords relevant to the content of a page/site. Adding what they believe to be popular search words like 'small firms', 'entrepreneurs' or anything similar to that in the meta tags will not fool search engines if these words do not appear visibly on the web page with enough density to warrant a true relevancy factor. In fact, the organisation is likely to be penalised. For a while, there was a very strong practice on the web of search engine optimisers simply copying the meta tags of a competitor's web site and placing them in their own pages in order to get the same ranking.

A number of companies have taken legal action against their competitors who have practiced this. A company could face legal action for what is deemed 'diversion of goodwill'. Unduly repeating words in meta tags will also result in penalties. How many times is too many? Only the search engines themselves decide that and their closely guarded secrets provide them with an element of product differentiation and competitive advantage.

<alt>

This tag is overlooked by many designers and developers and yet, in some cases, it can serve to give an extra push up in the rankings. The <alt> tag holds text that is used as a replacement (alternative) to images on a web page. It extremely useful for those people who 'switch off' the graphics in their browsers so they can get around the web much quicker. Instead of graphics loading into the picture 'place holders', you get text, ie 'picture of desert sunset' or whatever the image happens to be.

To spot these tags, all you need to do is hover your mouse pointer over a picture on a web page and if it has alt text, it will 'flag up' in a text box over the image. Designers and developers (quite diligently) frequently give images types of library references, like biglogo1.gif or even productshot6.jpg: many forget to add any <alt> text and those that do often just put the same description even in the <alt> tag. Some search engines do pay attention to alt text that can increase both keyword density and your relevancy factor. Try and use a sensible description of the image, but including specific keywords for that particular page.

<h1> to <h6>

These tags are are used to create page or subject headings. They work in reverse order, ie <h1> is a 'BIG' headline and <h6> is a smaller headline. They add important emphasis on certain keywords or phrases. So just as this little bit of formatting will help the words on the page 'jump out' at the visitor, in just the same way, a search engine will notice that emphasis.

As mentioned already, search engines may change their algorithm at any time and without warning so the effectiveness and structure of tags must be monitored and altered as necessary.

Fig 6.9 Example at Google (UK only) 04/10/2005.

- Type the single word 'guitars' into the search box – you will get a return of 17,500,000 pages!
- Type 'Fender guitars' and you will get it down to an easier to handle 2,410,000.
- Type 'Used Fender guitars' and you will get it down to a cosy 1,770,000.

Keywords

In the section above on meta tags, the terms 'keywords' and 'key phrases' are mentioned. Also mentioned is the importance of the <title> tag on your web pages. The right keywords in a title tag can greatly increase the chance of attaining a high ranking. Utilising the wrong keywords could mean that the target group is missed or the site appears in the millions of other pages trying to rank on the same words. People tend not to search on single words anymore, for the simple reason that too many pages get returned.

Using more specifically targeted keywords, keyword combinations or key phrases within the content of a web site can place it in a far less competitive situation.

One company could have a top 10 position and have thousands of visitors to their site. Another may have a top 10 position and very little traffic at all, simply because of the keywords they are using. One company is using the most popular, or common words. The other is using less popular words or phrases. It is easy to be inverted when it comes to the choice of keywords, particularly when companies are trying to reposition their image in a market place, or diversify into different products or geographical market places. Some companies involved in traditional industries attempt to improve their image by re-branding and introducing a whole new vocabulary into their corporate and promotional literature to make their business sound more hi-tech or interesting than it actually is.

It is essential to use the right words with the right density on the page for the search engine to give a good score. However, it is important to note that even if the keyword density was 100% perfect for the algorithm of all of the major search engines, if it is not a specific keyword or phrase that the target group are searching for it will not get traffic.

However, even if a company is described as being 'Eco-friendly, scalable, domestic waste disposal managers', with due respect to most people using a common vocabulary, you are still the dustbin men or the garbage collectors. An organisation needs to know what specific words or phrases their end users or potential customers are likely to use when they are searching for their product or service. Some of the most effective results come from forming company 'think tanks' to build keyword banks. Do desk research first, just like conventional marketing, ask people inside the business, and then people connected to the business such as existing customers and suppliers. It is advisable to check a competitor's **source code** and find out what they are using, but an organisation should only use the same if they have high-ranking pages. It is also important to consider the keywords that a competitor is *not* using. This may alert a company to a potential revenue stream.

When choosing keywords, search engine optimisers should try to avoid using precious keyword space with what are commonly known as 'stop' words. These are the words that are so common they are completely ignored by search engines. Words like *the, and, of,* and *to* are obvious ones. It is vitally important to make ensure that both 'keyword relevancy' and 'keyword proximity' is achieved to please search engines. If the keywords in the title or meta tags do not appear on the actual page itself, then they literally have no relevancy factor.

A search engine would not want to put words in places that their visitors cannot see, but not put them on the page where they could? This also causes a problem with keyword density, ie the number of times a word appears on a page, where they appear and how close together they are, sometimes referred to as **keyword stuffing**.

Sharp practice in search engine marketing

Many organisations will go to considerable lengths to achieve the objective of a top search engine ranking, often applying design and optimisation techniques that are underhand and aimed at fooling the search engine about the quality of their submission.

Doorway Pages

This type of page is designed around one specific keyword or phrase to gain a top rank on a specific word search known as doorway pages, hallway pages, hook pages, bridge, entry, jump, etc. Doorway or informational pages can sit on the organisation's own server, or on another server feeding back to them. They are more commonly known as 'informational pages' on an organisation's own server. They are highly optimised for a specific key word or words (one to three) on a specific search engine. Although effective, they are very much frowned upon by search engines.

Spamming

There are some people who seem to spend considerable time trying to figure out ways to fool search engines. Trying to find ways of manipulating a position in a search engine or driving untargeted traffic to a web site when they do not really want to be there is a pointless task. Time is better utilised getting quality content and highly optimised pages submitted correctly.

These are some of the over used 'tricks' that will get organisations into trouble with search engines when submitting pages in Fig 6.10.

Cloaked HTML

With a high scoring page, it is inevitable that someone will steal the code. In highly competitive consumer market places it is advisable for an organisation to protect their code. **Cloaking** is the only guaranteed way to do this. Cloaking is sometimes used for problem Flash sites. Although Flash technology can bring real interactivity and entertainment to a web site it is not recognised by search engines. Keywords or messages of any kind (other than title and meta tags) cannot be recorded, as the search engine spider views a Flash site, no matter how big or how much content it has, as it has nothing more than a graphic and moves on. Cloaking is used to feed the spider with a highly optimised text page and the visitor with the glossy graphics of the Flash site. However, search engines do not like this and a site caught cloaking is liable to be dropped from the search engine index completely.

Problem Pages

Although search engines use incredibly advanced search technology, in some areas they are not able to keep up with the pace of change on the web. Some web pages using high-end technology cause major problems for some search engine spiders. Sites that use Java, Flash and dynamically delivered content like Active Server Pages, Cold Fusion and even those just

---

Fig 6.10 Submission tricks

Keyword stuffing

Adding hundreds of keywords to your meta tags, comment tags or at the bottom of your pages. Spiders are trained to avoid sites where keywords are constantly repeated in an effort to get a high ranking. Where stuffing occurs, the chances of either being ignored or blacklisted are high.

Hidden text

Adding text to your pages in the same colour as your background, ie white text on a white background – not visible to the human eye but visible to spiders

Tiny text

Adding text in a tiny size font to your pages. Too much tiny text is just too much for search engines.

Refresh tags (page spoofing)

Using fast refresh tags to quickly move your visitor from one page to another. Search engine spiders can easily recognise this and you will see your site dropping in the rankings. Some Java techniques are used to avoid the HTML tag, but even when used for legitimate reasons they are still frowned on by search engines.

Pagejacking

Finding a top ranking site and literally cutting and pasting all of the code and graphics into your own page and then submitting it.

Bait and switch

You submit one highly optimised page and wait for it to rank . . . and then you pull it off the server and replace it with another page of your choice.

---

using frames, are all at risk of being ignored because search engine spiders may not understand them.

Fear of frames: Some search engine spiders have problems with web pages that are made using frames. A frames page is a similar to having a number of web pages open at the same time in your browser. The most common use of frames is to keep a navigation bar in view at all times for your visitors. It is advisable not to use frames but if necessary it is wise to use a <no frames> tag with some real content included for search engines to index. Even though <no frames> content is hidden in the HTML code, all major search engines recognise this tag to some extent and an organisation will not be penalised for its use. It is also possible also place meta tags, images, links and text inside the no frames tag.

Java gibberish: Java can add a lot of 'bells and whistles' to a site, but it also causes problems with search engine rankings. This is because 'pop-ups', scrolling text and animated 'roll-overs' fill the <head> of the document with too much text that cannot be indexed and pushes the text that can be indexed too low down the page. Important keyword-rich content should be placed as high as possible within the content of a page. One useful technique is to create a folder specifically for the Java script outside the head of the document. Any code that would normally appear in the <head> goes into a separate external .js file. This file contains all of the Java script code only – there should be no other HTML or anything else in the folder. Then only one line in the <head> of the document to is used call up the rest from the external folder. Not only does this help the search engines to find the desired content to be found and indexed but it also decreases the size of files, helping them download much more quickly.

Dynamic delivery: Until recently many search engines had difficulty sorting and ranking pages that had dynamically generated content. Such pages were considered to be search engine unfriendly and database driven sites problems had problems. Problem dynamic pages included Active Server Pages and Cold Fusion Pages amongst others. When a spider enters a site and wants to crawl deeper to determine which pages are suitable to index, if a page with a (?) in the URL is encountered, some spiders interpret this to mean that an endless permutation of URLs could end up delivering the same content. If this happens, without a clear idea of what to do next, the spider would either have stopped crawling or crashed. In the past sites that were dynamically powered tended not to get any rank at all in search engines because search engines could not index them in the first place. However, there have been major adavances in search engines' ability to index dynamic content recently. Not only are search engines able to treat dynamic content more favourably but companies that supply database driven web site software and content management systems (CMSs) have recognised the need to ensure that their clients' web sites are search engine friendly. Search engines have also developed products that help the process of indexing more dynamically generated web site content. For example, Google has a **beta** product called Google Sitemaps, an easy way to submit all URLs to the Google index. However, search engines continue to try and avoid what they call 'spider traps'.

I don't want to be in your search engine!

Where web space is set aside for development work, it is advisable that half finished pages are not available for indexing. Web traffic logs may be accessible without password protection and an organisation certainly would not want its competitors to read them. There could be a number of reasons why an organisation would not want a search engine spider to crawl certain pages of their site. One way to make sure that pages are restricted to both spiders and a human visitor is to password protect the specific pages.

It is also possible to restrict spiders by using the robots.txt protocol – a protocol that is recognised by all major search engines. For further information on 'Standard for robots exclusion' visit www.info.webcrawler.com/mak/projects/robots/norobots.html

6.7 Pay-per-click (PPC) search engine advertising

Pay per click advertising at search engines can be described most easily as follows: The placement of a small text only advert on the search results page which is triggered by a specific keyword or phrase being typed in a search box.

For example, carry out a search at Google for 'digital cameras' and look at the number of adverts that appear both above the 'organic' results and to the right hand side of the page. Now go back and do a search for 'digital camera memory' and note the different adverts that appear for that specific search. Programmes like Google AdWords provide real time advertising connections with targeted customers when they are keyword searching for a specific product on a cost per click basis. The advertiser chooses which keywords they want their ads to be linked with along with the daily budget for the campaign. The ads appear either on the right or side of the screen under 'sponsored links'. Google also provides keyword tools to help identify the similar words, phrases and synonyms that might also be targeted. Advertisers only pay when a prospect clicks through but they are getting a qualified lead. Analysis of those keywords that generate the highest click through rates (CTR) provides an indication of performance. This is because Google considers ads with a higher quality score, or high CTRs to be more relevant, and, just as with its organic listings, Google continuously strives to deliver best possible listings to searchers. Consequently Google AdWords was developed to work in a different way to Overture and Miva. Overture and Miva ads are ranked purely according to how much advertisers bid on keywords. Google AdWords, however, uses *both* maximum bid and historic CTR to determine a rank index by multiplying the two together. So, if more relevant and highly targeted ads can be devised that result in a higher CTR, ads may well appear above ads of competitors – and they may well be paying more for their clickthroughs. For example, suppose a competitor is bidding $0.20 on a keyword and you are bidding only $0.10 for the same keyword. If your historic CTR is 5% and your competitors is only 2% (because you are writing more appealing ads) then your ad will appear above theirs because ($0.10 × 5%) is greater than ($0.20 × 2%). That said, Google also adjusts the actual CPC downwards to ensure that an organisation is not paying more than necsssary to obtain a given ad position.

Google AdWords ads also appear on Google's partner sites in its Search Network which includes the likes of AOL, Ask Jeeves, price comparison site Deal Time and BT Openworld giving wider reach but to targeted, relevant markets. The key to success in using any PPC service lies in the richness of keywords themselves as well as the continuous testing of ads, such as using A/B split rotation of ads to determine which ads deliver the highest CTR. CTRs will usually be much less when keyword groups have too broad a range of keywords. It is better to ensure that keywords are grouped in such a way that each group is smaller and words within it are based on your understanding ofcustomer behaviour. Alongside Google's own keyword tools, online marketers can use the likes of Overture's keyword tool (www.inventory.overture.com) and Wordtracker (www.wordtracker.com) to track the most commonly typed in words to boost ROI.

6.8 Summary

The search engine is generally accepted as the vital vehicle for driving potential customers to web sites for the first visit. However, various studies agree that getting a listing on a major search engine is not enough and that top 10 rankings are vital for online success. Search engine positioning is of paramount importance if marketing objectives are going to be achieved.

Clearly, the overall quality of the organisation's web site will need to satisfy the ever-changing criteria set out by key search engines. Therefore, site content and links will determine not only the ranking achieved, but also whether a visitor will stay and consider the purchase. So, as has often been stated, 'Content is King!'

Marketing managers must address two fundamental problems. First, the marketing and budgetary implications of 'pay for performance' have to be thought through, with sales targets having to be re-assessed. Secondly, they must guard against the temptation of 'cloaking' and other devious tactics being applied, otherwise blacklisting by major search engines will ultimately result in online failure.

END OF CHAPTER CASE STUDY Pay-Per-Click boosts offline awareness for Kodak

Introduction

Kodak is a large multinational public company producing photographic materials and equipment. But in recent years digital cameras have become an increasingly important part of their business. Kodak UK operates three manufacturing facilities across the country in addition to its logistics control centre.

The Challenge

Christmas was approaching and Kodak set two main objectives for Christmas period:

1. Increase sales of their digital cameras and accessories
2. Increase market share in the digital camera sector.

However, discounting digital camera prices was not an option because they had to ensure this campaign did not adversely affect their strong relationship with their retail channel. Like many manufacturers, the retail channel is extremely important to Kodak and so they wanted to boost offline revenues by building awareness of the latest benefits and features of their digital cameras. Consequently Kodak's remit was to increase channel spend, recognising that for every £1 spent online, UK shoppers spend around £16 offline.

Proposal

Optimize, a leading UK search engine marketing agency, proposed a Pay per Click (PPC) campaign across all major UK PPC Providers, including Google AdWords and Yahoo! Search (formerly known as Overture) as well as other PPC service providers. The PPC campaign would have three primary goals:

1. Build brand awareness of Kodak's complete range of digital cameras.
2. Increase online sales of digital camera accessories.
3. Identify opportunities to grow the business of selling refurbished Kodak digital cameras online.

Optimize's Approach

As with all effective PPC campaigns, a tightly targeted list of keyword phrases provide the foundation for success. So, as early as the preceding summer work began on building a detailed picture of the highly competitive online digital camera market. It also involved obtaining an understanding the online search behaviour of those using search engines to research and buy digital cameras and accessories. This involved obtaining a better understanding as to how people searched at every stage of the buying cycle. The aim was to identify a list of target keyword phrases and marketing messages that could be tested throughout the pilot campaign.

A list of several thousand keyword phrases was identified. These were then categorised and, for each category of keywords, relevant ad text was developed to complement other Kodak marketing activities. Categories were either product-related (focussed around Kodak model numbers, for example), price-related (focussing on keywords that included 'buy', 'cheap', etc) or related to accessories. Once this had been done a month-long pilot campaign was launched during August.

Throughout the campaign, keyword bids were managed closely to ensure clickthrough costs were kept to a minimum. But, the most important objective of the pilot was to uncover variations in ad creative that encouraged the most clickthroughs. This was particularly important for Google since its AdWords PPC service 'rewards' advertisers who create high quality and relevant ads. AdWords treats high clickthrough rate (CTR) as a sign of relevancy, and hence high quality. Consequently, Google rewards ads with high CTRs with lower clickthrough costs and/or higher ranked ad positions (which in turn raise clickthroughs even higher). However, no campaign should be measured on clickthrough rate alone. Success can only be measured by maximising the return on investment (ROI), and the Kodak campaign was no exception.

Soon after the pilot campaign was underway, work began on identifying keywords and marketing messages that were most effective in driving the most valuable and profitable visitors to Kodak's web site. Based on these findings the campaign was optimised in preparation for the Christmas launch. This resulted in two major changes to the campaign. First, the number of target keywords phrases was more than doubled. Secondly, the segmentation of groups of keywords became much more detailed and highly targeted. Since the pilot campaign highlighted three and four-word phrases that converted well it was important to capitalise on this as longer phrases generally cost less. Also, since longer keyword phrases are much more specific they tend to convert more frequently. Lower cost-per-clicks (CPCs) and higher conversions help raise the ROI. Following on from this, most generic ad creatives such as 'Buy Digital Cameras' or even 'Buy Kodak Digital Cameras' were removed from the campaign and the creatives of hundreds of ads (many of which were new) were replaced with messages that were more focussed around their corresponding keyword group – using, for example, camera model numbers in the ad creatives.

Once all this preparatory work had been done the full campaign was launched at the beginning of November.

Searches for digital cameras are extremely popular throughout the year but in the lead up to Christmas the volume of traffic increases dramatically. During this period competition became ever fiercer. The sheer volume of visitors to the site provided an opportunity to analyse a high volume of representative data to understand which elements of the campaign were contributing most to its success. It soon became apparent that the campaign was delivering good results. Online orders for accessories and refurbished cameras were increasing and Hitwise was reporting a growth in market share of online activity. So, while the campaign continued to be optimised in the lead up to Christmas, work began on optimising the campaign for the New Year.

For the post-Christmas campaign a different approach was taken. The list of target keyword phrases was increased by a further 50% but the accompanying marketing messages were changed to place a much stronger emphasis on price. Price related keywords had a positive impact in the lead up to Christmas too but they became even more important in the New Year. In the pre-Christmas campaign some messages that helped to raise clickthrough rates emphasised guaranteed delivery dates. Such messages were less effective in the New Year campaign where typical clickthrough rates were much higher in ads that focussed on price and value.

Campaign Results

Overall the PPC campaign was a great success. The online spend for camera accessories showed a significant increase – December sales grew 51% when compared to November. Even though there were several marketing initiatives taking place in the lead up to Christmas, it was acknowledged that the PPC campaign played a significant part in this success.

The New Year sale was even more successful. Sales in January were 65% higher than the same month the year before. And despite the fact that most of Kodak's competitors were marketing aggressively during this period, the total UK online market share between September and January (as measured by Hitwise) grew by 8.8% for Kodak.

Kodak has consistently increased its market share among digital camera manufacturers. According to IDC, Kodak is the world's leading digital camera manufacturer, shipping over 4.9 million digital cameras in 2004 to surpass traditional digital camera giants, Sony (4.3 million) and Canon (3.5 million).

Case Study Questions

1. Why was testing so important in the early stages of the campaign?

2. What were the main benefits of identifying key word phrases?

3. Why do you think consumers' search behaviour changed leading up to Christmas and after the New Year?

Reproduced by kind permission of Optimize.co.uk.

DISCUSSION QUESTIONS

1. How important is search engine marketing in generating site traffic?

2. What is the difference between organic and sponsored results?

3. Choose a product that you are familiar with and develop a list of key word variations likely to be used by the target audience for that product.

4. What budgetary considerations should be taken into account when embarking on Pay-per-click campaign?

REFERENCES

Godin, S (2002) *The Big Red Fez*, Free Press, New York

Haig, M (2001) *The E-marketing Handbook*, London, Kogan Page Ltd, 61, 70

Mohammed, R et al (2002) *Internet Marketing*, McGraw Hill, New York, Higher Education, 408

Rayport, JF & Jaworski, BJ (2002) *Introduction to E-Commerce*, McGraw Hill, New York, 68

Revolution (2002) Paid for search benefits us all, 13 March 2002, 15

Revolution (2002) Search engine results are not good enough, 27 February 2002, 19

Revolution (2002) Both search engine optimisation and pay-per-click should be in mix, 6 March 2002, 38

Revolution (2002) Editors ensure search relevance, 13 March 2002, 15

Webber, S (2000) Using search engines to find business and economics information, in Bradley, P *The Business and Economy, Internet Resource Handbook*, Library Association Publishing, London, 13

Whalen, J (2002) www.rankwrite.com/linkpopularity.htm

www.makemetop.co.uk

www.Statmarket.com special report *Direct Navigation to Sites Rule, But Search Engines Remain Important*

www.jup.com/sps/research/ Search Engine Optimization, *Managing Risk in a Chaotic Market*

www.oveture.com/d/Usm/about/news/international.jhtmil

World Wide Web Consortium (2004), *OWL Web Ontology Language Use Cases and Requirements, W3C Recommendation*, 10 February 2004, www.w3.org/TR/webont-req/#onto-def

FURTHER READING

www.search-engine-book.co.uk: an e-book written by Mike Grehan, one of the contributors of *Online Marketing*. Recognised as a topical and authoritative text on search engine positioning and optimisation on both sides of the Atlantic.

www.wiley.com/legacy/compbooks/sonnenreich/history.html: Wes Sonnereich's search engine history.

Harrison, S (2002) *Mastering the PPC* (e-book).

WEB LINKS

www.w3.org/People/Berners-Lee Tim Berners Lee web site which gives a fascinating insight into the World Wide Web pioneer with archived material.

www.searchenginewatch.com the leading resource centre for everything relating to search engine positioning and optimisation hosted by SEO guru, Danny Sullivan.

www.paypemaster.com a site specialising in all aspects of pay per click search engine positioning, though most links relate to American sites, the UK does tend to follow American developments.

www.pandia.com/searchworld search engine news on web searching and search engine optimisation.

www.cadenza.org/search_engine_terms/srchad.html this site provides a detailed glossary of key search engine terms.

www.linkpopularity.com a site designed with the facility to test effective links between sites.

 Visit the Online Resource Centre which accompanies this book, for lots of interesting additional material, including self-assessment questions, internet exercises, and links for each chapter: **www.oxfordtextbooks.co.uk/orc/gay/**

Permission and Personalisation Online

7

Learning objectives

By the end of the chapter you will be able to:

- Appreciate the importance of online trust and relationships
- Evaluate how mass customisation has evolved online
- Understand the principles and practice of e-CRM
- Appreciate the philosophies of opt-in and opt-out underpinning permission based marketing
- Understand the developing model of Consensual Marketing
- Identify the different levels of 'personalisation' and their importance in online marketing
- Evaluate the technology and legislation impacting upon these developments

7.1 Introduction

This chapter addresses the underpinning online relationship models, practices and technologies that influence customer behaviour and confidence. The issues of Spam, permission and privacy are explored as international legislation is introduced to bolster fragile customer confidence. The chapter will also investigate the application of personalisation techniques as a means of developing successful individualised online interactions.

Life revolves around relationships whether it is in the workplace or our domestic and social situations. Our personal relationships are formed and dissolved through positive or negative experiences with individuals or groups. The way we communicate with close friends differs from the way we communicate with those less familiar. Knowledge, experience, understanding and trust shape the way we behave to each other and whether we are likely to develop brief or longstanding relationships. We form different degrees of loyalty based on our needs and desires.

In the world of B2C relationships, we can draw parallels about the need to know and understand customers' individual requirements, not just about products but how our entire communications exchanges impact on the association. Purchasing goods and services was less complicated three decades ago with fewer media channels and less competition. With limited choice, consumers were more loyal than they appear to be today. If a good brand experience were delivered, consumers would return with a smaller cut of the promotional budget spent on keeping them. They become 'advocates' or 'friends' of the business, but not everyone aspires to having such relationships and organisations should recognise this. Indeed, organisations may be selective and cherry pick their desired customers, eliminating others from a possible relationship.

In a changing business landscape, competition now comes from the four corners of the globe and customers are bombarded with aggressive offers. With brand loyalty being questioned, so too are the effectiveness of models such as the Marketing Mix. The legal challenges brought about by privacy, junk mail and Spam and so on has forced marketers to rethink their customer exchanges. For example, retention strategies have driven many organisations to focus on customer requirements supported database and software developments in a more customised, individual way, a way that seeks to add value to the customer experience. The emergence of **Relationship Marketing** (**RM**) as a modern philosophy and its subsequent evolution as a marketing function into **Customer Relationship Management** (**CRM**) and its digital offspring e-CRM has shifted the spotlight from hard transactional data to softer relational. This provides greater scope for the creative firm as well as challenges to win or retain profitable customers. Worryingly, many viewed this as a quick IT solution to a marketing and corporate problem. The transition over to a relational marketing approach has not been without its problems.

It should be noted that the RM, CRM and e-CRM terms can mean different things to different people, or for some people they can mean one and the same thing. We can provide simple distinctions and definitions. Relationship Marketing (RM) is a marketing philosophy aimed at developing added value experiences with customers and business partners through the effective integration of the business functions. Customer Relationship Management (CRM) is an enterprise wide business strategy focussing on the creation and retention of loyal and profitable customer relationships over the long term through the application of technology for timely and relevant communications. Electronic Customer Relationship Management (e-CRM) is the efficient handling of all customer relations by web-based methods integrated into an organisations back office systems.

By nature, the Internet provides its own unique test for marketers. Utilising an array of web metrics tools provides a rich view into online customer preferences and behaviour. The resultant data presents the chance for more tailored, relevant and timely offers in a way unimaginable *even* 10 years ago. The Internet has the potential to create a new level of customer intimacy. However, issues such as ethics and privacy mean that communications are more on the customer's terms as they grant 'permission'. Seth Godin's (1999) text on permission marketing brought new contact principles to the table. Now, new methodologies such as consensual marketing are emerging to recognise and act upon consumer preferences more effectively. Marketers must not lose sight of the Internet's two-way interactive dimension and its role in enhancing online brand building. Hopefully the 'new deal' produces benefits for customers and marketers alike. These issues will be explored during the course of this chapter. The models and concepts discussed in this chapter are interrelated and represent a paradigm shift in marketing thinking facilitated by changing technologies.

7.2 The evolution of relationship marketing and CRM

The fundamental role of marketing is the development of rewarding customer exchanges. Relationship marketing has focussed on the importance of loyalty and retention with the inclusion of customer lifetime values as a key metric. The notion of RM emerged during the nineties, mainly from the writings of the Swedish School of relationship marketers such as Gronroos and Gummesson together with Jones and Sasser (1995), Peppers and Rogers (1996) and Reichheld (1996) in America. Evolving from research into services marketing, the Swedish School believed that the old transactional marketing paradigm of the 4 P's was restrictive and had a limited shelf life in markets where customers sought added value in different ways. The expanded Marketing Mix, which incorporates People, Physical and Process dimensions, added cross-functional service delivery modes to enhance customer satisfaction. Jones and Sasser (1995) found that there was a significant correlation linking the frequency and value of repeat purchasing to the level of customer satisfaction. For example, respondents marking their satisfaction at 5 (Very satisfied) were six times more likely to buy again compared to those marking their satisfaction at 4 (satisfied) one level below. Peppers and Rogers espoused their new marketing philosophy in *The One to One Future* with more effective use of personalised promotional messages. Reichheld's research was a catalyst for many organisations to change their focus from chasing new business and instead, put the time and effort into keeping existing customers happy. He demonstrated that a 5% improvement in retention rates could improve return on investment by up to 95%. This can have a significant impact on marketing expenditure and the resultant profitability.

The plethora of seminal works in the mid-nineties brought a sea change in marketing philosophy and practice of both academics and blue chip organisations. Gone was the transactional business focus, which had dominated for decades, to be replaced by retention and loyalty strategies, based on effective customer segmentation and database marketing. This paradigm shift emphasised the importance of longer-term relationships and the lifetime values created by learning more about selected customers. Many observers consider the traditional transactional model to be past its sell by date. However, it could be argued that it may still suit some time starved modern consumers who have limited time or interest in materialism if marketers do not provide added value. O'Malley et al (1997) defines the RM philosophy as follows:

LEGAL EAGLE BOX 7.1 US Can Spam Act

The US CAN SPAM Act of 2003 (Controlling the Assault of Non-Solicited Pornography and Marketing Act) sets out key requirements for organisations sending commercial e-mails and penalties for failing to adhere to the regulations.

The four key requirements are as follows:

1. It bans false or misleading header information and requires accurate identification of the person initiating the e-mail.

2. Deceptive subject lines are prohibited. Subject lines must not mislead the recipient about the purpose, or the content of the message.

3. An e-mail opt-out mechanism must be incorporated in any outgoing e-mail messages. This allows the recipient to request ask for no further e-mails to be sent and this should be respected.

4. All commercial e-mail must be identified as an advertisement and include the organisation's physical postal address.

For a full explanation of the Act, consumers and businesses can visit the US Federal Trade Commission's web site at www.ftc.gov/bcp/conline/pubs/buspubs/canspam.htm

For *each* violation of the Act, commercial e-mailers can face fines of up to $11,000.

> Relationship marketing involves the identification, specification, initiation, maintenance and (where appropriate) dissolution of long-term relationships with key customers and other parties, through mutual exchange, fulfilment of promises and an adherence to a relationship norms in order to satisfy the objectives and enhance the experience of the parties concerned.

This definition takes us through the whole selling process from prospecting and profiling of profitable segments through the transaction process itself and beyond into online customer service, cross selling and repeat purchases. It is worth noting the importance of word-of-mouth recommendations resulting from positive customer experiences, and in the online world the power of viral marketing should not be underestimated. Interestingly, the definition also recognises that some customer relationships are not always profitable and should be terminated. However, in e-business, the reduced transaction and communication cost makes this less likely.

In the world of digital technologies, e-mail marketing emerged rapidly as a key tool in developing relationships via personalised and customised messages an ongoing dialogue. However, it has been used and abused, and in a privacy conscious world it is now constrained by legislation on both sides of the Atlantic with the CAN SPAM Act and the European Communications and Privacy Directive. Consequently, practices like permission based e-mail marketing, which were recognised three years ago as 'good practice' are now required by legislation. The Legal Eagle Box One outlines the key elements covering commercial e-mailers in the US.

Kotler et al (2001) suggest that potentially five different levels of relationships exists with customers and an understanding of these will shape the communication strategies employed. An analysis of the levels should take into account current profitability of different segments, their future potential and their propensity to respond to the organisation's campaigns. The five levels are as follows:

- Basic – this is purely transactional, with no attempt to achieve repeat business.
- Reactive – in the post purchase phase, customers are offered after sales support, but in a passive way.
- Accountable – immediately after a purchase, the organisation makes a conscious effort to get the customer's opinions on their product and service levels but usually as a one-off.
- Proactive – at this level, the organisation elicits customer opinions on products and services over a longer time period but often infrequently.

MINI CASE 7.1 Netflix.com

Netflix, established in 1999, has grown to be the world's leading internet DVD entertainment subscription service with over 3 million subscribers and $600 million of rental revenue by the end of 2004. At the heart of Netflix's success is an obsession with enhancing the customer experience via its customised technology which facilitates individual customer profiling and personal movie recommendations based on their stated preferences, likes, dislikes and rental behaviour. Its new 'Friends Network' allows members to see what their friends have watched recently as this can be a significant influence. Compared to its main competitors who generate their revenue primarily from new releases, Netflix

carries over 55,000 titles in its catalogue to satisfy the appetite of the keenest film buff. RSS feeds now alert members to new releases and catalogue additions which match their profiles.

Add to this next day free countrywide delivery, prepaid return envelopes, no due date returns, consistent innovation and a whole host of other interactive site features generates customer satisfaction levels in excess of 90%.

Sources: www.netflix.com
www.theregister.co.uk/2004/01/27/netflix_the_fly/
www.digitalenterprise.org/cases/netflix.html
www.clickz.com/news/article.php/3443651

The home page of the Netflix web site
Reproduced by kind permission of Netflix.com

- Partnership – the organisation stays extremely close to its customers, and actively encourages ongoing dialogue on all aspects of its business, as it seeks to achieve competitive advantage and superior business relationships (see Mini case 7.1).

Typically, we could expect organisations offering low-value items such as CDs, to be found at the basic and reactive level and organisations that offer higher ticket items to be present at the proactive and partnership levels. This is a sweeping generalisation, and the relationship between an organisation and its customers will depend heavily upon the philosophy and culture of the organisation and how this is reflected in its day-to-day service delivery. Relationship successes will be influenced by the organisation's orientation, be it product,

Fig 7.1 Boots Advantage card

sales or customer centric. Both product and sales oriented firms tend to be pre-occupied with the pre-sale and sale phases, and spend most of their marketing communications budget in these areas believing they have some superior product value which generates repeat purchases and customer loyalty. However, with the increasing sophistication of database marketing software, more targeted usage of loyalty and privilege discount schemes eg Tesco Clubcard and Boots Advantage (see Fig 7.1), have been employed with varying degrees of success to increase customer allegiances.

More astute companies place as much significance on the post purchase/after sales period to bond with the customer and provide a platform for future opportunities. The danger for many companies, is the fact that consumers may switch allegiance as a result of any negative experience with the company. Alternatively, companies may believe that some of their customers are loyal. But the reality is that customers may select from a pool of companies to get the best deals regardless of their positive experience with an organisation.

Two basic determinants of a customer relationship exist.

1. Whether a customer actually wants a relationship with your organisation.

2. Whether the organisation actually want a relationship with that customer.

First, it is a naive organisation that expects all customers to desire a rich ongoing dialogue and brand experience. Customers connect with organisations and have different desires and motives at different times. Many charities, for example, have sought to develop relationships, and of course increase donations with their supporters through targeted communications outlining project successes in the belief that the donors would bond more readily with the charity as they received news on how wisely their donations have been spent. However, some donors make it clear that they do not wish to receive any such communications, but they are happy to support the charity's work on an annual basis, without any further contact.

Buttle (1996), put forward five essential ingredients for the successful implementation of a relationship marketing strategy:

1. A supportive culture – this will often require a champion within the organisation if a changing culture is necessary.

2. Internal marketing – the underlying principles and implementation of relationship marketing need to be disseminated across all functions within an organisation who can influence the customer experience.

3. Understand customer expectations – this is core. An organisation must understand what is important to the customer.

4. Database sophistication – this is essential if the organisation is to provide timely and relevant to communications to carefully targeted segments, as well as providing quality customer service with information on issues such as stock availability and delivery dates.

5. Devise new organisational structures and rewards – in line with (1) and (2) culture and systems may have to change with a new cross-functional operation. New metrics may be necessary to measure a whole host of the relationship factors other than sales and profitability such as reduced attrition rates and customer satisfaction surveys.

Evans et al (2004) discuss the nature of relationships, and in particular, draws the analogy with a successful marriage whilst making reference to the works of Levitt (1983) and McCall (1966). If we consider a traditional western marriage, then we are talking about the long-term monogamous relationship, which may have to have time and effort invested in it for the mutual satisfaction of both partners. However, modern relationships are different for some people as divorce rates suggest, marriages and partnerships may perhaps be more open and people less faithful. The idea of customers being unfaithful, has concentrated the minds of marketers for many years now, as they seek to improve customer retention and loyalty.

Evans goes on to outline key components of a successful relationship that can be relevant to the online marketplace. They are as follows:

• Trust – will emanate from the organisation's ability to keep its promises on its deliverables to meet customer expectations. This became especially important in the dot.com boom for pure player companies for any future success. Trust is essentially a process with different elements (eg brand experience, satisfying customer expectations, verified payment systems, etc) varying in importance at the acquisition and retention phases. E-trust has become a key focus for academics and practitioners alike (see section 7.9 below for a more detailed discussion).

• Commitment – relationships rely on mutual commitment from both parties though the investment needed may be onerous.

• Loyalty – has been the strategic focus for many marketers during the last 10–15 years but varying degrees of loyalty exist based on measures such as lifetime values (LTV) and direct marketing segmentation and scoring tools such as RFM Analysis (Recency, Frequency and Monetary Value).

• Mutual goals – should be identified to achieve satisfaction for both parties in the exchange process. As Evans points out, the goals do not need to be same. For example, Tesco.com (www.tesco.com) aims to contribute to the profit and market share goals of Tesco plc. For the online consumer, it provides choice and convenience as part of a 24:7 lifestyle.

- Social bonds – whilst this refers primarily to personal relationships, it may be extended to the mutual interests of company and consumer. For example, the two parties may have similar interest and values with regard environmental issues.

- Structural bonds – this predominantly relates to buyer-supplier relationships. For example, a PC manufacturer may transfer specific aspects of customer support to their suppliers of printers, monitors and other peripherals.

- Adaptation – can consider the design and flexibility in organisational systems such as ordering and distribution. Are they designed for the convenience of the customer or the organisation or for mutual benefit?

- Satisfaction – both consciously or sub-consciously, consumers ask 'What's in it for me?' and satisfaction must be gained during the exchange process initially and throughout the customer lifecycle in the longer term.

- Cooperation – this can take many forms such as volunteering information such as survey participation, writing online reviews or involvement in new product development.

- Non-retrievable investments – Evans suggests that these have no worth unless there is a possibility of a longer-term relationship. Direct marketers know statistically from back data the likely length of a relationship and how much they should invest at the front end of any relationship.

- Attraction – what attracts a man to a woman, and vice versa? It can be simple and it can be complex. Business relationships can vary similarly. From a consumer's perspective, the attraction may come from the status and prestige attached to the brand, its reliability or street credibility. Online players like Amazon and eBay have benefited from the kudos from first mover advantage.

Brondo and Moore (2000) cited in Sargeant and West (2001) suggests the four main assets that are essential for relationship marketing on the web. These are:

- **Identify** consumer details such as their habits and interests by the regular capture of information.

- **Differentiate** the site content, by tailoring it to the needs of different users.

- **Interact** with customers by various methods such as writing online reviews or the ability to track orders online, for example, provide added value.

- **Customise** the product or service to meet the customer's exact requirements', which helps to build relationships, and enhance the customer experience. For example, we now take for granted the facilities to design our own personal computer or to specify the extras such as alloys and CD auto-changers we require when purchasing a car online. These elements are discussed later in this chapter.

To come back to the analogy of the western marriage – in years gone by, the gentleman would seek **permission** from his father-in-law to be, to wed his intended. This showed respect, and hopefully long-term commitment. In modern business relationships, we must also ask permission of the customer and respect them. We will also explore this as a critical issue in a later section of this chapter.

So far we have concentrated on the company/customer relationship, but Adam et al (2002) also suggest that in the modern era, the relationship management function focuses on players in the marketing logistics supply chain involved in the two-way flow information on goods and services. In the world of e-business, intermediaries and infomediaries

have formed critical alliances and partnerships. For example, the likes of World Pay (www
.worldpay.com) and Pay Pal (www.paypal.com) play a fundamental and secure role in the
authorisation of online payments and integration with store builder products. Consumers
often take such systems for granted, but they fulfil a critical role in providing reassurance,
speed and security which helps build a trusting relationship with customers. Adam's study
also recognises the importance of online customer service systems in the relationship management function. This can have a positive or negative effect on the customer experience. In
addition, organisations are moving steadily towards multi-channel customer service operations as consumers seek greater choice and flexibility.

7.3 **CRM and one-to-one marketing**

Alan Tapp (2005) observed that:

> 'CRM is important because rarely in history has so much money being spent by so many clients
> on improving their marketing. The sheer size of the budgets has concentrated the minds and
> the attention of CEOs and directors on marketing like never before.'

We could also add that rarely has one subject had so many column inches in marketing
and broader business publications devoted to it. A March 2003 article in *Marketing Direct*
begins: 'If your company's cash flow problems are getting you down, there's nothing like a
good story about the millions of pounds of company has wasted on the field CRM system to
cheer you up'. CRM does seem to have the ability to arouse very strong feelings and divide
opinion on its merits and payback. It emerged in the mid-nineties as a customer centric software application, which would manage all interactions at a time when organisations faced
increasing competition on a global basis. Typically, vendors described CRM as a strategic
business and process issue and not just as a technology solution. Undoubtedly, technology
has enabled a greater capacity for effective management of customer data but the root of
many CRM problems was the fact that many organisations had forgotten the customer!
Instead, discussions were stalled over the merits of various software applications, database
solutions and emerging e-commerce technologies. Many organisations became embroiled
in implementing the technology and more dangerously, were focussed on hitting internal
deadlines instead of improving the customer experience. The benefits of CRM will only accrue
when the technology supports the buying experience in the role of a facilitator, rather than
dictating it. CRM should be viewed as a business philosophy, and not as an IT solution. The
benefits to the organisation will of course be seen through improved customer value and
profitability. The criticisms have been levelled when systems have been purely automated or
when they have formed part of a multi-channel delivery approach.

In theory, focussing on the most profitable segments will generate increased customer
value. For many organisations, especially those in the financial sector, the Pareto 80:20 rule
identifies key customers who respond positively to individual promotions and make the cost
and effort of such campaigns worthwhile. Masters (2000) stresses the importance of these
key accounts, and how CRM can be used to nurture them. He goes on to suggest that they
can be subdivided into three key groups:

1. The most profitable current customers – we should focus on improving their customer
   experience and develop their brand loyalty, which in turn should increase their lifetime
   value and share of wallet.

2. New customers with long-term potential – having identified this group's profit potential, they should experience superior service levels so that they stay long enough with the organisation to achieve a healthy return on investment.

3. The most profitable customers in the past – even though they spend less than they have done in previous years, they remain very loyal and require little effort and investment in terms of marketing. On the ladder of loyalty they are on the top rung, and as advocates, they can be very helpful through word-of-mouth and supporting sales and marketing initiatives.

Reed (2002) emphasises that customer and prospect data has traditionally been scattered across an organisation. CRM is a recognised as the point where marketing meets technology. If we are to market more effectively, then the data held should be accessible to all. Reed suggests three options:

1. Data warehousing – which provides an integrated data storage facility across the organisation were intelligence and analytics capabilities to drill down for marketing purposes. This is high cost and high maintenance.

2. Data mart – provides similar data facilities but on a more limited scale and usually for a specific functional purpose, eg marketing. This is a cheaper alternative.

3. Database – provides local data solutions, designed for marketing purposes on a needs to know basis, with specific fields for a specific purpose. As Reed points out, they do not have to be integrated, and within an organisation various databases may exist, causing inefficiencies through duplication and resulting in customer irritation.

The one-to-one marketing philosophy of Peppers and Rogers (www.peppersandrogers.com) reinforces the concept of relationships and dialogue. The success of the philosophy relies heavily upon higher levels of customer interactions with key customers, who by nature may be the most profitable or perhaps have the most potential. One-to-one marketing is about collaboration and trust, which provide an essential platform for any relationship. Hence, the organisation must take a longer-term view of its relationship with individual customers if it is to exploit lifetime values. Mass customisation provides the ability to meet particular needs and tailor products accordingly. In markets where products have become commoditised, mass customisation delivers a degree of competitive advantage and differentiation. This can be important in the online world, where price comparison-shopping is commonplace. The knowledgeable shopkeeper of the early 1900s, is being replaced by the knowledgeable IT system of the 21st century in order to achieve the same purpose; customer satisfaction at a profit.

CRM systems give companies the opportunity to manage the customer lifecycle through every stage from prospecting to acquisition, cross selling and up selling based on customer data to develop longer, more profitable relationships. The added value is generated from the integration of front and back office systems, which handle customer queries such as product availability and despatch, with speed and accuracy. In sectors where products are fairly homogeneous, this service dimension becomes a critical from of differentiation and competitive advantage. Taking all of these different customer interactions into account means that CRM has a fundamental role to play in brand building any product or service. In Fig 7.2, Persil demonstrates how the Internet and CRM can be used to develop a relationship, way beyond the original dimension of the core product, which is to wash clothes clean. Where marketers communicate through integrated channels, the brand proposition must be delivered in a consistent fashion to ensure brand values and relationships are not undermined.

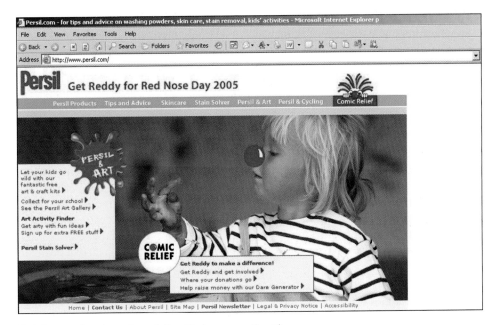

Fig 7.2 Extending the online relationship (www. persil.com)

Frederick Reichheld in his text, *The Loyalty and Effect and Loyalty Rules*, has carried out numerous studies into the impact of customer service on profitability. Reichheld observes that attitudes towards loyalty are primarily driven by the customer's perception of value. This is determined by customer experiences relating to marketing, sales, distribution and service activities. In theory, an enterprise wide CRM system, which is fully integrated, should result in improved loyalty. Reichheld devised a simple rating tool to evaluate online loyalty, based on customer recommendations. Customers are asked to rate the organisation on a scale of 0 to 10 and the percentage of customers giving a score of 6 or below are subtracted from the percentage of customers, giving a score of either 9 or 10. Getting high referral ratings requires high levels of performance across the whole range of business functions and how the customer actually perceives the performance. The service gap between customer expectations and actual performance can be significant.

7.4 Front and back office CRM systems

A multitude of CRM software solution providers have emerged in recent years such as Salesforce.com (www.salesforce.com), Siebel (www.siebel.com), E.Piphany (www.epiphany.com) and Sales Logix (www.saleslogix.com) providing on-demand, off the shelf or customised applications. Most offer online demonstrations which provide insightful viewing for students who are unfamiliar with CRM capabilities.

CRM systems have two elements to them referred to as front and back office systems, or alternatively operational and analytical CRM.

- **Front Office** systems manage the main points of direct customer contact, or what has become known as 'customer touch points' and is all about how we merge customers with products or services. 'Front office' covers three primary marketing related functions:

  1. Automated Marketing – this is primarily outbound activity with roles such as triggering automated e-mail communications, pop-up surveys and delivery or PR/Marketing materials such as white papers and newsletters. Automated marketing has involved from database marketing with the objective of understanding customers on an individual basis. Segmentation enables monitoring and modification of marketing campaigns to targeted individuals or groups.

  2. Sales Force Automation – tends to focus on outbound sales related activities. It provides efficient contact management systems in the areas of sales promotions, order entry transactions, handling account relationships and lead tracking. With more sales staff, both office based and in the field, connected via wireless laptops and various handheld devices, CRM systems provide real time information on product ranges, stock availability (linked to back office) and special offers such as the Sales Logix 'Dash Board' in Fig 7.3.

  3. CRM also offers vital support mechanisms for more effective and timely customer communications via letter, phone, e-mail or SMS. Many web sites integrate their sales and customer service activity by offering 'Call-back Services'. For example, Virgin Cars (www.virgincars.com) offer a call back service where the customer can specify when

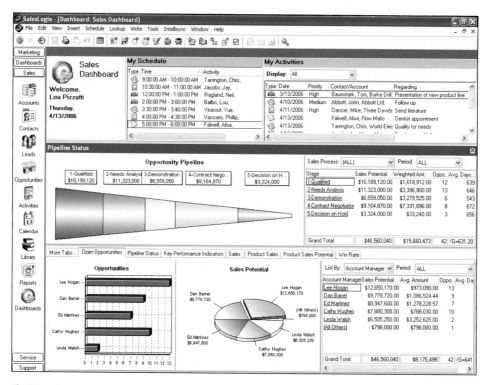

Fig 7.3 'Sales Force Automation' (www.saleslogix.com)

they want to receive a call from a sales representative. More importantly, CRM systems hold individual customer transactional and service records. This naturally provides greater confidence and empowerment for a sales person in a face-to-face situation and ultimately delivers a faster, more accurate and responsive service to the client.

4. Customer service – can support a two-way dialogue between customer and seller. The CRM customer service element has focused primarily on call centre management functions, but as more individuals and businesses have moved online the development of knowledge management and online help systems have developed a greater importance and sophistication. Customer centric support systems, or e-service as it is becoming known, provide convenient and accessible knowledge for customers removing the joys of call centre queuing. The success depends upon the quality, relevance and simplicity of the content. Organisations are seeing online self-service as a means of reducing direct contact with agents and customers. The content can vary from fairly rudimentary frequently asked questions to more sophisticated knowledge databases, which intelligently seek to answer customer queries. The data gathered on all customer interactions can be analysed to trigger appropriate communications.

- **Back office systems** – provides a repository for the collection, recording and analysis of all activities occurring via every customer touch point through the front office system. Back-office systems handle business administration processors such as accounting, invoicing and shipping information. At an analytical level, they provide business intelligence and produce regular or ad hoc reports for management on current performance and predictive reports on future trends, and opportunities. This requires effective data capture, storage, processing and report production. This may be generated at a functional or enterprise wide level.

It seems obvious and essential, that front and back office systems should be integrated. However, for many organisations setting up online this was both time-consuming and problematic because of the disparate systems that were being employed. In some cases, back-office systems were still operated manually by departments who rarely shared the customer-focused vision. Whichever way the CRM system is set up, online marketers must be sure about its analytical marketing capabilities and its functional usability. A traditional operational structure is illustrated in Fig 7.4 where there is a clear functional divide between those customer facing activities carried out by sales, marketing and customer service and the back office functions which are mainly internal in focus.

Observers of e-business merchants troubled with systems integration believed that too many were preoccupied with front end systems and focussed on the storefront design and usability issues to the detriment of back office systems. Consequently, they failed to deliver in more ways than one.

Traditionally, such structures have resorted in silos of information, with little or no linkage between functions. In addition, the structure lacks transparency throughout the supply chain, and consequently fails to provide the information desired by a modern online customer. In Fig 7.5 the enterprise wide CRM database integrates all key functional areas and provides the ability to offer top class service through all phases of the selling process.

In this integrated CRM structure, the central customer database provides a pivotal role and linkage with all customer touch points. To draw an analogy, the database is like an engine management system in a modern car which sends out information signals to ensure optimum performance, without which the car cannot function. The CRM system enables an

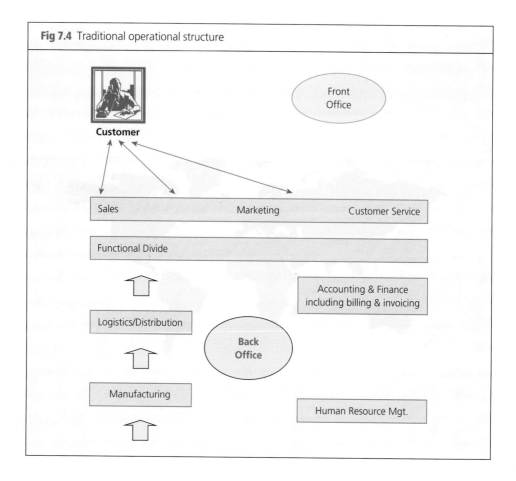

Fig 7.4 Traditional operational structure

organisation to follow changes in purchase behaviour, responses to campaigns by channel, customer complaints and credit histories, for example. Typically, it can also trigger promotional communications, which are event driven such as birthdays or annual membership renewals. However, data mining techniques provide the tools for marketers to be far more creative than this.

Openness, trust and transparency are facilitated by the system to enable successful inter-actions with external suppliers, distributors and resellers. This is critical, for example, in the area of stock replenishment when product availability is an important element of competi-tive advantage. For the customer, CRM provides value and benefits that both the pre-purchase and post purchase phases. In the pre-purchase phase, customers may ascertain the current stock levels of a particular product, held by the company, or if there are stock outs, when the new stock will arrive. Once an order has been placed, customers can then be informed when the goods will be dispatched, who the courier will be together with the likely delivery time.

In a Sistrum CRM Management Insight it was suggested that up to 35% of development time and resources can be taken up developing interfaces and points of integration between new and existing systems and their data sources, not to mention systems purchased from

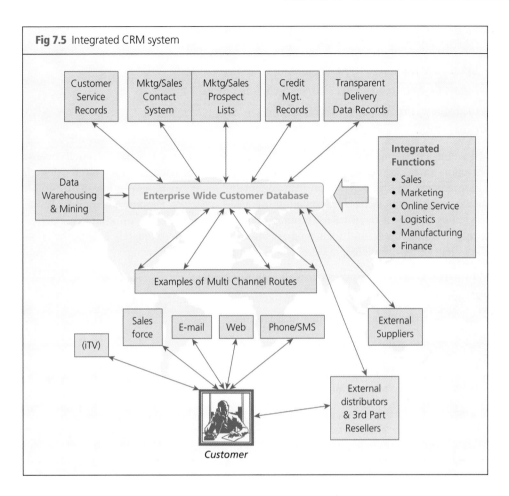

Fig 7.5 Integrated CRM system

different vendors. The problem is further compounded when organisations working with supply chain partners need to share distribution, inventory and customer transactional information. Inevitably, partner systems will not always be compatible with the host organisation's infrastructure. So integration issues can be both internal and external but the need for each system to talk to the other is critical in an information driven business. However, we must not lose sight of the practical problems of implementation, which are not just IT related but are often cultural, political and resource driven if seamless online and offline activities are to result in higher levels of customer satisfaction.

A joint White Paper produced by British Telecom and the Economist Intelligence Unit (2004) entitled, 'A Turning Point for CRM – where next for the customer focused business?' surveyed 172 senior UK executives and identified some of the major barriers to the successful implementation of CRM systems. These were as follows:

- Difficulties in capturing the right customer data (47%)
- Failure to analyse customer data properly (38%)
- Failure to integrate software and back-office systems properly (38%)

- Lack of training for people using CRM applications (34%)
- Insufficient input into CRM design from business units (31%)
- Insufficient input into CRM design from customers (27%)
- Failure to measure customer satisfaction, effectively (27%)
- Inadequate corporate networks (16%)
- Other (10%)

The problem of seeing information technology as a shortcut to success has been well covered but many of these problems revolve around the effective data capture, culture, design, measurement and implementation. Fundamentally, many organisations have failed to set themselves clear objectives when adopting CRM systems. Despite the rather dismal reflections on CRM so far, the BT/EIU report questioned the executives on what were referred to as, CRM milestones, and their progress towards them. Approximately half of the companies had either completed, or were close to completing the following:

- A single view of the customer across all points of contact
- Genuinely personalised, one-to-one marketing
- Real-time visibility on all customer interactions.

Companies had made less progress in the areas of:

- Customer sales and servicing capabilities
- Multi-channel CRM communications.

This reinforces the view of many organisations that customer service is a cost to the organisation rather than an important element in the development of relationships and brands. With regard to multi-channel technology, Bob Thompson of CRM Guru.com (www .crmguru.com) argues that the technology is still in its infancy, but the main problem lies in the fact that most companies rarely have a champion with responsibility for the whole customer experience. He suggests that executives are preoccupied with their own internal channels and silos, making integration difficult. Without a CRM flag bearer, the buy-in at board level is problematic resulting in well-documented deficiencies.

Clark et al (2002) cited in Baker (2003), put forward a number of preconditions that need to be considered and satisfied prior to commencing the implementation of a CRM strategy. In particular, they focus upon both the organisational and the customer perspective. The former is considered under the heading of Proposition Flexibility. The organisation must reflect upon its ability to customise its value proposition to the target market, especially by means of its manufacturing capability, distribution and service delivery. As Baker suggests, the core product and the complexity of its variants will influence this. This may require structural reorganisation is in the manufacturing and logistics functions to achieve business agility. The customer dimension is referred to as the Market Granularity. This considers the extent to which customers within the marketplace are comfortable with a narrow range of products or whether they are very demanding and require a diverse range. As Baker observes, this will depend whether customers have similar motivations and whether there is a high degree of heterogeneity. Whilst many writers have focussed on the technological CRM implementation, marketers also have to contend with a consumer who is wiser and more cynical towards marketing offers no matter how timely and relevant some marketers perceive them to be.

MINI CASE 7.2 Web service takes off

Who needs to use an overseas contact centre when you can solve 99% of your customers' queries online? This is the enviable position that airline, British Airways (BA) finds itself in having implemented a number of changes to its web site. Other benefits include a 60% reduction in the number of e-mails received, and an extra 3,500 hits on the booking pages of the site each week.

BA credits many of these improvements to the work it has carried out with RightNow Technologies, an online customer service specialist, which it began working with in 2001. RightNow made three best practice suggestions that have aided the improvements.

'First, a book now' button has been added to the support area of the site, which has been effective in driving sales, because customers often have a query they wish to address before booking.

The second change has been the introduction of Smart Assistant, a RightNow product that reads incoming e-mails and fires back logical solutions depending on the content of the mail before an agent even reads the mail. Nick Doran, head of global direct operations at BA says that benefits brought about by implementing Smart Assistant have been, 'astonishing', adding that the service is likely to be extended so that all incoming mails are checked by it.

The final change is to link RightNow knowledge technology across the whole of the BA Web network, meaning that customers can now search every online record to find an answer to their issue.

Source: Customer Service News, December 2004, volume 7, issue 7, 3.

Online operators possess a greater degree of flexibility now, with specialist services offered by innovative suppliers of technology. In the mini case below, we can see how the development of British Airways' web service designed by Right Now Technologies has resulted in significant self-service benefits for both customer and company.

7.5 CRM metrics – what should we measure?

As we have already pointed out, CRM has many doubters and critics, often because it has not delivered the level of ROI expected. Part of the problem is that companies have difficulty deciding what they can measure and what they needed to measure in terms of CRM metrics. CRM consultant, Bill Brendler (2004) suggests that many executives focus too heavily on measuring operational efficiencies, rather than key indicators of customer satisfaction at an individual and aggregate level. Organisations are often preoccupied with measures to influence the market to shareholders such as turnover and profit, and then at an operational level, to reflect on channel profitability, sales analysis, revenue per sale, fulfilment and back-order performance.

Naturally, these metrics are important, but they largely ignore customer behaviour by segment, individual account, acquisition or retention. Brendler argues that the real value from a CRM strategy emanates from the ability to get more out of each customer, whilst acquiring new customers without the need for large sales and marketing expenditures. Consequently, we can measure aggregated data or drill down to customers at an individual level using RFM Analysis (Recency, Frequency and Monetary Value).

CRM metrics will cover a variety of functional areas due to the enterprise-wide nature of evolving systems. However, if we focus upon, the main front office functions of automated marketing, sales force automation and customer service linked to either acquisition or retention strategies, examples of key metrics can be identified applying the following matrix (Table 7.1):

Table 7.1 Acquisition and retention activity in CRM

	Automated Marketing	Sales Force Automation	Customer Service
Acquisition	• No of new enquiries by time period • No of new customers by time period • Campaign measures against offers/incentives, etc • Banner ads • Profile(s) of respondents • Sales generated by customer, segment and total • Leaking pipe issues eg shopping cart drop-out	• Lead qualification, management and routing • Sales conversion rates by channel (e-mail, Internet, etc) • Channel integration • Quote to conversion • Sales forecasting • Pipeline management – transforming prospects into customers • Territory and account management	• No of prospects visiting site • E-mail responses to prospect questions • Cost reduction in enquiry handling • Levels of customer satisfaction
Retention	• Brand loyalty • Retention rates • Attrition rates • Performance by channel • Improvements in Lifetime Value (LTV) by customer, segment and total • Success of loyalty programmes • Visitor behaviour • E-mail deliverability	• Transaction logs • Ongoing real time – problem resolution • Ongoing real time reporting through the sales cycle • Contact history • Lead prioritisation • Integration of multi-channel campaigns	• Customer feedback • Customer queries are often best dealt with by e-mail or web self-service, fax or even letter • Incidence tracking, reporting and resolution records • Knowledge base queries – numbers/percentage leading to successful resolution • Call centre accuracy and response times • Order management performance

7.6 Permission marketing

As both the online and offline worlds are becoming increasingly cluttered with marketing messages, consumers today have become far more discerning about the messages they will choose to pay attention to. The task for marketers has been to initiate new ways of communicating with customers to cut through this clutter. The clutter is often referred to as 'interruption marketing'.

Long before words like permission, opt-in and Spam became part of our everyday online language, the distinguished UK direct marketer, Drayton Bird wrote his authoritative direct marketing text, entitled, *Commonsense Direct Marketing*. Bird suggest three simple steps to success in direct marketing:

1. Locate a prospect
2. Make that prospect a customer
3. Turn the customer into a friend

In 1999, Seth Godin introduced the concept of **Permission Marketing (PM)** in his seminal text, *Permission Marketing – Turning Strangers into Friends and Friends into Customers*, where communications messages are personal, relevant and anticipated, when the targeted customer has given permission (opted-in) to receive such messages from the sender. Godin argues that:

> 'Permission marketing encourages consumers to participate in a long-term, interactive marketing campaign in which they are rewarded in some way for paying attention to increasingly relevant messages.'

If we return to the work of Drayton Bird, we can see where the origins of relationship and permission marketing have evolved from. Online marketers are recommended to consider his general observations on direct marketing. He asks, 'What is the purpose of direct marketing?' Bird believes simply that we should aim, 'to isolate your prospects and customers as individuals and build a continuing relationship with them – to their greater benefit and you'll greater profit'. He puts forward his Three Graces of direct marketing, and we can consider the first two:

> 'First of all, when you isolate someone as an individual. This automatically implies that you discover what differentiates them from other individuals. What are their peculiar characteristics? And by speaking to them as individuals, using the knowledge you acquire about them and their relationship with you, you will be able to make appeals which are far more convincing to them. You can do this by placing that knowledge on a computer database.'

> 'The second grace: you can build a continuing relationship with these people by offering them services and products, which your knowledge of them told you are likely to appeal. This will bind them to you for a longer period. And since in most commercial activity your most expensive activity is recruiting the customer, the longer you can keep that customer, the better'.

Bird's early observations are highly relevant to Customer Relationship Management, Permission Marketing and Personalisation with the delivery of benefits (to the customer) and profits (to the company) through individual offers and communications emanating from knowledge accumulated at a personal level.

Seth Godin observes that we have limited time, and a limited attention span to soak up a plethora of on and offline communications that bombard us on a daily basis. It is extremely difficult for consumers to make informed buying decisions when faced with a raft of time sensitive offers. We also face another problem generated by the rate of new product development and increased competition, resulting in homogeneous and commoditised products. Consequently, there is little product differentiation in the market and so communications, brand and service can emerge as key differentiators. Companies have been dependent on big budgets for mass media content to get their message across but amidst the clutter this has become less effective and cannot guarantee satisfactory response rates and sales.

Godin suggests that PM provides the customer with the opportunity to volunteer to be marketed to. In traditional direct marketing terms, the customer is a hand raiser, who has signified their interest in your products or services. As a part of a multi-channel contact strategy, it is very useful to get the customer to indicate their preferred contact method (eg e-mail, phone, SMS, etc). As they have volunteered basic segmentation data and perhaps personal lifestyle data, then they are more likely to pay attention to the message being sent. If the messages are relevant, then Godin believes that this will encourage participation over the longer-term via interactive messages. The three fundamental elements for success in PM interactions are that they should be:

- **Anticipated** – eg if the customer has signed up for a weekly or monthly e-newsletter, then they *should* anticipate arrival and look forward to the content.
- **Personal** – eg the communications *should* be personalised by name, and by past behaviours (eg transactional).
- **Relevant** – the communication *should* be related to a product or service that the customer has previously expressed an interest in.

Research from Tezinde, Smith and Murphy (2002) showed that most e-mail recipients felt positive towards the concept of permission marketing and negatively towards Spam. Permission tackles privacy issues as the consumer has shown willingness in providing personal details to the organisation, and also helps with segmentation. However, the concept of permission alone is futile if the messages are not relevant to the needs of the consumer. If a company sends out more e-mails than consumers are capable of digesting, the consumer may feel the need to differentiate between opt-in e-mails and Spam. Rosenspan (2001) suggests a major problem exists with Permission Marketing in that it is usually built around the marketer's schedule, and not the consumer's. Therefore, it may have little relevance to the consumer. Potentially, this has a damaging effect, as it may affect relations between consumer and organisation and the former may resent future communications. He suggests that Permission Marketing is only the beginning of a genuine interactive marketing strategy, and that Participation Marketing is the way forward in the future. Marketers should take advantage of the opted process and find out as much as possible about the consumer. He argues that organisations should question their consumers on:

- The goods or services, they are most interested in
- The key influences in their buying criteria
- Their preferred method of contact

His guiding principles of Participation Marketing are as follows:

1. Really understand your customer
2. Encourage feedback at every opportunity
3. Involve customers as much as possible
4. Market to them on their timetable – not yours!
5. Make them feel related to your success

Distinguished American direct marketers, Ernan Roman and Scott Hornstein (2004) put forward the new philosophical and strategic process with regard to customer engagement in their practical and readable text, *Opt in Marketing*. They refer to this process as **Consensual Marketing** and it takes opt-in marketing to a higher relational level with the application of VOC (the Voice of Customer Research). Roman and Hornstein argue that the new model results from first-hand experience of increasing customer dissatisfaction with irrelevant marketing messages. The philosophy is an obvious and sensible one based on the belief that customer advice is best, an idea that many organisations appear to pay lip service to. The authors extol the virtue of a partnership between company and customer based on how the customer actually defines the value. The main vehicle for the voice of customer research has been a 45-minute long telephone interview on key aspects of the company/customer relationship for the initial data capture. However, data capture by e-mail and Internet are vital, especially as part of the retention strategy. The key questions addressed during this dialogue concern:

- Information needs
- Timing requirements
- Contact information
- Media preference and aversion issues

Roman (2003) suggests that organisations 'don't send stuff – send value'. Armed with the database populated with this information, marketers can send communications of significant value to the customer. To track changing customer habits and preferences during their work with IBM, customers received event updates every three months and provided the opportunity for them to refresh their profiles. The Internet and e-mail provided a fast and cost-efficient method for updating. In the Fig 7.6, we can see how effective the Consensual Marketing approach has been in practice:

Different levels of permission and participation exist in the relationships between the organisations and customers. It is tempting to believe that permission encourages participation, and that it will boost response rates to a degree. However, we must question the commitment of customers opting in with the simple act of signing up, and the likelihood of this resulting in increased sales and loyal relationships. How many times have you deleted an e-mail from your inbox after little or no thought? The true relationship will rely upon participation by both parties and a genuine two-way dialogue may emerge to the benefit of both parties when customers become involved with the development of new products and services. Some marketers believed that there is a need to incentivise the customer at every stage of the relationship in order to acquire, maintain and develop permission. This could be necessary as some customers are deemed to be mercenaries. However, other customers are true advocates of the organisation, and simply bonding with the brand maybe a fulfilling experience when valuable feedback from customer service questionnaires or other touch points is acknowledged and rewarded.

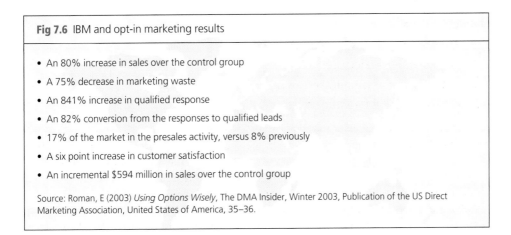

Fig 7.6 IBM and opt-in marketing results

- An 80% increase in sales over the control group
- A 75% decrease in marketing waste
- An 841% increase in qualified response
- An 82% conversion from the responses to qualified leads
- 17% of the market in the presales activity, versus 8% previously
- A six point increase in customer satisfaction
- An incremental $594 million in sales over the control group

Source: Roman, E (2003) *Using Options Wisely*, The DMA Insider, Winter 2003, Publication of the US Direct Marketing Association, United States of America, 35–36.

Ernan Roman believes that within the domain of the marketing, Permission is a single medium tactic, whereas Consensual Opt-in Permission Marketing seeks to initiate and develop a sustained dialogue with customers, which builds trust (see section 7.9), and will lift the levels of permission, making it a much more valuable marketing and corporate asset. In a short period of time, opt-in permission marketing became the standard for online marketers. Among its other benefits, PM served to focus attention on the problem of Spam, which was out of control and in danger of fatally wounding 'the killer app' (e-mail) before its potential had been realised. Direct e-mail marketing is effective for advertising to potential consumers, but the problems arise when bulk mails flood the Internet with communications that are intrusive, untargeted and sometimes abusive. If e-mail is used without much thought, most people consider it to be an ineffective marketing strategy, resulting in intrusion and privacy problems, whilst damaging customer relations. As Roman and Hornstein conclude, 'the customer experience is central to Consensual Marketing and the effective deployment of all e-media. An excellent customer experience provides compelling competitive differentiation'. However, we should recognise that the philosophy is based upon the effective integration of all media channels, and that e-mail and Internet have a vital role to play in customer interactions. It does promote a more genuine two-way dialogue, rather than permission, which in practice seems to be an excuse to capture your **e-mail address** for future promotions.

Whilst permission and opt-in marketing offers greater control for the consumer, it also provides three key motivations for organisations:

1. Marketing communications are better targeted: theoretically a win-win situation for both consumers and advertiser as the consumer gets the mail they expected and the advertiser is therefore more likely to achieve high response rates.

2. Profitability: opt-in will probably attract more profitable customers.

3. Customer databases are used effectively: CRM means building relationships and maximising the value of these. Effective opt-in and permission marketing is essential for this, ensuring customers are listened to, then providing them with what they want.

LEGAL EAGLE BOX 7.2 Opt-in regulations

The motivations for using opt-in are still relevant in 2006 but now they must also be considered alongside the regulatory framework set out in the *European Union's Privacy and Electronic Communications Directive (2003)* designed to tackle the growing problem of global spamming. The provisions of the regulations deal mainly with the sending of commercial e-mails, wireless and SMS messages together with outbound telemarketing communications. It also regulates the use of cookies, location and traffic data and publicly available directories. Under the new law, no unsolicited messages can be sent without consent and prior relationship (where the customer has opted-in). The unsolicited electronic communications can be sent without opt-in if the prior relationship fulfils three criteria:

1. Where contact details have been acquired through the sale or negotiation of a product or service.

2. Where the communication concerns similar products or services offered originally by the sender.

3. Where the individual is clearly offered the opportunity to refuse the use of their contact details for communications purposes from the time when the data is initially gathered and any future communications opportunities.

The regulation also gives an individual a permanent right to 'opt out' of receiving future unsolicited communications. An important element in this is that any sender must not try to disguise their identity and should always provide a current valid contact address. It should be noted that if an organisation is using existing lists, (contact details collected prior to 11 December 2003) then only a valid company address is needed for opt out purposes. However, it is still good practice to provide a clear opt out option rather than have customers struggle to remove themselves from a list.

MINI CASE 7.3 Euro Directive on e-mail regulations ignored

Following the introduction of the European Union's Directive on Privacy and Electronic Communications in December 2003, many UK companies are not adhering to the new opt-in regulations for e-mail marketing, according to a recent research study. Communications experts, Pitney Bowes, carried out the research into the online promotions of 50 leading companies across five consumer sectors.

Percentage of Top 50 Firms per Sector, Complying with EU e-Mail Privacy Regulations

Telecoms	66
Publishers	57
Banking	50
Insurance	46
Retail	42

Source: Pitney Bowes, May 2004.

The research specifically looked at whether the sites of these companies gave non-customers the chance to opt-in to any subsequent e-mail communications. In the survey, an average of 48% of companies failed to comply.

The new legislation puts a greater onus on organisations to maintain a higher standard of data collection and stewardship than previously existed. Nevertheless, it seems sensible only to send communications to individuals or organisations that wish to hear from you. The direct marketing industry in general has made valiant attempts to self-regulate marketing activity. It therefore seems ironic that many leading organisations are ignoring the new legislation, according to research carried out by Pitney Bowes.

7.7 Permission based e-mail marketing lists

Traditional direct marketers have always argued that the best list is the 'in-house' list. This has become increasingly important, since the introduction of the European legislation, as concerns exist about the purpose and accuracy of bought-in third-party e-mail lists. Individuals frequently changing their e-mail addresses, or moving to new Internet service providers causes another fundamental problem for e-mail marketers. As trust and privacy emerge as key consumer issues, e-mail filters and blocks are more prevalent. Consequently, e-mail deliverability is a growing area of concern if organisations cannot reach their intended target.

Online marketers must take a far more proactive approach in acquiring and maintaining e-mail contact lists in the post-EU Directive and CAN SPAM Act era. Marketers must demonstrate what value consumers will receive in return for opting in. Once permission has been obtained, all contact details, including e-mail addresses, together with communication preferences (text-based or HTML) and relevant interests should be captured. The company should also consider effectively using all customer touch points to enrich their in-house e-mail lists. This can be done offline via the phone, mail or even the humble guarantee card. Online options include incentives to opt-in such as free white papers or introductory discounted offers, for example.

Harvesting the Internet for new e-mail addresses requires greater creativity and ingenuity. Loren McDonald, at E-maillabs.com (www.emaillabs.com) suggests 28 ways to build permission based e-mail lists. These include:

• Featuring a sign-up form on each page of your website
• Adding opt-in check boxes on all demo requests, white paper and registration forms
• Including opt-in messages and check boxes on shopping cart pages
• Promoting your e-mail and newsletters in trade and consumer publications and establish credibility

Interestingly though, many of McDonald's suggestions involve offline activity to get people to sign up. This reinforces the growing importance of integrated marketing communications across channels, as consumers desire more choice and flexibility to cope with their modern lifestyles.

7.8 Personalisation, privacy and trust

These three issues are considered together in one section, as they are inextricably linked to the future of relationships in an online selling environment. All three have been responsible to a degree, for the more cautious uptake in online activity by consumers, compared to the extravagant forecasts of the late nineties. Many writers and researchers have observed that they are important and influential issues affecting online consumer relationships. Organisations may choose to ignore them, pay lip service to them or take them very seriously and devise policies and practices that respect customer concerns and needs.

In his book, *Intelligent Selling – The Art and Science of Selling Online*, Ken Burke, the US web practitioner suggests that **personalisation** is crucial for commercial success because we (consumers) have different needs and tastes, which need to be satisfied. Burke goes on to say that personalisation can make a generic web site relevant to the individual's interests. Regarding the web experience, he believes the goal of personalisation is to increase the customer experience and make that customer feel that the web site has been specifically designed for them.

Marketers, and in particular direct marketers have sought to personalise communications for decades with targeted offers and messages, eg, by using database and a mail merge to personalise sales letters. The same can be done effectively today by e-mail in a faster, more flexible and cost efficient manner. Personalisation relies heavily upon the willingness of individual consumers to volunteer increasing amounts of personal data. Online personalisation is merely utilising this information via software capabilities to segment niche markets, to enable more precise target marketing strategies primarily through the use of cookies. Whilst one-to-one marketing is becoming a possibility, the current applications focus on smaller, more definable clusters of customers based on past behaviour (eg site visits, pages viewed, products bought, etc) and key demographic/lifestyle segmentation criteria. In addition, other personalisation technologies can be applied such as collaborative filtering based on purchasing patterns of users with matched profiles. Whilst this appears to generate both fascination and results amongst buyer and seller, perhaps online marketers should ask customers direct what they want rather than rely on technology to make suggestions for them.

However, Jakob Nielsen (1998) believed that personalisation was overrated and that we should not rely on computers to second guess consumer preferences through artificial intelligence (modeling) rather than natural intelligence from consumers themselves. Nielsen

MINI CASE 7.4 Early adoption of personalisation for competitive added advantage

Tesco.com in 2000 (www.Tesco.com), were quick to recognise the convenience benefits of personalisation for their online customers. A key plank in the development of its online activities was the role played by Tesco Clubcard in gathering customer data. This was vital in shaping and informing its online activities as Tesco saw the potential for cross-selling and up-selling its range of products. To support this personalisation process, the automated shopping agent enabled them to identify what customers wanted based on previous transactions. The recording and production of tailored tick lists of grocery purchases added further convenience and provides a good example of customer centric CRM software applications that we now take for granted.

makes a critical point that consumer preferences can change frequently, and a lot of consumers do not wish to be stereotyped. Therefore personalisation strategies require consumer information and preferences to be refreshed on a frequent basis, perhaps even to reflect their changing moods. Nielsen suggest that consumers may not be willing to invest the time in setting up personalised preferences if they perceive it to be of limited value to them.

Combemale (2002) sees the personalisation of e-mails as a fundamental element in a successful e-CRM programme. He makes the basic point that personalisation provides the e-marketer with the ability to transform previously intrusive communications to those welcomed by the consumer because of their relevance and perceived value. In Fig 7.7, Combemale provides examples of personalisation in e-mail marketing.

Fig 7.7 Personalisation in e-mail marketing

Content personalisation
Vary according to database variables, depending on personal preferences.

Offers personalisation
Give different incentives to as many segments as you feel appropriate.

Permission levels personalisation
Speak to a prospect as often as they will allow you.

Format of personalisation
If they want text, AOL or HTML, give it to them in the right format.

From, to, subject fields personalisation
No restriction on what you may want to create to boost response.
   The content of each message that you can send can be individually personalised according to the information contained in your customer database. An advanced analysis will allow you to target messages accurately.
   Examples of personalisation strategies that may be considered are:

– **By spend**
Customers who have spent up to £300 in the last six months get message A; customers who have spent more than £300 get message B.

– **By product**
If behaviour profile says they buy children's books, they get offer C; if behaviour profile says, they buy rock CDs, they get offer D.

– **By interest**
If they like golf, give them message E; if they like tennis, give them message F; if they liked neither, give them message G.

Reproduced by kind permission of the Institute of Direct Marketing.

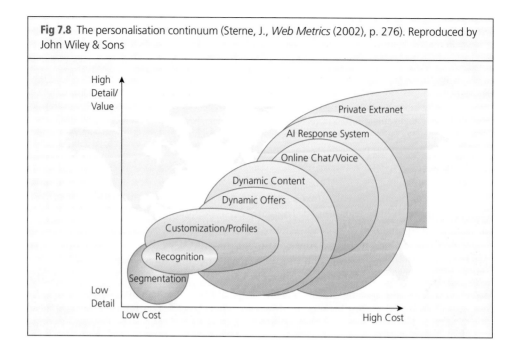

Fig 7.8 The personalisation continuum (Sterne, J., *Web Metrics* (2002), p. 276). Reproduced by John Wiley & Sons

Jim Sterne (2002) indicates the varying levels of personalisation available online in Fig 7.8. The degree of application will depend upon:

1. Perceived added value accrued by consumers from personalisation.

2. The degree of homogeneity that exists across an organisation's customer base.

3. Organisational resources to plan, implement and evaluate personalisation campaigns.

Ken Burke illustrates the development of different personalisation strategies by segment in his text, *Intelligent Selling*. In Table 7.2, Burke suggests a personalisation strategy for existing customers.

Personalisation, also provides added value for customers visiting web sites providing them with greater control, interaction or relevant offers. Increasingly sophisticated software facilitates better online relationships with improved ROI. The two Mini cases below, from Virgin Wines (Mini case 7.5) and Portland Holidays (Mini case 7.6) illustrate how personalisation can be employed effectively in the pre-purchase phase.

In the second example, the new Portland web site provides greater functionality which enables an improved personalised experience for the consumer.

The potential ROI for personalisation applications is immense but as yet is largely untapped. Soltoff (2004) cites the Jupiter Research Analyst, David Daniels who claims that in the US only 4% of e-mail marketers personalise messages even though personalisation is shown to increase response rates noticeably if other criteria other than 'name only' are applied.

Governments and trade associations have sought to influence organisational behaviour towards the protection of consumer **privacy** through legislation and good practice guidelines including ethical dimensions, especially as the press imply public paranoia about fraud and identity theft intensifies. General fears about online security and cyber crime also have a detrimental effect on e-trust. Citing one parliamentary lobby group, Will Sturgeon (2005)

Table 7.2 Personalisation strategy: previous buyers in the 25–35 age group

Site Area	Images	Kickers/Offers	Featured Product/tools	Market Goal
Home Page	Young people, mixed genders	Kicker/offer on product designed to appeal to segment	Specials and closeouts, good deals, items aimed at young professionals	Reinforce relationship, foster continued sales, increase average order size
Gateway Page	Young adults using items	Segment lead item	Seasonal category item Special 'Gateway' page for target group. Targeted cross sell items	
Product pages/ Product index pages	Targeted cross-sells	Choice of $10 off or free shipping w/minimum order	Seasonal targeted items targeted at young adult/active group	
Content pages	Put targeted content first	Offer discount on items referred to in content	Direct customers to 'Active Adults' section	
Shopping cart/ Thank you page	N/a	Free item	Offer free gift for signing up to 'Specials' email list	

Source: Burke, K (2002) *Intelligent Selling, 43*.
Reproduced by kind permission of Ken Burke.

comments that 'criminals are using computers more than crowbars'. In the same article, Philip Virgo of the European Information Society Group (EURIM) indicates that e-mail has become a vehicle for financial scams. He voices his concerns that people will avoid putting themselves at risk if they perceive the Internet to be a dangerous place to do business and more needs to be done. Jacques (2005) cites the 2005 Identity Fraud Survey Report produced by Better Business Bureau and Javelin Strategy & Research suggesting that 'Phishing' fears (see below) are out of proportion. The report suggests that by managing bank accounts done to fight cyber crime. A notorious phenomenon over the last two years has been the act of 'Phishing', which relates to identity theft or fraud. Replacing an 'f' with 'ph' is a hackers' convention going back to telephone hacking in the seventies. Phishing is a process of stealing personal data such as passwords and credit cards, by luring people to seemingly legitimate web sites and requiring verification of personal details that allows them to raid online bank accounts. The spoof sites or e-mails can be fairly sophisticated but rely on a degree of gullibility and naivety on behalf of the consumer. Opinion on the scale of the problem appears divided. A Symantec Internet Security Threat Report for the last six months of 2004 cited in South Africa's Independent Online (www.iol.co.za) suggested that 'Phishing' had increased 366% compared with the previous six months. Similar figures emerged from the Anti-Phishing Working Group with Phishing increases of 52% per month in the UK. However, a VNUNET article by Robert online provides the ability to detect fraud earlier than by normal monthly paper based statements. Most credit card fraud actually occurs offline when card details are physically copied or skimmed. Whatever the real situation is, online operators must empathise with potential negative perceptions that exist and put security systems in place for reassurance and offer practical advice for consumers. John Leyden (2005) from the

MINI CASE 7.5 Virgin's Wine Wizard

The competition in the online and mail order wine market is intense. Virgin offers over 10,000 different wines through its web site and getting the right wines and offers to the right people is essential for sales and repeat purchases. To emulate the experience and knowledge of a wine merchant, they deployed their Wine Wizard, incorporating personalisation software.

The Wizard asks online shoppers about their wine preferences so appropriate offers can be tailored. With every subsequent visit, purchases are recorded and their profiles refined further. Data analytics enable marketers to identify key profile and pur-

chased indicators, which differentiate their customers from one another. This may show significant or subtle differences in the type of customer who buys a mid ranged mixed single case compared to those buying multiple cases, for example.

Virgin can also add extra information to the customer database from other sources such as contact centre feedback and e-mails. This can be overlaid to produce a rich picture of individual customers. It has also enabled them to make the site more user-friendly and interactive, thereby improving its stickiness. For Virgin, personalisation has brought significant benefits with repeat purchases in excess of 50%.

The Virgin Wine Wizard

Reproduced by kind permission of Virgin Wines (www.virginwines.com)

online news source, The Register, highlights industry fears that identity scams and fraudsters could move on from banks and target supermarkets in the near future. Retailers like Tesco, Ocado and Sainsbury have moved swiftly to put anti-fraud strategies in place.

A Silicon article (2004) 'Agenda Setters 2004 – the battle for privacy', contrasts the focus of individuals and organisations using the Internet. It highlights, 'The ongoing battle between the struggle of the individual to keep himself to himself and those who see electronic identity as an open book.'

Here, we witness the modern consumer paradox or as Evans (2003) refers to it as the 'Privacy Paradox', in that we (consumers) are supposed to desire personalised and customised products and communications, which are both timely and relevant. To achieve this, the

MINI CASE 7.6 TUI personalises Portland website

Travel group TUI UK is planning a major CRM initiative or at Portland holidays direct brand.

The holiday group has created a web site enabling customers to access a personalised Micro site containing information tailored to their holiday. It is hoped that this will encourage customers to book their next Portland trip online.

The web site is divided into six sections: your holiday, tailor your holiday, travel details, your resort, your holiday account and useful information.

Users are able to access a range of services online, including negotiating deals on flights and accommodation, ordering taxis and maps of their destination.

UK marketing manager, Naomi Wilkinson said the company developed the initiative in response to a significant increase in Portland's online bookings.

Source: www.clickmt.com

LEGAL EAGLE BOX 7.3 Tackling online fraud

Following US proposals under the Anti Phishing Act of 2005, the UK government has moved to tackle online identity thieves in a reform of the Fraud Bill. Under the proposed legislation those found guilty of Internet crimes such as stealing personal information, copying, stealing or falsifying credit card details, could face jail sentences of up to 10 years.

According to the UK Attorney General, Lord Goldsmith, 'This reform is needed to enable prosecutors to get to grips with the increasing abuse of technology, particularly in relation to fake credit scams and personal identity theft which costs millions of pounds every year.'

organisation wants to know as much about the individual as possible. Unfortunately, the individual is becoming increasingly concerned about the use of personal data, and the intrusion into his privacy. Peppers and Rogers (2001) believe that personalisation and privacy should not conflict in a genuine relationship. They believe that privacy abuse will occur when organisations collect personal data for the sole purpose of selling what is in their current portfolio and *not* for relationship building. Patricia B Seybold (1998) suggested that privacy was not a topic that was under debate by those operating online as it was sacrosanct not to divulge customer information to third parties. If only this was true. Of course it happens, not only online but in the trading of information gathered through offline channels. More often than not, a company's approach to privacy and security is a reflection of its business philosophy and respect for its customers both on and offline. A fine example of this is Lakeland Limited (www.lakelandlimited.com), the creative kitchenware company with its home base in Windermere, who reassure customers in their calm, open and understated way that they will not pass on information to any third parties whilst being transparent about their security policies and cookies usage. The company has always prided itself on achieving high levels of customer satisfaction and trust in its traditional mail order and retail operations and this has been successfully integrated into its online business.

Privacy is increasingly demanding the attention of all stakeholders in the information society with many public and corporate initiatives and strategies emerging. The World Wide Web Consortium (www.w3.org/) through its Platform for Privacy Preferences (P3P project) is developing industry standard policies to make privacy and data gathering more transparent and understood across the international community (www.p3ptoolbox.org/guide/section1.shtml). For its part, the European Commission has been funding research into privacy and identity management through it PRIME project (Privacy and Identity Management for Europe) with the objective of empowering individuals to manage their privacy in cyberspace (www.prime-project.eu.org/) in a more safe and secure manner. The two driving principles in the project are **data minimisation** and **privacy by design** aimed at reducing the amount of personal data required for disclosure whilst building in privacy preferences. Privacy by design is gathering momentum with organisations incorporating privacy dimensions into their product and service design. For example, HP are implementing a 'Design for Privacy' initiative which recognises that some HP products or services require personal consumer information for activation such as online inkjet reordering. Based on their stated privacy preferences, customers only receive product and software information of relevance.

Respect for individual privacy and consumers' desire for choice control is beginning to be used to differentiate one company from another in the marketplace and to build brand values and customer loyalty.

Patton and Josang (2004) posit that, 'Trust is a catalyst for human cooperation'. Trust is vital for any form of exchange. It is easier to develop trust through verbal and non-verbal cues when consumers are accustomed to face-to-face interactions with sales and service representatives. Consumers also gain assurances about the product as they can touch, feel, see and taste the tangible product. Online merchants need to think differently and develop different cues and techniques to facilitate trust in the digital domain. The expected rapid adoption of online shopping in the late nineties did not materialise due to a lack of confidence and trust by consumers. This lack of faith was fuelled by two general factors. First, scare mongering from the media on issues like security, privacy and credit card fraud led many to perceive the Internet as a high risk method of shopping. The lack of online trust was a major barrier to growth. Secondly, there was a significant gap between the expected and actual online customer experience. The successful early online innovators sought to allay the fears of prospective customers by addressing these key issues and developing trust.

Trust can mean many things to many people. When we buy a product online, we enter into an agreement of trust and expectation that the organisation will deliver on its promise. However, even before consumers, part with their hard earned money, online merchants must establish credible credentials to instil confidence and reduce consumers perceived level of risk. A classic example is the existing reputation of eBay amongst the online community but it does not rest on its laurels as it seeks to overcome the concerns of new 'members' through 'eBay explained' and make online auctions and easier and less daunting experience (see Fig 7.9).

The influential US web expert, Sean Carton (2003) stresses the importance of trust for online marketers. In the Clickz.com article, 'Consumer Trust and the Internet', Carton argues that 'trust is probably the most important element in commerce and marketing. It builds relationships and expectations, reduces anxiety, paves the way for acceptance of new products, and clears communication pathways between companies and their customers. Trust is key to everything marketers do, from getting consumers to give up their credit card numbers or signing from newsletters to creating long, satisfying, loyal relationships with our customers.' With consumers becoming more security and privacy conscious, Merrilees and Fry (2003) believe that trust is a key factor in developing any company's reputation and that it is even more important in the context of e-retailing. They believe that trust can be established, where the consumer believes that an organisation will look after and respect the interests of the consumer in all its activities.

Urban (2003) suggests that trust is a process and that the tactics of developing it will differ depending upon the marketing strategy, be it acquisition or retention. He argues that potential customers will seek out elements of a website that will provide evidence or reassurance to them about the organisation's reputation and credibility, and its ability to deliver the offer. Web features such as testimonials from satisfied customers, press releases, positive media coverage, privacy and guarantee policies may all help to develop trust in the pre-purchase phase. Urban believes that the company must deliver on, or exceed customer expectations in

Fig 7.9 Explaining how eBay works

Reproduced by kind permission eBay.co.uk

the retention phase. To sustain trust, an online merchant must understand what the customer values. This could be fast, efficient ordering, unbeatable product choice, or exceptional customer service, which could differentiate the business from the competition and provide competitive advantage. These are all important functional trust elements but often trust is developed through an emotional attachment to the brand which Jenkinson refers to as 'emotional bonding'. Online consumers are less likely to purchase from an unfamiliar, small online retailer, compared to the familiar, well-established brand. Trust is often based upon experiences and maybe affected by a consumer's offline encounters and the brand's reputation.

Einwiller (2003) identifies three key trust elements for the online shopping environment:

1. Vendor trust

2. System trust

3. Self attitudes

In assessing the attributes of a trustworthy partner (the vendor) the key components are identified as their competence, predictability, benevolence, reliability and honesty.

System trust emanates from the individual's belief or perception that buying online is a safe, convenient and low-risk activity. Online trust in an organisation is determined by the individual's confidence in their own online knowledge and competence to complete transactions in an e-commerce context in a fast and convenient manner. Reputation also plays an important role in establishing online trust. The reputation can be real or perceived, often resulting from carefully coordinated and sustained marketing communications activity, and in particular public relations across a range of issues of importance to the consumer. In the online world, greater attention has been paid recently to the effects of viral and word-of-mouth (WOM) marketing. For example, despite the use of good web site design and clever copy, consumers place a high value on third-party information such as web site testimonials and customer reviews. Rumours abound that unethical web marketers have recognised this and often plant disingenuous reviews to win over prospects. However, such practices generate suspicion and may undermine consumer trust in the organisation. Building trust takes time but it can be quickly destroyed.

So what can online players do to engender trust as a means of building long-term relationships between customers and organisations? Here are some suggestions for developing online trust:

- First and foremost deliver on your promises and provide solutions to customer problems.
- Establish your credentials through your company history, philosophy, successes and awards.
- Make the web site as human as possible through images, tone, content and interaction.
- Do not be too pushy in the sales environment but provide unbiased information upon which consumers may base their decisions.
- Develop a genuine interactive dialogue where customer feedback is received and acknowledged.
- Devise clear service expectations, eg to answer e-mail enquiries within 24 hours. Failure to answer e-mail enquiries is bad practice not to mention a waste of a lead!
- Use and promote reputable third parties with their trustmark seals within your site to facilitate safe and secure online transactions (eg World Pay, PayPal and Verisign). Also display the SSL padlock for extra reassurance.
- Set out transparent pricing structures so the consumer knows the full price and will not get any unwanted surprises.
- Develop customer friendly returns and cancellations policies to provide reassurance.
- Develop partnerships/co-branding with reputable parties in your sector.

Establishing trust was very important in the early dot.com years for the growth and adoption of the Internet and it has taken on a greater importance in an increasingly privacy conscious world.

7.9 **Summary**

The Internet, and particularly e-mail, has been proclaimed as a marketer's dream tool for customer relationship building. However, just like its offline forerunner, direct mail, it has been used and abused, resulting in restrictive legislation and industry self-regulation to provide consumer protection. Permission Marketing (opt-in) has become the base level for starting online communications. Organisations are developing higher levels of permission approval from individual customers as the latter volunteer personal information and preferences. This enables, at least in theory, more effective marketing communications. In return, a customer expects added value, choice and control from the relationship with the expectation that his/her privacy and security will be safeguarded. It is difficult to develop trust online without these elements being incorporated into any e-strategy or even considered in a practical sense across all customer touch points.

END OF CHAPTER CASE STUDY A Real Ale relationship dialogue

Using CRM to connect with customers

(To protect the commercial identity of the brewery and its brand, fictitious names have been used in this case study)

The Northern cask ale brewer, Hilltop Brewery had achieved sustained growth since the 1992 Beer Orders had opened up the market for its core products. Its main product, Golden Drop had achieved a legendary status in the sector alongside brands like Marston's Pedigree and Theakston's Old Peculiar. However, Hilltop directors believe that it needed further development of Golden Drop's brand and product differentiation, if it was to achieve wider national distribution.

Like many brewers in the sector, Hilltop had healthy working relations with free-trade landlords and the companies. But Hilltop did not really know or understand the end user – the consumer. Who were they? What did they to drink, and how often, what did they like and dislike about Golden Drop and life in general? Did the profile of their consumer match the typical real ale drinker or CAMRA member? On a more fundamental level, they needed to know whether drinkers actually wanted a relationship with the brewery.

The conundrum for the Hilltop was how to gather data from the disparate target market, with whom there was no direct contact. A fundamental plank in the brand development strategy was the introduction of a customer relationship management programme. Individual breweries and the chains have often tried boosting sales through sales promotions and competitions. The Hilltop however, recognised the potential of the Internet and e-mail in developing an ongoing customer dialogue even though it did not have the capability to implement a full CRM application. At the same time, it was conscious of the potential irritation and damage to the brand caused by spamming. It had to come up with a plan that would capture the customer data needed to populate the CRM database and drive future communications in a more personalised way. With their agency, Hilltop devised a phased e-mail marketing campaign entitled 'Tipple Talk' which sought to develop their customer insight whilst building an online community for lovers of Golden Drop and the communities in which it is served.

The brewery believed that it had a loyal following of male drinkers aged 45 and over, who were a mix of B, C1 and C2 socioeconomic groupings with traditional male interests such as football, rugby and horse racing. It was hoped that the Tipple Talk programme would confirm or clarify these instincts. Hilltop felt the need to offer drinkers the opportunity to respond by either e-mail or a paper-based questionnaire. Everyone purchasing a pint of Golden Drop in a participating pub completed a brief questionnaire requesting basic contact details and permission for Hilltop to approach them within seven days by their preferred contact method. In return, each drinker was entered into a prize draw to receive free beer for one calendar month. Significantly, 67% initially expressed a preference for e-mail communications, 18% paper based communication and 15% said SMS if it was available.

Hilltop did not want to alienate its customers with a lengthy registration and questionnaire. In the first instance, they asked customers about their drinking behaviour and basic demographic information. For example:

- Which pub did they consider to be their 'local'?
- How many nights per week did they visit the pub?
- How many pints of Golden Drop did they drink per week?
- Pick three words that describe Golden Drop to them.
- Did they drink any other beers? If so which beer(s), how much and how often?
- Would they like receive more regular news about Golden Drop (eg weekly bulletins, monthly newsletters or both)
- An open dialogue box gave respondents the opportunity to provide feedback.
- How old are you?
- Where do you live (including postcode)?
- When is your birthday (opportunity for event triggered communications)?

The public houses, both managed and free houses, offering Golden Drop were the initial focus, on both sides of the bar. The brewery were conscious of the important roles played by landlords in serving Golden Drop to cask marque standards, recommending it to customers and supporting promotional activity at the sharp end of the business. Whilst it was in the interests of the landlords to support the campaign, Hilltop decided to further incentivise the promotion by entering participating establishments into a monthly prize draw after 50 or more customers had registered online. The winning landlord would have the choice of either visiting a premier sporting event of their choice all-expenses-paid OR receiving audio-visual equipment to the value of £1,500 for their pub.

The initial results of the campaign were very encouraging, with over 4,000 e-mail responses, indicating considerable brand loyalty towards Golden Drop and a strong affinity towards their local public house and its place in the community. The quality, strength and pedigree of the beer were emphasised time and time again. The high numbers, requesting regular communications with many suggesting the need to set up a Golden Drop Admiration Society, also encouraged Hilltop. Interestingly, some 16% of respondents were women.

On the back of this successful foray into CRM, Hilltop felt confident enough to ask more personal questions about how their customers spent their leisure time and what was important to them. The first edition of 'Tipple Talk' was scheduled for six weeks time, and e-mail reminders were sent in the weeks leading to the issue to build up anticipation and interest. A link through to another short questionnaire was placed in 'Tipple Talk'. In an attempt to retain high response rates, whilst boosting off trade sales of Golden Drop bottles, e-vouchers for a free bottle were sent on completion of the questionnaire. The data generated more useful customer insights:

- Their customers were slightly younger (35 yrs +) than they had previously thought.

- 57% only drank Golden Drop in establishments where it was available. 23% drank either Golden Drop or the premium guest ale on offer. Few would drink Golden Drop when they were driving because of its strength.

- People loved talking about the beer.

- Customers were more family-oriented than they had previously thought and regularly ate out.

- They were active in a number of outdoor activities (eg walking, football, rugby and golf).

- They had regular short breaks during a year within 100-mile radius of their home.

- 92% of respondents used the Internet at home, and 38% had broadband connections.

As a result of the feedback, Hilltop developed their online community based on shared interests and information. The meeting place for the community was entitled 'The Snug' to reinforce the brand's heritage and community focus. The Snug proved to be a lively forum for ideas and discussion, varying from the beer itself, comments on pubs and their landlords, pub food to issues of wider social and geographic interest.

Emanating from the information generated, Hilltop began to investigate various relationship building ideas using their web site and e-mail including:

- The formation of the Golden Drop Connoisseurs Society.

- Ongoing Golden Drop promotions linked to sporting and local events.

- Coded birthday communications with drinks and food vouchers.

- Pub of the month features.

- Targeted e-mail campaigns promoting the brewery's flagship public houses, where accommodation is available, especially those in areas of outstanding natural beauty with a 15% discount for society members.

- A central online accommodation booking service linked to individual public houses.

- Monthly competitions for the best country walk from a Hilltop public house.

- Developer links to beer related and tourist information web sites.

- An online shop selling a range of branded merchandise.

The Hilltop also wanted to develop a sense of community amongst its landlords. An intranet was created for online ordering and customer service to together with a forum to disseminate ideas and good practice. Area sales representatives have reported a positive reaction from both landlords and customers to these new relationship initiatives.

Results so far

- Beer sales have increased by 4.2% compared to the same period last year.

- 5,237 people have signed up to receive a monthly e-mail newsletter. 12% of these are from people living outside of the Hilltop territory but who have stayed in Hilltop pubs.

- 3,840 have signed up to receive the weekly news alert.

- Visits to the Hilltop web site have increased by 27%.

- Hilltop has received enquiries from national beer wholesalers.

Questions

1. How useful is this type of CRM activity for creating customer value, and brand building purposes?

2. Why was it important for Hilltop to consider different stakeholders?

3. Suggest ways in which Hilltop may segment, and target its e-mail communications.

4. Suggest ways in which Hilltop may develop its CRM activity online, what data could be collected and how it could be kept current and accurate.

DISCUSSION QUESTIONS

1. How can a web site be utilised to build loyalty and effective relationships?
2. Why is 'trust' so important in this process?
3. Is the concept of 'relationship marketing' a passing fad or a fundamental philosophy for business success in the digital world?
4. Have legal pressures driven permission marketing, or does it make good business sense?

REFERENCES

Adam, S, Muyle, R, Deans, KR & Palihawandana, D, E-Marketing in perspective: a three-country compassion of business use of the Internet, *Marketing Intelligence and Planning*, Vol 20, No 4 (2002), 248

Baker, S (2003) CRM in the context of new consumer marketing, *Interactive Marketing*, Vol 4, No 4, April/June 2003, The International Journal of the Institute of Direct Marketing, 326–327

Bird, D (1993) *Commonsense Direct Marketing* (3rd edn), Kogan Page, London, 34–35, 43

Brendeler, B & Bellemare, T (2004) *Tool Metrics vs. People Metrics*, www.crm2day.com/cgi-bin/crm-library

Brondo, HP & Moore, G (2000) *The Engaged Customer: The New Rules of Internet Direct Marketing*, Harper Business, New York

Burke, K (2002) *Intelligent Selling – The Art and Science of Selling Online*, Multimedia Live, 625 Second Street, Suite 100, Petaluma, California, US, 43

Buttle, F (1996) *Relationship Marketing – Theory and Practice*, Paul Chapman Publishing, London, 11–13

Carton, S (2003) *Consumer Trust and the Internet*, www.clickz.com/experts/ad/lead_edge/print.php/3067571

Combemale, C (2002) E-Mail, the growth of e-mail marketing, *The Interactive and Direct Marketing Guide*, The Institute of Direct Marketing's Practitioner Guide, Ch 4, 10–17

Clark, M, McDonald, M & Smith, B (2002) *Achieving Excellence in Customer Relationship Management*, Report of the Cranfield CRM Research Forum, Cranfield School of Management

Einwiller, S (2003) When reputation engenders trust: an empirical investigation in business to consumer electronic commerce, *Electronic Markets*, Vol 13, No 3, 198, Routledge, www.electronicmarkets.org

Ernest Jones, T, ((ed.) Lofthouse, G) (2004) *A Turning Point for CRM – Where Next for the Customer Focused Business?* British Telecom/Economic Intelligence Unit White Paper

Evans, M, O'Malley, L & Patterson, M (2004) *Exploring Direct and Customer Relationship Management*, Thomson Learning, London, 212–220

Godin, S (1999) *Permission Marketing – Turning Strangers into Friends and Friends into Customers*, Simon & Schuster UK Ltd, 43

Independent Online (2005) Web site phishing up 366%, 22 March 2005 www.iol.co.za/index.php?set_id=1&click_id=31&art_id=vn20050322112316129C102926

Jacques, R (2005) *Online ID Fraud Fears 'Out of Proportion*, 26 Jan 2005 www.vnunet.com/news/1160796

Jones, T & Sasser, WE Jnr (1995) Why satisfied customers defect, *Harvard Business Review*, Nov/Dec, 88–99

Leyden, J (2005) *Supermarkets Next in Line for Phishing Attacks*, 14 March 2005, www.theregister.co.uk/2005/03/14/supermarket_sweep/

Masters, T (2000) Have we lost our way? *Direct Marketing Week*, 7 November 2000, 19

McDonald, L (2004) *28 Ways to Build Permission Based E-Mail Lists*, E-maillabs.com – articles

Merrilees, B & Fry, ML (2003) E-Trust: the influence of perceived interactivity on e-retailing users, *Marketing Intelligence and Planning*, Vol 21, No 2 (2003), 127

Nielsen, J (1998) *Personalisation is Overrated*, www.useit.com/alertbox/981004.html

Patton, MA & Josang, A (2004) Technologies for trust in electronic commerce, *Electronic Commerce Research*, Vol 4, 9–21, Kluiver Academic Publishers, Netherlands

Peppers, D & Rogers, M (1996) *The One to One Future*, New York, Doubleday

Peppers, D & Rogers, M (2001) *Are Personalisation and Privacy Really at Odds? Inside 1 to 1*, www.1to1.com/PrintView.aspx?DocID=20286, 26 November 2001

Reed, D (2002) Connecting technology and marketing, *The Interactive and Direct Marketing Guide*, IDM, Middlesex, London

Reichheld, FF, *The Loyalty Effect*, Boston, Ma, Harvard Business School Press

Roman, E and Hornstein, S (2004) *Opt in Marketing – Increase Sales Exponentially with Consensual Marketing*, McGraw-Hill, United States of America

Roman, E (2003) Using options wisely, *The DMA Insider*, Winter 2003, United States of America, 31

Rosenspan, A (2001) Permission is not enough, *Interactive Marketing*, Vol 2, No 3, Jan/March 2001, IDM

Sargeant, A & West, DC (2001) *Direct and Interactive Marketing*, Oxford University Press, Oxford, England, 400–402

Silicon.com (2004) *Agenda Setters, 2004 – the Battle for Privacy*, www.siliconagendasetters.com/analysis6.htm

Sterne, J (2002) *Web Metrics*, John Wiley & Sons, New York, 276

Sturgeon, W, Silicon.com (2005) *Bring Crime Fighting into the Internet Age*, www.software.silicon.com/security/prnt.htm?TYPE=story&AT=39128918-3902465, 22 March 2005

Tapp, A (2005) *Principles of Direct and Database Marketing* (3rd edn), FT, Prentice Hall, Essex, England, 215

Tezinde, T, Smith, B and Murphy, J (2002) Getting permission: exploring factors affecting permission marketing, *Journal of Interactive Marketing*, Vol 16

FURTHER READING

Burke, K (2002) *Intelligent Selling – The Art and Science of Selling Online*, Multimedia Live, 625 Second Street, Suite 100, Petaluma, California, US – a lively and informative practitioners' guide to selling online with good chapters on different aspects of personalisation.

Newell, F, *Loyalty.com – Customer Relationship Management in the New Era of Internet Marketing* (2000) McGraw Hill International, US – visionary text applying CRM online.

Patton, MA & Josang, A, Technologies for trust in electronic commerce, *Electronic Commerce*, Vol 4, Nos 9–21 (2004) Kluiver Academic Publishers, Netherlands.

Roman, E and Hornstein, S (2004) *Opt in Marketing – Increase Sales Exponentially with Consensual Marketing*, McGraw-Hill, United States of America – extols the virtues of 'voice of customer' research beyond the permission boundaries.

WEB LINKS

www.crmguru.com – is the world's largest CRM portal.

www.dma.org.uk – offers up to date news, views and best practice on legal aspects of direct and interactive marketing.

www.E.piphany.com – web site of leading US CRM software vendor with excellent white papers and case studies.

www.1to1.com – the web site of the Peppers and Rogers Group with great content on one-to-one marketing.

www.permission.com – the web site of permission guru, Seth Godin.

www.privacylaws.com – provides excellent UK and international insight into legal issues, especially data protection.

 Visit the Online Resource Centre which accompanies this book, for lots of interesting additional material, including self-assessment questions, internet exercises, and links for each chapter: **www.oxfordtextbooks.co.uk/orc/gay/**

8 Web Site Development, Design and Content

Learning objectives

By the end of the chapter you will be able to:

- Recognise the various models for trading online
- Understand the role of portals and community web sites in the commercial web presence
- Appreciate the importance of setting marketing objectives for web sites
- Understand how a web site is developed
- Critically evaluate best practice in web site design
- Recognise the difference between web site copy and content
- Recognise best practice in copy and content development

Chapter-at-a-glance

8.1 Introduction

This chapter considers various elements of the commercial web presence. It is not intended as a narrative on web site design per se, but rather a study of those elements which combine to make a successful web site. The study is made from the point of view of the customer who uses the web site. Web site design should be customer-led and consideration is given to how the organisation publishing the site can achieve its online objectives. Various interactive features may stimulate the customer such as ease of navigation and product choice but marketers must also incorporate elements that engender trust, privacy and security as these constantly emerge as key consumer issues.

There are some aspects of the organisation that will have a disproportionate influence on their customers' perception, and the phrase 'you are your web site' is particularly apt. A poor web site does not necessarily equal a poor company, but that could well be the perception of potential customers for whom the web site is the first experience of the organisation. We also consider how the organisation can best use its web presence to not only develop its brand, but how to stand out from the millions of competitor web pages and get a return on investment whilst delivering a great experience and offering better value than the competition. As Nielsen (2000) argued, 'with about 10 million sites on the Web in January 2000 (and 25 million by the end of the year, and a hundred million by 2002), users have more choice than ever. Why should they waste their time on anything that is confusing, slow or that doesn't satisfy their needs?' Huang and Christopher (2003) suggest that web designers must understand the key stages and influences in the purchase decision if they are to design an effective e-commerce application.

Many references cited come from publications around the turn of the century. There is a reason for this. The late nineties saw the development of the Internet for commercial use and during this time there was experimentation from those seeking benefits from the new medium. It was also the period when graphic designers and programmers wielded an unhealthy influence over web site development, with a concentration on technology itself rather than its effective use. The failure of so many dot.com companies at the end of the nineties helped focus attention on what actually works online from a business perspective. Practitioners began to publish the results of empirical experiences and, to a lesser extent, academics began to publish theoretical research. That few writers, practitioners or academics, have subsequently produced little that either significantly adds or contradicts the basic concepts and models from this period owes more to the quality of those publications than the lack of research and/or publications since.

8.2 The commercial web presence

The commercial web presence considers the online offerings of businesses, not-for-profit organisations, or public institutions. Whilst much of the content is relevant to other web sites, family or hobby sites for example, the emphasis is on those sites seeking a return on investment. Its development will be determined by its strategic and tactical use by the marketer.

Cripps (2002) suggested five basic site typologies:

1. **Brochurewear** – typical of many early sites that transferred information eg catalogues, from offline to online, and were static in nature. They have matured in many cases to customer friendly interfaces.

2. **Transactional** – sites whose main function is revenue generation. Cripps cites Amazon as a prime example of this typology and illustrates from a design perspective its use of a three-column grid model. The focus is the content in the centre column supported by various tools and customer cues on the outside.

3. **Entertainment** – a diverse range of online broadcast media exists and is typified by their interactive nature for consumers' entertainment and participation. For example, YouTube (www.youtube.com) offers a place to engage in new ways of video viewing and sharing.

4. **Community/Portal Websites** – meets the needs of special interest or hobby groups (see section 8.3 below). Many pop groups, such as The Red Hot Chilli Peppers have used the Internet to establish an online community to develop their fan base.

5. **Relationship** – in its truest sense, this refers to relationship building sites such as Friends Reunited (www.friendsreunited.co.uk) and Where Are You Now? (www.wayn.com). However the interactive and informative nature of the Internet has enabled commercial sites to build their customer relationships more effectively through relevant content, advice, customisation and personalisation whilst building the brand. For example, companies selling pet insurance, often provide useful pet health, travel tips and links to specific sites such as The Kennel Club in addition to policy information. Pop groups and bands such as Snow Patrol referred to in chapter 1 (Fig 1.9), have also utilised the Internet and developed their own web sites to build stronger relationships with their fan base with the latest news, tour dates, individual profiles, merchandising and other features.

US Internet pioneer, Ken Burke (2002), suggests that the purpose of an e-commerce site is to build a good relationship with your customer so they choose to buy from you, and 'everything your website does should have the sole aim of "wrapping your arms" around your customers, anticipating their needs, providing the products and information they want, and addressing their concerns in a respectful, thoughtful fashion.' So rather than being purely transactional, customer focussed web design provides the opportunity to develop meaningful consumer relationships through improved functionality.

No web site can be successfully developed without clear organisational objectives for the web presence. According to Young (1999) 'There are probably as many different reasons for wanting to publish a site on the Web as there are Web sites'. In section 8.3 we will consider key web site objectives.

Online trading business models

The different forms of web presence listed above summarise the ways in which on and offline business can use the web as part of the organisation's overall strategic aims. For the pure players, the web site is their business and so the development and maintenance of that site becomes fundamental to their existence. In chapter 2, we outlined a number of ways in which an online-only business can make money such as those outlined by Paul Timmers (1999). These include e-shops, e-mall, e-procurement, information brokers and third party marketplaces. Such models typically seek to generate multiple revenue streams via sales, advertising, subscriptions and commission.

The subsequent acceptance of the Internet by the businesses community has resulted in some aspects of the models being adopted by offline business. For example many '**bricks and mortar**' retailers now trade online as well (e-shops model) and some newspapers allow access to their online content through subscription (subscription model) or registration (information brokerage model).

Portals and community web sites

Whilst the development of portals and community web sites are normally an aspect of an online business models in themselves (ie to generate advertising or infomediary income), they can be used by businesses as part of their online presence.

What is recognised as a portal has changed over the years. Portals were initially seen as the 'home' or 'entry' page for users, the page that first appears when the user opens a browser on their PC. In its truest sense, this page then becomes the user's portal (dictionary definition; entrance, gateway or access to a place) to the World Wide Web. As the web developed, the term portal has been applied in many contexts. Although still operating as portals, many web sites act as gateways to limited information rather than the entire web. As the subject content of these 'sub-portals' is finite, they attract specific interest individuals and/or groups (a geographic location, sport, or hobby for example) and develop into online communities. Organisations quickly realised the potential of these virtual communities. Creating a direct dialogue with customers could not only help maintain loyalty (Armstrong and Hagel, 1996), but also if commercial portal/community providers could create a 'club' mentality amongst customers, it could become a new source of competitive advantage. The two most common types of portal are those of providers (eg AOL) and shopping (eg Kelkoo). These portals are businesses in their own right, but there are other categories that organisations can develop to attract potential customers. These include:

- **Geographic portals** – where the product or service has a geographic association. A bed and breakfast or independent hotel might include, as part of its web site, descriptions of, and links to, all the attractions the locale might have to offer.

- **Special interest portals** – normally associated with a sport, hobby, or pastime. Such sites could be product related. A grass seed vendor might host a web site on lawn care that could develop into an online community, with users (or members) asking questions, raising issues, or providing solutions to others' problems. Such is the nature of these sites that users have been described as partaking in the practice of 'social networking'. The portal and portal provider do not have to share a product category. An example is that of Kingfisher team F1 (see Mini case 8.1). Such commercial online communities rely on the intrinsic connection that members feel toward one another and difference from others not in the community (Muniz and O'Guinn, 2001). As with geographic portals, such sites can be presented as if they are sponsored by the selling organization, rather than published by them.

- **Information portals** – commonly used in B2B trading, such portals attract workers in specific industries or users of certain products (see Mini case 8.2). Taken out of a direct competition environment, it is not unusual for businesses to be willing to offer help to other businesses. This is particularly true with owners and managers of the small to medium enterprise (SME). Like many individual consumers, managers like to feel they are one of a crowd, facing shared problems, but often working in isolation. Offline, this issue is addressed with networking meetings, conventions and industry associations. Online there are B2B information portals. Often set up by market leaders in their given industry,

MINI CASE 8.1 Kingfisher Team F1

Kingfisher is India's largest selling beer with some 40% market share. Although India has a number of legal restrictions on the advertising of alcohol, Kingfisher has cleverly used other elements of the promotional mix to become widely associated with sporting activities such as cricket, football and horse racing.

In 2002 Kingfisher decided to develop a branded community on the increasing popularity in India for Formula One (F1) racing. 'Kingfisher Team F1' was to be a community of beer drinkers who shared a passion for F1.

Original recruitment was by a team of 'promotion executives' who visited pubs where the enthusiasts gathered to watch F1 races on big screen TVs. The recruitment team approached race watchers who were drinking Kingfisher beer and explained what the club was and took details of interested parties – including e-mail addresses. All contact from there on in would be on the Internet.

Using the tag line 'If F1 is your religion . . . get baptized!', the first e-mail gave details of the advantages of becoming a member of the club and how to join. A second e-mail to those who opened the original but did not take up the offer was more aggressive in its sale pitch, using a headline 'BEER AND RACING BENEFITS'. Recipients who responded to this e-mail brought the overall take-up rate to 87%. The total of 4,200 members was close to double the original target of the Kingfisher marketing team.

Building a membership of a 'community' is one thing, keeping it is another. To this end, Kingfisher created a fortnightly newsletter – 'Irregular Pulse'. This offered fairly standard fare: news, driver profiles, car specifications and computer wallpaper downloads. Most popular though – and hardly surprising given the target segment profile – was the 'Pit Babes' section.

In the week leading up to a weekend race day, Kingfisher Team F1 members received e-mails with a race preview, circuit information and a very popular 'predict the pole positions' competition. This was followed up by another e-mail on the Friday before the race with information on where the race could be viewed and what benefits awaited members at the various pubs. The day after the race e-mails with comprehensive post-race details and analysis went out.

Offline activities included (obviously) the encouragement of members to interact in the pubs at the time of the race, but also activities such as go carting events during the F1 off-season.

MINI CASE 8.2 A discipline specific portal helps professionals in multiple industries

The portal site of Strategiy.com (www.strategiy.com), launched in April 2004, is a dedicated marketing, advertising and media portal for the Middle East. Marketing and advertising professionals in industries such as FMCG, airlines, banking, consumer electronics, IT, automobiles, foods and beverages as well as media and ad agencies are encouraged to access the free portal. Content includes; latest news; discussion forums; agency databases; latest marketing campaigns, exhibitions, and events calendar; interviews and features on Middle East business leaders; appointments and recruitment services.

The home page of Strategiy.com (www.strategiy.com)

these portals must operate as independent entities to maintain their credibility. Cisco Systems set up this kind of portal. In its early days, they included on its web site a 'technical questions' section. Cisco's customers were encouraged to offer advice to their fellow consumers. Its impact was two-fold; it helped Cisco develop a community spirit amongst its customers, and reduced the investment needed for its customer support provision.

8.3 Web site development

As a medium, the Internet has expanded far more quickly than any other in history and as a result web site development has had a steep learning curve. Not only did the developers have to struggle with how best to utilise the new technology in business terms, but also that technology was advancing on an almost daily basis. There was an even greater impediment to the development of successful business applications for the Internet – the issue of whom in the organisation 'owned' and championed the organisation's web presence. It does require much more of team approach than imagined with various marketing, IT, finance, logistics and customer services involved in the final design and implementation.

IT vs marketing vs amateurs

Early commercial web site development was accessed on computers and the Internet was seen by the Information Technology (IT) departments as being their responsibility, their 'property' even. In the main, management was happy to let them take it. This created problems as the Internet is a medium used to market the organisation. For the new online only businesses, it was not only the primary method of marketing, but also the only way of conducting transactions. Herein lies the problem. Although there were some notable exceptions, people trained in IT (be that systems engineering, programming, networking, software, or **graphic design**) often had limited business or marketing skills, knowledge or training. As a result, web sites were designed with only limited consideration for their audience.

The main reason management was comfortable with IT taking responsibility for the organisation's web site was that few had IT and computing expertise. The situation has improved but things are still far from perfect. A study into Internet campaign effectiveness published in 2005 by SciVisum (www.scivisum.co.uk) revealed that 26% of marketing departments fail to alert IT departments about impending campaigns. This lack of communication was partially to blame for 73% of the same survey's sample organisations experiencing web site failures during online marketing campaigns.

The most successful and groundbreaking web sites did not fall into this 'us versus them' trap, and allied IT and Marketing in their web development. The most significant issue was IT staff's focus. It was the nature of web site developers to want to 'showcase' their skills in the use of the latest technology available in the media. Unfortunately, this was rarely to the benefit of the web site's objectives. According to Katz (2001) it is a guarantee for web site failure to 'focus on the technology, not the business'. Similarly, Loizides (2003) states that 'One of the worst offences marketers can make is using technology for technology's sake.' Many developers made the mistake of 'over-designing' web sites, with too much emphasis on visual stimulation and use of the latest, or most fashionable technology. This was a mistake on commercial sites. In a review of business sites, e-commerce web site Grokdotcom concluded that the most successful, including Amazon, Dell and eBay were, in a design sense, 'boring'. This is a compliment not a criticism. The argument is that these sites do not exist to entertain or as a testimony to the designer's ability, they exist only to generate income. Nor does this 'boring' design happen by chance; 'Tons of research and attention have gone into the process of making sure these sites do the job they are supposed to do.' (Grokdotcom 2003). Others are more direct in their criticism of undisciplined use of technology. Targeting specific software applications, online marketer Cory Rudl (quoted in *Opportunity World Magazine*, April 2003) states: 'lengthy, pointless flash presentations do not work' and Dr RF Wilson (2003) defines 'Splash' pages as 'home pages with dancing logos powered by Macromedia Flash technology designed to annoy and turn away visitors before they reach the real home page.' Both of these writers have a wide and successful track record of running online businesses and writing on the subject.

The third prominent group in early web site design was the enthusiastic amateur. The amateur web site designer normally had an IT background or qualification. Most school, college or university computing courses offer an element on 'web site design'. Such courses range from basic HTML, through what-you-see-is-what-you-get (WYSWYG) type software to full-blown Internet design. After taking such courses, many can create something perfectly acceptable online. However, with a very few exceptions, such web sites are rarely of a commercial standard. As Long (2002) says: 'owning web software doesn't mean good results [in developing a web site] any more than owning a camcorder means you can write, produce and edit your own TV commercials.' The point is well made, there is far more to creating a successful commercial web site than writing HTML. The upcoming section discussing the web site development team takes this argument forward.

Web site marketing objectives

In the business world any expenditure must be justified. A web site is not cost-free, and it must give return on investment (ROI). To do so it must achieve the objectives set for it. Objective setting is not only essential to determine ROI, it is fundamental in web site design. No web site can be successfully developed without there being clear objectives for the organisation's web presence. Many web sites are designed without the important question of web site objectives being answered.

Although there are specific goals, there are just three primary marketing objectives to any Internet presence:

1. Brand development – where the online presence complements and enhances the offline branding efforts of the organisation. Applications of this might include:

   - Provision of company information/details including: staff history, PLC annual reports, student related information
   - Corporate image promotion
   - Product information over and above that available in other media
   - Public Relations
   - Human resource information such as vacancies/job details/application forms
   - Promotional campaigns that utilise cross media advertising ie TV adverts that refer you to the web site of the advert where the web site becomes part of the development of the brand in its own right

2. Revenue generation – where the online presence increases revenue into the organization by:

- Sales, where payment is made at the time of purchase or an order is generated online, with an invoice to follow

- Prospect generation – with the web site as an advert for the company and/or product or the web is used as a medium for advertising (on other sites)

- Direct marketing – following all models of offline DM, but using the Internet instead of other media as the medium of communication

3. Customer service/support – the web is used to enhance the service and support offered to customers, and potential customers, at significantly reduced costs. Applications include:

- Pre-sales information – over and above simply promotional text that helps buyers to buy, FAQ pages, for example

- Post-sales information such as comprehensive fitting instructions or usage advice like recipes for foodstuff

- e-CRM – the use of technology to develop and manage relationships

- Personalisation – perhaps the holy grail for marketers, where sellers communicate with buyers on a one-to-one basis

Such is the nature of the World Wide Web that one site, correctly developed, could address any or all of the three primary marketing objectives.

There is a fourth *business* objective; that of cost savings and the use of technology to replace human involvement and/or traditional methods of communication. An example of this would be the posting of job vacancies on the organisation's web site, complete with an online application form that can be 'vetted' by software developed to identify and/or reject pre-determined parameters. Such examples of 'automation' makes more efficient use of staff time in that it frees up staff to focus on 'value-added' tasks. It should be noted, however, that in the example given here, the 'recruitment' section of the web site should still conform to the criteria laid down in this chapter for web site design and presentation.

In May 2005 the research company, ForSee (www.foreseeresults.com) published details of a survey of 11,000 online consumers. The study looked at online consumer satisfaction and concluded that navigation, function, performance and site capabilities all affected the conversion rate of users.

The development team

It is important that responsibility for the web site's development is correctly allocated. As stated earlier, an organisation's web presence is often still considered to be part of the job description for the IT department rather than Marketing's task. This is not best practice if a web site is to meet its objectives but it is less IT driven than before.

Morphy (2001) suggests that to be truly effective 'a web site should be developed using a variety of skills – IT, design, marketing, copy-writing. The key is assembling the right team and giving that team the tools and resources it needs'. A 'dream team' for web site development might include:

- Programmers – to make the technical aspects work

- Graphic designers – to address aesthetic issues

- Web usability specialists – to make sure the site is easy to use

- Content writers – to put the information in a format suitable to the media

MINI CASE 8.3 A team approach

In the US Credit Union Marketing Council awards of 2002, to create a dynamic, interactive and fully functional web site requires a teamwork approach according to Elizabeth Thompson. The team should include key players, including a project manager, from the functional areas of marketing, IT, web services and your external design agency, if appropriate. Teams should openly discuss what is sought-after and achievable based on the credit union's strategic objectives before deciding on how to get there. Brainstorming sessions can be creative and motivational. By being inclusive and assigning key tasks at key stages of development and maintenance, different people can be responsible for updating different pages and keeping the content fresh.

Adapted from: Thompson, E, 'Award Winning Web Sites', Credit Union Magazine, August 2002, www.cuna.org.

- Copy writers – to write sales copy
- Marketers – to ensure that the web site meets online marketing objectives and that online efforts are integral to offline strategies
- For an online shop, an experienced retailer

A number of these elements may be addressed by the same person. An experienced and qualified 'web designer' might be an expert on both programming and usability, for example. However, it is unlikely that a programmer can write good content or successful copy or an experienced marketer an expert on writing HTML. Depending on the organisation, this team could be in-house, or as is more often the case, these skill sets would be an integral part of an authentic web design company.

The issue of the importance of a variety of skills input is not one often visited by academic writers, but practitioners of e-marketing are more aware of its significance. One such practitioner, Lorraine Johnston (2003), writing on the e-marketing web site Grokdotcom (www.grokdotcom.com) states: 'The design of a web site requires the input of many specialists, including technical programmers, information architects, copywriters, designers, usability folks, marketers and people who understand the consumer psychology of selling and buying.'

There is a strong argument that the project should be overseen by a marketer, preferably a senior marketer. After all, this is the only element of the organisation's marketing mix that is available all around the world, 365 days a year. However, there is an acceptable case that as the web is a form of publishing then the project manager could be someone who is experienced in publishing.

Another group who should have significant input on web site design are the customers, both existing and potential. Carragher (2002) advocates that no web site should be developed without both current and potential customers being consulted. Their consultation might take the form of pre- or post development counsel. Market research into what target customers might expect or require from a web site would be undertaken before development starts. When the site's development is complete selected customers should be asked to test-use it prior to the site being made live on the web. Such practice would be considered the norm for any market-oriented organisation prior to implementing any marketing initiative – adverts or promotional material, for example. Carragher concludes his web site development guide with the warning that 'web sites are too important to be left to "techies"'.

An interesting and consistent element raised is that of *gender* in both the development of web sites and its potential visitors. Building on research into the differences between the production and preference aesthetics of men and women, Moss et al (2005) looked at whether female users preferred web sites designed by women and males those designed by men. When web sites were rated against 23 criteria spanning navigation, visual and linguistic elements, the research showed that men look for linearity, formality and a not too colourful look while women look for more colour, more informality and less linearity. The language used is also different, and the sites women create also have more links than those created by men. A subsequent step measured the extent to which certain industry sector web sites used the masculine or female web aesthetic. In all cases, the overwhelming majority of web sites emerged as being rooted within a masculine design paradigm. When respondents were asked to rate a number of male and female-produced web sites the result was an extremely strong tendency towards own-sex preference, with men rating the male-produced sites much more highly than the females, and vice versa for the females. In an industry that is dominated by men, Moss's research showed that around 75% of web designers are men. This raises a note of caution for those organisations whose web sites target the female market(s).

Web site preferences are demonstrated by these two web sites included in Gloria Moss and Rod Gunn's web log (www.designpsych.weblog.glam.ac.uk/). One site was designed by a male and the other by a female. Overwhelmingly, the two genders preferred the site designed by someone their own gender. Compare the images in Figs 8.1 and 8.2 below.

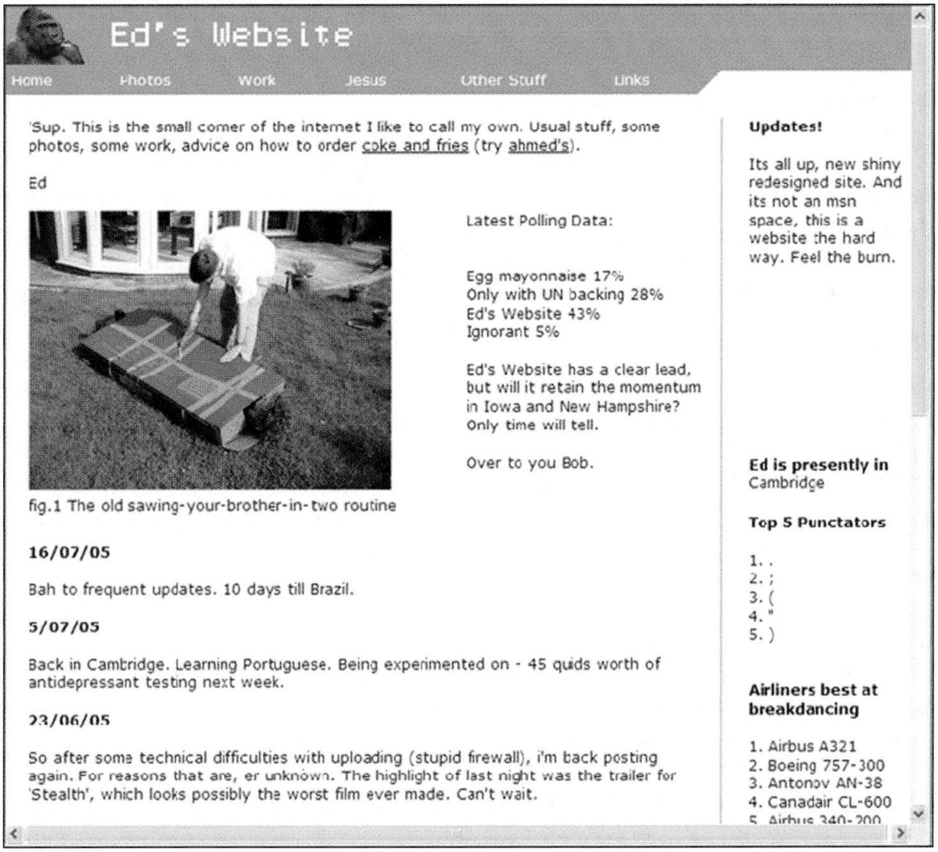

Fig 8.1 The male web site featured in Moss and Gunn's research into gender preferences

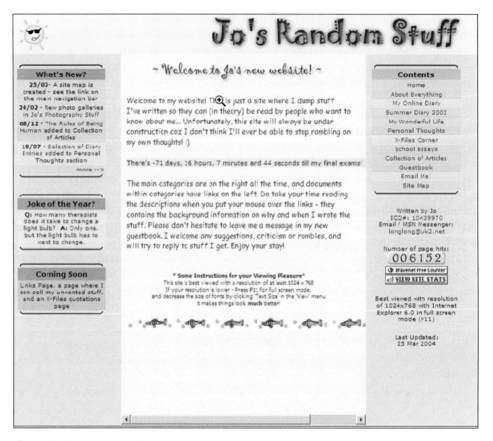

Fig 8.2 The female web site featured in Moss and Gunn's research into gender preferences

The development process

The development of an organisation's web presence should be a carefully planned phenomenon, and not an ad hoc event. Eisenberg and Eisenberg (2005) suggest a six-part framework for a successful web site:

1. Planning – how success will be measured

2. Structure – how the content is placed in context

3. Momentum – how people are moved along the buying process

4. Communication – how value is communicated

5. Value – how value is actually provided

6. Accountability – how each of the above are measured, tested and optimised.

Whilst this gives the development team a good basis for what is required, it does not offer a comprehensive planning model. An appropriate model is offered by the founder of gotomedia.com, Kelly Goto (2001). The recently redesigned web site of J. Barbour & Sons (www.barbour.co.uk) in Fig 8.3 addresses the needs and aspirations of its many 'publics'. Goto presents an effective series of phases that a web site design should go through (see

Fig 8.3 www.barbour.co.uk.

Reproduced by kind permission of J. Barbour & Sons Ltd.

Fig 8.4). It is comprehensive, and a sound model for would-be development teams. To omit any of the stages is to take a risk on the web site not being successful.

One thing that is intrinsic, but not specific, in the Goto model is quality control. It is also something that is often forgotten in the rush to get a web site 'live'. Often the development of a web site is considered to be a project of finite duration, which ends when the site goes 'live'. To do this is a serious error. No matter how small, a web site is a continuous undertaking and should never be considered 'finished' (again, see Fig 8.4).

Quality control

Quality control is too frequently missing from the development of the organisation's intangible product, its web presence. Commenting on the importance of Quality Assurance (QA) online media practitioner, Jeremy Lockhorn suggests a QA process should have four steps. This is shown in Fig 8.5.

Although this represents a more rigorous process than most web sites undergo prior to going live, a final step is omitted. That is testing by members of the public, preferably from the market segment at which the site is aimed. This is necessary as anyone who has been involved in a site's development can become too familiar with the site, and so overlook faults that become obvious when an outsider uses the site. Although it is probably part of stage three of Lockhorn's model, an additional, and advisable check would have a specialist review all the textual content for spelling or grammatical errors as well as simple typographical errors.

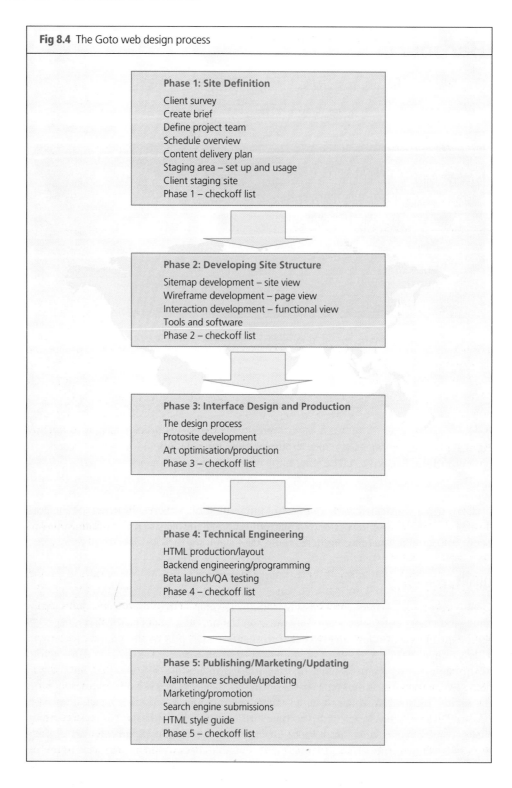

Fig 8.4 The Goto web design process

Phase 1: Site Definition

Client survey
Create brief
Define project team
Schedule overview
Content delivery plan
Staging area – set up and usage
Client staging site
Phase 1 – checkoff list

Phase 2: Developing Site Structure

Sitemap development – site view
Wireframe development – page view
Interaction development – functional view
Tools and software
Phase 2 – checkoff list

Phase 3: Interface Design and Production

The design process
Protosite development
Art optimisation/production
Phase 3 – checkoff list

Phase 4: Technical Engineering

HTML production/layout
Backend engineering/programming
Beta launch/QA testing
Phase 4 – checkoff list

Phase 5: Publishing/Marketing/Updating

Maintenance schedule/updating
Marketing/promotion
Search engine submissions
HTML style guide
Phase 5 – checkoff list

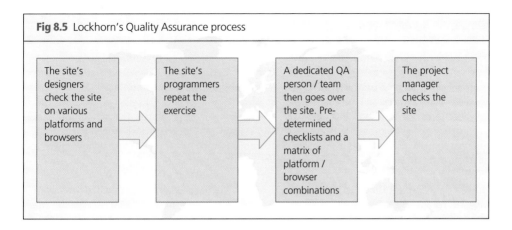

Fig 8.5 Lockhorn's Quality Assurance process

| The site's designers check the site on various platforms and browsers | The site's programmers repeat the exercise | A dedicated QA person / team then goes over the site. Pre-determined checklists and a matrix of platform / browser combinations | The project manager checks the site |

8.4 Web site design

The design of a web site is not an end in its own right, it is a means to an end. In the same way that a bricks-and-mortar store's layout and merchandising is designed to sell more product, so the web site should be designed to take the buyer through the different phases of the buying process. Traupel (2002) suggests that a good web site should act solely as an appetizer for a four-course meal – whetting the appetites of the viewers and motivating them to take some action that moves them forward in the marketing process such as contacting the company or registering via the web site for more information.

Navigation

Navigation is how the user moves around a web site by clicking on the various **hypertext** links built into that site. It is how the Internet works. For the commercial web site, however, good navigation is more critical than simply having links on a page that can take visitors to another page on the same site.

Eisenberg (2003) suggests that the goal of each web site page is to persuade. He says that '. . . all pages should link together, in a step-by step-fashion, to guide visitors through the process of buying from you. Lead them though, one page at a time, and constantly anticipate their every move. Make them feel comfortable and in control.' This concept of designing the site's navigation so that users are guided from arriving on it, through to taking a desired action has been labelled 'Persuasion Architecture'. The concept of Persuasion Architecture (PA) is about developing the structure of a web site so that it focuses on persuading visitors to take an action. Like much of online marketing, it was born in the offline environment. Brick-and-mortar shops have incorporated persuasive architecture in stores for decades, with retailers planning shop layouts to attract attention and stimulate desire in customers by persuading them to navigate the store in a desired way. Online, each element of the site's navigation should persuade the user to intuitively follow a path that is pre-ordained by the developers and one that will result in the customer's needs being met and publisher's object-ives being fulfilled. As such PA is a complex undertaking, with all potential user actions

---

MINI CASE 8.4 The Law of Convenience

Jerry Michalski, former editor of 'Release 1.0', a popular news-letter during the personal computer revolution, coined the phrase, 'Law of Convenience', saying that 'Every additional step that stands between people's desires and the fulfilment of those desires greatly decreases the likelihood that they will undertake the activity.' In terms of web site usability, this means that every click a user has to make on a web site to meet their needs reduces the chances of their actually meeting those needs.

An example of the Law of Convenience in action is that of the initial foray of bookseller, Barnes and Noble (B&N) into online trading. Prompted by the success of Amazon.com, B&N launched its own e-commerce site, expecting much of the site, which offered twice the number of books as Amazon – a company that, at the time, had nothing like the brand recognition of market-leaders, B&N. Optimism turned to dismay however, when the B&N web site (www.bn.com) generated only a tenth of book sales achieved by Amazon.

Deferring to offline marketing experiences, B&N's initial response was more promotion, but without success. Eventually, B&N's marketers looked at their web site and discovered that consumers using Amazon could find a book in two clicks, but at bn.com they had to click through around 11 levels of marketing and promotion pages to reach a book.

B&N's site violated Michalski's Law of Convenience – at each successive link required on the B&N web site the potential customer grew more weary of using the site and so was more likely to leave without making a purchase. Amazon, who subsequently introduced their 'one-click', recognised the value of the Law of Convenience and developed their site accordingly.

---

having to be considered and factored in to the site's design. To help effective PA design, response models such as AIDA (covered in chapter 5) can be utilised. To be successful, PA must be an integral part of the web site, being a prime consideration from the beginning of the planning process. It is the consideration of the numerous micro-actions that a user will make from arriving at a web site to their taking the ultimate action, the purchase. The failure to do this is illustrated in Mini case 8.4.

Taylor and England (2006) considered web site navigational design in a two-year study of a tourism-marketing organisation. In the study, they reflected on the usefulness of story-boards and hierarchy charts in the design of web site structures and concluded that they do not necessarily offer the most convenient navigation experience for the consumer. Instead they found that identifying and ranking the most commonly required content ensures that the grouping of this content facilitates a more uncomplicated user experience.

Usability

Web usability has its origins in the sciences of graphical user interface (GUI, pronounced 'gooey') and human computer interface (HCI) and is all about making the web site user friendly. Even big brand names are losing substantial revenues because their sites are too complicated for customers (Carroll 2003). According to web usability guru Jacob Nielsen (2001), 'usability means making technology easy and approachable for people, making tech-nology adapt to the way people behave, not the other way round.' Nielsen is perhaps the best known evangelist on usability, securing his place over a number of years of outspoken comments against such things as frames ('they suck') and 'Flash' technology ('99% bad'). Although Nielsen's critics argue that he takes too radical a stance on the subject, designers of the most successful web sites would appear to support the ideas he promotes. Nielsen's site (www.useit.com) (see Fig 8.6), itself an exemplar of simplicity in web design, includes a wealth of advice based on his experience and research.

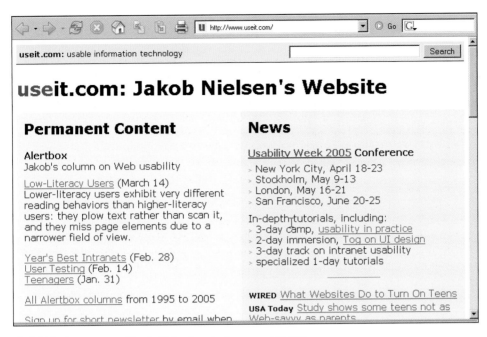

Fig 8.6 The home page of Jacob Nielsen's web site www.useit.com

Of all Nielsen's teachings, one is of particular interest to those looking to achieve any objective from a web site. In an article on usability in 2003 he says:

'If a website is difficult to use, people leave. If the homepage fails to clearly state what a company offers and what users can do on the site, people leave. If users get lost on a website, they leave. If a website's information is hard to read or doesn't answer users' key questions, they leave.'

Speaking on usability, Carragher (2002) supports Nielsen's views on the primary purpose of any web site, saying that 'commercial web sites exist only to extract a response from their users . . . and ultimately, commercial web sites exist to extract money, directly or indirectly, from visitors to the site.' Whilst Nielsen uses the term usability to encompass all aspects of web site design, it can be difficult to identify where usability starts and other elements of web site design begin. Good navigation, for example, is an integral part of good usability and yet it is discussed as a separate issue. Eisenburg (2004) argues that usability is subjective – in the same way that his 64 ounce glass mug is perfectly usable for him, it is not for his two-year old daughter – a web site's usability is in the eye of the beholder. He says, 'when users land on your web site, they bring their own needs, wants, perspectives, and motivations. They're volunteers on your site and choose whether they'll continue interacting with your site. If they feel you don't understand them, if they can't figure out what to do, or if you're just not providing the value they want offered, they're one click away from your competitor's Web site.' If this is the case, then usability could be argued to be part of the segmentation process that drives the development of a web site to suit the target visitor, in this case to make it intuitive for the wants needs and desires of that target audience. Weil (2001) has a view of usability that best suits the ethos of this book, she says that it is 'all about customer-centric site design'.

Fig 8.7 12 tests for effective web performance

1. How many mouse clicks to a phone number when starting at the home page?

2. Is there an opportunity to give feedback/pose questions and is this achieved using external e-mail addresses or online forms?

3. Is there animation on the site? If so, does this slow down progress within the site and prove to be gimmicky or is it useful?

4. Does the site use fussy backgrounds that distract from the text?

5. Are there typing errors or spelling mistakes held within the text of the site?

6. Does the site contain broken or dead links?

7. Are there misleading headings/links that do not wholly correspond to the pages they describe?

8. Does the site contain 'orphan' pages (pages with no content eg returning a '404' message)?

9. Does the homepage have a fast (under 5 seconds) or slow (over 5 seconds) download time?

10. Does the web site display links on its home page that are one-way?

11. Does the site contain pop-up windows that appear without the request of the user?

12. Does the web site contain an internal search engine that will locate specific information within the site?

Design guides

Early web site development was predominantly based on designers' intuition, with a problem being that there was a general lack of cognitive guidelines and little theoretical or experimental validation for web design (Dalal et al, 2000). As the web has formalised, theory, practice, and user expectations have stabilised the design of popular web sites.

A number of design guides exist. The BBC's Training and Development section offers a guide that is both well researched and presented. As part of an ongoing assessment of companies' web performance, they conducted a survey of 62 web sites, benchmarking them against key criteria of what the authors consider to be good web site design. Those criteria were based on 12 different and common faults as advised by the unit's manager of New Media Training, Jonathon Hall. The report (2002) does not seek to judge the sites, but simply to see if they fall foul of the '12 sins'. For the 12 tests that formulate the guide see Fig 8.7.

Although the 12 points do not address all aspects of a commercial web site, they do provide a good basis for assessment. If such basic issues as these have been incorrectly executed, then it is likely that other elements of the site would be faulty also.

Bryan Eisenberg (2001) uses the acronym KISS – keep it simple, stupid, when introducing his advice for web site design. He says that the key to successful web site design is not sophistication, it is simplicity. His tips are:

- The best web sites load in about 10 seconds at 28.8 Kbps

- On the web, visitors look first for relevant text, not graphics

- The best web sites have simple and consistent navigation

- Respect the conventions of the web

- Make everything obvious

- Never leave your prospect stranded anywhere on your site

- The best web sites do not assume the client is expert
- Keep in mind that visitors are looking for a reason *not* to trust you
- Keep it short and sweet

Another insightful guide comes from Nick Nichol (2000). Nichol's list is delivered as a warning of 'what not to do'. It states that the following should not be found on a business web site:

- Large useless graphics
- Phrases like 'Welcome to My Site' – they are self-serving statements that only cloud your message
- Blinkers, spinners, page counters, etc
- External links on your home page – this is equivalent to having an office or storefront that leads to a choice of doors that go to other businesses
- Just about any award logo/banner – they are self-serving space-wasters that should be replaced with visitor-focussed information that gives people a reason to stay at your site
- Typographical or grammatical errors
- Over use of we, our, us, my, me, mine and your company name – these are self-serving words that turn off readers. Instead, you should use words like you and your.
- Frames – many search engines do not index them properly. Many frames require scrolling to read the text and activate links. Frame scrolling bars take up precious real estate. Frames do not bookmark properly
- Under construction signs/notices – what good does a page that is not finished do for your visitors? It just wastes their time and could frustrate or annoy them
- Broken Links – they are annoying, frustrating and unprofessional. Why make your visitors angry?
- Missing graphics
- Incomplete contact information – it is amazing how many companies try to remain anonymous and then expect people to do business with them
- Home Page that scrolls into oblivion – give visitors links and benefit-related teasers that lead to separate pages
- Plug-ins/JavaScript pop-up windows – most people will not take the time to load plug-ins to view or do something at your site unless you give them a great reason to do so. They will just click away

Like the guides of the BBC and Eisenberg and others, Nichol covers issues that seem to be rather obvious to many. This is an indictment of some of the poor practices in web site design that existed at the time of their writing. That the guides are still relevant when assessing a web site suggests that some web developers have failed to learn from the errors and practices in the years since the commercial web site came of age.

Credibility

In the same way that an offline customer would be reluctant to hand over cash to a vendor with no credibility, so the web customer must perceive the online business as being credible before they are willing to commit to any transaction. All elements of web design can add or detract from the organisation's credibility, however it is such an important issue that it is worth addressing in its own right.

Assessing the credibility of a web site could be described as a bridge between computer science, HCI for example, and more practical applications of web presence design. From a marketing perspective, for a web site to be commercially effective it must be credible in the eye of the customer. Most criteria for credibility are also valid for business web design.

The value of online credibility is well presented by Poirier (2003). He says: 'Web visitors form impressions about your company based on the totality of the experience they have navigating through your site. On a rational level they are looking for facts and information about your products, but on an emotional level, they are influenced by other relevant cues: the logic of content architecture, ease of navigation, clarity of writing, quality of customer service and professional visual presentation of material. Substandard delivery on any of these can have a significantly negative effect on how prospects rate your company against competition.' Professor BJ Fogg (1999) describes credibility as: 'A perception based on two factors: trustworthiness (unbiased, truthful, good, honest) + expertise (experienced, intelligent, powerful, knowledgeable.' Fogg went on to present a 'web credibility grid' of elements that increase credibility and a similar grid for elements that decrease credibility. This grid is presented in Fig 8.8.

Fig 8.8 Fogg's web credibility grid

	Presumed credibility	Reputed credibility	Surface credibility	Experienced credibility
Elements that increase credibility				
Web site provider	The provider is a non-profit organisation	The provider is recognised as an expert by others	Users are familiar with the provider outside of the web content	Users with questions receive quick and helpful answers
Web site content	The site has ads from reputable companies	The content has been approved by an outside agency	The site appears to have lots of relevant information	The site's content has always been accurate and unbiased
Web site design	The site was created by an outside design firm	The site won an award for technical achievement	The site has a pleasing visual design	The site is easy to navigate
Elements that decrease credibility				
Web site provider	The site tries to recruit advertisers but has none so far	The provider was sued for patent infringement and lost	The site's URL does not match the provider's name	The site does not give contact information anywhere
Web site content	The site shows only a few hits on their web counter	The content got bad reviews from an outside agency	The site seems to have more ads than information	The site has typographical errors
Web site design	The site has no security protocols for transactions	The site is reported to have copied the design of another site	The text font is either too large or small to read comfortably	The site has links to pages that no longer exist

Although a useful guide, the grid has potential flaws. For example, is it likely that a member of the public would know if 'the provider was sued for patent infringement and lost'? Similarly, respondents were not required to make their own judgement on the issues raised. On the issue of advertising, respondents were simply presented with an identical web page with or without a banner ad across the top and asked to choose which they thought to be most credible. Asking the respondents to comment on the credibility of the site based on how the ads were presented, or who the advertisers are, might give a better indication of their perception of credibility.

Stanford University's Persuasive Technology Lab has applied its scientific research to the web by accessing the credibility of web sites in the Stanford Web Credibility Research Centre. This centre compiled 10 guidelines on credibility based on three years of research that included over 4,500 people (Stanford University 2002). They are:

1. Make it easy to verify the accuracy of the information on your site
2. Show that there is a real organisation behind your site
3. Highlight the expertise in your organisation and in the content and services you provide
4. Show that honest and trustworthy people stand behind your site
5. Make it easy to contact you
6. Design your site so it looks professional (or is appropriate for your purpose)
7. Make your site easy to use – and useful
8. Update your site's content often (at least show it has been reviewed recently)
9. Use restraint with any promotional content (eg, ads, offers)
10. Avoid errors of all types, no matter how small they seem

Although there is an element of subjectivity to some of these points (eg number 6 – what is 'professional'?) this is a very useful checklist for developers to use when accessing the credibility of their web site.

The global web presence

Former German Chancellor, Willy Brandt once said, 'If I am selling to you, I speak your language. If I am buying from you, dann müssen Sie in meiner Sprache sprechen.' (translation: then you must speak my language). For the domestic organisation that sells globally or the international company that trades from bases around the world, the staging of their web presence is an essential consideration. There are, effectively, three types of global web site.

1. The single web site of a domestic organisation that caters for a global audience, normally in English, though verbatim translation of some or all pages into other languages may be included.
2. The domestic organisation that develops different web sites for global users, often using the domain names of the local countries. The content of these sites would be mainly translations of the 'home' site, though the presentation and content may be adapted to address local issues.
3. The global organisation that develops local web sites for each country in which it has a physical presence. In this case each web presence would have a standardised corporate design and structure but content would be localised, such as HSBC or Hewlett Packard in Mini case 8.5.

MINI CASE 8.5 Hewlett-Packard's global web presence

Many commercial giants approach their global web presences in a similar way. A good example is HP, which has 73 country specific sites. Each site is developed from the same template, so all look similar even though their content is country specific.

English is the most common language, but there are another 29 others – and UK and American English are different. Multi-language countries are also considered, the Canadian site, for example, is available in French and English.

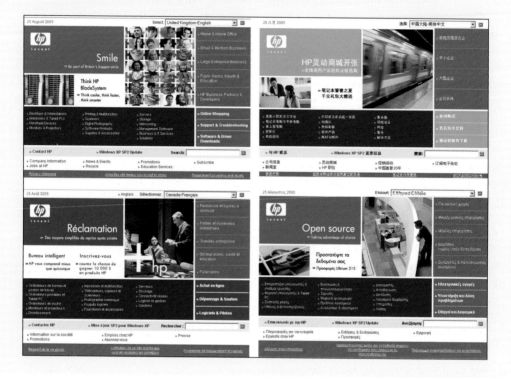

Whatever the size of the organisation, or its web presence, the globalisation of web sites should not be a budget operation. It is important because poor translation into a local language, for example, might be seen as laziness at best or an insult at worst. Either way, the customer is likely to shop elsewhere.

Considerations for global web site development include:

• Have translations done by a native speaker of the 'new' language, and then have it read by another. Literal translations rarely work, particularly of the thousands of idioms that can be found in the English language, and often wording or phrases need to be changed to suit local nuances. For example, 'change hands' should become 'change ownership' and 'do everything possible' should replace 'bend over backwards'.

• Make a decision on whether sites in 'English' will use UK or US spelling norms. Colour or color, for example, or organisation with an 's' or 'z'. In truth few users will object to either, but there should be consistency on each site.

• Any translation should also include consideration of meta-data for search engine optimisation. Users do not search in English only – Google has 97 language interfaces. Literal translations may not accurately represent key words or phrases used in other countries or languages.

- Have a clear template that can be easily used for all country sites. Such a template should take into consideration all issues that might arise in the various countries being targeted. For example, a site using leading edge technology might be fine in the US, where **broadband** is prevalent, but users in other countries might still rely on dial-up connections.
- If all country specific sites are available from the 'home' site, consider the links. The link to the German site should say 'Deutsch', not 'German'. Flags are an option, but beware of using the UK's Union Flag for English language sites, not all English speakers are from the UK.
- Ensure country specific practices are catered for. For example, forms need to be considered carefully when designing fields for users to complete. An obvious example is the reference to 'zip codes' that only exist in the US. Also, in many Asian countries, the first name is the family name, so offering separate fields for first name and last name is a prescription for confusion.
- Measurements and dates can also present problems. If you are selling dolls' houses for example, will the customer be more at home with metric or imperial units (eg centimetres or inches). If in doubt offering both is a good solution. Similarly, provide temperatures in both Fahrenheit and Celsius on a site describing holiday destinations. With dates it is always best to spell out the name of the month. In the UK 4/9/2005 is 4 September, in America and other parts of the world, it would be 9 April.
- Some offline issues need to be considered when featured online. For example, regional product standards should be a consideration when selling globally. With electrical products, for example, electricity supplies vary around the world. The most common around the world are 110V and 220V, but the UK uses 240V, and plug sockets differ also. Similarly, video standards vary, and most DVDs are artificially restricted to play only in limited countries.

Nielsen (2000) recommends using 'international inspection' to ensure the international usability and acceptance of a web design. In simple terms, this should consist of a panel of people, ideally with usability experience, in every country in which the merchant is planning to trade. Apart from basic language issues, culture and local ways of doing business need examination and testing.

Web design in practice

There are a number of elements of web site design that either have a basis in offline custom or have developed from web design practice over the last 10 years. The following are some of those elements.

- In web design, familiarity breeds acceptance. When people visit a web site they have a mental map of how their 'ideal' web page should be. What the 'ideal' site looks like, is not only open to debate, it is subjective. Early texts on the web site design encouraged creativity. Typical of the time was Young (1999), who commented, 'The web is a great source of inspiration if you're having trouble choosing a design. By looking at existing pages, you can get an idea of what you do and don't like when it comes to web page design.' Budding developers would come across a myriad of web site designs. The same exercise now, would reveal that the most-visited commercial web sites all follow a similar

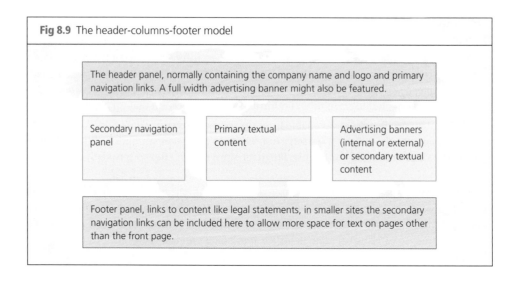

Fig 8.9 The header-columns-footer model

The header panel, normally containing the company name and logo and primary navigation links. A full width advertising banner might also be featured.

| Secondary navigation panel | Primary textual content | Advertising banners (internal or external) or secondary textual content |

Footer panel, links to content like legal statements, in smaller sites the secondary navigation links can be included here to allow more space for text on pages other than the front page.

design format. Although there is no definitive design for commercial web site success, a common design model has emerged used by sites that are also popular with users. This model has benefited from a virtuous circle, the more it is used the more it is accepted, and so in the minds of users, it is 'ideal'. Although the specifics are being constantly tweaked to achieve business objectives, this popular design-style is the 'header-columns-footer' model shown in Fig 8.9. Depending on the objectives of the web site, and the content to be presented, the number of columns can be adapted to suit. Sites that consistently appear in the most-visited lists use this model, including the BBC (www.bbc.co.uk), AOL (www.aol.co.uk), MSN (www.msn.com) and Amazon (www.amazon.com). As with many elements of web site design, this model learns from offline publishing – the similarity to newspaper presentation is obvious. Although this model is particularly suitable for information driven sites, it is a good starting point for any web site concept.

- **Download** times. The technology of the Internet means that web pages do not appear instantaneously on demand. The reasons for this are manifold. Some are beyond the control of both user and designer such as **bandwidth** and how busy the network is. Beyond the control of the user is the site design. Beyond the control of the site's developer are the configuration and specification of the user's PC. Research by Rose et al (2000) has determined that the longer it takes for a web page to download, the less interested the consumer is. Users typically wait around only eight seconds for a home page to appear before moving on. In business terms, this means your competitor is only eight seconds and a click of the mouse away.

The **home page** is where visitors normally arrive on a site, so that page's download time is paramount. In an attempt to guarantee fast download, the best practitioners of web site publishing aim to keep their home page size between 40 and 45,000 bytes. Table 8.1 shows the download time for a page totalling 40,000 bytes. The BBC's web design team aim to always stay below this limit for the corporation's **front page**. It should be noted that if a page includes **banner** ads provided by a third party those ads might have a high byte-count, particularly those that are animated. In this case, the organisation might lose visitors because the ads are slowing the download times.

Fig 8.10 Travel site ebookers' front page is an example of the header-columns-footer model

Table 8.1 Download times

Connect rate	Connect time in seconds
28.8K	17.90
56K	12.91
ISDN 128K	6.11
T1/broadband 1.44 M bpd	3.19

Although the use of broadband has increased significantly, developers designing only for broadband users are risking failed business objectives. Consider the UK in June 2005, for example. At that time more than 7.4 million users had high speed broadband connections – exceeding those using dial-up services for the first time (*Sunday Times*, 5 June 2005). However, this still leaves a large number of customers on 'dial-up'.

- The use of colour on web sites. Although convention says that there are 256 colours from which to choose for a web site, the best sites follow simple principles, namely:

  - Text should be dark

  - Backgrounds should be light

  - Pre-existing corporate colours should be the primary colours for that organisation's web site

Beyond these basics, designers have a wide choice of colours, even on a site in 'corporate colours' there will be a requirement for other colours to be used. Developers should be aware that colours have different significance in countries across the globe.

Some considerations will be scientific: green is the colour that can be differentiated in more shades than any other colour and blue can create an optical illusion that images are farther away than they actually are. Other considerations will be influenced by convention. For example, on traffic lights red means stop, yellow caution, and green go, translating into the colours being associated with danger and safety. The meanings of other colours are more inspired by custom or tradition: pink for baby girls and light blue for boys for example. Other uses are based on psychological influences, blue evokes confidence and trustworthiness, perhaps explaining why so many corporate colour schemes include blue.

- Different **browsers**. Although there is much communality, not all browsers read standard web site code in the same way. What this means is that a web site designed specifically for one browser. Internet Explorer (IE) for example, will not appear on a Firefox or Mac browser in exactly the same format as on IE. Research published in 2005 by web-testing firm SciVisum (www.scivisum.co.uk) revealed that 7% of the 100 leading consumer sites they assessed included non-standard code recognised only by Microsoft's browser and that one in 10 UK web sites failed to work properly on the Firefox web browser. Firefox is an **open source** alternative to Microsoft's Internet Explorer (IE) and has proved popular since its launch in November 2004, in its first six months gaining 8% of the market. Although there is business logic to making web sites IE-only compliant as IE is the most widely used browser, offline businesses would think twice about locking their doors to 7% of customers, so why is it commonplace online? It is generally accepted as good practice that if more than 1% of a web site's visitors share a certain techno-graphic trait, that group must be considered when designing a web site (Omniture, 2005). The message for developers is this. Although only the most basic HTML code will work on all browsers, designers should strive to make their web site readable on as many browsers as possible, and if this means a compromise in design criteria, so be it.

- A degree of compromise is also necessary when setting web page width and length. Whilst most design work is done on computers with big screens, not all users have monitors that are as big. Fifteen-inch screens are, for example, the size of choice for most universities, libraries and other public access providers. Add to this the fact that the user's own toolbar preferences will reduce the actual viewable space means that developers should consider designing for the lowest common denominator when setting screen size. Screen size issues include:

- Get the message on screen – users do not like scrolling across a page

- Offering a fixed or flexible width. It is possible for the designer to have pages re-size themselves to suit each user's screen. However this means sacrifices in other design elements and the trade-off should be considered carefully.

- Most printers' default setting is 600 pixels wide. Therefore, if it is likely that web pages will be printed (and many are) a page designed wider than that will not print the entire width of the page on the same piece of paper.

As mentioned earlier, 'familiarity breeds acceptance' and users accept certain design norms. Designers should look at the most visited sites to see how they handle page sizing, and follow suit.

- **Readability of text.** Lessons learned in centuries of print show that humans read best lines that are no longer than 2.5 alphabets long. In the Latin alphabet used in English, this equates to around 65 characters. Books will rarely have lines that are longer than 65 characters, no matter what size the font and this applies online also. Bear in mind that because it is presented as a collection of dots (pixels), the human eye has more difficulty reading text on a screen than on paper. On-screen, it is very difficult to read long lines of text, hence one of the reasons the previously described 'header-columns-footer' model is so successful and modelled on traditional newspaper layouts.

- The presentation of text on web pages is also an issue. Worthy of consideration are:

  - **Font type.** Because of the way they are formed on-screen (in pixels) sans serif fonts (those without 'tails' eg Arial) are more easily readable than serif fonts (those with 'tails' eg Times New Roman). In print, the reverse is true.

  - **Font size.** Designers should consider the web site's target market carefully before making the font size fixed. For example, in the UK, almost two thirds of people coming up to retirement are using the Internet compared with just one third in 2001, signalling a growth in the number of these so-called silver surfers (The Future Foundation, 2005). For the majority of people, as they get older, their eyesight deteriorates, making a larger font desirable though many sites offer the facility to change font sizes to suit the user.

  - **The use of bold, underlining, and italics.** Bold can be used to emphasise words or phrases as long as the colour is consistent. Online, a word in bold that is a different colour to its surrounding text is normally a link. The same applies to underlining. Breaking convention will confuse users. Italics should be avoided online – again it is the pixel construction to blame – as the words become almost illegible.

  - **Non-standard characters** that not all browsers can read. This is a browser issue similar to that described above, the subscript ™ for example, does not appear as such on some browsers.

Landing pages

Landing pages serve a specific purpose in any web presence. They are part of the web site, but have no links going to them *from* that web site, all links to them are not only from external sources, but those sources are restricted by the organisation's marketers. Landing pages can be described as the entrance doors to a web site that only selected customers are directed to. They are used when the marketer wants the user to visit a web site, but for a particular purpose, and where entering through the home page would detract from that purpose. Usually developed for particular promotions, the landing page URL is used in marketing messages link from any page to another, and not everyone will enter the site through the front page. McAlpine compares the web to hundreds of millions of pages blowing in the wind, with people picking them up at random. Each page has to be self-explanatory and make sense by itself. By definition, this means that not only must the content must be high quality, but it must signal the context and purpose of every page.

Writing for the web

Online, users read content on a web page differently to the way in which they read content on paper. Not only is the context different, the mode of reading is different. Humans find it hard to read on a computer screen. Even with high-resolution monitors prolonged, reading on a computer screen can be painful. As a result, users rarely read a web page content in full. They scan the text, picking out keywords, sentences, and paragraphs of interest and skipping over other text that has no appeal to them. The web writer must indulge this practice by writing content that uses descriptive headers and sub-headers, short paragraphs, bullet points and content that gets to the point quickly using fewer words than would have been used offline. Hypertext links can be used to not only emphasise elements of the text, but also lead readers to further information and act as a call-to-action.

Research conducted by Morkes and Nielsen (1997) attempted to measure the effect of improving web content to a format more suitable to the medium by developing five versions of textual content of a web page. They then used four measures of performance – time, errors, memory, and site structure – to assess how well the pages performed when viewed by users. The results of the study are shown in Fig 8.12. Although the focus of the research was to observe the results rather than the reasons for those results, Morkes and Nielsen conjecture was that what they refer to as 'promotional language' imposes '. . . a cognitive burden on users who have to spend resources on filtering out the hyperbole to get at the facts'.

Segmentation is now an accepted and essential marketing task with few products appealing to all members of society. It is essential, therefore, that the content is written in such a way that it appeals to the site's target audience, or audiences. According to Tomsen (2000) the key to a successful web site lies in meeting the net user's goals and expectations. The textual content should, therefore, be what they expect to see, what they are comfortable with and what they find satisfaction in. Technologies such as collaborative filtering and customisation facilitate greater relevancy and targeting. However, misleading statements must be avoided (see Legal Eagle Box 8.2).

The web is, by its nature, self-segmenting of the market. This is because the web is a pull rather than push medium. The web-user chooses to visit a web site, they 'pull' the content to them rather than having it 'pushed' upon them involuntarily as with a TV or billboard advert. This phenomenon means that the user arrives at the web site with an increased expectation of the content of that site. However, each web site will attract different sub-segments. As in the hotel example in the earlier section on landing pages, the only people that visit the hotel site are those seeking accommodation in that locale, although those people might represent several segments in their needs such as business or casual travellers, short or long stay. Web sites attract different users. McGovern (2002) suggests that there are four types of commercial traffic that designers should be aware of, and cater for. They are:

- First, perfect **prospects** who know exactly what they want.
- Second, prospects that sort of know what they want.
- Third, prospects that are not sure they want anything but might buy if what they want were to appear.

on all media where the customer is directed to the web site. If a promotion is featured in a particular magazine, then a specific URL is given in 'x' magazine. When the user arrives at that landing page the content is not generic (as the home page will be) but specific, the user can be greeted as the 'x' magazine reader and reference made only to the offer in question. In this way there is more chance of the prospect becoming a customer. Landing pages can also be used to segment customers before they arrive at your site, depending on how they find and access it. For example, a city centre hotel might have potential customers arrive at its web site from:

1. An e-mail campaign aimed at high end business users
2. A sponsored add on Google when the search phrase is 'budget weekend accommodation'
3. A banner add campaign on a number of suitable web sites targeting the family holiday maker

If each of these linked to the hotel's **front page** the user would have to search the web site to find the suitable pages – or they might simply click away to another hotel's site.

Using three different landing pages, however, the content of each could reflect the buyer behaviour of each customer segment. In offline terms, the 'sales approach' is different. Whilst each landing page still has a 'corporate' design style, the key message will be different. In the examples above the landing pages might highlight:

1. Fast track check-in and electronic check-out facilities, networked communications in every room, ultra-comfortable beds with a choice of pillows for a good night's rest
2. Rooms from £45 per night, or buy two nights and get the third free over the weekend
3. Safe location, indoor swimming pool, games room, Sky Box Office and TV games in every room

Each of the three segments of customer could then be directed to the sites 'book now' page or to the pages of the web site that give further details of the particular benefits. The text on landing pages is normally 'copy' rather than 'content', with calls-to-action prominent. Pitched correctly in response to adverts or promotions as described above, the landing page should be the equivalent of the close of a sale.

Access for the disabled

Generally speaking, accessibility is taken to mean the design or modification of '. . . . web sites to allow access to people with disabilities' (IBM, 2000). As more countries pass laws stating that web sites must be accessible to blind and disabled people, the issue of making a web site accessible to *all* Internet users has moved from moral to legal grounds. As other sections in this chapter suggest, however, accessibility is also good business practice. The Royal National Institute for the Blind (RNIB) suggest three arguments in favour of making web sites accessible (RNIB, 2001), namely:

• It makes good business sense
• It is the law
• It is fair

Addressing accessibility issues to indulge social pressure or respond to legal enforcement would suggest that the organisation's web site development has not followed best business practice in the first place.

LEGAL EAGLE BOX 8.1 Web accessibility laws: Disability Discrimination Act 1995

Organisations are legally obliged to ensure that their web site is accessible to disabled people under Part III of the Disability Discrimination Act 1995 as it falls within the definition of a service under the terms of the DDA. The Act was effective from 1 October 1999. A service provider has to take reasonable steps to change a practice which makes it unreasonably difficult for disabled people to make use of its services. What services are affected by the Disability Discrimination Act? An airline company provides a flight reservation and booking service to the public on its web site. This is a provision of a service and is subject to the Act.' However, many organisations have failed to achieve universal access. This has led the Disability Rights Commission (DRC) conducting a formal investigation into barriers to web access for disabled people. The resulting report, *Web Access and Inclusion for Disabled People*, indicates that 97% of organisations stated that it was an important issue but 81% had made no noticeable effort to address the problem. DRC has now commissioned the British Standards Instituion (BSI) to produce new guidelines in PAS 78: *Guide to Good Practice in Designing Accessible Web Sites*. The Commission has the powers to investigate 'named party' cases when organisations fail to meet the guidelines and will support individuals taking test cases against the failing organisation.

As the compelling case for accessibility has become more widely understood, and the introduction of relevant legislation, many organisations have been working to provide guidelines to assist with the development of accessible web sites. The Worldwide Web Consortium (www.w3.org), under the auspices of its Web Accessibility Initiative, has produced a comprehensive set of guidelines for the creation of accessible web sites (Chisholm et al, 1999). These guidelines are organised to allow for three levels of compliance:

- Level 'A' when all priority 1 guidelines are met
- Level 'AA' for meeting priorities 1 and 2
- Level 'AAA' for meeting all of the guidelines

The W3C guidelines have been widely adopted and are now 'recognised as a de facto global standard for the design of accessible Web site' (EC, 2001). Given the widespread adoption of these standards, developers are probably best advised to follow this path unless specifically required to adopt other standards.

Accessibility requirements have generated an increasing number of tools and resources to help organisations ensure that their sites follow relevant accessibility guidelines. Probably the most popular of these is free, the **'Bobby'** verification service (www.webxact.watchfire.com). This tool allows a site to be checked for compliance against the W3C accessibility guidelines for compliance at any of the three levels. Sites that pass these tests are allowed to display a 'Bobby Approved' logo.

Bobby is an automated online tool where pages must be submitted for checking via the Internet. From a developer's perspective, it is quicker and easier to be able to run checks locally, ideally using the same software package that is used to actually create the pages. Some of the most popular HTML editing tools provide extensions to allow this (Macromedia, 2001). These tools alone will not make a site accessible; the nature of the various guidelines (Chisholm et al, 1999; NCI, 2001) is such that some human evaluation is recommended. Bobby can identify elements of a web site that need attention, sometimes these can be easily fixed but because of the individual nature of each web site, 'Bobby' should be taken as a guide rather than gospel.

When considering accessibility design in practice there are a number of common faults in web design that reduce access for the disabled user. These include:

- Incorrectly assigned ALT text – the screen readers used by disabled users rely on the ALT text on images to describe those images, so the text should do just that.

- Non-resizable text – users with partial or poor sight need to be able to enlarge the text on web sites for the information to be accessible to them. Many sites present text in a fixed, usually small, size.
- When images are used to display text, the text is not resizable and so not accessible to users with poor sight. In addition, text embedded in images appears pixelated and blurry when read through a screen magnifier.
- Link text that makes no sense when read out of context – visually impaired users often browse websites by tabbing from one link to the next, so for maximum accessibility all link text should stand alone. 'Click here', for example means nothing without the pro- or pre-ceding text.
- Separate 'accessible' versions of web sites – often mistakenly considered to be the best solution, the W3C say they should be used only as a last resort 'if all else fails'. Separate accessible versions are strongly advised against because they usually have less functionality than the main web site, are rarely kept as up-to-date as the regular web site and can be seen as excluding disabled people from regular society.
- Nielsen (2002) also suggests utilising sound to support visually impaired site visitors, and where audio clips are an integral site element, transcripts of the clips should also be made available for those with hearing problems. We have multimedia tools available, we should use them for the benefit of all customers.

Footnote

Research by Lindgaard et al (2006), seeking to ascertain how quickly people form an opinion about web page visual appeal, came back with results that not only have implications for all elements of web site design, but that should be compulsory reading for all web developers. The findings were that in just one-twentieth of a second, less than half the time it takes to blink, people make aesthetic judgements that influence the rest of their experience with a web site. Lead researcher, Gitte Lindgaard, a psychology professor at Carleton University in Ottawa, commented in a Reuters interview, 'It really is just a physiological response, so web designers have to make sure they're not offending users visually' and that 'if the first impression is negative, you'll probably drive people off'. Ominously for designers, the research did not show how to get a positive reaction from users.

8.5 Web site content

The visitor to the commercial web site is there for one reason, to gain information that is of some benefit to them in meeting their wants or needs. It is possible that data can be gleaned from pictures, but on the web when we consider information we are talking about textual content. If that content is presented correctly then the result for the site owner will be the fulfilment of their objectives. Textual content is, therefore, the most important aspect of the organisation's web presence. Straub (2003) makes the point that 'The bottom line for web site development is to have content on sites that appeals to serve only as users. Good content can overcome a lot of other drawbacks to a web site'. Design and aesthetics are still important, but on a commercial web site, form should serve function, not the other way around – art rarely serves utility. In the same way as some TV adverts are entertaining and win design awards but fail to increase sales of the product being advertised, so web sites should not overshadow the message. 'If people are talking about the design of your web site instead of the message that your web site is delivering, then you have put the cart before the horse' (Morris, 1999). The most important aspect of content is whether it actually brings any value to the reader. Web content specialist, Nick Usborne comments in his book, *Net Words* (2002) that too many businesses fill their web site with comments about themselves rather than what the customers wants to know. Phrases like: 'Our mission is to ensure that our customers accomplish theirs' might be acceptable in a mission statement, but on a web site it is self-serving and sycophantic. 'Online, a competitor is only a click away' is a common phrase used to describe e-commerce activity. Web sites are relatively easy to develop so it is likely that a company's competitors will all have a web presence. As Usborne says 'Online, only words will set you apart'. It is, therefore, essential that those words are the right ones and that they are presented in the correct manner.

An Oxford Internet Survey report in June 2005 (www.oii.ox.ac.uk) listed 20 reasons why users go online. Table 8.2 lists each reason with the percentage of people who said

Table 8.2 The importance of online content

Reason for going online	% of people doing so	Author's comment on the importance of content and its presentation
Seek product information	87	In this context the importance of content and its presentation is absolute
Surf/browse	83	Depends on the reason for surfing, someone simply amusing themselves might put up with poor content
Look up facts	78	To be understood, the facts must be presented in a clear manner
Plan travel	77	Whilst pictures might add to this content, again it is the words that will provide the information
Buy online	74	In this context presentation and content that encourages a purchase are essential
Seek information on local events	66	Information must always be transparent
News	61	News is news, not entertainment. The clarity of its presentation is paramount
Instant messaging	56	Not normally commercial, so slang or short cuts can be used, with little attention to grammar
Download music	53	The instructions should be obvious
Play games	48	As above, and the language should be that expected by the potential user
Bank online	45	Mistakes here can cause problems for user and financial services provider, so development of good content is essential
Look for jobs	42	Provision of information that must be specific and clear
Study material for education	40	In most subjects this will be textual information, so clarity is vital
Download or watch videos	33	Prominent, clear instructions
Listen to the radio	33	Instructions
Chat	26	See instant messaging above
Genealogy	22	Information, presented clearly
Distance learning	21	See study material above
Read blogs	17	Should be written in the language of the target reader

they accessed the web for that reason. Not part of the Oxford survey, but added for this text, are comments on the importance of good content. The list is presented to emphasise how the development of good content permeates all aspects of the commercial web presence.

For the commercial web site to achieve its objectives, content on the commercial web site should be professionally written. To do any other is to limit the site's potential for success. If the web site offers online sales then the content should be sales 'copy', and should be written by an expert in such. As writer on web site content, Gerry McGovern (2002) says, 'creating content is not a mundane task. The objective of content is to communicate knowledge that will either reinforce or change behavior. This is a huge challenge that demands tremendous intelligence and skill.' Bly (2003) addresses the question 'should you write your own copy?' with an enthusiastic, if ironic 'yes', but then adds the caveat – 'but only IF these three conditions exist:

- you are an excellent copywriter,
- you enjoy writing copy and
- you have the time to write copy.'

MINI CASE 8.6 The amateur content

Although not a strictly a commercial site in its own right, Matt Barrett's Athens survival guide (www.athensguide.com) does include Google generated ads, so presumably it does generate some income. A portal, this site is included here as a showcase of how 'amateur' writing can exhibit a passion that can be missing in commercial sites. Though he might not realise it, Matt displays a considerable skill in writing both content and copy. The site is enhanced by the idiosyncrasy of what appears to be a labour of love by its author. Developers beware however, this is a rare exception to the rule of having content written professionally that actually works.

The restaurants page of Matt Barrett's, *Guide to Athens*.

Content and copy

Textual content of a web site can be made up of copy or content, it is important to distinguish the two writing formats.

- **Copy**, according to Collin's English Dictionary, is 'the words used to present a promotional message'. For the online marketer this definition is insufficient, with online copy serving two purposes:

  1. **Acting as a 'call-to-action'**. A call-to-action is a word or phrase that encourages the user to take an action desired by the writer. Fig 8.11 shows examples of 'actions' that a commercial web site might have as part of its objectives. However, online copy is not limited to encouraging that conclusive action, so in this application, the term 'sales copy' is inappropriate. Online, call-to-action copy is the text that drives user actions, taking them from the front page of a web site to the desired conclusive action. This could be as basic as a banner ad that says 'click here to go to this week's special offers' to being used as part of persuasive architecture where navigation links are calls-to-action. For example, the link that says 'products' is actually saying 'if you want to find out more about the products that might be of benefit to you click here'. Giving the product link (it might be a text or a button), any other name reduces the chances of the user making it to the conclusive action.

  2. **The provision of promotional material** that helps visitors achieve their intended goals. In chapter 5 we introduced the concept of 'helping the buyer to buy', and copy is part of that process. In this application 'sales copy' can be a valid term for the text. This

Fig 8.11 Actions that a web site might desire of its visitors in order for site objectives to be attained

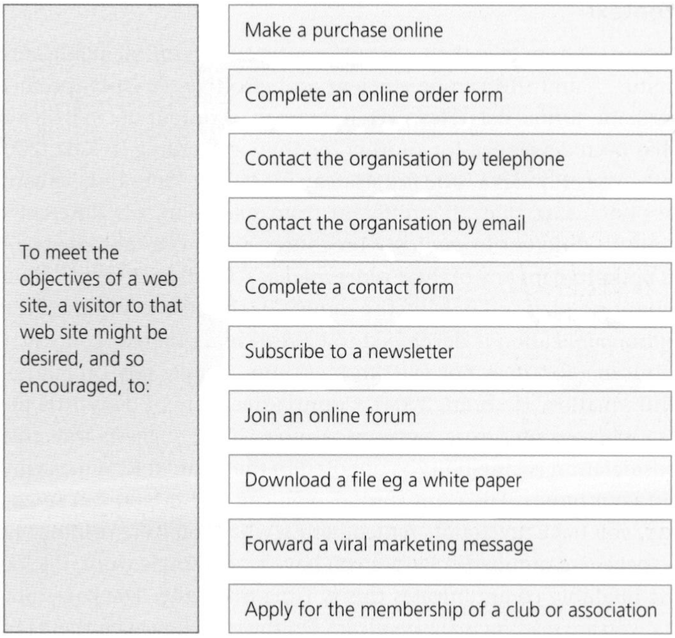

To meet the objectives of a web site, a visitor to that web site might be desired, and so encouraged, to:

- Make a purchase online
- Complete an online order form
- Contact the organisation by telephone
- Contact the organisation by email
- Complete a contact form
- Subscribe to a newsletter
- Join an online forum
- Download a file eg a white paper
- Forward a viral marketing message
- Apply for the membership of a club or association

copy is the text which helps the buyer in their decision-making process. A description of the product, a reassuring message about privacy and a clearly stated no-quibble returns policy are all part of the copy that will encourage the user to become a buyer.

The good copywriter will be able to combine both of these purposes into the same text.

• Content. Where *copy* is primarily persuasive, *content* is informative. It comprises of longer bodies of text that readers might need, or wish, to read. Content might include such things as legal terms and conditions, papers or articles. The history of stained glass windows on a web site promoting courses on glass making is, for example, content. Perhaps the most obvious example of content, as opposed to copy, would be news stories featured in an online newspaper. Product descriptions might have an element of 'copy' in them, but would primarily be 'content'.

Although the online marketer should be able to differentiate copy and content, for the user – the potential customer – all text is content. This creates a problem for the web site developer.

Copy cannot be used simply to move the user to the next section, page or objective without regard for content. Similarly, content cannot be developed without attention being given to the copy that is necessary to help the site meet its objectives. Historically, copywriters and content writers trained and worked in their own environments. Newspapers, for example, employ journalists to write news stories – the content – and copywriters to compose promotional copy. Successful writing for the Internet requires copy and content to blend seamlessly, interacting to meet the needs of the user and the objectives of the site's publisher. However, there is a shortage of writers who have the skills, and inclination, to combine the two elements of online text. There is little doubt that the acceptance of the Internet as a legitimate, and increasingly significant element of marketing strategy, will see an increase in people willing and able to write effective web site content.

Content in context

Many organisations simply take their web site content from offline publications and other corporate literature – and this can be efficient and effective. Product specification, for example, is rather static, formal data. However, it is rare that content sits well on a web site when that content has been developed for another medium. According to Katz (2001), to simply duplicate what works offline is a 'sure fire strategy for failure'. Speaking on content development, Nielsen (1997) says that, 'It's different from television, it's different from printed newspapers, and it's different from glossy brochures, so you cannot create a good website out of content optimized for any of these older media. The old analogy still holds: movies are not made by filming a play and putting the camera in the best seat of the theatre.' Content written for offline publication is developed to be read in a different context than it is on a PC monitor. 'Information does not exist in a vacuum. People rely on context in order to comprehend information' (Gahran, 2004). Context-free content does little to give the web site visitor a satisfactory user experience. McAlpine (2001) suggests that the key issue in contextual consideration is tangibility as opposed to the intangible. A magazine, she says, is '. . . material in your hands. The form is solid. You can feel it, you can smell it . . . If your attention strays, you have no trouble remembering what you were reading. The front page has a title. The pages are numbered. Before you have read a single word, the look and feel of Time magazine infallibly communicates this is Time magazine. The pages are stapled. The context of what you are reading is always clear'. On the web, however, these tangible aspects of the publication do not exist. Print content is linear, such that page 7 is linked to page 6 and page 8. Web content on the other hand can have multiple links, meaning the reader can

Fig 8.12 How textual content can improve results on web sites

Site Version	Sample Paragraph	Usability Improvement (relative to control condition)
Promotional writing (control condition) using the 'marketese' found on many commercial websites	Nebraska is filled with internationally recognised attractions that draw large crowds of people every year, without fail. In 1996, some of the most popular places were Fort Robinson State Park (355,000 visitors), Scotts Bluff National Monument (132,166), Arbor Lodge State Historical Park & Museum (100,000), Carhenge, (86,598), Stuhr Museum of the Prairie Pioneer (60,002), and Buffalo Bill Ranch State Historical Park (28,446).	0% (by definition)
Concise text with about half the word count as the control condition	In 1996, six of the best-attended attractions in Nebraska were Fort Robinson State Park, Scotts Bluff National Monument, Arbor Lodge State Historical Park & Museum, Carhenge, Stuhr Museum of the Prairie Pioneer, and Buffalo Bill Ranch State Historical Park.	58%
Scannable layout using the same text as the control condition in a layout that facilitated scanning	Nebraska is filled with internationally recognised attractions that draw large crowds of people every year, without fail. In 1996, some of the most popular places were: • Fort Robinson State Park (355,000 visitors) • Scotts Bluff National Monument (132,166) • Arbor Lodge State Historical Park & Museum (100,000) • Carhenge (86,598) • Stuhr Museum of the Prairie Pioneer (60,002) • Buffalo Bill Ranch State Historical Park (28,446).	47%
Objective language using neutral rather than subjective, boastful, or exaggerated language (otherwise the same as the control condition)	Nebraska has several attractions. In 1996, some of the most-visited places were Fort Robinson State Park (355,000 visitors), Scotts Bluff National Monument (132,166), Arbor Lodge State Historical Park & Museum (100,000), Carhenge, (86,598), Stuhr Museum of the Prairie Pioneer (60,002), and Buffalo Bill Ranch State Historical Park (28,446).	27%
Combined version using all three improvements in writing style together: concise, scannable, and objective	In 1996, six of the most-visited places in Nebraska were: • Fort Robinson State Park • Scotts Bluff National Monument • Arbor Lodge State Historical Park & Museum • Carhenge • Stuhr Museum of the Prairie Pioneer • Buffalo Bill Ranch State Historical Park	124%

LEGAL EAGLE BOX 8.2 Misleading online statements

Misleading online advertisements in the UK are partly regulated by the Control of Misleading Advertisement Regulations of 1998 as amended by the Control of Misleading Advertisement (Amendment) Regulations 2000.

A misleading online advertisement is one which deceives or is likely to deceive its readers and affect their economic decision-making. An online statement will affect the economic decision-making of the recipients if it persuades them to part with money. An online advert will be regarded as deceptive if it:

• Contains a false statement of fact;
• Conceals or leaves out important facts;

• Promises to do something but there is no intention of carrying it out;
• Creates a false impression even if everything stated in it is true.

The Committee of Advertising Practice (CAP) has also produced a British Code of Advertising Sales Promotion and Direct Marketing (the CAP Code). This Code applies to e-marketing communications in the following areas:

• Online advertisement in 'paid for' space such as online banner and pop-up advertisements
• Advertisements in commercial e-mails, and sales promotions wherever they appear online.

MINI CASE 8.7 Personalised information for new and expectant parents

A site that does an excellent job of offering well-written, personalised information is that of BabyCenter (www.babycenter. com). Being a new or expectant parent is one of the most meaningful life changes a couple experiences, and this site addresses all the issues about which the parents-to-be might wonder. The web site offers answers to the numerous and varied questions that new parents have. Furthermore, the company starts the process by asking one simple question: 'When is your due date or baby's birth date?' Personalised emails inform parents of what's going on during the pregnancy or with the new baby, based on the child's age. By offering highly relevant information to customers at a critical stage of their lives, BabyCenter has become a trusted resource for millions of new and expectant parents. Information is drawn from both experts and the opinions of the parent community, meaning that BabyCenter offers a range of credible information for customers – which they use to evaluate the company's online store offers.

• The fourth group are not prospects, nor are they qualified to take advantage of the product or service. They are there by mistake.

With the exception of the latter, each group will require something different from the web site. Not to consider all three is to neglect the purpose of the web site. It is in the textual content, rather than the design elements of the web site, that the web site can be made to appeal to the different segments as illustrated in Mini case 8.7.

Content management

Giving textual content the attention it deserves is a good start if the web site is to stand any chance of achieving its objectives. However, web site content is dynamic rather than static. Content must, therefore, be managed. Content management, as the title suggests, is about *managing* the content of the web site. In printed publications, the job title of someone who undertakes such duties is the editor. The editor's job is to ensure that the right content is getting to the right reader at the right time at the right cost. This is the same job that the web site content manager takes on. Seizing on the commercial opportunity, a myriad of software vendors have produced applications that offer the organisation 'content management'. To describe such software as content management tools is misleading. It does little more than provide a method of accessing web sites and changing the content, though as such it has its benefits. This is, however, the limit of any *management* that it offers. It does not

---

MINI CASE 8.8 Demystifying content management

'Content management' is a new name for publishing. The core objective of publishing is to get the right content to the right person at the right time at the right cost. Publishers manage publications. Key staff include authors and editors. Authors create content. Editors decide what content should get published and how much editing that content requires.

When the printing press was invented, the process of printing was difficult and complex. The very act of printing was as fascinating as what was being printed.

So too with the web. It was invented by Tim Berners-Lee as a publishing tool. That is why we have HTML, a publishing markup language. That's why we have web 'pages.' Content management is web-based publishing.

The early years of Web publishing, like the early years of printing, were very dependent on the programmer/developer (the printer). Publishing a large web site was a major technical feat.

Many people like to make their discipline sound complex because it makes them appear more valuable to the organisation. Web publishing sounded very complex.

However, web publishing technology is becoming streamlined and standardised. The focus is moving away from tools and toward content. If you understand content, this is your time to shine. Publishing content is a centuries-old discipline. The basic rules and concepts are the same, whether you are publishing in ink or on the web.

Let us take a publishing perspective to a sample of content management terms:

- Content toxicity: A pretty ridiculous name for out-of-date content.
- Dynamic content: Usually content published from a database. However, whether or not content is published from a database is not relevant. What is relevant is the content is accurate, well written, and up to date.

- Static content: Content published using static HTML. Again, a largely irrelevant term.
- Interactive content: Another irrelevant term. People interact: content informs.
- Content re-engineering: A mechanical name for editing.
- Content master: An editor or author.
- Content manager: An editor.
- Content strategist: An editor.
- Information architecture: The discipline of managing the organisation and layout of web content. In print, editors have managed information architecture-type challenges for centuries (table of contents, indexes, etc.)
- Knowledge harvesting: A weird name for what editors do when they select good content from all the poor stuff they get.
- Content weeding: The act of editors weeding out poor content.
- Personalised content: Published content. Publishing is, by definition, an act of personalisation. The *New York Times* has a specific scope and focus. *Sports Illustrated* is about sports. *Fortune* magazine is about business. If you edit a web site, you are by definition creating personalised content. As with much about the web, personalisation has been vastly over-hyped.

I have yet to come across a content management issue that cannot be understood from a publishing perspective. If you are managing a web site, thinking like a publisher can help you clear away the fog of hyperbole. You can focus on what you really need to do to achieve success.

McGovern, G (2002) Available on: www.clickz.com
Copyright 2005 Jupitermedia Corporation All Rights Reserved.

commission, source, select, proof read or reject content. It does not act as an editor. It does not replace an editor – or anyone – with an editor's duties. The content must still be developed before the 'content management' tools can do their job but at least from the customer's perspective, there is a better chance of the content being fresh, topical and relevant if the software is user-friendly.

8.6 Design tips for increasing web sales

In our introduction, Huang and Christopher (2003), argued that designers must understand online buyer behaviour. For a commercial site, generating and increasing revenue is a fundamental objective. Numerous tools and opportunities present themselves throughout a web site's pages. Here we consider a number of design opportunities that simplify the customer's shopping experience and increase the prospect of a profitable transaction.

- Make the category navigation tabs clear and representative of the product, eg books, DVD, CD, digital cameras, etc.

- Provide a link to the shopping cart. CD WOW provides a 'Floating Cart' making it permanently accessible as you browse different pages.

- Provide concise, informative and descriptive product copy. For example Fresh Soap Deli succinctly describes its Triple Lemon soap as 'An explosion of energy with lemon, bergamot, lemongrass and fresh lemons, will revive and stimulate' (www.freshsoapdeli.com).

- Alongside product descriptions, include 'call to action' buttons that prompt the customer. These include 'more info' and 'buy now'.

- Provide links that display items previously 'bought' and 'viewed'. This is useful for repeat purchases and when consumers are evaluating alternatives from different sites.

- Provide links to other channels for ordering. Some consumers may use different channels for different purposes eg Internet for information, and the telephone for ordering, especially if they have security concerns about online fraud.

- Provide a user-friendly and flexible shopping cart and checkout function that enables consumers to add quantities, delete and recalculate, and complete the transactional process smoothly.

- Make sure you get the customer to input their e-mail address at the checkout for future communications and incentivise them to sign up to your newsletter.

- At the checkout, use cross-selling opportunities. Eg if the customer is purchasing a Photo Printer, this should be a trigger to offer deals on printer paper, memory cards or other accessories.

- Use high quality photography and other visual images to promote and sell your offer. Remember a picture paints a thousand words.

- For a variety of reasons, including bad site design, merchants may find carts abandoned with items entered. Timely reminders by e-mail that may ascertain if the consumer has encountered any site problems could reactivate a significant volume of sales at the checkout, and a link back to the site via the e-mail will also help.

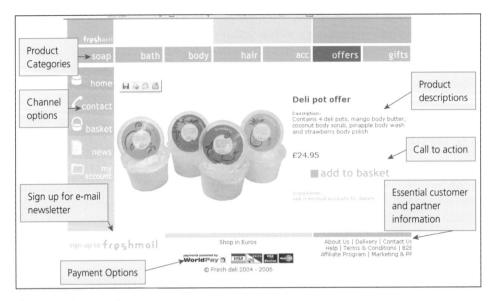

Fig 8.13 Fresh Soap Deli

In Fig 8.13 we see the simple yet effective design of the Fresh Soap deli web site.

Web site development is an ongoing process. Testing, evaluating and refining every element is essential for revenue generation, added value and competitive advantage. Having designed an effective site for the various 'publics', they must accept and adhere to the terms and conditions stated on the legal elements. See Legal Eagle Box 8.3.

LEGAL EAGLE BOX 8.3 Web-site legalities

1. The use of a web site should be subject to acceptance of some Terms of Use, Privacy Policy, and Disclaimers as well as other notices posted on the web site from time to time. The 'look' and 'feel' of any site should be subject to intellectual property law. Users of a web site should be required to read and adhere to copyright/trade mark notices.

With interactive sites the site owner should protect and keep personal information transmitted through it secure and confidential. Before transmitting personal information site users should be referred to the Privacy Policy by clicking on a link. Personal or confidential information collected through web sites should not be disclosed to third parties.

Every effort should be used to keep web-based communications secure. Individual web site users should also be required to take appropriate steps to protect their personal information when using a web site. Web site owners should reserve the right to deny access to a user where there is reasonable suspicion of violation of any law by that user.

Users' Conduct

Users of a web site should be prohibited from:

- Disrupting or interfering with the security of the site or otherwise abusing any service provided on the site or linked web site.

- Disrupting, interfering or abusing any other user's enjoyment of the site.

- Obtaining unauthorised access to any part of the site that is restricted from public access.

- Defaming, abusing, harassing, threatening or otherwise violating the legal rights of others.

- Impersonating another person or entity or falsifying anyone's attributions.

- Restricting or prohibiting any other user from using the web site.

8.7 Summary

For the Internet user, a web site is simply something that makes up the World Wide Web. For the marketer it is much more. The development of a web site is now an essential element in any strategic marketing effort – whether that is as a medium for promotion, a lead generator, or part of an after sales service. This means that web site development must be given the same respect as any other aspect of the marketing strategy. After examining the different online trading models and how organisations can use portals as part of their online presence, the chapter concentrated on three aspects of commercial web sites. The first element looked at how the web site is developed, considering issues such as what the objectives of the site are, who is responsible for its development and how it should be developed. The second element considered the usability of a web site and how poor usability will reflect badly on the organisation, or brand, that publishes it. Design guides were considered, as was online credibility before design practice is examined. The final element emphasised the importance of good content to a web site, also raising the issue of content management systems.

END OF CHAPTER CASE STUDY One of yours?

A news clip just informed me: a phenomenal 80% of all purchasing decisions are made or influenced by women! I can not actually verify that statistic for you (the talking head certainly sounded credible enough), but I can tell you that women – in one way, shape or form – are behind the majority of actions people take on your web site. The question is, are you helping these economically powerful people accomplish their tasks on your web site? Do you really know what they need? How would you even start? Your web site's persuasion architecture must begin with an understanding of your audience, not in the aggregate, but in the specific. So, meet Danielle. A specific if there ever was one!

Big Picture Stuff

We have discussed with you the four different categories of visitors that land on your site:

1. The one who knows exactly what he/she wants and nothing is going to get in their way. They are highly motivated and goal-oriented.

2. The one who has a pretty good idea of what he/she wants and would buy if presented with the right item, but is still in the process of narrowing their final decision. They are quite motivated, but you have room to work some persuasion magic.

3. The one who does not have anything specific in mind, but would buy if you could hit the right button (think window-shopper). They are only mildly motivated and your persuasive skills have to be operating at peak efficiency.

4. The one who landed on your site by mistake, has zero motivation and will probably click elsewhere.

As a bare minimum, your web site must incorporate navigational and persuasive structures that account for these fundamental mindsets. The second and third types constitute the great untapped gold mine of your audience. The best-performing web sites, however, take this framework much farther: they incorporate personas. A persona is a construct, a character fleshed-out from demographic, psychographic and topological factors, for whom you design a specific navigation pathway through your site. And because no one persona characterises your entire audience (humans are definitely not one-size-fits-all), you need more than one persona construct, hence more than one way to navigate through to the goal. The process of constructing a persona begins with understanding an individual.

Back to Danielle

Danielle (untrained in the nuances of persuasion architecture) was a mystery shopper for our forthcoming Online Retail Study for Customer-Focused Excellence. A 20-something, single mother, Danielle describes herself as a micro-manager and works an entry-level management job. She is an urban dweller (she shares an apartment with several others to keep her costs down) who does not own a car or know how to drive. She works hard so she can pay her debts and find a place where just she and her son can live together. Detail-oriented, Danielle enjoys getting the most out of life. Generally frugal in her purchasing, she rarely buys for the sake of buying, although she has been known to be impulsive and justify an expensive purchase for personal reasons. More often than not, though, she thinks carefully and researches her options before spending lots of money. Got a nice mental picture of this person? Now read her reactions to shopping online. They are truthful, honest and something you need to internalise. Pay very close attention . . . your potential customer speaks:

In Danielle's Words

In the world today, evolving technology is supposed to provide us with the conveniences to make our everyday lives easier. It enables us to be continually connected to our home, job, family and friends – including the people we do everyday business with like the butcher, baker and candlestick maker. But is the Internet going to replace the physical store? Probably not, at this rate. Why? Because in their quests to simplify my life, they set up their shops in such a way that the whole process of online shopping ends up taking longer and aggravates me more than getting up early on a Sunday morning, hopping on the train or bus and schlepping to the store itself. In the end it just makes me want to scream 'I NEVER EVER WANT TO SHOP ONLINE AGAIN'! When I was given my assigned web sites to shop on, I found I had lots of clothing and accessory sites. I love to shop for clothes and accessories, so I logged on with a mission to find the perfect little black dress (I am not really a window-shopper; when I shop I normally have something in mind that I want). I thought having a target would help me with navigation and the entire process, but I was wrong. Instead, I was helped to a serious dose of frustration. I was assigned the Land's End web site this year, and I can see why it won last year's survey: there's descriptive copy, it is in plain spoken English, they even give you a virtual model! Two things about this site bothered me, though. The first – it took about a minute to load up a product page. While it is great to be able to enlarge the pictures, there has got to be a way to make the upload faster. The second – copy was scattered all over the place; some of the copy was on the top of the page, and if I wanted to know more about the product I had to scroll down. When I am reading about a product I do not want to look for the copy. What is worse than having to scroll down to the bottom of the page for copy is having no copy at all – just a blurb. This was my experience on many other sites. I mean, I am on the site looking to spend my money. The very least they could do is try to convince me. Don't let the pictures speak for themselves. Pictures never really do a product justice to begin with. Tell me where I could wear this. Since I cannot feel the fabric, tell me what it feels like. For example, although the Newport News web site describes a material as 'plush', they leave the picture to sell the product. And in most pictures, I can barely see the product, so how can the combination of a picture and a brief blurb of copy convince me to buy this item? It does not. I want to know: Why should I buy this?

Have you ever been to a department store like Macy's and found the perfect dress, but you were not sure whether to buy it or not? So you decide to keep looking and then if you really want it, you figure you can go and order it on their web site since it is part of their new line. This happened to me. I actually found that little black dress in Macy's department store, but I wanted to see if I could get it cheaper somewhere else. I kept looking around, but then I got this assignment so I decided it was fate that I buy this dress. So I log on to macys.com and look at the categories at the top of the page, it looks easy enough – all the categories are clearly listed. So I click on 'Women'. Then it brings me to the next page, where there are more categories, also clearly listed and since I am looking for that black dress I so badly wanted, I click on the obvious category of 'Dresses'. Easy, I think to myself. After I click on Dresses, there are more categories to choose from if I wanted to narrow it down more: All Occasion, Bridesmaid, Daytime, Evening, Juniors and Sundresses. I do not really know what my dress would be under so I decide to look through all the dresses.

I never found my dress. I even searched for it by choosing a brand. So I felt grumpy because they did not have the dress online; moreover, I could not shop by brand because they did not have their own store brand available to shop by. Before I looked I wish they had a disclaimer saying that not everything in stock at the store is available on the web site or even better still; make all their common stocked merchandise available on the web site. Unfortunately Macy's web site is just as confusing as their department stores.

Another thing that really got on my nerves when I was doing my mystery shopping was having to search for policies. To view most policies, you have to scroll to the bottom of the page and find a link. I do not want to scroll to the bottom for these things. I want to see this information when I first get on a product page, maybe on the side of the page. When I finally find the link to policies, I often find the policies are so vague and legalistic that I even have to think about who pays the shipping if I have to return something. How hard can it be to say, 'We'll take back any product you are not satisfied with. If you ordered the wrong size or don't like it, you're responsible for the return shipping. If we made a mistake or the product is inferior, you won't be charged for shipping'?

Then, when I finally decide to buy something, the checkout process takes too long. Many of these sites have an indicator letting me know how long till my purchase is completed, but it is not always accurate. Sometimes it says there are only four steps to an easy check out, but each step winds up having three pages of data I have to fill in. I will not shop on these sites again because I feel they are being dishonest – as if I am in a horse race and my rider is sitting on top of me dangling a carrot in front of my face for three hours saying 'One more step and we'll be done'.

Pattern for Persona

Think you have got someone like Danielle coming to your site hoping to do business with you? Delightfully unique though

Danielle is, she is also an average Jane. Listen to what she has to say. Think about how your site might better help all your Danielles accomplish their goals. Then, when you think you understand Danielle really really well, start thinking about Kevin! And Elizabeth! And don't forget Carlos!

Bryan Eisenberg, 2004, Reprinted from the GrokDotCom Newsletter with permission, copyright 2004, Future Now Inc. www.futurenowinc.com.

Questions

1. How might a clothing retailer develop its web site to better serve 'Danielle'?

2. Develop at least one other 'persona' and then consider how a web site selling a product for which your 'persona' is a target customer. Hint: why not use the persona of a member of your family or someone you know well?

3. What are the drawbacks to developing a retail site to suite specific personas?

DISCUSSION QUESTIONS

1. What is the concept of 'usability' and why is it so important?

2. Apply the BBC's 12-point check to a web site of your choice – your employer or place of study for example. Assess the validity of each point for that particular web site.

3. Section 8.4 suggests that users have a mental map of how their 'ideal' web page should look and that many web sites have adopted the header-columns-footer model, so making this the 'ideal' format. Present arguments that support and counter this 'ideal' format.

REFERENCES

Armstrong, A, Hagel, J III (1996) The real value of on-line communities, *Harvard Business Review*, Vol 74, No 3, 135–41

Bly, B (2003) Should you write your own copy? *Bob Bly's Direct Response Newsletter*, September 2003

Burke, K (2002) *Intelligent Selling*, Multimedia Live, CA, US, 1

Carragher, J (2002) *Why Web Sites Don't Work*, Trinomics Ltd

Carroll, M (2003) Usability and web analytics, *Interactive Marketing*, Vol 4, No 3, Jan/March 2003

Chisholm, W, Vanderheiden, G & Jacobs, I (1999) *Web Content Accessibility Guidelines 1.0*, Worldwide Web Consortium

Cripps, M (2002) *Making the Web Work for You*, The IDM Practitioner's Guide, Middlesex, London, Ch 7.3

Dalal, NP, Quible, Z, Wyatt, K, (2000) Cognitive design of home pages: an experimental study of comprehension on the World Wide Web, *Information Processing and Management*, Vol 36, No 4, 607–21

Eisenberg, B (2001) *KISS your Customers if You Want Them Back*. Available online at www.clickz.com/article.php/841041

Eisenberg, B (2004) *Are You Designing for Usability or Sales?* Available online at www.clickz.com/experts/crm/traffic/article.php/3297211

Eisenberg B, Eisenberg J (2005) *Call to Action: Secret Formulas to Improve Online Results*, Future Now Inc., New York

Fogg BJ (1999) *What Variables Affect Web Site Credibility*, CSLI IAP Conference, Nov 1999

Gahran, A (2004) *Contextual Editing: Not Yet Dead*. Available online at www.Contentious.com

Grokdotcom a Anon 2003 *Boring Giants?* Available online at www.grokdotcom.com/ website-design-that-sells.htm

Halls, J (2002) *The 12 Deadly Sins of Site Design*. BBC Training and Development. Available online at www.bbctraining.co.uk. Accessed November 2002

Hirsh, L (2001) *10 Surefire Tips for Driving Customers Away*. Available online at www.crmdaily.com/perl/story/14291.html

Huang, AS, & Christopher, D (2003) Planning an effective Internet retail store, *Marketing Intelligence and Planning*, Vol 21, No 4, 230–238

Johnston, L (2003) *An Architect's Secret for Marketers'*. Available online at www.grokdotcom.com/architectformarketers.htm

Lindgaard, G, Fernandes, G, Dudek, C, Brown, J (2006) Attention web designers: you have 50 milliseconds to make a good first impression! *Journal of Behaviour & Information Technology*, Vol 25, No 2 / March-April 2006, 115–126

Lockhorn, J (2003) *The Importance of QA*. Available on www.clickz.com/experts/ad/ad_tech/article.php/2237231

Loizides, L (2003) *Lesson in the Art of Flash*, INT Media Group. Available online at www.clickz.com/mkt/capital/print.php/2240791

Long, BS (2002) How to avoid common web mistakes, *Public Relations Tactics*, Vol 9, No 11

McAlpine, R (2001) *Web Word Wizardry*, Ten Speed Press

McGovern, G (2002) *Information Architecture Versus Graphic Design*. Available online at www.clickz.com/design/site_design/article.php/945631

McGovern, G & Norton, R (2002) *Content Critical*, Pearson Education

Morkes, J & Nielsen, J (1997) *How Users Read on the Web*. Available online at www.useit.com/alertbox/9710a.html

Morphy, E (2001) *Memo to Companies: You Are Your Web Site*. Available online at www.crmdaily.com/perl/story/14288.html

Morris, C (1999) *Good Page, Bad Page*. Available online at www.wdvl.com/Authoring/Design/Pages/good_bad.html

Moss, G, Gunn, R & Kubacki, K (2005) Optimising web design across Europe: gender implications, *International Journal of Applied Marketing*, in press

Muniz, AM Jr & O'Guinn, TC (2001) Brand community, *Journal of Consumer Research*, Vol 27, No 4, 412–32

Nielsen, J (2000) *Designing Web Usability*, New Riders Publishing, Indianapolis, US, 11, 308, 309

Nielsen, J (1997) *Top Ten Mistakes of Web Management*. Available online at www.useit.com/alertbox/9706b.html

Nielsen, J (2003) *Usability 101: Introduction to Usability*. Available online at www.useit.com/alertbox/20030825.html

Nielsen, J (2001) Source interview with Martina Bosshard, published on www.credit-suisse.ch 31/07/01

Nichol, N (2000) *20 Things That Should Never Appear On Your Web Site*. Available online at www.webgrammar.com/m10-f.html

Omniture (2005) *The Conversion Funnel & Persuasion Architecture*, Omniture Inc

Poirier, P (2003) *Can Your Site Stop Your Telephone from Ringing?* Available online at www.MarketingProfs.com

Rappa, D (1998) *Managing the Digital Enterprise*. Available online at www.digitalenterprise.org

RNIB (2001) *Why Should I Make Information Accessible?* Available online at
www.rnib.org.uk/seeitright/whyaccess.htm

Rose, GM, Staub, DW & Lees, JD (2000) *The Effect of Download Time on Consumer Attitude Toward the Retailer in E-commerce*. Proceedings of the Sixth Americas Conference on Information Systems, Long Beach, CA, 2000, 1352–1354

SciVisum (2005) *Campaign Effectiveness Study*, SciVisum Ltd

Stanford University *Guidelines for Web Credibility* (2002) Available online at
www.webcredibility.org/guidelines/index.html

Straub, D (2003) *Foundations of Net-Enhanced Organizations*, Wiley

Taylor, MJ & England, D (2006) Internet marketing: web site navigational design issues, *Marketing Intelligence and Planning*, Vol 24, No 1, 2006, 77–85

Timmers, P (1999) *Electronic Commerce, Strategies and Models for Business to Business Trading*, John Wiley & Sons Inc

Tomsen, MI (2000) *Killer Content: Strategies for Web Content and E-Commerce*, Addison Wesley

Traupel, L (2002) *Marketing to today's 'distracted' consumer*. Available online at
www.internetday.com/print/0,,1381_963161,00.html

Usborne, N (2002) *Net Words: creating high impact online copy*, McGraw Hill

Weil, D (2001) *Top tips on what makes a user-centric site*. Available online at
www.imakenews.com/wordbiz/e_article000100489.cfm?x=238915,0

Wilson, RF (2003) *12 web site design decisions your business or organisation will need to make correctly*, Web Marketing Today 9 July 2003. Available online at www.Wilsonweb.com

Young, ML (1999) *Internet: The Complete Reference*, Millennium Edition, Osborne/McGraw Hill

FURTHER READING

Carragher, J (2002) *Why Websites Don't Work*. Available online at
www.trinomics.com/publications/whywebsitesdontwork.pdf – an excellent web site evaluation from a business perspective.

IBM (2000) *Understanding Disability Issues When Designing Web Sites*. Available online at
www-3.ibm.com/able/disability.html

IBM *Web Design Guidelines*. Available online at www-3.ibm.com/ibm/easy/eou_ext.nsf/Publish/572. See comments on Keeker, below.

Keeker, K (1997) *Improving Web-site Usability and Appeal*: Guidelines compiled by MSN usability research. Available on www.msdn.microsoft.com/library/default.asp?url=/library/en-us/dnsiteplan/html/improvingsiteusa.asp – both the IBM guidelines and these by Keeker have flaws, but overall they are an excellent starting point for web designers and marketers alike.

Krug, S (2000) *Don't Make Me Think – A Common Sense Approach to Web Usability*, New Riders – the title of this book says it all for this practical text.

McGovern, G & Norton, R (2002) *Content Critical* Pearson Education – the sub-title to this text is: 'Gaining competitive advantage through high-quality web content', my advice would be to prefix this with 'if you are serious about' and add 'read this book' at the end.

McGovern, G, Norton, R & O'Dowd, C (2002) *The Web Content Style Guide*, Pearson Education – the text's sub-title describes it well: 'An essential reference for online writers, editors and manager'.

Nielsen, J (2000) *Designing Web Usability*, New Riders – considered overly simplistic by those designers who tend to design for themselves (and not their clients, or more importantly, the web site users), this book should be compulsory reading on all web design courses.

Seybold, P (1998) *Customers.com*, Random House – an excellent text on how e-technology can be used to meet customer needs. The section on how American Airlines adopted the web is a case study of how it should be done.

WEB LINKS

www.bobby.watchfire.com/bobby/html/en/index.jsp – Bobby, a free service that allows developers to test web pages for accessibility and encourage compliance with existing accessibility guidelines, such as the UK Disability Discrimination Act and W3C's Web Content Accessibility Guidelines (WCAG).

www.Contentious.com – news and musings on how we communicate in the online age from Amy Gahran.

www.Doctorebiz.com – the author of this site, Dr Wilson, is something of an evangelist in more ways than one (e-business and religion) and his presentation is a bit twee, but there is some good content, with particularly sound practical advice.

www.E-consultancy.com – research, information, training and events on best practice online marketing and e-commerce. Included on this site is a guide to accessibility (**www.e-consultancy.com/publications/accessibility**).

www.excessvoice.com – Excess Voice provides articles and advice from Nick Usborne, a leader in the field of online copywriting. The web site is the home of the Excess Voice newsletter. Not only is the newsletter free, but signing up qualifies readers to receive a series of excellent 'writing for the web' guides.

www.Gerrymcgovern.com – this site's title is 'web site content management solutions', though it is actually about content development. McGovern explains that the title attracts more consulting work than simply 'content development'. A sad reflection of how much online content is undervalued by businesses.

www.searchengineformarketers.com – This is Larry Chase's Search Engine for Marketers and it does what it says on the tin, offering reviews and links to the top sites in 40 marketing categories.

www.marketingexperiments.com – offers free copies of the extensive research results of **www.Marketingexperiments.com**.

www.Marketingprofs.com – excellent e-marketing content. Note however, the terminology used and models/theories quoted mean the articles are mainly for readers with a background in marketing.

www.Usabiltynews.com/news/article1008.asp – a framework for analysing the user experience.

www.Useit.com – usability guru Jakob Nielsen's web site is full of useful tips based on research and practice.

W3C Web Accessibility Resources – comprehensive information and advice on web accessibility from the W3C (**www.w3.org**).

Wordbiz – advice and tips from long time expert in e-newsletter and blogging, Debbie Weil (**www.wordbiz.com**).

 Visit the Online Resource Centre which accompanies this book, for lots of interesting additional material, including self-assessment questions, internet exercises, and links for each chapter: **www.oxfordtextbooks.co.uk/orc/gay/**

The Online Product

9

Learning objectives

By the end of the chapter you will be able to:

- Appreciate the significance of the product to online marketers
- Understand the implications a product's attributes have on their potential for successful online marketing
- Understand how the concept of the augmented product can be applied in the online environment
- Critically evaluate the role played by the Internet in the concept of mass customisation
- Understand key issues in online branding

9.1 Introduction

This chapter addresses the key elements of how the 'product' element of the marketing mix transfers online and the issue of the suitability of a product (or service) for marketing online is explored. In addition, we address the continued importance of effective branding as a top management priority and investigate the difference between the 'online brand' and the 'brand online' as well as considering how branding decisions can be influenced by the Internet.

Offline product identification is a straightforward exercise. Online however, marketers have had to re-evaluate just what the term 'product' means as well as making the fundamental decision on whether their product is suitable for online sales. The Oxford English dictionary (OED) offers three definitions of 'sold'. The first refers to 'the disposal of or transfer to a purchaser in exchange for money or other consideration' and forms the main focus of this chapter. The other two OED definitions are (1) to promote or facilitate the sale of objects, property, etc and (2) to persuade to accept or approve of – these are the objectives of far more web sites than those which have the objective of actually taking buyers' money in an online transaction. This is particularly true of B2B sites, where it is the norm for goods to be invoiced whereas public sector and not-for-profit web sites seek to promote and persuade stakeholders to utilise their services or support their cause. In chapter 5, a purchase behaviour matrix was presented (Table 5.1) which demonstrates how customers might use any combination of on and offline facilities in the buying process. Communications channels are becoming increasingly integrated. We also suggested that (potential) customers do not just use the web to *choose* a product, but also to *research* it in the first phase and during the process of researching a product, selling opportunities emerge. Few consumer-buying decisions for products of significant value are made purely at the point of sale. In most cases the decision is made, or at least influenced, before the shop (on or offline) is entered.

Many of the key product management and strategy decisions, such as introduction or deletion in the product lifecycle management, and penetration and diversification in models such as Ansoff's Matrix, are all relevant online as well as offline. The reality of the new economy for marketers is that these decisions have to be taken at speed and provide greater flexibility, agility, customisation and added value to an expectant marketplace.

Molenaar (2002) in discussing strategic business choices suggests a number of online considerations have emerged surrounding the nature of products sold, their delivery and their communication. These include:

1. Analysis of the benefits of increased product standardisation over customisation.

2. How market reach of the Internet may influence choices in (1). Reaching markets further afield may make standardisation from a production and communications perspective more attractive. However, Molenaar suggests smaller markets tend to demand more customisation.

3. If customisation is sought, what additional service elements are required to serve the chosen target market? Customisation suggests a more marketing oriented approach.

4. How does the nature of the product and the Internet's interactive dimensions facilitate new delivery modes? For example, the product may be capable of delivery over the Internet or partners in the supply chain may provide a new function.

In addition to these issues, marketers need to consider the role played by the Internet in relation to the brand building experience via the organisation's web site through different stages of the buying cycle. Is the objective to create brand awareness, to provide information, to generate leads and integrate with other channels or to sell online? The customer experience of the web site becomes a product in itself to influence present and future relationships. As Jim Sterne (2001) warns, 'your Web site is the window to the soul of your company.'

9.2 Product attributes and web marketing implications

Jobber and Fahy (2003) describe a product as 'anything that has the capacity to satisfy customer needs'. Blythe (2001) classifies consumer products in the following way:

1. Convenience products eg low-value products, bought habitually through intensive distribution channels with minimal promotional effort such as newspapers, soft drinks and everyday groceries like milk and bread.

2. Shopping products eg infrequently purchased items usually requiring some search effort from the consumer. Typically, the products may be household appliances or 'white goods' like fridge freezers and washing machines or personal computers which traditionally required personal selling and cooperation between retailers and manufacturers.

3. Speciality products eg items which have been thoughtfully researched and planned for by the consumer especially in relation to the product category and brand. They tend to be high-ticket items with limited distribution, superior outlets and levels of customer service to support all phases of the buying process.

4. Unsought products – these are products that consumers rarely seek out, instead they are aggressively promoted and sold. Blythe cites products like life insurance or encyclopedias in this category.

Regarding the four classifications and how they transfer online, we can make some general observations. The first classification contains goods that would rarely be purchased in isolation online because of their low value, and it would be unrealistic to fulfil such small orders online. Typically such products can form part of bigger orders through online grocery operations. In the second category, the combination of offline product searches and improved online product information has increased sales considerably. In addition, this classification has lent itself more readily to being sold online rather than in the high street for some organisations. For example, W.H. Smith & Sons tried selling personal computers in their high street stores but abandoned it due to the floor space taken and the cost of staff training, yet they could be sold successfully online with quality home installation instructions backed by telephone support. In the third category, virtually any *speciality* product can now be found online from hot tubs to gourmet food, from designer clothing to speciality flags. More high-ticket items are being bought online as customers grow in confidence and merchants refine their operation. The final category is an example of how the power has shifted from seller to buyer online. For example, consumers can 'search' and compare financial products quickly using price comparison sites without feeling any initial pressure from sales staff.

We can also make the distinction between physical products having tangible features such as a car or a computer, and service 'products' which are intangible, such as a life assurance policy or veterinary service. Some products combine both elements as in the case of a car. Added value is provided through style and performance and customer confidence is reinforced by a three-year warranty, free servicing provision and financing. The customer receives a bundle of benefits. The challenge for all marketers is the quest to harness the unique technological and communications assets of the Internet to provide additional online value through the total product offer with personalisation, customisation, interaction and comprehensive product information.

Three broad product categories can be sold online:

1. Physical or tangible products eg an iPod

2. Service or intangible products eg e-tickets or travel insurance distributed online

3. Digitised products eg digitised or e-books or downloaded software or music

The Internet can facilitate the success across related categories as in the case of the Apple iPod that largely relies upon the seamless link with its iTunes store for commercial success (see section 9.2).

As the Internet developed through the mid nineties it became obvious to many that selling products online would become a viable proposition. However, early predictions of the imminent demise of bricks and mortar retailers as shoppers flocked online proved unfounded. It also became obvious that not all products were ideally suited to electronic shopping (ES) due to the sensory dimensions in the buying phase such as those that required touch or feel prior to purchase – clothes or fresh food, for example. However some commoditised products readily lent themselves to ES – Amazon soon proved that books and CDs did. Molenaar (2002) argued that the most successful online products are those purchased on impulse, requiring a certain amount of interaction, and which are low risk and 'emotional' products. During this period many bricks and mortar retailers were cautious, and waited to see if the new medium was simply a passing fad. Other retailers were concerned that they could not operate both physically and electronically without one cannibalising the other. In attempting to assess the issue of cannibalisation, Michael de Kare Silver (1998) devised a framework to help determine a product's online aptness. The 'test' should be considered against the rate of consumer adoption of the Internet that was sporadic at the time. It was, and still is, a useful tool when contemplating *how* to sell online.

de Kare Silver's Electronic Shopping Test

The ES Test consists of three elements, each of which must be addressed to determine the product's suitability for online sales.

1. Product characteristics – what are the product's primal appeal to the senses? Does it need to be touched or tried before buying? Products that appeal to sight and sound senses make good candidates for ES. Books and music fit these. Products that appeal to touch, taste and smell are less likely to suit ES. Clothing, food and perfume were examples offered by de Kare Silver.

2. Familiarity and confidence – to what degree does the customer recognise and trust the product (and the merchant), and are they likely to repurchase it? The more familiar the product – or brand – is to the customer, the more confidence they would have in any repeat purchase of it. Brand strength is a critical issue for online retailers when seeking sustainable customer relationships. Similarly, engendering trust is another fundamental plank for online success.

3. Consumer attributes – what are their underlying motivations and attitudes towards shopping? Is it convenience or value? Do they like to experiment with new products, or

ways of purchasing them? Do they prefer to purchase environment friendly goods, from organisations that conduct ethical practice? Do they like the theatre of shopping and therefore have little enthusiasm for going online, or are they the new hybrid, multi-channel shopper?

When de Kare Silver's developed his ES Test (in 1998) his observations were generally well received, reflecting what many practitioners had learned at the 'coal face' of e-commerce. There was a tendency to concentrate on the first element – the characteristics of the product itself – in isolation. Hindsight has shown that the product itself is not the determining factor in its being suitable for sale online. For example, both food and flowers would fail the first element of the ES test, and yet both are successfully sold from web sites (eg Flowers.com, Tesco.com) as long as orders can be efficiently fulfilled. The key lies in de Kare Silver's second two elements being far more decisive.

The second element concentrates on 'familiarity and confidence' in the product or brand, though de Kare Silver focuses primarily on the 'repurchase' of goods. Although this is important, the contemporary online store cannot survive on repeat purchases alone. It needs to sell products that the buyer is purchasing for the first time to develop a critical mass. Since the ES test was published, the purchaser's 'familiarity and confidence' in the vendor, or its brand name, has become equally important and based on customer experiences. For the well-known bricks and mortar store that has gone online, the perceived values and trust of the offline organisation are taken to the online presence. Nigel Swaibey, Managing Director of one of the UK's leading direct marketing operations, Scott's of Stow (www.scottsofstow.co.uk) acknowledges the importance of the Internet experience as a complementary brand building channel to Scotts' other direct marketing activities. Commenting in *Direct Response*, April 2005, he says, 'We try to make the online experience richer by providing information, products and offers not available in our catalogues. Previews, special web-only offers sale features, are increasingly popular with our online customers.' Such features help develop online brand affinity and advocacy. Established offline retailers with a sound customer base had a significant advantage in terms of customer confidence and brand awareness compared to new online retailers.

For pure players with limited offline exposure, their actual web presence is an essential element in developing confidence in the mind of the customer especially with issues such as privacy, security and trust influencing buyer behaviour. Evidence of the importance of the credibility of the seller over-riding product characteristics can be taken from history. From 1893, Sears and Roebuck sold goods ranging from cookers to ladies' hats from their mail order catalogues. Families living in remote areas of the American Midwest had not heard of the manufacturers nor seen or touched the products, yet they trusted the company. Naturally, the non-availability of the goods in local (physical) stores added to the attraction of catalogue purchasing – something we address later in the chapter.

The third element of the ES test is 'consumer attributes' and the enthusiasm, or lack of it, of different segments towards the online experience, not to mention their IT competence levels. As well as the valid points raised by de Kare Silver about online buyer behaviour, the contemporary online marketer must also consider the developing role of the Internet and how it is deployed through the different phases of the overall buying process.

De Kare Silver was concentrating on the B2C online market. In B2B transactions, the suitability of the product to be sold online has additional considerations. One is that the product is likely to be a raw material or component part of a finished product. The specifications of the product will be such that a simply 'select > click > buy' procedure is not appropriate.

Perhaps more significant, however, is how B2B purchases take place in practice. Few are paid for in cash, therefore discussion on terms, lead times, delivery and so on is necessary and if credit facilities are to be offered, references must be taken up. There is also the issue of trust. Few businesses would initially spend money on a product that might be essential to that business without first being confident that those goods will be delivered on time, on budget and as specified. The confidence required for such a B2B purchase is unlikely to come from a visit to a web site alone. It is significant, however, that once that confidence is established, a web site is an ideal vehicle for making repeat purchases.

The digital product

Digital goods and services are 'products' that can utilise the Internet as a delivery mechanism. Digitisation provides many benefits for both consumers and organisations. For example, lower distribution costs, order tracking and opportunities to personalise product offerings can extend the product.

Digital products can come in one of three categories:

1. Products that are digital by composition
2. Products that can be presented in digital format
3. The product is information (which can be presented in electronic format)

The first category refers to products that exist only in a digital state and so make them ideal for sale and distribution via the Internet. Products that fall into this classification include software, computer games, and music. Whilst the transfer of software via the Internet was one of the first uses of the new medium as a channel of distribution, the latter has gained much public attention in recent years. Prior to the launch of MP3, iPod and similar digital music players, music always had a physical form, be that as a record, tape, or CD. The contemporary music collector no longer needs the storage space for the physical product, whole music collections can be stored in digital format on their PC, or even a device that fits in the palm of their hand. The recordings are downloaded directly from the Internet and played randomly if desired. With the rate of product change, consumers quickly take the features and benefits of many new products for granted.

The second category is the product that can be presented in digital format. These can be broken down into two sub-categories, those that exist only in digital format and those that can be digitised.

1. Products that exist only in digital format are those that have a tangible element, but the customer's 'ownership' is intangible. An example of this is in the travel industry, where a customer buys a flight but they do not take physical possession of the aircraft or any associated services. They do, however, need some kind of evidence of purchase to present before they are allowed to board the aircraft. Most airlines now offer ticketless check-in for flights. When the customer books, and pays for, a flight online they are issued with an e-ticket number. Consumers obtain value and convenience with the ability to select their seat choice, check-in, and print out their boarding pass. Upon arrival at the airport the passenger, if they have only carry-on baggage, can go straight to the departure lounge without having to queue at the check-in desk. For the airline, substantial cost savings are achieved with no staff involved in the ticket issuing process. The digitisation can be extended further. The airline passenger might also have booked a hotel room and car hire. As with the flight ticket, the presentation of a reservation number to the relevant service

provider is all that the customer needs in order to access those services. The product has never been tangible but paperwork, and its distribution, was previously required. Zhang (2004) summed this up in a paper that investigated the Japanese travel industry: 'Digitization can also reduce delivery cost. The products and services offered by the travel industry are easily digitized. Unlike physical products, reserved tours can be digitized and delivered via the Internet.' The proliferation of successful online travel agencies like Lastminute, Expedia, Deckchair, and Travelocity is a testament to the advantages to both vendor and purchaser of the digitised nature of holiday purchases. With a user-friendly offering, the customer can quickly become comfortable with the new digital purchase and delivery. Customers soon take such service elements for granted and they become part of the expected service for all carriers so further differentiation is needed to maintain some sort of competitive advantage.

2. Products that can be digitised are those that can be presented in physical format offline, but also be adapted to an online presence. Because of the nature of their development – they exist in a digital format before being produced as a tangible entity – newspapers are a perfect example. A newspaper can be printed on paper and sold as a physical product or its content can be presented digitally on a web site. Early predictions that the Internet would have a dramatic effect on sales of printed newspapers have not materialised, though the papers have still to decide on the best business model for their online offering and what to charge for. Many remain totally free to the online user. Some, like the *Financial Times* (www.ft.com), offer generic content for free, but more specific content is available only to subscribers. The *New York Times* (www.nytimes.com) offers a mix of free headlines, with full stories available to those who have completed the free registration process, and from September 2005, more specialised content on a subscription basis.

3. The third category is that of information *as a* product. People have always been willing to pay for information that benefits them or meets their needs. In this context, information has a monetary value and can be considered to be a product in its own right. The Internet can be used as the medium for the transmission of that product. Dann and Dann (2001) argue that information as a product lends itself to being sold over the Internet as it is expensive to generate but cheap to replicate. The Internet is an ideal medium through which information can be replicated indefinitely without distortion.

Types of information that can be sold as a product online can be broken into three main models:

(a) Information developed for offline purposes but transferred using the Internet as a medium for transmission. This would also include information that prior to the Internet would be available only in hard copy; Mintel (www.mintel.co.uk) and Keynote

---

MINI CASE 9.1 The price of the mag is to read the ad

Although the technology has been around for a couple of years, December 2005 saw *Time Magazine* become the biggest brand to date to try out a model for giving access to content previously only available through subscription. Time.com site visitors were given 24 hours' access to the celebrated 'Person of the Year' cover story, as well as the magazine's archive of articles. The cost? View an online multi-paged, full-screen interactive ad from Chrysler to gain entry to that part of the site featuring the premium content. *Time*'s hope is that the 'free' premium content will drive enough traffic to attract advertising income that will surpass that from subscribers. Part of a major sponsorship, the Time-Chrysler deal crossed over onto *Time*'s print edition.

(www.keynote.co.uk) market research reports that are familiar to many marketing students would fall into this category.

(b) Information prepared and presented purely for online transmission. For example, white papers that are written not only to disseminate information, research findings, and opinion, but also as a promotional tool for the person or organisation responsible for publishing it. A second example is e-books. These are often of a specialised nature and unlikely to be published in the traditional printed format (where a significant print-run is required) but are made available to be purchased and downloaded from a web site. However, leading authors such as Stephen King and Frederick Forsyth have forayed into the online world, and organisations like Online Originals (www.onlineoriginals.com) offer e-book opportunities to readers and budding authors.

(c) Information prepared in response to an online request and transmitted using Internet technology (though traditional methods of delivery could also be used). This could be any request for information where personal contact or presence is not required and the Internet is replacing traditional forms of communication. The information might be of a generic nature where the content is drawn from previously researched data or the customer might have requested specific information that had to be researched, analysed, and presented as a bespoke report. An example of this in the B2B market is Pira International (www.piranet.com) in Fig 9.1. On their web site users can use:

- The 'Enquiry Service' where Pira's 'information scientists' who have specialist knowledge of Pira's industry sectors and a unique collection of publications and electronic resources carry out search requests as well as desk research from published information.

- The 'Bespoke Information Service' that allows organisations to define their specific information requirements and determine the format and delivery of the information requested. Pira then collates, organises and distributes this information according to the organisation's predefined specifications.

Fig 9.1 The home page of Pira International (www.piranet.com)

The online service

A natural extension of information as a product is the intangible product – the service. As with the concept of information as a product, many online services (or e-services) are included as part of the organisation's overall offering, and not as a specific product to be paid for in itself. Pre- and post-sales services are perceived as part of the promotional effort or the augmented product (see next section) and not separate entities. Services that can be sold online are split into two fundamental groups:

1. those that can be paid for online and delivered offline, and
2. those that can be paid for *and* delivered online.

Services in the first group far outnumber those in the second. The payment for many services can be divorced from the actual performance of the service. Any service that can be paid for 'remotely' eg by telephone/credit card could also be paid for online. The web is being used as a benefit for both buyer (the convenience of being able to use the web as a medium for payment) and vendor, for whom online payment saves on the human resources required for other methods. Third party payment solutions operations such as PayPal and WorldPay provide trusted and secure payment facilities.

Services that are in the second group – those that can be paid for and delivered online – are less common. Effectively they are limited to services that can be delivered/presented in digital format. This type of service falls into two categories:

(a) Those that are a function of e-technology. For example, many businesses offer some kind of web site evaluation. An example of this is the 'Bobby' verification service offered by Watchfire (www.watchfire.com) that allows a site to be checked for compliance against the W3C (www.w3.org) accessibility guidelines for disabled users. The service, once initiated by the user, is conducted and delivered online.

(b) Those where the results of a performed service can be transmitted on the Internet eg a requested report is compiled offline, but transmitted by e-mail as a 'word' document, rather than being presented or delivered in 'hard' format.

The hard to find product

There is one other product that sells well online. In marketing terminology, this is commonly known as the 'niche' product – to the consumer it is the 'hard to find' product. It also has a close relative – the 'didn't know it existed' product. 'Hard to find' has almost become a generic search or brand term online, for example Hard to Find Records based in Birmingham (www.htfr.com).

Before the advent of the Internet there were many products that were difficult to find, even with the help of Yellow Pages! An antique hunter would have contacts, exhibitions, catalogues, and sales in which to seek out particular items. A keen angler would probably be a member of a club and subscribe to magazines where products might be advertised or featured. In a B2B context, there would be trade associations, industry journals and conferences to seek out contacts that might help source a product. But for many people such avenues did not exist. If suppliers were not listed in the local telephone directory, sourcing many products was problematic. Now, if you want a copy of an out of print book, a brake part for your 15-year old Japanese sports car, a holiday villa on a remote Greek island, or the nearest cinema showing an obscure French movie – simply typing the relevant phrase into a search engine should ensure that a solution is found.

With the exception of big online retailers, perhaps the most successful online businesses are those that offer the 'hard to get', niche products. Here are a few examples of such online product sites:

- Blackwell's the long established publisher and book retailer has its own rare book site at www.rarebooks.blackwell.co.uk.
- www.scotchwhisky.net is a site that helps satisfy the thirst and knowledge of whisky connoisseurs seeking a rare tipple from independent bottlers across Scotland.
- For boys who do not grow up, Slotcars Online (www.slotcarsonline.co.uk) offers enthusiasts the chance to source rare Scalextric cars.
- Sites like Trevena Cross Nursery (www.trevenacross.co.uk) offer gardening enthusiasts the opportunity to purchase rare and exotic plants.

In addition, small, specialist companies were unable to reach prospects outside their immediate geographical market. In some cases, they did not exist at all because the means to reach the market simply did not exist. Now a medium is available that can promote their product around the world. Such companies will normally have low overheads and as the products are rare, high selling prices are achievable. This means that a business with a relatively small turnover can still make a healthy profit. The Original Gift Company (www.theoriginalgift.co.uk) in Mini case 9.2 is good example of a specialist firm reaching out to a wider market.

MINI CASE 9.2 Help in finding an original gift

A company that takes the 'hard to find' concept a stage further is the Original Gift Company (www.theoriginalgift.co.uk). Not only can customers source unusual products, but the site also helps buyers in their search by allowing them to search for a gift under the criteria 'person', 'lifestyle', 'occasion', or 'type of gift'. The latter allows further search by such criteria as 'express', 'personalised', or by how much they wish to spend.

This phenomenon was first broached by Jakob Nielsen in 1997 and has been well addressed by Chris Anderson in his article, 'The Long Tail' (2004). Although focussed on the entertainment industry, Anderson's concept is relevant to nearly all sectors of business. In essence the model takes the 80/20 rule (also known as 'Pareto's principle' after Vilfredo Pareto, an Italian economist who devised the concept in 1906) that 20% of products are responsible for 80% of sales, a stage further. Anderson says that the 80% of sales come from high-maintenance-low-profit lines and that the remaining 20% can make high profits for niche operators. That 20% is the 'long tail' of sales. Anderson's article addresses the Internet's role in his model, making the 20% easier to market, and uses the following example from the music industry: 'For instance, the front screen of Rhapsody (www.rhapsody.com) features Britney Spears, unsurprisingly. Next to the listings of her work is a box of 'similar artists.' Among them is Pink. If you click on that and are pleased with what you hear, you may do the same for Pink's similar artists, which include No Doubt. And on No Doubt's page, the list includes a few 'followers' and 'influencers,' the last of which includes the Selecter, a 1980s ska band from Coventry, England. In three clicks, Rhapsody may have enticed a Britney Spears fan to try an album that can hardly be found in a record store.' This encapsulates how astute marketers can use the technology of the web to take potential buyers to web sites where they can buy niche products, but they might also purchase products that they did not even know existed.

Aggregation of products

In the past the customer would have to visit a number of retail outlets in order to meet their shopping needs (the origin of the term 'market'). Now we have 'one-stop-shopping', where one outlet supplies a wide range of products under one roof. Effectively, this is the story of the growth of local supermarkets through to the current out of town flagship stores. Although this may have benefits for the consumer, it can bring problems as well as advantages for the retailer. The most significant problem is that of aggregation of products involving logistics and inventory control issues. A retailer may carry 10,000 lines, they all have to be identified, sourced, ordered, received and displayed. This stock represents 'dead' money until it is sold. The Internet brings the major advantage of not having to carry that amount of stock. This was, and still is a major advantage for Amazon over its bricks and mortar book-selling competitors. Even a relatively small bookshop will hold thousands of books, many of which could be on the shelves for lengthy periods before they are sold. Yet without a wide range of books few customers will enter the shop to browse and purchase (the 80/20 rule mentioned above). Online, Amazon, Waterstones and Barnes and Noble can 'display' thousands of texts at very little variable cost, yet they need to stock only the most popular titles with others being ordered from publishers when the customer places an order. Neither do the 'virtual' books advertised deteriorate in the same way as the physical editions do when left on a shelf to be thumbed by browsers.

The definitive example of this concept is the **virtual business** where goods are promoted online, the purchases made online, and the order passed to a supplier who delivers directly to the customer. At no time does the virtual shop owner take possession of the goods, or even see them. The supplier invoices the virtual shop for the goods and delivery, which should be less than the customer has paid the online entity. This results in profit for the virtual business, profit for the supplier and satisfaction for the customer. In a service sector such as the hotel industry, many virtual businesses operate as an intermediary in the sale of hotel rooms such as eBookers (www.ebookers.com), Expedia (www.expedia.com) and BestStay.com (www.BestStay.com). Similarly, many online merchants take orders for 'white goods' (fridges, freezers, etc) without holding stock and the manufacturer aggregates the incoming orders to achieve efficient production runs. Though this business model was much hyped in the late nineties, success has not been easy for many truly virtual businesses.

9.3 The augmented product concept (APC) and its application to the web

Kotler (2003) suggests that each product has a hierarchy of customer value (Fig 9.2) on three levels that culminates in the 'augmented product'.

The three levels are as follows:

1. The core product – describes the fundamental benefit derived from the product. A car is primarily provides a mode of transport.

2. The actual product – describes the tangible and intangible elements incorporated into the product that present the total offer to the consumer. Kotler suggests that five elements can be built around a tangible product and these are:

   • Quality level

   • Features

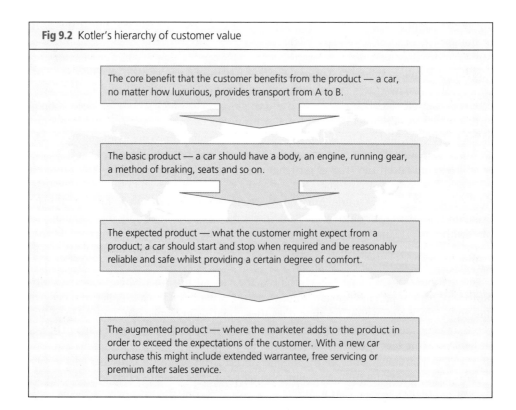

Fig 9.2 Kotler's hierarchy of customer value

The core benefit that the customer benefits from the product — a car, no matter how luxurious, provides transport from A to B.

The basic product — a car should have a body, an engine, running gear, a method of braking, seats and so on.

The expected product — what the customer might expect from a product; a car should start and stop when required and be reasonably reliable and safe whilst providing a certain degree of comfort.

The augmented product — where the marketer adds to the product in order to exceed the expectations of the customer. With a new car purchase this might include extended warrantee, free servicing or premium after sales service.

- Styling
- Brand name
- Packaging

3. The augmented product incorporates additional features and service elements that deliver extra customer satisfaction and provide points of differentiation over competitor offerings. For example, a car with a five year warranty as standard would have a distinct selling advantage over those without. Aaker (2002) argues that in mature product categories there is a degree of 'sameness' and he believes that the Internet offers considerable to scope to differentiate products and services. He cites the example of how Pampers differentiated itself from its key competitors like Huggies through a variety of online programmes using its web site. The programmes included parenting advice through the Pampers Parenting Institute, a loyalty reward programme with Fisher Price Toys and customer competitions. It is clear that the augmented product level is inextricably linked to the brand experience.

In earlier additions of Kotler, a fourth element was also included, namely *the forecasted product*. This is where product managers utilise marketing research and apply their own intuition to take the product forward into the future, either through incremental modification or new product development.

With the exception of the first point, the core benefit, there are other issues that will affect the customer's definition of each stage. The cost of the product is an obvious influence. Staying with new cars as an example, the purchaser of a £60,000 Mercedes would expect air conditioning as part of the 'basic' product. The same could not be said of a £5,000 Hyundai. Brand, or brand perception, would be another issue. Again, the owner of the new Mercedes will have an expectation of after sales service that the Hyundai buyer might consider to be augmented. Place of purchase might also have influence, particularly on after sales service, though the price is likely to be higher in an 'up-market' store compared to a factory outlet. The marketer should also consider buyer behaviour, with all its intangibility. Put simply, some people expect more than others who are more easily satisfied. To complicate the issue further, some people expect more of some products that others – though this is likely to be influenced by branding as well as learning, attitude or culture.

APC application to the web

To examine how the model can be applied to products sold online, let us consider each stage in turn.

1. The core benefit. For the product purchased online, the method or location of purchase has no effect on the core benefit of that product.

2. Similarly, the actual product is not normally affected by the purchase being made online but this may depend upon customer expectations. For example:

    (a) If the online buyer has been made aware, not only of the product, but the problem that the product will solve, then the buyer's expectations of that product will be influenced by the mode of purchase.

    (b) If the buyer uses the web to extensively research the product prior to purchase, then it is reasonable to suggest that their expectations of that product will be enhanced. In an age when consumers have the means, the inclination and the incentive to research products prior to purchase, producers should take this increased expectation into consideration when developing their product offering. Providers of services should take particular notice of this point. Take hotel accommodation, for example. Fifteen years ago a traveller booking a holiday would have their expectations limited to the information provided in a brochure, the descriptions by a travel agent and the traveller's own imagination. Today, the Internet provides the traveller with access to web sites offering not only independent ratings and tourist information but also the hotel's own web site including 360 degree tours which provide more detail and images than a brochure ever could.

(c) The product can be augmented by the web if there is an additional service offered through the Internet that is not available offline. This might be fitting, usage or application advice on a web site or e-mails to inform of service requirements.

We have considered the web site as the product and it is pertinent to do so again in the context of the APC. In chapter 5 we reflected on buyer behaviour 'when using the web to make a purchase, is the buyer demonstrating the benefits sought from (a) the product; or (b) the method of purchase. Is the convenience of using the technology offered over-riding the benefit they seek from the purchase? For the buyer, is the benefit of home shopping and the subsequent delivery of an inferior product more important [to them] than the offline – and more inconvenient – purchase of a superior product?' Is it possible that the 'web site-product' is more important than the actual purchased product? Do some customers purchase only what is available on a web site, rather than what is the most suitable product to meet their needs? Interactive service quality has become an area of interest for many academics such as Singh (2002), Cai and Jun (2003), Svensson (2003), Jun, Yang and Kim (2004) and Rahman (2004).

9.4 Customising the product offering

The Industrial Revolution introduced the concept of mass production that brought to the customer a product that had reasonable quality and price, Ford's Model T car being the stock example. At the other end of the supplier-customer spectrum is the bespoke product made specifically for an individual customer – made to measure suits for example. Somewhere in the middle of these two extremes lies customisation, where a standard product is customised to the buyer's preference. BMW adopted this concept when they launched the new Mini in 2001. That a wide variety of 'packages' and options that could be added – at a cost – to the standard car mean that there are very few identical Minis on the road. BMW's Mini customisation strategy is an example of mass customisation. In the presentation of his concept of 'mass customisation' Pine (1993) argued that people were not always willing to sacrifice their product preferences for lower prices (essentially, what mass production offers) but were willing to pay extra for products that met their individual needs. Hart (1995) later commented that mass customisation consists of cutting-edge management methods and tools that give companies the ability to produce customised, affordable, high-quality goods and services, but with the shorter cycle times and lower costs historically associated with mass production and standardization. Avlonitis and Karayanni (2000) make the point that the Internet leads to faster discovery of customer needs, greater customisation of the products to customer needs, faster product testing and shorter product life-cycles.

As with the Mini example cited above, Pine's mass customisation model still requires extensive contact between the seller and buyer, normally face to face. Any one-on-one sales interaction can be expensive for the vendor, and time consuming for the purchaser. The advent of the Internet meant that consumers could customise their product remotely – not only from the comfort of their own home or workplace, but without any pressure or influence from a salesperson. Another significant benefit was that because online selection and ordering was relatively inexpensive for the vendor to offer, the price of customised products decreased. The concept of using the web as a medium for mass customisation has limited application. Not least is the issue that manufacturers are so used to dealing with customers through intermediaries such as wholesalers/retailers/agents that they are often ill equipped to deal directly with end-users. Also, manufacturers soon learned that selling direct to customers online could alienate offline distribution channels partners, so compromising offline sales. In essence, there are only two types of business that can benefit from using the web in a mass customisation strategy:

1. The manufacturer that has no bricks and mortar distribution channel, and

2. The intermediary that takes component parts of a product from various suppliers and offers the buyer a choice of multiple combinations.

Dell Computers (www.dell.com) is perhaps the most successful example of the practice of online mass customisation with no physical retail outlets. Dell allows customers to design their own computer online. The computer is then assembled and dispatched to the customer.

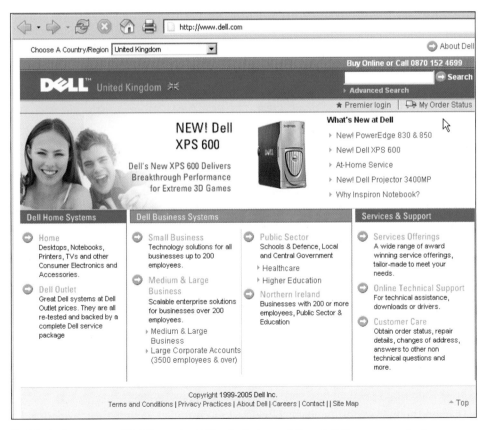

Fig 9.3 The home page of Dell Computers' UK web site (www.dell.com). Dell are exponents of mass customisation.

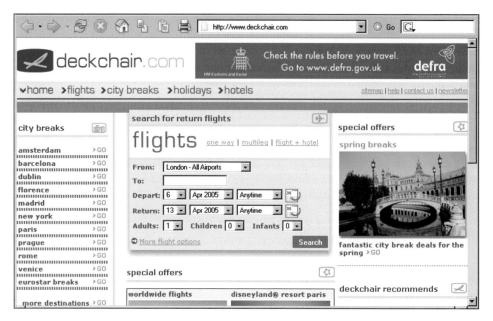

Fig 9.4 The home page of Deckchair.com's web site (www.deckchair.com)

All elements of the final products are supplied by Dell, having been supplied to them to meet the customer's specifications.

Mass customisation through an intermediary is well practiced by the travel/holiday industry. A standard seat on an airplane flying from point A to point B is a commodity (Christensen et al, 2000). However, companies like Deckchair.com (www.deckchair.com) allow the customer to choose not simply the flight but any combination of holiday duration, departure airport, destination, flight, hotel, and car hire from those made available on the web site. According to customer research, that they do not have to pay for product features they do not want and the opportunity for price adjustment are the two most favoured advantages of mass customisation (Bardakci & Whitelock, 2004). Unlike the manufacturer-to-customer example, Deckchair.com does not own the various airlines, hotels, or car hire companies: they merely act as a conduit between suppliers and customers. The Internet, combined with the growth of 'budget' airlines, has seen an increase in this 'dynamic packaging' – so dubbed by the holiday industry – which provides a greater range of travel solutions, to the detriment of the package (mass produced) holiday.

Individualisation of products

Individualisation of products takes the mass customisation concept a stage further by offering individually manufactured products to the end user. Examples of this practice include:

- Timberland's 'Bootstudio' (www.timberland.com), where buyers can 'build a boot as original as you are', including adding your own monogram;
- Nike ID (www.nikeid.com) which allows customers to control the look of their made to order shoes and view their final creation from five different angles;
- Diamond.com (www.diamond.com) which lets customers design their own ring by selecting the shape, price and carat range of the diamond and the metal and style of the

setting. Once the buyer has indicated the size, the selected ring is displayed in front and side view;

- The National Gallery's web site (www.nationalgallery.co.uk) which allows users to create 'print on demand' customised calendars and greeting cards featuring products from the collection;

- Lab21 (www.lab21.com) which brings customisation into the new millennium by creating individually formulated skin-care products based on customers' DNA. That customers must take a DIY at-home DNA test means this is not totally an online offering, but once the questionnaire on the health of their skin is added to the DNA results, lab21's Skin Profiler System then creates a custom formula to treat specific conditions.

The success of this concept is still to be proven however. In June 2005, for example, Procter & Gamble closed down the 'Reflect' web site (www.reflect.com), its once highly touted experiment in mass customisation of beauty products. Launched in 1999 with much fanfare as a stand-alone company backed by P&G and venture-capital firms near the height of the dot.com bubble, Reflect's web site offered users individually developed and labelled hair, skin and cosmetics products. The closure left observers asking the question 'if a company like P&G can't make this concept successful, who can?'

9.5 Branding dimensions

Brands have existed since early Roman times, but branding as a marketing tool is only about 120 years old (Tedlow, 1990). Many famous brands have evolved over many decades, even centuries, such as Marks and Spencer, General Motors, Nestlé and Levi. It is therefore amazing to consider that online brands that have become household names like Google, AOL, Amazon and eBay have barely existed for 10 years. Their presence demonstrates the power and influence of ICT alongside traditional media applications in the brand building process. Developing online brands can take different forms from developing a new brand as part of a new online operation to adapting a traditional brand to the online world or as part of an integrated strategy. This is where most dot.coms suffered as they lacked the skill or investment to build their brand quickly. This is in contrast to bricks and mortar operations that benefited from consumer awareness of their brand allowing them to concentrate resources on other strategic and tactical issues. Whittle (2000) argued that bricks and mortar had lower online acquisition costs because of their brand equity. She cited branding as *the* top management priority for 91% of dot.com companies whilst 71% of bricks and mortar organisations focussed on profitability as their main priority. Whittle went onto claim that dot.coms spent 76% of their revenue on marketing their web site compared to 13% of traditional businesses. The role of branding in establishing an online business is crucial.

There are numerous definitions of branding. Kotler (2003) says that 'a brand is an offering from a known source . . . a brand name carries many associations in the minds of people . . . these associations make up a brand image'. The Chartered Institute of Marketing states: 'Successful brands create a special relationship with customers because they are based not just on tangible benefits but on intangible attributes that evoke strong emotional responses.' Jobber and Fahy (2003) describe branding as 'the process by which companies distinguish their product offerings from those of the competition.' A brand has numerous, often complex dimensions such as its name, symbols, logos, personality, perceived quality, reputation, brand philosophy, associations and positioning which combine to establish a desired brand identity. Brand management involves developing rational and emotional elements to engender consumer feelings towards the brand; feelings that tend to reflect their self-image and develop for all customer touch points. These brand perceptions result from the value derived by the consumer. Hollenson (2003) observes that leading B2C and B2B organisations have implemented business strategies to develop dominant global brands through mass advertising and distribution but now 'remote links' through the Internet will have a significant influence on brands, especially awareness and equity. This is determined by the consumer's relationship or experience with the brand in an online environment and how it rates against their expectations. Gaffney (2005) suggests that the engagement with the brand is the difference between a changeable relationship where the customer is less loyal and an intense bond and advocacy is developed. It really depends upon whether a brand meets the aspirations of its target market and fosters a level of anticipation and interest. The question for marketers is how far the brand can go in terms of extensions, establishing credibility and setting out clearly understood values that connect with the customer and reflect their own aspirations.

Rayport and Jaworski (2002) provide a 10-step framework for managing the online branding process:

1. Clearly define the brand audience – segmentation is fundamental to all marketing activities in terms of defining the market potential and needs of the segment(s) chosen. This understanding helps shape the online offering and define brand values.

2. Understand the target customer – online marketers should develop a more detailed understanding of the target market's consumer behaviour, especially in a multi-channel environment. What drives the customer, what are their values, their lifestyle characteristics and their problems?

3. Identify key leverage points in customer experience – what are the key drivers or critical success factors that influence and stimulate their behaviour in the buying process. Could it be the site convenience, the diverse product range and integrated services, the level and speed of interaction or the competitive prices?

4. Continually monitor competitors – primarily for price and product comparisons, but also other aspects of the offering that need constant review, evaluation and action. In the online world, loyalty or betrayal is only the click of a mouse away.

5. Design compelling and complete brand intent – the brand philosophy should be clear, pervade all elements of the web site and support the proposition. For example, the easyGroup (www.easy.com) that incorporates easyJet amongst others sets out its group proposition in its brand values (www.easy.com/values/index.html). The initial easyJet brand has provided an effective platform to extend the house brand in many diverse sectors (see Fig 9.5).

6. Execute with integrity – this covers all aspects of the online offering and must enhance the brand reputation by developing a trustworthy and credible offering that stimulates consumer behaviour through acquisition and retention phases. Are the brand philosophy and the inherent values meaningful, realistic and achievable? What online (and offline) activities and elements should we deploy to support it? eg product, prices, sponsorship, co branding, communities and other interactions.

7. Be consistent over time – brands take time to establish but their message and values should be unswerving so that the target market(s) understands what the brand stands

---

Fig 9.5 easyGroup brand values

The easyGroup strategy
We will build on our brand values:

1. great value

2. taking on the big boys

3. for the many not the few

4. relentless innovation

5. keep it simple

6. entrepreneurial

7. making a difference in people's lives

8. honest, open and fun

We will protect our brand from internal and external threats and manage appropriately the business and other risks inherent in venturing. We will develop our people and ensure their reward is aligned to realised shareholder returns.

The easyGroup mission statement
Our mission is to manage and extend Europe's leading value brand to more products and services, whilst creating real wealth for all stakeholders

The easyGroup vision
easyGroup will develop Europe's leading value brand into a global force. We will paint the world orange!

Reproduced by kind permission of easyGroup.com.

---

for. Mixed messages can cause confusion and brand schizophrenia. As Rayport and Jaworski suggest, in the online world, consumers may have different interactions with the brand so their experiences may differ. In addition, consumers may desire slightly different things from a brand but as long as the underlying values and experiences deliver higher levels of satisfaction then longer-term profitable relationships are a distinct possibility.

8. Establish feedback systems – marketers now have versatile and sophisticated analytics software at their disposal to monitor the brand against promotional activity in real time. However, organisations should also monitor and encourage feedback in two other ways. First by physically monitoring chat rooms and forums where softer, qualitative data is in the public domain about the brand and how people perceive it. Secondly, rather than just having a 'Contact Us' navigation tab, organisations should actively encourage customer contact, and perhaps even incentivise the feedback.

9. Be opportunistic – organisations should capitalise on opportunities to build the brand. The multimedia formats available through the Internet offer greater creative scope to develop and reinforce the brand message. Brands like the Mini and Sony Playstation have utilised the Internet to create exciting content and features in line with their vibrant brand images. Beyond the site content, organisations should also be opportunistic through public relations, co branding, sponsorship, placement of banner advertisements and other activities in appropriate domains that reach the desired audience, both current and potential.

10. Invest and be patient – Rayport and Jaworski included this key step at the time of investor anxieties over dot.com businesses and emphasised the need for a longer-term view with sustained investment in the business and the brand. This is just as relevant today and requires effective and innovative business and marketing planning.

There is some debate as to whether the Internet is a benefit or threat to branding. That most customers are aware of how a favourable brand provides comfort, satisfaction and familiarity, and trust for them offline or online (Ha, 2004) supports the argument that the lack of physical interaction of online shopping makes online branding more important than offline. The variety of brand experiences increase the consumer's familiarity with the brand and positive experiences determine web site allegiance and purchase intentions. Others argue that customers will use the Internet to gather detailed information on products and services and make their own judgement on the suitability of a product, thereby making brands superfluous (Rowley, 2004). There is no finite answer to this issue. For some products the value of a brand could diminish as a result of the Internet, but then many products have always sold without the benefit of branding – successful budget grocery stores such as Aldi, for example, sell no branded goods. Other products will benefit from their brand being enhanced by the Internet such as Dell Computers. It all depends on the product, the vendor, and – most importantly – the customer.

In this section we will consider three aspects of online branding:

1. The brand online – how the offline brand can use the Internet as part of its overall branding strategy

2. The online brand – where the offline business uses a different brand for its online presence

3. The pure online brand – how the pure online entity can be developed as a brand.

The brand online

A particular problem for early adopters of the web as a brand communication medium was that of differentiation or uniformity – should the web presence mirror offline-branding efforts, or should the online brand differ from that offline?

Some organisations simply took offline branding efforts and transplanted them, unchanged, online. However, translation of corporate brand values from market*place* to market*space* is often problematic, leading to inconsistencies in the way that the brand values are interpreted (Stuart & Jones, 2004). Others argue a new theory of the concept of branding is not needed between the on and offline environment, but rather a different approach to executing the brand's essence (de Chernatony, 2001). de Chernatony (2004) builds on this by saying that a brand is a brand, regardless of its environment; and what is different is the way the brand's promise is executed. Rubinstein (2002) supports the premise that new technology has not changed the basic principles of branding, but that it has 'highlighted a shift in emphasis from the belief that branding is all about communications to the belief that real branding is about creating relationships with customers.' She goes on to cite the interactive nature of the Internet as being the driver of this change.

Flores (2004) raises the issue of measuring the impact on sales of 'brand web sites'. He argues that quantitative metrics such as visitor counts or advanced clickstream analysis do not provide insights into how a brand web site visit might affect attitude and behaviour towards the brand. In his paper, Flores goes on to stress how important the user's web site experience is in developing brand acceptance. McLean and Tunnicliffe (2004) comment on the role of web sites in branding and take it a stage further, saying that 'the web site reveals everything about a brand, its values and priorities, its best intention and worst habits . . . the overall role of any brand web site is to be a window into the brand's soul.' A further consideration is that due to the very nature of the medium – pull rather than push – Internet users may not be as receptive to the brand message online as they are offline. Research conducted by Jones et al (2005) suggests that brand name recall is substantially lower for online respondents than offline. Ultimately, the brand manager should aim to have the web presence reflect the culture, ethos, personality, and values of the brand while meeting the needs and perceptions of an online audience. For example:

- Buitoni (www.buitoni.co.uk) extols the Italian passion for food and life
- www.jackdaniels.com reinforces the heritage and folklore surrounding the famous Tennessee bourbon whisky
- Euro Disney (www.disneylandparis.com) promotes the dreams and magic of the Disney experience in Europe
- Tag Heuer, the Swiss manufacturer of precision watches (www.tagheuer.com) effectively combines the brand history, product innovation and sports and celebrity collections and endorsements to reinforce its up-market brand positioning through its site.

A brand's standing in the eyes of stakeholders will influence its success in due course. A 2005 survey by Envisional produced some interesting branding results in Mini case 9.3.

There are inherent risks when a successful offline brand seeks to utilise the online channel. After 20 years of successful retailing the fashion label, 'The Duffer of St. George' (www.thedufferofstgeorge.com) launched its first web site in 2004 as it sought to determine the brand potential of being online. Apart from a range of interactive features on the company and brand history, product ranges, details of stockists and key projects, the site also builds interest and anticipation with insights into its forthcoming collections before they appear in-store. The site was originally designed as a brand building and CRM vehicle without an online store but it now includes a user-friendly e-commerce store.

The online brand

The Internet is now an integral part of any marketing strategy, but this was not always the case. In its early commercial development, a web presence was an often isolated rather than distinct element in the marketing mix. One of the reasons for this was that early adopters represented very specific segments of the market. Some organisations saw the early Internet community as 'geeks' or 'nerds' whilst others saw a young, affluent and trend-setting segment attracted to the informal, novel and interactive nature of the web. It was members of this group that were targeted by offline businesses who felt that the web offered them a channel to new customers who would not normally be in their customer profile. For these businesses the web gave them the opportunity to develop a new – online – brand identity.

Probably the best proponents of adjusting the brand to better suit the new medium were the high street banks. Historically, banks had a conservative, staid image that was suitable as a brand for a high street bank. This was reinforced with commercials of bowler-hat wearing managers and a customer base drawn predominantly from the middle classes. In the late eighties this was changing as a new generation of customers sought different things from their bank. Changes were already taking place in high street banking when, following in the

MINI CASE 9.3 The best and worst perceived brands online

Research published by Internet monitoring company, Envisional (www.envisional.com) in April 2005 revealed the top 20 most prominent, most positively and most negatively regarded brands online. Although all those brands that appear are well known, where they all sit in the charts is not always as expected. One thing that is rather surprising is that not one travel-related company appears in the results in Table 9.1 below.

Table 9.1 Online brand perception

Top 20 most prominent brands online	Top 20 most positively regarded brands online	Top 20 most negatively regarded brands online
1 Microsoft	eBay	McDonalds
2 Google	HP	Coca-Cola
3 Yahoo!	Dell	Walmart
4 Sony	Mini	Nestle
5 HP	UPS	Unilever
6 eBay	Nokia	Microsoft
7 Apple	Virgin	Pepsi
8 Disney	Amazon	Burger King
9 BBC	Federal Express	Red Bull
10 UPS	Toyota	GlaxoSmithKline
11 Amazon	Sony	ICI
12 Reuters	Apple	Starbucks
13 Nokia	Cadbury Schweppes	Ikea
14 Samsung	Hilton	Danone
15 Ford	Ford	BP
16 Dell	Samsung	PowerGen
17 American Express	Honda	EMI
18 BT	BMW	AstraZeneca
19 Mini	Tesco	Shell
20 Walmart	Yahoo!	Nike

Reproduced by kind permission of Envisional, 2005.

footsteps of Citibank in the USA, First Direct (a UK subsidiary of the Hong Kong and Shanghai Banking Corporation) developed the first telephone banking service in the UK. This business model was a natural predecessor of Internet banking with no face-to-face contact. For the banks and their customers, the Internet emerged at the right time to provide added value. The segment of their customers that wanted to distance itself from the traditional

MINI CASE 9.4 CompUSA learns the hard way

Whilst the banks represent successful examples of re-branding for the online presence, this is not always the case. To create a new brand is to disregard the effort and time that has gone into developing the offline brand and start again with the new brand. Even the banks made no secret of whom the parent company of the new offline brand was, albeit in the small print at the bottom of the page. In 1999 American computer retail giant, CompUSA launched its own online brand – Cozone. Not only was the brand different, but also it had its own product lines and management.

The aggressive and expensive advertising campaign featured several sporting and business celebrities, but made no mention of the parent company. The lesson was hard-learned. With visitors and sales well below those required to sustain the venture, Cozone closed after only six months. CompUSA subsequently launched CompUSA.com – the online version of the well-earned offline brand.

Adapted from Clauser, RC (2001) *Offline rules, online tools*, Brand Management Vol 8, Nos 4 & 5, May 2001.

banking image was the same group of customers that were early adopters of the Internet – ABC1 professionals who were comfortable and familiar with the technology.

The plethora of online services, including credit cards, that emerged in the late nineties were all part of traditional banking establishments, but had undergone 're-branding'. In the UK, a number of banks re-branded or created separate online divisions to appeal to the early adopters such as:

- The Cooperative Bank and Smile (www.smile.coop)
- The Prudential and Egg (www.egg.com)
- The Halifax and Intelligent Finance (www.if.com)
- Abbey National and Cahoot (www.cahoot.co.uk)

The web sites were less formal and offline advertising matched this by being humorous and entertaining – not something that suited the old image of banks. As the popularity of Internet banking increased, so did the gap between the on and offline models. Influenced by the success of their more informal online approach to customers, the banks realised that it was vital that the offline brand structure be designed in a manner compatible with the online environment (Strebinger & Treiblmaier, 2004). It is interesting that in many ways the banks' current offline branding models are more akin to their online presence than those of the bricks and mortar predecessors with greater emphasis on customer convenience and flexibility through multiple channels.

The pure online brand

Not only does the Internet provide a medium for marketing, it can be used as a channel for sales. This means that an organisation can trade as an online entity only, and those businesses can also be a brand. Two of the most prominent online brands, Yahoo! (www.yahoo.com) and Amazon (www.amazon.com), were both launched in the early days of the web. This may be relevant – successful online branding is, in no small way, due to a brand's early appearance in the net's history (Lindstrom, 2001). There are two main reasons for this:

- As the Internet became popular in the mid nineties the new media became news. TV and the print media ran features on the new phenomenon and highlighted successful exponents – in this way brands like Yahoo! and Amazon were known by people who had not even accessed the web.

- In the early days there were not many quality web sites for users to visit. Yahoo! was the pre-eminent portal directory (it was not a search engine at that time), Amazon was *the* example of online shopping. For new users, visiting these two sites was almost obligatory.

Developing the online brand should be no less considered than that of the offline brand. Because a new medium of communication is being used there is no reason for branding lessons learned offline to be cast aside. As Clauser (2001) states: 'The fundamental rules of brand building have not changed. Business should stick to the traditional, tried and true rules of branding while using the new technology and strategic tools now possible on the Internet. Follow them carefully, break them cautiously.' Rowley (2004) suggests that an online brand development strategy should comprise of seven stages (see Fig 9.6).

A final, ongoing, stage is the reviewing, evolving and protection of the brand. Whilst this is an excellent model, it does not differ significantly from the stages of an offline brand development strategy. This provides further evidence that the e-marketer should not discard lessons learned over time in 'traditional' marketing. Brands also offer legal protection and their protection in international trade has become increasingly important due to misuse such as counterfeiting. Other dimensions in online brand protection are considered in Legal Eagle Box 9.1.

Because the Internet provides a point of contact between customer and vendor the importance of that web site's development can be emphasised with the comment that for many organisations, 'you are your web site'. Poirier (2003) states that 'web visitors form impressions about your company based on the totality of the experience they have navigating through your site.' De Chernatony & Christodoulides (2004) suggest that the online brand promise must include such issues as web site appearance and navigation. As suggested earlier, in the mind of the customer, the web presence *is* the organization. In these circumstances, to segregate the organisation from the brand is to be pedantic. As with the offline brand, however, the online brand's web site should reflect the ethos, culture, and service quality of the business itself. A good example of this is online office supply wholesaler, LaserMonks (www.lasermonks.com). As the name suggests, the business operates from a monastery with its success owing much more to its brand, and all that it represents, than it does to the products that it sells (see Fig 9.7).

Rowley (2004) says that there is evidence to suggest that it is difficult to communicate an online brand in the absence of preconceptions already established through other channels. She goes on to make the point that many of the early dot.coms failed because they needed to establish presence and reputation quickly and the huge marketing budgets that this required undermined their financial stability. As the LaserMonks example suggests, however, with the

---

LEGAL EAGLE BOX 9.1 Online brand protection

Although the Internet has enhanced the exposure of e-marketers' brands, it has brought about an unprecedented rate of brand risks as protecting online brands against misuse can be an uphill task. Generally speaking digital rights protection over the Internet is a difficult matter. In recognition of this several companies such as Microsoft, Verisgn and IBM have produced software that manages online brands and digital rights.

By using this software, marketers are able to protect themselves from loss of traffic through misuse of brand in their competitors' meta tags or hidden site texts. Such software can, for example, prevent unauthorised use of a company's trademark or logo.

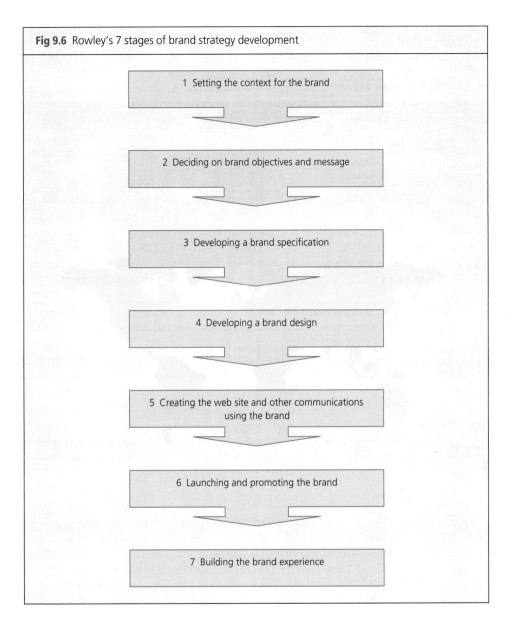

Fig 9.6 Rowley's 7 stages of brand strategy development

1 Setting the context for the brand

2 Deciding on brand objectives and message

3 Developing a brand specification

4 Developing a brand design

5 Creating the web site and other communications using the brand

6 Launching and promoting the brand

7 Building the brand experience

right brand – and product – the e-marketer can use both offline (PR) and online (viral, newsletter, and e-mail) marketing methods to develop the brand without spending disproportionate sums on advertising.

Co-branding

Establishing partnerships in the supply chain to increase site traffic has become commonplace online. Partnerships in the form of co-branding have also taken on greater

Fig 9.7 The home page 9 the Laser Monks' web site (www.lasermonks.com)

Reprinted with kind permission of Laser Monks, Inc.

importance. Online alliances occur when complementary brand offerings come together to cross promote and reach a wider audience with similar profiles. The web auctioneer QXL (www.qxl.co.uk) has adopted this approach to boost brand awareness first with the internet travel agency, Ebookers (www.ebookers.com) and then with Manchester United (www.ManUtd.com).

Co-branding can also be effective at the times of major events such as the partnership between ITV (www.itv.com) and the worldwide foreign exchange company, Travelex (www.travelex.com) during the 2002 World Cup, the year's biggest sporting event. The online campaign highlighted in the ITV sales case studies (www.itvsales.com), generated high post campaign brand awareness for Travelex rising from 25% before to 45% after. In addition, those who agreed that Travelex was a trustworthy brand rose from 35%–50%.

Brand equity is closely linked to profitability and shareholder values and so the management and measurement of the brand performance is important for all organisations, both on and offline. Monitoring of the online brand can take many forms online:

• Web forums and communities which may influence brand opinion and purchase decisions

• Monitoring positive and negative coverage such as the best and worst performing online brand surveys such as those carried out by Envisional (www.envisional.com)

• Brand loyalty based on site traffic and purchase behaviour

• The effectiveness of brand communications through different channels such as e-mail and search engine marketing. For example, how many customers captured through a search engine do not convert? How effective are banner ads at brand building?

- Brand awareness can be monitored for market share against key competitors via industry research and media analysts such as NielsenNetRatings (www.nielsen-netratings.com)

Branding in international markets

The global nature of the Internet has generated significant export market opportunities for many organisations. It does provide a low-cost market entry strategy, especially for SMEs. Online cross-border, international or global commerce requires a thorough understanding of the issues affecting any business involved in overseas trade such as legal, language and cultural factors. The strategic development of online global or international brands is influenced by consumers' experience in their home country and the level to which marketing communications, web site content and processes like payment and distribution are adapted to local conditions. Some established global brands like Coca Cola, Cadbury's and Procter and Gamble have traditionally tweaked their products and marketing communications to meet the tastes and culture of specific markets. Marketing strategists need to decide on the level of standardisation to be applied to sites across borders. Okazaki's (2005) study of top US brand web sites in European markets showed that a localisation strategy and tailored content for each country was adopted even though there was conformity in relation to corporate logos, layout and colours. The 'Glocal', globalisation strategy of adapting global brands to local conditions seems to be commonplace. A case study on the Hong Kong and Shanghai Bank (www.hsbc.com) cited in Blythe (2006) illustrates this approach with each country in which HSBC operates having a web site based on local needs, and in some cases local culture and law, but all under the corporate branded strap line of 'The World's Local Bank.' The bank also allows countrywide freedom for marketing communications purposes. This approach allows tremendous reach to diverse cultures across the globe. However, tailoring means much more than just translating your domestic web site into the language of the chosen country. In the case of the US dating agency, Match.com (www.match.com) cited in the May 2005 issue of the marketing executive online resource, *cmomagazine* (www.cmomagazine.com), Orr states that the effective US corporate strap line 'Love is complicated, Match.com is simple' failed to hit the mark when transferred to overseas operations. It was not just the translation but a range of cultural nuances that produced a poor response. So internationalising the product and the web site is important but to what extent should it be done? In the same article, Jeff Swystun, global director of Interbrand recommends that 70% of content should be consistent across all web sites and 30% local content. Clearly, organisations must maintain some control and set minimum brand requirements otherwise the brand values could easily be undermined by maverick local content.

Domain names

When considering the web site as the brand, an important consideration is the domain name of that site. Domain names consist of two parts, the name and the suffix, each warrants consideration.

- The name. For major brands this needs little consideration – the name registered is the brand name. Not only does this make marketing sense, but legal sense as well. The brand name will, almost certainly, be a registered trade name and so will be protected by law from having anyone else use it (see Legal Eagle Box 9.2 below).

LEGAL EAGLE BOX 9.2 Domain names

One of the main controversies over the use of domain names is the use of trademarked names that belong to other companies. If an organisation owns a trademark that pre-dates a domain name of another business, it may give rise to a successful court action.

With domain names there is also the possibility of an action for the tort of passing-off. This occurs when one business appears to the public to be another business that has established a good name or reputation. It is, therefore, prudent to check and ensure that your domain name is not the same or very similar to the name of an existing business before using it for e-marketing.

- The suffix (or 'extension' as they are known in the USA). Technically, the Top Level Domain (TLD) of the naming authority with whom the name is registered, the most common suffix is .com (dot com) which is the US suffix for a commercial organisation (originally .com was for commercial organisations and .org not for profit entities but this distinction was never enforced). In essence, the .com *should* denote a US company, with other country specific suffixes representing organisations from those countries (eg .uk for the UK, and .fr for France). In reality, because the Americans were the first to register domain names, .com has come to be perceived as the suffix for a global domain – a business that trades throughout the world. For the global brand .com is the suffix that should be selected. For the local brand, the local suffix is sufficient.

Choosing the domain name of a pure online business is more complex. For the offline brand the domain name mirrors the brand name. For the pure online entity the domain name is the brand name, and vice versa. What comes first is down to inspiration, creativity and often impulse and luck. As 'dot com' is likely to be part of the brand name there is unlikely to be a major problem in selecting a term that is already used by an offline company (lastminute.com could not be confused with, for example, last minute taxis). The name can, therefore, be selected for its merits as a brand name, eg Lastminute.com, Deckchair.com, eBay.com and so on. A problem arises if the online brand is to be known by its name only, without the suffix. The online entity of the Royal Bank of Scotland for example, is Mint, with its domain name being Mint.co.uk. In this instance it is possible (indeed, likely) that the Royal Bank of Scotland had to obtain the generic 'mint' domain name from whoever owned it. The problem of acquiring generic domain names has resulted in a number of new online businesses inventing words that do not exist in the English language, so ensuring the word has not been registered as a domain. An example of this is the flight booking site of Opodo. A Pan-European travel company owned by nine of Europe's leading airlines, Opodo means nothing, it is a word made up by the company's marketers. Apart from not being registered as a domain name anywhere in the world, its only merit seems to be that it reads the same when seen upside down.

Issues relating to the suffix are the same as those for offline brand domain names – with one exception. If the domain name *is* the brand name, it has been generally accepted that dot com be used. This relates to historical practice how the term (dot com) was used to describe the pure online business created in the late nineties. Though the situation may change over time, for the majority of users, Lastminute.com is a business; Lastminute.co.uk is a web site address.

9.6 **New product development online**

New Product Development (NPD) is an important process for all organisations to nurture the right culture to achieve their future success. Numerous writers including O'Connor et al (2004) have commented on the Internet's influence on 'accelerating' the NPD process. In fast moving technology industries, the pace of product development can be critical in achieving competitive advantage. Indeed, public sector organisations have recognised the role the Internet can play in developing a culture of innovation. Philips (2003) cites the part played by Scottish Enterprise in fostering diverse e-business applications through its 'Connecting Scotland' initiative.

As part of the NPD process, the Internet performs two primary roles:

1. It provides interactions with consumers to provide ideas, feedback and testing on new product concepts.

2. It provides a real time platform for collaboration for all supply side participants in the design, delivery and promotion of new products.

In the information age, the sharing of knowledge and participating in collaborative projects using the Internet has spawned many successful new products and has provided firms in the manufacturing sector with key benefits in terms of creativity and cost and speed efficiencies. Digital channels and software developments facilitate file sharing amongst design teams that quicken the NPD introduction cycles and illustrate the impact of design changes in real time to each functional area and external collaborative partners. Software developments such as Windows Sharepoint Applications provide an effective collaborative tool for product development teams to share all forms of project contact information. In such collaborations, the consumer will rarely see the work involved but the end product should deliver extra value in some way. For the marketer, any new introductions should consider the dynamic marketing environment in which the organisation operates. Analytical models such as Porter's Five Forces can generate a useful market assessment.

Bickerton, Bickerton & Pardesi (2000) suggest that the Internet is a powerful, though public tool in the NPD process that can be integrated into the traditional six-stage NPD model (Fig 9.8).

1. Idea Generation – Both Bickerton and O'Connor discuss the advantages offered through the Internet of having development teams contributing ideas from more than one location in real time. This can generate creative and innovative ideas as design teams spin off and stimulate one another. The Internet can also stimulate new ideas simply by observation and monitoring or relevant sites and their content. Screening, or filtering of ideas is an important activity at this stage in the process and the combined knowledge of the design teams can make informed decisions in faster times.

2. Concept Testing – the Internet offers flexible, cost efficient concept testing capabilities. Virtual prototypes can be developed providing 360-degree visual representation with feedback obtained by various online survey methods such as online focus groups, e-mail surveys and word association techniques to gauge customer reactions. Dahan and Srinivasan (2000) make a key observation that the virtual prototypes are significantly cheaper to produce than physical prototypes and more product concepts can be explored as a result. This should lead to the elimination of weaker concepts at this stage. Marketers may also

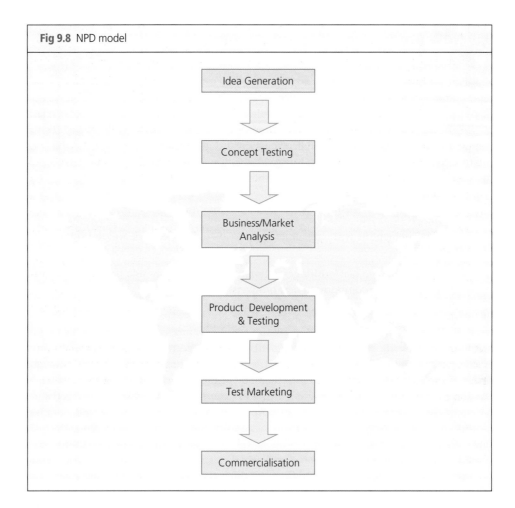

Fig 9.8 NPD model

test other aspects such as brand values and promotional messages via online concept boards or video streaming of proposed campaign ideas.

3. Business/Market Analysis – With only serious product ideas remaining, the Internet can provide an effective platform for assessing project costs in conjunction with all internal departments and external supply chain partners involved in design, procurement, manufacturing and marketing. Bickerton et al give the example of tendering online where suppliers respond with costs, service level agreements and implementation plans in relation to the specifications laid out in a tender document.

4. Product Development and Testing – Bickerton suggests that the Internet may have limited application at this stage, especially with physical products where sensory elements play a key role in the research process. However, the Internet can be a valuable research tool when it is combined with offline test samples delivered in the home. One of the UK's leading online research organisations, Virtual Surveys (www.virtualsurveys.com) offers a coordinated product testing service where products are distributed to carefully selected prospects who then respond online. They claim a number advantages such as quicker,

more honest feedback, better countrywide geographic sampling and reduced costs. Online product testing comes into its own when the product is digital in nature. For example, a holiday company can test the usability of a new website prior to launch by getting potential users to use the site as if they were booking a holiday. This can test the ease of use, quality of information, special features such as 360-degree virtual tours as well as the effectiveness of the booking process prior to the site going live.

5. Test Marketing – The Internet again offers a cheaper and quicker alternative to test marketing in the physical world. A temporary site could be set up for a period of time, say a month, to gauge the market potential for the products on offer and the effectiveness of promotional communications to the target audience(s) such as e-mail marketing and responses from generated different search engines.

6. Commercialisation – Prior to the Internet's introduction, the commercialisation stage was a costly, physical process with products being stockpiled prior to their launch based on forecasted data in conjunction with launch campaigns. In the offline world, the timing of a product launch can be critical but online support is increasingly important as a first port of call for prospects. Regarding product availability, O'Connor et al stress the importance of information and communications technology throughout the manufacturing, warehousing and logistics functions in providing customised product offerings with flexible delivery to meet increased customer expectations.

Mohammed et al (2002) include the launch of a new website as an example of a new product in the commercialisation stage but as long as the other key stages in the NPD process have been covered the site should be functional and capable of handling the volumes of customer traffic hopefully generated by a successful awareness campaign.

 ## 9.7 Summary

As one of the principal elements of the original marketing mix concept – the 4Ps – the product has always been central to any marketing activity. The development of the Internet as a viable marketing tool has, however, required marketers to re-visit their understanding of what the product is. Not only is there a consideration of whether or not the product can be *sold* online, but which are most suited to the medium. We have seen the development of the online product – is it a brand new classification of product or is it simply something that was previously available offline, but technology has allowed it to become *online*? Whether the product is an online product or not, part of any product is the issue of branding. Again the marketer must consider whether or not the off and online brand should be synchronised, and whether there is such a thing as the online brand as well as how any brand is considered online.

END OF CHAPTER CASE STUDY Sell experiences, not products

A few weeks ago, I was on a panel with Information Systems (IS) executives to discuss the 'Future of the User Experience' at Forrester's annual Automotive Summit. It was a thought-provoking day and the inspiration for today's column.

The automotive industry is one of the online biggest marketers. Several research studies find roughly 70% of car buyers perform research online before buying a vehicle. Most consumers in the market for a high-consideration product or service, be it a car, home, engagement ring, computer, or new bank or brokerage firm, conduct a significant amount of online research to inform their purchase decisions. Because of this, $8.4 billion was spent in 2004 in online advertising, according to Jupiter Research (a Jupitermedia Corp. division). This figure is expected to double by 2009.

Where does the money go? Much of it is intended to position products or services in very crowded marketplaces. With so much money pouring into online advertising, it is amazing how slow most industries are to respond to customer inquiries or leads. According to Jupiter Research, 40% of automotive leads, 37% of travel leads, and 25% of retail leads take three or more days to respond to.

If I were CEO of a company producing high-consideration products or services, I would invest in improving the buying experience from initial impression to final close. While I was at it, I would reinvent the product or service, in the spirit of creating the 'Purple Cow,' Seth Godin endorses (Godin, S, 2002, *Purple Cow: Transform Your Business by Being Remarkable*, Penguin Group). If you are thinking about reinventing your customers' total experience, look outside your industry for inspiration.

Last year, I bought an iPod at an Apple store. It was more beautifully and luxuriously packaged than a Rolex watch. Opening the box, I felt as if I had bought something truly wonderful. What I bought was not a product, but a total experience that was seamless from beginning to end. Here is what makes the iPod exceptional (and enables Apple to command a premium for the product):

- Holistic marketing. Every detail of the marketing mix is synchronized beautifully and obsessively. The advertising, web experience, product, store, and packaging all feel connected. Each is beautiful on its own. That is why opening the box feels like a rite of passage.

- A total experience perspective. ITunes' business model ensures the experience extends beyond purchase and becomes an integral part of the customer's lifestyle. Beyond iTunes, communities have sprouted around podcasting and play list sharing.

- Great service after purchase. Many brands fail with service. I was concerned about this when I had trouble connecting

my iPod to a new computer. I went online to sniff around but required human contact to sort out the problem. Apple has a Genius Bar in its stores, and customers can sign up online for an appointment.

This very highly sophisticated experience is for a product that costs under $500. A nicely appointed business laptop is $3,000. The sticker price for a good car now runs north of $30,000. Luxury cars cost twice that. Should we not expect more from the experience of buying some of the most expensive, highly considered purchases in our lives?

Learn from Apple. Think about how to make your customers' experience exceptional. Here are a few items that I discussed on that panel for your consideration:

- Think experience. It is not just about the car. After the home and workplace, it is where many Americans spend the most time. Apple thinks experience. The iPod is not an MP3 player. It is a complete experience; together with iTunes, it is a command central for buying, enjoying, and sharing music.

When I am looking for a neighborhood retail store, I go to Citysearch to find it. I print out a map with directions, carry it to my car, and either input the destination into my navigation system or read the printed directions. I am solving a transportation problem, but I do not do it on an automotive site. I must cobble together the experience myself. It would be great to visit my car site, get directions, and click a button to transmit them to my vehicle's navigation system. Navigation is just a small part of the overall transportation experience the auto industry could solve. The Internet could easily be command central, and an automaker could own it.

Make the Internet work harder. When my car needs service, I call the dealership to schedule an appointment. This should happen online, or the vehicle could let me know and put me in touch with my local dealer. Many telematics companies are working on these kinds of solutions.

- Make the purchase process transparent. Car buyers are frustrated by the process of finding a dealer, getting quotes on the desired vehicle, then negotiating a fair price. They arm themselves online with competitive pricing information to do battle with a dealer. The manufacturer's suggested retail price (MSRP) provided on OEM (original equipment manufacturer) sites often differ from the actual price paid, and this can confuse consumers. The OEM that cracks the code on online local pricing information will have a winning proposition.

- Reinvent the vehicle around the user. My computing experience is customised to my needs technically, in terms of basic functionality, and aesthetically. My desktop is a photo of a recent vacation; I smile every time I see it. My Yahoo! has the news and information I want to read. How customisable is a car? Not very. I would like the car's interface to reflect my desire for simplicity. The dashboard could be a screen I can easily customize on my computer by dragging and dropping the controls I want to see. Memory controls on the seat and mirror positions are a starting point, but there is much more that can be done to make the transportation experience exceptional.

Regardless of your industry, we can all learn lessons from Steve Jobs, and Virgin's Richard Branson, as we strive to reinvent the product and the purchase/ownership experience. I enjoy your feedback, so please share your opinions on how the Web can reinvent the personal product experience.

Mark Kingdon Available on: www.clickz.com
Copyright 2005 Jupitermedia Corporation All Rights Reserved.

Questions

1. The case study starts by making the assertion that 70% of car buyers use the Internet to research vehicles prior to purchase. Using a (new) car of your choice, first visit the web site of its manufacturer and consider whether there is enough information presented to influence your buying decision. Then search for and read other web sites that might offer a more independent assessment of the same car. Consider whether or not the content of this kind of site has more or less influence over your buying decision?

2. The author originally addressed his comments to executives in the Automotive Industry, and concludes by offering some advice to them. Using that advice as a basis, consider how online marketing can 'make customers' experience exceptional' for an organisation or industry of your choice – your university/college, an airline, or holiday company for example.

DISCUSSION QUESTIONS

1. In this chapter the travel industry is used as an example several times. Why is it the case that travel and the Internet are such good partners? As well as aspects of marketing you should also consider the relevant elements of an environmental analysis eg culture.

2. In the section on 'the long tail' the focus is on the entertainment industry. List three other industries or product lines where the phenomenon might exist.

3. Choose a brand that is well known to you and write down three things that the brand means to you (eg, Volvo might be 'safe', 'boring', 'good value for money'). Now visit the web site of that brand and judge whether the web site matches your perception of the brand. If perception and web site reality are not in tune, why not? Is the problem with your perception or the brand's web site?

REFERENCES

Aaker, D (2002) The Internet as an integrator, *Strategy & Business*, 3rd Quarter, 2002, a quarterly management magazine published by Booz Allen Hamilton and available at www.warc.com/77205p.asp

Anderson, C (2004) *The Long Tail*. Available at www.wired.com/wired/archive/12.10/tail_pr.html

Avlonitis, GJ & Karayanni, DA (2000) The impact of Internet use on business-to-business marketing: examples from American and European companies, *Industrial Marketing Management*, Vol 29, No 5, 441–59

Bardakci, A & Whitelock, J (2004) How 'ready' are customers for mass customisation? An exploratory investigation, *European Journal of Marketing*, Vol 38, No 11, 1396–1416

Blythe, J (2006) *Essentials of Marketing Communication*, 3rd edition, FT Prentice Hall, Pearson Education, Harlow, UK

Bickerton, P, Bickerton, M & Pardesi, V (2000) *Cybermarketing*, 2nd edition, Butterworth Heinemann, Oxford, UK, 128–131

Cai, S & Jun, M (2003) Internet users' perceptions of online service quality: a comparison of online buyers and information searchers, *Managing Service Quality*, Vol 13, No 6, 504–519

Christensen, M, Johnston, C, Overdorf, M, Barragree, A (2000) *After the Gold Rush: Patterns of Success and Failure on the Internet*, Innosight LLC. Available at www.innosight.com

Clauser, RC (2001) Offline rules, online tools, *Journal of Brand Management*, May 2001, Vol 8, No 4–5, 270–287(18)

Dahan, E & Srinivasan, V (2000) The predictive power of Internet-based product concept testing using visual depiction and animation, *Journal of Product Innovation Management* 2000, Vol 17: 99–109

Dann, S & Dann, S (2001) *Strategic Internet Marketing*, John Wiley & Sons

de Chernatony, L (2001) Succeeding with brands on the Internet, *Journal of Brand Management*, February 2001, Vol 8, No 3, 186–195(10)

de Chernatony, L, Christodoulides, G (2004) Taking the brand promise online: challenges and opportunities, *Interactive Marketing*, Vol 5, No 3

de Kare Silver, M (1998) *E-shock 2000*, Macmillan Press

Flores, L (2004) *Measuring the Sales Impact of Brand Websites*, The World Advertising Research Centre. Available online at www.warc.org

Fogg, BJ (1999) *What Variables Affect Web Site Credibility*, CSLI IAP Conference, Nov 1999

Gaffney, J (2005) Superbrands, advocacy, obsession, *1 to 1 Magazine*, A Peppers & Rogers Group Publication, October 2005, 20

Gummerus, J, Liljander, V, Pura, M, van Riel, A (2004) Customer loyalty to content-based Web sites: the case of an online health-care service, *Journal of Services Marketing*; Vol 18, No 3; 2004

Ha, H-Y (2004) Factors influencing consumer perceptions of brand trust online, *Journal of Product and Brand Management*; Vol 13, No 5; 2004

Hart, CWL (1995) Mass customization: conceptual underpinnings, opportunities and limits, *International Journal of Service Industry Management*, February, Vol 6, No 2, 36–45(10)

Haig, M (2001) *The E-marketing Handbook*, Kogan Page Ltd

Hollerson, S (2003) *Marketing Management – A Relationship Approach*, FT Prentice Hall, 479

Jobber, D & Fahy, J (2003) *Foundations of Marketing*, McGraw Hill, Maidenhead, Berkshire, 129, 131

Jones, MJ, Pentecost R, Requena G (2005) Memory for advertising and information content: Comparing the printed page to the computer screen, *Psychology and Marketing*, Vol 22, No 8, 623–648. Published Online: 20 Jun 2005

Jun, M, Yang, Z & Kim, D (2004) Customers' perceptions of online retailing service quality and their satisfaction, *International Journal of Quality & Reliability Management*, Vol 21, No 8, 817–840

Kotler, P (2003) *Marketing Management*, Prentice Hall Harlow, UK

Lindstrom, M (2001) Corporate branding and the Web: A global/local challenge, *Journal of Brand Management*, May 2001, Vol 8, No 4–5, 365–368(4)

McLean, K & Tunnicliffe, D (2004) *The Life of Brands Online*, Market Research Society Conferences. Available online at www.warc.org

Mohammed, RA, Fisher, RJ, Jaworski, BJ & Cahill, AM (2002) *Internet Marketing*, McGraw Hill International, 305

Molenaar, C (2002) *The Future of Marketing*, FT Prentice Hall, Harlow, England, 133, 212–214

Nielsen, J (1997) *Do Websites Have Increasing Returns?* Available online at www.useit.com/alertbox/9704b.html

O'Connor, J, Galvin, E & Evans, M (2004) *Electronic Marketing*, FT Prentice Hall, Pearson Education Limited, England, 247

Okazaki, S (2005) Searching the web for global brands: how American brands standardize their web sites in Europe, *European Journal of Marketing*, Vol 39, No 1/2, 87–109

Orr, A (2005) Lost in translation, *CMO Magazine*, www.cmomagazine.com/read/050105/lost_translation.html, May 2005

Philips (2003) *E-Business Strategy*, McGraw Hill Education, Berkshire, England, 180–181

Pine, BJ, Joseph, B (1993) *Mass Customization: The New Frontier in Business Competition*, Harvard Business School Press

Poirier, P (2003) *Can Your Site Stop Your Telephone from Ringing*? Available online at www.MarketingProfs.com.

Rahman, Z (2004) E-commerce solution services, *European Business Review*, Vol 16, No 6, 564–576

Rayport, JF & Jaworski, BF (2002) *Introduction to E-Commerce*, McGraw Hill International, 259–262

Rowley, J (2004) Online branding, *Online Information Review*, February 2004, Vol 28, No 2, 131–138(8)

Rowley, J (2004) Online branding: the case of McDonald's, *British Food Journal*, March 2004, Vol 106, No 3, 228–237(10)

Rubinstein, H (2002) Branding on the Internet – moving from a communications to a relationship approach to branding, *Interactive Marketing*, Vol 4, No 1, July/September 2002

Singh, M (2002) E-Services and their role in B2C e-commerce, *Managing Service Quality*, Vol 12, No 6, 434–446

Smith, PR & Chaffey, D (2002) *EMarketing Excellence*, Butterworth Heinemann

Svensson, G (2003) A generic conceptual framework of interactive service quality, *Managing Service Quality*, Vol 13, No 4, 267–275

Stanford University *Guidelines for Web Credibility* (2002). Available online at www.webcredibility.org/guidelines/index.html

Sterne, J (2001) *World Wide Web Marketing*, (3rd edn), John Wiley & Sons, 381

Strebinger, A & Treiblmaier, H (2004) E-adequate branding: building offline and online brand structure within a polygon of interdependent forces, *Electronic Markets*, June 2004, Vol 14, No 2, 153–164(12)

Stuart, H & Jones, C (2004) Corporate branding in marketspace, *Corporate Reputation Review*, Spring 2004, Vol 7, No 1, 84–93(10)

Swaibey, N, cited in Papas, C (2005) Online On target, *Direct Response,* Haymarket Publications, April 2005, 33

Tedlow, R (1990) *New and Improved: The Story of Mass Marketing in America*, Harper Collins

Whittle, S (2000) *Never Mind the Profits, Feel the Branding*, www.vnunet.com/Analysis/601597, 3 April 2000

Zhang, Z (2004) Organizing customers: Japanese travel agencies marketing on the Internet, *European Journal of Marketing*; Vol 38, No 9; 2004

FURTHER READING

Charlesworth, A (2003) Choosing a domain name, *International Journal of e-Business Strategy*, Vol 4, No 4, May/June 2003 Winthrop Publications – a guide to selecting a suitable domain name for a 'bricks and mortar' organisation.

Chaston, I (2001) *E-Marketing Strategy*, McGraw-Hill.

Sterne, J (2001) *World Wide Web Marketing*, Wiley.

WEB LINKS

Larry Chase's Search Engine for Marketers (**www.searchengineformarketers.com**) – this site does what it says on the tin, offering reviews and links to the top sites in 40 marketing categories.

Marketingexperiments.com (**www.marketingexperiments.com**) – offers free copies of their extensive research results.

Marketingprofs.com – excellent e-marketing content, though terminology used and models/theories quoted mean the articles are mainly for readers with a background in marketing.

 Visit the Online Resource Centre which accompanies this book, for lots of interesting additional material, including self-assessment questions, internet exercises, and links for each chapter: **www.oxfordtextbooks.co.uk/orc/gay/**

Pricing Issues on the Web

10

Learning objectives

By the end of the chapter you will be able to:

• Comprehend the new influences impacting upon online pricing strategies and tactics

• Understand how traditional pricing models apply in digital markets

• Comprehend how the Internet has provided consumers and organisations with greater power in the buying process

• Evaluate the way in which new pricing models are being applied, and their implications for online marketers and consumers alike

Chapter at a glance

10.1 Introduction

The Internet has a created a fluid and challenging pricing environment. It has empowered buyers with purchase information and more choice to transact with sellers with few geographic restrictions. In many product categories, customers are more price sensitive, especially users of price comparison sites (or shopbots). Price comparison sites like Kelkoo (www.kelkoo.com) have become important international online brands in their own right operating right across the European Union.

Rapid price changes are driven by dynamic pricing software. Consumers are reacting in different ways and perceive unfairness when sharp prices rises push up the selling price at short notice. Consumers tend to expect online prices to be up to 20% lower than offline, largely through the removal of intermediaries. However, Meriden (2002) suggested that Internet inflation was running at twice the level of the economy as a whole. This indicated that the heavy discounting of the dot.com era was over.

The Internet has changed organisational cost structures and provided the capability to maximise profits. Conventional pricing strategies and tactics are relevant online, but marketers must swiftly develop an insight into buyer-seller interactions. With greater price transparency than ever before, frequent monitoring of competitor prices is critical. These and other issues will be explored within this chapter.

10.2 Online pricing strategic guidelines

McKinsey Marketing Practice (2000) in their paper, *Internet Pricing, A Creator of Value – Not a Destroyer* posits three fundamental ways in which online marketers may benefit from the flexibility that electronic pricing provides:

1. Precision in price levels and price communication whereby companies can identify customer sensitivities to price movements within a range.

2. Time adaptiveness in response to market changes with real time reactions to shifts in demand.

3. Segmentation of prices with the overlay of multiple sources of customer data to segment the market with greater precision and then price to the specific segment.

McKinsey argue for the following elements to be present if an online pricing strategy improves return on investment:

1. Identify degrees of freedom consistent with strategic objectives and brand values, so whilst online pricing provides greater flexibility it supports overall corporate objectives such as entering new markets and market penetration.

2. Build appropriate technological capabilities to support e-pricing, which are relevant, and responsiveness to changes in customer demand eg dynamic pricing.

3. Build an experimenting and nimble pricing organisation based on constant testing and monitoring of demand shifts resulting from price changes and customer reactions to promotions.

MINI CASE 10.1 Leading way to lower prices

Internet access could be vital for independent garages seeking approved repair status, according to the Retail Motor Industry Federation. The EU Block Exemption Regulation allows some independent garages to source information on vehicles direct from the manufacturer. This gives motorists the opportunity to get their cars serviced and repaired at garages at competitive prices rather than franchised dealers who currently have a virtual monopoly. The whole after-sales market will be shaken up.

Manufacturers argued that cars needed fully equipped franchised dealers with specially trained technicians for optimum performance. They believe that after investing vast sums in the development of new models, the dealer networks they support should keep lucrative servicing and repair work. Many are actually owned by the manufacturers themselves.

Under the new EU regulations, manufacturers will be forced share their technical secrets with approved independent garages outside of the network to increase competition and keep prices as low as possible.

This information is expected to be made available online, as it is seen as the most credible distribution method. Bob Hood, RMI independent garages director, says, 'Manufacturer provision of equipment, training and technical information will be available to all who need it, for a price. It is vital that independents get an online connection. Apart from the possibility of receiving manufacturers' technical information, they can also access the industry and market information already available online.' Mr. Hood adds, 'It is almost inconceivable that motor manufacturers would choose a medium other than the Internet to distribute technical information.'

This has provided a great opportunity for independent garages such as Unipart Automotive, with their network of Car Care Centres. It remains to be seen how quickly car owners desert main dealers for the independents and the speed and level to which prices will fall.

Adapted from: Hughes, S, *Newcastle Evening Chronicle*, 16 May 2003. (www.icnewcastle.co.uk)
Garages fight off challenge from Europe, Independent Online, www.motoring.independent.co.uk/features/article16622.ece; www.twobirds.com/english/publications/newsletters/upload/16070_1.pdf

Whilst technology is now available for organisations to improve profit maximisation online, consumers also have more tools at their disposal and have become more powerful in the search for products and information that represent value to the individual.

In Mini case 10.1 we see how the Internet can influence pricing and cost structures and apply downward pressures on prices directly and indirectly.

10.3 Influences on pricing strategies and tactics

Many marketing chapters on price recognise that it is the only revenue-earning element amongst the marketing mix elements. Customers demonstrate their propensity to pay for the value offered by the product or service. Price should be developed as part of a cohesive and consistent offering with the other P's, and carefully positioned in the consumers mind to meet the needs and aspirations of the target market.

Revenue determines the health and wealth of an organisation in terms of its profitability. Organisations must not neglect opportunities to maximise profit in circumstances where the customer may be willing to pay more than the intended selling price. As Doyle (2002) observes, 'Low prices rarely provide a sustainable basis for competitive advantage in today's competitive markets', as most organisational objectives should aim to develop the 'added value' package and brand positioning. In simple terms, a high quality product that is retailed at below average prices will invariably do three things:

1. It will not generate sufficient revenue for the organisation.

2. It will generate suspicion and confusion amongst the target market.

3. It is likely that it will only attract price conscious bargain hunters who provide little opportunity for repeat business at attractive margins.

However in the online world, the core product may often be significantly cheaper compared to traditional channels but other revenue streams such as affiliate marketing contribute effectively to total revenue. Probably the most well-known affiliate scheme is run by Amazon but any organisation can participate. In Fig 10.1, a new, exciting handmade soap

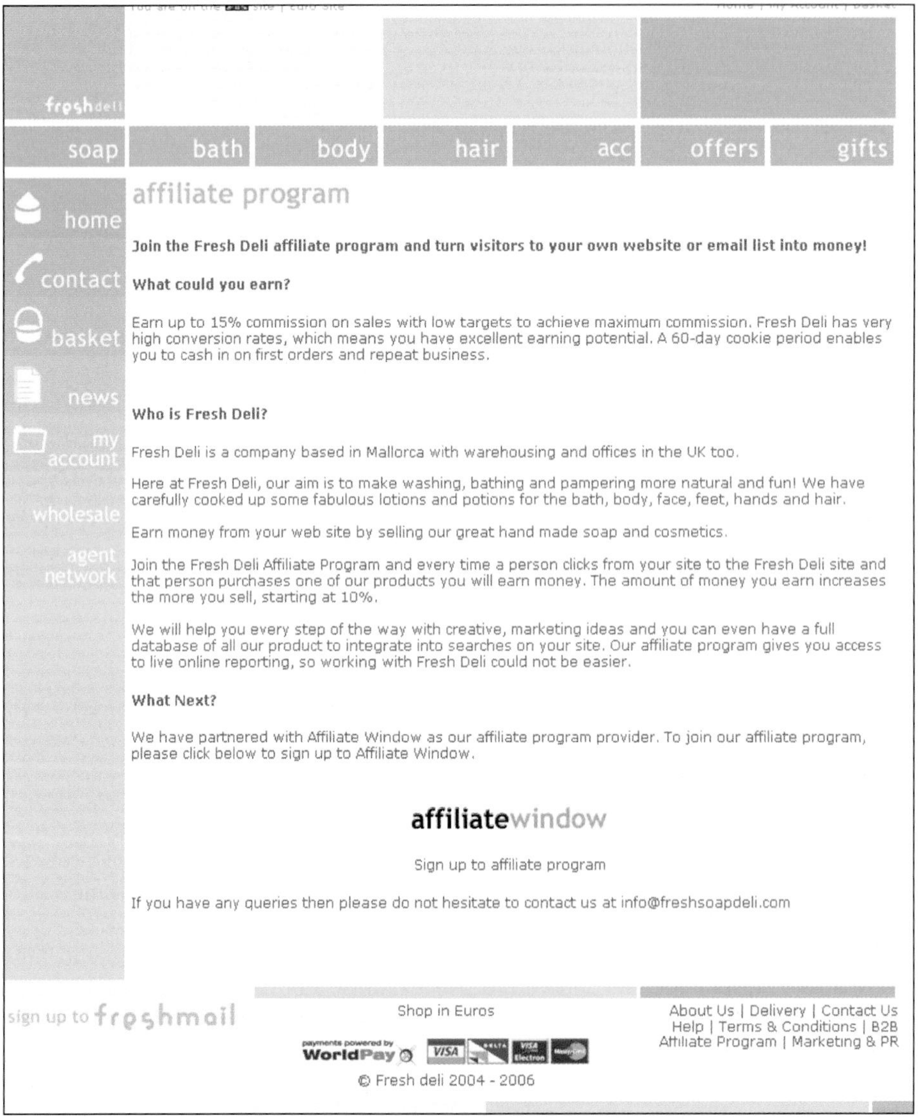

Fig 10.1 Fresh Del Soap affiliate

venture, Fresh deli Soap, takes advantage of a scheme operated by Affiliate Window Ltd (www.affiliatewindow.com).

Unfortunately, many businesses, especially SMEs, rely on the safe but restrictive **cost-plus** method of pricing. Understandably, cost focus is a fundamental concern for fledgling businesses aiming to be lean and mean in their formative years. However, cost-plus is applied in an inflexible way with prices often being set over many months. This can have a detrimental effect on profitability as changes in current or future consumer demand, materials price and inflation are largely ignored and opportunities for price maximisation missed. A walk into any high street retailer or supermarket provides hundreds of price applications designed to seduce, persuade and coerce the consumer into parting with their cash or plastic, most have online applications also. Value means different things to people or segments, and marketers have to wrestle with the problem of unearthing motivations and desires of potential prospects. For the product or service provider, the headache comes when attempting to establish the right price in the chosen market place. Will the consumer give you the thumbs up or down? Has the Internet really brought about a mass market of bargain hunters or do consumers seek other benefits from it?

Setting prices

Whether it is on the web or on the high street, there are key considerations that apply in establishing price:

- Pricing objectives related to broader corporate and marketing objectives
- Pricing strategies often determined by market sophistication and segmentation
- Customer value and perception
- External and competitive influences

For example, an organisation may adopt a penetration pricing strategy online to achieve a dominant share of the market or to attract a significant list of prospects or affiliates. Typical tactics involve things like free membership e-mail sign-ups in return for specific member discounts and offers.

Pricing objectives

Pricing objectives must be consistent and inextricably linked to broader corporate objectives that set specific and measurable targets such as sales and profit figures, market share in new or established markets. Price can have a significant influence on the attainment of such objectives.

Many leading writers cite four main strategic objectives to influence price setting:

1. **Maintaining Market Share** – eg often where there is longer term potential in the sector or perhaps a channel has to be defended. Despite consumer expectations of cheaper online prices, John Lewis often price more aggressively in-store to defend its position against local high street competitors.

2. **Growth** – eg often achieved by aggressive, penetration pricing such as Tesco.com.

3. **Harvesting** – eg in mature markets when competition has intensified but core segments remain loyal, the strategy seeks to maintain price or increase volume whilst market share declines. For example, Amazon often sells products at competitive prices but they tend to be higher than those offered by newer partners in the Amazon Marketplace.

4. **Repositioning** – eg in the marketplace where companies may desire to go up or down market, change image or appeal to a new target market. For example, lower Internet costs enabled the traditional financial services giant, the Prudential, to reach a younger, affluent market with the launch of Egg (www.egg.com).

For some companies, the Internet provides an important revenue stream for those facing stiff competition in traditional markets. Attracting new customers via a new channel may enable the company to maintain its overall market share.

MINI CASE 10.2 How does the easyJet fare structure work?

easyJet operates a very simple fare structure. All fares are quoted one way to allow customers the flexibility to choose where and when they would like to fly. easyJet does not stipulate any restrictions to qualify for the cheapest fares (unlike most traditional airlines who will only offer cheap flights if the customer stays a Saturday night, therefore a cheap fare will not be available for a day-return business or shopping trip). The way we structure our fares is based on supply and demand and prices usually increase as seats are sold on every flight. So, generally speaking, the earlier you book, the cheaper the fare will be. Sometimes, however, due to market forces our fares may be reduced further.

Our booking system continually reviews bookings for all future flights and tries to predict how popular each flight is likely to be. If the rate at which seats are selling were higher than normal, then the price would go up. This way we avoid the undesirable situation of selling out popular flights months in advance. That gives you the flexibility to decide last minute and still get a better deal than if you flew with other airlines at the same time for the same journey.

easyJet is committed to offering the lowest fare amongst all our competitors for any given flight.

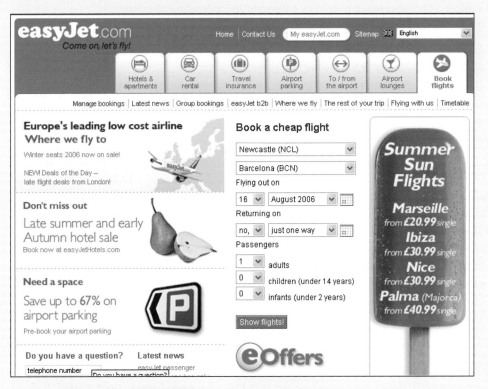

The home page of the easyJet.com web site
Source: www.easyJet.com
Reproduced by kind permission of EasyJet.

The Internet has proved to be an ideal vehicle for companies following rapid growth strategies. Prime examples are the low cost airlines such as easyJet and Ryanair where the Internet has been a primary component in their cost efficiency and revenue generation strategies, which has allowed them to achieve their objectives. The Internet can be used effectively to harvest profits by making archive material available to interested parties. A specialist IT reseller could reposition itself by revamping its web site as it starts attracting a wider audience rather than just the IT savvy customer. This would give greater buying power and more scope for variable pricing on a more extensive product and service range. Mini case 10.2 taken outlines Easyjet's pricing policy.

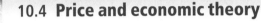

10.4 Price and economic theory

Let us take some time to consider some price issues and economic principles that determine demand curves and how they may impact upon price setting on the web.

Classical economists made the assumption that the laws of demand and supply determine price. In a perfectly competitive world if one supplier raises price then the market becomes more attractive and profitable. Other suppliers outside of the industry enter to capture some of this extra profit. On the other hand, a fall in market demand will reduce the number of suppliers because they will be operating at below economic profit. The less financially viable will 'go to the wall' and the market becomes a less attractive proposition. Over time, the market will settle and a position of equilibrium will emerge where quantity consumed will match the quantity supplied and firms will only make 'normal' returns.

The scholars rely on a number of suspect assumptions that should be appreciated by marketers. The demand and supply model assumes that:

- Perfect market knowledge exists and that the consumer knows where to purchase the best deals. Price comparison sites have improved consumers' search abilities. In addition, powerful search engines and growing customer experiences will enhance market knowledge.

- Consumers buy more of a product when it is cheaper and that price is the motivating factor in all purchasing decisions. The myth that web shoppers are a homogeneous group of bargain hunters has been dispelled by numerous studies, which identify various non-price factors influencing purchase behaviour, such as time, convenience, brand image and product availability.

- Suppliers are offering identical products in the marketplace. In markets such as books and CDs this is the case, as they are selling a homogenous commodity. However, in the majority of markets there are many product variants within the same product category. For example, in the personal computer market which is extremely competitive, direct manufacturers such as Dell, Mesh and Evesham may offer different components such as motherboards, game cards, scanners and printers across similar bundled or price ranges on the web. Conversely, many buyers like to customise their PC online to meet specific personal or business needs.

The price charged for a product will normally reflect the 'value' placed on the item by the buyer and depending upon the circumstances at that time such as urgency and scarcity. For marketers and sales forecasters alike, setting price levels to satisfy both buyers and sellers can be methodically researched or a result of gut feel or entrepreneurial inspiration. The price set can have a significant impact on demand and growth as the product moves through key stages of its lifecycle.

For economists and marketers, the information generated from demand and other marketing research activities attempts to estimate the effect of price movements up or down on the sales volume of a particular commodity. The subsequent demand levels have a knock-on effect with suppliers, distributors externally as well as having internal financial and other resource implications for the organisation.

Both price setters and economists want to know sales at any given price (**Demand**). What is the effect on sales volumes of any price changes? The measurement of such changes is referred to as **price elasticity** and indicates how sensitive buyers are to price movements. So if we increase the prices of our CDs by 10% from £10 to £11, do our sales decrease, remain static or even increase? Some product categories or segments can be very sensitive to price changes with resultant shifts in demand. There inevitably comes a point when further price falls will not influence demand. This is illustrated Mini Case 10.3 on Ryanair.

If demand is inelastic then raising prices will lead to an increase in total revenue. Few consumers actually know the exact price of many necessities, hence this gives the retailer the opportunity to vary and often maximise price without alienating the consumer.

Economists suggest that perfect competition and market knowledge exists when in reality this is virtually impossible to achieve, certainly prior to the emergence of e-commerce. In addition, Mohammed et al (2001) suggest that demand curves will be influenced by other factors such as:

- The types, prices and availability of substitute products eg non-branded printer cartridges.

- The prices and availability of complementary products from which demand is derived, eg the demand for CD rewriteable discs will be derived from the cost of putting in CD drivers in PCs, the ease of copying and the public perception that audio CDs are overpriced.

- Income effects when it increases demand usually increases where the product is price/income elastic eg luxury goods such as long haul holidays.

MINI CASE 10.3 Ryanair could not find takers for 100,000 free seats

Ryanair, the Irish low-cost airline, failed to give away 100,000 free tickets over Christmas 2002.

A November promotion giving away 500,000 free tickets for use during December and January resulted in only 400,000 ticket sales. The rate of take-up has fallen since a similar promotion in September when Ryanair tried to give away 1 million free tickets but was left with 130,000 on its hands.

Airline industry analysts have questioned the low-cost business model that believes more people will fly the cheaper seats are.

'The airline industry is mature, there is a limit to the amount of times a year people want to fly, they haven't got any more holiday and they can't afford it when they are out there', one analyst said.

A Ryanair spokesman said: 'I don't think it indicates less demand, it is more to do with when people want to travel such

as at the weekend. It indicates a lot of people want to fly at the same time'. The giveaways still helped Ryanair post a rise of 64% in passengers carried in December.

Chris Avery, airlines analyst at JP Morgan said: 'There are just some locations in the depth of winter that even free seats won't attract people to. The question is whether Ryanair should have so much capacity to these places in winter'.

Perhaps it is the case, that the novelty of cheap seats is diminishing and there is both a time and income limit to the number of times people can travel. Also the choice of destination is vast but clearly some cities are far more attractive than others and airline capacity requires astute management.

Adapted from: *The Sunday Telegraph*, Business, 3, 12 January 2003.
www.thetravelinsider.info/16nov01.htm
www.accaglobal.com/publications/studentaccountant/2455131

- Increased market size has the effect of increasing the demand for the product, eg as more people take early retirement, the demand for all year round travel options increases.

- Changing consumer tastes are a key variable affecting demand, eg recent health concerns have lead to many consumers to seek out low salt food products.

If the Internet has brought one key ability to the price setter, it is the sheer speed by which they can test consumer sensitivities to price movements literally in real time by individual transactions or even by log analysis of site navigations. When discussing price sensitivities, Verma et al discuss the substitute awareness effect. A product becomes decidedly price sensitive when purchasers are conscious of substitutes and their availability in the market place. Many shopbots can generate a plethora of alternatives, and many also state whether they are 'in stock'.

It has been argued that the mechanisms of the Internet leads to perfect competition and the emergence of a **frictionless economy** where the Internet decreases both search and transaction costs in market places with no restriction on time or location. More competitive information is generally available to customers, not to mention that 'switching costs' are virtually zero. In theory, these factors should intensify competition across most sectors. So is the Internet ' The Great Equalizer', as referred to by Brynjolfsson & Smith (2000)? Do the conditions of perfect competition outlined by Formica in Fig 10.2 below, via digital technologies enable the *ideal* market price to be achieved?

Price is only one element in the decision-making process and clearly some of the elements in Fig 10 are not met or achievable in every marketplace or product category, nor can we underestimate the importance of branded web sites that visitors often return to even though there is no significant price advantage. Web bargain hunters will have the best price as their key driver, whilst other buyers may value other elements in a web site's total offer, such as fast, flexible delivery, confidence from customer reviews, trust in terms of payment security, or fast and efficient shopping carts. Clearly those online merchants who have been innovative in developing features that provide a unique user experience reap the rewards of their endeavours with the customers' propensity to pay higher prices.

So why do we have market distortions occurring in the so-called frictionless economy? Concerns over these developing market issues have been raised by the Office of Fair Trading in its paper, 'E-commerce and its implications for competition policy' (2000) regarding market power which readers are recommended to view. Issues such as first mover advantages, excessive pricing, vertical restraint, collusion, price discrimination, product differentiation

---

Fig 10.2 The world of perfect competition (Formica, 2002)

- Products are identical
- Free entry/exit: no barriers to entering or leaving the market
- Large number of buyers and sellers
- Full information about supply and demand
- Customers are perfectly informed: no search costs, no time wasted seeking the right product
- Every buyer would be matched with the supplier that could best meet his/her needs
- Prices would be at exactly the level that would keep supply and demand in equilibrium
- Sales are priced at the marginal cost of production

Table 10.1 Price transparency	
Issue with Price Transparency	**Strategies to Overcome Price Transparency**
• Reduces margins	• Be innovative: Create new products and services that will enhance customers' lives
• Commoditisation	• Bundle your products and services: Offer customers 'added value' not obtainable elsewhere
• Reduces customer brand loyalty	• Be creative: Use different pricing models based on the way customers buy from you
• Creates poor customer perception	• Reward customers for repeat purchasing by enabling them to create an account and only see 'their' specific pricing based on previous purchase history

Source: Matthewson, JA (2002) *e-Business*, Butterworth Heinemann, 49.

and access to online marketplaces all have the potential to distort the market, making the hypothetical dream of perfect competition in the digital world a distant dream.

We shall briefly address the interrelationship between three key elements-**price transparency**, how 'perfect' shopbots are, and **price dispersion** on the web.

The Internet does provide a massive amount of free information on products and prices for both buyers and sellers. This is an important point in the discussion of price transparency, as it has long been assumed that the beneficiary would be the buyer but clearly sellers may also obtain competitive advantage via price transparency as they can monitor competitive price movements and react. For example, CD-Wow often gives a price comparison with three of their major competitors when you select a CD or DVD. Matthewson (2002) states price transparency also brings risks attached and reduces the 'opportunity to communicate the values of your product and justify your premium prices'. He suggests four main issues with price transparency and strategies to cope with them in Table 10.1.

Shopbots have become an integral part of the web landscape and have become destination sites in their own right. They allow price sensitive and less brand loyal buyers to select the best deals on the web, at least in theory. Efficient search technology software gives the buyer new found power to trawl the marketplace at speed to compare a vast array of suppliers. For the price conscious consumer driven by reduced transaction costs rather than relationships, they are an essential port of call. The leading innovator in price comparison sites was mySimon (www.mySimon.com). The Internet is becoming heavily populated with similar sites such as www.kelkoo.com and www.dealtime.com and for financial products www.moneysupermarket.com. Price comparisons may be helpful but the results generated are not as 'perfectly informed' as we would like to think. In the first instance, the results are open to the vagaries of search engine marketing such as meta tags, algorithms and cloaking (see chapter 6 on Search Engine Marketing). If the design process and submission is not carried out professionally, some better-priced sites may not appear. Many shopbots now have trader links, affiliate schemes, sponsorship and paid priority listings that may lead to top rankings for preferred partners rather than generating genuine results. Price sensitive consumers are becoming more aware of these weaknesses and allegiances of certain comparison sites and becoming less trusting and thus searching elsewhere for their desired deal. Some shopbots are claiming that they are truly independent with verification coming from industry bodies such as regulators. An example of this is Uswitch (www.uswitch.com), which will search for and calculate the best deals on offer for key utility services such as electricity, gas and telephone services. In June 2003, Uswitch achieved accreditation from the telephone regulator Oftel, for adhering to its strict code of practice that ensured independent and accurate data on price comparisons. Perhaps other shopbots should seek similar accreditation if, as many commentators observe, trust is a key issue for sustained Internet growth. Inefficiencies and imperfections with shopbots exist otherwise price dispersion would be minimal when comparing identical offerings but sites will differentiate in other ways.

Recent studies by Smith, Brynjolfsen and Bailey (1999), Brynjolfsen and Smith (2000), Clay et al (2000), and Ancarani and Shankar (2002) have identified significant price dispersion across various product categories and channels. Differences have emerged between pure players and clicks and bricks retailers compared to traditional offline retailers. For example, Ancarani and Shankar found that when price lists, often referred to as posted or menu prices, were considered, traditional retailers were generally more expensive than their multi-channel and pure player counterparts. However, when delivery costs are added, the picture changes with the multi-channel retailers emerging as the most expensive followed by pure players with traditional retailers offering the best prices. This has price and strategic implications for all retailers in various ways. Driving down the cost of logistics will provide competitive price advantage for some e-tailers whilst others may view postage and packing as an extra contribution to revenue through overcharging. Certainly the Internet is all about information, speed and efficiency but today's consumer is a fast learner via the web's forums and mainstream media and should be treated with more respect than currently afforded to him/her. Other tried and trusted promotional tools can be applied online such as loyalty schemes, price matching or quantity discounts. For the traditional high street operator battling against online businesses, the delivery cost issue provides more promotional ammunition to add to the attractions of the physical shopping experience. Research from *Web User* in the Mini case 10.4 compares the different practices.

10.5 Pricing methods

The approach to price setting may be influenced by the organisation's focus of influence internally, whether it is cost driven or market driven, or both. Alternatively, the focus of its price setting could be the effect on demand of competitors' prices where competition is intense and aggressive. Consequently, many writers suggest three main determinants or approaches to price setting:

1. Cost orientated pricing
2. Competition based pricing
3. Market oriented pricing

We will consider the first two briefly, as detailed discussions of these are beyond the scope of this chapter, and devote more time to the third method.

Cost oriented pricing

Revenue is inextricably linked to some cost factor and an understanding of the organisational cost structures and how they behave in different market situations will influence the price set. Marketers should have a fundamental understanding of the main cost concepts

MINI CASE 10.4 Price wars – high street v the Internet

Is price the sole motivator in the purchasing decision? Are there other factors that influence the great British public? If so, how does this influence what they buy and how much they pay for it?

It has often been assumed that consumers get a better deal buying online but is this really the case? Certainly we can compare prices more easily by keying into Google but various newspaper articles claimed that UK consumers are paying more than their European partners for many goods, especially electrical items. To add to the frustration, it is suggested that multi-national companies have blocked them from accessing their cheaper web sites in other countries.

According to The Times Online, back home in the UK, leading up to Christmas in 2005, the consumer was caught in the middle of a price war between high street retailers and their online counterparts. Major electrical manufacturers such as Sony, Panasonic and Sharp offered discounts to high street retailers after intense lobbying caused by significant growth in online sector sales at the expense of the traditional outlets. The traditional retailers argued that they had to contend with much higher overheads and provided better service compared to the online merchants. For their part, they contend that the move by the manufacturers was anti-competitive. Ultimately the consumer benefited, at least in the short-term.

A 2003 survey by Web User, the UK's biggest selling Internet magazine, generated some interesting price results for the common online purchases, books and CDs. The survey acknowledged the online attraction of sellers like Amazon who offer an immense catalogue with convenience, reviews and recommendations, and of course consistently low prices. In contrast, they recognised the high street benefits of book browsing, 3 for 2 deals and what they referred to as 'pre-postman tension' when waiting to collect your letter box-unfriendly Amazon parcel.

The survey looked at the pros and cons of the selling price and the total price when face with delivery charges by comparing Amazon with WH Smith and Borders high street operations.

Web User bought five recently published books whose list price (no discounts) totalled £64.95 from Amazon. They then compared the Amazon saving with price and availability of the same books at London branches of Borders and WHSmith.

Their results found significant variations across the five texts and three book merchants, prices, deals and deliveries against the full cost cost of £64.95. The overall findings are summarised below:

1. Amazon	(Super saver delivery)	£39.95
2. WHSmith	(including 3-for-2 deal)	£42.96
3. Amazon	(standard delivery if all books ordered together)	£44.66
4. WHSmith	(not using 3-for-2)	£47.95
5. Amazon	(each book ordered separately)	£53.30
6. Borders		£58.95

Basket 1 qualified for Amazon's free Super Saver Delivery and produced a saving of £25.40 (39%) off the list price. Even if the books had been ordered together using Amazon's standard delivery (£2.16 per order plus 59p per item) the total would still have saved than £20 on the list price but if ordered separately from Amazon, the total cost would have increased significantly.

WHSmith were quite competitive with Amazon, though three of the five books qualified for the 3-for-2 deal. Borders' similar promotion covered fewer titles and its prices were generally higher.

The survey concluded that buying from Amazon made good sense as long as you were buying in bulk.

Sources: www.rip-off.co.uk/archives/internet shopping 18 12 04 .htm *Web User*, Issue 57, 15–28 May 2003, 18–21
www.timesonline.co.uk/article/0,,2103-1874365,00.html,
Why the high street struggles to match the web in price war, 16 November 2005

such as fixed costs (rent, rates, etc), variable costs, marginal costs and total costs (fixed and variable costs).

Many normal business costs also apply to online businesses such as rents, rates, electricity, sales, marketing, administration and distribution costs. Marketers must be aware of some cost nuances for an online operation and how they may impact on the final selling price. For budgeting purposes, the organisation will have to assess the current and future importance of the Internet in relation to offline channels, if appropriate and weight the budget accordingly. Many marketers are playing follow the leader and allocating a certain percentage, say 15%, of the promotional budget based on other players in the market.

Strauss, Ansary and Frost (2003) put forward the useful distinction between the **upward** and **downward** pressure on prices created by different web related costs.

Upward price pressure

- **Distribution**: Particularly for many online retailers, eg online food retailing, both niche and mainstream, the distribution function is a significant element in their cost structure. Naturally the cost will depend on the product category but you can expect at least 10% of the selling price for a physical good to be taken up by the elements of distribution such as warehousing, inventory control and delivery. In the UK, the failure of merchants to meet delivery promises in the early dot.com era (indeed, many stories abound about the failure to deliver at all!) caused considerable customer disenchantment resulting in the loss of repeat business. Marketers must be aware of customer responses to excessive delivery charges) that could just be a decisive sting in the tail when they reach the site's checkout and decide to spend their cash elsewhere. It is apparent that some online operators charge delivery rates above the carrier's costs in order to recover their distribution costs, it can make a useful additional revenue contribution. Whilst it is acknowledged that distribution can force up the total cost to the customer, they may not react adversely to the delivery charges if it means that either, they have still made a significant cost saving against the alternatives, or the distribution provides some other key benefit to them such as time saved. The speed of distribution can create competitive advantage in certain markets and to certain customers.

- **Affiliate marketing**: these schemes have become a powerful tool in creating a vital network of intermediaries who can drive traffic and generate sales. Commission is then paid to the affiliate for the link, which takes their site visitor through to the sponsor's site with payment made, usually by the number of visitors or actual sales. The cost consideration is the level of commission paid which can be as low as 3% and as high as 70%. Amazon, with 400,000 affiliates (Smith & Chaffey, 2002) generates over a quarter of its revenue through such schemes and pays 15% commission. The 15% commission must be carefully factored into their pricing in what is already a price competitive market. Amazon openly welcomes anyone from portals to individuals to become affiliates. This 'mass affiliate' approach will differ from say an author's e-book on a specialist subject that would depend upon carefully selected partners with credibility and standing within that domain. Commission rates given for this type of knowledge based product will usually be lower as the end-user will place a higher value on the information contained within so 5% of £149 generates more than 15% of £16.99. The monthly running total of affiliate commissions must also monitored carefully for against our cash flow.

- **Site development and maintenance costs**: these also impact upon the final selling price and will be dictated by the complexity of the site and the need for frequent updates and management of the site. In the UK, web sites with no dynamic content can be bought for around £1,000 but if dynamic content is deemed a necessary you can start at around £7,000 with no upper ceiling. Other costs includes site maintenance charges though with training this can be done in-house with the likes of Dreamweaver and web hosting packages which can start from as little as £1.99 plus VAT depending upon the level of service support necessary www.OneandOne.co.uk. Some web hosting operations specialise in the needs of industry sectors such www.openworld.co.uk which provides packages for the hotel industry.

- **Search marketing costs**: this is an important factor in the online marketer's promotional cost calculations. Organisations must evaluate the traffic generated by specific search engines against the cost and decide which sites they must submit to. These could be the main search engines such as:

- Google
- Yahoo!
- MSN
- Ask Jeeves
- Lycos
- AltaVista
- Overture
- Miva (formerly Espotting)
- AOL

New revenue models seeking to achieve improved return on investment are replacing the old models of free submissions to search engines. Now, pay for inclusion, pay-per-click (PPC) and search engine list bidding have all to be costed in and their importance will depend on how many people arrive at your site via a search engine. For those companies submitting sites, it is vital that they effectively forecast site traffic and budget accordingly otherwise a surge in unexpected site traffic could cost the company dearly. Agencies now incorporate a pay-for-performance element within their schedules for clients. This model enables better budgetary control in the customer acquisition process as the agency lodges fixed amounts with the fee or bid price deducted from the budget allocation every time a lead is generated.

- **Fiscal and anti-competitive measures**: these will impact either upwards or downwards, but organisations must be aware of their effect. For example, this year we have seen the introduction of new European Tax Laws referred to as the Directive on the Taxation of Digital Sales which requires non-EU based companies selling digital content to charge Value Added Tax (VAT) depending upon the country where the customer lives. The Directive seeks to reduce the customer opportunity to go outside of the EU to access downloads of music, e-books and other information 'goods' which placed EU based companies paying VAT, at a disadvantage. If an EU resident purchases digital content from a non-EU based seller, say in the US, then the seller would have to add VAT to the invoice price at the rate applicable in the specific EU country. So some of the perceived benefits of the global market are undermined, as consumers will be hit by higher prices. Awareness of such legislation is essential. They may also be affected by regulatory bodies, such as Oftel in the UK who monitor anti competitive behaviour such as excessive price-cutting by dominant market powers.

Downward price pressure

The application of information technology has been a primary driver to streamline business processes and reduce costs. Some of the cost benefits of digital technologies over offline processes are briefly considered below.

- **Transaction costs of order processing** are significantly lowered online, with estimates of around one-tenth of the offline costs associated with staff costs and paper based administration. In B2B trading exchanges, the cost of data flows between trading partners is reduced. For example, electronic data interchange (EDI) provides a lower cost method of exchanging transactional records. This is not without its technical problems, many of which have been overcome with the growing adoption of eXtensible Markup Language (XML). Not surprisingly many companies are actively encouraging customers to transact online to the benefit of both parties. For example, many low-cost airlines offer customers a 10% discount if they book online. British Airways previously charged customers £10 more if they visited www.ba.com for flight information and then booked offline. The use of 'e-tickets' via e-mail provides a fast and efficient distribution method when compared to traditional methods via the postal service.

- **Online customer service** is becoming more refined and adept at handling customer queries in a more customer focussed way that the early FAQs on web sites. Companies like Right Now Technologies (www.rightnowtech.co.uk) are providing tailor-made online customer service solutions for both private and public sector organisations that not only reduces the cost of customer handling but frees up call contact centre staff to deal with more specific customer service issues as the web handles most of the regular queries.

- **Online direct mail** is appreciably cheaper, more flexible and faster than its traditional offline counterpart. If we consider e-mail 'the killer app', mailing costs are around one-fifth of those sent by ordinary postal services, though the effect of spamming on response rates will influence ROI. The production costs associated with the printing of product catalogues is again cheaper with the online equivalent, for once the front end costs have been amortised, the running costs and maintenance of an online catalogue is minimal. In Fig 10.3, the European virtual factory outlet Haburi.com (www.haburi.com), combines a functional online catalogue with effective e-mail marketing to sell designer labels online.

- **Overheads** of online businesses will be lower than those faced by a bricks and mortar retailer. The online business has lower distribution and warehousing costs, and, as location is not an issue with them, cheaper business premises and rates can often be sourced where links to key transport networks exist, improving cost efficiency further. With better logistics operations and real time deliveries, stockholding costs are at a minimum. In some cases, the inventory does not exist until orders are received.

Fig 10.3 Haburi.com

- **Digital delivery** now allows many products such as music and software publications to be made available online or digitally via downloads, which is much cheaper than the production and delivery of these products in their physical form.
- **Online surveys** also provide marketers with a major saving in their research activities. The advent of data collection software removes the need to draft surveys, speeds up and increases data entry accuracy.

Competitor based pricing

The organisation bases its prices on what the competition charges for products similar to their own rather than focus on its costs or market demand. This assumes that most buyers will make both product and price comparisons before arriving at the purchase decision. The comparisons usually revolve around 'the evoked set', which are the main competitors in that product category. For example some one considering the purchase of a new vehicle in the UK may consider the offerings from Vauxhall, Ford, Peugeot and Honda before making their initial brand choice. From here they are likely to search out the best pricing options amongst dealerships offering which specific manufacturer's model.

There are two main forms of competitor based pricing: *Going Rate Pricing* and *Competitive Bid* or *Sealed Bid Pricing*.

Going-rate pricing is where firms charge more or less the same as other players in the market, though there is an element of follow the leader if a dominant player exists in the marketplace. If the product in question is basically a commodity, the firm may seek to develop some form of differential advantage that appeals to the buyer. So for an online CD merchant, differentiation may come from better site design, superior delivery service, better customer ratings or a wider catalogue of artists for example which result in superior sales when compared with the competition. Despite greater price transparency and comparison-shopping resulting from better software technologies, a number of studies have suggested that **price dispersion** exists online.

In **Competitive Bid or Sealed Bid Pricing**, contracts are won or lost on the basis of pricing work to meet a buyer's specifications. Whilst some entrepreneurs may have a gut feel for pitching at a price to satisfy both parties in the process, business modelling has been used to determine the *expected profit* from such contracts and the likelihood of being successful in a bid tender. This is derived from the bid price minus costs multiplied by the probability of securing the contract.

However, as with many models, the expected profit concept has limitations, the primary one being the need for quality information regarding the competitors and their past and current bidding intentions, which in reality is not the easiest of tasks.

A number of issues have arisen over online protocol in sealed bid auctions. Liao and Hwang (2001) questioned the assumption that the auctioneer is fully trusted by those involved in the bidding process, though there maybe new participants in the auction so trust may not be established. Traditional auctioneers like Sotheby's have a proven track record that instils confidence in the participants. Similarly, eBay, with its strict online auction protocols has established trust. Liao and Hwang also highlight a number of key differences with online and traditional offline sealed bid auctions such as the physical opening of bids in the presence of the bidders that is not possible online. They argue that auctioneers colluding with bidders to secure a contract with the lowest bid could leak submitted bids. The authors cite various papers on sealed bid auctions, which identify four key criteria for their successful operation:

1. **Validity** to determine the largest bid cast as the winner
2. **Privacy** to ensure no conspiracy could occur
3. **Fairness** to ensure that all bids remain confidential and the winning bidder guarantees their bid
4. **Efficiency and Security** to ensure that no eavesdropping can take place which could lead to the interference of bids during the process

As players on both sides of the online sealed bid process become more experienced and comfortable with the protocol, the concerns over the above criteria should be reduced.

Market oriented pricing policies

Once an organisation has set its pricing objectives, it should now be in a position to consider its pricing policies and how they support the other marketing objectives and mix elements. We will consider some of the traditional market oriented pricing mechanisms, which remain valid for online markets.

Skimming

This refers to the price set for a new, innovative product, which usually has a technological advantage over existing competitor offerings seeking to maximise short-term profits. To recoup research and development costs and to 'position' the product to reflect its uniqueness, the price will be set high initially and targeted to the company's profiled 'innovators'. Once demand has been satisfied within that customer layer, the price is adjusted, usually downwards, to meet the demand of the next layer who would be the 'early adopters'.

Certain conditions must be in place for this policy to be effective. There should be a reasonable lead-time before competitors can produce a similar product, market entry for competitors is not easy and product quality and image should generate sufficient demand so profits outweigh cost substantially. For example, price skimming was possible with the introduction of DAB (digital audio broadcasting) radios.

Penetration pricing

This is where the organisation identifies long-term market potential and sets a low price initially in order to penetrate the market and build up a critical mass of customers in the short to medium term. Many companies implemented this strategy during the web's infancy with incentives and discounts well below high street retail prices to drive consumers online in the hope that they would stay there and generate repeat purchases. As mentioned by Doyle earlier in this chapter, a low cost strategy is rarely sustainable in the medium term unless efficient purchasing policies exist.

Psychological pricing

As the term suggests, this plays on the psychological, subjective and emotional responses that the buyer has to a purchase rather than a rational, economic approach. This represents fundamental differences in consumer and organisational buyer behaviour so psychological pricing is prevalent mainly in consumer markets, especially retail. The ethics of psychological pricing can be questioned. It creates cynicism in some and confusion in other customers. A recent article in a reputable US online marketing newsletter, which shall remain nameless,

Fig 10.4 Prestige pricing (www.singlemaltsdirect.com)

was quite blunt in some of its dubious pricing recommendations such as 'charge a staggering high price and they'll think it's better; create a fake price and then give a fake discount'. Marketing draws from social sciences but with many observers suggesting that the modern consumer is more sophisticated and discerning, perhaps there is a need for more intelligent pricing which does not leave the customer feeling deceived.

Prestige/status pricing

This plays on these psychological and emotional responses to justify higher prices which buyers deem to be key indicators of quality. It is strange what goes on in the deepest recesses of the consumer's mind – sometimes rational, sometimes irrational, and sometimes a combination of both but the perceived value to the individual which reflects the quality of the product is often derived from the brand image, the purpose of the product and its overall usage. Rare and expensive malt whiskies have found a niche online, especially in export markets, to satisfy connoisseurs of the 'tartan medicine'. www.singlemaltsdirect.com (Fig 10.4) is one of a number of sites devoted to single malts.

Brand power and image have taken on a greater importance in the last two decades, with market leaders and innovators such as Nike, BMW, Callaway and Diesel persuading consumers that are some inherent product qualities that will enrich the individual's life in some way. Such high-ticket products may prove difficult for some customers to pay in full by credit. However, a number of third party finance intermediaries like Able2Buy (www.able2buy.com) and V12 Finance (www.v12finance.com) provide fast interest free credit approval to facilitate such transactions.

Odd-even pricing

This predominantly sets prices below key pricing points in an attempt influence the buyer perception that the product is significantly cheaper than it is. Pricing with odd numbers is more common then pricing with even numbers eg £9.99 instead of £10. However, Wilson (2002) states that studies by direct marketers have found that sales are better at key pricing points such as $197, $297 and $397 when compared with prices set marginally higher or lower.

Bundle pricing

This is a technique that lends itself to online marketing for the time-starved, cost conscious consumer. Verma and Varma (2003) suggest that numerous online suppliers 'are aggressive users of bundling'. Some may bundle a product and a service together such as a game with free online support. Others may offer more than one product, often complementary, sold as a package to the benefit of both buyer and seller. Online retailers of digital photographic equipment such as Pixmania (www.Pixmania.com) and Warehouse Express (www.warehouseexpress.com) bundle cameras, memory cards, batteries and other accessories together.

Differential pricing

This is when the seller charges different prices for the same product to buyers in different locations, different segments or by purchase quantity. The variations may take into account additional distribution costs such as transport or postal costs to different 'regions'. In the case of the Internet, the regions may be different continents and normally the extra charges should be passed on to the consumer and reflect the different cost structure. However, location can provide significant cost advantages with more cheaper labour costs and attractive fiscal regimes. Online merchants such as CD-Wow source originally sourced cheaper CDs and DVDs from the Far East to offer extremely competitive prices to its UK market.

However, the company was pursued in the High Court by the British Phonographic Industry (BPI). They claimed that its members were the owners or exclusive licensees of the UK copyright of CDs being offered for sale and imported without their consent. An out of court settlement was agreed between the two parties with CD-WOW agreeing not to sell CDs obtained outside of the EU to the European market. The online merchant may also have to consider other 'local' conditions such as the legal, economic and regulatory frameworks that apply. Differential pricing may also involve pricing the product differently to different segments based on the value they place upon the product or perhaps the timing of their purchase. For example, a senior citizen maybe quite flexible and cost conscious with regard to his train arrangements, whereas a business person travelling to a scheduled meeting will need to travel on a specific train. So the price paid by both parties will be significantly different.

Traditionally, differential pricing needed to have a number of conditions prevalent in order for it to work effectively. First, the seller should know the strength of demand between different markets to price accordingly. Secondly, the different segments should be geographically apart and isolated so that buyers remain unaware of the price differences to avoid an adverse reaction from key customers. This occurred when US customers of Amazon learned that the company was employing individual price segmentation techniques to optimise price but to the detriment of many overcharged customers. Whilst price setting on a geographic basis exists and log analysis will recognise the customer's IP address by country (eg .de=Germany, .fr=France, .uk=United Kingdom) within economic areas such as the European Union there are risks attached to such pricing policies especially as **price transparency** via currency in the form of the euro and shopbots enable better shopping comparisons.

Price lining

This refers to the method of applying a limited number of prices to products within a specific range (eg budget) and higher prices in the next band (eg mid-range) and top prices for the top of the range items (eg premium range). The price differences are sufficiently distinct as part of a careful positioning strategy to meet the needs of specific segments. For example, many tyre manufacturers, such as Dunlop, brand their products in this way with the India and SP ranges. Similarly, processor manufacturers such as Intel (Pentium and Celeron) and AMD (Athlon and Duron) and producers of digital memory cards combine product and price to meet the performance requirements and propensity to buy of their different segments.

Price lining assumes that demand for products within each range is relatively inelastic with buyers rarely responding to any price alterations. It assumes that buyer behaviour changes little but buyers may acquire more market and product knowledge, or simply over time they have more disposable income and move up a range. For example, many online wine merchants carefully price line their range starting with introductory cases at round £40 followed by cases at just under £60 and £80 followed by their fine wines top of the range. The seller would hope to move the customer up the range where margins are higher though it may depend on their entry point into the range. A bargain shopper may come in for the introductory case but rarely go beyond the £60 case as they have a customer expectation or ceiling of £5 per bottle. Incentives may be used to introduce the buyer to the next range up as well as hoping they become a loyal advocate in the process. Fig 10.5 illustrates possible demand for different ranges of wine. On web sites, many products are grouped by price, as well as product category, to make the purchase decision easier for consumers influenced by certain price brackets. The drop down price menu is a fundamental part of web design.

Consumers may limit their purchase selection by price due to income limits or the value they place on the product. In this case many web sites offer price as a key search criteria.

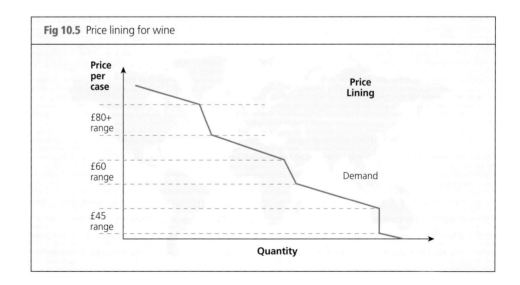

Fig 10.5 Price lining for wine

Promotional pricing

This is the meeting of two of the four marketing mix variables. Price is different to the other mix elements as it is a revenue generator whilst the others are costs. It is also linked to the promotional element, as many pricing policies are promotionally driven, especially sales promotion. Numerous promotional pricing techniques exist in the marketer's armoury and a few preferred options will be explored. **Price leaders** are when a firm applies low prices usually below their normal mark-up, possibly at cost on a limited and carefully selected group of products. The aim is to entice customers into a store be it on, or offline, in the hope that the customer will buy other merchandise at normal or above average mark-ups. The effect of this tactic is to compensate lost profits on the price leader with an overall increase in revenue from other purchases. Printer manufacturers offer what appears to be low cost technology but make up their margins through the print cartridges.

Other techniques include **special event pricing** or **time specific mark down pricing** where organisations will link price to special situations such as seasonal sales, end of season or one day events which can generate significant consumer interest, reduce the risk of purchase for the customer and increase total sales volume. For example, *The Financial Times* (www.ft.com) uses e-coupons to increase the purchase frequency of *FT Weekend* by occasional buyers. Alternatively, some merchants may use such price promotions as a means of rewarding customer loyalty based on past purchases or for purchase quantities. For example, Amazon (www.amazon.co.uk) used this to encourage multiple purchases at Christmas 2004. If the customer purchased goods that totalled more than £39 they would receive free delivery. The result is a win-win situation for both buyer and seller. The offer has the effect of tying in the customer to the one site instead of web site hopping to save a pound or euro here and there especially as Amazon seek to develop itself as a one-stop shop for gifts. They have identified a minimum purchase figure as a key threshold. It would be interesting to find out what percentage of customers who normally spend below this amount who subsequently spend just enough to take advantage of this seasonal offer. **Internet service provider** Pipex offers loyal users of their broadband service an Xtras Reward scheme, highlighting customer lifestyle as shown in Fig 10.6.

Another promotional pricing strategy is referred to as **experience curve price** when a company is confident of its ability to have a significant cost advantage over the competition and to maintain this advantage as it becomes leaner and meaner through knowledge and experience. So for some e-commerce operations, first-mover advantage was significant in their survival and consolidation phases. For example, Lastminute.com went through a steep learning curve initially but now have the brand dominance in their sector to achieve economies of scale and significantly pull in more partners to make the Lastminute proposition even more attractive.

10.6 **Pricing and market sophistication**

Prices will also be influenced by the degree of market sophistication both on the part of the product and the target market. Two classic marketing concepts provide useful tools for marketers when establishing prices, namely the Product Life Cycle Concept (PLC) and the Diffusion of Innovation Model (Rogers 1962) often referred to as the Product Adoption Model.

Your Free Reward

Dear Mr R GAY

PIPEX Xtras has now been running for a few months, and lots of our customers have been treating themselves to a night at the theatre, a massage or even a free case of wine. However, some customers haven't redeemed a reward yet. What about you? Maybe you don't have enough points, or you're saving up points for a bigger reward, or perhaps you haven't had the opportunity to really explore the website. Whatever the answer, we think you will like this – a chance to try out PIPEX Xtras and sample the rewards absolutely free without using up your points!

Claim your FREE reward

To thank you for choosing PIPEX we have put together a range of our most popular rewards for you to select from and don't forget, whichever reward you opt for, it will not affect your points balance.

Your PIPEX Xtras points balance at 10/08/2005 is: 25pts and don't forget, your points total won't be affected by claiming your free reward.

Choose from one of the following:

Claim NOW - this offer is only available until 30th September! Simply click on an image of your choice for more information and once you've made your decision, just follow the instructions.
You will be emailed your free voucher. All you need to do is print this off and book your reward according to the instructions on the voucher.

A Vast Range of Rewards

PIPEX Xtras has a huge range of rewards available to suit all tastes. There are health and beauty rewards, flights, dining, sports lessons, days out, theatre tickets... and there's more to come soon. Just make sure you visit the PIPEX Xtras website regularly so you don't miss out.

And there's even more from PIPEX...

Don't forget you can get free broadband with our Refer a Friend Scheme.
Or how about cutting those phone bills with the new PIPEX Talk service.

Enjoy your FREE reward

PIPEX Xtras

Fig 10.6 Online rewards schemes

Reproduced by kind permission of PIPEX Communications plc.

For most products, the prices set should change for a variety of strategic and tactical reasons, as the product moves through different phases of its product lifecycle. For example, if a company introduces a product that has apparent technological advantages over the competitors' offerings and research suggest that there is a demand for it, then the marketing effort will be targeted towards 'Innovators' during the 'Introduction' phase. The 'Innovators' usually possess both the resource in the form of disposable income, and the desire for the product. Hence, they are usually willing and motivated to pay the higher prices for reasons such as prestige, status, 'street cred' or even snob value as well as the superior product performance. Organisations are naturally keen to target this group in order to recoup as much of their promotional, research and development costs as possible in the early stages of the PLC. For example, ADSL or broadband connections were initially expensive to the individual and the costs outweighed the benefits. The target markets were business users who benefited from the faster connections and capabilities. Another example is where Ford customers were willing to pay above the intended market price on advanced orders for the trendy new Ford StreetKa as product availability was controlled.

Such markets are less-price sensitive at this stage, as the product is a 'must have item' for the target group. However, presuming the product is well received by the marketplace, as it moves into its 'growth' phase it will become more desirable to 'early adopters', 'early majority' and so on who tend to be more price sensitive. The organisation will generally reduce prices to continue the sales momentum. The price reduction is balanced out by an increase in sales volume as the product reaches mainstream markets. Prices face ongoing downward pressure until a point is reached where sales begin to decline. At this stage, marketers may extend the PLC, often by product modifications or increased promotional spend. Alternatively, products often 'past their sell buy date' will be sold at heavily discounted prices, sometimes below cost to reduce inventory costs and improve cash flow. The Internet has provided merchants with a fast and flexible outlet for getting rid of end of line items such as end of season clothes, bin end wines or other warehouse clearances.

The use of PLC and the Production Adoption model in relation to pricing and other mix elements, focuses marketers minds on the value placed on the product or service by different customer groups. A fuller discussion of pricing by segmentation on the Internet will follow in section 10.8 of this chapter.

10.7 **Price and customer value**

The Oxford English Dictionary provides one definition of '**value**' as 'the material or monetary worth of a thing'. Dibb and Simkin (1997) discuss value for money as 'the benefit consumers perceive to be inherent in a product or service, weighed against the price demanded'. In the majority of purchase decisions, the buyer reflects upon the total product offering and assesses whether or not the package offered by one organisation is superior to the bewildering array of other product and brand choices from other suppliers in the sector. Customers seek to obtain the maximum amount of value from a purchase as they consciously, or subconsciously, ask 'What's In It For Me?' As we are in the Age of Celebrity with many of the public consuming celebrity gossip and admiring their idols, online fashion retailer ASOS (www.asos.com) has capitalised to offer value presenting the stars' outfits and the latest gossip.

The ability to maximise price maybe limited by two key factors: first, the search costs involved in identifying products in the evoked set, a selection of brands from which the

Fig 10.7 ASOS

individual or organisation may make their purchase decision. Search costs may involve time and money in traditional markets as consumers may move from store to store or city to city to make the comparison. Secondly, the purchase decision may also be affected by the buyer's market knowledge, which could be less than perfect as they lack awareness of all product offerings that exist across the sector.

The Internet has caused a fundamental shift in the power possessed by any buyer as various shopbots allow an immediate comparison of product attributes and prices enabling rapid search facilities, for example with regard to searching for the best personal loans, the best rates on credit cards available or price flights. In addition, most shopbots provide a direct link to the specific lender allowing rapid application processing that previously could have taken many days. A further development of interest has been the emergence of cross border shopbots across Europe. For example, www.bookchecker.com compares the prices of books across nine European countries including shipping costs. Another shopping agent, www.uk.pricemind.com compares consumer electronics prices in the UK, Denmark and Sweden. Various surveys have suggested that people in EU countries are comfortable with the euro since its introduction in 2002. From an e-commerce perspective, this multinational currency lends itself ideally to the concepts of price transparency and online comparison.

Collier (1995) recognises that price is only one of a number of factors in the 'value for money' assessment process and that the buyer will consider both **objective** and **subjective** factors. To a certain extent, these factors mirror the left-brain right brain appeal where logic and emotion may combine to arrive at a purchase decision. The personality, motivations and other traits will influence whether an individual responds more to a logical promotional

LEGAL EAGLE BOX 10.1 Clarity of pricing information

The law requires online price information to be given at the following points:

1. in the product description where the product price and possible limitation of liability are to be clearly stated

2. in the shopping basket or online order form where the product price, secondary costs and total price should be provided

3. in the order confirmation stage where the product price, secondary costs and total price should be given.

Where the online supplier is providing a price comparison, information on which it is based should be made available online in a clear form with regular updates. Online price information should be stated in the national currency of the supplier. Where price information is also stated in other currencies due to the wide market focus of supplier, a link to a conversion table may be given.

Table 10.2 The buyer's 'value for money' assessment for a personal computer
(Adapted from Collier, RA (1995) Butterworth Heinemann, 163)

Objective Factors	Subjective Factors
• Price	• PC manufacturer's reputation
• Payment terms	• Brand image of manufacturer
• Product bundle	• Style and design, eg iMac
• Customised product	• Site content and usability
• Speed of delivery	• Choice of peripherals
• System performance	• Levels of customer care
	• Support provided by hardware and software 'partners'

---

appeal or one that is more emotive. Therefore, a fundamental understanding of the target market is essential for site design and content. The objective factors relate to those dimensions that can be measured such as price and performance whereas the subjective elements are more often personal to the individual such as reputation, brand image, product styling and the customer experience. Furthermore, online issues such as trust, fulfilment and site usability may significantly influence the price the consumer is willing to pay.

In Table 10.2 we suggest possible purchase criteria when buying a personal computer.

10.8 Pricing and segmentation

Segmentation has been discussed in detail in chapter 5 where we recognised how effective new technologies have become in analysing the many different transactions and characteristics of online consumers. During the formative years of e-commerce, online merchants used price as the basic competitive weapon as they sought to build up a viable customer base by price penetration. Iyer et al (2002) argue that web users are no longer a homogeneous group of bargain seekers and convenience shoppers, the obvious implication being that eSure, the Internet insurance arm of HBOS, segments its market effectively with a groundbreaking policy of only insuring drivers with four years' no claim discounts. The company keeps its claims down by insuring good, responsible drivers and rewards them with higher no claims discounts of up to 75% for a total of 10 years' no claims.

people go online for a diverse range of reasons. They go on to suggest that there is a need for better systems of segmentation to allow a better appreciation of Internet users' need and wants.

Technologies already provide a range of segmentation tools such as sophisticated lifestyle systems and log analysis to segment and target in ever decreasing clusters of consumers. Companies continue to search for the holy grail of Peppers and Rogers one-to-one marketing ideal with data mining techniques enabling promotions on an individual level as personalisation and customisation programmes offer tailored products. **Collaborative filtering** is a primary technology applied for more effective customer profiling and matching of buyer behaviour patterns. This links your profile to the profiles of similar customers and makes product suggestions based on recent historical transactional data of those with similar profiles. These future product projections, based on the sophisticated analysis of back data, should generate offerings that resembling individual tastes and interests and more importantly, willingness to spend.

In some markets, price discrimination has occurred as online merchants have deployed price segmentation deepening upon the consumer's route to the checkout. For example, selling prices are often cheaper via a price comparison site as visitors to such sites are more price sensitive.

10.9 Pricing strategies and tactics: the new influences

Dynamic pricing

Srivastava (2001) defines dynamic pricing as 'the buying and selling of goods and services in free markets where the prices fluctuate in response to supply and demand.' Wind, Mahajan and Gunther (2002), in their seminal text, *Convergence Marketing*, refer to the two distinct angles in dynamic pricing as:

1. **Flexible Seller-Initiated Pricing** where prices are raised and lowered in real time in response to the buyer's price elasticity. As they point out, the fundamental constraint with this model is the buyer's reaction to these changes and their willingness to accept them.

2. **Buyer-Initiated Pricing** where the customer sets the price agenda making bids or offers through various new technology-driven models such auctions and exchanges.

In recent years, both academics and practitioners have focussed mainly on how dynamic pricing has been applied in the new digital business models with particular reference to the various forms of online auctions such as eBay and QXL, and Business-to-Business (B2B) exchanges like Covisint in the automotive sector. In fact, many observers suggest that these real-time, convenient and innovative processes are the real drivers of the new Internet economy for both buyer and seller alike.

In this section, we will consider these models with relevant exemplars as well as other dynamic pricing applications and how they can be implemented for the benefit of buyer and seller alike.

A broader definition of dynamic pricing comes from Kannan and Kopalle (2001), who refer to dynamic pricing as 'a pricing strategy in which prices change either over time, across consumers, or across product/service bundles.' On closer examination, this is how traditional pricing strategies have been applied in the physical world, certainly for most of the twentieth century under the guise of *variable pricing* or a form of price discrimination Prices *should* change over time for a whole variety of internal and external reasons such as inflation, changing consumer tastes and material prices. Marketers will price for different consumer segments, perhaps on the basis of disposable income or location where differential pricing is applied with different prices to different countries, assuming that price transparency does not exist otherwise customers may react badly. Manufacturers may also change prices as they bundle or unbundle product packages depending upon their objectives.

The essence of dynamic pricing in the virtual world lies in its speed, flexibility and responsiveness for improved communications, tracking of competitor prices and reactions to shifts in demand resulting from recent advances in technology. Dynamic pricing can make significant improvements in yield as part of revenue management processes designed to improve ROI from different customers and often for the same product at the same location, such as a hotel room. Some may be paying full business rates, some taking advantage of last minute deals, others may be discounted as a result of a members' club rewarding loyalty. Unless you engage everyone in the hotel over dinner and ask them individually what they paid, the consumer is often none the wiser with regard to such differential pricing applications, as transparency does not exist. For the hotel, though, it can increase it revenue streams by customer category. Dynamic pricing allows more precise tailoring of offers with mass customisation.

Yield Management (**YM**) techniques, which have been applied predominantly in the airline sector in years gone by, are now being applied across a number of sectors. Kimes (1989) defines yield management as 'allocating the right capacity to the right customer at the right time at the right price in order to optimise revenue or yield'. The process lends itself to those sectors where there is a fixed capacity or supply, either of a product or a service, and the revenue potential of the item will diminish over time, It assumes that the early purchasers are more price sensitive than later buyers. YM as an application is also appropriate in those markets that are very competitive and there is an early-anticipated demand. Iyer et al (2002) cite the online holiday markets where incentives are given for early bookings. Similarly, with CDs and DVDs, many merchants offer discounts for pre-release orders that help anticipate demand whilst generating early revenue, which in turn can improve buying power. In Fig 10.8, CD-WOW are offering pre-release deals on anticipated DVDs and CDs.

Biller et al (2005) investigated dynamic pricing and the Direct-to-Customer (DTC) Model as a means of automotive manufacturers and dealers combating the threat from automotive e-tailers. They argue that integrating dynamic pricing with inventory control and production offers significant opportunities for profit maximisation and improved supply chain management.

Customer reaction and perceived fairness

Adamy (2000), cited in Kung, Monroe and Cox (2002) highlights the potential problems and PR disasters with differential or dynamic pricing. In America, Amazon's customers

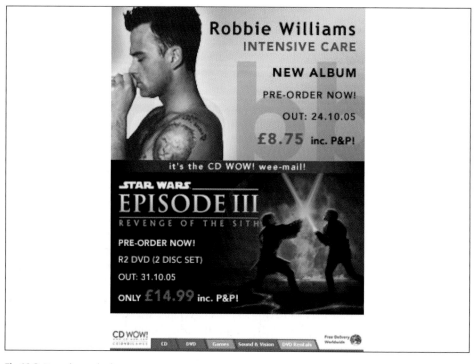

Fig 10.8 Pre-release deals
Reproduced by kind permission of CD-WOW!

exposed the e-tailors pricing practice of selling the same products (DVDs) at different prices to different customers based on their purchase history. For a full season set of X Files DVDs, prices varied between $80–$100. The company was deluged with complaints but stated that it was just testing customer responses to different price levels. Amazon was stung by the adverse reaction and removed its differential pricing and made refunds to those who had been charged the higher prices. Interestingly though, Kung et al suggest that it was not just the issue of the different prices being charged that caused the furore but the fact that personal shopping patterns had been applied in this exercise which was deemed to be an intrusion of privacy and thus unethical.

Merchants will have to be more sensitive to customer reactions if they are going to implement price applications in this way otherwise trust, which is essential for online success, could be destroyed. Online businesses should note that many consumers are getting wiser. Huang, Chang and Chen (2005) give a fascinating insight into customer perceptions of pricing fairness amongst consumers in Taiwan. Most online pricing mechanisms such as auction models and discounting to loyal customers were deemed to be fair. However, rapid price changes effected by yield management and price discrimination where surfers received best prices via shopbots were deemed unfair. Respondents also believed online prices to be fair if they were around 8% lower than offline. As customers become more knowledgeable, they may question the ethical dimension of an organisation's rapid price changes and discrimination and take their business elsewhere. Marketers must seriously consider customer reactions to online pricing tools and how it impacts upon sales and loyalty.

10.10 **Other Internet pricing influences**

Affuah and Tucci (2003) posit that there are five main types of pricing and suggest the influence of the web upon these models:

1. Menu pricing

2. One to One bargaining

3. Auction pricing

4. Reverse auctions

5. Barter

Menu pricing

This presets the prices of goods and services and there is no scope for negotiation on the price so the fixed price is the price everyone has to pay. Due to the costs associated with changes in prices such as printing and administration, many organisations, particularly in the retail sector, alter prices fairly infrequently. Is there anything wrong with this? A key weakness with fixed pricing is that it does not always enable price maximisation as the buyer may be willing to pay more, or have expectations to pay more than the set price, hence vital revenue could be lost. Alternatively, without an understanding of consumer expectations the price could be set above their pricing points. Consequently, customers and prospects could decide to take their business elsewhere.

Price set is largely dependent upon the rules of demand and supply and for an offline business the process of monitoring price sensitivities can be both time consuming and cumbersome in a physical marketplace. Testing might take place against every 30 or 50 customers on site visits to help forecast sensitivities. Kannan and Kopalle (2001) argue that the Internet is well suited to dynamic posted pricing strategies as many online retailers change price at least on a daily basis aided by price comparisons of competition and falling menu costs, but when do posted prices become dynamic? The customer is likely to have certain expectations about how long the price will remain static but this will vary from sector to sector and partly due to customer knowledge and awareness of those sectors. If the frequency of price changes is greater than the customer expectations, the more there is the likelihood of customer alienation and trust breaking down.

We have highlighted a number of pricing practices of the airline industry that along with commodities like CDs and books, have been the learning ground for online marketers. Merchants have to consider customer reactions and sensitivities to rapid price movements. How many customers may they alienate when a product price is reduced significantly within hours of that customer's purchase being made? To what extent will it change their purchase behaviour perhaps by speeding up or delaying their decision based on previous experience and judgement of the merchants price movements. Various authors have outlined the importance of branded sites that people return to time and time again but perhaps as the customers become more web-wise and sophisticated they may become less loyal and switch as many people have done offline with financial services products.

On 19 March 2003, Amazon mistakenly priced a HP iPAQ Pocket PC at £7.32 when it should have been retailing at £287, and a less powerful version which normally retails at £192 was priced at £7. Not surprisingly, Amazon was inundated with frantic bargain hunters

LEGAL EAGLE BOX 10.2 Mistakes in pricing

Although one of the advantages of doing business online is the speed with which goods/services can be advertised to a global marketplace, input errors are potential problems with online pricing.

The issue of mistake in pricing information attracted a great deal of interest in September 1999 when Argos, through its website, offered a Sony television for £2.99 by mistake whereas the true price was £299. Argos refused to honour orders that flooded in based on the erroneous advertisement.

In another case in January 2002, Kodak offered, through its Shop@Kodak website (www.kodak.co.uk) a digital camera package including the camera, a docking station, memory card

and paper. The package was advertised as a 'special deal' and mistakenly at the price of £100 with the actual price being £329. Over the few days following the advert Kodak received a great number of orders and the customers who placed the orders received an automated confirmatory e-mail.

On realising the error that had occurred Kodak wrote to the customers purporting to withdraw the offer and claiming the mistake had vitiated any agreement made. Kodak faced a large number of highly organised complaints and court proceedings were instituted on behalf of some customers later that month. At the end of January Kodak agreed to satisfy all orders that had been confirmed.

as the news spread around chat-rooms and offices. There were rumours that people in the City ordered 50 at a time. On realising the mistake, Amazon closed down its site and withdrew the items stating that it was not legally bound to supply the items ordered as its terms and condition clearly stated that no contract exists between Amazon.co.uk and the customer until an e-mail is dispatched confirming the order. Contractually, Amazon was on reasonably firm ground but it antagonised many customers. Technology is a great thing but 'internal errors' like this are very costly both in terms of profits and PR gaffes that damage long-term customer relations.

One to One Bargaining

Affuah and Tucci posit that one-to-one bargaining is when the buyer and seller negotiate to reach a point at which the consumer pays the price that, in their eyes, reflects the value that they are receiving from the good. This naively assumes that the seller is familiar with each buyer's demand curve. In an online world, web metrics provide the data for individual customer analysis enabling better yield management.

Auctions and exchanges

Auctions and exchanges, especially in the B2B marketplaces, have warranted significant attention from academics and practitioners alike, as they exemplify the streamlined benefits of speed, efficiency and reduced costs that digital technologies purport to provide for both buyers and sellers. For example, the automotive online trading activities by the Covisint Group (www.Covisint.com) established in US have revolutionised the e-procurement process between major manufacturers and suppliers, resulting in car production costs being reduced by between 7–10%. (For a fuller discussion on e-procurement and Covisint, see chapter 12.) In consumer markets, other auction models developed by the likes of Priceline.com (Name-your-own price model) and the web phenomenon, eBay (www.eBay.com) have successfully pioneered new buyer-seller relationships. eBay is now recognised as the UK's most visited web site by Nielsen NetRatings (2003) toppling Amazon for the first time since Internet audience measurement began in March 2000. In March 2003, over one billion pages were viewed on eBay's site, so clearly Britain's growing online community have caught the bid bug.

Whilst dynamic pricing aims to achieve optimised prices for all parties, they inevitably force downward pressure on prices to the point where margins may be so low that it is not viable for suppliers to participate in such activities. Chris Philips, European marketing director of e-marketplace company, Commerce One says, 'There is nothing like savings of 15 to 20% to focus the mind' but 'you are not going to see savings of 20% the next year and the year after that; the supplier market will not bear it'. In addition to the B2B, C2B and B2C markets, online auctions are now reducing the public sector procurement bill with everything from basic stationary, computers to energy supplies up for more competitive sourcing.

For any player considering involvement in an auction or exchange it is imperative that they are conversant with the trading protocols and rules applicable in the chosen market-place, as this should influence their strategies and tactics employed. Klein (1997) cited in Chaffey (2002) illustrates four potential roles or applications for auctions:

1. **Price Discovery** – whereby the offer or bid prices submitted may determine a market price where the seller may have been uncertain as to the market's willingness to pay a certain price.

2. **Efficient Allocation Mechanism** – online auctions provide an ideal channel for disposing of excess stock such as discontinued lines that offline utilise valuable floor space eg Comet have established their own auction, www.clearance-comet.co.uk for such purposes and interestingly have achieved selling prices close to those of the original retail price.

3. **Distribution Mechanism** – organisers of auctions may use the process to draw up a list of approved suppliers who are capable of meeting the order specification. This saves time on filtering out those organisations submitting bids when they are unable to fulfil some aspect of the order such as volume, speed or product specification. *Supplier readiness* to the requirements of online auctions is acknowledged problem and buyers often offer 'process' training to suppliers.

4. **Coordination Mechanism** – an intermediary can manage the purchase on behalf of a number of buyers. This was the idea behind the now defunct, Energy Auctions Online, who sought to aggregate the utility power needs (electricity, gas, etc) of groups of manufacturers and then seek optimal bids from power suppliers.

Reverse auctions

So what is an auction and what forms can they take? 'An auction occurs when there is a "one-to-many" trading scenario' and usually involves one of two situations: first where there is only one seller and numerous buyers or alternatively one buyer and many sellers, that latter is usually referred to as a *reverse* auction. Two general types of bidding process can distinguish the auction further:

1. **The English Auction** where the initial base price is set below the expected final selling price. Higher bids are submitted, outbidding the last one with the top bid being successful when the auction closes. Most online auctions work within specified time limits. Traditionally, auctions would be held in an auction house at a specific location eg Sotheby's or

Christies' for items of high value to a fairly exclusive market. With the Internet platform, the auction goalposts have moved significantly with items of all descriptions and value and few geographic boundaries. Will clearing out the cupboard under the stairs and going on eBay get a better price rather than venturing to the car boot sale? The revenues generated in this English auction will reflect the value placed on the single item by the highest bidder.

2. **The Dutch Auction** is where the auction intermediary sets an initial high price. Lower bids are submitted until a level is reached which is acceptable to the bidder. The main problem for the selling organisation is setting the initial price right. It can be problematic when new products are being auctioned or new markets are entered without a full understanding of what the market is willing to pay. The main variation on this model is the Reverse Auction in the C2B market, sometimes referred to as first price sealed bid-auctions, employed by the likes of priceline.com (www.priceline.co.uk). Consumers bid for items with a limited shelf life and availability such as airline tickets and hotel rooms and submit their credit card details. Bids are submitted and checked to ensure that they are within the partner's pricing structure and against the quota of rooms and seats made available at certain times. For Priceline, it generates revenue from the ticket commission and a percentage on the product cost and the successful bid price.

The latitude of consumers' bids in this type of model has generated significant interest amongst researchers. With this being a relatively new phenomenon, consumers seem to be going through a learning curve, as they are inexperienced. The resultant bids are spread well above and below the mean price. Where the lowest bid is accepted as the contract, then it follows that margins are likely to be squeezed and this price may become the norm to the point where the item is undervalued. The trick, and key to success for eBay and Priceline is not carry any stock and the associated costs but for the technology to enable their intermediary role.

Online exchanges and hubs have also attracted much interest as they were viewed in the dot.com era as one of the leading edge purchasing applications capable of delivering significant cost benefits in the B2B sector. Leading UK food retailers such as Sainsbury and Tesco have been prominent players in the new global exchanges (eg CPG, GlobalNetXchange, Transora and WorldWide Retail Exchange). Reductions of around 10% off procurement bills as well as improving the efficiency of the supply chain in terms of purchasing, IT and logistics have been expected. However, apart from the big hitters in these markets, the adoption of these exchanges has been slower than expected members signing up. Most players are aiming for around 10% of their tendering process to be online within the next eighteen months. The concern for most suppliers is that prices are driven down to the point where the commodity virtually becomes worthless.

Some of the potential and the pitfalls of the auctions are outlined in Mini case 10.6.

Barter

This is the ancient practice of trading goods without exchanging money for them. Instead the parties exchanging the goods had to agree to value at a similar rate for the deal to be done. This can be particularly attractive to small firms enduring cash flow difficulties. In the early online days, bartering attracted limited interest but barter exchange web sites are becoming more commonplace on both sides of the Atlantic with intermediaries emerging to facilitate the trade such as the International Barter Alliance (www.ibabiz.com).

Interview with Clare Waters, Sales Director, Albion Chemicals, 23 May 2003

ONLINE AUCTION EXPERIENCE

1. **How many online auctions have Albion Chemicals taken part in and when was the first one?**

   Unfortunately we have not retained a record of the number of auctions in an 'easy to get at' format, however, I would estimate the number to be around 90. Often, companies advise us that they will be hosting an Internet Auction when it is in fact simply an Internet-based tender.

2. **How often do they take place?**

   We have seen an increase in Internet Auctions over the past 12 months. The trend appears to be for Auction Agencies to manage the buying portfolio in line with cost saving programmes and supplier rationalisation. On average we may receive one to two auctions per month, split over several days dependent upon the number of product lines/auction rooms.

3. **What is the typical value and length of the contracts being auctioned?**

   The variety in both value and length of contract is significant. Some companies use this medium to re-auction their entire portfolio every quarter; others may auction one product only for a period of three years. It is impossible to see any particular trend in this area.

4. **Is this typical of the type of contract normally entered into offline?**

   Generally it is typical, however, I would suggest that some companies, having set up the system online, are now using this medium to tender their business more regularly than they used to do when the process was a more manual one.

5. **Are all the online auctions that you have participated in run by existing customers only or have you entered into auctions with new prospects?**

   We have only ever participated in those run by 'known' companies, albeit they may not be currently trading.

6. **Do all online auctions involve the same terms and conditions and bidding processes?**

   There are a number of independent agencies heading up Internet bids: Albion Chemicals have dealt with CPG Markets/ Chemconnect/Abbreviate/Procuri.Com. Bidding processes are of a similar nature, however conditions are dependent upon the agency and customer requirements. There are several types of auctions, ie Reverse Auction/Rank Auction/ Pricing Only.

7. **What are the key determinants influencing your bidding?**

   Generally we will know the customer and our bid will be based on whether the product/volume combination included in the auction is of strategic interest to us. We also know our own strengths so, for example, if we are asked to bid for a product sold in large volume bulk tankers, we would be unlikely to bid as this sort of business would lend itself more readily to a producer rather than a distributor like ourselves. Our bid would also be determined by the market sector, eg strategically we wish to grow our sales into the Personal Care market, but have little interest in Textiles.

8. **Does your online approach differ in any way to your offline tenders?**

   Yes. Offline tenders are generally requested by customers with whom we either already have a relationship or with whom we are in the process of developing one. The tender process is carried out in detail by our sales team with a great deal of time spent with the customer understanding their requirements relative to health and safety, manual handling of the chemicals, service and logistic needs, etc. We are then able to shape the tender according to the appropriate service provision. With Internet Auctions there is generally very little additional information given by the customer – even to the extent that they often do not include product specifications, so we are not able to be certain that we are quoting for the correct grade of product or whether they take the product packed or in bulk. Generally, we offer a price but it is subject to a great deal of discussion following the award of the tender and further knowledge of the customer's needs means we often have to change our tendered price.

9. **What are the good things about online auction from Albion Chemicals point of view?**

   Really very little, apart from sometimes giving us the opportunity to quote for a potential account where we currently have no business and no relationship. However, where this has happened and we have been awarded some business, it has proved almost impossible to implement, as the local site nearly always prefers to retain their current supplier. Quite often Internet Auctions are imposed by the Finance Director, etc, and there is little or no buy in from those who actually place orders for products.

10. **What are the bad points?**

    Internet Auctions have the ability to drive down prices within a market whilst the customer still expects the same level of service previously provided. Thus, distributors become the 'middle man' and are forced to continuously reduce their cost base to sustain this whilst the producer of the product will not, in turn, reduce their input price to the distributor.

Internet Auctions can also be used to 'off-load' surplus cheap products, which is not a sustainable situation. The cheap product is used up, the customer goes back out to tender, but by this stage their price expectation is considerably lower than it had previously been.

However, my main concern is that business awarded on price generally ignores the health, safety and environmental concerns inherent in the safe delivery of what can be dangerous products. Customers driven by price only do so at their own risk; distributors who operate at these levels will not have a sustainable business as contributions are often below re-investment cost and erode shareholder value.

Customers who operate over the Internet are also generally the first customers to be let down in times of shortage due to the transactional nature of their buyers and the low levels of supplier loyalty that they generate due to this cost only approach.

11. **Do you expect an increase in the number of online auctions and are you likely to participate?**
Although in the short term I believe we will see an increase, ultimately the number of chemical auctions will inevitably decrease. With increasing legislation, those able to offer distribution of hazardous chemicals will reduce in number, therefore, the barriers to entry will be higher, in which circumstances the customer is unlikely to achieve the breadth of interest in his online auction purely based on a price reduction exercise.

Online loyalty schemes and promotions

Loyalty schemes have existed in various guises from Green Shield stamps to Clubcard and Nectar though not all have achieved their desired objectives. The successful schemes have adopted integrated database software to track changes in purchasing behaviour whilst creating an effective ongoing dialogue. Operators have been desperate to build up a critical mass of regular customers through rewards or loyalty schemes which offer added value through differentiation. E-metrics provides more measurable response data then ever before tracking redemption vouchers both coded offline and online e-vouchers, e-coupons, reward schemes and responses to other price-related promotions. These types of schemes are now commonplace amongst etailers so they must think again to differentiate themselves further. This requires the development of coherent programmes that engage the target audience. These may be as diverse as simple charity donations of accumulated points to broader rewards based schemes (eg MyPoints and iPoints) including online auction loyalty programmes involving complementary trading partners. In 2003, eBay took over Fairmarket, a leading technology platform innovator in this sector to offer points as the effective auction currency replacing money (see www.anythingpoints.ebay.com). Bidders utilise their accumulated points from third parties in the bidding for the categorised prize type. The customer experience is far more interactive and engaging than ordinary reward schemes and with the prize options limited there is less danger of a Hoover flights scandal. The US experience also suggests that this is an important brand-building tool that increases site stickiness. The added value represented by such schemes should improve uptake by consumers.

Information and entertainment goods

The Internet is a perfect delivery mode for the effective and efficient dissemination of digital content. As Daupa and Kapur (2001) observe, 'information goods are particularly well suited to migrate to online markets' as distribution costs are a fraction of the cost of the equivalent physical good.

A tactic employed by online newspapers and periodicals has been to offer part of the site or its content for free whilst the added value elements are chargeable. Similarly, leading industry research groups offer free executive summaries of key report findings with the aim

Table 10.3 Examples of information goods	
• Online newspapers	*Wall Street Journal*, *FT.com*
• Electronic Journals	Ingenta, Emerald, Oxford Reference Online
• Newsletters	Motley Fool
• Software	Microsoft downloads
• Online infopedia	Encyclopaedia Britannica
• e-books	*Riding the Bullet* by Stephen King

of persuading the reader that there is sufficient content in the main report to justify the full report price. Online publishers are devising more innovative content tailored to customer needs. Specialised academic publisher of legal books, Cavendish offers chapter-by-chapter online delivery and purchase of key texts to appeal to the financially challenged student. The costs are front ended and quite high for these content creators but the mode of delivery is both efficient and highly cost effective. Whilst the selling price is reduced, total revenue should grow, as the text is more accessible and sales volumes increase. Many online news and media groups have slowly started adopting e-subscriptions as the preferred revenue model as consumer resistance to charging slowly thaws.

The Internet is also an effective delivery model for entertainment goods such as music and games downloads, at least in the eyes of the public. The buyer behaviour of the music listener has changed considerably with a significant decline in the sales of CDs contrasted with the growth of file swapping as copying becomes so user-friendly. It is not so much a case of music declining in popularity but rather that the technology had devalued it. To illustrate the scale of the problem, in 2000, 67 million registered users with Napster were swapping files. To combat this revenue and price problem, the recording industry has done two things. First, there has been the development of 'copy controlled' discs. Second, like the newspapers, major labels such as Sony, are now adopting subscription models like iTunes.

An alternative pricing approach has been applied by Lycos in the games market. For the casual gamer, typical costs of £30–40 per game, are prohibitive. In an attempt to increase take up amongst this segment, Lycos has introduced a 'Pay for Rental Games' model where members can purchase a time limited game DVD which also incorporates e-vouchers to be retained against future online purchases and hopefully move the casual gamer up the ladder of loyalty in due course.

10.11 **Summary**

Has the power really shifted from sellers to buyers? The Internet has tossed many pricing theories into the air and new models have emerged. Online marketplaces, auctions, affiliate marketing, technology enabled information goods, shopping agents, price transparency and other technological developments have altered the pricing landscape significantly but have they brought about the expected changes of perfect competition and a frictionless market? The majority of studies suggest that this is not the case with market power and other tactics distorting the market. As the Internet has matured since the dot.com crash, prices online have generally risen faster than offline despite the much-heralded cost benefits of integrated technological applications. Marketers are licking their lips with such technology at their disposal. Fast and frequent price changes are easily within the financial grasp of most e-tailers allowing them to react swiftly to changes in demand and maximise profits. Whilst the Promised Land appeared to be getting closer, net savvy customers are getting wiser, if not marginally disenchanted with the constant, albeit smaller incremental price changes of the dynamic pricing model to the point that some companies are returning to fixed pricing in order to re-establish customer trust, unless they benefit from mass customisation and collaborative filtering.

The myth that all web-users are a posse of bargain hunters is far from accurate and consumers are looking for other web benefits such as time and convenience. This has to be the case, as online price inflation has risen faster compared to offline prices and when shipping costs are included there are generally few differences between the two. It is noticeable that on and offline buyer behaviour is similar in terms of brand allegiances. Even though lower prices are usually available at smaller niche web sites, many online consumers gravitate and return to those sites with a prominent brand presence which they trust and respect, like Amazon and Lastminute. As with most premium brands, above average prices are usually achievable.

Despite much attention being given to the e-procurement process in driving down costs, evidence suggests that the take up in online marketplaces and auctions has been far slower than expected, possibly because of the failure to effectively factor in nonprice issues. The reality is that the technology for online buying in the B2B sector has raced ahead compared to the speed of cultural change amongst buyers. The difficult decision for many suppliers is whether to participate in a process that reduces their margins even further. Certainly, the view amongst many suppliers in the food and grocery sector is that prices may be squeezed by major retailers to a point to render the commodity virtually valueless. The impact of the web will be felt throughout the supply chain.

END OF CHAPTER CASE STUDY – Online subscriptions models the online news stand – roll up and buy your content here!

In the world of publishing and new media, the world of traditional newspapers and new online delivery models are evolving strategies to satisfy the needs of different readers whilst generating new revenue stream to compensate for declining advertising revenues.

As the Internet evolves from its infant headaches, online newspapers have refined and developed their content, providing added value to the reader experience. Apart from current affairs, many offer financial information, sports updates, property, heritage, culture and even online dating services. For the most part, access to online newspapers has been free as they sought to build up a critical mass coupled with the expectation of reasonable online advertising revenues. However, in the post 9/11 era, the decline in revenues from mainstream print advertising forced media groups to reconsider the open access strategy and test subscription and other models to reverse the losses accrued by online newspapers. As one web editor, cited in Hayward (2002) commented 'the longest free trial in history' was coming to an end.

What strategies and tactics can be implemented to bring online newspapers into profitability with online advertising failing to produce the desired return on investment (ROI)? Various options have been suggested such as site sponsorship by compatible partners or selling site content to other online publications but many have grasped the stinging nettle and introduced subscription charging. Online marketing strategists have had to wrestle with a number of key questions. Should we charge for full site entry or for just specialist sections with perceived higher value content? Will readers formerly used to free content sites now be willing to pay? Could the application of charges drive them away from the site and have a negative impact on future online advertising revenues as click rates decline?

Hayward observes that most readers are unwilling to pay for general news content that is readily available from a variety of free digital and non-digital media sources (eg www.bbc.com). He argues that the broadsheets and business newspapers can charge for content because of the greater value placed on the speed and convenience by recipients such as those in the City and other professions. Add to this the fact that it can be claimed as a business expense, and then the outlay can be justified. Unless a member of the public has a specific interest and the site provides 'unique' information not contained elsewhere, it would be difficult to justify the subscription cost.

Crosbie (2003) suggest that most publishers would prefer to charge for full access due to its simplicity and software implementation, and perhaps it might maximise revenue from subscriptions. He contests that most visitors will want access to a limited number of pages but few will want to view everything. The offline analogy is the sports mad male purchasing a newspaper primarily for the quality of sports content and little else. Consequently it can be argued that a standard subscription charge may deter visitors period. Site traffic reductions will have a negative effect on net site revenues including other revenue streams such as affiliate revenues. As Crosbie argues 'free content creates the traffic flow from which paid subscribers are drawn'.

Returning to the issue of 'value', it becomes critical to test and research exactly what people will subscribe to and the value they place upon the chargeable content. For example, accurate and relevant sector reports frequently produced is more likely to persuade payment to be made. Crosbie supports this by arguing that if you must charge, then the best strategy is to charge for more exclusive or specialist items where research suggest consumers of such information may be less uncomfortable with having to pay, whilst those not requiring such information can access the free, mainstream content. No one is alienated, subscriptions revenues may reduce marginally but with traffic maintained, overall site revenues should be sustained.

A variety of subscription strategies have been applied both in the UK and the US. In Britain, we can look at the paid content strategies of two leading media players, the *Financial Times* and *The Independent*, who have moved online with differentiated offerings distinct from their hard copy editions. In 2002, FT.com introduced a two-tier subscription pricing strategy. *Level One* (£75) gives subscribers access to a range of new products, a front page preview of the FT for the following day and full archive access. *Level Two* (£200) provides the same plus two key research information tools, *World Company Financials* and *World Press Monitor*. FT.com indicate that that 80% of their content remains free to access and that subscriptions will account for at least 10% of revenue by the end of 2002. By comparison, the online brother of *The Independent*, *Independent Digital* charges for some specific content together with tailored usage subscriptions. The main content covering the likes of current affairs, sport, education and the arts remains free whilst access to influential correspondents, archives and crosswords incur charges and are sold individually as distinct packages in themselves. Subscribers have the option of paying for daily, monthly or annual subscriptions by package or full access.

In the US, the esteemed *Wall Street Journal* decided on the uncomplicated strategy of charging for everything, which may be attributed to the maturity of the American online market, the needs of WSJ's corporate readers or both. Hayward contrasts this with *Le Monde Interactif* in France 'where the strategy has been to differentiate the web site experience and content of the free access areas compared to the subscription areas. He reports that Bruno Patino, *Le Monde Interactif*'s Chief Executive is keen to give the subscriber a superior offering and makes the analogy between flying business and economy class. A visit to www.lemonde.fr will introduce the visitor to the content rich site differentiated in terms of style and multimedia from it free content areas for a mere 5 euros per month. Clearly, diverse subscription policies are being applied in different locations depending upon the brand, assessment of would-be subscribers and the desired content.

Two cautionary points needs to be addressed by marketers of subscription models. Cited in Hayward's article, Rebecca Ulph at Forrester Research queries whether the online information brand offers sufficient quality and experience to persuade visitors to subscribe, so where does the '*added value*' come from? The other dilemma that is inextricably linked to the branding issue revolves around customer acquisition and retention strategies. What are the key profiling characteristics of potential subscribers? Do they match our current subscribers and how can we reach them? How much content are they willing to pay for? Which promotional offers will attract and keep them and how should the content be delivered in the future?

With more sophisticated software and lower costs associated with digital distribution, coupled with the relentless adoption of the web, there is an inevitability that the number of online subscribers will increase as fees reduce and content improves.

Questions

1. Identify the key drivers influencing on online media's implementation of subscription models.

2. Suggest how online newspapers might 'persuade' members of the general public to subscribe in terms of content and promotional activity.

3. Will the profile of a publisher's online and offline readership be one and the same? Discuss.

4. In your country, select *two* of your leading online newspapers, which charge for some, or all of its content. Compare and contrast the two sites in terms of subscription packages offered and the quality of the content user experience.

Sources: Crosbie, V *An All or Nothing Game*, www.clickz.com/design/freefee/article.php/2203341, 14 May 2003
Hayward, D *Curtain falls on 'longest free trial in history'*, *Financial Times*, FT-IT Review, 11, 19 June 2002
Sweeney, M FT.com introduces two-tier subscription service, *Revolution*, 7, 30 April 2002

DISCUSSION QUESTIONS

1. Is it true that online shoppers are a determined group of bargain hunters? Discuss.
2. Will Internet shopping and its prices kill off the high street?
3. What has been the impact of price transparency on buyers and sellers?
4. Are traditional pricing techniques applicable online? Discuss, with examples.

REFERENCES

Adamy, J (2000) E-Tailer price tailoring maybe wave of the future, *Chicago Tribune*, 25 September, section 4, 4

Affuah, A & Tucci, CL (2003) *Internet – Business Models and Strategies*, McGraw Hill, New York, USA, 60–62.

Ancarani & Shankar (2002) *Price Levels and Price Dispersion on the Internet: A Comparison of Pure Play Internet, Bricks and Mortar, and Bricks and Clicks Retailers*, June 2002, www.gunther.smeal.psu?cachedpage/11613/2

Brynjolfsen, E & Smith, M (2000) *Frictionless Commerce? A Comparison of Internet and Conventional Retailers*, MIT Sloan School

Brynjolfsen, E & Smith, M (2000) *The Great Equalizer? Consumer Choice Behaviour at Internet Shopbots*, MIT Sloan School

Chaffey, D (2002) *E-business and E-commerce Management: Strategy, Management and Applications*, Pearson Education Limited, 46–47

Clay, K, Krishnan, R & Wolff, E (2000) *Pricing Strategies on the Web: Evidence from the Online Book Industry*, Heinz School, Carnegie Mellion University

Coleman, A, *Financial Mail on Sunday*, 1 June 2003, 35

Collier, RA (1995) *Profitable Profit Management*, Butterworth Heinemann, Oxford, UK, 163

Daupa, A & Kapur, S (2001) *Pricing on the Internet*, Dept. of Economics, Birbeck College, London, March 2001

Dibb, Simkin, Pride & Ferrell (1997) *Marketing – Concepts & Strategies* (3rd European edn), Houghton Mifflin, 576

Doyle, P (2002) *Marketing Management and Strategy*, FT Prentice Hall, 218

Formica, P (2002) *Market Creation in the Dotcom Economy*, International University for Entrepreneurship

Huang, J-H, Chang, C-T & Chen, CY-H (2005) Perceived fairness of pricing on the Internet, *Journal of Economic Psychology*, Vol 26 (2005), 343–361

Hughes, S, *Newcastle Evening Chronicle*, 16 May 2003

Iyer GR, Miyazaki, AD, Grewal, D & Giordano, M (2002) Linking Web-based segmentation to pricing tactics, *Journal of Product & Brand Management*, Vol 11, No 5, 2002, 288–302

Kannan, PK & Kopalle, PK (2001) *International Journal of Electronic Commerce*, Spring 2001, Vol 5, No 3, 63

Kimes, Sheryl, E (1989), Yield management: a tool for capacity-constrained service firms, *Journal of Operations Management*, Vol 8, No 4, 348–363

Klein, S (1997) Introduction to electronic auctions, *International Journal of Electronic Markets*, Vol 4, No 7, 3–6

Kung, Monroe & Cox (2002) Pricing on the Internet, *Journal of Product and Brand Management*, Vol 11, No 5, 2002, 274–287

Liao & Hwang (2001) A fair and privacy-preserved protocol for sealed-bid auctions, *Electronic Markets*, Vol 11, No 3, 163–170

Matthewson, JA (2002) *E-Business*, Butterworth Heinemann, 49

McKinsey Marketing Practice (2000) *Internet Pricing, A Creator of Value – Not a Destroyer*

Meriden (2002) Still cheaper by half? *Internet Business*, May 2002, 28–29

Mohammed, R et al (2002) *Internet Marketing*, McGraw Hill, 319–321

Nielsen NetRatings's Report: *Property Level, UK at Home and Work Combined*, March 2002–March 2003

Rogers, EM (1962) *Diffusions of Innovation*, Macmillan, New York

Smith, M, Brynjolfsen, E & Bailey, J (1999) *Understanding Digital Markets*, MIT Sloan School.

Smith, PR & Chaffey, D (2002) *EMarketing Excellence*, Butterworth Heinemann, 81–82

Srivastava, A (2001) *Dynamic Pricing Models-Opportunity for Action*, Cap Gemini Ernst & Young Center for Business Innovation.

Strauss, J, Ansary, A el & Frost, R (2003) *E-Marketing* (3rd edn), Prentice Hall, 313–314

Sunday Telegraph, Business, 3, 12 January 2003

Turban, E, King, D, Lee, J, Warkentin, Chung, MH (2002) *Electronic Commerce – A Managerial Perspective*, Prentice Hall, 377–378

Verma, DPS & Varma, G (2003) On-line pricing: concept, methods and current practices, *Journal of Services Research*, Vol 3, No 1 (April–September 2003), 135–155

Web User, Issue 57, 15–28 May 2003, IPC Media, 18–21

Wilson, RF (2002) *Planning Your Internet Marketing Strategy*, John Wiley & Sons, 203

Wind, Y, Mahajan, V & Gunther RE (2002) *Convergence Marketing*, FT Prentice Hall, 162–164

FURTHER READING

Oxford Review of Economic Policy, Summer 2001, Arup Daripa and Sandeep Kapur

WEB LINKS

www.econ.bbk.ac.uk/courses/pdec/dkbib.

www.ebay.co.uk

www.managingchange.com – provides a good discussion on dynamic and ethical pricing

www.europa.eu.int/comm/competition/car_sector – European Union Block exemption pages

 Visit the Online Resource Centre which accompanies this book, for lots of interesting additional material, including self-assessment questions, internet exercises, and links for each chapter: **www.oxfordtextbooks.co.uk/orc/gay/**

11 Online Communication Tools

Learning objectives

By the end of the chapter you will be able to:

- Understand the role of the Internet in the marketing communication process
- Appreciate how the Internet can be used as a medium for advertising
- Appreciate how e-mail can be used effectively by the marketer
- Understand the advantages and pitfalls of using online viral marketing strategies
- Evaluate the significance to marketers of public comment web sites
- Critically evaluate the use of the Internet in public relations
- Appreciate how electronic newsletters can be used most effectively by marketers
- Understand blogging, what it is and its commercial value
- Understand how online sales can be automated and its benefits
- Understand how the Internet can be used as part of integrated multi-channel marketing strategies

Chapter-at-a-glance

11.1 Introduction

The Internet has had a significant impact on how buyers and sellers communicate. In a decade, numerous digital communications tools have emerged to offer greater creativity, precision and measurement for the online marketer to move buyers through the decision phases, either solely in the virtual world, or as part of an integrated campaign with tried and trusted offline methods. Two-way interactions provide a new challenge for developing effective customer relationships. E-mail, banner ads, interactive TV, webinars, blogging, podcasting, search engine marketing (see chapter 6), interstitials (pop-ups) and online communities have all become effective delivery mechanisms for the promotional message whilst providing the customer with greater control of what they receive, how and when. Yet in the late nineties many in marketing communications believed that the Internet would only have a minor impact on the world of advertising, with the traditional methods of print and TV remaining at the forefront. For example, Cartellieri et al (1997) found that many marketers did not believe that it would change their approach to advertising and that it would not significantly impact upon advertising delivery formats, expenditure and pricing. However, they astutely forecasted that as the technology developed then the Internet advertising spend would grow as 'the gap between this new precise, interactive marketing capability and conventional "fuzzy" passive media will widen'. Burns (2006) cites the 'This Year Next Year UK' media investment report forecast by the WPP Group that states that UK advertising spend will rise to £12.2 billon this year (2006) and is expected to reach £12.7 billion in 2007. Burns suggests that the Internet and other digital media are primarily responsible for this growth and are expected to outstrip print media expenditure by 2007.

This chapter looks at how the Internet can be used both strategically and tactically as an integral part of the organisation's strategic marketing communications effort. After considering the Internet's role in marketing communication, a number of online marketing applications are addressed. These include the use of e-mail in direct marketing and online viral campaigns, as well as how the Internet can be used as a medium for advertising. How the online marketer can use public comment web sites, the use of newsletters as a medium of communication and e-marketing applications of blogging are contemplated, as is the Internet's role in public relations. The chapter concludes by looking at the Internet as part of integrated marketing strategies.

11.2 The communications process

Any form of promotion requires a communication to take place. Before considering the Internet as a medium for promotion, it is important that we address the issue of the Internet as a medium for communication.

Whilst it has undoubtedly had an effect on the way in which many of us live and trade, early writers on the Internet over-egged the nature of those effects. Nicovich and Cornwell (1998), for example, talked of the Internet's 'ability to create different environments in which we can experience new forms of reality'. Although this is not inaccurate, the same description could also have been applied to the radio, TV, or even the printed word. Yes, the Internet does combine elements from other forms of media to create 'new forms of reality', but it is still primarily a form of communication. Many Internet evangelists have missed, and continue to miss, this basic point. The value is in the message, not its nature of transmission. However, the attraction is that the message can be customised and delivered or accessed on demand to the suit the receiver. Online communications is all about being relevant to the target audience.

11.3 **The Internet and the communications process**

The communications process (see Fig 11.1) consists of five outbound stages and one return stage. If any of the five outbound stages fails the message will not be successfully received. If the return (feedback) stage does not exist, the communication has failed.

The notion that the Internet is more than a medium of communication is dispelled by the analysis of the Internet's role in the communications process.

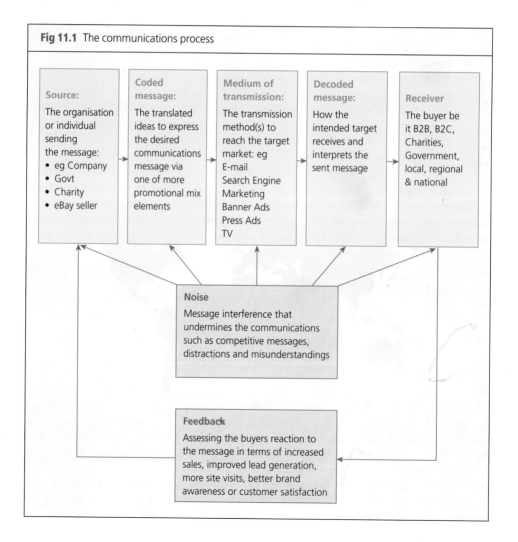

Fig 11.1 The communications process

Source:	Coded message:	Medium of transmission:	Decoded message:	Receiver
The organisation or individual sending the message: • eg Company • Govt • Charity • eBay seller	The translated ideas to express the desired communications message via one of more promotional mix elements	The transmission method(s) to reach the target market: eg E-mail Search Engine Marketing Banner Ads Press Ads TV	How the intended target receives and interprets the sent message	The buyer be it B2B, B2C, Charities, Government, local, regional & national

Noise

Message interference that undermines the communications such as competitive messages, distractions and misunderstandings

Feedback

Assessing the buyers reaction to the message in terms of increased sales, improved lead generation, more site visits, better brand awareness or customer satisfaction

- **Source**

The source of the message is the same for the online communication as in the offline world. In marketing terms it is the person who is wishes to communicate a marketing message, whatever that might be. The Internet has not spawned an entire species of people who did not have a marketing message prior to the Internet – they simply had no suitable medium to transmit that message. Source credibility is important. Building the brand and delivering the promise are fundamental in developing credibility and trust.

- **Coded message**

This could have two interpretations:

1. How the message is formed *grammatically*
2. How the message is formed *technically*

In the former, the online world matches the offline. In marketing terms this means a message being 'coded' in such a way as the target recipient will accept it. This could be simply the language itself (eg in English for English speakers), or the *use* of the language in terms of tone and formality. A message written in such a way as to appeal to 14 year-olds, for example, will not have the same appeal to 70 year-olds. As covered in chapter 8, the Internet provides a new context for messages to be received in, so web transmitted messages should have a different 'code' to the same messages transmitted in other media. Again, this has offline precedents – a copywriter would use a different textual 'code' for the same message on a TV (a visual medium) advert than one on the radio (a non-visual medium).

Certainly the Internet has brought a new technical language – that of HTML, though the concept of this type of encoding is not new. Telephone messages do not take the speaker's words and squeeze them down a wire or through the air, for example, they are 'converted' technically to enable the transfer to take place.

- **Medium of transmission**

This is the most obvious difference between the offline communications and that online as the Internet *is* the medium of transmission. An advantage to the Internet as a medium is that there is little or no distortion to the message as it is transmitted. Indeed the reason for its inception was to provide a dependable method of communication in the most adverse of conditions – a nuclear war. The medium of transmission should be the right vehicle(s) to reach the desired target audience and may include one or more elements of the Promotional Mix (see section 11.3). Online must consider issues like e-mail lists and potential non-deliverability as receivers change e-mail addresses or employ **spam filters** and spyware.

- **Decoded message**

The points raised above in 'coded message' are repeated here. The user's browser 'translates' the technical data in the same way as their TV translates its signal. Once translated by the browser, the target of the message either recognises, the language and grammar used, or they do not. Whether or not they accept or reject the message is down to the skills of the marketer who wrote the content. Again, the reader is referred to chapter 8, particularly the section on web site content.

- **Receiver**

As with the previous point, the issues are repeated, this time from 'source'. The target receiver has always existed offline, the Internet being the new medium. The species that did not receive marketing messages prior to the Internet does not exist.

• **Feedback**

Feedback is essential to assess the success of the communications and what can be learned to improve future communications. In the offline world the feedback can use a number of media, from a remote telephone call, to a personal visit. Online the same principle applies. The only thing new is that the Internet itself can be used to respond. But then the Internet can be used to respond to a non-Internet-transmitted message as well.

Some might argue that Internet-based technology can be used to track feedback without the receiver actually making a conscious response. This is not the case. The technology used to gather e-metrics (see chapter 5) can help to identify whether or not the message has been made available to the recipient but not whether or not they have *received* it – simply that a page has been downloaded or an e-mail opened, does not guarantee that the user has read its content. Any *actual* feedback must be consciously be initiated by the recipient, even if only to click on a single link (with the technology making the feedback complete). However, the interaction and informality of the Internet may enable marketers to monitor and capture feedback through online communities, forums and other mechanisms.

• **Noise**

Noise may occur when the communication is blocked, hindered or undermined. This can be down to competing messages, the wrong time or medium, legal aspects of permission marketing or factors like the non-deliverability of e-mails as previously mentioned. Some modes of communication are prone to technical interference. For example, site traffic and brand visibility may suffer because of search engine optimisation failings to secure top rankings.

The Internet provides significant cost advantages in the delivery of online messages compared to traditional methods but this has led to its over use and abuse. The difficult for the sender is the ability to be heard above the electronic din. The task is to learn how to embrace the new media tools and when to use them in line with expressed customer media preferences.

11.4 The promotional communications mix

The promotional communications mix consists of five main elements that marketers may use, control and combine as part of a coordinated campaign to produce a desired response from a target audience. The five elements are as follows:

• Advertising – non-personal communications using mainstream media
• Personal Selling – face to face interactions between sellers and prospects
• Sales Promotion – short-term incentives designed to stimulate quick sales
• Public Relations – creating a sustained positive image to an organisation's 'publics'
• Direct Marketing – uses customer databases for transactional and relational marketing through response and measurement

Online activities such as the Internet promotions, targeted advertising, search engine and e-mail marketing come under the direct marketing umbrella with database technologies driving timely and targeted communications. The other elements of the promotional mix all have a role to play in a successful campaign. The roles played may vary depending upon the level of integration of on and offline media. For example, offline advertising may play an important role in building the online brand or driving site traffic. Integrated Marketing Com-munications (IMC) may drive traffic both ways. Most major UK supermarkets use in-store activities to drive customers online whilst some online promotions may create interest in in-store events or promotions with market share being the key driver. Personal or telephone selling may play a key role in a high involvement purchase decision through an online channel, such as a car purchase. However, many organisations are effectively adopting sales automation to complete the buying phases. Both sales promotions and public relations tools have made a successful transition over to the online world and are being increasingly employed to stimulate, persuade and influence the online buyer. Rowley (2001) suggests that the level of integration of marketing communications and its role in e-commerce depended upon the stage of e-development, and that probably still holds true today. The content of the communications message will be determined by the nature of the target market. It will differ considerably if we are aiming at Internet bargain hunters or brand loyal repeat buyers. In addition, the message and tools employed may also differ depending upon the objectives associated with response models such as attention, interest, desire and action. Evaluation is a critical review process in any campaign and the Internet provides a plethora of web metrics to measure success against set objectives.

11.5 Online advertising

Even 12 years after it started (the first banner advert appeared online in 1994), the online advertising industry is still in a state of flux. Offline, if anyone wants to know the cost of advertising on any of the traditional media – TV, radio, print, billboard, etc – they will be referred to a 'rate card'. This will be an industry standard for the medium in question. Prices vary depending on such elements as size, length, and time. For example, a 30-second TV ad in the middle of a programme viewed by six million people will have a set rate. A full-page colour ad in the October edition of a monthly magazine with a readership of two million will have a set rate. Naturally, rates will vary depending on the business environment, economy and so on, but they will remain industry-wide.

Online, although there are moves towards a recognised unit cost, to date there is no equivalent to the offline rate card. There are a number of reasons for this absence:

- Early scepticism of the Internet as a marketing communications medium
- Continuing scepticism in the value of online
- Advances in technology
- The industry being fragmented with no recognised lead-body

There is not even a single recognised method for *assessing* the cost of advertising, although this is more due to the different applications than it is dispute amongst practitioners and publishers. There are three common models:

- **CPM (cost per thousand impressions)** – or pay per **impression** advertising. An impres-sion takes place when an ad appears on a web page when downloaded by a user. As with most offline advertising, just because the ad has downloaded does not mean the user has even consciously seen or noticed it. Advertisers pay an agreed fee for each thousand impressions downloaded. The cost will be higher the more targeted the advertising is. This model is most suited to brand advertising where repeated exposure is the objective. There

LEGAL EAGLE BOX 11.1 Legal requirements of online adverts

a) Online Terms of Sale

Where goods are marketed online with an online order form being used, the vendor should provide potential customers with online terms and conditions of sale of those products. Online suppliers should make the terms conspicuously available on their web sites and should bring them to the notice of the customers or potential customers. They should clearly indicate that the terms are an integral part of the contract.

Web-users should be instructed in plain language to review the terms and conditions before assenting to them and the terms should be easily retrievable/printable by the web site user. When designing a web site it is important to ensure that potential customers cannot circumvent the 'accept' dialogue button which they are required to click to indicate their acceptance of the terms. This is particularly important if the terms and conditions change from time to time.

b) Online Price Information

Where products are advertised online the web-vendor should state the pricing details in full and with a breakdown by:

- Product price (including VAT)
- Charges where necessary (such as custom duties, etc)
- Secondary cost (such as transport, packaging and insuance cost, etc)
- The overall total cost

Clear information on prices should be given at the following points:

- In the product description
- In the shopping basket
- On the order form
- In the order confirmation

Where the price is stated in the national currency of the online vendor a link to a conversion table or conversion service should be given to enable web-site visitors/potential customers to ascertain the price in their national currency. The web site vendor should provide clear and understandable information about the different payment method acceptable to him/her.

are potential problems for the advertiser in that there may be difficulties determining how many times the ad has downloaded and who has downloaded it. These issues are similar to those addressed in chapter 5 where **proxy servers** can distort **metrics**.

- **CPC (cost per click)** – or pay per click. With this form of advertising, the advertiser only pays (the publisher) if a user clicks on the ad. It is more suitable for direct marketing ads. Publishers cover themselves against an ad not being clicked on by having minimum fees for campaigns. CPC is the method of payment used by the search engines in their prioritised listing schemes.

- **CPA (cost per action)** is normally only associated with affiliate-type undertakings. In this model the publisher only receives payment if the click through results in an agreed action, normally a sale, but possibly a membership sign-up or similar (affiliate marketing is covered later in this chapter).

Other models may gain popularity as web advertising develops. One such candidate is **Pay-Per-Call (PPC)**. This is where the ad, or web site, features a toll-free number. Software tracks the number's use when customers are redirected to the advertiser's actual phone number. The fee charged for PPC is higher, but then the chances of the organisation achieving a sale are increased.

A caveat for anyone who agrees to pay for ads based on their click through rates is that they should be aware of the 'pay per click' scammers. It is not always customers who click on ads. Unethical companies might pay their own employees to click on competitor's ads. Online robots that are programmed to click on ads exist, but are normally spotted by software developed to detect them. The most common form of pay per click fraud is when people are

---

Fig 11.2 Click through scams

Business A makes money every time a particular ad for business B is clicked because business B will pay for every click. Business A could be an advertising agency or it could be the site's publisher. Let's say the fee business 'B' pays is 20p for every click on an advert that takes the user to their web site. The corrupt agency or publisher then hires surfers to click on the ads, paying them 5p every time they do so. Hey presto, 15p profit for each click for the unscrupulous business A. Not only does this mean a direct loss of money for business B – 20p per fraudulent click – but any future strategy based on **click-through-rates** or ad metrics will be seriously flawed.

---

paid to click on online ads. Although the exercise is widely practiced and reported in the Indian sub-continent, examples in other parts of the world are not unknown.

An example of a possible scam is illustrated in Fig 11.2.

Another issue of some concern to the e-marketer is the use of technology to interfere with ads. There are two main drivers behind such actions:

1. Those advertisers who seek to gain commercial advantage by less than scrupulous means. An example of this would be **adware** that has the ability to deliver competitive ads next to or on top of a site's existing ads without the user's knowledge or the publisher's permission.

2. Some people prefer ad-free web sites, and so are offered software to eradicate, or move, ads. The most common is that which prevents pop-up ads appearing, popular browsers such as Firefox and Internet Explorer have pop-up suppressors. Firefox goes a stage further by making available a browser extension called Greasemonkey that enables users to change the way particular web pages appear. For example, a Firefox user, with the Greasemonkey extension, visiting CNN.com would have the ad banners shifted to the bottom of the page leaving only the textual content untouched.

For both of these examples there is an ongoing battle between the programmers on either side of the fence. No sooner is technology made available from one side than it is counter-acted by software, or legal action from the other.

Types of online advertising

Like its counterparts in traditional media, online advertising is divided into two sub-groups:

1. Direct marketing ads that seek to elicit a direct action from consumers (eg 'click here to take advantage of this limited offer')
2. Branding ads that reinforce consumer opinion by frequent exposure

Direct marketing now dominates the online market with 66% of all ads with branding trailing on 34% (Nielsen/NetRatings 2003).

Where can online ads be placed?

Advertisers have a wide choice of the type of web publications on which they might wish their ads to feature, these include:

- **Portals**. A rich source of publications for advertisers, the major portals – such as Yahoo! and MSN – dominate online ad hosting with 51% of the market (Nielsen/NetRatings 2003). The remainder of the market is almost equally split between news and information sites (26%) and entertainment and society sites (23%). Not only are portals the most visited group of web site classification but they often allow for fairly specific targeting efforts – hotels on a travel portal for example.

- **Community web sites**. With social networking becoming one of the most popular applications of the web, those sites that cater for specific groups of people are prime targets for online advertisers. The communities could be related by hobby, interest or geographic region and provide excellent opportunities for targeted advertising. For example, Dogster (www.dogster.com), as the name suggests, is a web site for the dog-loving community, making it a suitable venue for ads promoting any dog-related products.

- **Search engines**. The concept of 'paid results' as a form of advertising is covered in the chapter on search engines. Some search engines, however, also carry banner ads on some if not all of their pages.

- **Shopping search engines**. Using a software application called '**shopping agents**', sites such as shopping.com, bizrate.com and price-guide.co.uk respond to user's searches by providing comparisons between online store's prices. The web page on which such comparisons are presented is a perfect opportunity for targeted marketing.

- **Chat-rooms**. Some companies provide free chat-room software and hosting in return for having ads placed on each page. This would not suitable for a business web site, but it would be fine for a not for profit or hobby/interest site.

- **Message boards** and online forums. Many of these are provided free to the user so, the publisher must look to recoup their expenses from somewhere. Placing ads on each page is an obvious course to follow. This has a number of advantages, primarily that each board and forum subject will have its own page, so increasing the advertising opportunities. The second major advantage is that the focus of the users' interest is defined by the theme of the subjects being discussed, so allowing for targeted ads to be placed.

- **Blogs**. Described in detail later in this chapter, many blog sites are provided free to the blogger with the business model of the provider requiring that the blog pages carry banner ads. As with other types of web publications featured here, blogs that are on specific subjects are ideal for targeted advertising efforts.

- **Podcasts**. Offer the marketer targeted opportunities for advertising, though without the aid of any images. As the use of podcasting increases so does the opportunity for advertising on the medium. An illustration of its potential can be seen in Mini case 11.1.

- **RSS aggregators**. RSS stands for 'rich site summary' and is an XML format used by publishers to put their content on numerous sources by syndicating it around the web. The way it works is for users to subscribe to a desktop or web-based application that allows them to opt in to RSS feeds from all kinds of publishers, from the *Wall Street Journal* to individuals' blogs. The RSS feeds come not from the individual publishers, but 'aggregators' who pull together the data and make it available to subscribers in subject areas of their choice. The feed aggregators deliver headlines and a little additional information that will link to the full version of the content. Think of it as a kind of search engine that is constantly looking for information on a subject of the user's choice, and delivering it to their PC. Traditionally (a strange term for an application that is only a few years old) RSS feeds were ad free, and many will seek to maintain their integrity by remaining so. Increasingly,

MINI CASE 11.1 Podcasting – the talking guidebook?

For some time, visitors at many museums have been given the option of having a personal spoken guide to their visit via head-set and tape/CD. However, these are limited to the museum being visited. Tourists to cities can still be seen walking the streets and feverishly dipping into their printed guidebook as they arrive at interesting places or buildings. The guidebook's days might, however, be numbered.

Although there are hundreds of travel-related podcasts pro-duced by keen amateurs, the podcast guide hit the mainstream of travel in August 2005 when Virgin Atlantic published its podcast guide to New York on its web site (www.virginatlantic. loudish.com). The guide consists of six-minute segments on subjects such as restaurants, shopping, essentials for first-timer visitors and off-the-beaten-track sights and activities. Eventually, Virgin plan to produce podcast guides to all its 26 destinations worldwide.

however, aggregators are looking to develop their activities as income streams by selling advertising space on requested feeds. For the marketer this presents an ideal (though at the time of writing, unproved) opportunity for targeted marketing in that each users has revealed their interests by signing on for information on specific subject areas.

- **Mobile devices**. As more people access the web 'on the move' advertisers can target them. The significant issue here is that the download capacity might be limited and the **viewable area** is much smaller than on the average PC or lap-top.

- **Searching pages**. On sites where a complex search has been initiated the page will norm-ally show a message saying that the search is being performed, often with some form of apology or reason for the delay. As well as this message, a targeted ad could be included. An example would be a flight search web site. It is not unreasonable for the user to wait for a comprehensive search of numerous airlines to produce results on a specific destination from a specific airport. The ad could be for other services for the host web site – hotel searches is an obvious example – or the space could be sold to third party advertisers. A 'searching' page from Travel Supermarket (www.travelsupermarket.com) is shown in Fig 11.3.

- Pages that are designed to be printed can be divided into two groups: (a) those which have content that users might wish to take away – maps for example, and (b) pages of text that are deliberately formatted for printing. For example, online newspaper articles that can be viewed (and subsequently printed) on a separate browser page. These ads have the advant-age that their lives are longer. An ad on a web site might only exist in the user's eye-line for a short time. A printed ad exists for as long as the content is useful so you can 'print this page'. A significant second benefit to advertising on such a page is that the ad can be tar-geted at the reader based on the content of the article in question. An even better use of ads on printable pages comes from online map provider Multimap (www.multimap.com) who include, for example, a discount coupon for a chain of motorway services on the hard copy of maps for the traveller en route. In Fig 11.4, there is an example of a 'printer page' from ClickZ, the online marketers' network.

In addition to web sites, e-advertisers can also place ads on the following:

- **E-mails** – advertising on emails rather than email as a medium for an advertising message eg Hotmail advertising their own service. Free e-mail providers must make a profit and placing ads on customer's e-mails is one way.

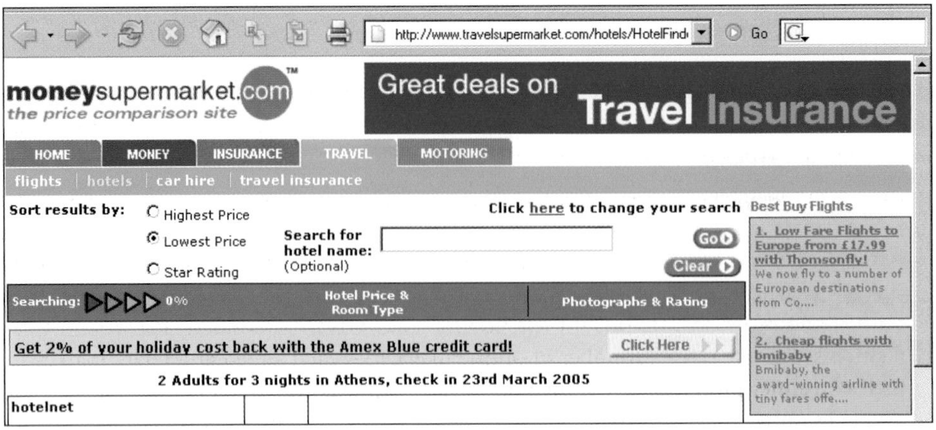

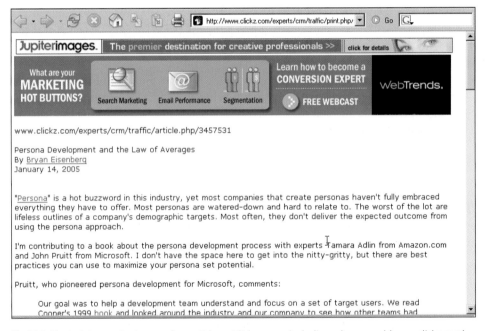

Fig 11.3 A 'searching' page from Travel Supermarket (www.travelsupermarket.com)

Fig 11.4 The 'printer version' page of an article on Clickz.com – including a banner ad (www.clickz.com)

Organisations should maximise e-mail ad opportunities to customers and prospects. A simple example is the e-mail 'footnote' that promotes the organisation, a product it provides, or simply the web site of that organisation or product. A more astute application is to use 'service' e-mails. One example is the order confirmation e-mail where an ad for an associated product could be included. Online auction site eBay (www.ebay.com) include ads on their service e-mails confirming the 'current highest bidder'. Such ads are not always targeted effectively with ads having no connection with the product on which the user is bidding.

- **Newsletters** – non-affiliated newsletters sell advertising space in order to cover costs or make a profit. These can be particularly good for advertisers as the content of the newsletter will have a specific theme, so making targeted advertising more accurate and relevant.

- **Online magazines** – similar to the special interest portal (covered in chapter 8), the online magazine could be described as one big ad, or at least one big ad forum. Not that this is how the user should perceive it. The concept is for a manufacturer (or distributor) to maintain a web site containing high quality magazine-like features, then add promotions, discounts, and other promotions for the publishing company's products. Practitioners like Procter & Gamble have a number of online magazines each aimed at a target market for their consumer products. These include 'Health Expressions' which contains advice and resources on wellness and treatment and 'Being A Girl' containing forums and guidance on youth topics. Both are, naturally, liberally sprinkled with ads and promotions for P&G products related to the subject matter.

Ad formats

The online advertiser has a choice of where they distribute their ads and also what format those ads can take. As with traditional offline advertising, the choice of format should best match the ad objectives, the target market, and the online publication on which it will be featured. For example, a rich media format would be best suited for an ad for a new games console featured on a web site aimed at teenage boys. Conversely, a static banner would be more appropriate for a site targeted at senior citizens. The main format options are; banner, pop-ups, floating, and rich media.

Banners

Banners were the first format of ad to appear online, and they are still the most popular. The first banner ad, for AT&T, appeared on 'Wired' magazine's Hotwired.com in October 1994 (see Fig 11.5).

Banner ads are normally described by their sizes, which in the main are fixed in order to web developers to design-in spaces for ads. Recognised banners sizes (in pixels) include:

- 468×60 – the most common, and so 'standard', size
- 234×60 – the 'half' banner
- 120×60 and 125×125 – 'button' size
- 120×600 and 160×600 – 'skyscrapers' that go at the side of a web page

Anyone with an interest in the way banner ads have developed over the last 10 years should take a look at the site published by Tari Akpodiete. The Toronto web designer has made public what she believes is the largest collecton of banner ads in the world. Her site, Banner Report, can be found on http://www.bannerreport.com.

Fig 11.5 The first banner ad 1994 – from US telecommunications giant, AT&T

Early banners were static but it did not take long before fairly basic **HTML** was used to produce banners that featured animated **GIFs** to produce moving or changing images. Both static and animated banners are still the most common form of online ads used today but as customer expectations rise rich media and online video are increasingly been adopted to offer a more stimulating multisensory experience. Regarding the use of animation in online banner advertising, Yoo and Kim (2005) studied the effects of animation on memory and attitudes towards ads. They said that marketers were resorting to the use of fast moving images in their banner ads to cut through the online clutter. They found that rather than having a positive impact, the high intensity animations inhibited had a negative effect and reduced recognition and retention of the ad.

Banners ads can be used for two primary purposes that of brand building and direct response campaigns that link through to a dedicated micro-site to take the consumer through the next stage of the buying cycle. Banner ads may also be used in conjunction with other online tools at key points in the buying cycle, as demonstrated in Mini Case 11.2.

Pop-ups

Before discussing their benefit, or otherwise, it is necessary to determine what a 'pop-up' is. Although universally recognised, and often derided, by the common term 'pop-up' the application's technical name is 'interstitial'.

Meaning *in-between*, an interstitial is an advertisement that appears in a separate browser window, usually while a web page loads. The pop-up appears 'over' the loading page, so making it visible immediately. A similar application is the one that produces a 'pop-under' – an ad that loads 'behind' a web site and so is not seen until the browser is closed. Although these are named 'superstituals', many define an interstitial as any ad that spawns a new browser window, regardless of whether the window comes to focus up-front or sits behind the active window, effectively, making no differentiation between pop-up and pop-under ads.

For many, pop-ups are second only to spam e-mails when it comes to online annoyance. Yet so many sites include them – why? The obvious answer is that they generate income for both the publisher hosting advert and the organization that conducts the advertising. But are they effective? A 2004 report published by e-Consultancy (www.e-consultancy.com) presenting the views of more than 2,000 UK web users confirmed that the majority (70%) found the ads intrusive, but that 84% of respondents had responded to an online advert. They are also not as common as many might think, only 3.5% of all online ad impressions are pop-ups.

MINI CASE 11.2 Banners in the buying cycle

Banner ads can be very effective when combined with specific consumer searches in moving individuals through the buying cycle.

Prior to the lamented corporate demise of MG Rover (MGR), they had successfully tested banner ads in conjunction with search engine company, Ask Jeeves. They tested placed MGR banner ads against specific automotive and sport search terms. Interviews were held with some 1,500 users who had seen the ad following their search together with a control group who had not. The results were quite significant. 55% of users inputting car searches were actually in the buying cycle and of them, 60% had not yet decided on their brand choice. Nearly half of those who had seen the ad had reacted positively, ie purchased, requested brochures, visited dealers, had test drives, etc. Those who had not responded said they would in the future. Sadly, too late for the iconic British brand.

Adapted from: *The Online Direct Marketing Guide* (2004) www.iabuk.net

When appraising the use of pop-ups, the e-marketer should consider the following:

- Use pop-ups judiciously and sparingly, do not bombard the user
- Do not display a pop-up every time the user opens a new page – or the same page (eg the home page that might contain the navigation bar)
- Make the pop-up window easy for the user to close, or have it close automatically when its originator-page is closed
- Make the pop-up window unobtrusive, not covering the whole screen
- Have a defined purpose for each pop-up

Floating ads

The **floating ad**, also referred to as a 'voken' (a virtual token), is a relative of the pop-up, but more sophisticated. This is the image that 'floats' over the top of a web page's content rather than appearing in a small browser box. Most are static images, but some move around the page – an aeroplane flying around or a car driving across the page, for example. Unlike the standard pop-up that appears and stays put, even the static-image floater moves around the page, often following the user's cursor. Although aesthetically more pleasing that standard pop-ups, floating ads come with all the negative aspects of their cousins plus the added irritant that the 'close' button is often difficult to locate. As with standard pop-ups, however, they can be effective if used judiciously.

Rich media

For some advertisers the static or animated banner cannot create the results they wish from an advertising campaign. Rich media ads are those that use interactive technologies like Java and Flash that allow advertising creatives to design ads that more closely resemble offline counterparts. According to a Nielsen/NetRatings report in 2003, of all rich media ads, nearly 90% use animated and static **GIFs** with only 5% of rich media ads using generic **Flash**, **Shockwave**, **streaming video** or **Real Audio/Video** technology. It is likely that, although more basic applications currently still dominate (as most web sites utilise the same rudimentary rich media technology as the ads), the use of rich media in advertising will increase. This is a result of two factors, one with a technical origin, the other based on marketing theory.

1. The wider availability of broadband access, with its faster download capacity, will facilitate an increase in the use of Flash technology in ads and downloadable video clips.
2. When delivered online, video clips of ads such as we are used to seeing on TV, can be targeted at much narrow segments than on TV.

Europe has been slower in its adoption of broadband than the US where more than 56% of Internet users have broadband at home (www.nielsen-netratings.com, 2005). Although the novelty element of rich media has been widely used to attract the attention of advertising overloaded consumers, it is B2B marketers that make most use of rich media advertising. The potential is illustrated in Mini case 11.3.

Advergaming

Whilst most formats of online advertising (as described above) are little more than traditional advertising performed using e-technology, one form of online marketing bears no relationship to the traditional offline models. That is **advergaming**. A close relative to viral marketing (covered in section 11.7) it relies on a viral element for the concept to be passed

---

MINI CASE 11.3 TV, the Internet, video, advertising or a mix of them all?

January 2006 saw Scripps Networks' launch of HGTV KitchenDesign, the first of its targeted broadband channels showing more than 200 streaming videos on design trends and kitchen makeover tips. President of Scripps Networks, John Lansing, said in a statement: 'By providing content that appeals to a whole new audience and introducing them to our established brands, we are creating demand for our networks and for the broadband service that our cable operator partners provide.'

HGTVKitchenDesign.com includes a video viewer that allows users to simultaneously receive further information about an idea or a product as the video plays, interactive tools to enable users to personalise their existing or new floor plan and share ideas about their kitchen design plans and products or services they have found useful.

This new broadband channel is the first of several that Scripp plans to launch. The others will also be related to lifestyle and be targeted at affinity groups.

---

from user to user on the web. Early advergaming efforts were sponsored web sites where users would visit and play arcade-type games online. An example is Kraft Foods' site, Candystand (www.candystand.com) launched in 1997. These sites often require registration suggesting that they have multiple marketing objectives, with user data being used for research and/or target marketing agendas. More recently, the advergaming concept has been developed, with 'alternate reality gaming' its latest manifestation. Though a direct descendant of advergaming, alternate reality gaming moves the concept closer to viral marketing. As a branding exercise, the concept can move away from being an advertising medium and develop into a concept in its own right – alternate reality gaming marketing.

Pioneered commercially by online campaigns for properties such as the film 'AI' and the game 'Halo 2,' these alternative reality gaming efforts blend 'hoax' like web sites that do not announce their affiliation with online quests, unfolding mysteries, and even real-world activities such as messages received at phone booths or pre-recorded calls to participants in the middle of the night (Carton 2005). Such efforts blended computer game play with pre-recorded webcams, phone messages, and other sinister-seeming 'intrusions' into gamers' real-world lives. So realistic were some games that one, 'Majestic', was closed after September 11, fearing that players would mistake the game for what was going on in the real world. Less menacing games have continued however, seamlessly blending together reality and fantasy using the Internet.

What works best?

In such a young media as the Internet, the jury is still out on what types of ads work best. Research on the subject is, however, ongoing. In December 2003 journalism school, the Poynter Institute (www.poynteronline.org), observed nearly four dozen individuals as they navigated their way through a number of web sites, tracking what they call 'user eye-flow' on those sites. The Poynter Institute was looking primarily at how users interacted with news sites, but it also looked at how users interact with ads before they click on (or away from) them. Their observations included the following:

- Users avoid certain ad formats, the seemingly ubiquitous 468×60 being one such format
- Whilst pop-ups are seen by 70% of users, they were generally ignored or closed within three seconds
- Borders around ads appear to deflect attention from the ad content
- Ads that are blended into textual content work well

- Placement within the page is important. Ads that appear in the upper left corner being seen most often (this hardly a surprise as Western text is read left to right, top to bottom)

Ad placement and control

When a marketer wishes to run advertising on television, radio or the printed media he/she will deal with the commercial representatives of each media. Although this could mean dealing with a number of people, that number is not high. But what if they wished to run a series of banner ads on popular web sites? This would mean dealing with the representatives of each web site to negotiate terms and technical specifications. And that is assuming that all the appropriate web sites have someone with whom to conduct the negotiations.

The majority of online advertising is facilitated through advertising network managers who represent web site publishers who wish to sell advertising space. These managers aggregate the available advertising 'space' and sell it to individual advertisers or to the buying arms of advertising agencies. As well as providing a service for the media buyers, the aggregators also provide an essential service for the web sites owners, but it does not come cheap, with the aggregators taking up to 50% of the sales revenues for the ads they serve (Nielsen/NetRatings 2003).

It is most common that ads are targeted so as to appeal to users who may visit a certain page. They are, however, inflexible within that parameter with every user seeing the same ad (or ads) on a web page. Other options do exist. These include:

- **Surround sessions.** First introduced to the online advertising industry by the *New York Times*' online edition (www.nytimes.com) in October 2001, a surround session is one in which a visitor to the site sees only the ads for one organisation. This may include '**sequential advertising**' where the advertiser controls the sequence in which ads are shown. No matter what pages on the site that a user visits, they are presented with a series of ads that will build a message and usually lead to a 'response' ad.

- **Dayparts.** The daypart session, or site session, is when a single advertiser dominates all the advertising on a publisher's web site for a pre-determined time of the day. Although the innovation is widely attributed to the *New York Times*, several organisations had already dabbled with the concept prior to NYT's adoption of it in the summer of 2002. MarketWatch.com, for example, had sold its Friday afternoon advertising space to Anheuser Busch, allowing the brewer to feature a Friday afternoon 'happy hour' on the site.

The dayparts are: early morning, daytime, evening, late night, and weekends. Daytime is the most popular, though some sites might peak at other times of the day. Global advertisers should also consider time differences. Early morning in London is around midnight in New York and even earlier in California. If this is an important issue for advertisers, publishers should consider having sites hosted on different servers around the world so that local times can be catered for.

11.6 E-mail marketing

Although it is the web that is synonymous with the Internet, it is e-mail that is the most popularly used element of the Internet. In a significant research project into consumers' e-mail use, IPT (2004) revealed that e-mail, at 99%, was the most common activity on the Internet, with using the web for price comparison (77%) and news (65%) the next most prevalent. In other research, this time into business use, over 80% of respondents cited e-mail as being a pre-requisite for doing business in the modern commercial world (Vile & Collins 2004). The marketing professionals respondents' element of the IPT (2004) research revealed that 92% currently use e-mail marketing as part of their marketing mix.

Despite its popularity, e-mail does bring with it what many would consider to be a curse – spam. Spam is bulk e-mail sent without recipients' permission or a prior business relationship. Reputable marketers do not use spam. They send e-mails only to people who have given permission to receive e-mails from that organisation. Unfortunately, legitimate e-mail marketers have suffered at the hands of 'spammers' but EU legislation is redressing the balance with the 2003 Privacy and Communications Directive. Such is the proliferation of un-requested e-mail that most Internet and e-mail service providers implement some form of 'filter' to block the spam before it reaches the in-box of the unwitting recipient. The technology behind 'spam filters' is still in its infancy and this, combined with the efforts of spammers to stay one step ahead of the filter developers, can mean that legitimate messages are blocked because they are perceived as spam.

E-mail offers a great potential for targeted and personalised communication (Merisavo and Raulas 2004) and so is a suitable medium of communications for a number of purposes, including:

- Newsflashes – these can be negative or positive, to announce special offers or to notify of urgent problems with a product
- New product announcements – a specific e-mail message that is integrated with offline promotional efforts
- New product availability – or increased availability of existing ones
- Promotional discount offers – the delivery speed of email can add urgency to the promotion
- Press/publicity releases – to reach a wider audience than conventional media
- Order confirmations – for offline as well as online orders
- Personalised greetings messages – as part of a relationship marketing strategy, wishing customers birthday or religious holiday greetings
- Reminders for event purchases – eg bouquets for Mother's Day
- Shipping status – particularly when an extended delivery period is quoted, customers are less likely to be frustrated if they are kept informed of delivery status
- Technical support for products and services – reduces the need for (expensive) call centre operations
- Newsletters – to keep customers informed of relevant happenings (see also section 11.11)
- Reminders for frequent purchasers – replenishment notification for consumable products
- Expiration notices – for subscriptions, guarantees, etc
- Customer surveys – for primary research
- Thank you messages – for purchasing a product, joining a **mailing list**, attending a function, returning a survey, or any other undertaking that the organisation should be grateful for
- Traditional direct marketing

It is worth noting that the same e-mail can address more than one of the issues listed above. For example, an expiry notice for a subscription could promote an enhanced service, technical support include an advert for a product associated to that about which the enquiry has been made, or a new product announcement include a promotional offer for that product.

The remainder of this section concentrates on the last application of e-mail in the list above – direct marketing. It should be noted, however, that many of the points raised with regard to direct e-mail marketing, can be applied to other applications in the list above.

Direct marketing using e-mail

According to the Institute of Direct Marketing, direct marketing is 'the planned recording, analysis and tracking of individual customers' responses and transactions for the purpose of developing and prolonging mutually profitable customer relationships'. Direct marketing using the Internet as the medium of communication is commonly referred to as 'e-mail marketing'. Marketers should be aware of this and not believe that the use of e-mail has introduced a brand new method of marketing. Indeed, the most successful proponents of 'e-mail marketing' are those who apply tried and tested direct marketing techniques to their trade. As with its offline predecessor, successful e-mail marketing consists of a number of distinct stages. These are shown in Fig 11.6.

In each stage of the email marketing process the marketer has specific issues to address if any campaign is to be successful. They are:

Stage 1 – Define objectives of campaign
Think strategically. Successful e-mail campaigns are not tactical, they are strategic. Is the objective of the campaign to increase sales, generate leads, build brand awareness, develop an integrated campaign,or a part of a relationship building retention strategy. Like any marketing campaign, unless the strategic objectives are clear any tactics are likely to fail.

Stage 2 – Determine target recipients
The two elements to this stage are:

1. Segmentation

2. The selection of *actual* recipients

Both of these issues are addressed by Seth Godin (Vice President Direct Marketing at Yahoo!) when he says that any e-mail should be personal, relevant and anticipated (1999). With regard to segmentation, this is an offline marketing practice that is easily transferred to online campaigns. The direct marketer must only send e-mails to recipients who are either current, or genuinely potential, customers for the product or service on offer. One advantage that the online campaign has over offline efforts is that recipients choose to receive certain information – effectively segmenting themselves. The targeting of actual recipients requires current e-mail address lists and constant updating. The development of mailing lists is covered later in this chapter but there are a number of issues to be addressed with regard to mailing lists, they include:

- Permission is everything – never send customers or prospects emails without their permission to do so.

- Use 'double opt-in' methods of gaining permission (the customer not only indicates an interest in receiving emails, but confirms such in a separate communication).

- Include an 'opt-out' facility – make it easy for recipients to unsubscribe, and honour that request.

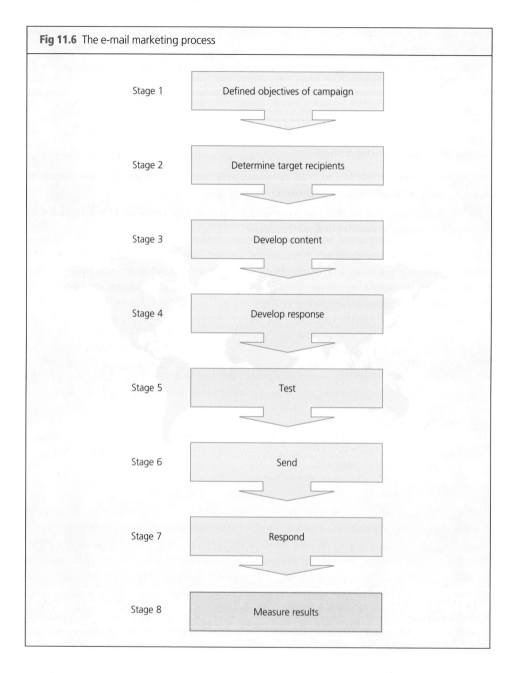

Fig 11.6 The e-mail marketing process

Stage 1 — Defined objectives of campaign

Stage 2 — Determine target recipients

Stage 3 — Develop content

Stage 4 — Develop response

Stage 5 — Test

Stage 6 — Send

Stage 7 — Respond

Stage 8 — Measure results

- Permission is a two-way street – the organisation must keep their side of the agreement by sending only e-mails containing interesting, relevant, and actionable information.

Stage 3 – Develop content

Like that of web site content (see chapter 8) the development of the direct marketing e-mail is best delegated to experts in the field. Issues for particular attention include:

- Use personal greetings – 'Dear Mr Jones' helps develop a relationship, 'Dear valued customer' does not
- Include a **'call to action'**, and get it right – make it easy for the recipient to act on whatever is being promoted, and offer some sort of incentive to do so
- Get the 'subject' line right – it is the key to whether or not a recipient will open the e-mail
- Get the 'from' line right – use an e-mail address/domain name that the recipient will recognise
- Get to the point – keep content concise with a link to a web site for additional information
- Put the important information in the first paragraph – newspaper journalists are trained to do this to grab the attention of the reader
- E-mail is an interactive medium of communication, use it as such – make e-mail and web site links obvious, include other contact details

When developing the e-mail the marketer must decide on whether to send the message in plain text or **HTML** format. The best option to address the issue is to ask users (when they register) to indicate which they would prefer. For the marketer, HTML offers greater flexibility, with the ability to include visual pages with links, images and graphics embedded without the need to be logged on to the Internet. In the absence of an expressed preference, the format that is most suitable to the recipient should be the one that is used. For example, a mailing to computer programmers would be best in HTML as the addressees would be certain to have the hard and software to accept the message. Conversely, for a mailing to a segment of the market who might use public access to the Internet, or if the e-mail is likely to be printed for offline reading, plain text is best.

Stage 4 – Develop response
The objective of any e-mail campaign must be to illicit a response from the receiver and the organisation should be prepared to react to any response. Issues for consideration include:

- Delegate ownership – someone must take responsibility for the campaign and all post-campaign actions ie tracking responses, replying to enquiries, etc
- Be ready to respond – have follow-up messages prepared in advance (eg Thank you for your enquiry)
- Develop unique landing pages for e-mail messages – never link to the front page of the web site
- Automate as much as can be budgeted for – the technology is available, it should be used if the organisation can afford to do so. It will save money if manual intervention is eliminated wherever possible. Be discriminating however, an automated e-mail to confirm a change in profile is perfectly acceptable, automated responses to specific enquiries or complaints will succeed only in sending customers to competitors
- Liaise with other departments (including technical) to ensure systems can cope with added workload resulting from planned e-mail campaigns

Stage 5 – Test
This stage can be divided into two elements

1. Testing the technology
2. Testing the message

- Technology
  - Test before sending – a test message should be sent to at least one 'test' recipient for each e-mail client and browser likely to be used by recipients eg Outlook, Outlook Express, Yahoo!, Hotmail, AOL, Mozilla, etc)
  - Check that the e-mail does not trigger any anti-spam software
  - Check that links in the message work
- The message
  - Test, and keep testing. Experiment with changes to various elements of the e-mail (eg subject line) and analyse responses to strive for an 'ideal' format. Similarly, the message itself can be varied. For example, what attracts more responses, a 30-day free trial or free shipping. For professional direct mail e-mail marketers this is an ongoing and never-ending task.

Stage 6 – Send

Before the message is sent, the direct marketer must consider the timing of the execution. Again, the actual decision will depend on the nature of the recipients, but considerations will include:

- The time of day. Is it better for the message to arrive when the recipient is at their desk, or to be waiting for them when they start work?
- The day. Business e-mails sent on Friday afternoon are likely to sit in the in-box until Monday morning, when the recipient is more likely to delete a whole stack of e-mails.
- Global time/date lines. Both of the previous points may be affected by time differences between the sender and the receiver.
- Local conventions. Scotland, for example, has different Bank Holidays to those in England and Arabic nations have Thursday and Friday as their 'weekend'.

Stage 7 – Response

Ensure that all plans made in stage 4 are implemented efficiently and effectively. The actual fulfilment of responses will be determined by the quality of the preparation.

Stage 8 – Measure results

There must be a return on investment (ROI) with any e-mail campaign. Specific metrics have to be consistent with the chosen strategy and must be related to the key performance indicators and objectives of the firm (Weischedel et al 2005), but issues of concern might include:

- E-mail delivery – did the message reach the addressees in box? A low rate would suggest problems with delivery. For example, incorrect addresses or spam filters blocking the e-mail.
- Open rate – having reached the in box, is the e-mail opened or deleted without opening? A low rate would indicate that either or both of the 'from' or 'subject' lines has no appeal to the recipient.
- **Click-through rate** – do recipients respond to the 'call to action', usually to click on a link to a web page? A low rate could be the result of a poor call to action, poorly written content or simply that the offer does not appeal to the recipient.
- Conversion rate – what percentage of recipients actually take up what is on offer in the message eg buy a product? Potential reasons for a low conversion rate would include a poor

---

MINI CASE 11.4 E-Mail shades it for Rimmel London

Communicating the launch of a new range of face founda-tion products was the challenge for Rimmel London (www .rimmellondon.com) and its e-mail agency, Iris Female. The range of foundations was aimed at women with darker skin principally in the 18–24 year old group with ethnic backgrounds. Using cold lists, they used e-mail to target 215,000 women in London and the Midlands close to flagship stores stocking the range. The campaign sought to promote the new range of shades and for prospects to register their details for a 10,000 full size sample giveaway. The communication was incentivised with the chance to win tickets to the MOBO music awards and after show

celebrity bash. An e-mail link led prospects through to a micro-site that invited them to submit personal details and colour preferences in return for the free sample and prize draw entry. Two hours after launch, over 3,000 people had registered. This rose to 27,000 by the end of the month providing a rich database of warm prospects.

Adapted: *Building a Strong Foundation*, Marketing Direct, June 2006, 29.
Email is one of the most effective and efficient ways to reach young women in a targeted way, www.eventtr.co.uk/evtpress/2006/05/ News bulletin 17 May 2006.

---

landing page, poor creative content of the web page, or a poor buying procedure. Another obvious reason is that the message was targeted at inappropriate recipients.

Mini case 11.4 illustrates how Rimmel London used e-mail to communicate its new range of face products, as well as drive traffic to its extrovert makeover site.

Results of individual responses should be retained to track future activity. It may be fea-sible that a recipient might be attracted by the e-mail's message but not act upon it until a later date.

Analysing metrics such as these can substantiate the tangible, but marketing is not a one-dimensional practice. Consideration should be given to measuring the intangibles. These are typically less simple to track, measure, and analyse. Customer research, such as surveys, questionnaires, and focus groups, can be insightful, particularly if research is con-ducted before and after the marketing initiative. Intangible results can include:

- Customer satisfaction
- Brand awareness and perception
- Brand preference
- Brand consideration
- Brand enthusiasm

Mailing lists

There are numerous ways of legally gathering the e-mail addresses of willing participants such as, for example, keeping the addresses of online buyers. Other methods mirror those used offline such as competitions and give-a-ways, whilst others use the technology of the medium – collecting e-mail enquiries, for example. Some businesses, perhaps those new to an industry or sector for example, have no access to such information and so need to buy-in e-mail lists of potential customers.

This is perfectly acceptable if the lists are garnered from reputable agencies. These agencies make a business from the collection and storage of the e-mail addresses of people who have given permission to receive 'relevant' e-mails. One method used for this is the 'tick this box if you are willing to receive information from third party companies who have products

![Legal Eagle logo] **LEGAL EAGLE BOX 11.2 E-mail marketing**

E-mail marketing is now regulated by the Privacy and Electronic Communications (EC Directive) Regulations 2003, Regulations 22 and 23. These Regulations define e-mail as:

'any text, voice, sound or image message sent over a public electronic communications network which can be stored in the network or in the recipient's terminal equipment until it is collected by the recipient . . .'

The Regulations provide that marketers should not transmit or instigate the transmission of unsolicited marketing material with the use of e-mail systems to individuals unless the recipients had consented to receiving such marketing material. Regulation 23 prohibits marketers from sending marketing information by e-mail to individuals unless they:

• Provide their identities as senders of the e-mail marketing material or,

• Provide a valid address to which the recipient can send an opt-out-request. In the online environment a valid address could simply be an e-mail address.

A marketer may, however, send e-mail marketing material to an individual without prior consent where:

• The individual's contact details were obtained in the course of a sale or negotiation for the sale of the sender's product or service;

• The e-mail marketing material is sent to the recipient for the purpose of advertising a product that is similar to that which has already been sold to the recipient or which has been negotiated for sale; and

• The recipient has been given a simple means of opting-out of receiving further marketing information.

pertinent to you' type of message included on some web sites. This is legitimate, the web site owner often benefits from the income gained by selling such details to the agencies. The web site owners should never pass on any user or customer details to a third party without their express permission (see Legal Eagle Box 11.2). In many parts of the world, this is considered to be bad business practice; in Europe, it is also illegal.

Bought-in lists can yield good results. A company selling a new type of modelling tool might purchase a list of e-mail addresses of model boat enthusiasts, for example. Other lists are practically worthless, often being simply a list of e-mail addresses gathered by a variety of methods, most of them nefarious. One such is the use of 'e-mail harvesters' described in chapter 5. This type of list is best left to purveyors of the more dubious products and services that frequently find their way into e-mail in-boxes and are quite rightly condemned as spam. Legitimate marketers should always stay away from generic e-mail lists. Not only are they a waste of money, but their use could ruin the reputation of the organisation or brand.

E-mail marketing: footnote

The content of this section is been dedicated to e-mails that have originated with the organisation as part of a marketing objective, be that direct marketing, relationship building, customer service or any one of a number of other initiatives. There are, however, two additional elements of out-going e-mail use that the e-marketer should be aware of:

• **The response e-mail**. If the web site is being used to generate leads, then the textual content of the web site will be designed to encourage the reader to contact the web site publisher often through an e-mail link from the web site.

• **The reply e-mail** is sent in response to an unsolicited incoming customer enquiry. In most instances the e-mail has been sent because the organisation has got something wrong. It could be a complaint about a service or product. It could be a product query raised because the information is not included on the web site. On the positive side, it could be a 'thank you' or compliment message.

Planning for both applications indicates the way in which the organisation goes about its marketing. The former is easiest to plan for, in that the reaction should be similar for all enquiries. The response will be determined by the nature of the product or service on offer, but it can be fairly resolute and dealt with by one of a number of pre-prepared formats. The latter is more difficult to deal with as the subjects may vary. There is also the problem that the incoming e-mail will not necessarily arrive in the in-box of the person most suited to deal with it. Although all eventualities cannot be fully catered for, forethought is again the answer. Members of staff should be allocated the job of either replying to this type of email or made responsible for re-directing the message to the right person. An interim message of 'your query has been passed onto (named person) and they will reply two working days' will normally appease the sender. If individuals or sections that address specific aspects of the organisation exist, then the web site should identify them, with specific e-mail addresses listed.

11.7 Viral marketing

Solomon et al (2006) refers to viral marketing as a 'marketing activity in which a company recruits customers to be sales agents and spread the word about he product.' Sterne and Priore (2000) refer to it as 'Word of Mouth on Steroids'. The term 'viral marketing' was originally penned in a newsletter by the venture capitalist behind Hotmail, Steve Jurvetson (see Mini case 11.5). He defined it as 'network-enhanced word the of mouth'. Since then the term has become 'a buzz word that is used, misused, abused, and co-opted to cover whatever marketers are trying to push' (Wilson 2000). Although the subject of the text is not strictly viral marketing, in his excellent book, *Unleashing the Ideavirus* (2001), Seth Godin uses the phrase 'digitally-augmented word of mouth'. In essence, viral marketing describes any marketing strategy or tactic that encourages individuals to pass on a marketing message to others. Successful execution means the message's exposure grows exponentially – like a **virus**. Another term used to describe the practice is **buzz marketing**, reflecting that the message creates a buzz as it is passed from person to person.

As with many online activities, it is based on a tried and tested offline business concept. Although Jurvetson used the phrase 'viral marketing' to describe an online phenomenon that was Hotmail, the notion has been around much longer. 'Word of mouth', 'referral marketing', and 'network marketing' are descriptions given to offline viral marketing. 'Turn your customers into your sales force' is another phrase that has stood the test of time. It is

MINI CASE 11.5 Viral marketing at its best

The classic example of online viral marketing is Hotmail (www .hotmail.com), which went from launch to 12 million users in less than 18 months. They spent less than $500K on marketing, advertising and promotion and grew the business by just adding 'Get Your Free E-Mail at Hotmail.com' at the bottom of each e-mail. The Hotmail concept was simple, develop a quality product, then give it away, but on every 'product' (e-mail) include a message advising readers on how to sign up for the same free service. The users did the rest.

interesting that when seeking to describe 'viral marketing' some authors use offline examples that pre-date Jurvetson's creation of the phrase. It is not difficult to see why this has happened.

Viral marketing depends on three criteria:

1. The sender is willing to receive, or they actively seek, the kudos that comes from forwarding the message.

2. The receiver must perceive value in the message (they should be pleased to receive it).

3. The originator of the message must benefit from its propagation.

Although the latter should be a given before the campaign is launched, a shortcoming in either of the other two will result in failure. For these outcomes to take place, the message must have perceived value, no one wants to be known for, or wants to receive, rubbish.

What the Internet brings to the word of mouth campaign is a medium of communication that allows people not only to communicate more easily, but one that allows the sender to communicate with more than one person at once and with the same ease. Both e-mail and the World Wide Web can be used to pass the message on:

• With e-mail, the sender needs only to type one message and with a few clicks of their mouse send that message to all 50 people in their e-mail address book. And they all get that message almost instantly.

• On the World Wide Web, a regular movie watcher could post her opinion of a new film on a number of web sites and have it read by thousands of people ('The Blair Witch Project' benefited from this). Ten years ago that same movie buff would have only been able to communicate her review to a close circle of friends.

The actual nature of the viral message will be determined by the objectives of the viral campaign. In the Hotmail example (see above), the objective is to promote the actual product and encourage users to sign up for the service themselves. More often the objective is one of brand building, with increased brand recognition being sought. The controversial 'SportKa' campaign in 2004 was aimed not only at raising the profile of the new model, but also making the car appeal to its target market.

Ford UK's campaign, called 'Evil Twin', comprised of a viral spoof (modelled on the movie, 'The Mothman Prophecies') in which the car, apparently tinged with evil, is shown on short video sequences playing evil tricks on innocent victims. These amusing 'sketches' were the 'viral' element, with viewers expected to forward them to friends. Naturally there was a link to a web site (set up by Ford) which featured free downloads of screen savers, wallpaper and posters. Unlike some viral spoofs, this one did not attempt to conceal the company behind the promotion.

The first film clip saw a parked SportKa whack a bird with its bonnet as the bird attempted to land on it. It created a minor furore from animal rights protestors, but that was nothing compared to the outcry when the second video, showing a curious cat being decapitated by the car's sunroof, hit the web. Both Ford and its ad agency, Ogilvy & Mather put out statements aimed at placating the protestors, but the subsequent publicity did little but increase further the amount of people who became aware of not only the campaign, but the new SportsKa.

The controversial element of many viral campaigns has resulted in consumer outrage over the marketing technique in some quarters. In an effort to address the issue before legislation, particularly in the US, makes the practice illegal, the Word of Mouth Marketing Association (www.womma.com) has formed an ethics committee to set up guidelines for marketers.

Ford's SportKa viral campaign is an example of common practice to include an element of controversy to attract both off and online media. This has spawned another phenomenon, the sub-viral. Sub-viral marketing involves advertisers deliberately releasing spoofs of their own ads to the web in an effort to generate online 'buzz'. An example of this was the spoofs of the Budweiser 'wassup?' advertising campaign. This involved high quality short videos that seemed to make fun of the brewing giant's global TV advertising campaign, including the UK's Royal Family taking afternoon tea and using the phrase 'wassup'. Despite their initial condemnation of the spoofs, it soon became clear that Budweiser were not totally unconnected in the sub-viral campaign.

The sub-viral depends on an aspect of both the off and online viral campaigns that is essential if the campaign is to be successful. That is the involvement of other media. Whilst viral marketing is built around consumers communicating with consumers, and the use of multiple e-mails obviously enhances this, the main conduit for a successful viral campaign is often the TV, radio, and the printed press. Reporters pick up the message and release the viral message through their own media. For a short while this has the effect of a virtuous circle. People see the story on TV, radio or in a newspaper (often as a news story, which means it meets the criteria of public relations when compared to advertising) and so seek the viral message online. They then forward it to their friends and colleagues and so the virus spreads even faster. In the longer time frame, however, this can be detrimental to the campaign. If any friends have already received the message when the media-fed user sends it out then the esteem in which the sender is held is reduced, the receiver perceives no value in the communication and so the originator receives no benefit. Hence, all three of the previously mentioned essential outcomes of a viral campaign are absent.

This is another example of how the e-marketer can draw from traditional marketing theory to aid them in their online campaigns. The brief description of how the marketing environment changes (for better and worse) as the campaign unravels is a mirror of the product life cycle (PLC) concept. In the PLC those customers who embraced the product in its 'introduction' phase, the 'early adopters' soon discard the product when it moves into the 'growth' phase. As the viral message works through its own life cycle so the nature of its audience changes. By the time the 'laggards' have received the message its effect has dwindled. By their very nature, the laggards have little interest in the message or the product (they are not actually part of the target market for the product), otherwise someone would have sent them the message earlier.

Viral marketing does not have to be as complex, however. The most common implementation is the web site or e-mail link that encourages readers to 'forward this to a friend'. Other low cost, but effective, viral efforts include:

- Signature lines on e-mails with a message so intriguing that users click through the link to a web page
- Free screensavers – there was a time around 1998 when every PC seemed to have a Guinness screensaver
- Humorous images, jokes or articles – these work best if they are industry, group or segment specific
- Desk top games – some of which involve the user 'registering' to play, so meeting a viral campaign's objective of gathering data on users.

Wilson (2000) suggests six essential elements required for a viral marketing strategy to be successful. They are that the campaign:

- Gives away something that is useful to the target market

- Provides for effortless transfer to others – obvious one-click links with text to prompt use

- Scales easily from small to very large

- Exploits common motivations and behaviours

- Utilises existing communication networks – like-minded people will use the media to communicate with their Internet community

- Takes advantage of other's resources – once launched, the viral message does not require any resource input from the originating organisation

There is, however, one significant drawback to initiating viral campaigns. Once the message is 'launched' the originating organisation has no control over it. Messages that are targeted at a particular segment, and found amusing or useful to them, can easily find their way into the in-box of another group of customers who find them to be offensive.

There is one more significant advantage that the Internet adds to traditional methods of viral marketing. Its results are measurable. Word of mouth or referral marketing can only be assessed by post-event marketing research where the people are asked whether or not the 'received or passed on a marketing message. Any message that travels over the Internet leaves a digital trail for the marketer to examine and analyse. Not only is there a trail to follow, but in many instances those participating in specific campaigns can be identified and targeted for other marketing efforts. And if the marketer wants to know what the public thinks of their, and others' viral campaigns, they can visit sites like the Viral Chart (www.viral.lycos.co.uk),

Fig 11.7 The front page of Lycos's Viral Chart

see Fig 11.7. This site tracks the hottest and newest viral campaigns and features them in top ten chart. There's also an archive and a newsletter to keep the marketer in touch.

As with other elements of marketing, both off and online, viral marketing rarely stands in isolation. Though it can be used strategically, it is more likely to be a tactical element of a wider strategy.

11.8 Public comment sites

The World Wide Web is made up of a number of different types of web site. Whilst the corporate and product site is the most common commercial web presence, these are not the only kind of site that the e-marketer can use. There are a number of sites that exist for, and thrive on, the public's interactive comments and partcipation. Sometimes referred to as 'Consumer Generated Media' (CGM), there are two types of these sites that the web marketer can consider:

1. The chat-room and/or bulletin board

2. The consumer protection site

Note, a third form of public comment site – the blog – is covered in section 11.12.

Community chat rooms, bulletin boards and consumer protection sites

Many of the community portals and web sites have bulletin boards and chat-rooms where the customers and prospects post their views on the organisation and its products. Pitta and Fowler (2005) state that online communities 'are essentially market segments whose interests are similar and much more specific that the population at large'. The e-marketer can use these in two ways:

1. Passively, purely as market research by way of monitoring customer feedback and analysing postings made by less than satisfied consumers. An extension to the concept of customers making comments on third party sites is the anti-company web site. These are sites that are usually set up by disgruntled customers. Whilst these sites can be annoying or embarrassing, they are hard to stop. Although legal recourse is available if the site includes libellous material the courts will do nothing if the site presents only facts and true events. The marketer can turn such sites to their advantage by monitoring the negative content and using it as customer feedback that can be analysed and then the appropriate action taken to address issues raised. A classic example of this is US fast food outlet Dunkin Donuts. As reported in the *Boston Globe* (25 August 1999) in an article titled, 'Big-business clout gets a dunking', the company's outlet managers were encouraged to monitor a site (www.dunkindonuts.org) set up by a disgruntled customer, David Fenton, and address issues raised in the online criticism. Dunkin Donuts eventually purchased the site from its founder to use as a mechanism for tracking negative feedback, although the content did turn into something more akin to cheery pro-donut propaganda before it was eventually closed. Even the ubiquitous Google has its detractors. Founded in 2002, the most substantial anti-Google site is Google Watch (www.google-watch.org). However, so well liked is Google that there is an anti-site for the anti-site – Google Watch

> **MINI-CASE 11.6 Beware of the public with the knowledge – and access to chat-rooms**
>
> Prior to the Internet the primary media outlets – the TV and radio – were immediately available only to the corporate voice. If a press release was a little miserly with the truth, the actual facts might never come out, or the time delay was such that the 'real' story never got the same exposure as the original flawed one. Times have changed, however, and the marketer should be aware that it has.
>
> In January 2006, a London investment bank alerted investors about the number of flights that Ryanair had cancelled, fearing that the cancellations could indicate financial problems at the budget airline. The airline responded immediately, saying that all of their flights that day (of the financial alert) had left 'as normal and on time'. This statement was picked up by airport workers and soon aviation-industry-related chat-rooms (eg the Professional Pilots Rumour Network, www.pprune.org) were reporting Ryanair cancellations and that the company's aircraft were sitting on runways at Luton, Stansted, and Liverpool airports.

Watch (www.google-watch-watch.org). Mini Case 11.6 illustrates the speed and dangers of the online grapevine.

2. Be proactive by posting their own comments. However, this must be practiced with caution. Internet users are astute and wise to marketers' efforts, and may perceive such action as opportunist sales promotion. If handled properly, the practice can produce positive results. Comments can be added either overtly or covertly.

- Overt comments would identify the organisation. For example, on a bulletin board on car repairs (there are many community, or portal, sites for specific makes of car) a user might post a message asking for advice on a specific problem. The answer might be to use a product sold by the organisation. The reply posted by the organisation would make the situation clear – the reply using the first person of the organisation – 'we make a product that will solve this fault' with contact details being included, preferably a link to a web page.

- The covert reply would take the persona of a third party (with specially registered hotmail-type e-mail address if necessary). In the example above the posting would read; 'I have had this problem and found a product that solved it quickly and easily, I bought the product online at . . .'. Again, this method should be practiced with caution. Any organisation that is caught out is likely to be black-listed by what might be a significant portion of its target market.

    This type of covert involvement can be even more dubious. Some marketers believe it is good practice to hire 'ambassadors' to push products whilst posing as consumers in chat-rooms. Similarly, the ambassadors might raise questions or usage issues about the product in order to procure market research data. Any organisation participating in such practices must weigh the potential benefits with the possibility of a consumer backlash if the practice comes to light.

Consumer review sites

Numerous sites exist that have been set up as consumer review forums. Two examples are Planet Feedback (www.planetfeedback.com) and My3Cents (www.my3cents.com). Both web sites encourage consumers to 'to learn, interact and voice opinions regarding companies, products and services' (my3cents) and advocate that companies use the sites for consumer research. A third example, Epinions (www.epinions.com) encourages customers to comment on goods and services they have purchased. An additional factor with Epinions is that it is a wholly-owned subsidiary of shopping.com (a shopping search engine), so the site also

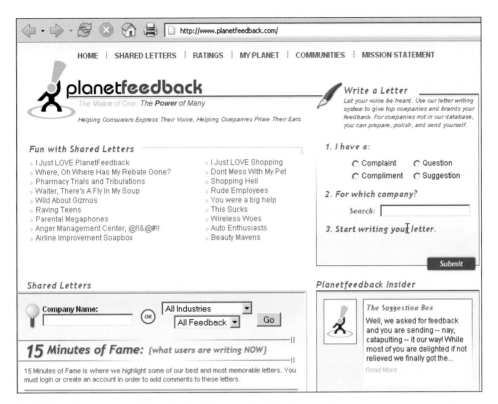

Fig 11.8 The home page of Planet Feedback (www.planetfeedback.com)

becomes a series of endorsements for the products featured on the parent company's site. Submitting reviews to such sites is a popular pass-time for many web surfers. The instantaneous nature of the web encourages people to submit comments to review-type sites such as PlanetFeedback. Research published in the US in 2004 (Raine & Paul Hitlin) suggests that around 25% of web users have submitted such comments. Table 11.1 gives further details of user rating practice.

Some of these review-type sites monitor responses from criticised organisations and publish their own comments on those responses. Those responses could be by way of a direct on-site reply to the criticism or simply to make operational changes that address problems raised. Either way, it is a smart organisation that takes these sites seriously. Any that ignore them take the chance of incurring the wrath of consumers or wasting some great free customer feedback.

11.9 Affiliate marketing

A direct relative to, but an extension of, online advertising is the use of affiliates to increase sales. With UK affiliate sales for 2006 expected to exceed £2 billion in 2006, according to E-consultancy's *Affiliate Marketing Network Buyers Guide* (2006), and an estimated 20% of online retail sales originating with affiliate marketing (AM) this is big business.

Table 11.1 Use of online rating systems

The percentage of Internet users in each category who say they have rated a product, service, or person online.

Men	29%
Women	22%
Generation	
Generation Y (Ages 18–27)	30%
Generation X (Ages 28–39)	28%
Trailing Boomers (Ages 40–49)	23%
Leading Boomers (Ages 50–58)	23%
Matures (Ages 59–68)	20%
After work (Ages 69 and above)	11%
Household Income	
Less than $30,000/yr	22%
$30,000–$50,000/yr	24%
$50,000–$75,000/yr	27%
More than $75,000/yr	33%
Education Attainment	
Less than High School	17%
High School	20%
Some College	29%
College +	30%
Internet Access at Home	
Dial-up Connection	24%
Broadband Connection	32%

Although the phrase did not exist when they first started out, Amazon stands as the epitome of successful affiliate marketing. The idea is for business A to have other businesses sell their products for them. This is, however, a rather simplistic description because it gives the impression that business A is the manufacturer of the goods. If this were the case this description would depict simple distribution of products. AM is more akin to the distribution of the 'parent' organisation, arguably a form of franchising. E-marketing writer and practitioner, Tig Tillinghast (2001) offers a more concise definition of AM, stating that affiliates 'put up banners or other types of links on their own sites in return for a proportion of the commerce generate'. Essentially, AM is an online referral programme with partners in the affiliate agreeing to a referral fee that is paid when a referred customer completes a transaction.

For an affiliate programme to work successfully, the affiliated organisation (the one publishing the sites containing the links) must be proactive and vigorously promote the product or service on offer. Ad banners are passive, sitting on the web page waiting for the user to click on them. Far more '**clickthroughs**' are made from textual links than from ad banners. For example, a football coaching web site could include an ad banner for David Beckham's autobiography. Alternatively, they could include a link in the text, something like: '. . . this is an issue that is a common problem for professional footballers, as David Beckham comments in his autobiography, the solution is not easy'. The link to the affiliate would be from the words 'David Beckham's autobiography'. Not only would the link take the user to the bookseller's site, but to the exact page for that book, meaning that the user can easily become a buyer.

Successful affiliate marketing is a partnership between advertiser and publisher, and so should be considered from both sides of the alliance. For the likes of Amazon, affiliate marketing is a significant part of their strategic marketing plan with affiliates being considered as part of the service's channel of distribution. For the affiliates, being an affiliate produces a form of direct income, in much the same way that selling space (on a web site) for advertising does.

Good practice

Organisations that are serious about using affiliates to increase sales should make every effort to help publishers generate sales from their sites. In much the same way that franchisees must help franchisers if a franchise partnership is to be mutually beneficial, so the affiliating company must help its affiliates if any affiliate partnership is to succeed. There are a number of things the advertiser should do if they are to attract quality publishers into forming an alliance through AM. The advertiser should:

- Offer a judicious affiliate programme that rewards publishers promptly and fairly

- Provide real-time online reporting of commissions earned

- Offer greater rewards for more specific referrals that are more likely to result in a sale. For example, if the referral link simply goes to the front page of the advertiser's web site then a lesser commission is paid than if the link goes to a distinct CD of a particular artist

- Offer 'lifetime' commission for referred customers. If a publisher refers a customer for a software program, then if the customer updates the program in subsequent years, the publisher should receive commission on that subsequent transaction

- Restrict the amount of affiliates employed. Although recruiting every publisher on the web might be fine for Amazon, for most advertisers it is not advisable. If an affiliate is one of thousands they are unlikely to give the required dedication to selling the product as if they are one of a 'selected few'. Again, recruitment to the programme will be endorsed by a selection procedure and an 'only the committed should apply' type recruitment campaign

- Treat affiliate publishers as part of the sales team and consider tactics used in offline sales (newsletter, promotions, gifts to top sellers and so on). Similarly, use the affiliates for feedback on products and services, again the same as organisations use sales staff or agents

- Offer support to publishers, perhaps a dedicated section of the advertiser's web site or direct e-mail or telephone contact

- Provide quality-advertising materials eg banner ads in various sizes

- Provide help with advertising 'copy' to be included within the publisher's own content. This might also include free articles or information on the product, or copies of press releases or references to web sites or offline publications that feature positive reviews of the product

- Access to the product or service eg the way a book is presented online – description, reviews, etc

- Tips on search engine optimisation. Publishers are likely to be experts in their own subject so search engine marketing training provision has a double benefit in that the publisher is happy to have an improved search engine presence, and the advertiser gets multiple entries on the search engines. There is a caveat to this point however. Using affiliates to swamp results is frowned upon by the search engines and may result in having the advertiser's site black listed.

11.10 **Public relations**

If advertising and sales promotions are aimed purely at potential and actual customers, public relations has a more diverse target. 'Not only must the company relate constructively to customers, suppliers, and dealers, but it must also relate to a large number of interested publics' (Kotler 2003). In this definition, 'public' refers to any individual or group that may have an effect on how the organisation conducts its business. Although traditionally, it is recognised that a function of public relations is 'corporate communications', it is not unusual for the role to be reversed. Many modern organisations have a corporate communications director/department that has 'public relations' as part of its function.

It is generally accepted that in a marketing context the abbreviation PR stands for 'public relations'. However, for the online marketer – as well as some who ply their trade purely offline – the same abbreviation should also be applied to 'press relations'. The two are linked, but need to be considered separately by the e-marketer.

e-public relations

Public relations communications can be split into two main categories.

1. Announcing good news
2. Counteracting bad news

In the first the marketer can be proactive. If a new extension to the factory or increase in the workforce is being announced, the event does not happen overnight, with considerable time going into the planning. With bad news the PR effort is often reactive. This means there is less time to react, and it is more likely that the 'public' will come looking for information. In the Internet age, their first stop is likely to be the organisation's web site. Following the alleged terrorist plot to blow up a number of transatlantic planes on 10 August 2006, and the subsequent disruption to air traffic, Easyjet moved quickly and e-mailed its customers to advise its passengers on new security measures, whilst seeking patience with the inevitable check-in delays.

It is important that the organisation has the appropriate content on the web site. This is in addition to published press releases and should be written for a more general public than press releases that are written for a specific audience such as journalists. The PR information can easily be integrated within the 'normal' web site content. There might be a 'news' link on the front page, or the front page could be designed so that PR-type content can be naturally included. For a company that regularly launches new products or services then there could be a 'new products' section. If an organisation has recurring problems, for example environmental issues, there could be a permanent, and updated, section of the web site that addresses PR issues without actually being given the title of 'public relations'.

e-press relations

The press, from whichever media, are often the conduit between the organisation and its 'publics'. The organisation must pay for any content that appears in newspapers or on TV or radio (which makes it advertising) but it does not pay for anything that a journalist might write in those media. The organisation should make it easy for the journalist to access information. The traditional method was for the organisation's PR department to send press releases to pertinent journalists. Previously, this would be by post, then by 'wire' or fax when there might only be a dozen newspapers that organisations might want to contact. However, the increasing volume and diversity of media made it difficult to get public relations communications to all appropriate publications and individuals in a timely and efficient manner. With the advent of the Internet, the media outlets expanded further, but the new media presented an opportunity for the PR professional as well. Enter the online and email press release.

In the early days of the Internet, the organisation simply included on its web site a 'press releases' section where all releases were presented in full. This developed into a more comprehensive section with an archive of past releases for researchers to access. Whilst key journalists could still be contacted directly, the web page made the information available to a much wider audience. The concept has additional advantages in that the press releases form a history of the organisation that can inform potential customers, suppliers or partners who might be researching the organisation. Similarly, enquiries from students, potential employees or other interested parties will be reduced if information can be accessed online.

The 'electronic press rooms' have evolved from their early days as simply a PR page on the web site. The best now include 'virtual press kits'. Designed to facilitate the journalists' thirst for easily available information, as well as the press releases, a kit will include such content as:

- An up to date list of individual press contacts within the organisation
- A frequently asked questions section
- Downloadable company logos – different sizes to suit all publications
- Details of the company, including a concise history
- Details of company locations
- Descriptions of the products or services offered by the organisation. If a press release is about a product, a 'background' to that product would be included
- Short biographies of significant staff
- A photo library – all relevant staff, products, head office, manufacturing centres, distribution centres, etc
- If the press release has been communicated verbally, audio and video clips of the event can be included. A transcript of what was said should also be available

Readers might recognise elements of an earlier chapter within the virtual press kit. In chapter 5 we considered how the web can 'help the buyers to buy'. To do this the web site should provide customers with the information that helps to meet their needs. In the press kit scenario, the journalist is the customer and the information is the product.

To cater for the growing number of online publications, each press release should be available on its own web page so that the e-journalist can include a **hyperlink** to that page in their article.

In addition to publishing on their own web site, the organisation's PR team can also make use of another online service, the news wire. Although a fee is normally involved, the online news wire services such as www.prnewswire.com makes each release available to all journalists. This service is useful for industry specific stories where journalists will check regularly for current releases or use archives for research into subjects for articles they might be writing.

Press releases should be written by those properly trained and experienced. Developing knowledge and contacts within a sector is vital for PR practitioners to achieve better coverage for their clients. Jane Lee of Dexterity (www.dexterity.co.uk) specialises in media relations for the IT industry. In Fig 11.9, Lee offers practical tips for the effective use of the Internet for PR.

Fig 11.9 PR Tips for Internet marketing

Since 1994 Jane Lee has worked under the name of Dexterity as a solo PR practitioner specialising in press relations for IT companies. During this period the Internet and e-mail have become prime tools in every aspect of the work. Here is some practical advice for using the web effectively in PR.

1. Nowadays 99% of journalists prefer press releases by e-mail, but a handful may want news on paper, so ask, do not assume.

2. Paste the text of the release into the body of the email – do NOT send as an attachment. And do not call to check if the release has arrived and/or will be used.

3. Although most journalists have a broadband connection, some (especially freelancers) are touchy about unsolicited attachments as they could be infected. Always check before sending files and keep them small.

4. Send your releases as personalised e-mails, or at the very least put your list of addresses in the BCC field of the e-mail software.

5. Journalists are bombarded with press releases so keep yours short and punchy. Consider giving the first paragraph and then a URL link to the full details and photographs.

6. Every press release should contain an 'Unsubscribe' option. And when you get such a request, update your list promptly, confirming you have done so to the sender.

7. Monitor blogs covering your client and its sector for what others think. Then you can spot trends and stave off negativity.

8. Make it your business to know which journalists prefer e-mail contact only and which are happy to be offered ideas by phone. Imagine how irksome it is if you are concentrating and the phone rings. An e-mail in contrast, is not intrusive.

9. The Internet is a fantastic research tool, so even if you have not seen a hard copy of a magazine you want to target, find its web site to work out what angle or content the editor might be interested in.

Reproduced by kind permission of Dexterity.co.uk.

MINI CASE 11.7 Online PR at Cisco

The turn of the new century saw Cisco's PR department make significant changes to its web presence. At that time the networking giant's PR content consisted of simply posting press releases, to change things they created news@cisco.com (www.newsroom.cisco.com).

The site had four goals: control the message across international borders; reach opinion leaders globally; communicate with one voice; and enhance productivity with reduced expenses. The site now consists of sections dedicated to: media resources, corporate news, product and technology news, global news, customer news, partner news, community & philanthropy news,

news releases and feature articles, and even a video archive. There is also the almost obligatory 'corporate overview'.

The content is presented with a high level of honesty, something that has resulted in favourable press coverage for events that are not always good for the company, product recalls, for example. Terry Anderson, the director of Corporate Public Relations at Cisco, estimates that the department saved approximately $5.1 million in FY04 by reducing print costs and time spent faxing news releases, answering reporters' calls, and distributing press kits.

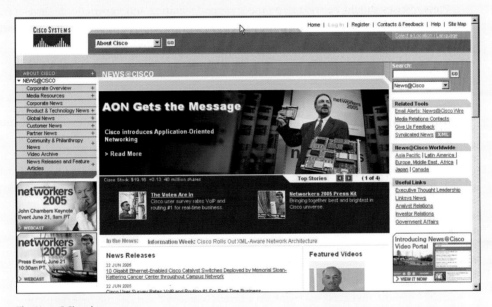

The News@Cisco home page

If releases are to appeal to journalists, they must be written in a format, with content, that will appeal. For smaller, local newspapers where journalists may be required to write on subjects outside their field of expertise, it is not uncommon for the press release to be presented almost verbatim in a publication. In these cases, a well-written 'article' is more likely to appear in the press. Mini case 11.7 illustrates the efficient side of corporate PR at Cisco.

Disaster recovery

Contingency planning, or disaster recovery, is an essential task of any PR practitioner. It is certainly true that elements of a contingency plan, such as data recovery and hard and software issues, belong in a more technically based book than this one. There is, however, a public relations aspect to any such disaster recovery plan and so the exercise should not be left to the IT department.

MINI CASE 11.8 The cost of web site down time

On 9 June 2005 Amazon.com had a complete outage lasting 41 minutes, with its homepage returning a browser error from all 15 of their worldwide locations. As Amazon.com's net sales for its first fiscal quarter, ending 31 March 2005, were $1.90 billion and with 90 days in the quarter (2,160 hours) the online retailer's income was around $8.8 million an hour, this means the shut-down could have cost them about $6 million. That figure could be higher, however, as the site was down at lunch time on the East Coast of America – prime online shopping time for office workers.

The 'disaster' might be a technical problem (like servers going down), security issues (hackers accessing customer data), being the victim of 'spoofing' (where an innocent organisation's domain name is used for spam e-mail), or operational predicaments (such as a misplaced decimal point reducing the cost of a product from £599 to £5.99). Naturally, the size of the organization and its dependency on the Internet for its income, will dictate any PR response.

For a small business that generates half a dozen leads a month from its web site, having the site 'down' for a couple of days is hardly significant. For the B2B pipe welding company, a mistyped price is more likely to generate humorous ribbing than legal initiatives. But if a company like Amazon went offline for a day or if a bank makes customer data available to third parties on their web site (and these cases have happened), then they have a potential commercial disaster on their hands (see Mini case 11.8).

Although a loss of income has to be addressed as a short-term one-off event, far more damaging is the potential loss of trust and damage to a brand name and this must be addressed by the PR team. For the smaller company this could simply be an e-mail to exist-ing customers, 'sorry for the inconvenience. . . .', but for larger companies not only should a message be included on the web site, but releases might be necessary for local, national and sector media. If you are the PR director for eBay and the site experiences problems, expect phone calls from the BBC and CNN asking when you can be interviewed. Any contingency plans should include pre-developed web site content. When required, the content could be added to an existing corporate site or it could actually be on a separate site already sitting on a server but not 'live' to the world. There might even be a number of sites developed to address different 'disasters', each one on a carefully selected domain name; companyname-infosite.com or companyname.info perhaps. Content should include such things as appro-priate contact details for customers, press releases for media use and a FAQ-type page would address the main issues that worried customers might raise. A 'contingency site' is not purely the domain of the pure online business. Such a site should be part of the offline business's response to any disaster or even adverse publicity. The contingency site's URL would be included in any response featured on any media. Whatever the scale of the disaster, or how-ever limited or comprehensive the response, it is wise to have the response prepared in advance as events arise at the most inconvenient of times. Larger organisations should have staff available on 24-hour call out to address any disaster. Although loss of brand confidence or income can never be compared to loss of life, organisations should hold airline Pan American's Lockerbie bombing experience as a worst practice example. Following the fateful explosion on board one of their jumbo jets just before Christmas 1988, rather than address-ing the needs of relatives of those involved, Pan Am remained silent for hours. This silence was followed only by a denial of any responsibility. The company's inept handling of the situation is widely considered to have been the last straw for the ailing airline. Enveloped in financial turmoil, it went bankrupt in 1991.

LEGAL EAGLE BOX 11.3 Disaster recovery

It is vital that organisations take the development and mainten-ance of the disaster recovery plan seriously. It is not a task that can be left until someone finds enough time to deal with it. A serious incident can of course occur at any time. A major part of the disaster recovery planning process is the assessment of the potential risks to the organisation which could result in the dis-asters or emergency situations themselves.

Many pieces of UK legislation impact upon information secur-ity, and require UK companies to have in place secure data man-agement and recovery solutions. Certain industry sectors are subject to Codes and Standards that require specific additional disaster recovery processes. In putting disaster recovery plans in place, it is necessary to consider all the possible incident types, and the impact each may have on the organisation's ability to continue to deliver its normal business services.

Focus areas in any disaster recovery plan should include the following:

- E-commerce processes
- E-mail based communications
- Other online services
- Production processes
- Information technology services
- Marketing and public relations
- Quality control mechanisms
- Customer service handling
- Sales and sales administration
- Business planning activities

11.11 **Commercial newsletters**

E- newsletters are vital communications tool for all organisations regardless of size or status. They provide a diverse range of PR information to stakeholders and are a vehicle to promote products, services, events and sponsorship. Clubs and societies send e-newsletters to mem-bers. Marketers can use them as a medium for adverts, but they have no control or influence over their content. Commercial newsletters, on the other hand, can be effective as part of the organisation's overall communications strategy by providing a terrific mechanism for com-municating a highly personalised blend of information, entertainment, and promotions (Brondmo 2000). In some aspects newsletters are a natural extension of an e-mail marketing campaign. The significant difference is that newsletters are not sales vehicles. Although the ultimate objective of any marketing effort must be to generate sales, a newsletter is very much 'below the line' and unlikely to be perceived as being beneficial if the content is merely sales copy. Both the sender and the receiver should be aware that a newsletter is not regular promotional e-mail. A carefully constructed newsletter should include, and can address more than one of the following objectives:

- **Brand building** – to supplement off and/or online branding strategies
- **Relationship building** – as part of a relationship marketing strategy
- **As part of a membership subscription** – perhaps as a lower cost option to a printed and posted version
- **As a supplement to a dynamic web site** – users having a regular newsletter of new stories/features to save them from having to visit the web site every day. Headlines or abridged stories are linked to the full item on the web site
- **An income stream** – rather like the advertising income model for web sites, newsletters can carry (paid for) ads or they can be sponsored. For example, a fisherman's guide might be sponsored by a fishing rod manufacturer

- **After sales service** – where the product and/or service or industry might be dynamic and so users would appreciate updates on uses or developments, eg computer games
- **Marketing research** – in exchange for regular, useful, information, subscribers may be willing to offer (more) details about themselves and their buying habits

As with e-mail mailing lists, the strength of a newsletter lies in its subscription list. Newsletters are only of value if specifically requested by the recipient. Subscriptions will only be maintained if the content of the newsletter brings something of perceived value to the subscriber. Therein lays the key to successful newsletters: they must have a consistent quality of content that is of value to the subscriber, and that is not easy to achieve. The newsletter is an important element in developing successful online relationship marketing. For registering, opt-in subscribers should be rewarded with content that they value and get pleasure from.

The production of newsletters is not something to be taken lightly by marketers. Even a monthly edition will require significant input to the content perhaps from dedicated members of staff to write and source content. Such is the commitment required, that newsletters should be considered at a strategic, rather than operational, level. It is the content that takes up the person-hours. Naturally, the content of some newsletters is more straightforward to develop than others. For example, a weekly newsletter from a travel agency web site could, effectively, be a compilation of items from their web site. For some organisations, putting together a series of interesting articles for a weekly or monthly publication requires dedication and committee otherwise it can become a dreaded chore and a sure recipe for a spiral of decline in quality, and so, subscriptions.

As well as the content, the technical elements of the newsletter must be addressed. This is almost always better if outsourced to organisations offering professional services in the field. Sending out newsletters on multiple 'blind copies' (BCC) does not present a professional approach to subscribers as they might not even get past 'spam-filters'.

The last word on the subject goes to newsletter expert Alexis Gutzman (www .alexisgutzman.com): 'Every newsletter you send out is a test of your professionalism, and a reflection on the competence of your organization'. Succinctly put, rarely observed.

11.12 **Blogging**

One of the latest developments suitable for use by the online marketer's is the 'weblog', or 'blog' – a kind of online personal journal. Although the term 'weblog' was first used by Robot Wisdom in December 1997, with the term 'blog' being introduced in 1999, the practice dates back to the early 1990s. At that time there were far fewer web sites, but without search engines, it was not so easy to find them. Bloggers were individuals who surfed the web and listed, or logged, web sites they found interesting. When the bloggers added their own comments or reviews of the sites other web users would then access influential bloggers' pages for their opinions on those web sites. The focus of the blogs very quickly moved on beyond other web sites to encompass any and all subject areas that took the interest of the bloggers. Webopedia (www.webopedia.com) defines a blog as 'a web page that serves as a publicly accessible personal journal for an individual. Typically updated daily, blogs often reflect the personality of the author'. The last six words of this definition are the key to blogging. Bloggers have attitude. They have an opinion on everything, or a specific subject, and they are not shy about letting others know their views. Companies upset bloggers at their peril – a blog is another example of consumer generated media (see Mini case 11.9).

MINI CASE 11.9 Caveat venditor. Consumer-generated justice – blogger style

When Thomas Hawk (a pen name) purchased a camera online at PriceRitePhoto.com just before Christmas 2005, the online store said the camera was in stock. Shortly afterwards he received a phone call – seemingly as part of a **bait and switch** type strategy – asking if he wanted accessories and extended warrantee to go with it. When he declined the camera suddenly became out of stock. When Hawk told the company he intended to write-up his experience on his blog, the PriceRitePhoto representative '. . . went ballistic', threatening, amongst other things, police and legal action. Hawk put his story in his blog and the story spread like wildfire, with the offline media picking it up as well as numerous online publications. In the two days following his blog, Hawk's web site had 125,000 visits – a substantial increase on the normal 5,000 visitors per day. The resulting furore saw PriceRitePhoto.com being delisted on Yahoo! Shopping and PriceGrabber.com and angry consumers attacking the store's web site. Howard Baker, a manager with PriceRitePhoto is reported to have said that the business had suffered 'millions of dollars' worth of damages in two days.

Footnote: A few weeks later, PriceRitePhoto tried a solution, re-branding itself as BarclaysPhoto.com. The strategy was not totally successful, however, as Hawk outed the company in his blog.

The blog on which this case is based is on www.thomashawk.com/2005/11/priceritephoto-abusive-bait-and-switch.html

The boom year for blogging was 2002 as it moved from minority interest into the mainstream of the Internet. Setting up a blog also became easier as online hosts, for example, www.blogger.com, provided would be bloggers with a free web-based tool and web space. 2005 saw a boom in commercial organisations using blogs as part of a marketing strategy.

The blogging phenomenon also benefited from the development of an XML based software application called **RSS**. RSS stands for either **'Rich Site Summary' or 'Really Simple Syndication'**. Whilst the former is probably the original 'technical' definition, the latter is more commonly accepted probably because it helps describe what RSS is. RSS is a way of distributing and receiving content online without using email and provides great convenience for the receiver. Publishers use RSS to distribute a 'newsfeed' to readers who have subscribed to receive that newsfeed. The term newsfeed suggests the original concept of RSS. News media providers would provide the content and subscribers would be notified whenever there was an update to the content via a desktop application. This came in the form of a short summary with a link to the full text. The BBC enables interested parties to subscribe to, and select RSS feeds via its 'Feed Factory pages (www.bbc.co.uk/feedfactory). Many organisations are now making product offerings available through RSS feeds. An example of this is Tesco's Deal of the Day. The big advantage of RSS technology is that messages are transmitted on the Internet without the use of email. In addition, because the individual signs up for the distributed content, it is a permission-based channel that overcomes legal problems with total opt-in. Although news sites like CNET (www.cnet.com) and the *Guardian* (www.guardian.co.uk) have published RSS feeds for a while, it is adaptation of the technology by bloggers that has seen RSS become popular.

Although each blog is by definition personal, their proliferation has seen the development of 'community blog' sites. Often developed by the publishers that provide the bloggers with free web space, these sites are communities of blogs on a specific subject. In Fig 11.10, an example of this New York City Bloggers (www.nycbloggers.com), a web site that features more than 3,500 locally written weblogs that are organised by subway stops. These portals of aggregated weblog sites are often more to do with developing a site that will appeal to advertisers than they are about providing a community service.

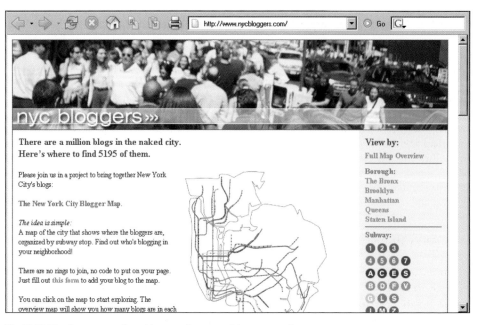

Fig 11.10 The front page of nyc bloggers (www.nycbloggers.com)

For the organisation a blog can be used as part of its online marketing efforts. Effectively, the commercial blog replaces the individual's views on life with the organisation's views on anything it wishes to. The business web log could be made available:

- On the Internet where all consumers could read the content – suitable for both B2B and B2C organizations

- On an intranet – ideal for workplace communication

- On an extranet – B2B companies can use this to keep customers or distributors informed of new developments, product uses and so on

- As a 'podcast' – incorporating any or all of the above, the information being made available in an audio format that allows listeners turn that audio content into MP3 files, which are easily downloadable on iPods (hence podcasting) or other MP3 players. This allows users to listen to blogs at their own convenience or whilst undertaking other tasks without the need to be tied to the PC. Podcasts also provide other commercial applications with feeds having the ability to carry advertising, providing presentations on specific topics or supporting the sales function with current product and price information. News and entertainment value can be enhanced with downloads such as The Times Online use of comedians and football fanatics, David Baddiel and Frank Skinner's 2006 World Cup podcasts.

For all of the above, the blog can be used to present information in a much more informal manner than is suitable in other forms of communication. Though the nature of the industry, market, or product will ultimately dictate how appropriate it is for the organisation to publish a blog, blogging can be suitable for both commercial and not-for-profit organisations.

MINI CASE 11.10 The 'Raging Cow' blog debacle

In March 2003, beverage manufacture Dr. Pepper's sought to take advantage of the blogging phenomenon by having teen bloggers feature their new 'Raging Cow' soft drink. A select group of teen bloggers and their parents were flown to Texas where they were showered with gifts and indoctrinated on how to blog the new beverage. However, this went against the ethos of blogging and when the story got out bloggers united to publicise the scam. A boycott of Raging Cow was advocated

– which may or may not have hit sales – and soon the global media were covering the 'Raging Cow blog debacle'.

The blogging plot (rightly) backfired. But did the marketing strategy?

In some quarters having the global media help announce the introduction of a new product would not be considered a bad thing.

As with web content in general, e-mail marketing and newsletters, the content of any organisational blog must be considered carefully, and therein lies the main problem for organisations considering this form of marketing communication. Blogs are easy to start, but difficult to maintain. Writing coherently is a difficult and time-consuming task. Writing with a passion is even more so and blogs should show 'attitude' or they are simply press releases. A comprehensive blogging strategy is not, therefore, a cheap option. For the commercial organisation, a blog would be a permanent, almost full time, job for a member of staff – plus back-up to cover holidays, illness, etc. In some organisations, outsourcing the blog to a professional might be the best option. Any expense comes from the marketing budget. As with web site content, the commercial blog should also be part of a managerial process in its publishing, with some kind of editorial control included. After all, like a web site, for the customer the blog *is* the organisation. Leaving the global reputation of the organisation to an unskilled member of staff is not good business.

As with **chat-rooms** and **bulletin boards** the e-marketer can use blogs as a source of information. Bloggers are usually evangelists on their chosen subject, but they are also very often early adopters who spread the word on new products. Offline market researchers spend a lot of time and money identifying and finding out the views of early adopters. Online they identify themselves and make their opinions freely available (see Mini case 11.10).

11.13 **Online sales promotions**

Strauss et al (2003) refer to sales promotions as 'short term incentives of gifts or money that facilitate the movement of products from producer to end-user.' Bickerton et al (2000) recognise that a successful online selling environment is important but the buying process itself must be effectively promoted. Sonal and Preeta (2005) suggest that the interactive nature of the Internet provides marketers with the opportunity to design sales promotions that are innovative, exciting and enjoyable. The customer involvement increases as a result the relationship between the customer and the bond is strengthened. Other advantages of net based promotions are that they can be customised and provide a faster, cost effective acquisition tool compared to traditional sales promotions primarily due to the Internet as a distribution channel. For the consumer they can download what interests them (rather than be bombarded through their physical letterbox) at a time to suit them. Like other elements of the Promotional Communications Mix, sales promotions should be designed to stimulate or achieve pre-determined goals and objectives such as:

- Building product awareness – associated with a product launch
- Generating interest – to drive web site traffic perhaps via e-mail
- Offering product information – or a product trial which serves to inform
- Generating demand – such as price reductions which can invigorate sales
- Brand building – through repeat purchases or special rewards for loyalty

Typically customers responding to a sales promotion are rewarded by marketers with more (added value) or less (reduced prices) for their purchase. Sales promotions are often linked to mainstream advertising and take advantage of such things as:

- Free products or services trials
- Competitions, prize draws, games, etc
- Seasonal discount, volume discount, introductory discount, cash back and e-coupons
- Free gifts
- Loyalty schemes including rewards schemes

However, in the UK, practitioners must abide by the British Code of Advertising, Sales Promotion and Direct Marketing, which came into force on 4 March 2003. The Institute of Sales Promotion (www.isp.org.uk) provides best practice guidelines on all aspects of sales promotion and should be followed. The Institute also offers a legal advisory service for any organisation contemplating a sales promotion campaign.

Bickerton et al split sales promotion into two main types:

1. **Strategic Sales Promotion** – where timely activities are designed to support key campaigns scheduled in the marketing plan. Sampling is a valuable strategic tool in terms of changing purchase behaviour or introducing new products. The Internet has been used effectively by various cosmetics to survey females about hair and skincare products and with the data gathered, relevant product samples are sent to respondents. However, with the digital nature of the Internet it lends itself especially well to digital products such as software or music where demo versions of software or track samples can be offered to entice a customer into purchasing the full product. For gaming enthusiasts they can trial the latest offerings at web sites like www.worthdownloading.com.

   In an interesting turnaround for the photographic industry, obtaining prints from digital cameras and their memory cards has become a phenomenon in 2006. Companies like Snapfish (www.snapfish.com), part of HP, and Pixmania (www.pixmania.com), part of the Fotovista group, have heavily promoted their photo downloading services. The typical introductory offer to entice prospects into trying the service for the first time has been the offer of 20 prints to try out the service. Will they become established brands to rival Kodak and Fuji?

2. **Tactical Sales Promotion** – is more short term and reactive to markets, competition and objectives. Sampling, e-coupons, price reductions, free gifts and competitions are the main tools applied online. Britain has been known as a nation of coupon clippers but now we are beginning to download increasing volumes of e-coupons. They can be used in various ways. First, e-coupons can be downloaded and printed to redeem in-store. Second, they often have a code incorporated that can be redeemed at the online check out

and discounted against the advertised price. Alternatively, some online merchants also provide vouchers with the despatched order to reward loyalty and to encourage repeat purchases. Again, the value of the voucher is redeemed using a code at the checkout stage. The merchant must make the terms of the coupon usage clear both the consumer and retailers or any other third party involved. For example, is there any minimum order value, the actual monetary value (eg 0.001p) or a limited time period offer or any fulfilment costs associated with its usage. Third party intermediaries like e-Coupons (www.ecoupons.co.uk) and Vouchercodes.com (www.vouchercodes.com) trawl the Internet for voucher codes and deals that the consumer can benefit from online. Vouchers are open to abuse by counterfeiters and unscrupulous consumers and retailers. Blundo et al (2005) discuss a whole range of issues regarding secure e-coupons such as protection from e-coupon double spending and proof of purchase that require security checks such as verifying individual voucher serial numbers against the individual customer it was issued to.

Sales promotions can also offer timely seasonal discounts. In Fig 11.11 Cottages4You (www.cottages4you.co.uk) provided a topical offer during the 2006 World Cup whereby each customer received a £20 discount of their booking for every goal England scored in each game. This was quite a safe gamble on their part following Sven Goran Eriksson's defensive-minded squad selection. Whilst there is a tendency to focus on sales promotions role in product adoption, brand building and market penetration, it also has another role to play at the other end of the sales cycle when it can be used to shift excess stock on less than successful lines.

Fig 11.11 Cottages4You

11.14 **Automation for online sales**

The final step in the buying process online is the completion of the sales transaction. The amount of effort that the organisation puts into selling its product(s) is dependent on the nature of the product and the market in which it trades. For a potato crisp manufacturer the emphasis is on distribution. Once the crisps are on the retailers' shelves the goods, with the aid of advertising and appropriate packaging, they sell themselves. For white goods manufacturers, distribution and advertising are also important, as is the direct selling in the showroom. For an original equipment (OE) car component manufacturer there is no self-service element, and distribution issues only arise after the sale is confirmed. With this kind of product, in this kind of market, a long and complex negotiated sales agenda must be undertaken. Naturally then, some products lend themselves to automated online purchasing, and others do not. In chapter 5, we considered the buying process models that customers might go through in order to make a purchase. Depending upon the product, customers are either willing to make an automated online purchase, whilst for other products they might research the product online but make the purchase in-store.

In the B2C market, the success of certain online retailers gives a clue to what products might be sold automatically, without human inputs in the process. Books and CDs are obvious examples of products that are easy for the buyer to self-select online. (See also the section on de Kare Silver's ES test in chapter 9). The latest Dan Brown, Nick Hornby or Kathy O'Beirne book cannot be mistaken as anything else, and a fan is unlikely to mistakenly purchase a book by a different author. Humans only get involved at the packaging and dispatch stage. Intangible products like domain name registrations, for example, lend themselves to sales automation. The seller's software is set up so that buyers can only register valid names, the buyer chooses a name, when its availability is confirmed payment details are taken and e-mail confirming completes the transaction.

For the B2C consumer, automated online sales bring convenience and speed, but they rarely repeat their purchases. One copy of a specific novel would normally be enough for even the most ardent fan of the author. An exception to this is grocery shopping, where a significant percentage of a monthly 'shop' is repeat purchases. The online retailer assists the consumer by allowing automated 'baskets' to be set up by the shopper. Once established the shopper actually has no need to peruse all the products available, they simply click on the 'confirm order' button – adding non-repeat purchases if they wish.

Automated sales in B2B markets provide value to both the buyer and vendor. In the earlier example, the original sales negotiations for an OE car component might take months, but once the car manufacturer agrees the deal, they will want frequent repeat orders for 'just-in-time' operations. In many B2B transactions the sales procedure is more likely to be one of 'order acquisition' rather than one of a true sales nature. It is this notion that sales are not one-off events that is fundamental to the e-business concept. Kalakota and Robinson (1999), e-Business: Roadmap for Success, make this point by saying that 'By approaching sales or "order acquisition" as a process rather than as a function, companies will begin to see things from their customers' point of view'.

The automated order acquisition process is of great value to the industrial buyer. The advantages come in three guises:

1. The fully automated sales process, where the buyer places an initial order online then sets repeat delivery dates. Any changes can also be made online.

2. The semi-automated process, where the buyer sets up their own 'order sheet' and then only needs to visit the web page and enter quantities for the order to be processed.

3. The brochure-type site where the buyer, in their own time and convenience, scrolls through the products available and enters quantities for the goods they want providing a workplace form of self-service.

There is another 'fully' automated method of purchase, but one that is more part of a distribution process than a sales procedure. Using an Internet connection, the buyer's computer places an order with the vendor's computer when a pre-determined stock level is reached. After the stock quantity is determined there is no human input to the process.

11.15 Integrating multi-channel strategies

Although the title of this section refers to 'strategies', the content is divided into three sections, only one of which carries the term 'strategy'. The reasoning behind this is that although the first two elements (retailing and communications) are actually parts of an overall marketing strategy, they can both be strategic in their own right.

Multi-channel retailing

In chapter 5, buying process models were discussed in some depth. The purchase behaviour chart included in that section suggests there are around 30 options available to the buyer in the way in which they research, purchase, and take possession of (ie collect or have delivered) products. That chart highlights the fact that the contemporary retailer must consider the Internet as part of any retail strategy. Even if the retailer has no web presence, it is likely that they will carry stock that is reviewed, described, or sold online.

Success in pure (online only) Internet retailing is rare. Amazon is the one obvious example, but few others spring readily to mind. Even successful online niche retailers – an aspect of business that has benefited enormously from the way the Internet has opened up new markets – are usually based on an existing offline business, be it bricks and mortar or mail order.

Although slow to recognise, and accept, the Internet's impact on their industry, traditional retailers are still fragmented in their use of the new medium. Famous names like British Home Stores (www.bhs.co.uk) have a web presence but do not sell products online, whilst others such as Halfords (www.halfords.co.uk) offer far fewer products online than they have available in-store. There are, however, a number of notable examples of how off and online retailing efforts can be combined to provide customer satisfaction (lest we forget, the objective of all businesses). Perhaps the UK retailer that has taken the Internet most seriously is grocery giant Tesco (Fig 11.12), with its online grocery business – tesco.com – topping annual sales of more than £1,000m in 2005. However, whilst the major retailers have accepted the Internet, only 3% of smaller retailers trade online. (Computerweekly.com 17/8/04)

Successful pure online retailing is determined by the nature of the product. For example, books and CDs are easily identified by, and distributed to, customers. For successful **clicks and bricks retailers** – those that have a combination of physical and web based stores – the nature of the product seems to have little influence. The main reason for this is that such

Fig 11.12 The front page of the Tesco web site (www.tesco.com)

businesses can 'sell' their goods online and have the customer collect them from a bricks and mortar outlet. This takes on board both recognized definitions of the term 'sell'. A web site can *sell* a product by (a) giving potential customers the information and advice they need to make a buying decision and/or (b) conducting a transaction.

According to a joint study in the USA by Fry Inc., comScore Networks Inc. and the E-Tailing Group Inc (2005) – described by them as the 'first evolution of the multi-channel consumer study' – one third of consumers often 'shop the web', then go to a store to make a purchase. Also in the USA, retail giant Sears has operated what it calls 'fusion retailing' for several years, letting customers shop online with the option of home delivery or collection from a local store. Around 40% of Sear's business is conducted this way, with the ratio going up to 60% for some high value items such as sporting goods and garden products (Cebuhar 2003). What is more, almost a quarter of all customers who collect online orders make additional purchases worth $200 while they are at the store collecting those goods.

Obvious contenders for integrated retailing are the so-called 'catalogue' stores. Prior to the Internet, Argos for example, sold its goods by giving away catalogues listing all their products and then having customers call at a shop to purchase and collect their pre-selected goods. This method is still their primary way of conducting business, but now the customer can go online to view products (instead of reading the printed catalogue). As well as going to the store to purchase and collect their selections, they now have the additional options of purchasing online and having goods delivered and purchasing online and collecting goods. For selected goods, in-store availability can be checked online so as to prevent wasted journeys for out of stock items.

The offline-online experiences of Argos and Sears are just two examples that have helped alleviate retailer's fears in the early days of the Internet – that the web does not cannibalise offline sales. Indeed, as these two examples testify, used properly the Internet can complement offline sales efforts.

Multi-channel communications

This represents yet another aspect of marketing that is perceived by some as being born of the Internet era, but that has been around for a while. For example, in the fifties and sixties the Disney Corporation used what they referred to as 'synergy' to coordinate marketing applications in print, films, TV, merchandising and the company's theme park near Los Angeles. Each element of the organisation's marketing mix was cross-promoted to build the brand and increase income.

At the time of writing – and probably for a few more years to come – there is one main barrier to integrated off and online communications strategies. And no, technology is not the guilty party. Humans are. Or more accurately, the human nature of those working in the advertising industry is to blame. In too many instances online advertisers and offline advertisers (currently) sit in separate camps. And they do not speak to each other. One thinks the other is an upstart newcomer who owes everything to the traditional advertising industry. The second sees the other as a dinosaur whose days are numbered. Both are wrong. Online advertising is a natural offspring of traditional marketing, it is not a brand new blank canvas with no laws or guidelines. Those laws or guidelines come from the offline marketer. Traditional marketers have much to offer the online advertiser. In an evolutionary way, traditional advertisers will adapt to the new challenges coming their way. They have done so before (print to radio, radio to TV) they will do so again. But the traditional marketers need a push. That push is coming (and will continue to come) from quality research that proves that not only does Internet marketing work, but Internet advertising in tandem with offline marketing works as well.

Independent research company Dynamic Logic (dynamiclogic.com), for example, have conducted cross-media research that suggests that brand awareness can increase by 50% when online is combined with TV advertising.

Integrated marketing strategies

There are a number of ways in which the marketer can combine use of the Internet with other elements of the marketing mix. For example:

- Using a web presence to enhance a marketing message made in other media
- Using sponsorship of offline events to publicise web sites
- Using referral to web sites from ads in other media to:
  - Reinforce the marketing message
  - Provide potential customers with further product information
  - Further explain availability eg locations of retail outlets where the product can be purchased

Fig 11.13 Marmite (www.marmite.com)

- Provide a point of purchase
- Create interest, or intrigue, offline with potential customers being directed to a web site to satisfy their curiosity – rather like a 'teaser' campaign
- Using a web site as a point of contact for applying for a promotional offer
- Using e-mail to:
  - Reinforce a marketing message originating in another medium
  - Confirm an order made in another medium
  - Respond to an enquiry or complaint made in another medium
- Buy search engine placements to coincide with offline promotions. For example, potential customers might catch only part of a radio advert or PR-generated news item and revert to the world wide web to make further enquiries, typing into the search engine the catch-phrase, tag line or any prominent element of the piece they have heard
- Using a web presence to develop a relationship with customers that has been initiated offline

Integrated campaigns can work particularly well if they utilise the less formal nature of the web that encourages a light-hearted approach. A good example of this is meat paste product Marmite, which – mirroring the offline campaign – actually makes fun of itself on its own web site. Since around 1996 Marmite have run a successful 'love-hate' marketing campaign. Early in 2005 they extended this to the Marmite web site (www.marmite.com). The landing page (Fig 11.13) offers users the choice of entering the love or the hate site. The 'love' site offers different ways to enjoy Marmite, the 'hate' site provides joke recipes and cartoon graphics of people being sick.

One thing is certain, inclusion of the Internet in any marketing strategic of the future, or even the present, will not be optional.

11.16 **Summary**

This chapter considered the role of the Internet beyond that of a promotional vehicle with its role being considered in the context of both strategic and tactical marketing communication efforts. A significant advantage that the Internet has when used in a sales capacity is its ability to automate the sales process, particularly in a B2B environment. Particulars of this were covered before a number of key elements of how the Internet can contribute to marketing strategies were addressed in detail. First, how e-mail can be used as a medium for direct marketing, followed by the concept of viral marketing. Online advertising was addressed in detail with aspects covered including; how online advertising space is purchased, the types of online advertising, where ads can be placed and what formats they can take. The marketer's use of the web's facility for hosting public comments is examined next with Internet applications for public relations also being addressed. The scrutiny of web-based communications concludes with a look at email newsletters and the marketing potential of a new phenomenon, the blog. The chapter concludes with a reflection of how the Internet can be used as part of an integrated multi-channel marketing effort.

END OF CHAPTER CASE STUDY The web: magnifying the power of word of mouth, says BuzzMetrics

Lest marketers forget, a new study by research firm BuzzMetrics Inc. is a reminder that the online channel is more than a sales and product research vehicle, it is also a public forum where consumers exchange unedited information that can have a powerful effect on brand. The research firm's study showed that a consumer watchdog group's 2003 lawsuit against Kraft Foods over its use of controversial trans-fat in Oreo cookies – for a time – focussed virtually all online consumer mentions of the product on trans-fat.

The takeaway for marketers is that while word of mouth has always affected brand perception, it has greater power now because society is more networked via the web – and because in the online environment, word of mouth can now be measured, says John Carson, CEO of BuzzMetrics.

'Before the lawsuit, the talk about Oreos online was a smattering of different things – Oreo recipes, coupons and promotions, Oreo mentioned as a vice by people who were dieting,' he says. 'After the lawsuit, the discussion involving Oreos was 90% about trans-fat. If you look at the influence on the overall talk value – what gets people talking about a product – it was a huge shift, and not a positive one for the brand overall.'

The answer for marketers is to get involved in the online discussion – with caveats. The biggest challenge to marketers is to view online discussion such as blogs, user group forums and the like not as marketing channels, but as a conversation channel. Because brands are so actively discussed online, the brands themselves have a place in those discussions, but brand participation must be on consumers' terms, Carson says.

Consumer backlash against brand participation in online consumer forums can be avoided if the brand's representative enters the discussion clearly identified as a brand employee, with his or her presence in the discussion – for instance, to be an informa-

tion resource on behalf of the company – clearly explained, Carson says. As examples, he cites the software and auto industries. For years, he says, they have employed advocates to meet consumers on behalf of the brand in real life, such as at user and customer meetings. Today they represent their brands in online discussions as well.

BuzzMetrics supports word of mouth brand positioning with proprietary software that tracks what consumers are saying online. Its spidering software crawls blogs, online user groups, and other public online forums to find mentions of its clients' brands, data it puts into a standard format and then uploads to a database. A team of human editors then uses software-aided search of that database to sort brand mentions by date, location, user ID and other markers, to develop a detailed picture of how the brand is being discussed online. The Oreo study, for example, drew from more than 2.6 million comments from 120,000 consumers. Carson says, 'The shift now is that marketer need to think about not just the messaging they are putting out there, but also about what is going to happen to that message – how will consumers take it, make it their own, and pass it forward'.

Reprinted from InternetRetailer.com with permission, copyright 2004, Vertical Web Media LLC.

Questions

1. Consider how many elements of marketing strategy are touched on – directly or indirectly – in the narrative.

2. Consider the last sentence in the case study. Now pick an organisation of your choice – your employer or university for example – and comment on the implications of the sentence's sentiments on that organisation.

DISCUSSION QUESTIONS

1. Spam e-mail is universally disliked. Discuss the notion that no reputable organisation would use it as part of their marketing strategy.

2. The most successful viral campaigns are those that include an element of controversy that might be damaging to the brand. Discuss why famous brands (like Ford) take the risk of using such strategies.

3. Why do so many organisations misuse or ignore the Internet as part of an integrated communications strategy? Discuss.

REFERENCES

Bickerton, P, Bickerton, M & Pordesi, V (2000) *Cybermarketing*, 2nd edition, Butterworth Heinemann, Oxford, UK, 243

Blundo, C, Cimato, S & De Bonis, A (2005) Secure e-coupons, *Electronic Research*, Vol 5, 117–139

Brondmo, HP (2000) *The Eng@ged Customer: The New Rules of Internet Direct Marketing*, HarperCollins Publishers

Burns, E (2006) *U.K. Ad Revenue Driven By Online*, www.clickz.com/news/article.php/3610186.

Cartellieri, C, Parsons, AJ, Rao, A & Zeisser, MP (1997) The real Impact of Internet advertising, in Sheth, JN, Eshghi, A & Krishnan, *Internet Marketing*, (2001) Harcourt Inc, Orlando, FL, US, 291

Carton S *Alternate Reality Gaming and You* 21 March 2005. Available on www.clickz.com/experts/ad/lead_edge/article.php/3491191

Cebuhar, C (2003) cited in *E-tailers Send Shoppers Back to the Mall*, available on www.Internetnews.com/ec-news/article.php/3289541

E-Consultancy (2006) *Affiliate Marketing Networks Buyers Guide*, www.e-consultancy.com/publications/affiliatemarketing-networks-buyers-guide/

Godin, S (2001) *Unleashing the Ideavirus*, Do You Zoom Inc

Godin, S (1999) *Permission Marketing*, Simon & Schuster Adult Publishing Group

IPT Email Marketing Survey (2004). Available on www.ipt-ltd.co.uk.

Kalakota, R & Robinson, M (1999) *E-Business: Roadmap for Success*, Addison Wesley

Kotler, P (2003) *Marketing Management*, Prentice Hall

Luthi, J (2004) *Affiliate Marketing: A Buyer's Guide*. Available online at www.e-consultancy.com accessed April 2004

Merisavo, M, Raulas, M (2004) The impact of e-mail marketing on brand loyalty, *Journal of Product & Brand Management*, Vol 13, No 7, 2004, 498–505

Nielsen, J (2004) *The Most Hated Advertising Techniques*. Available online at www.useit.com/alertbox/20041206.HTML

Nielsen/NetRatings (2003) *The State of Online Advertising*. Available on www.nielsen-netratings.com

Nicovich, S & Cornwell, TB (1998) An Internet culture?: Implications for marketing, *Journal of Interactive Marketing*, cited in Richardson P, (2001) *Internet Marketing*, McGraw-Hill

Pitta, DA & Fowler, D (2005) Internet community forums: an untapped resource for consumer marketers, *Journal of Consumer Marketing*, Vol 22, No 5, 265–274

Raine & Hitlin (2004) *The use of Online Reputation and Ratings Systems*, Pew Internet & American Life Project. Available on www.pewInternet.org.

Rowley, J (2001) Remodelling marketing communications in an internet environment, *Internet Research, Electronic Networking Applications and Policy*, Vol 11, No 3, 203

Solomon, MR, Marshall, GW & Stuart, EW (2006) *Marketing: Real People, Real Choices*, Pearson Education Inc., Upper Saddle Road, New Jersey, US, 371

Sonal, K & Preeta, V (2005) Practices, perceptions and avenues of Net promotions, *Electronic Research*, Vol 5, 401–424, Springer Science & Business Media

Sterne, J & Priore, A (2000) *E Mail Marketing*, John Wiley & Sons, New York, 201

Strauss, J, Ansary, AI & Frost, R (2003) *E-Marketing* (3rd edn), Pearson Education Inc., New Jersey, 382

Tillinghast, T (2001) *Tactical Guide to Online Marketing*, Tactical Guides Publishing

Vile, D and Collins, J (2004) *Email: Business or Pleasure?* Quocirca Ltd Available on www.theregister.co.uk.

Weischedel, B, Matear, S, Deans, K. (2005) A qualitative approach to investigating online strategic decision making, *Qualitative Market Research: An International Journal*, Vol 8, No 1, 2005 61–76

Wilson, RF (2000) *Demystifying Viral Marketing*. Available online at www.wilsonInternet.com/ebooks

Yoo, CY & Kim, K (2005) Processing of animation in online banner advertising: the roles of cognitive and emotional responses, *Journal of Interactive Marketing*, Vol 19, No 4, Autumn 2005, 18–34

FURTHER READING

Godin, S (2001) *Unleashing the Ideavirus*. Do You Zoom Inc. – this book takes the concept of viral marketing several stages further. A very good read for both budding entrepreneurs and viral marketers.

Seybold, P (1998) *Customers.com*, Random House – an excellent text on how e-technology can be used to meet customer needs. The section on how American Airlines adopted the web is a case study of how it should be done.

Sterne, J & Priore, A (2000) *E-mail Marketing*, John Wiley & Sons, New York

Tillinghast, T (2001) *Tactical Guide to Online Marketing*, Tactical Guides Publishing – although the title suggests that the book addresses all aspects of online marketing, it actually concentrates on online advertising. It does provide, however, a very 'hands-on' account of using the world wide web as a medium for advertising.

Weil, D (2004) *The Beginner's Guide to Business Blogging*. Available online at www.BeginnersGuideToBlogging.com.

WEB LINKS

Alexis Gutzman (**www.alexisgutzman.com**) – advice on producing newsletters

Dafermos George N *How Weblogs are Turning Corporate Machines into Real Conversations* – a combination of theoretical contemplation and practical advice from an ex-student of the author. Available on **www.opensource.mit.edu/papers/dafermos3.pdf**

E-consultancy (**www.e-consultancy.com**) – research, information, training and events on best practice online marketing and e-commerce

Larry Chase's Search Engine for Marketers (**www.searchengineformarketers.com**) – this site does what it says on the tin, offering reviews and links to the top sites in 40 marketing categories

Marketingexperiments.com (**www.marketingexperiments.com**) – offer free copies of their extensive research results

Marketingprofs.com – excellent e-marketing content, though terminology used and models/theories quoted mean the articles are mainly for readers with a background in marketing

The Institute of Sales Promotion – **www.isp.org.uk/** provides best practice advice on all aspects of sales promotion

Wilsonweb.com – the author of this site, Dr Ralph Wilson, is something of an evangelist in more ways than one (e-business and religion) with some good content and sound practical advice

Wordbiz – advice and tips from long time expert in e-newsletter and blogging, Debbie Weil (**www.wordbiz.com**)

www.warc.com The World Advertising Research Center offers news, information and cases on all aspects of marketing communications

 Visit the Online Resource Centre which accompanies this book, for lots of interesting additional material, including self-assessment questions, internet exercises, and links for each chapter: **www.oxfordtextbooks.co.uk/orc/gay/**

Online Distribution and Procurement

12

Learning objectives

By the end of the chapter you will be able to:

- Describe the main issues in distribution channel management
- Understand the impact of e-commerce upon the place element in the mix
- Comprehend the affects of the Internet and related technologies upon the value chain and supply chain
- Understand the importance of the fulfilment function for successful online relationships
- Evaluate the benefits and processes associated with e-procurement

Chapter at a glance

12.1 Introduction

This chapter will consider traditional issues associated with the management of the distribution function. The transformational effects on distribution strategies and policies of new technology applications in electronic markets will be addressed. We will also reflect on the demands of the new interactive market and the challenges that it brings in terms of real time customer expectations and 24:7 opening for the distribution and logistics functions. We will also address the added value, performance and cost efficiencies created by disintermediation, reintermediation outsourcing and e-procurement. Intranets and Extranets play vital roles in the new distribution networks such as disseminating HR policies and knowledge management internally whilst linking supply chain partners externally such as Tesco's Information Exchange.

The distribution function has traditionally concentrated on the movement of goods but the Internet has facilitated the movement and flow of information and services, as well as providing a new channel of distribution. This is highlighted in Mini case 12.1 of the National Health Service IT programme below:

MINI CASE 12.1 NHS Goes digital

The National Health Service (NHS) has gambled £6.2 billion (€9.067 billion) on technology to deliver a new integrated IT system to modernise patient care for England's 50 million residents. The project could serve as a model for other countries in the industrialised world.

The NHS is bureaucratic and particularly backward in terms of IT. The government vision is for a modern, efficient health service 'designed around the patient'. The NHS IT programme, the National Programme for IT (NPfIT) is embarking on one of the biggest information technology projects ever tackled. The aim is to wire every hospital, clinic and doctor's office across England with every resident's records stored on a central database, accessible via broadband across the country. The NPfIT aims to use the Internet as a means of information distribution between different NHS organisations. Doctor appointments, referrals and prescriptions will all be done online with links to pharmacies (Electronic Transmission of Prescriptions (ETP)).

The ambitious integration of disparate systems is the responsibility of the Department of Health agency, NHS Connecting for Health. Secure, accurate data will enable faster diagnosis and treatment of patients. The provision of a centralised e-mail allows rapid transfer of patient information. A Picture Archiving and Communications System (PACS) support this with digital imaging such as X-ray and scans providing quicker and better diagnosis. The system provides a key link between hospital and general practitioner for better post-operative care. It is intended that the patients themselves will eventually have Internet access to their entire NHS records via a secure NHS gateway.

The US and European governments are taking a keen interest in how the project may improve efficiency. One key advantage has been the cost savings generated by central purchasing of core systems, estimated at £3.8 billion (€5.5 billion), from the main service providers such as BT, Computer Sciences Corp, Accenture and Fujitsu. However, cost control for such a massive

programme is essential and Richard Grainger, Head of the NPfIT has informed suppliers that overruns will not be tolerated and they could be dropped from the project.

Patient confidentiality is an important issue and the NHS overcame potential problems by creating an 'audit trail' to show which part of the patient's record was accessed, when and by whom. They will also be able to control the sensitive or personal aspects of their records that they do not want every medical practitioner or health care worker to see such as mental health problems or an abortion.

By the end of 2008, the system is expected to handle 5 billion transactions a year, including electronic appointments, prescriptions and access of patient records. In the 2005 annual report, Richard Granger, the NHS IT Director General reported on project achievements such as:

– February 2005 saw the first electronic prescription issued.

– Over 30,000 clinicians are registered NHS Care Records Service data users.

– The Quality Management and Analysis System (QMAS) providing IT support for General Practitioners (GP's) has over 20,000 registered users across 8,800 practices.

In 2006, this mammoth project is not without its difficulties and it remains to be seen whether the vision of the patient centred system will materialise.

Sources: NHS IT programme set to ditch failing suppliers, www.management.silicon.com/government/ 0,39024677,39128976,00.htm
www.egovmonitor.com/node/1420
NHS Connecting for Health Fact Sheet, www.connectingforhealth.nhs.uk/publications/toolkitjuly05/ corp_brochure_guide_to_npfit.pdf
The *Wall Street Journal*, Europe, A1 & A6, 3 December 2003.

MINI CASE 12.2 It's in the post

A 2001 survey of 102 web-based operations by West Midlands Trading Standards found the following disturbing results about distribution and fulfilment performance:

- 33% failed to confirm receipt of order
- 50% failed to confirm despatch
- 38% did not arrive on time
- 17% did not arrive at all

12.2 Internet distribution issues

Distribution, logistics and purchasing activity have been at the cutting edge of information technology and interorganisational relationships, especially within the B2B sector with exchange and auction business models. The Internet is an effective distribution channel for the delivery of digital products by electronic means with minimal costs through a virtual network. However, attention has focussed on the changing channel interactions between manufacturers, service providers, suppliers, distributors and consumers of physical products. Many web visionaries predicted a far-reaching reformation of the supply chain with the elimination of layers of intermediaries (**disintermediation**). This reduced transaction costs as customers went 'direct'. However, other layers have emerged (**reintermediation**) with cybermediaries or infomediaries performing distribution activities especially information exchange, brokering and selling information products.

Electronic markets have the potential to carry out numerous channel activities from the provision of promotional product information to payment transactions and post-sales support. Linking front and back office operations across functions and any location through systems integration is critical for effective internal and external operations. Data integration is increasingly important in the multi-channel world that now exists. Information flows are essential for the effective management of customer relationships (CRM). However, the Internet has not been without its channel problems. For example, many early online operators failed to meet customer expectations as they lacked the logistics expertise and established infrastructure of physical firms. Failure to deliver on time is inexcusable and damaging. Findings from a West Midlands Trading Standards Survey in 2001 (Mini Case 12.2) illustrate the well-publicised service problems of new Internet players from 1999–2002. Whilst the distribution function for most online players has improved significantly, and indeed is extremely efficient in some cases, some are slow and lack transparency in tracking orders.

The Internet also raises more fundamental problems of channel conflict as traditional partners are removed. Consequently, the added value offered by the Internet as a distribution channel must be offset against negative factors. As Reynolds (2001) argues 'a robust, fail-safe logistics and fulfilment management system (LFMS) is the only way for an e-business to be successful in this new competitive landscape'. Speed to market will be critical.

12.3 The distributive environment

Brassington and Petitt (2003) state that, 'Part of the responsibility of marketing oriented organisation is to get the product to the customer in the right place at the right time' In modern cost-driven economies, we can also add 'at the right price' to incorporate the purchasing function generally, and e-procurement specifically.

Channel decisions are inextricably linked to other 'mix' decisions. They impact upon on the availability and storage of goods, total cost, final selling price, and promotional activity. It has tremendous commercial potential to drive out costs whilst delivering competitive advantage. Creativity and innovation in channel decision-making is every bit as important as any product, price and promotion decisions. Marketing is no longer a discrete functional area or silo, but an important element in the value chain now supported by web services. As both online customers and competitors are regularly described fast and unpredictable, the focus for organisations and management writers has been on **'business agility'**. Cited in Mason et al (2002) Veermani and Joshi define the concept as 'the ability to respond quickly and effectively to satisfy customers'. Harvey (2003) cites the Unisys survey of European business executives where 70% believed that companies with the capability to respond fastest to shifting business models, technologies and processes would beat those driven purely by cost efficiencies. There has been a shift from traditional batch production due to shorter product lifecycles and increased product customisation. Consequently, the pressures on the supply chain are intense. IT systems provide better communications and real-time information sharing across functional areas and with supply chain partners. The organisation has a better chance of satisfying the consumer seeking choice, availability and value. Glazer in Sheth et al (2001) discusses 'marketing in an information intensive environment' and the value of what a firm knows to help the exchange process. He cites three sources requiring integration:

1. **Downstream**: between firms and customers, including channel intermediaries (distributors)
2. **Upstream**: between the firm and its suppliers
3. **Internal**: information held internally within the organisation and ideally shared and accessible across functions

Glazer argues that as information value increases, then the traditional support role played by intermediaries becomes more important. Resellers have closer relationships with customers through transactions and interactions such as communications and customer service. The future of these relationships depends upon the organisation's ability and desire to eliminate channel layers.

12.4 **Traditional distribution management issues**

The Place element within the Marketing Mix revolves around the physical movement of goods and decisions on intermediaries. However, the distribution function is complex and includes a diverse range of activities outlined below:

Typical Intermediary functions

- **Marketing information** – collecting, distributing and analysing marketing research information such as historical sales data about the players within the organisation's marketing environment.
- **Facilitating the exchange process** – identifying buyer's needs in terms of product categories, quantities, range, etc and devising manufacturing, inventory and packaging schedules to fit.
- **Linking many suppliers** to facilitate extra consumer choice
- **Promotional activities** – setting promotional objectives and activating the various elements of the marketing communications mix and measuring their effectiveness. This includes identifying and communicating with prospects

- **Pricing** – establishing terms and conditions of sale at each stage of the value chain such as prices, leasing or rental arrangements
- **Managing risk** – analysing and sourcing the resources needed for involvement in the channel, the degree of control and influence and the potential benefits such as revenue and profit generation
- **Physical Distribution Management** (PDM) – managing the transportation, all aspects of warehousing management and information flows

Intermediaries execute the activities described above linking producers, other intermediaries and end-users together. In order to reduce channel competition and conflict, a channel member may seek greater control through merger, acquisition or alliance at different channel levels. This is referred to as a **vertical marketing system** (VMS). Ford (US) was famous for purchasing key automotive suppliers in the US to control costs and guarantee the availability of key components. Organisations may withdraw from a vertically integrated market by choice or by legislation such as Whitbread's in the brewing industry. Industry restructuring increased international competition and the 1992 Beer Orders meant the sectors financial returns were no longer attractive. Concentration on core competences has been a management mantra in the last decade. The investment and expertise required to sustain vertical integration is onerous. Firms are looking more to connect the skills and proficiency through the development of robust channel partnerships and networks, for example through third party direct despatch, which reduces inventory costs. As Kotler and Armstrong (2004) suggest, the argument is not about whether these channel functions have merit but who actually carries out these roles and how much added value or efficiency will they create fro company and customer. These offline issues are just as important in the online world. Figs 12.1 and 12.2 indicate the potential efficiencies gained by using an intermediary.

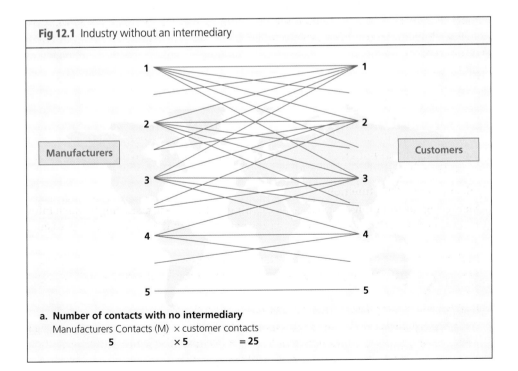

Fig 12.1 Industry without an intermediary

Manufacturers

Customers

a. **Number of contacts with no intermediary**
Manufacturers Contacts (M) × customer contacts
    5   × 5   = 25

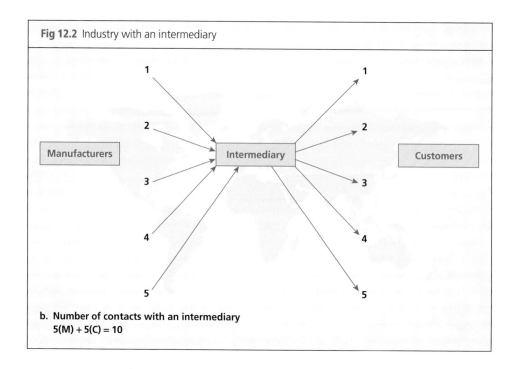

Fig 12.2 Industry with an intermediary

b. **Number of contacts with an intermediary**
   5(M) + 5(C) = 10

The figures above illustrate the efficiencies generated by intermediaries that benefit both manufacturers and end-users through reduced of customer interactions. Intermediaries can reduce industry distribution costs by providing storage and distribution facilities for a number of producers. The number of intermediaries involved in channel length will vary from B2C and B2B markets as well as by product or service. In many cases, new online channels, especially those suited to the networked economy (eg banking, music downloads and publishing) have produced added value through speed, time saved and convenience.

12.5 **Channel management behavioural issues**

Efficiency in the distributive process relies on the working relationship between channel partners. They should be mutually beneficial and not adversarial. It is easy to lose sight of the fact that real people make management decisions, woo partners and make agreements with them, design strategies and so on. Like all relationships, it can be harmonious, distant and formal, or break down altogether. Blythe (2001) discusses three key elements in channel management.

Channel co-operation

This is required both for the channel partners involved and ultimately, the customer. Blythe suggests that members should agree on the market segments to approach. Common strategies and tactics can then be addressed and implemented. Each member's role in the distribution channel should be clearly defined to ensure no duplication of effort or mixed messages to the

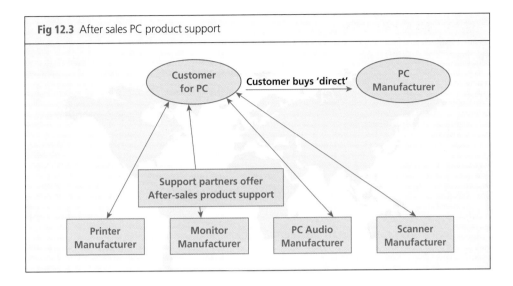

Fig 12.3 After sales PC product support

end-user. In the physical world, British Airways (BA) works tirelessly at developing coopera-tion with its global network of suppliers from ranging from food to fuel suppliers. Supplier conferences are held where BA sets out its goals and objectives in a spirit of mutual coopera-tion. Of course the nature of cooperation will be influenced by the respective powers and dominance of different players.

Co-Marketing

This is the partnership between channel members and how they support one another. This can be facilitated by joint promotions or marketing research, for example:

- Joint mailings, post and e-mails
- Co-branding
- Financial remuneration eg bonus payments for hitting targets
- Commission for affiliate programmes (usually determine by the dominant player eg Amazon)
- After sales service arrangements, see Fig 12.3

Many PC manufacturers have recognised that their peripherals' suppliers can provide more detailed product knowledge than the manufacturer themselves. For example, Epson or Hewlett Packard provide printer expertise, Ilyama and Samsung may provide monitor expertise and so on. The consumer then has to ring the peripheral support partner direct for assistance. However it is a bone of contention with many PC owners about the telephone rates charged for such support not to mention the length of time you are left dangling in a queue. Another key issue could be the number of times it takes to resolve a problem. If the support partner is not effective, they will not only damage their brand but also that of the original manufac-turer of the system.

The presence of an intermediary would create efficiencies in the number of contacts but in the PC example, the consumer could potentially be contacting several different support partners when things go wrong, not to mention long waits on premium rate support lines.

MINI CASE 12.3 Distribution and channel partners

Levi's, in an early online foray, recognised the potential of the web to secure orders and communicate direct with its target markets. Levis set up their own web site, which in effect, cut out their retail partners who had supported them over the years. Not surprisingly, there was a backlash from the retailers who threatened to stop stocking Levi merchandise. As a result Levis revised the site and signposted customers to their nearest stockist and peace was restored.

Channel Conflict

Conflicts can arise within channels for a variety of reasons such as:

- Changes in commission rates
- Poor service or performance by an intermediary
- Changes in channel power base

12.6 Traditional operations going online

The UK's online shoppers spent a record £1.7 billion on the Internet in November 2003 because of time starved pre-Christmas shoppers according to IMRG, the e-tailers trade association (*FT* 12 Dec). This growth contrasted sharply with the gloom on the high street. Regarding particular product categories site visits grew by 43% in electronics and appliances, and 21.4% in the grocery and alcohol sites indicating a healthy increase of traffic towards the Internet as consumers become more comfortable with it. Glen Drury, MD of Kelkoo commented that the number of top retailers moving online helped fuel the healthy growth in online sales.

Examples of UK Retailers Making Strides Online

- Department Stores   www.JohnLewis.com
- Chemists   www.boots.com
- Electrical appliances   www.Comet.com
- High street banks   www.hsbc.com
- Food retailers   www.tesco.com
- Sports retailer   www.jjbsports.com

Campaign (2002) believes that Tesco's online success has resulted from integrated thinking and its effective logistics model on which analysts poured scorn initially. Fulfilling orders in-store via personal shoppers did not appear to be the leading edge of Internet practice but it works. In the background supporting the system is the Tesco Information Exchange (TIE), a secure, collaborative B2B exchange providing real time sales, logistics and finance information through Tesco's EPOS data.

In both the B2C and B2B markets, traditional channels are characterised by linearity as goods and services are 'pushed' through the system. The linear relationship model changes in a variety of ways where intermediaries disappear or emerge, or demand for customised products increases.

Table 12.1 Internet rivals – how the online supermarket services compare

Company	Tesco.Com	Sainsbury 2You	Asda.co.uk	Ocado
Online Overview	Its internet grocery operation has utilised its existing home delivery service from its main stores. Staff controlling large trolleys in-store carry out order picking. Tesco offer two-hour delivery slots.	Tried a van style depot system and built warehouses in Park Royal, London and Manchester but it proved too expensive. They shut the Manchester depot and switched Sainsburys2You to a store based picking system similar to Tesco.	Asda tried and discarded a depot-based system when it closed its original two fulfilment centres in Croydon and Watford. It now picks 30 from its 259 stores nationwide, which deliver greater efficiency.	Operates out of a single depot in Hatfield, originally covering the western side of the M25 plus parts of Surrey and Hertfordshire. By 2005, it covered 10 million households across the South East, the Midlands, and the North West. Key feature is that Ocado offer one hour delivery slots.
Delivery Charge	A fee of £3.99 for off-peak times is payable, rising to £5.99 during peak periods	Up to £5 delivery charge and a £25 minimum order value.	£4.95 but there is no minimum order.	Free orders over £75 and a minimum order of £25
Sales	£577m in 2003–04	Undisclosed	Undisclosed	£70m (2004)
Profits	£28m	Losses of £29m	Undisclosed	Not yet (2004)
Orders per week	120,000 per week and rising.	33,000 customers per week.	Undisclosed	12,000 customers per week.

Note: The other major UK player in the grocery sector is Morrisons plc but as yet it shows no sign of trading online though it is becoming more active with its More4Baby (www.more4baby.co.uk) pages with partners and affiliates.
Adapted from: *The Independent*, Business, 2, 15 Friday August 2003.
www.asda.co.uk
www.tesco.com
www.ocado.com
www.sainsburytoyou.com

12.7 Traditional value added functions of channel members

Manufacturers and service providers have relied on channel intermediaries to make their offering available to the end-user. The selection of channels, and management of inter-mediaries, is of significant strategic and financial importance to the firm. Doyle (2002) states that 'marketing channel costs and margins' can account for up to 50% of the final selling price. For the extra cost, intermediaries should provide expertise or efficiencies that the man-ufacturer deems to be uneconomic to provide or unavailable. Online operators have the choice between performing a variety of distributive functions themselves sometimes referred to a 'pick, pack and ship' or utilise the expertise of a specialist logistics firm such as Exel (www.exel.com). Brassington and Petitt (2003) categorise the value added as follows:

• **Transactional value** – where the intermediary considers risk associated with taking the title and addresses such issues as:

– How effectively they position and promote themselves to their target market?

– Are the intermediaries likely to be more effective in the market place than the producer or other intermediaries?

– How effective are they in connecting buyers and sellers and matching needs?

One of the fundamental advantages of the Internet lies in connectivity as it facilitates communications betweens between buyers and sellers, service/information providers to information 'seekers'. One basic advantage of the Internet that we now take for granted is being 'open for business' all day everyday. Though in reality many online merchants operate 'high street hours' with human support services backed up by out of hours automated services.

Manufactures may use the Internet as a promotion and information site for their products. This directly connects prospects to approved distributors. Manufacturers of kitchen appliances and cars incorporate a store or dealership locator facility within its site. This is helpful to the prospect but also provides support to the distributor with better channel relations.

Automated technologies also bring communications benefits both in terms of costs and speed for both parties in the exchange process. Simons, Steinfield and Bouwman (2002) discuss the importance of the cost-benefit ratio in channel management. They estimated various costs per transactions across a number of different sectors to illustrate the efficiencies of Internet related channels against traditional channels.

However, Simons et al state that efficiencies are usually achieved at high volumes and the estimates do not cover start-up costs, which can vary across sectors. They go on to outline two value paradigms originating from various writers (Bucklin 1966 & 1972, Stern et al 1996 and Lynn 2000), which can be summarised, in Table 12.3.

Clearly, there are many channel design issues to be considered if value is to be added at each stage of the chain. The nature of the channels and the support required will vary for the following reasons:

• The complexity of the products on offer

• Their monetary value

• The competitive advantage offered by the channel

• Known customer service expectations

In terms of promotional activity, the Internet also provides transactional value through its ability to communicate effectively with interested parties (eg by e-mail) often with co-branded or timely campaigns to add impact. In Fig 12.4, Pet Planet (www.petplanet.co.uk), a leading

Table 12.2 Differences in price per transaction across channels

Channel	Price per transaction indication*
Web/EDI based	$1
Telephone/Call centre	$10
Retail	$50
Personal Selling	$200

* Estimates based on high volume channels
Source: Simons, Steinfield and Bouwman (2002).

Table 12.3 Online value paradigms

Distribution Paradigm	Buying Process Support Paradigm
• Spatial convenience	• Local inventory provided by channel members
• Lot size to match the consumption process. Requires effective forecasting	• Sales process support through all phases of the buying process including pre-sales, sales and after-sales support
• Waiting and delivery times to meet customer expectations	• Order handling, pick, pack and ship, inventory updates and billing, especially real-time expectations
• Product variety (specialist or broad range)	• Credit provisioning with credit risk absorption

Source: Adapted from Simons, Steinfield and Bowuman (2002).

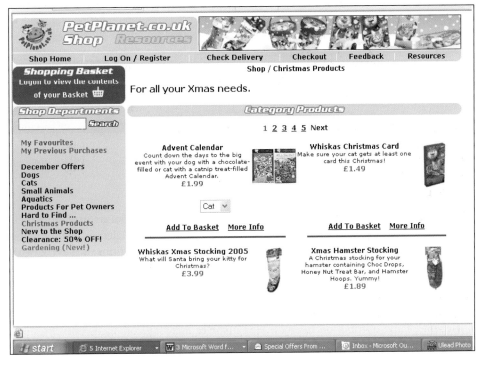

Fig 12.4 Pet Planet.co.uk

www.PetPlanet.co.uk

online pet retailer communicates with its database of e-mail customer leading up to Christmas.

Tracking and measuring campaign responses has always been a key direct marketing activity. Software developments have provided marketers with a diverse range of e-marketing measures to determine 'virtually' any aspect of a web-related campaign (eg log files, click through rates, etc) Similarly fulfilment companies can produce fast tracking throughout the order handling and despatch process. Real-time reporting for both these activities adds value for customers. Another real time dimension of the Internet is the area of price negotiations where dynamic pricing and online auctions take place.

Fig 12.5 Tiscali home page
Reproduced by kind permission of Tiscali.co.uk.

Internet Service Providers (ISP's) such as Tiscali (Fig 12.5) and Yahoo! are extending their technology role significantly to incorporate a range of information, telecom and shopping services. The shopping channel brings together a range of pure player firms such as Figleaves (www.figleaves.com) and sites with their traditions on the high street such as John Lewis (www.johnlewis.com) and Argos (www.Argos.com). The careful selection of key partners brings together significantly increases brand awareness, increased site traffic for each channel member and additional revenue streams for the ISP.

The role of the distribution function also involves matching products, both in range and quantity, to the buyer's needs. This role is increasingly performed by search engines and price comparison sites such as Pricerunner (www.pricerunner.com) and Kelkoo (www.kelkoo.co.uk).

From direct and database marketing came the Spiral of Prosperity Model. The model presumes that, the more we know about a customer, the more we can offer tailored and relevant solutions. If we add classic 'direct' profiling techniques and believe in the premise that 'birds of a feather flock together', then the application of **collaborative filtering** software has considerable potential for communicating appropriate product suggestions. People with similar profiles using bases for segmentation like age, sex, income and lifestyle *should* have similar likes and dislikes. It will depend upon the knowledge and understanding of the segment and sub-segments.

- **Logistical Value** – focus on how intermediaries source a range of goods and services relevant to the needs of their customers. This involves storage, bulk breaking and transportation of physical products, often through established channels. The Internet comes into its own with:

- The distribution of services (eg travel related) through new channels or by new inter-mediaries (reintermediation)

- The distribution of digital content such as subscription newspapers, software or music downloads formerly delivered physically

- The Internet public and private sector also provides costs effective and flexible delivery with e learning. (An example of this is illustrated in Mini case 12.4 below.)

The Internet also facilitates **aggregation**. This occurs in three ways. A traditional logistics function performed by an intermediary is the coordination and promotion of products or services offered by numerous suppliers to increase customer choice. Various online car sites (eg www.jamjar.com) bring together a range of manufacturers products such as Ford, Renault, Toyota and Vauxhall within their web sites. Some vehicles are being 're-imported', therefore locational factors such as close proximity to motorways and North seas or Channel ports are important. Many online merchants use the 'Drop Ship' distribution model whereby they carry no stock and merely facilitate orders for manufacturers or distributors at a lower channel level. The Internet also offers aggregation of information as search engines and price comparison sites generate information from diverse sources at rapid speeds. For example. Infoseek.co.uk attempts to offer 'the best of the best' site results by drawing together results from twelve of the UK's top search engines. Jim Sterne (2001) looks at a different Internet dimension, which he refers to as **aggregate attitude** whereby market information can be aggregated rapidly through online surveys. This can be carried out effectively at the point of sale to monitor customer satisfaction. However, as Sterne points out, not every site survey is working with, or for, the online operator and negative PR may be generated which is tricky to control and influence.

MINI CASE 12.4 Online training scheme provides flexibility and access in the Highlands

The Highlands of Scotland Tourist Board has responsibility of the promotion of a massive area covering 10,000 square miles that includes Skye, Aviemore, Strathspey, Inverness and the Northern Highlands (www.highlandsofscotland.net). Tourism is crucial to the regional economy with over 2 million visitors per year, (80% from overseas) generating revenues of £420m.

TRAINING

The board regularly uses e-marketing and has specific web sites such as walkingwild.com and escapetotheedge.co.uk, together with its host intranet which is an integral part of the corporate communications. It now has an online training programme spe-cially developed with Learndirect Scotland for Business (lds4b).

'They offered a new approach to our training needs,' said Elaine Mackay, the board's assistant customer services manager. 'Instead of staff from remote offices being sent on courses they can pick a quiet moment in their day and just log on'.

The board signed up for courses in coaching skills, active listen-ing, time management and effective questioning. 'The courses

we picked don't take very long so staff can do small chunks at a time'.

'At first, some were a bit sceptical about online training just as we were coming into the season but they have been surprised how easy it is to fit around their existing workload. They don't waste hours travelling to a training centre, they just log on and get started, 'Mackay continued.

Staff can also sign up for e-commerce and spreadsheet courses.

'They like the fact the courses provide all of the information they need in one place without them having to research or study at home. All the courses end with a multiple-choice test so every-thing is there'.

'It gives out staff a chance to develop their skills and move up the career ladder. Climbing the customer service rankings is also important for us', she concluded.

Adapted from: *Scotland on Sunday*, 7, 7 September 2003
www.highlandsofscotland.net

- **Facilitating Value** – through financing operations instead of producers facilitating multiple accounts, servicing, training and provision of market information. For example, companies like Able2Buy (www.able2buy.com) and V12 Finance (www.v12finance.com) offer hassle-free online credit facilities.

Security is a major issue for many buying and selling online. Building customer trust and confidence is essential for the development of a critical online mass, especially the online 'late majority' or 'laggards' groups who are likely to be more resistant to Internet adoption. This could be due to resistance to change in shopping habits and limited online experience and so on. The online 'feel good factor' will increase, as safe and secure transactions become the norm at the point of sale and tabloid scare mongering about credit card fraud decreases. We must not focus solely on the consumer's security but also on the merchant's ability to process and gather payment for goods and services sold either directly or indirectly through specialised third parties to a genuine customer.

Any web-based transactions containing private and sensitive information needs a secure server utilising public key encryption where software facilitates connections and information with other computers. **Secure Sockets Layer (SSL)** developed by Netscape is the Internet protocol application used to encrypt computer connections using digital signatures or certificates for purposes of verification. Certification authorities produce and issue digital certificates to organisations seeking to establish their credibility and web integrity. This is especially important during the acquisition stage of any online campaign as certification guarantees the merchant's authenticity when checked against the issuing authority's database.

Thawte (www.thawte.com) is one of a number of well-established certification authorities. Their approval mark is visible on many mature online players. Click on the link and Thawte confirms the trader's credentials (see Fig 12.6).

New intermediaries are also playing vital roles in two other key areas of the purchasing process:

1. Shopping Cart Services
2. Payment Service Provision

1. **Shopping Cart Services** – early online shopping experiences were characterised by droves of prospects exiting sites at various points up to and including entering their credit card details. Complexity in site design, poor usability and unwieldy order forms led to site drop out rates of up to 70%. Wendy Hewson of the Hewson Group (www.hewson.co.uk) has generated important research findings into the concept of 'The Leaking Pipe'. This research attempts to pinpoint those areas where prospects choose to leave a site before completing a transaction.

Shopping carts perform two fundamental functions. First they enable, consumers to purchase more than one item at a time offering a convenient link with your online catalogue. This sounds rather obvious but nevertheless important if you consider the alternative of numerous single purchase transactions between buyer and seller especially as online shoppers may also wish to browse around different online 'departments'. Secondly, most shopping cart services incorporate secure order forms and transaction facilities with safe, convenient storage of credit card numbers. Payment by credit card remains the most popular method. Internet based transactions require firms to set up a **merchant account** separate to the firm's bank account to provide a unique identification number to the **Payment Service Provider (PSP)** who collect the card details and forward onto the acquiring bank for authorisation.

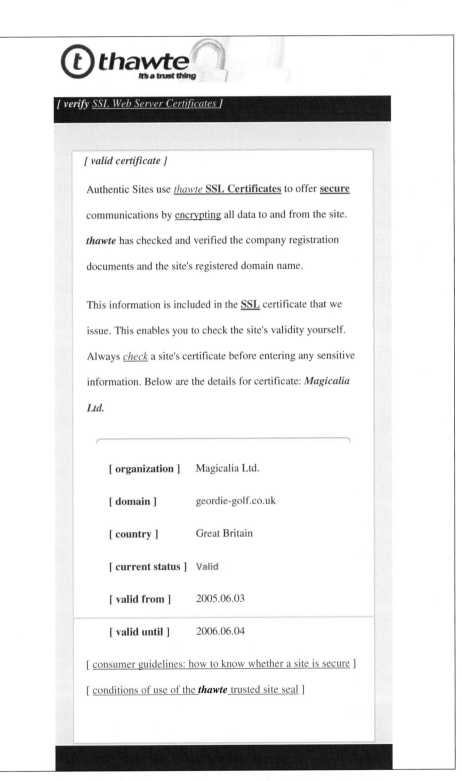

Fig 12.6 Thawte SSL Web certificates.

Reproduced by kind permission of dabs.com.

Many e-commerce software companies, particularly those with expertise in shop design incorporate shopping cart software coupled with integrated functionality payment processing systems. For example, Electronic Retail Online (www.erolonline.co.uk) offer a range of flexible shopping cart system for SMEs with linked facilities to leading payment gateways such as Netbank, Paypal and World Pay (see below) which provides ease of use to customers. Most web site hosting operations also offer fully integrated, secure shopping packages to speed online business access (eg www.webcentre.lycos.co.uk). Online merchants should also consider other shopping cart facilities. For example, secure e-mails for order confirmation and card acceptance, multi-lingual and currency capabilities for true cross border or global transactions, real-time inventory information and back office integration for the logistics function, be it in-house or outsourced.

2. **Payment Service Providers** – numerous payment solutions are now available from separate arms of established financial institutions or new online intermediaries. World Pay (www.worldpay.co.uk) the Internet payment operation set up by the Royal Bank of Scotland is an example of a market leading intermediary with global merchant accounts and more than 12,000 strategic banking and e-commerce partners. Consumers take the products and services offered for granted but they provide fundamental functions that influence the continued expansion of e-commerce. World Pay provides facilities to handle payment by instalments, which can be very important in a purchase decision online. Not surprisingly, many decision-making units like to spread payments and budget with higher value purchases. The majority of online businesses did not offer this facility in the early dot.com days and lost business to the established high street stores who did.

Other PSP services usually include:

• Secure cardholder and address verification systems

• Multi-channel payment acceptance (eg Internet, phone, fax, etc)

• Multi-currency and multi-lingual systems designed to support global transactions.

The payment management market promises to be more competitive with PayPal, eBay Inc's online payment system establishing European headquarters in Dublin. PayPal handles some 31 million accounts.

Brassington and Petitt (2003) state other intermediary activities also add value such as the provision of market information. Intermediaries may obtain valuable information sources, aggregate the information or be closer to the end-user to facilitate important feedback.

LEGAL EAGLE BOX 12.1 Payment Service Providers

In September 2000, two Directives on Electronic Payment – Directive 2000/28/EC and Directive 2000/46/EC – were adopted which provide the rules for the issue of e-payment by credit institutions. The framework set up by these Directives works to safeguard the financial integrity and stability of e-payment institutions. In April 2002 these two Directives became part of UK Law and the activities of e-payment providers were brought under the Financial Services and Markets Act 2000 by the Financial Services and Market Act 2000 (Regulated Activities) (Amendment) Order 2002.

E-payment providers have certain contractual obligations in relation to their customers. Customers are to be given comprehensive information about a provider's e-payment products and such information should include the date beyond which the e-payment ceases to be valid. Users should also be informed of their liabilities in the event of third party misuse, loss, malfunction, theft or damage to any electronic device on which their electronic payment is stored.

Many online market analysts have emerged such as Forrester (www.forrester.com) and Nua (www.nua.com) to provide in-depth surveys covering online industry and consumer trends. Appetising abstracts are used to entice organisations to purchase full reports. Other rich sources of information are available from established media sources such as the *Financial Times* (www.ft.com) and newer sources such as Silicon (www.silicon.com) and ZDNet (www.zdnet.com) provide frequent online briefings. Many technology-based companies have used white papers to inform their 'publics' about their leading edge applications. Other online resources can be useful for marketers in targeting key customers as outlined in Mini case 12.5.

12.8 Channel strategies

McDonald and Christopher (2003) discuss the growing range of strategic distribution options offered by the ICT enabled world. They suggest five hybrid distribution systems, described below.

Single Channel Strategy

This is where the main thrust of an organisation's marketing effort is through one channel. Typically pure players such as Firebox (www.firebox.com) and Easyjet (www.easyjet.com) utilise the Internet.

Channel Migration Strategy

This is where organisations have operated in one channel but now seek to persuade custo- mers to visit another channel that could provide organisational benefit such as reduced costs or reach new markets. Comet (www.comet.com) differentiates between on and offline prices to encourage Internet shopping as a new distribution channel as illustrated in Fig 12.7.

Integrated multi-channel strategies

These will incorporate both (1) channels describing the mode of product and service dis- tribution and (2) media channels which disseminate the organisation's communications messages. In multi-channel operations the organisation recognises the emerging multi- modal customer whose behaviour seeks channel flexibility. For example, First Direct who revolutionised direct banking in the eighties via the telephone, offer Internet banking with

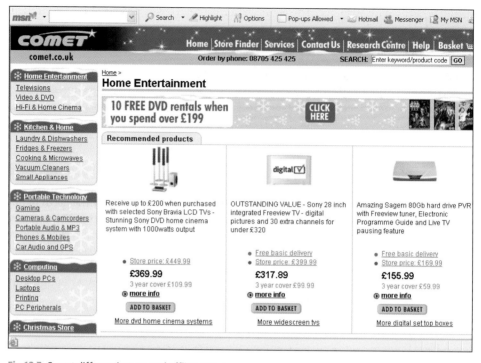

Fig 12.7 Comet differentiate on and offline prices

SMS support. Customers may also use the high street network of First Direct's parent company, HSBC together with branches within a shop at supermarket chain, Morrision's. A cost benefit analysis of each channel should be undertaken to monitor its customer usage and impacts on other marketing activity such as cross selling and up-selling. Database technology underpins any multi-channel strategy especially where the availability of real time information gives competitive advantage and these linkages between front and back-office are critical.

Wilson et al (2004) discuss the dilemma for marketing managers in optimising multiple channels in a world where the array of IT enabled channels meets the time starved, convenience seeking customer. The rapid growth in the purchase of mobile devices and wireless applications in the UK provides marketers with new challenges and opportunities. Wilson et al emphasise the need to consider not only the customer preferences of one channel over another but also the role that each channel may play in the actual buying process. Many consumers utilise the Internet for product information searches because of ease and low search costs, yet still prefer to have some human contact either face to face or by phone when ordering. Wilson makes a critical observation on consumer behaviour, that new channels will be accepted if they are in the consumers' interests and benefits accrue. Interactive television (iTV) is recognised as a powerful new communications medium because of its armchair convenience and flexibility. Garnier hair products have implemented interactive TV campaigns on channels such as UK Living and UK Style to target female segments with the aim of populating their database and offering trial products via a secure site. With a growing proportion of the UK population 'on the move', mobile devices will inevitably grow in importance offering new channels. Trials of mobile barcode systems incorporated in text messages have worked effectively. Receivers of SMS messages are directed to trial stores where the barcode is read and discounts obtained. The use of such channels is likely to appeal to the IT gadget savvy consumer. New channels therefore depend on the target audience's receptiveness. In Europe, acceptance and penetration of mobile channels is high and growing quickly. This contrasts starkly with the US surprisingly, where analysts seriously question the viability of mobile marketing, at least for the next five years. The demand for 'online anywhere' connectivity is increasing rapidly as purchases of mobile devices for work and play and wireless applications see rapid growth. Successful multi-channel marketing will require a seamless integration between phone, e-mail, in-store, fax, mobile and web-based customer touch points for the multi-modal customer through to transparent, integrated back office systems.

Needs-based segmentation strategy

This is where the organisation makes different channels available to satisfy the needs of different market segments or clusters, based on their preferences or behaviour. This strategy may be limited by resource constraints or profit potential.

Graduated customer value strategy

This is where different channels are used depending on the worth of different customers to the business. This is the underlying principle of Key Account Management (KAM) when senior account executives are tasked with servicing and selling to major, high value customers. Their business is critical to the organisation in terms of strategic importance, prestige and profitability. Accounts of lesser value may be handled by more cost efficient methods like the Internet, telemarketing and sales force automation (SFA).

12.9 **Disintermediation**

Strauss, El Ansary and Frost (2003) describe **disintermediation** as 'the process of eliminating traditional intermediaries' from existing distribution channels. Many business analysts expected that the Internet would create new business models that would result in channel partners disappearing as both suppliers, distributors and ultimately customers could buy direct. Cutting out the middleman was quite appealing. Some saw this as a way of redressing the power balance between manufacturers and food retailers.

Hollerson (2003) observes that the Internet, and falling technology costs, has brought information structures within the grasp of the public and not just organisations. There are benefits for both producers and consumers. Hollerson suggests that producers can benefit from going 'direct' by obtaining better margins where previously, the intermediary would add on their costs. The value generated (speed, time, convenience, etc) by the direct route could enhance the brand and increase customer loyalty. Alternatively, the Internet provides the consumer a massive marketplace in which to shop. It provides global reach and puts the purchasing decision wherever a connection exists. With wireless technology that means anywhere. In the travel and tourism industry, disintermediation has taken place with more consumers bypassing the traditional high street travel agent and purchasing through online merchants such as Lastminute and Expedia. We have not quite seen the demise of the travel agent, though their long-term future looks insecure. Amazon has bypassed the retailers of CDs and books. Similarly, there were predictions that the future of the traditional car dealership was under threat. We were expected to beat a path to the Internet car retailers and buy predominantly on price. Price sensitive consumers have bought through organisations like Jamjar (www.jamjar.com), Autobytel (www.autobytel.co.uk) and Broadspeed (www.broadspeed.com). However, increased competition has brought down car prices generally making it difficult for the under-resourced online dealer to get established.

Chaffey (2002) describes how manufacturers such as Vauxhall sought first mover advantage selling online but found that the results have initially been disappointing. Whilst price is a key element in the consumer's choice criteria, clearly when it comes to a major purchase such as a car, other value added activities performed by channel members remain an important consideration. The test drive, salesman's product knowledge, trade-in negotiations and on going after sales care provided by factory trained technicians provide confidence and reassurance during all phases of the purchasing experience. Some automotive sites are attempting to overcome this buyer behaviour problem by arranging test drives and servicing with dealerships. It remains to be seen whether such arrangements will be win over consumers where personal service is a vital ingredient in high value purchases.

The term 'transformational marketing' has been applied to the impact generated by the changing market structures and relationships. Hollerson acknowledges that whilst the Internet may have removed some traditional intermediaries, a process of **reintermediation** has emerged. New channel members have replaced the old and carry out new channel roles. Traditional channel models emphasised the intermediary's role in enabling transaction and delivery efficiencies. They would coordinate the outputs of several producers and offer them in more manageable quantities to players in the next level. In the new economy, aggregation revolves around the availability of information and its value. Intermediaries take over the marketing role on the web and provide an interface between buyers and sellers. Some may offer services across the value chain whilst others may provide specific functions in the value chain such as payment processing or e-fulfilment. Alternatively, the Internet also enables services to be offered in a quicker and more sensitive way. Friends Reunited has extended their provision to include online dating allowing those seeking romance to do it in a more impersonal but private way than previously possible.

Starkov (2003) discusses how new intermediaries in the US hotel industry have been more successful than established hoteliers from the offline world in securing online room sales. Starkov suggest that hotel groups tend to be some of the smartest direct marketers in the offline world with direct mail and telemarketing efforts but when it comes to the Internet they have found it difficult to maintain market share against the emerging intermediaries such as hotels.com (www.hotels.com). He cites their failure to develop clear Internet strategies, and their failure to appreciate the potential of Internet distribution networks and the needs of net savvy consumers. In the UK, online hotel intermediaries have emerged and established themselves as key sellers of hotel rooms providing discounts and price comparisons. Many achieve higher search engine rankings than the named hotel group themselves.

12.10 **Logistics management**

The Place element has traditionally centred on design and management of channels together with physical distribution (PDM). PDM focuses on the efficient handling and transportation of goods from the point of manufacture to the customer. Movements are carried out by the manufacturer's own transportation or by third parties. However, logistics has developed as a discipline in its own right and is a meeting point for marketing and purchasing functions. Brassington and Petitt (2000) state that it is 'concerned with inbound raw materials and other supplies and their movement through the plant as well as with the outbound goods. It also covers strategic issues such as warehouse location, the management of materials and stock levels and information systems'. It should be appreciated how the logistics function affects customer satisfaction and value. The level of service is determined by corporate and marketing objectives and competitor offerings. The design of logistics systems should focus on the needs and behaviour of the end-user. However, there may be trade-offs due to:

- Costs eg adoption of new systems
- Barriers to entry
- Availability of suitable partners
- Constraints placed by powerful players in the chain, eg minimum orders.

As McDonald and Christopher (2003:414) observe 'quick logistics has become the aim of many organisations, enabling them to achieve the twin strategic goal of cost reduction and service enhancement'.

The relationships between buyers and sellers in the supply chain have changed in recent years from adversarial to partnership. The objective is to achieve more reactive inventory systems for the retailer, especially the need to eliminate costly 'stock-outs'. **Efficient customer response** (ECR) is the term given to this desired integration. Partners will employ continuous replenishment systems such as vendor-managed inventory (VMI) that relies on real-time data via extranets. **Cross-docking** may also be applied which partly eliminates the need for costly inventory costs. The successful implementation depends upon coordinating partnership transport information as products are transferred from one vehicle to another at distribution centres without physically entering the warehouse and stock system. For ECR to work, the usual channel member issues of cooperation, compatibility and conflict apply. The linkages are illustrated in Fig 12.8.

Warehouse management systems (WMS)

Warehouse management technology has progressed significantly in recent years with information and automation developments. The traditional role of stock management (eg acceptance, storage and movement of materials) has often functioned as an operational silo. Now warehousing, whether in-house or third party is at the heart of the supply chain. As Reynolds (2001) claims 'a best-of-breed WMS gets product or material in and out of the door faster, for less money and with fewer errors. For the merchant, it means fewer lost sales opportunities, less brand damage and increased customer satisfaction'. Typical WMS activities involve receiving goods in, effective management of space, automated and customised order picking for faster response. As WMS has become more integrated new technologies such as Radio Frequency Identification (**RFID**), together with bar-coding is used for product authentication, tracking and data collection within the warehouse, the enterprise or extranet. Wireless speech recognition systems, e-paper solutions and mobile printers all increase outputs within the warehouse whilst reducing errors. Web-based transport management systems, including **factory gate collections** (FGC) and routing systems are being adopted to maximise transport efficiencies and eliminate what is referred to as 'empty mileage' where delivery vehicles normally return empty. Firms involved in transportation are beginning to see the benefits of accepting other firms' goods on return journeys though some swallowing of pride change in

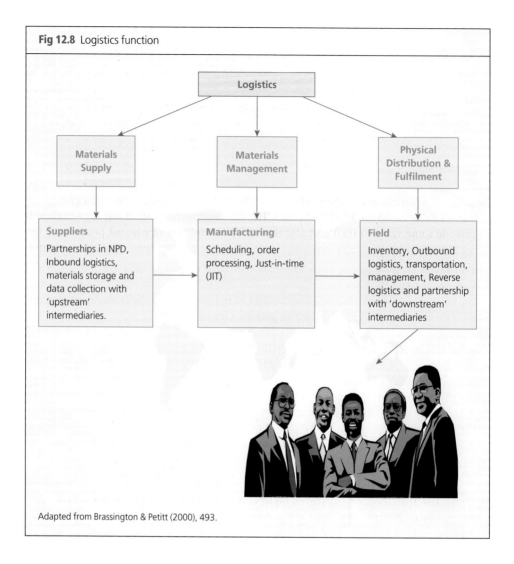

Fig 12.8 Logistics function

Logistics

Materials Supply → Materials Management → Physical Distribution & Fulfilment

Suppliers
Partnerships in NPD, Inbound logistics, materials storage and data collection with 'upstream' intermediaries.

Manufacturing
Scheduling, order processing, Just-in-time (JIT)

Field
Inventory, Outbound logistics, transportation, management, Reverse logistics and partnership with 'downstream' intermediaries

Adapted from Brassington & Petitt (2000), 493.

attitude to some business relationships may be need. 'In-cab' wireless technologies are also being introduced in to the UK's truck fleets to provide another rich source of information. Lewis (2002) describes some of the potential applications:

- To eliminate paperwork in mundane tasks such as proof of delivery
- To communicate delivery to trigger electronic payments
- To alert consignees that a delivery vehicle is soon to arrive, this can speed up goods inward
- Route tracking of vehicles when using routing programmes to optimise speed and fuel efficiencies. Alternatively, it may identify 'unusual' movements off route or where a vehicle is stationary for a long period indicating something wrong (eg theft or breakdown).

All of these web or wireless technologies are enabling firms to improve deliveries, speed up loading and unloading and generally improve supply chain efficiencies. This should lead to improved customer satisfaction and loyalty.

Reverse logistics

Reverse logistics relates to the management and handling of returned goods. These can be either faulty, damaged unwanted by the customer or excess stock from a retailer. This can be a particular problem for online businesses where the customer cannot use basic senses such as touch and smell when buying and relies on the accuracy of web descriptions. Dissatisfaction may occur on receiving the despatched goods. Traditionally, goods have been returned to the point of purchase (eg a local store) and then transported on to a regional distribution centre or collection facility. Online it is different, as goods will have to be collected individually by the seller or a third party. This can be costly and time consuming, and undermines the efficiencies gained through the forward supply chain with under-utilised vehicles. Logistics companies are wrestling with best strategies for this element of e-commerce.

Porter's value chain model (1985) posits that the fundamental role of any organisation is to provide some value to their end user through the provision of relevant products or services. The vehicle for the value generated is via the internal value chain. This is a set of interconnected activities on both the supply side (eg logistics system) and demand side (sales and marketing of products). The activities are carried out by the organisation, if vertically integrated, by intermediaries, or both. Each activity generates information and requires expertise. Players in the value chain have the opportunity to maximise efficiencies and thus add value at each stage. This ultimately creates an offering of real or perceived value for which the customer is willing to pay the selling price.

Chaffey (2002) suggests some fundamental limitations in the *internal* value chain concept relating to e-commerce:

- The generic value chain is more relevant to goods rather than services.
- The chain tends to 'push' through from supply to the customer instead of being designed around customer needs.
- The internal value chain does not underline the importance of networked relationships.

Zahay and Handfield (2003) discuss the use of the value chain concept and its use at improving key aspects of interactive marketing such as customer relationship management (CRM), new product development and supply chain management. They believe that customers buy 'value' predominantly for one of two reasons:

1. Low prices produced by operational efficiencies
2. Differentiated product features or service processes (eg customised).

Zahay and Handfield (2003) give US case study examples of how technology may support the virtual value chain:

- **FedEx** introduced real-time package tracking compared to delayed tracking offered by competitors to differentiate it.
- **Wal-Mart and Target** utilise pertinent web site design to complement their particular positioning strategies. Wal-Mart's strategy of everyday low prices (EDLP) is reflected in a simple but fairly cluttered site. Target on the other hand offers more value to its more affluent customers through more prestigious site design that contains added value facilities such as its online gift registry.
- Telecom company **Nortel**'s fulfilment and distribution strategy has incorporated unique customer focussed order houses together with logistics 'houses' located near key customer

Fig 12.9 The value chain

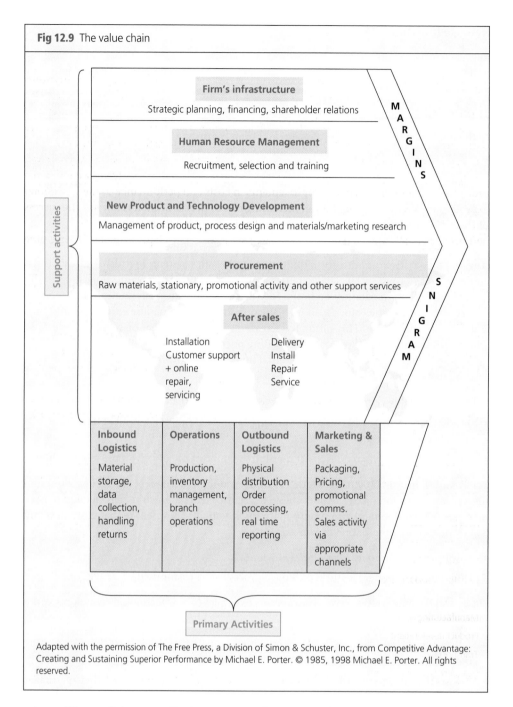

bases. The result is a cost effective system with guaranteed product availability and faster delivery times relevant to customer requirements.

• **General Motors** (GM) has radically restructured its global component supply chain to provide speed and flexibility in manufacturing. This gives GM the capability to produce customised vehicles in the same way as PC manufacturers like Dell offer, in much shorter lead times.

12.11 Supply chain management

Supply chain management (SCM) has evolved from the value chain concept. Organisations are not only looking to redesigning the networks to increase customer satisfaction, but also to drive down costs, increase response times and flexible capability across functions and partnerships. SCM takes a more critical look at supplier and distributor relationships and their role in achieving customer satisfaction. Doyle (2002) describes the new relationships and demands on channel partners in the design of customer focussed 'value delivery system'. He suggests such a system should ensure rigorous quality standards, delivery as and when promised, continuous efficiency improvements in costs and performance to meet customer expectations. Technology has had an increasing role to play in SCM. It is not just the success of the main player(s) in the supply chain (eg Ford, Tesco, etc) that is important but also the performance of all supply chain members against other supply chains which will determine collective success.

Williams, Esper and Ozmet (2001) describe the electronic supply chain as 'SCM organisations that are linked within and between their trading partners by the Internet and/or EDI to buy, sell, mover products/services and cash flows'. They argue that the eSC is fluid and dynamic in nature and provides organisations with the flexibility needed to achieve business agility. Sahay and Mohan (2003) researched the criticality of supply chain processes and their importance in alignment with business strategy in India. Table 12.4 indicates the relative importance of each in achieving business objectives. The first two elements emphasise the growing move towards customer oriented supply chains.

Reddy and Reddy (2001) differentiate between the **market economy model** and the **network economy model**. The market economy model with its origins in mass manufacturing

---

Table 12.4 Criticality of supply chain processes

Supply Chain Process	Criticality Score
Customer service	4.38
Demand management	4.22
Inventory management	4.19
Order processing/fulfilment	4.05
Manufacturing	3.97
Product development	3.53
Transportation	3.43
Distribution management	3.43
Import export management	3.32
Promotion planning	3.18
Warehousing	3.08

Sahay & Mohan (2003) 'Supply Chain Management practices in Indian Industry', International Journal of Physical Distribution and logistics Management Vol 33, No 7, 2003, 582–606.

relies heavily upon the operational efficiencies generated by technological applications. Tighter, more vertically integrated supply chains have emerged *'pushing'* the product to the customer with output determined by forecasted demand. Japanese just-in-time (JIT) and Kanban systems have been adopted to provide more responsive manufacturing and inventory functions. A WIPRO Technologies (www.wipro.com) white paper, *'E-manufacturing & SAP-Creating Responsive Shop Floor in the Supply Chain'* by Kulkarni and Oak (2003) argue that the manufacturer's shop floor has often been neglected as firms have focussed more on initiatives such as CRM and SCM. They argue that the manufacturing function adds real value but has had to be more responsive to increased customer demands, shorter lead times and the decline in batch production. E-manufacturing is put forward as a critical element in the seamless integration of the entire supply chain often requiring a complete rethink on plant design, processes, IT systems and staff deployment to enhance operations. Reddy and Reddy suggest that information systems and Internet adoption has fuelled agile systems to meet the needs of individualisation or mass customisation where demand is often volatile. The network economy model configures orders to impart added value through individualisation and fast delivery to meet rising customer expectations. It moves away from the traditional batch or process methods of manufacturing to a loose network of suppliers, manufacturers and infomediaries bonded together by interconnected information systems. Bennett (2006) illustrates The network economy relationship in Fig 12.10 and describes how various information and manufacturing functions are carried out by channel members utilising digital technology. The brand owner coordinates assorted activities resulting in customised products that increase customer satisfaction.

It illustrates how different business partners may offer different functions such as customer service, warehousing and shipping and customised component manufacture. In the case of Nike, the brand owner, they concentrate their energies on their areas of expertise, which are marketing and new product development. Their supply chain partners provide the manufacturing and logistics expertise and flexibility in supplying Nike's ever-increasing range of sporting goods, with shorter lifecycles, at speed to retailers and consumers. Mason et al (2002) argue that supply chain agility is a defining competitive characteristic of industry today with *demand driven* market sensitive forecasting producing more efficient responsiveness. This relies on real time information sharing. Two important issues impacting upon supply chain agility are:

• Outsourcing

• Inventory management control

• **Outsourcing** 'is the purchasing of a function or functions once administered in-house from another business – an independent contractor – and usually applies to a complete business process' (Wright 2004). Hollerson (2003) suggests that the cost of staying 'leading edge' across a multitude of value chain activities has become financially onerous for many firms, hence the focus on core competences and outsourcing of other activities. Global competition and information technology has also been responsible for this trend. Competition has intensified across most sectors. The Internet is an effective vehicle in bringing potential buyers and sellers together across the globe for promotional, transactional and information exchange purposes and opening up outsourcing possibilities. It may be viewed as a cost effective route to specialisation, accessing expertise, innovation and enhancing goods and services but like any business relationship many issues have to be considered such as contractual arrangements, flexibility and ability to integrate at a physical, cultural and IT level. Global sourcing has become a growth area. It may be attractive to source

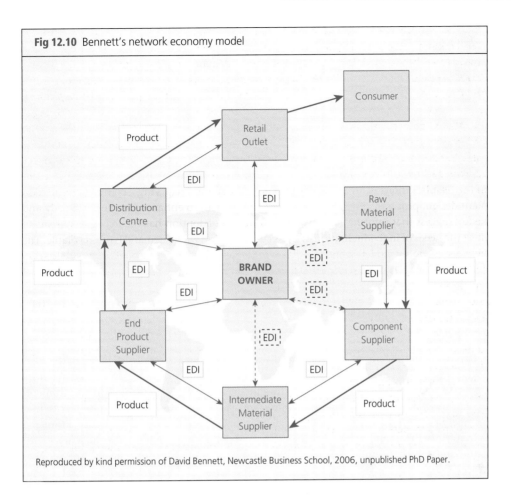

Fig 12.10 Bennett's network economy model

Reproduced by kind permission of David Bennett, Newcastle Business School, 2006, unpublished PhD Paper.

components from the Far East or Eastern Europe because of cheaper labour and other manufacturing costs but this has to be considered against the costs and speed of transportation from remote locations where less developed infrastructures exist. In addition, firms have to consider various marketing environments such as cultural, legal and political frameworks, which may differ. Physical goods still have to pass through customs.

Digital technologies help facilitate outsourcing of services generally and IT related services specifically. Many firms are contracting out functions online like customer care, payroll systems, and stock replenishment and order fulfilment, eg www.netfulfilment.com. Location is not usually a factor as systems communicate using EDI or XML. Marketers may consider these to be mundane administrative functions with fixed costs associated. E-documentation drives labour time and errors out of the system. Firms may also outsource 24-hour network systems security provided with the latest utilities and firewalls continually upgraded remotely. Enthusiasm should be tempered, as the business world is full of expensive systems failing to deliver or integrate. Table 12.5 consider the advantages and disadvantages of outsourcing.

Table 12.5 Advantages and disadvantages of outsourcing

Advantages	Disadvantages
• Benefit from other firms' experienced staff	• Potential loss of customer ownership and information
• Gain from other firms' areas of expertise	• Loss of skills in the area of outsourcing
• Set and monitor performance indicators of 'partners'	• Innovation gains go to the outsourcing company
• Pay or penalise on performance	• Possible lack of attention if outsourcing company has a large portfolio of products and clients
• No cost of ownership	• Issues of back sourcing if problems occur
• Reduce purchasing activity (eg raw materials)	• Underperformance from the outsourcing company
• Eliminates capital spending	• Failure to deliver on promised solutions
• Greater budgetary control	• Open to scrutiny in public sector outsourcing

Adapted from Wright, R, *Business to Business Marketing*, 2004, FT Prentice Hall.

• **Inventory management** has traditionally revolved around the trade-off between the costs and satisfactions of carrying too much or too little stock (stock-outs). Modern inventory management in real time takes on extra dimensions such as continuous replenishment, shipping validation, product traceability and theft detection. Two developments that impact on inventory management and the broader supply chain are **Vendor Managed Inventory** (VMI) and RFID. VMI is a method of optimising supply chain efficiencies with the onus on the supplier for managing and maintaining inventory levels. The supplier accesses the firm's inventory and forward sales position via an extranet. This enables them to decide whether they need to ship specific product lines to maintain optimum stock levels. This reduces stock outs and also allows the buyer to hold reduced inventory levels as a form of just-in-time (JIT) is applied. Even though the goods may have been delivered, the supplier keeps ownership of the goods until they are consumed, then electronic payment can be made by accessing the buyer's bank account, known as self-billing. Once consumed, inventory levels are immediately adjusted. The access to sales data makes forecasting and replenishment easier and more accurate for the supplier but they have to be focussed. The buyer benefits from the reduced costs and efficiencies and end-user satisfaction is achieved through timely product availability.

RFID is attracting a phenomenal amount of attention as a more durable and information rich alternative to the barcode. RFID tags can be embedded into the majority of products, though limitations still exist eg refrigerated products. They can be used for shipping and receiving confirmation, supply chain tracking, theft detection and inventory management. With antennae and computer chip, they vary in range capability from anything up to 1,000 feet. Strategically placed **middleware** readers identify them as they pass through the supply chain. Up until now the costs of tags, and no definitive standards, have hindered their adoption but this is quickly changing. In the US, Wal-Mart has informed its top 100 suppliers that they need to place RFID tags on all palettes and cases by January 2005. However, the adoption race is not without difficulties as identified in Mini case 12.6 below.

MINI CASE 12.6 Metro AG tests RFID tags

Leading German retailer, Metro AG announced plans for a roll-out of a wireless inventory tracking system, expected to eventually replace barcodes. The project at Metro AG underlines the growing deployment of radio frequency identification technology in the retail and grocery sector.

Metro AG planned to rollout RFID in November 2004 across 250 stores and 10 central warehouses in Germany within the 12 months and involve 100 of its biggest suppliers, representing 65% of all its sales in Germany.

The Metro rollout followed a pilot RFID project at one of its supermarkets known as the Metro Extra Future Store (www.future-store.org) in Rheinberg, Germany, begun last year. Proctor & Gamble Co, Kraft Foods Inc, and Gillette Co have already put RFID tags on some goods they supply to the Future Store.

The tags should cost between 30 US cents and 40 US cents each. Suppliers will attach tags to pallets and cases of goods supplied to certain stores and central warehouses. Wireless readers will detect those tags as they move in and out of the warehouses and into the stores. The system will allow better monitoring of its supply and inventory, cutting down on lost, stolen or destroyed products. In addition, it should ensure no stock outs but with possible staff reductions. Suppliers will be able to track their goods through Metro's systems using a computer system supplied with RFID generated data.

Alain Benichou, distribution sector vice-president for IBM Europe, the Middle East and Africa claims that inventory carrying costs can be reduced by up to 20% representing billions of euros. German software maker, SAP AG and US semiconductor maker, Intel Corp also have lead roles in developing the technology that aspires to produce benefits for customer and companies alike. However, civil liberties groups in Germany have protested over hidden tags tracking customer movements and broader privacy issues. Other major retailers like Wal-Mart are taking a very keen interest in the proceedings.

Sources: www.spychips.com/metro/overview.html; www.future-store.org; www.rfid.ie

Delaney, KJ, *The Wall Street Journal Europe*, 12 January 2004, A5.

The use of RFID tags has also been applied in the clothing retail sector in the trendy Prada store in New York. As well as the real-time inventory benefits described earlier, RFID tags also have interesting promotional and relationship applications. A customer selecting a tagged item to try on can run it past a changing room reader. The reader can trigger a video promotion of the garment, check availability, show different colour ranges and suggest other accessories. This adds value and novelty to the in-store customer experience.

- **Handling and fulfilment** services have their origins back in the days of mail order and have steadily increased in performance and importance as direct marketing emerged as key marketing activity during the nineties. McDonald (1998) suggests 'the core activity of fulfilment is filling a customer's order after it has been received; thus, fulfilment encompasses order forms, receiving orders, processing orders, inventory management, warehousing, customer service and planning and control'. Reynolds (2001) states that for the e-business, 'logistics, fulfilment and customer service can constitute an unbeatable partnership' for a high level of online customer experience based on speed, accuracy and transparency. Stephen Bentley, chief executive of Granby Marketing services believes that the term 'handling and fulfilment' does not adequately reflect the range of activities involved in the modern fulfilment industry and that it is offers far more that the outdated view of a pick and pack' industry. He argues that the term 'marketing response management' is a better reflection of an industry emerging as outsourcing specialists for a variety of sectors.

- **SCM meets CRM.** Integration of partners and systems in the supply chain is an essential component in achieving competitive advantage for e-businesses. For marketing departments, customer relationship management (CRM) tools have been hailed as the direct marketer's holy grail in boosting profits and loyalty, when applied effectively. However, rarely have the two applications been applied and integrated effectively on an enterprise wide basis. Few marketers saw the potential marriage of the front office (CRM) to back office (SCM) until recently. However, the likes of Deloitte Consulting, Forrester Research and the Peppers and Rogers Group have all highlighted the common sense business advantages of integrating the two rather than operating them as isolated functions. Estimates for improvements in return on investment (ROI) run as high as 40%. CRM targets, promotes and sells timely offers whilst SCM sources, manufactures and fulfils the order. Linking the two produces numerous benefits such as:

- More accurate demand led forecasting
- Better enterprise wide information flows and visibility
- Better integration of marketing, production (eg build-to-order), customer service, distribution and other enterprise wide planning for optimised operational efficiency
- More efficient inventory management
- Real time information for all customer touch points leading to increased customer satisfaction
- Prioritising these functions based on customer value and importance

Leading software vendors like Oracle, recently incorporating PeopleSoft (www.oracle.com), SAP (www.sap.com) and Siebel (www.siebel.com) are all developing such integration solutions along with various technology partners.

12.12 **Online marketplaces**

The emergence of online marketplaces, exchanges, hubs or extranets, especially B2B, has generated considerable media and academic coverage in the last five years. Many Private Trading Networks (PTNs) have existed for many years but online public exchanges have emerged to change the procurement process. This coming together of buyers and sellers, often beyond normal trading areas and networks, has resulted in significant benefits to those organisations participating. For example, estimates for cost savings produced by automotive market exchanges like Covisint (www.Covisint.com) range between $3–4,000 per vehicle. In a business world where 'driving out costs' has become *the* strategic corporate obsession, price reduction via e-marketplaces has exciting possibilities. Organisations are starting to realise that the potential goes way beyond price and extends to the entire supplier relationship affecting the end product. This includes dimensions such as customer service levels, delivery and product quality which all 'add value' in the chain.

Signing up and participating in online marketplaces is not as straightforward and quick as you may think. The size and complexity of exchanges vary considerably. The operating systems, protocols, rules and administrative processes also vary. Organisations need to assess whether they have both the systems capabilities and physical capacity to participate and meet the demands of other players, particularly if there are dominant participants involved. For example, to what extent are trading tasks (eg ordering and invoicing) automated and integrated between exchange partners? This will influence the level of supply chain integration.

Sawhney and Kaplan (2001) identify two types of exchanges or hubs that have emerged in the B2B online marketplace. **Vertical** and **horizontal** hubs meet different market needs.

- **Vertical hubs** are where commercial arrangements exist with organisations operating within a specific sector. The hub can involve a single dominant company wielding power, or more likely where a number of players form a trading consortium.

Whilst some exchanges and auctions have been slow to take off they are now gathering momentum. For example, Internet Retailer (2003) reported that the GlobalNetXchange (www.gnx.com) for global retailers such as Sainsbury, Sears and Roebuck reported a 77% rise in the number of transaction in the year up to September 2003. Since its launch in 2000, GNX claim to have organised some 18,000 auctions with an estimated value of $12 billion resulting in members of savings of around $1.2 billion. Apart from the procurement savings, other efficiencies are gained as members strive for improved supply chain collaboration. Other examples of vertical hubs are IMXExchange (Financial services/mortgages) and e-Steel (steel industry).

- **Horizontal hubs** are where non-industry specific products and services are sold across a range of industries. Typically office supplies and MROs (Maintenance, Repair and Operations) are traded in such marketplaces where homogeneous items are needed by every organisation.

Philips and Meeker (2000) offer a different categorisation emerging from the creator of the trading place:

1. **Buyer-managed** – usually where vendors of considerable size join forces to form large hubs

2. **Supplier Managed** – typically where purchasing agents and aggregators develop exchanges to bring smaller buyers together and increase their purchasing power eg utilities markets

3. **Distributor/market maker** – these are independent or neutral exchanges or auctions from the buyers and sellers. They play a role in matching orders eg Priceline or Chemdex

4. **Content Aggregators** – who gather content from different sites across the World Wide Web, often for redistribution and resale according to customer needs eg news aggregator www.Moreover.com

Whilst the B2B sector has witnessed most of the marketspace activity, various consumer models have emerged such as eBay who sell across a diverse range of product categories. However, the Internet has also provided opportunities for niche markets. A classic example that effectively combines businesses and consumers in its simple but very effective model is Golfbidder (www.Golfbidder.co.uk). Golfbidder is Europe's biggest exchange of second hand golf equipment. Golfers notoriously keep old clubs, especially putters that once upon a time made their owner do a good impression of Tiger Woods but the magic suddenly disappeared. For many golf professionals, second hand clubs acquired in trade-in deals clog up their shop with old stock. Golfbidder identified a new market opportunity in acting as an intermediary between the golf professionals and would-be buyers of the equipment. They concentrated only on premium brands such as Mizuno, Callaway, Ping and Taylor, made to attract better margins and establish an upmarket brand. Professionals were given guaranteed prices by Golfbidder valuers to eliminate any risk and improve cash flow and the appearance of their retail premises. Visitors to the exchange were given reassurance by the provision of a 12-month warranty. Clubs are auctioned off as lots in the case of sets or instant buys on individual items such as market leading drivers. Many golfers find it difficult to justify £399 for a new weapon but getting it mint second for 50% of the RRP is an attractive proposition. Last year, Golfbidder achieved sales of £2.7 million and has become the PGA's (Professional Golfers Association) official golf club exchange.

12.13 E-procurement

E-procurement represents a classic function of electronic commerce. Its development has afforded the procurement function similar benefits achieved by other business sectors. E-procurement is the use of e-commerce technology to aid the traditional business practice of procurement. The importance of procurement and the subsequent management of its function must be considered before e-procurement is considered in any depth.

Procurement is a key stage in the ideal supply (or value) chain. Stephen Rinsler (2003) (director of Compass Logistics Ltd and Chairman of the Supply Chain Faculty) argues for the necessity of including procurement as one of the key factors in any healthy business supply chain. Many businesses still compartmentalise the purchasing function as an individual operation, offering procurement insignificant consideration.

Without procurement playing an active role in the supply chain, incomplete knowledge is likely to result in poor purchasing decisions. For example, order quantity calculations in purchasing businesses are often hastily made from the supplier's point of view. In effect, the procurement department of a given business pays more attention to the supplier's needs than the needs of their own business. This is a direct symptom of isolating the purchasing department and offering insufficient information to make sensible purchase decisions. Rinsler argues that a far more effective and commonsense approach is for purchasers to understand the *real* demand, by looking at purchasing decisions from a supply chain point of view. In this instance, forecasted risks and errors can be accounted for with a holistic understanding of the company's operations and requirements.

Procurement's integration into a well-run supply chain is an essential precursor to the consideration of any e-procurement effort. Procurement is as fundamental as any business process, and will cause major business inefficiencies if it is not managed effectively. No technological developments can substitute this managerial responsibility.

Just as procurement is a component of the traditional supply (or value) chain, e-procurement is a direct component of the virtual value chain concept. The virtualisation of the traditional value chain seeks to exploit the benefits of e-commerce and its associated technologies. Each stage of the supply chain can benefit from technological developments brought about by e-commerce technology. Procurement is a particularly time consuming, cumbersome (and therefore costly) process in the value chain. These characteristics make procurement an ideal candidate for improvement through technology. While there are many tangible and intangible benefits of e-procurement, Fisher (2000) cites four key benefits as identified by The Butler Group:

1. The ability to aggregate purchasing across multiple departments without removing individual control.

2. Reducing 'rogue buying' to ensure goods are bought to specification or 'approved' suppliers are only used.

3. E-procurement creates a more reactive purchasing policy to find the best price or quality from a wider range of suppliers.

4. E-procurement also illustrates the disparities between pricing, quality and delivery.

The technology driving any e-procurement effort offers the opportunity for purchasers to easily locate the most competitive deals from a vast range of suppliers. Whether the e-procurement system is simply a primitive use of online catalogues, or indeed a complex purpose-built solution, the potential to reduce cost of goods through *choice* is great.

E-procurement can be used to offer a much greater choice of supplier, which obviously creates an opportunity to reduce the cost of goods, by making for informed and frugal business purchase decisions. This is in part due to the opening of the global marketplace for purchasers within businesses of any size. Traditional procurement often relied upon the trading reputation of a small number of suppliers, or sometimes their locality. The new age of e-procurement allows specific information regarding the quality and price of goods offered from a potentially unlimited number of suppliers to be available, continuously, quickly and universally.

Industry portals and increasingly complex e-procurement systems are now offering very specific supplier search facilities. These methods present those companies engaging in e-procurement with industry-specific search tools. While basic Internet searches tend to return a great deal of inappropriate results, e-procurement systems, often incorporating B2B portals, are limited to the scope of a business. This basic premise ensures that finding suppliers through most e-procurement systems is a relatively efficient process. Fine-tuning of supplier and product characteristics becomes more in-depth with the growing complexity of e-procurement systems, to the point whereby the entire process can be automated.

The advantage of having a diverse range of suppliers is easily understandable, the more suppliers, the greater the competition. There is, however, another side to the e-procurement supplier argument. With so many suppliers available, building up a good working relationship with a supplier becomes difficult. Similarly, it becomes increasingly complicated to administrate a vast array of suppliers. It is with this in mind that e-procurement technology can, therefore be alternatively used to *reduce* the number of suppliers to a business.

While this notion may appear to contradict one of the main 'selling points' of e-procurement, this is not necessarily the case. The key to effective supplier management through e-procurement is to create the optimum balance between financial benefits offered by an extensive supplier base, and controlling the management of those suppliers. A good balance could be achieved by initially selecting a set number of competitive suppliers from the global marketplace, and introduce them to the present supply chain. Healthy competition is bred, the global marketplace has been scoured for the best suppliers of the time, and relationships can be effectively built, controlled and administrated.

Auctions and various methods of *combined purchasing* can also be used in e-procurement to drive down the cost of goods. The theory behind combined purchasing relies upon the spending power of a group of purchasers rather than one individual purchasing company. By joining forces with several companies who each share similar purchasing needs (often business sector rivals) purchasers can drive down the price of goods by making large bulk purchase orders. In such cases, the supplying company is keen to make a major deal with a group of businesses in their industry, while the purchasing companies reap the rewards of negotiating extremely competitive prices.

In terms of industry supplier/purchaser auctions, the procurer is able to make the most cost effective deal at any given time. Much in the same way as a customer can compare prices at EBay for a CD they wish to buy, the industry purchaser can compare prices of stock they need to purchase, choosing the most competitive. For example, nine Northern local authorities in Lancashire and Yorkshire have established their own online trading hub known as the Roses Marketplace for e-tendering, contract management and e-catalogue based purchasing. Local and regional suppliers are invited to join the hub that not only streamlines procurement but also has potential economic benefits for numerous SMEs.

These methods of e-procurement are presently most frequently associated with industry-related stock and equipment purchases – otherwise known as *direct goods*. The premise of simply purchasing stock items in this fashion is somewhat lacking in the true scope of the procurement function. Indeed, the purchasing of so-called 'indirect' goods is an equally important task of the procurement function, and one that can also obtain value from the benefits of e-procurement.

Indirect goods such as maintenance, repair and operations items have traditionally been procured in a separate manner from direct goods such as manufacturing stock. The lines between direct and indirect goods in terms of procurement are however becoming less prominent, with the growing acceptance and adoption of e-procurement. Why should a company purchase only direct stock in a competitive and efficient manner when indirect but necessary goods like stationary, heating systems and electricity can reap the same benefits?

E-procurement seeks not to define certain purchase items as indirect or direct, but to assume that all commodities with a requirement of *being purchased* should be considered in the same light, and be afforded the same benefits.

Hewlett Packard (www.hp.com) was one of the first companies to develop an e-procurement system, and remain forerunners of the medium. HP implemented a major e-procurement facility whereby both direct and indirect goods are purchased. The use of an all encompassing purchasing system allows for standardisation within the organisation, which leads to ease of use, less confusion and a comprehensive, efficient purchasing system understood at many levels.

It is generally considered by most market analysts that even a small improvement in the cost of purchased materials can have a significant effect upon a company's profitability. The reduced costs of purchases brought about directly from the benefits of e-procurement are often enough of an incentive to drive businesses towards adopting such a system.

While the significant reduction in business purchase prices is a valid benefit, e-procurement's value increases further when the economies of administration efficiency are considered.

Traditional procurement was information heavy, as indeed its electronic counterpart is now. This meant that a lot of resources were consumed in the administration process of procurement. *Information heavy* as it happens, is what e-commerce does best. The medium of e-commerce has been built on the principle of electronically exchanging business information in the most efficient way possible. With this in mind, the major burden of procurement's transactional administration can be significantly alleviated with the appropriate use of e-procurement.

The potential for automation in terms of procurement is major. From re-order levels, to finding the lowest price supplier, through to transaction payment and receipt, automation can and does occur at all stages of the procurement process. Various companies choose to implement e-procurement to varying degrees, but it is possible to run a virtually paperless procurement system.

MINI CASE 12.7 **BMC**

BMC West, a former division of office products company, Boise Cascade, have introduced an e-procurement system from Optika. While the system began with teething problems, the company saw a real return on investment within 13 months. Since upgrading the system, BMC West have seen a reduction in administrative paperwork so significant that they now use only one filing cabinet compared to 33 previously. Another key improvement is the elimination of extremely high numbers of telephone calls with their network of suppliers.

Adapted from: AK Reese, *Paperless Procurement*, www.isourceonline.com

MINI CASE 12.8 Crown Cork

One company that has honed in on a direct e-procurement strategy is Crown Cork & Seal Co, a Philadelphia manufacturer of containers. The company sources a wide range of products and materials such as metals, solvents, resins, motors, belts and machine parts from over 1,400 suppliers. Previously, the purchasing department coordinated masses of orders from the organisation's 70 facilities and according to Daniel J Donaghy, VP of procurement, 'There was no time to focus on strategic procurement'. In February 2001, the firm put in place an end-to-end sourcing solution that uses a procurement aggregator and service provider. Now Crown Cork & Seal buyers search items, generate requisitions and approve them online. The system streamlines the company's accounts payable process by letting users view electronic invoices and search them by company or other criteria. The pay back is impressive. Crown Cork & Seal has generated savings of between 12–23% across its purchase requirements. The software paid for itself in 90 days and and nearly 100% of suppliers have adopted the web-based system.

Source: Greengard (2002) Originally printed in December 2002 issue of *Business Finance*.

E-procurement is not simply about automation. Automation is a small part of e-procurement, but not the most essential. The electronic exchange of information at the procurement level can be utilised to maximum effect by businesses that make best use of the medium. A matrix of information can be installed, offering data pertaining to the relevant parties at a precise level of detail, accuracy and volume. At the very best level, e-procurement can provide the information and tools to make and execute exceptionally informed and timely purchasing decisions.

E-procurement has a long way to go before its integration to widespread business can be described as anything like an overall success. Teething problems are inevitably found in most newly set-up e-procurement ventures, although most of the time these problems are insignificant enough to be overcome in the long run. As with any technological or theoretical advance in business, there are common examples of inappropriate or poorly managed adoptions of e-procurement systems. However, the success stories of e-procurement are now spawning some potentially equally successful imitators. The perceived success of e-procurement may not be particularly strong today, but current opinion and exemplar suggest that e-procurement is the way forward.

12.14 **Dominant technologies**

Shore and Venkatachalam (2003) discuss the criteria for selecting potential supply chain partners based on their information sharing capabilities. They suggest that the evaluation should assess the supplier's internal IT infrastructure and their application of key technologies such as:

- Enterprise Resource Planning (ERP)
- Supply Chain Management Systems (SCM) (previously discussed)
- Electronic Data Interchange (EDI)
- Extensible Markup Language (XML)

ERP

Enterprise resource planning systems provide integrated software for the effective management of information flows. Systems like those developed by SAP, Peoplesoft and Oracle provide organisations with the capability of integrating internal systems and processes that were previously incompatible. The benefit of ERP is the ability to coordinate internal functions such as human resources, manufacturing, purchasing, logistics and sales and marketing in real time. Duncan Gourlay of PWC, cited in Philips (2003) suggests three fundamental changes in ERP as a result of software development and systems integration:

- Organisations are employing systems which are more customer and demand driven.
- Organisational systems are evolving as firms increasingly seek supplier interactions via the Internet.
- Organisations seek the rewards and efficiencies generated by amalgamating disparate systems to provide seamless information flows to optimise upstream and downstream activities.

As Reynolds (2001) points out, many companies have invested heavily in sophisticated and customised ERP tools. Now they are faced with integrating the systems with their online site that can be an onerous task. There are significant benefits associated with web-based ERP especially with regard to inventory management efficiencies. However, Reynolds goes on to highlight the risks and failures with spiralling costs and failure to meet project deadlines. The harmonisation of IT systems is critical for a customer focussed real time management system. However, ERP has been criticised because of its focus on internal systems. With the development of new middleware products to connect front and back office systems, customer relationship management (CRM) software, SCM and database technologies can be added to provide a much needed external systems perspective.

Electronic Data Interchange (EDI)

Hollerson (2003) defines electronic data interchange (EDI) as: 'The transfer of structured data, by agreed message standards, from one computer to another by electronic means.'

Traditional EDI has existed since the early eighties in the B2B sector to link product or service suppliers to pivotal intermediaries. Strauss et al (2003) emphasise its importance in establishing structural network relationships. Typical examples of EDI applications are given in Table 12.6 below.

EDI has the benefit of reducing administrative costs (time and human error) as the need for physical documentation is removed and faster data exchange processes emerge (eg buying, ordering and delivering). On the downside, EDI is expensive and complicated to implement.

Table 12.6 Traditional EDI network applications

Industry	Example of application
Banking	Funds transfers between financial institutions
Travel	Real time reservation systems linking tour operators and travel agents
Automotive	Ordering systems linking manufacturers and supply partners

LEGAL EAGLE 12.2 Electronic data interchange

Despite the usefulness of EDI to the commercial world for tracking routine business documents and reducing errors in commercial exchanges of data, the use of EDI raises a number of legal issues.

The most common concerns for parties using EDI are those of security and protection from alteration of data so transmitted.

Apart from the issues of security and confidentiality, the problem of identifying the moment and place at which an electronic data interchange is concluded can be a difficult one. To be used with confidence, EDI must be able to thwart intrusions by hackers and provide some level of transactional authenticity and evidence.

Consequently, its adoption has been largely restricted to larger blue chip companies and their private value-added networks (VANs) with smaller firms being unable to participate. *Business Week*, cited in Hollerson, estimates the cost of adding new partners to a traditional EDI network at $50,000 compared with $10,000 for an Internet based EDI system. EDI has tended to be limited in its applications to purchasing and invoicing largely because of its security advantages. In Legal Eagle box 12.2 above, we highlight key issues over data transmission with EDI.

Extensible Markup Language (XML)

Whereas EDI has largely been the domain of larger companies, technology standards based on Extensible Markup Language (XML) are creating greater openness and flexibility in web based communications with positive implications for all interactions. The language was created by the World Wide Web Consortium (www.w3c.org).

Whilst HTML (Hypertext Markup Language) defines the presentation of web pages, its applications are limited as the Internet spawns an increasingly diverse range of information types. For example, dynamic pricing systems, database supported CRM systems and flexible online product catalogue information requiring effective integration between both internal and external systems. XML not only provides instant program-to-program communications across numerous platforms, it also facilitates visual content presentation. It is rapidly emerging as the key language for information flows between different systems operated by organisations of all sizes. Ron Schmeizler (2002) consultant with Zap Think, an XML and web services research firm, enthuses in *Tech Republic* about the merits of XML in that it marks data so that multiple systems can agree on the XML format and read the data so there is little concern where the information originates from.

A key advantage of XML lies in its flexibility to allow developers to create customised tags and codes to identify any objects relevant to corporate, customer or supply chain needs. As Bandho-padhyay (2002) asserts, the use of XML tags makes the sharing of information between front and back office systems easier. The XML database structures also make for more efficient search engine retrieval results. For supply and value chain enhancement, industry sectors are their own agreed XML codes and dictionaries. This creates the possibility of information exchange between all players at different value chain points. The sheer volume and value of Internet based B2B transactions should ensure ongoing adoption and development of XML technology standards.

In reality, companies will have heavily invested in EDI and will seek benefit from that investment. If XML is going to be more than the latest buzzword, it will have to coexist with EDI for the foreseeable future. To enable this, software developers are writing translation and transformation codes to allow data exchange and achieve cost efficiencies.

12.15 **Summary**

It is very easy to remember the criticism levelled at new online businesses a few years ago about the obsession with front end systems and total ambivalence towards its back end systems, and believe that life in the world of distribution and fulfilment is now rosy. It is true that many organisations have begun to seriously address the need for better designed, more transparent and flexible delivery systems if customer satisfaction is to be achieved in the final mile. Good online systems offer speed and convenience at both ends but it is increasingly evident that to achieve this companies need to redesign and realign their processes with new partners in strategic alliances and outsourcing agreements. These offer cost and performance efficiencies that help to achieve competitive advantage. Underpinning these developments are increasingly sophisticated software tools and platforms that integrate buyers and sellers seamlessly. It is true that the Internet has impacted upon traditional distribution intermediaries though new players have emerged to step into their shoes.

Finally a cautionary tale: 'I have a friend' who ordered two CD-ROMs from his ISP loyalty programme for his daughter's Christmas present in mid-December and was quoted 8–10 days for delivery. Santa came and went, three e-mails flew to customer services in early 19 January and received no reply. The CD-ROMs arrived on 19 January. Why?

END OF CHAPTER CASE STUDY e-fulfilment system makes Edinburgh Crystal shine

Slick integration between Edinburgh Crystal's web site and its manufacturing enterprise system provided a successful backbone for the company's e-commerce – and a 1,000% increase in sales.

Challenge:

To use e-commerce to build a global, but sustainable marketing presence, to increase sales and margins and to improve service

Solution:

To build an automated on-line web store, linked to Internet banking, to the firm's ERP systems and to the contract shipping company's third party logistics system

Cost:

- ERP system: £43,000
- Web system: £12,000

Edinburgh Crystal, the UK's leading £22 million revenues crystal glass brand, has integrated its manufacturing and logistics systems with an Internet-based global customer sales facility, and it is working brilliantly. Its site is Number One on Yahoo's Scottish gifts search and the firm has seen its proportion of sales across the Internet rise a staggering 1,000%. Why? Edinburgh Crystal did e-commerce the right way.

IT manager Andy Thompson says the keys are threefold: having good, accurate foundation manufacturing and business systems (ERP) in place; thinking carefully about integration with the web front end; and heavily promoting the web site across the web search engines and the rest. For Edinburgh Crystal this meant linking its new web sales system to its McGuffie Brunton Impact Encore ERP system and, via its event management system, developing automated processes to drive independent payment and distribution management company systems.

Impact Encore was installed two years ago at the firm's Edinburgh site, replacing an earlier Unix-based bespoke green screen system, and handling financials, aggregated demand driven manufacturing and warehouse management, stock control, work in progress, etc. It was a somewhat complex implementation, having to handle the vagaries of mixed craftsman and machine-based manufacturing (with issues like scrap and rework), and a sales order processing front end managing some 120 concessions and 12,000 customers, *plus* a separate forecasting system.

Thompson says the firm had gone for largely 'vanilla' ERP software, deliberately reducing its bespoke content from 60% to just 5%, and involving considerable business process re-engineering to achieve this. He also says that following 'go-live' and the usual bedding in, the system had been augmented with Open Database Connectivity (ODBC) links to a Microsoft Access database to allow for easier user queries and ad hoc reports.

Among key results of this work was the fact that stock accuracy was raised from 96% to 99.8%, while inventory was reduced from £6.5 million to £4 million. Beyond this, the lengthy material ordering process cycle from sales order entry through weekly MRP and purchase order raising – which previously took two weeks – was reduced to overnight electronic transactions. Also, the Edinburgh Crystal store concessions product replenishment cycle moved initially from six weeks down to two, and more recently down again to just four days, hugely improving customer service.

In short, manufacturing and business management had become integrated, slick and efficient. And it is this important development that provided the company with the firm foundations it needed for its more recent implementation – the Edinburgh Crystal e-commerce sales site. It meant that web-based buying could work without the problems of manual re-keying into multiple systems that so often let such initiatives down. Instead, the web order entry system could link directly into the existing internal ERP and be configured to work with new external systems so that everything from order processing, through product picking and documenting to despatch was automated to ensure prompt, low cost fulfilment.

This is how it works. Consumers place orders on Edinburgh Crystal's 'on-line store', and all credit card transactions – authorisation and processing – are automatically undertaken via a link from the site to the Netbanx (Internet banking) site. Orders are collected by the firm's Internet service provider (ISP) UUnet and, at the end of each day, all data (held in an Access file) is e-mailed to Edinburgh Crystal. The file is then imported into the ERP system where the orders are processed: 30 minutes later the picking lists are released. Also, through Encore's Event Management module (which enables users to monitor triggers in Encore and associate actions to events), a Visual Basic routine is triggered. This collects all order detail information, such as product price, duty, weight and customers' addresses and feeds it into a local Federal Express PC, using ODBC.

That in turn creates a manifest file and prints off the FedEx shipment documentation ready for the next morning despatch. It also dials up and downloads the manifest into a secure site on CompuServe, accessible by FedEx's central US computer, which in turn provides FedEx with invoicing and dispatch information, and instructions for product pick up.

Finally, the invoice generated by Edinburgh Crystal is used as despatch documentation and for ledger update. The Netbanx site sends credit card details back to Edinburgh Crystal, which are then processed by another Visual Basic programme to update the sales/general ledgers.

There is more to come. Currently, Edinburgh Crystal is preparing to move from it Impact Encore v3.0 ERP system up to v5.0 primarily to gain the Microsoft SQL Server database in place of its existing flat files. Thompson says that benefits will include access to business, manufacturing and logistics information by more staff, since they will no longer have to wait for slow ODBC connections. Instead they will be able to link information directly into their Microsoft Office systems for up-to-the-minute reports.

It is also investing in McGuffie's human resources (HR) module in v5.0. Thompson says that this will further reduce operating costs by ensuring that staff tracking, training and documentation are improved, achieving the dual benefits of better-motivated personnel and better management of people across manufacturing and the support roles.

For the future, Edinburgh Crystal will also be looking at integrating real time shop floor data collection, possibly using IEGL's Total Factory to get better plant visibility, production scheduling and stock control. Thompson says this would also improve manufacturing accuracy, costs and business responsiveness by making it possible to drive the business directly from demand via EPOS terminals at the concessions, 75 of which have already been installed.

'While the rapid take-off of e-commerce has created the opportunity to increase our global market presence, it is the implementation of Impact Encore, with its additional functionality, that has provided us with the internal capability to maximise this opportunity,' says Thomson. It has done so 'by enabling us to effectively integrate an e-commerce operation into our existing business framework.'

Keywords: e-fulfilment, ERP, Business process re-engineering

Questions

1. What did Andy Thompson describe as the three key planks in Edinburgh Crystal's e-fulfilment system integration?

2. Describe the key benefits accruing from this integration and how each would 'add value' in the supply chain.

3. How do these back office systems result in front-end customer satisfaction?

First published in Manufacturing Computer Solutions (www. mcsolutions.co.uk), a Findlay Publications journal, courtesy of Findlay Publications and Edinburgh Crystal.
Visit www.edinburgh-crystal.co.uk/

DISCUSSION QUESTIONS

1. Why has the distribution function taken on greater importance for online marketers?
2. Why do you think there were so many problems with the deliveries in the early days of the Internet?
3. Select a sector of your choice. In what way has the Internet affected the 'Place' element in that sector?
4. What impact has the Internet had on the value chain?
5. The role of the intermediary has taken on greater importance in the online world. Explain why, with examples.

REFERENCES

Bandho-padhyay (2002), *E-Commerce, Context, Concepts and Consequences*, McGraw Hill Education, Maidenhead, Berhs, UK, 158–159

Blythe, J (2001) *Essentials of Marketing*, (2nd edn), FT Prentice Hall, Harlow, London, 160

Brassington, F & Petitt, S (2000) *Principles of Marketing*, FT Prentice Hall, Harlow, England, 490

Brassington, F & Petitt, S (2003) *Principles of Marketing*, FT Prentice Hall, Harlow, England, 471, 480–483, 484

Bucklin, LP (1972) *Competition and Evolution in the Distributive Trades*, Prentice-Hall, Englewood Cliffs

Bucklin, LP (1966) *A Theory of Distribution Channel Structure*, IBER Special Publications, Berkeley, CA

Delaney, KJ, *The Wall Street Journal Europe*, 12 January 2004, A5

Doyle, P (2002) *Marketing Management and Strategy*, FT Prentice Hall, Harlow, England, 83, 311

Financial Times, 12 December 2003, 3

Fisher, A (2000) *Financial Times*, Business Supplement, Understanding e-procurement, Winter 2000

Glazer, R (1991) Marketing in an information-intensive environment: strategic implications of knowledge as an asset, in Sheth, JN, Esghi, A and Krishnan, BC (2001) *Internet Marketing*, Harcourt Inc, Orlando, 35

Gourlay, D (PWC), cited in Philips (2003) *E-Business Strategy*, McGraw Hill, Maidenhead, England, 171–173

Greengard, S (2002) E-procurement grows up, *Business Finance Mag.com* [online]. Available from: www.businessfinancemag.com/magazine/archives/article.html?articleID=13925&pg=2 [02/12/03]

Harvey

Hollerson, S (2003) *Marketing Management – A Relationship Approach*, FT prentice Hall, Pearson Education Limited, Harlow, England, 92, 402, 422–423

www.techrepublic.com.com/5100-6313-1052105-1.html, 28 June 2002

www.internetretailer.com/dailyNews.asp?id=10618

Kotler, P & Armstrong, G (2004) *Principles of Marketing*, 10th edn, Pearson Education Inc, New Jersey, 401

Kulkarni, S & Oak, V (2003) *E-manufacturing & SAP-Creating Responsive Shop Floor in the Supply Chain*, WIPRO Technologies White Paper

Lewis, C (2002) *E-logistics*, March 28–30

Lynn, F (2000) The dynamics and economics of channel marketing systems, in the *2000 Handbook of Business Strategy*, Faulkner and Gray, New York, NY

Marketing Direct Daily, IDMF Show review, Issue 4

Mason, SJ, Cole, MH, Ulrey, BT & Yan, L (2002) Improving electronics manufacturing supply chain agility through outsourcing, *International Journal of Physical Distribution & Logistics Management*, Vol 32, No 7, 2002, MCB UP Limited, 611

McDonald, M & Christopher, M (2003) *Marketing- A Complete Guide*, 2003, Palgrave, Basingstoke, England, 389–392, 414

McDonald, WJ (1998) *Direct Marketing – An Integrated Approach*, McGraw Hill, International Edition, 400

Philips, C & Meeker, M (2000) *The B2B Internet Report – Collaborative Commerce*, New York, Morgan Stanley Dean Witter, April 2000

Porter, M, (1985) *Competitive Advantage*, Free Press, New York

Reddy & Reddy (2001) *Supply Chains to Virtual Integration*, McGraw Hill, 6

Reese, AK (2001) *Paperless Procurement*, Supply and Demand Chain Executive [online]. Available from: www.isourceonline.com/article.asp?article_id=597 [10/12/03]

Reynolds, J (2001) *Logistics and Fulfilment for e-business*, CMP Books, New York, 1, 19, 346, 410–412

Rinsler, S (2003) *Why Procurement Must Be Connected to the Supply Chain*, Supply Chain Planet [online]. Available from: www.supplychainplanet.com/e_article000180322.cfm [27/11/03]

Sahay & Mohan (2003) Supply chain management practices in Indian industry, *International Journal of Physical Distribution and Logistics Management*, Vol 33, No 7, 2003, 582–606

Sawhney & Kaplan (2001) Business-to-business Internet marketing, in Richardson, P (ed) *Internet Marketing – Readings and Online Resources*, McGraw Hill, New York, 265–271

Scotland on Sunday, 7 September 2003, 7

Shore, B & Venkatachalam, AR (2003) Evaluating the information sharing capabilities of supply chain partners, *International Journal of Physical Distribution & Logistics Management*, Vol 33, No 9, 2003, 804–824, MCB UP Limited

Simons, LPA, Steinfield, C & Bouwman, H (2002) Strategic positioning of the web in a multi-channel market approach, *Internet Research: Electronic Networking Applications and Policy*, Vol 12, No 4, 2002, 339–347, MCB UP Limited

Starkov, M (2003) *The Internet: Hotelier's Best Ally or Worst Enemy?* www.4hotleliers.com/4hots_fsh.php?mwi=89, 12 April 2003

Stern, LW, El-Ansary AI & Coughlan, AT (1996) *Marketing Channels*, (5th edn), Prentice Hall, Englewood Cliffs, NJ

Sterne, J (2001) *World Wide Web Marketing*, (3rd edn), John Wiley & Sons Inc, New York, 345–348

Strauss, J, El Ansary, A & Frost, R (2003) *E marketing*, (3rd edn), Prentice Hall, Upper Saddle River, New Jersey, 333, 345

The *Wall Street Journal Europe*, A1 & A6, 3 December 2003

Timmers, P (1999) *Electronic Commerce: Strategies and Models for Business-to-Business Trading*, John Wiley & Sons, Inc

Veeramani, D & Joshi, P (1997) Strategic production-distribution models: a critical review with emphasis on global supply chain models, *European Journal of Operational Research*, Vol 98, 1–18 cited in Mason, SJ, Cole, MH Ulrey, BT & Yan, L (2002) Improving electronics manufacturing supply chain agility through outsourcing, *International Journal of Physical Distribution & Logistics Management*, Vol 32, No 7, 2002, MCB UP Limited, 610–620

Williams, LR, Esper, TL & Ozmet, J (2002) The electronic supply chain, *International Journal of Physical Distribution & Logistics Management*, Vol 32, No 8, 2002, 704

Wilson, H, Hobbs, M, Dolder, C & McDonald, M (2004) Optimising multiple channels, *Journal of Interactive Marketing*, Vol 5, No 3, 252–268, January – March 2004, Henry Stewart Publications

Wright, R (2004) *Business to Business Marketing*, FT Prentice Hall, Pearson Education Limited, Harlow, England, 289

Zahay, DL & Hadfield, RB (2003) Using the value chain to improve interactive marketing, *Journal of Interactive Marketing*, Vol 4, No 4, 343–354, April/June 2003, Henry Stewart Publications

FURTHER READING

Kuglin, FA & Rosenbaum, BA (2001) *The Supply Chain Network* @Internet Speed, AMACOM, New York

Reynolds, J (2001) *Logistics and Fulfilment for e-business*, CMP Books, New York, US

Trade publications

Logistics Manager

Intranet Strategist

WEB LINKS

Small and medium sized enterprises can get useful guidance on electronic payments via UK online for business at **www.electronic-payments.co.uk**

For an insight into the ongoing XML developments visit the World Wide Web Consortium at (**www.w3c.org**).

UK Online and DTI project, *Supply Chain-UK Electronic Trading Hubs*, **www.com-met2005.org.uk**

 Visit the Online Resource Centre which accompanies this book, for lots of interesting additional material, including self-assessment questions, internet exercises, and links for each chapter: **www.oxfordtextbooks.co.uk/orc/gay/**

Online Marketing Legal Issues

13

Learning objectives

By the end of the chapter you will be able to:

- Understand the key issues of online contract formation and authentication of online transactions
- Appreciate the insecure nature of the global network and the prevalent confidentiality/security risks
- Understand the legal requirements for protecting personal data
- Recognise the availability of different types of e-payment systems for online transactions

Chapter at a glance

13.1 **Introduction**

As we have discussed in other chapters in this text, many organisations' early 'e' focus was with front end systems and site design. Latterly, back office systems have caught the attention of the connected business as they strive for greater efficiency and customer satisfaction. However, the ease with which marketers share information and transact in today's electronic age highlights the main characteristics of the new economy. Despite the advantages of going online there are legal risks associated with e-marketing thus making it necessary for marketers to address the legal issues appropriately to guard against potential legal action, bad PR and being seen to act in an ethical and lawful manner. This chapter will consider the nature of the legal environment in general and specifically related to key cyber legal issues. It also reminds the reader of the need to abide by existing legislation such as the Sale and Supply of Goods Act 1979 and the Trades Description Acts 1968 and 1972 as well as codes of practice such as those of the Advertising Standards Authority (www.asa.org.uk) and trade bodies like the former E-Mail Marketing Association known as eMMa that developed its own charter before merging with the DMA, which may apply.

Marketers must be aware of the threats and opportunities provided by legal frameworks and in Mini cases 13.1 and 13.2 we give two examples.

MINI CASE 13.1 Gambling online

In the UK, a liberalised framework and helpful tax regime towards online gambling enabled the online sports betting exchange Betfair (www.betfair.com) to expand rapidly and achieve around 90% share of the world's online gambling revenues. However, Betfair understands concerns about online gambling and respects national laws that make it illegal. For example they do not take bets from the US where Internet gaming is banned in the majority of states. In addition, betting exchanges like Betfair have to operate within the tighter guidelines of the 2005 Gambling Act that covers 'remote gambling' on issues such as licensing and advertising. In addition, the EU allows governments to ban cross-border online gaming on moral grounds.

MINI CASE 13.2 Apple versus Apple

Apple Computer has been in legal wrangles with Apple Corps, the Beatles' holding company that has controlled Apple Recordings, regarding their shared name and logo for nearly 23 years.

The wrangle has flared up again thanks to the phenomenal success of iTunes. Apple Corps which is owned by Paul McCartney, Ringo Starr and the widows of former Beatles, John Lennon and George Harrison argue that Apple Computer is in breach of a 1991 trademark agreement but Apple Computer claim that the distribution of digital entertainment content was permitted under the agreement.

Under the agreement, the Apple Computer company were forbidden from using any trademark for any application 'whose principle content is music'. Apple Corps claim that the iTunes online service infringes their trademark, and industry experts forecast that the payout could far exceed the $30 million that they paid back then for a breach of an earlier agreement allow-ing the company to use the Apple trademark only for computer sales.

From an NME article, a top entertainment lawyer told the US magazine, *Daily Variety*: 'People are expecting this to be the biggest settlement anywhere in legal history, outside of a class action suit. The numbers could be mind-boggling.'

In a High Court judgment, Mr Justice Mann ruled that Apple Computer used the Apple logo in association with the online store and not the music it sold, and therefore did not breach the agreement. The ruling surprised many observers and the Beatles company was facing a legal bill of £5 million though an appeal was likely.

So at the time of writing, the Fab Four will not be available on iTunes.

Sources: www.nme.com/news/109877.htm
'Why morons recognise iTunes', Metro, 31 March 2006, 26.

When using the open network or other electronic devices to provide services, marketers have to take the necessary steps to develop trustworthy e-environments by addressing the legal issues and considering how they impact upon various stakeholders. This chapter also focuses on the areas of law that affect e-marketing. It highlights the legal framework and requirements that must be addressed in order to promote trust in the e-marketing environment, which is critical for the continued adoption of the Internet.

13.2 Direct marketing and database management

Direct marketing is the communication of any advertising or marketing material that is directed to particular individuals. Direct marketing has been controlled by a number of Codes and Regulations.

The British Code of Advertising, Sales Promotion and Direct Marketing (the CAP Code)

The CAP Code covers the obtaining, compiling, processing, management and use of personal data for the purpose of marketing products and services to the public through targeted mail. The Code covers three key areas.

1. **Processing of Personal Information**

When collecting personal information for marketing purposes, marketers should provide their names and the general purpose for which the individual's details are being collected. Where the recipient of such personal data has the intention of disclosing it to a third party, that should be clearly stated, thus giving the potential customer the opportunity to object to the collection.

   The information should be used only for the stated purpose to which the potential customer had given consent. Where the marketer later decides to use it for a different purpose, further consent should first be obtained.

2. **Corrections and suppressions**

Individuals' circumstances change from time to time. Where there are changes in individuals' personal details, and they request that their personal information be corrected, marketers should act on such requests within 60 days.

3. **Withdrawal of consent**

Consent, when given, is not indefinite as it could be withdrawn at any time. On request, marketers are required to delete individuals' names and addresses from their database. They should also stop future mailing to those individuals. One of the legal requirements is that marketers should ensure that their lists are accurate and up-to-date.

Sanctions Under the CAP Code

The CAP Code is backed up by sanctions, which include the withdrawal of trading privileges, and loss or suspension of the Royal Mail's mail-sort contract that can work to increase the cost of postage for an organisation. Where there is persistent offending by a particular marketer, the case can be referred to the Information Commissioner or the Director General of Fair Trading.

The Data Protection Act 1998

When effecting direct marketing, if the information contains personal data, the marketer is required to comply with the Data Protection Act 1998. That Act defines personal data as any data that can be used to identify a living individual, including names, addresses, personalised e-mail addresses and video images of such individuals.

The 1998 Act provides that when personal data is processed in the course of a direct marketing activity, such processing must:

- Be fair and lawful
- Be for a specific purpose or specified purposes
- Be relevant, adequate and not excessive
- Be accurate and up-to-date
- Not be kept for longer than necessary
- Give effect to data subjects' rights
- Take adequate measure to prevent the loss, damage or destruction of such data
- Ensure that where personal data is to be transferred to a non-European Economic Area (EEA) country, adequate protective measures are in place.

The Privacy and Electronic Communications (EC Directive) Regulations 2003

These Regulations apply to direct marketing effected by electronic means such as by telephone, fax, e-mail, and text messages, automated calling systems and image messages (such as video). Marketers are required to comply with the provisions of these Regulations when sending direct marketing by electronic means. This section will focus on telephone marketing, fax marketing and automated calling system. Due to the growing importance of e-mail marketing and text messaging using wireless mobile networks these two will be dealt with separately.

Telephone marketing

When marketers are effecting telesales calls, they must identify themselves and on request provide a valid business address or freephone telephone number at which they can be contacted. If the services of sub-contractors are used (such as call centres), the identity should be that of the organisation on whose behalf the calls are made. Even where a subscriber consents to receiving telesales calls, that consent can be withdrawn at any time.

Once a subscriber has opted out of a telesales call, that request must be given effect. Such a request need not be in writing. However, it is prudent to have such a request in writing in case of any future complaint to the Information Commissioner. On opt-out such individuals' details should be suppressed and not deleted for the purpose of checking new directories against opt-out lists/numbers.

Telephone Preference Service (TPS): This is a list of telephone numbers of which the telephone owners or subscribers have registered an objection to receiving unsolicited telesales calls. The TPS list is a statutory requirement and marketers must regularly clean their database against this list. However, those that have registered on the list may give specific consent to telesales calls that relate to specific products.

Fax marketing

When marketers are effecting direct marketing with the use of a fax system they must provide their identities and a valid address or freephone number at which they can be contacted. Direct marketing with the use of fax is now regulated by the Privacy and Electronic Communications (EC Directive) Regulations 2003. Under these Regulations to send an unsolicited fax message for the purpose of direct marketing, a marketer must first obtain the consent of the potential recipient of the fax message.

Even where a marketer uses a sub-contractor to send fax messages for direct marketing, the liability will still be that of the marketer if the sub-contractor infringes any legal rule. In order to protect themselves against such legal liability marketers should put appropriate contracts in place to guard against breaches by their subcontractors.

Fax Preference Service (FPS): There is now a statutory list of fax numbers where the subscribers to those numbers have registered a general objection to receiving unsolicited marketing faxes on those numbers. Marketers should not send or instigate the sending of an unsolicited marketing fax to any number listed on the FPS register. A marketer can, however, send unsolicited marketing faxes to an FPS registered subscriber if the subscribers have notified the marketer that, for the time being, they do not object to receiving such calls.

Most sections of the Regulations that refer to consent indicate that such consent is to be given *'for the time being'*. This simply means that although consent is given for direct marketing materials/information to be sent to a particular individual, such consent cannot be taken to be indefinite. If there is good reason to render such consent as no longer valid, the consent will be deemed nullified. Where the recipient is happy to continue to receive marketing information, the consent will remain valid.

Automated calling systems

An automated calling system is any system that is 'capable of automatically initiating a sequence of calls to more than one destination in accordance with instructions stored in that system'. Normally such systems transmit sounds that are not live speech for reception by persons at the destinations called. Automated calling systems do not cover marketing by text/picture/video message, fax, or e-mail.

Generally speaking, marketing material cannot be transmitted by such a system without the prior consent of the subscriber. Any marketing material sent by the use of an automated calling system must include the identity of the caller and an address or a freephone number at which the caller can be contacted.

Where 'silent calls' are concerned, the natural assumption is that the call is made with malicious intent. Although 'silent calls' are disturbing, the Regulations do not apply to them, as they do not transmit marketing material. Where it is proved that 'silent calls' are made with malicious intent by an individual, the Data Protection Act will allow disclosures that are necessary for the prevention of such calls.

If a subscriber is able to demonstrate to a court that the provisions of the Regulations have been breached in the course of using automated calling system, and that the breach has caused quantifiable damage, the subscriber may be able to claim compensation.

MINI CASE 13.3 Data disclosure

Company A sets up a database on its intranet in order to make the details of customers who are bad credit risks accessible to all its employees. It also extends access to its intranet to companies B, C and D so that they can identify bad risks. This infringes Principle 1 of the Data Protection Act 1998, as the individuals are not notified of the further disclosures to third parties.

Database management

An organisation's database usually contains personal data, which is data that can be used to identify a living individual. Any organisation that makes use of a database must put procedures in place to safeguard the way such personal data is used, stored, shared, cleaned and destroyed.

Data matching using databases

Organisations should only process personal data in databases in line with the purpose for which the data was collected. Where personal data was collected for a particular purpose, it should not be matched with data obtained for another purpose in order to create a new set of data for the purpose of using it in a totally different way.

Data cleansing for accuracy

Principle 4 of the Data Protection Act 1998 provides that personal data must be accurate and, where necessary, kept up to date. For this principle to be fulfilled personal data has to be cleansed on a regular basis. Data cleansing is the process of removing errors and inconsistencies from data held in a database. When data is being cleansed, the process must be carried out carefully. Data cleansing can include running checks against the names, surnames and addresses held on a database.

An organisation's marketing database should be kept separate from the main customer database with the latter being cleansed on a regular basis. The marketing database should then be screened against the customer database regularly to ensure accuracy and consistency. In the process of cleansing and screening all inaccurate data should be amended. Data storage systems should be such that enable stored data to be easily changed and corrected thus ensuring compliance with Principle 4.

Sometimes it will be necessary to completely delete data when the need to hold it no longer exists. In addition, processing of certain personal data may be stopped if it causes the individual undue damage or distress. The processing can be prevented if the Information Commissioner or the Court gives an order requiring the processing to be stopped. Organisations' data processing systems should, therefore, be capable of supporting the complete deletion of personal data if compliance with the Act is to be achieved.

Using databases for marketing

Data subjects have a legal right to object to the processing of their personal data for marketing purposes. To give effect to this right marketers should have a way of identifying and recording the individual data subjects who have shown their objection to the use of their personal information for marketing campaigns. Such objectors' personal data should not be deleted from the system but simply suppressed. The suppression of the names, addresses

---

Fig 13.1 Database actions points

1. Identify marketing information that needs opt-in and that which needs opt-out.
2. Suppress personal data of objectors.
3. Screen your database against the preference service lists.
4. Develop systems that will enable suppression and screening of personal data.

---

and telephone numbers of objectors will enable future 'bought-in' lists to be checked and screened against those that have already objected to receiving marketing material.

Before using its database to market its goods or services an organisation should screen it against the telephone, fax and mail preference services lists. In order to screen their databases against these different preference services lists organisations will have to build certain facilities into their systems design. Key elements are recommended in Fig 13.1.

Security and confidentiality of databases

Principle 7 of the Data Protection Act 1998 provides that personal data must be protected from unauthorised or unlawful processing; accidental loss, destruction or damage by appropriate technical and organisational measures. Since database contains personal data, it is essential that it be processed securely to ensure compliance with Principle 7. To enable such compliance both technical and organisational security measures must be taken.

The technical measures will include the use of firewalls and passwords to ensure that the database is protected from outside access and internal attacks. Although there are grave concerns over outside attackers breaking into a computer system, security threats from insiders should not be overlooked as they already have access to the network and might find it easier to obtain unauthorised access to secured parts of the system.

Staff should be made aware of database security requirements and the seriousness of security breaches. Appropriate security mechanism should be put in place to ensure that unlawful and unauthorised attempts at breaches can be detected and prevented. Data management systems that store databases should have audit trail functionalities to allow the identification of individuals that access the database at different times.

13.3 E-mail marketing and spamming

E-mail marketing has become a very powerful yet inexpensive way of contacting existing and potential customers. The main reason for the growth of e-mail marketing is that it can be targeted to specific individuals and organisations. Apart from using an e-mail list of existing customers, marketers can buy e-mail lists from dealers, thus allowing them to direct e-mails to recipients who have consented to receiving such e-mails.

This ease of use has made e-mails an important means of exchanging information, working, learning and marketing goods/services. The new methods of marketing using this channel include:

- Sending direct promotional information to existing customers about new products or services.

- Sending advertisement material to individuals in an attempt to acquire new customers.
- Sending e-mails to existing customers to encourage customer loyalty and enhance customer relationship.
- Placing promotional information or advertisements in e-mails sent by other people or organisations.

Types of e-mail marketing

There are three main types of e-mail marketing:

1. Direct e-mail marketing

This is the sending of advertisement information in the form of e-mail directly to the individuals to either market goods or products or to announce special offers.

2. Retention e-mails

These are normally in the form of regular e-mails known as newsletters aimed at developing long-term relationships with recipients of the newsletters. The newsletter may contain promotional messages or advertisements or it may aim to provide recipients with good value information on various areas of business and activities in the society.

In order to market effectively with the use of e-mail newsletters, marketers have to find out what readers are interested in. Some readers have indicated that they are interested in information that helps them do their jobs better as well as information that can be used to raise the profile of their companies. To make e-mail newsletters interesting, it is, therefore, important to include useful articles on topical issues that affect businesses. Once in a while an e-mail newsletter marketer needs to make a bold assertion or take a stand on recent community or national developments. It is also important to challenge the readers on such issues by finding out their views.

3. Advertising in others' e-mails

This can be a very effective way of marketing ones goods and services especially where the advertisers have large e-mailing lists. The main advantage of marketing with the use of others' e-mail is that a very small amount is paid for the e-mails to be sent to the advertiser's subscribers. It should, however, be checked that the advertiser has the consent of the recipients to send the email and that they have been given the opportunity to opt-out of further marketing information.

Sending effective e-mails

Individuals respond better to e-mail marketing when they feel special and unique and respond differently if they feel that they are just treated as part of a large group. The most important thing, therefore, is to make your e-mail marketing material personal and specific. For example, where a marketing e-mail is being addressed to an individual consumer, 'Hi Sue' is a good way to start off. This reflects the type of relationship that exists between the sender and the recipient of the e-mail. Where the e-mail is directed to a business recipient then 'Dear Mr Brown' or 'Dear Ian Brown' can be used.

Another technique is to keep e-mails short. Today's age is a fast moving one and the new medium of communication is substantially different from the verbose, long-sentenced practice of paper-based communication. Short sentences, bullet points and short messages are vital to effective e-mail marketing. E-mail marketers should always bear in mind that their e-mail recipients might have to read hundreds of other e-mails in addition to their own.

Making e-mail marketing as conversational as possible helps to give it an informal feel and enables quick responses. Informal, lively and conversational e-mails are likely to be read and remembered. At the same time, it has to be remembered that e-mails are now legally binding documents, thus they need to be clearly articulated with the emphasis placed at the right point.

In e-mail marketing, it is important that appropriate punctuations are used to convey the right meaning, as the content is mainly text. The subject line of an e-mail is extremely important, as it must captivate the attention of the recipient. Using an attractive and descriptive subject line increases the chances that a marketer has of getting the e-mail message read by the recipient. In responding to enquiries on an initial marketing e-mail sent by them, marketers should always refer to the context of the initial e-mail in order to refresh the memory of the reader.

E-mail marketing and personal data

E-mail marketing is now regulated by the Privacy and Electronic Communications (EC Directive) Regulations 2003, Regulations 22 and 23. These Regulations define e-mail as:

> 'any text, voice, sound or image message sent over a public electronic communications network which can be stored in the network or in the recipient's terminal equipment until it is collected by the recipient . . .'

These Regulations provide that marketers should not transmit or instigate the transmission of unsolicited marketing material with the use of e-mail systems to individuals unless the recipients had consented to receive such marketing material. Regulation 23 prohibits marketers from sending marketing information by e-mail to individuals unless they:

- Provide their identities as senders of the e-mail marketing material, or
- Provide a valid address to which the recipient can send an opt-out-request. In the online environment a valid address could simply be an e-mail address.

A marketer may, however, send e-mail marketing material to an individual without prior consent where:

- The individual's contact details were obtained in the course of a sale or negotiation for the sale of the sender's product or service.
- The e-mail marketing material is sent to the recipient for the purpose of advertising a product that is similar to that which has already been sold to the recipient or which has been negotiated for sale.
- The recipient has been given a simple means of opting-out of receiving further marketing information.

Under these Regulations marketing by e-mail to sole traders and unlimited partnerships are regulated by the same rules as those regulating marketing to individual subscribers. Where partnerships are concerned, consent should be obtained from the individual partner to whom the marketing material is targeted before unsolicited e-mails are sent to the individual. A person, such as the personal assistant or secretary, who can be reasonably expected to act on that individual's behalf, can give such consent. Where consent is to be obtained from third parties, marketers should ensure that such third parties have the authority to provide the consent.

To ensure that consent is properly provided and personal data of partners/officers are well protected, the key frontline staff such as receptionists, secretaries, administrators and personal assistants should be trained on data protection and e-security/confidentiality in relation to disclosure of personal details of partners/officers. It is noteworthy that corporate subscribers, unlike individual subscribers, do not have an enforceable right of opt-out under the Regulations. However, where e-mail marketing materials are sent to individual employees of a company, Section II of the Data Protection Act 1998 gives such individuals the right to object to the marketing information being sent to them.

Although there are clear advantages of e-mail marketing, the use of e-mails has serious data protection and personal data management implications. Concerns over the use of e-mail for marketing purposes arise from the fact that e-mails:

- frequently contain information about individuals in the form of personal data;
- sometimes such personal data are not those of the sender or recipient of the e-mails and more often than not, the third party is unaware of the existence of the e-mail;
- are mostly sent without any supervisory check of their content;
- may be easily forwarded and retransmitted to others across the globe with relative speed and minimal cost;
- once sent, become permanent records, as they cannot be easily erased, even if they are deleted from the desktop system as they can be retrieved from the service provider;
- are easily copied, printed and redistributed manually;
- can be easily stored for later use, easily amended and quickly discarded.

The resulting effect of these characteristics is that e-mails have the potential to be used inappropriately. It is, therefore, important to address data protection effectively in the management of e-mail marketing and key elements are highlighted in Fig 13.2.

Fig 13.2 E-mail action points

- When your e-mail marketing material contains personal data, ensure that the e-mail recipients are aware of your identity.
- First obtain the consent of individual recipients before sending marketing information by e-mail to them *unless*:
  - you are advertising a similar product; and
  - the recipient has been given a simple means of opting out.
- Ensure that all personal data in e-mail marketing are accurate.
- Establish retention and destruction policies and procedures that include e-mails and ensure that your e-mails are destroyed in line with such policies.
- When sending e-mails that contain personal data, process such e-mails with due regard to the rights of data subjects.
- All e-mail marketing material that contain personal data must be kept secure in compliance with the seventh data protection principle.

Management of e-mail marketing

An organisation's e-mail list is one of the most valuable corporate assets in today's age. If companies are to derive maximum benefit from their e-mail marketing, they must implement good e-mail management practices. When the risks surrounding inappropriate use of e-mails are taken into consideration it becomes vital to establish good e-mail practice that is organisation-wide.

Staff should be given appropriate training and supervision on the use of e-mails, and e-communications systems as a whole. Guidance documents should be provided to staff on the issues of sending, receiving, keeping and disposing of e-mails in line with Data Protection Laws and other related legislation.

To manage e-mail lists effective the following should be implemented:

- Once consent has been received from potential recipients of your e-mail marketing material, add the details to your e-mail list immediately so that they are included in the next e-mail marketing exercise.

- Take appropriate steps to suppress the details of those who have opted out of your e-mail marketing information. Apart from the fact that sending marketing material to those that have opted-out is anti-marketing, it also exposes marketers to potential legal problems under the Privacy and Electronic Communications Regulations 2003.

- Ensure that the content of your e-mail marketing materials is appropriate and well targeted.

- Attract individuals to sign on to your e-mail list by offering some incentive such as useful information for the running of their businesses.

- Remove any inaccuracies in your e-mail list immediately in order to keep an accurate record of those to be sent e-mail marketing information. This will help you to project the effectiveness of an e-mail campaign more accurately.

Part of effective e-mail management is the use of appropriate disclaimers. E-mail disclaimers should provide some indication of the extent of responsibility that an organisation is willing to assume on the use of its e-mail facilities. For examples of e-mail disclaimers that may be used by organisations see Figs 13.3 and 13.4 below.

Fig 13.3 E-mail disclaimer

This e-mail contains confidential information and is intended solely for the addressee(s). If you have received this e-mail in error, please delete it immediately as you may not use or copy the content or attachment in any way.

The e-mail contains information believed by the sender to be accurate and reliable, this organisation will, therefore, not accept any responsibility for changes made to this e-mail after it was sent.

Fig 13.4 E-mail disclaimer

This e-mail message and any attachment contain privileged and confidential information that is intended for the exclusive use of the addressee(s). If you receive this e-mail by mistake, you are prohibited from distributing, disclosing, reproducing or disseminating it in anyway.

13.4 **Electronic contract formation and validation**

The basic requirements for creating a valid contract are offer, acceptance, consideration and intention to create legal relations. Acceptance becomes effective when it is communicated to the offeror. With the wide range of communication methods for the acceptance of electronic contracts the question has been when an electronic acceptance is deemed communicated. The United Nations Commission on International Trade Law (UNCITRAL) Model Law for Electronic Commerce stated that an electronic message should be deemed received when it has entered the designated information system of the recipient. The risk with this position is that the recipient may not actually collect or read the message for a long time. To avoid this problem an electronic offer should stipulate a date by which it should be accepted.

With regard to contract validity, parties may enter into a contract in such a manner and under such terms as they wish. The fact that a contract is entered into electronically will not make it less binding on the parties. According to Glatt (1998), it is of no legal consequences that a computer program completes a contract. However, it is desirable that electronically negotiated contracts be concluded in writing for the purpose of providing evidence on which parties may rely. Such written evidence provides legal safeguards to electronic contracts thus reducing the risk of subsequent repudiation of the contract by any of the parties.

Although some of the legal rules for the formation of contract apply to online contracts others do not go so well with them. To start with, where products are advertised on a web site the question that has to be answered is whether such an advert is an offer or simply an invitation to treat.

In the physical world, a display in a shop window has been deemed to be an invitation to treat rather than an offer. This principle is well illustrated in the case of *Fisher v Bell* [1961] 1 QB 394 – marked flick knife was displayed for sale in a shop window. The seller was prosecuted under the Restriction of Offensive Weapons Act 1961, which made it an offence to offer to sell such items and was acquitted. The court held that the display of the item on the shop window was merely an invitation to treat.

One could view a web site as similar to a shop window and, therefore, by analogy regard the description of the goods on a web site as a mere invitation. A justification for this would be that the web site owner might be bound by more contracts than he has goods in his stock. This point was illustrated by the Argos incident when Argos accidentally advertised its 21-inch televisions for £2.99 on its website instead of £299. Almost £1 million of orders were taken before the mistake was noticed. Argos declined to fulfil the order. The question was whether the price on the web site was an 'invitation to treat' so that the customers' orders actually constituted the offer or whether the display of the price on the web page was an offer which the customer could accept to form a binding contract. The former was the case so that a potential buyer makes an offer to the web site owner.

The next important element is the acceptance of the offer. English law requires that an acceptance must be a final unconditional expression of assent to all the terms of the offer. The expression of the assent to the offer must be in response to the offer and must match the exact terms of the offer. In Hyde and Wrench (1840) 3 Bear 334 – W offered to sell land for £1,000. H wrote back offering £950, which was refused. H later wrote stating that he was prepared to pay £1,000. **Held:** that the introduction of a change in the terms of the offer had nullified that offer.

For a contract to be properly formed acceptance must be communicated although the party that made the offer (the offerer) may waive the requirement of communication.

Communication of acceptance requires some form of external manifestation of the acceptance to the offeror. Communication is said to have taken place when the acceptance is actually brought to the noticed of the offeror by the offeree or his authorised agent.

With online contracts the legal issues of formation of contract have become more important and complex. Issues that have to be resolved in today's electronic age are when and where are online contracts formed? To determine when acceptance of online contracts are communicated such contracts have generally been divided up into two categories: web-based contracts and contracts effected by e-mails.

Web-based contracts

Where contracting parties are communicating on a web site over the Internet and the acceptance is effected by clicking a button on the web seller's page, the parties are directly and constantly connected to each other. An important factor is that such parties will almost inevitably recognise it if a connection has been interrupted and they would always know when their messages have not been transmitted. It is this knowledge of successful transmission or non-transmission that constitutes one of the characteristics of instantaneous communication.

With a web-based contract there is normally a direct link between the visitor and the web seller and if that direct link is lost parties should become aware of that fact immediately. Thus a web site acceptance will normally amount to instantaneous communication and will not be effective until it has actually been received by the offeror.

Contracting through e-mails

Where a contract is effected through e-mails the question of when acceptance is communicated to the offeror is an important one. An acceptance by e-mail is not normally regarded as an instantaneous communication. This is because e-mails differ substantially from instantaneous means of communication such as fax and telephone. E-mails are not normally sent directly from the offeree to the offeror but from one service provider to another and need to be picked up by the message recipient at the provider's server. Thus, the users of e-mail systems entrust their messages to independent third parties who then transmit those messages on the senders' behalf.

Apart from this third party factor in messages sent by e-mail, it is difficult for the sender to know whether and when the e-mail was received and whether the message was complete at the time of receipt. With e-mail acceptance the question is whether acceptance is effected when the message leaves the sender's mailbox, when the recipient collects the mail or when he actually reads it? All these point to the fact that an e-mail message is not an instantaneous acceptance of an offer.

The practical solution to the problem of formation of a legally binding online contract is to specify in advance how offer and acceptance are to be effected and where/when the contract will be deemed formed. E-marketers should:

- Ensure that messages are actually received by the recipient, as a message will only be valid when it is received. There should be an express statement of what will be regarded as received.
- Spell out when acceptance will be deemed to have taken place, as this will determine when the contract is actually formed and when parties are bound by their various obligations.
- Ensure that online confirmation of the receipt of an order is not mistaken for acceptance of the order.

> **Fig 13.5** E-commerce regulations 2002 – Key Provisions
>
> - The different steps to be followed for concluding a contract electronically shall be set out in such a way as to ensure that parties can give their full and informed consent.
> - Contract terms and general conditions which are to bind the consumer must be made available in a way that allows the consumer to store and reproduce the information.
> - The procedure for correcting errors prior to order placement must be made available to the consumer in a way that allows him to identify and correct handling errors and accidental transactions before the conclusion of the contract.
> - Receipts of orders shall be acknowledged by e-merchants without undue delays and by electronic means.
> - An e-merchant or e-service provider should indicate any codes of conduct to which they subscribe and information on how those codes can be assessed electronically.

To ensure that a contract formed online will be legally binding an e-merchant is required to state the procedure to be followed by the other party for the contract to come into existence. To this effect the E-Commerce Regulations of 2002 establish a coherent legal framework for the development of e-commerce in the UK. The key provisions of the Act are outlined in Fig 13.5.

13.5 Electronic authentication

In the physical world parties who wish to enter into a contract must show the intention to do so. Such intention can be given through a variety of ways orally, in writing or evidenced in writing. Where the contract is in writing parties are normally required to sign the contract document in order to give it authenticity. This has made the traditional paper signature an important element in commercial transactions. As the Internet develops as a means of global communication and a channel of international trading the important issues of contract formation and authentication have generated a great deal of debate.

It has been realised that in this information age commerce no longer involves trading in physical goods but also trading in information. This realisation has moved different systems to identify and provide ways of ensuring authenticity, integrity and non-repudiation of electronic contracts. Traditionally a signature serves several purposes, the most important of which are:

- It authenticates a writing by identifying the signer, therefore, creating a link between the signer and the signed document.
- It represents an approval or authorisation of the information or content by the signer, binding him/her legally to the contents of the signed document.

A signature on a contract document imports a sense of finality to the transaction and may work to lessen subsequent inquiries beyond the face of the document. Murray (2003) in his work clearly identifies the key functions of a signature.

Fig 13.6 Digital signatures

To serve these purposes a signature should be effected in a way that ensures it is impracticable to falsify or alter it without detection. The question that has been asked is whether digital signatures (Fig 13.6) enjoy the same authenticity and integrity as the traditional paper form.

An electronic signature is a block of data that enables a message to be tagged with a unique identifier, created by a secret key and can be recognised by the recipient of the message. It serves as a means of authenticating an electronic message, both in relation to the identity of the person that signed it and as to the content of the message. According to Brice different systems and business communities are now developing modern technological practices for ensuring that documents signed electronically are secure and authentic.

The issue of contract authenticity in cyberspace is being given due consideration as steps are being taken in various jurisdictions to ensure that electronic signatures are given the same level of recognition as paper signatures. Two clauses of the UK Electronic Communications Act will have far-reaching implications. Under Clause 7 electronic signatures are to be accorded the same level of authenticity as paper-form signatures. Clause 8 provides that the appropriate government minister will have a discretion to elect that references in any Act of Parliament to a requirement that a particular thing has to be 'in writing' or 'by deed' no longer means that and that electronic documents which are authenticated electronically shall suffice.

The United Nations Commission on International Trade Law (UNCITRAL), which is the body that promotes the progressive harmonisation and unification of the Law of International Trade, adopted a Model Law on Electronic Commerce in 1996. The aim of this Model Law is to enable individual States to modernise their legislation by bringing them in line with modern electronic technology in the area of commerce. Article 6(1) of the UNCITRAL Model Law on Electronic Commerce provides that where the law requires information to be in writing, that requirement is met by a data message if the information is accessible so as to be usable for subsequent references. Article 7(1) of the UNCITRAL Model Law on Electronic Commerce states that where the law 'requires a signature of a person, that requirement is met in relation to a data message if:

a) a method is used to identify that person and to indicate that person's approval of the information contained in the data message; and

b) that method is as reliable as was appropriate for the purpose for which the data message was generated or communicated, in the light of all the circumstances, including any relevant agreement.'

It will, therefore, be left to the court to use its discretion to determine the weight to be attached to electronic signatures and whether to regard a particular electronic transaction as a valid contract. So far, consumers have not adopted electronic signatures widely as they still prefer to physically sign cheques or debit or credit card receipts. However, the acceptance of digital signature based systems in the B2B and G2G sector has produced significant improvements in efficiency. Hamilton (2002) claims that the shifting of contracts to the electronic form has reduced the European Commission's annual paper bill by some €2 billion (£1.23 billion). Similarly, a digital signature based system has reduced the claim processing time from 50 to 20 days and costs by $350 million between brokers and insurers in a global insurance company. The future expansion of global Internet business will require digital signatures to be accepted in international law.

The technology

Digital signatures are created and verified by cryptography. Cryptography is the science that transforms messages into unintelligible forms in order to hide its information content, establish its authenticity, and prevent its undetected modification. It also prevents the message from repudiation, prevents its unauthorised use and can turn it back into the original form. Cryptography therefore provides very important functions, namely:

- Identification
- Authentication
- Non-repudiation
- Privacy

Identification: an electronic signature identifies the signer with the signed document. It verifies that the sender of the electronic message is really who he claims to be as the distinctive marks or digits attribute the particular symbol or mark to the signer.

Authentication: the signature guarantees that the message sent has not been tampered with or altered. This makes it impracticable to falsify or alter the message transmitted without detection. It ensures that messages and communication are protected from unauthorised viewing and use. With the use of cryptography personal and confidential information, which can easily be stored, analysed and reused, may be shielded.

Non-repudiation: it provides assurance that the sender will not subsequently deny that a message had emanated from him/her. It prevents parties from denying that a message had been sent or received. These important uses of cryptography make it an essential tool in today's e-world where the global network allows vast quantities of data to be transmitted, copied, stored, used, and distributed worldwide. Customer trust and confidence is provided by trusted third parties such as TrustAssured (see Fig 13.7).

Privacy: Cryptography employs an algorithm, which, in turn, uses two different but mathematically related keys. One of the keys is used for creating a **digital signature** or transforming the original data into seemingly unintelligible form (**the public key**) and the second key is used in verifying the signature or returning the unintelligible message to its original form (**the private key**). Where the public key, which is disclosed to the public, is used to encrypt a message it can only be decrypted by the corresponding private key. For encryption to work properly parties sending and receiving the message have to know the rules or the secret used to transform the original information into a coded form.

There are, however, some types of cryptography that are based on a single key with the parties encrypting and decrypting data with the same secret key. This is called secret key or symmetric encryption. Where symmetric encryption is used both parties must agree on a

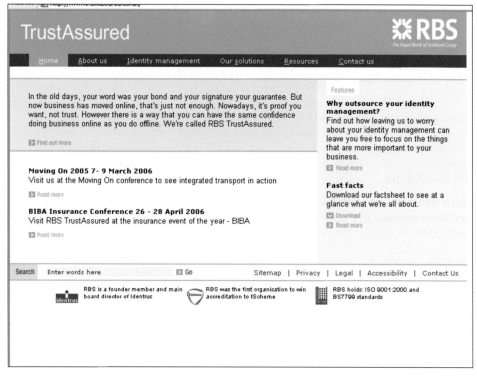

Fig 13.7 TrustAssured

Reproduced by kind permission of www.TrustAssured.co.uk

shared secret key. One of the main problems with symmetric encryption is that of authenticity. This is because as both parties possess the same key, there is the possibility of creating a message and then claiming that the other person sent it.

Verification

It is important that electronic signatures are checked through a robust verification process. After an electronic message has been signed with the use of a private key to encrypt it, the public key must be used to verify the signature. Where many people need to verify the signer's digital signature, the public key must be made available or distributed to all of them. The main advantage of the pair key system is that, although many people may know how to extract the message with the public key, they will not know how to sign with the signer's private key, therefore, making forgery difficult.

A **hash function** is another process used for creating and verifying a digital signature. It is an algorithm that does not use a key. It simply uses a formula to convert a message of any length into a single string of digits called a message digest. A hash function, therefore, creates a digital representation called a hash value or hash result of a standard length that is normally smaller than the message but unique to it. Any alteration of or change to the message produces a different hash result. The use of a hash function, therefore, ensures that there is no modification of the message from the time of signature. As the message is sent in plain text (although in a shorter form) the drawback is that there is no privacy in relation to message content.

13.6 **Electronic information and confidentiality**

The fact is that the Internet was not developed with privacy and security in mind thus it has brought about global interactions which have presented opportunities and risks to merchants and consumers. Although consumers enjoy the convenience of this new mechanism, they are also aware of the fact that the '**information superhighway**' collects, processes and distributes enormous amounts of personal data. Internet users have two key areas of concern about the security and privacy of their information. The first is unauthorised use of sensitive personal information, which has properly been given out, while the second is misuse of information by third parties who gain unauthorised access to it. This position has moved different systems to promulgate data protection laws for the purpose of regulating the processing of personal data in the public sector.

There has been a general consensus that the automation of information processing in today's digital era makes it essential to ensure information security through confidentiality, integrity, authenticity and non-repudiation of such information. By its very nature, the Internet makes global e-commerce fast and inexpensive but with an openness which makes it difficult to secure. To this effect the United Kingdom Department of Trade and Industry has defined e-commerce as:

> 'using an electronic network to simplify and speed up all stages of the business process, from design and making to buying, selling and delivery'.

With the openness of the Internet there are risks that an electronic message may not have been sent by the apparent sender, the message may have been manipulated or modified in transit or the sender may have repudiated the message with a possible loss by the message recipient. This has resulted in the development of mechanisms to ensure the reliability and confidentiality of electronic information, one of which is the mechanism of encryption.

Encryption

As online players transact electronically they need to be completely confident that all their communications are private, confidential and secure. Encryption is the process of disguising a message in a manner that hides its substance and original form. The process of encryption generally involves transformation of data from its original form into a form that is extremely difficult to read without the knowledge of the appropriate mechanism (the key). The encrypted text is normally referred to as cipher text and ensures privacy of information by protecting electronic data from being viewed by anyone for whom it is not intended. Encryption has, therefore, become the critical enabling technology used to ensure that sensitive and personal information is protected in the open network.

Decryption is the reverse of encryption. It is the transformation of encrypted data back to its intelligible form normally referred to as plain text. The processes of encryption and decryption can be effected in two main ways:

1. Private key system (or symmetric algorithms) and
2. Public key system (or asymmetric) algorithms.

Private key system

The private key system, which is the more traditional method of encrypting data, uses one key for both encryption and decryption. With the use of this system, parties agree on a key before commencing their electronic transaction. The security of this system, therefore, rests on the key, as anyone with access to the key will be able to decrypt the electronic message. The important thing with secret key encryption is that parties must not disclose the secret key to third parties. The main problem with private key encryption is, therefore, that once the key is accessible to a third party the message is compromised. In view of this problem, proper key management is an important issue in the use of single key encryption, as the private key has to be transmitted to the intended recipient in a way that keeps the key confidentiality.

There are advantages and disadvantages of using this encryption mechanism. One of the main advantages is that it is inexpensive, thus parties can use the single key system to encrypt large files of information without incurring large expenses. Another advantage is that it is faster than the public key encryption system that makes it attractive to e-merchants who need to transact at a fast rate. One of the major disadvantages of this system is that the private key must be distributed in secret, as access to the key will render the accompanying message public knowledge. The unauthorised possessor of the private key can decrypt the message and impersonate one of the parties by sending false information to the other party. Another disadvantage is that separate keys are needed for each pair of users on the network. The implication is that the total number of keys will drastically increase as the number of users increase. The result will be appropriate key management problem and the possibility of message compromise.

Public key system

To overcome the problem faced by users of the private key system with regards to transmitting the secret key without unauthorised interception the public key encryption was introduced. A public key encryption employs an algorithm, which uses two different but mathematically related keys – the private key and the public key. The private key has to be kept secret and must only be known to the designated owner. The public key has to be disclosed to the public but is associated with the particular owner.

As there is no need for a third party to know the owner's private key, this system eliminates the key exchange problem faced by the private key system. The public key technology can be used in two different ways. The first way is one whereby the private key, which is only known to the owner, is used to encrypt a message while the public key is used to decrypt it. The second use is one whereby the sender of a message uses the public key to encrypt the message while the key owner uses the private key to decrypt it. This ensures confidentiality of electronic transmissions as a message encrypted with one key can only be decrypted by the appropriate mathematically related key.

Although the use of the public key system enables two users to communicate securely without exchanging a secret key, the heavy usage of computing power required for this type of encryption makes it relatively slow. As the computations used to encrypt data under the public key system requires more time encryption of large messages with this method is impractical. Apart from the above public-key systems are vulnerable to chosen-plain-text attacks and are quite expensive to use.

With the slow and expensive nature of the public-key systems, the practice has been to use a combination of the private key and public key systems in transmitting electronic information.

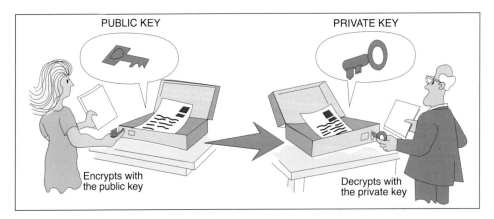

Fig 13.8 Public and Private Key

This is done by encrypting the actual message with the use of a secret key system while appending a digital signature using a public key system and encrypting the secret key with the private key of the public key system. Where the there is joint use of the secret and public key systems, privacy is guaranteed as only the user's public can be used to decrypt the secret key which in turn is needed to decrypt the actual message. Authentication is also achieved as the digital signature provides evidence that the originator generated the plain text message. Apart from privacy and authentication, data integrity and non-repudiation of messages are also achieved through the use of digital signatures. Clarke (1997) recognised the importance of the key pair very early on when he stated that a practice is emerging of using separate key pairs for encryption of message content and for digital signature (see Fig 13.8).

Electronic certificates

As the public key used in public-key-encryption of electronic data and the encryption of signatures have to be made accessible to members of the public some mechanism must be put in place to verify the identity of the holder of the private key. This is effected through the use of an electronic certificate. An electronic certificate is an electronically signed document that attests to the connection of a public encryption key to an individual or entity. The public key encryption system is based on the presumption that the public key really belongs to the signer. There is still the possibility of a person signing an electronic message in the name of someone else.

Message or data recipients, therefore, need to be certain that the public key they are using actually belongs to the correct person. An electronic certificate provides the assurance that a particular public key belongs to the purported owner. An electronic certificate will normally contain a public key, the name of the person or entity that the key belongs to and the whole package is authenticated by a digital signature. The main purpose of an electronic certificate is, therefore, to confirm that the information on the certificate has been verified and attested by a reliable and trusted third party. The attestation works to establish the confidentiality and authenticity of the message that is decrypted with the public key.

An electronic certificate can contain every type of information necessary to identify the creator of a public key encryption or digital signature. Apart from the name of the originator and the owner's public key such a certificate can also contain the expiration date of the certificate, a serial number and any other information deemed necessary. All electronic certificates have to be digitally signed by a trusted third party who checks and verifies the identity of the user and a Certificate Authority normally undertakes this function. This verifies the certification of origin and is approved by the British Chamber of Commerce. 'As well as allowing you to send tamper proof, private e-mail and documents, ChamberSign will allow you to use (*e-Cert*) which is the new way of remotely sending electronic Certificates of Origin and invoices to your Chamber for verification and endorsement, saving you waiting time". This especially useful to SMEs operating in export markets (www.cambschamber. co.uk/services/chambersign/index.asp).

13.7 Electronic information security

Cyber crime

It has, however, been recognised that although the Internet offers marketers greater access to information and opportunities, it provides criminals with a new channel for committing fraud. Although the concept of 'cyber crime' has not yet been given a generally accepted definition, it conveys illegal activities largely or completely performed using a computer connected to the Internet. The vulnerability associated with the Internet has put users at risk as the open network has become a virtual breeding ground for attackers, some of which are malicious and have the potential of causing damage.

Common security threats

Criminal activities on the Internet are in different forms most of which are effected in order to obtain unauthorised access to computer systems and manipulate confidential information. The following are some of the common types of crime committed on the open network.

- **Hacking**: Hackers are those who hunger for details about computer systems and use devious or even illegal means to satisfy their curiosity. According to Chaffey (2002), hackers can use techniques such as spoofing to hack into a system and find credit card details. By using software tools, hackers can break into computes to steal data, plant viruses or work any other mischief. Manipulation and disruption of electronic information by hackers through access to voice-mail, e-mails and long-distance telephone connections are costing companies in the US more than $1 billion every year.

It has been noted, however, that although hackers are causing tremendous damage, online companies are often reluctant to report attacks by hackers for fear of discouraging business and encouraging other hackers to take their turn.

- **Software piracy**: The advent of powerful, inexpensive computers together with easy access to information on the web have brought about illegal copying and distribution of software on the Internet. Computer software companies have, as a result, suffered at the hands of pirates who copy software without authorisation and sell them for significantly lower prices. With the ease that the digital age provides in distributing copyright work, Internet users are exposed to the risks of computer viruses and fraudulent software purchases. In addition, Internet software piracy may work as a drain on national economies as the reduce prices of the pirated software may bring about lost of national income. Apart from the issue of national economies, digital piracy also infringes owner's economic and moral rights.

- **Password attacks**: Password sniffers are programs that monitor and record the names and password of Internet users as they log on to the network. With the use of the password sniffer the installer impersonates an authorised user. Through this means he logs on to the system, has access to restricted documents and can manipulate information held therein as he wishes.

- **Denial-of-service attacks**: This involves sending large amounts of traffic to a web site which blocks it, preventing normal users from gaining access and making it inaccessible to the outside world. Laudon and Traver (2001) described a denial of service attack as an act which floods a web site with useless traffic with the result that it overwhelms the network. This kind of attack can bring down an enterprise's network thus causing disruption and damage. In February 2000, the US networked world realised the disruption that can be caused by this sort of attack when cyber criminals blocked services to and from major US companies such as eBay, Amazon.com, CNN.com and Yahoo!. Lo (2003) identifies two main types of denial of service attacks – operating system attacks which target bugs in specific operating systems and networking attacks which exploit inherent limitations of networking.

- **Spoofing (Masquerading)**: Spoofing occurs where an attacker runs software, which creates electronic messages that appear to come from a computer that is trusted by the victim. When two computers trust each other, they may exchange sensitive information that would not normally be available to other computer systems. The attacker would normally take advantage of this trust by masquerading as the trusted computer in order to gain access to confidential areas. Information that is commonly compromised by spoofing are account details, credit card details and social security numbers.

Protection against e-security risks

During the course of transactions, organisations send, receive, use and store electronic information for different aspects of their business. As the computer and network systems are vulnerable to a variety of risks, mechanisms have to be put in place to ensure that those systems are protected. The following are ways of securing e-communications systems.

- **Systems Access Control**: Organisations involved in e-marketing should ensure that their electronic data is only available to those individuals and groups that need to access it for normal business. This can be effected by the use of user IDs and passwords. Effective use of IDs and passwords should ensure confidentiality and protection of e-information from unauthorised access and tips are offered in Fig 13.9.

Reasonable efforts should be used to safeguard workstations in order to protect them against unauthorised access to workstations, network and data.

- **Intrusion Detection**: This is the art of detecting inappropriate activities on a computer or network system. Its main function is to detect an intruder breaking into a network system. Although it is generally believed that the outside world poses the greatest threat to online security, statistics shows that a large percentage in intrusion comes from within the organisation. Intrusion detection enables the collection of information about intrusion

---

Fig 13.9 Password don'ts

Password Don'ts

- Don't reveal your password over the telephone to anyone
- Don't reveal your password in any e-mail message
- Don't reveal your password in a questionnaire or security form
- Don't share your password with family members
- Don't give your password to a colleague for purposes of checking your e-mails while you are on holiday

---

techniques for the purposes of strengthening intrusion prevention facilities. Where an intrusion is detected quickly enough, the intruder can be identified and ejected from the system before damage is done or e-assets compromised.

- **Firewalls**: A firewall is a device that prevents unauthorised users from accessing a marketer's network system. For the purpose of online security, a firewall is essential but requires a certain level of expertise to ensure that any gap that may enable unauthorised access is closed. Firewalls can be configured to only accept links and communications from trusted systems.

Hazari (2000) provides a good analogy to the operation of firewalls when he states:

> 'We can think of firewalls as being similar to a bouncer in a nightclub. Like a bouncer . . . firewalls have a set of rules, similar to a guest list or a dress code that determines whether the data should be allowed entry. Just as a bouncer places himself at the door of the club, the firewall is located at the point of entry where data attempts to enter the computer from the Internet.'

- **Secure Electronic Transactions (SET)**: This is a security protocol based on digital certificates and digital signatures, which allows parties to a transaction to confirm each other's identity. Through the process of encryption SET scrambles electronic information exchange between parties thus ensuring integrity, security and confidentiality of such information.

In any SET protocol there are normally three or more parties: the customer, the merchant and the payment processing company such as WorldPay (www.worldpay.com) and PayPal (www.PayPal.com). The Set protocol uses digital certificates and encryption to secure transactions thus providing a PKI-based authentication system for payments over the Internet. SET provides three key services:

- It provides a secure communications channel among all parties involved in a transaction.
- It enhances trust through the use of digital certificates and digital signatures.
- It ensures privacy by making relevant information only available to the parties involved.

Although SET was launched in the late nineties, its uptake has been quite slow. In more recent times the SET protocol is being incorporated into several payment options such as smart cards, digital cash, and electronic cheques for the purpose of making these payment systems more secure.

13.8 Data protection

Data subjects have certain rights over the use of their personal information and these rights need to be taken into consideration in off-line as well as online processing. Many organisations use a variety of e-communications methods to effect their business transactions and, therefore, need a clear knowledge of their legal implications. Marketers rely on information volunteered or captured from consumers. The legal management and stewardship of this information is critical for future trust and openness from consumers for better-informed decision-making to take place.

The principles

If your organisation collects, processes and stores data about individuals then you are a data controller and have key responsibilities under the law. These responsibilities maybe summarised under eight fundamental principles, which you must fulfil.

These provide that personal data must be:

- processed fairly and lawfully
- processed for specific purposes and in an appropriate way
- adequate, relevant and not excessive
- accurate and up-to-date
- kept for no longer than necessary
- processed in line with data subject rights
- adequately secure
- only transferred to non-EEA countries that have suitable data protection controls
- Fair and Lawful Processing: To fairly obtain and process information you must provide the data subject with:
  - the identity of the person(s) processing the information
  - the use to which the data will be put
  - those that will have access to the data

Fairness has to do with informed consent and transparency in the processing of personal data. Birkinshaw (2001) in his book provides a detailed discussion of the conditions for lawful processing of personal data.

- Specific purpose: The purpose for which personal data is processed and kept by you must be specific and clearly stated and you should only process data in the manner compatible with the purpose. Your organisation should:
  - Notify data subjects of the purposes of collecting and keeping their data
  - Ensure that such purposes are lawful
  - Record the different types of data that are kept and the purpose of each
- Adequate, relevant and not excessive: Data processed and kept by your organisation should be just enough to enable you to achieve your purpose for using the data. Data should not be kept 'just in case there is a future need for it'. To determine whether data is

relevant and not excessive the question you need to ask yourself is, 'Is the data just what I need and is it necessary for my business?' If the answer is 'no' then you have infringed this particular principle.

- Accurate and up-to date: Your organisation is required to ensure that data is processed and kept up-to-date. To this effect you should have adequate clerical and computer procedures to ensure a high level of accuracy to stored data. This can be achieved by periodic circulation of data update forms to your data subjects, and periodic review/audits of data held on your system.

- Kept for no longer than necessary: This requirement places an obligation on your organisation to clearly state the period of time within which specific data will be kept and the reasons for the retention period. To fulfil this requirement, regular reviews of stored information has to be undertaken for purposes of deletion and data retention period guidelines must be available for use.

- In line with data subject rights: Every individual whose personal data has been processed has certain rights under the law. The first is the right of access to his or her personal data that has been processed. Apart from access rights, data subjects also have rights to have their personal data removed from a direct marketing or mailing list, to have inaccurately processed personal data corrected or erased and can also complain to the Information Commissioner or sue for compensation.

- Adequate security: Your organisation should take adequate security measures against unauthorised access to, disclosure or accidental loss of processed personal data. The level of security measures used will depend on the confidentiality and sensitivity of the particular data. Steps should be taken by your organisation to ensure that all employees and agents are aware of the security measures and comply with them. You should have periodic reviews of the security devices that are in place to ensure its continuous effectiveness.

- Transfer to non-EEA countries: There are specific requirements that have to be met before your organisation can transfer personal data outside the European Economic Area where the recipient country does not have an adequate level of data protection law. There are, however, a few countries, which have met this adequacy test, they are Switzerland, Hungary and Canada. The 'Safe Harbour' arrangement, which is a voluntary code of practice for US organisations, has also been approved so that any US company that signs up to that Code is regarded as having met the adequacy requirement.

Where a recipient country does not have appropriate levels of protection, one of the following conditions must be met:

- The data subject has consented.
- The transfer is required by law.
- The transfer is for the performance of a contract with the data subject.
- The transfer is for entering into a contract on behalf of the data subject.
- The transfer is necessary for obtaining legal advice.
- The transfer is necessary to prevent injury or serious damage.
- The data is an extract from a statutory public register.

For more information on these principles and how they work, see (Fig 13.10) the Information Commissioner's Office web site at www.informationcommissioner.gov.uk.

Fig 13.10 The Information Commissioner's office (www.informationcommissioner.gov.uk)

E-privacy issues

The Directive on Privacy and Electronic Communications 2002 aims to take account of technological changes to ensure that appropriate privacy rules apply to e-mails, the use of the Internet and other types of e-communications. The Privacy and Electronic Communications Regulations of 18 September 2003 have now transposed this Directive into UK law.

The new Regulations, which are to be cited as the Privacy and Electronic Communications (EC Directive) Regulations 2003, took effect from 11 December 2003 and on that date businesses were expected to change their current data processing and e-communication practices to reflect the requirements of these Regulations. The Regulations recognise that although electronic communications hold immense benefits for public and private organisations, they bring about risks to individuals' personal data and privacy.

Amongst other things they provide new rules on confidentiality, security, retention of data, use of cookies, unsolicited communications, traffic/location data and subscribers directories. The e-Privacy Regulations, therefore, aim to protect the fundamental rights of individuals to the privacy of their personal information.

Confidentiality of electronic communications

The new Regulations require the providers of electronic communication services to ensure the confidentiality of electronic communications.

They prohibit the interception and surveillance of such online communications except where authorised for purposes of:

• National security
• Law enforcement or related purposes

- Recording evidence of a commercial transaction
- Recording other transactions, or where it is authorised under national law.

Where electronic information is intercepted for the purpose of monitoring a business transaction, the parties involved in the business transaction should be informed of the information collected/recorded, the purpose for which it is collected and the duration of the storage period.

Security of electronic communications

Where electronic personal data of individuals are processed, the data controller and subsequent data processors must take appropriate technical and organisational measures to safeguard the security of the data. When taking such security measures the data controller or processor should ensure that the steps taken are commensurate to the security threat/risk. Some of the risk areas are online interfaces, communication channels, and third party risks. The security measures include access control devices, having appropriate policies in place, the use of firewalls and intrusion detection devices. Your organisation should have security procedures to identify and authenticate authorised users of your network systems. These procedures should be tested periodically to ensure effective functionality and compliance with legal requirements.

Storage of electronic communications

As electronic communications are processed and used in the daily operations of your organisation, they have to be stored in a way that retains authenticity, confidentiality and integrity while ensuring protection from alteration or destruction. Due care and appropriate procedures must be used to ensure that stored electronic data genuinely reflects the original transaction, which it purports to document. This includes:

- Carrying out a risk assessment procedure to determine the level of security required for the purpose of preventing unauthorised access, loss or damage to data.
- Using appropriate technological devices to carry forward electronic information from previous systems into more modern systems.

When communication networks are used to store electronic information or gain access to electronic information, clear and comprehensive information must be provided on the purposes of such storage and the data subject concerned should be offered the right to refuse such processing and storage.

Cookies and similar devices

The new Regulations do not prohibit the use of cookies, web bugs or any other hidden identifiers but simply impose certain rules on their use. Wacks (1998) describes cookies as text files written to a user's hard disk without his knowledge. Any individual or organisation that uses any device to gain access to information stored on a user's terminal equipment must provide clear and comprehensive information on:

- the type of device used
- the purpose for which it was used
- the right to opt-out of its use

Information on the type, and purpose of a cookie can be provided in the privacy statement/policy, and posted on conspicuous points of the web site.

Unsolicited communications

The 2003 Regulations have changed the position on the use of e-mail and SMS for direct marketing purposes. Such communications to potential customers will only be allowed on an opt-in basis (in other words, with the recipient's consent). This is a fundamental consideration in the application of any **permission marketing** campaign, as is the unsubscribe option.

Where promotional e-mails to existing customers who had purchased or negotiated for the purchase of similar products are concerned, the requirement is that customers are to be given the opportunity to 'opt-out' of such direct marketing exercises.

The concept of 'similar product' has been given a broad interpretation to include the marketing of any product, which the recipient of the marketing information would reasonably expect to receive.

Traffic data

Traffic data is any data that is processed for the purposes of conveying communications or for billing purposes. Before traffic data is processed, subscribers and users must be explicitly informed of the type of data that is being processed. There is also an obligation to inform subscribers and users about the data processing implications of any value added services before obtaining their consent.

Traffic data must be erased or made anonymous when it is no longer needed for the purpose of the transmission of the communication. When traffic data is used for the purpose of a user's billing or other payment, the processing of traffic data will be allowed to the end of the period during which the bill may be lawfully challenged or payment requested. In such a case the service provider must, before obtaining the user's consent, inform the user of the type of traffic data being processed and the duration of such processing.

Even when consent has been obtained for the processing of traffic data, the processing must be restricted to persons acting under the authority of the provider to deal with such data. The data processed must be restricted to what is necessary for the purpose of the particular activity.

Location data

Location data is any data processed in an electronic communications network that indicates the geographical position of the terminal equipment of a user of a public electronic communication service. Location data can only be processed anonymously or with the individual subscriber's consent. Before individuals are asked to give their consent they must be provided clear information on:

- The type of data to be processed
- The purpose of processing the data
- The duration of the processing period
- The potential recipients of the processed data

Where outsourcing of e-documentation and fulfilment activities, all supply chain partners must adhere to the legislation.

Even after they consent, the individuals must be given the opportunity to withdraw their consent at any time. They must also be provided with a simple means of preventing the processing of that information. Where data is to be transmitted to a third party for the purpose of providing a value added service, the service user must be adequately informed of that fact.

The processing of location data has to be restricted to persons acting under the authority of the service provider and also to the processing that is necessary for the activity in question.

Subscriber directories

Before individuals' personal data are included in a directory they must be informed of the purpose for which the directory is to be used. The data subjects must be given the opportunity to consider whether their personal data should be included in the directory.

Where individuals' personal data have been included in a directory, they must be given the opportunity, free of charge, to verify, correct or withdraw their personal data that has been processed. Where a request to verify, correct or withdraw personal data has been made, it will only apply to editions that are published subsequent to the request.

A corporate body can indicate that its details should not be included in a directory. Where that is the case the request must be given effect to. All these requirements on subscribers' directories apply to both printed and electronic forms of directories.

Prevention of calling line identification

Where presentation of calling line identification is available, the service provider is required to offer the caller a free and easy way of preventing the presentation of the calling line identification on a per-call basis.

The service provider must also offer a called subscriber a free and easy way of preventing the presentation of the calling line identification of incoming and outgoing calls.

Itemised billing

At the request of a user, a service provider shall provide that user with bills that are not itemised. In exercising its duties the Office of Communications (OFCOM) is to have regard to the need to reconcile the rights of subscribers to receive itemised bills with the right of users. Public electronic service providers are to make sufficient alternative privacy-enhancing methods of communications or payments available to their users and subscribers.

Exemptions

A service provider will be exempted from the requirements of these Regulations where exemption is required for the purpose of safeguarding national security. A certificate signed by a Minister of the Crown will constitute conclusive evidence of an exemption under this category.

Where compliance with the provisions of these Regulations would be inconsistent with a requirement imposed by or under an enactment or by a court order, or in connection with legal proceedings, the service provider will be exempted from the requirements of the Regulations.

The service provider will also be exempted from the requirements of the Regulations if compliance is likely to prejudice the prevention or detection of crime or the apprehension/ prosecution of offenders.

Enforcement

Any person who has suffered damage as a result of an infringement of these Regulations can make a claim for compensation. The Information Commissioner has the power to enforce the provisions of these Regulations. In exercising this enforcement power the Information Commissioner may receive advice from the Office of Communications on technical and similar matters.

13.9 E-payment systems

The explosive use of the commercial Internet in recent years presents both opportunities and challenges to businesses as it gives them access to a worldwide market. Where commercial transactions are concerned, goods and services have to be paid for and this has, traditionally, been done with cheques, cash, postal orders and travellers' cheques. A payment mechanism is, therefore, a means by which economic value is transferred between two parties, sometimes using some intermediaries.

Internet buying and selling mostly involves the use of electronic payment. An electronic payment is a paperless method of payment with the advantage of being quicker and more cheaply effected than the paper form of payment. Where payments for goods and services are done electronically then security and trust become keywords in such transactions. For any type of electronic payment to be effective it should be secure, easy to use and should have low transactional costs. The risks that are inherent in electronic payments are quite substantial. Where payment is effected by an electronic means the message containing the financial information of the purchaser is capable of being intercepted. Where this occurs the interceptor may use the financial details to take a turn on an electronic shopping spree. The result would be that consumers who are shopping electronically might be paying for goods that they have not ordered or received.

The supplier, on the other hand, may face the risk of shipping goods to a purchaser who is fraudulently using the financial details of another person. This position has affected consumer confidence in e-commerce but it is hoped that as security on the Internet improves, it will have a positive effect on consumers. To combat this problem of insecurity significant initiatives have been made worldwide with the aim of reducing the risks inherent in electronic payments. The following electronic payment methods are available to consumers and suppliers of goods and services:

Digital cash

The digital cash is an attempt to replicate the benefits of cash in the off-line world. Such as micro payments. The user will normally install a 'cyber wallet' on the hard disk of his computer. A message is then encrypted to his bank asking for an amount to be deducted from his account. The bank reads the message by decoding thus verifying that the right customer has digitally signed it. The bank encrypts a message, signs it with its digital signature and sends it back to that customer who stores it. When the user makes a purchase, the vendor sends the coin to the user's bank for verification and the amount is credited to the vendor's account. Two of the main advantages of using digital cash are that the user can engage in direct person-to-person transactions and the system provides a high level of anonymity.

Electronic credit/debit card payment

Consumers are normally willing to make purchases with credit/debit cards in the physical world. Credit and debit cards are also becoming popular as payment methods for electronic commerce purchases. Most credit/debit card modes of payment use the Secure Electronic Transaction (SET) specification, which was jointly developed by the Master Card and Visa. The SET specification is based on public key cryptography and digital certificates. A **digital certificate** is an electronic document or affidavit issued by a trusted organisation, like a bank,

Fig 13.11 Electronic cheques

that vouches for the identity and the authority of an individual or business to conduct any transaction over the Internet. According to Markose (2003), innovations in payment systems underpinned by electronic technology are transforming the monetary landscape of many countries.

When a consumer makes a credit card purchase from an Internet merchant (see Fig 13.11), the consumer transmits encrypted financial information to the merchant along with the digital certificate. The merchant sends the information to a payment gateway where it is decrypted, processed and verified by a certification authority. The payment gateway routes the transaction back to the financial institution that issued the credit card for approval. The merchant is then advised electronically that the purchase is approved and the cardholder's account is debited while the amount is credited to the merchants account.

An electronic cheque is a digital substitute for the paper cheque and just like the ordinary paper cheque, it is a legally binding promise to pay. Chandran describes an electronic cheque as an electronic image of a paper cheque. Instead of a hand-written signature, which is the normal way of endorsing a traditional paper cheque, an electronic cheque uses a digital signature. One of the advantages of using an electronic cheque is that since it will follow the same payment stream as the paper counterpart it is normally issued from the same cheque account therefore avoiding the need to create a new payment instruction. It is, therefore, designed to fit into the current practice of payment by cheque with minimal effect on the payer, payee and intermediaries.

An electronic cheque payment is effected by the payer issuing a cheque by creating an electronic document with all the information required to be on a cheque and appending a digital signature. The payee receives the cheque, verifies the payer's signature and endorses the cheque with a digital signature before sending it out to his bank. The payee's bank verifies the payer's and payee's signatures, credits the payee's account and forwards the cheque to the payer's bank for clearing and settlement. The payee's bank verifies the payer's digital signature and debits the payer's account.

Smart cards

A smart card is a plastic card, which contains a microprocessor chip that holds large amounts of information and is tamper-resistant. It is normally used to store up specified monetary value enabling a holder to use it as a substitute for cash. Holders are mostly able to control the amount of money loaded on the card by recharging or reloading the card with money from the their account.

Smart cards have many potential uses and the main concern is that of security as it is capable of storing a great amount of personal and financial information. They are widely used, despite this security risk, due to the advantages that they have. These include ease of use, rechargeability and use with a variety of currency. The main question is what limits if any, are to be placed on financial information sharing among organisations that issue these cards. It is possible for the personal details of customers to be passed on to another organisation for marketing purpose without the consent of the customer. Another area of concern is that of stopping payment for a particular transaction. Consumers need to know whether a counter electronic message can be used to stop payments. Even where cryptography is used to keep personal and financial messages secret extra care should be taken of the public key to ensure that customers' confidential information is not misused.

Adequate information should be provided on the payment system that the consumer is expected to use. As the payment and rules governing it are crucial to instilling consumer confidence in electronic commerce, the level of security of the specified payment system should be described. In choosing a payment system e-merchants should, therefore, give due consideration to the security of the system. As the security of communication over the Internet is not yet guaranteed, transmission of payment over this open network is of great concern globally. In Europe, although there is no Directive so far which specifically addresses the issue of electronic payment, the European Commission's Recommendation concerning transactions by electronic payment instruments and in particular the relationship between issuer and holder, requires consumers to be furnished information on the terms, conditions and use of electronic payment instruments.

It also provides that where losses arise as a result of loss or theft of the electronic payment instrument, the consumer's liability should:

- up to the time of notification of the loss or theft, be limited to €150 except where the consumer has acted with extreme negligence or is fraudulent;

- not be liable for any loss after notification of the theft or loss;

- not be liable for any loss where the payment was effected without the physical presentation or electronic identification of the instrument itself.

The consumer is, however, required to take all reasonable steps to keep the electronic payment instrument safe and must notify the issuer of the instrument after becoming aware of the loss or theft of the electronic payment instrument. Such notification should also be given to the issuer where the instrument holder's account contains recordings of unauthorised transactions or contains errors or other irregularities. The consumer is entitled to cancel a payment where there is evidence of fraudulent use of his payment instrument. There should be a facility for re-crediting the consumer's account with sums paid out in the event of fraudulent use of the instrument.

The guiding principle for enhancing consumer confidence in electronic payment systems is that e-merchants should ensure that payment on the Internet does not entail a greater risk to consumers than the risks connected with other means of payment. Thus the fact that a consumer has decided to use electronic payment in his online transaction should not make it more difficult for the consumer to have defects remedied or have the contract cancelled. Internet payment should not put consumers to greater information security risks or data protection risks than off-line transactions. Third party solutions such as ePayments, PayPal and

WorldPay build trust and confidence in consumers whilst carrying out a secure function on behalf of merchants.

13.10 Summary

The Internet has brought about huge advantages to e-marketers as it provides ease of advertising, possibility of increased sales, fast/convenient ways of effecting electronic contracts and access to a global marketplace. However, the use of the open network by marketers has brought about concerns over the protection of personal data of customers, associates and partners.

Marketers have to address issues of e-confidentiality and e-security effectively as there is a potential risk that electronic messages may be manipulated or modified in transit. Where e-transactions are not properly authenticated, there is the risk of repudiation with a possible loss to a party. To enable secure, valid transactions, e-marketers should put arrangements in place to ensure the authenticity, confidentiality and reliability of their online transactions. Consumers should be given the freedom of choice in e-payment methods and such methods should be easy to use, secure and with low transactional costs.

END OF CHAPTER CASE STUDY E-mail marketing

Benzies Business Development Agency

Benzies Business Development Agency was established in 1984 and supports local business in Bombay, India. The Agency assists businesses to expand by part-funding the employment of new staff and their marketing campaigns.

Benzies had realised that it needed to get information on its services out to a wider public, as most businesses were not aware of the services that the Agency provided. In the past only micro businesses had used its services and statistics showed that retailers, financial institutions and most SMEs had rarely used these services.

The Agency decided to launch an e-mail campaign programme to all sectors. The e-mail communication was created in an HTML format and was to be sent out to all local businesses, business owners, local solicitors, all micro businesses, SMEs, large and multi-national organisations in Bombay.

Why Did Benzies Choose E-mail Marketing?

Benzies Business Development Agency had used direct marketing channels in the past to market its services to the public. The processes that the organisation went through with direct marketing included:

- Designing the flyer that was outsourced to an external organisation. The time used for the designing phase of the flyer was out of their control. Initial proofs had to be produced first for the Agency's approval before the work was carried out. Where the designer was busy, this could take up to two weeks.

- Production of the flyer was the next step. That again was outsourced to a printing company. The proofs had to be produced and sent to the Agency for approval before the bulk of the flyers could be produced.

- The next stage was mailing of the flyers and this was the most tedious stage as the flyers had to be enveloped and stamped individually. Where a large number of direct mailing was planned, the time and efforts used for mailing the flyers was quite substantial.

Strategies for E-Mail Marketing Success

On deciding to replace direct marketing with e-mail marketing, Benzies Business Development Agency thought of two strategies that would help it achieve good results:

1. Online Registration Form
2. Stronger Customer Relationships

Online Registration Form

To help its e-mail marketing campaign Benzies Business Development Agency posted an online registration form on its web site. Registration on the Agency's web site allows registrants access to some white papers on e-business. The online form has short easy-to-use screens and requires name, full postal address and an e-mail address.

The registration form is normally encrypted and sent over a private channel to create a registrant's profile. It contains a data protection statement as follows:

'Any information that you provide will be used by Benzies Business Development Agency for informing you of the services that we provide and for responding to enquiries. All reasonable steps will be taken to ensure that your personal information is secure.'

Since posting the registration form on its web site, the Agency has 120,000 registrants on its database. Every month Benzies Business Development Agency sends out e-mail marketing communications to 30,000 organisations using this database. The Agency always includes an opt-out box in every marketing e-mail message which reads:

'Please tick this box or contact us if you wish to be taken off our mailing list'.

The opt-out box allows customers to unsubscribe from the marketing database at any time.

The monthly e-mail marketing communications generate about 6–9% responses and some further enquiries about services provided by the Agency. Statistics show that out of these enquiries, 3–5% result in the use of the Agency's services.

Stronger Customer Relationships

Benzies Business Development Agency also decided that for its e-mail marketing campaign to succeed it needed to build stronger relationships with its existing customers. Having realised that selling services to new customers is much harder than selling them to existing customers, the Agency decided to put in the hard work on its existing customers. With this in mind the Agency decided to:

- Research its existing customers' needs.
- Keep in touch with existing customers by sending them information on tenders in their areas of activities.
- Understand their customers' expectations.

- Convert knowledge about their existing customers into better services and measure the level of uptake of these improved and customised services.

By keeping in touch with their customers and sending them information on tenders, the Agency went the extra mile. These various steps taken by Benzies Business Development Agency helped with the building of its relationships with its customers. The effect of this closer relationship was that any e-mail sent by Benzies to its customers was regarded as useful information that had to be read.

The Result

The e-mail campaign launched by Benzies Business Development Agency has enabled the Agency to reach a wider audience quickly and conveniently. The Agency is now in a position to better leverage its resources. One of the key benefits of the e-mail marketing campaign is that the organisation can actually see the results of its efforts.

The Agency has a particular software built into its e-mail marketing device that indicates whether an e-mail has actually been read and when. With this the Agency can identify the type of information that interests its existing and potential customers.

For Benzies Business Development Agency, e-mail marketing turned out to be the most cost-effective, reliable, quick and convenient method of disseminating its marketing information to its recipients. With e-mail marketing the Agency is now able to use very few staff to take full advantage of its e-mail facilities to market its valuable services to the business community in Bombay.

Questions

1. Compare and contrast mail marketing and e-mail marketing. Identify the issues that must be taken into consideration by an organisation that is embarking on an e-mail campaign.

2. What data protection issues may arise in the use of an online registration form?

3. How did Benzies Business Development Agency build stronger customer relationships and what were the benefits?

DISCUSSION QUESTIONS

1. Describe the main differences between web-based contracts and contracts formed through e-mails.

2. An employee at Zel Ltd sent an e-mail with an attachment containing A's financial details to another employee. An incorrect e-mail address was used and the e-mail went to an outsider. What are the legal implications of this situation?

3. The Secure Electronic Transactions (SET) protocol that was launched in the late nineties provides three key services, what are these?

REFERENCES

Birkinshaw, P (2001) *Freedom of Information, The Law the Practice and the Ideal*, Butterworth, 347

Brice, W *Electronic Signatures in the Real World* at www.messageg.com/security/brice.html

Chaffey, D (2002) *E-Business and E-Commerce Management*, 457, 459, Prentice Hall

Chandran, K *Electronic Cheque – The Emerging Payment System* at www.indianbanksassociation.org/home/bulletin

Choi, S *Electronic Payments and the Future of Electronic Commerce*, Center for Electronic Commerce, The University of Texas at www.cism.bus.utexas.edu/works/articles/cyberpayments.htlm

Esen, R Electronic signatures and US initiatives, *The Journal of Electronic Commerce Law and Practice*, Vol 20, 200/2001

Esen, R (2002) Cyber crime: a growing problem, *The Journal of Criminal Law*, 66(3), 269 – where she highlights that the lawlessness on the Internet may lead to lack of trust on the part of consumers

Essinger, J (2001) *Internet Trust and Security*, Addison-Wesley, 205

Glatt, C (1998) Comparative issues in the formation of electronic contracts, 6 *Int. JLIT*, 34

Hakal, D Moving money on the Net: it's getting easier – but is it safe?, *Newsday*, 10 Nov 1996, A-67

Hazari, S *Firewalls for Beginners*, 6 November 2000 at www.securityfocus.com/focus/basics/articles/fwbeg.htm

Jay, R & Hamilton, A (2003) *Data Protection: Law & Practice*, Sweet and Maxwell

Laudon, K & Traver, C (2001) *E-Commerce*, Addison Wesley, 245

Lo, J (2003) *Denial of Service or 'Nuke' Attacks*, at www.irchelp.org/irchelp/security

Manuel, C (1999) *Debit Cards: Beyond Cash and Checks*, National Consumer Leagues at www.natlconsumersleague.org/debitbro.htm

Markose, S How far towards a cashless society, *The Economic Journal* 2003 at www.res.org

Molner, D Signing electronic contracts, *ACM Crossroads Student Magazine* at www.acm.org/crossroads/xrds7-1/contract.html

Murray, J Public key infrastructure digital signature and systematic risk, *JILT* 2003 Vol 1

Nestel, D Online orders: electronic contracts can deliver unwelcome surprises, *Houston Business Journal* at www.houston.bizjournals.com

Nicholl, C (1998) Can computers make contracts, *JBL*, Vol 35, for a discussion of web-based contracts

Palmer, G & Nash, A *Firewalls* at www.freebsd.org/doc

Peikari, C & Chuvakin, A (2004) *Security Warrior*, O'Reilly

Press, J *An Introduction to Public Key Systems and Digital Signatures* at www.users.breathe.com/jpress/papers/pkc.htm

Price, K *Intrusion Detection* at www.cs.purdue.edu/coast/intrusion-detection

Sax, M (1998) *Encryption: Secure Methods of Communication and Commercial Transactions*, International Electronic Trade

Schoeter, A & Willmer, R (1997) Digital money online – a review of some existing technologies, *Intertrader*, UK, 33

Stalling, W (1995) *Network and Internet Work Security*, Prentice Hall

Stallings, W (2002) *Introduction to Secure Electronic Transaction (SET)* at www.informit.com

Wacks, R The death of online privacy, paper presented at the 13th Annual BILETA Conference: *The Changing Jurisdiction*, March 1998, Trinity College, Dublin

FURTHER READING

Kinsella, NS & Simpson, AF (eds), *Online Contract Formation*, 2004, Oceana Publications

Carey, P *Data Protection: A Practical Guide to UK and EU Law*, 2004, Oxford University Press

Kinnard, S *Marketing With Email*, 2000, Independent Publishers Group

Schellekens, MHN *Electronic Signature: Authentication Technology from a Legal Perspective*, 2004, Asser Press

Turban, E, King, D, Lee, J, Warkentin, M & Chung, H *E-Commerce Security in Electronic Commerce: A Managerial Perspective*, 2002, Prentice Hall Publishers

Warren, P & Streeter, M *Cyber Alert*, 2005, Fusion Press

WEB LINKS

www.asa.org.uk: This is the web site of the Advertising standards Authority that ensures that advertising meets the requirements of the advertising codes.

www.trustassured.co.uk: Trustassured manages public key infrastructure and digital certification processes.

www.worldpay.com: WorldPay is a payment service provider for online transactions.

www.securityfocus.com: This web site is a good source of e-security information and security-related news.

www.informationcommissioner.gov.uk: The Information Commissioner's web site provides extensive information on data protection.

www.dma.org.uk: This is the web site of the Direct Marketing Association, UK, which is Europe's largest trade association in the marketing sector.

 Visit the Online Resource Centre which accompanies this book, for lots of interesting additional material, including self-assessment questions, internet exercises, and links for each chapter: **www.oxfordtextbooks.co.uk/orc/gay/**

1G/2G/2.5G/3G/4G The series of generations of wireless technology, 4G is still awaited. 1G was analogue only and the latest, 3G, supports rich media

3PAS see **adserver**

404 File not found message An HTML error code that indicates that a requested web page was a dead link

Above the fold The part of a web page that is visible in the user's browser without their scrolling down

Access provider see **Internet Service Provider**

Accessibility see **web site accessibility**

Accountable marketing Term used to describe to pay per click advertising – as opposed to the unaccountable nature of corporate marketing

Active content Content on a web site that is either interactive or dynamic

Active server page (ASP) a dynamically created web page that uses ActiveX scripting which is processed before being served to the user – mostly used for online query forms

Ad impression The downloading of a specific advertisement banner

Ad inventory The number of ad impressions that a web site sells over a set period of time

Ad rotation The changing – rotation – of displayed ads on a web page

AdSense Method of web site ad distribution from the Google organisation

Adserver A third-party ad server (3PAS) that stores adverts and delivers them to web site visitors, normally used by an online advertising network

Ad space The area of a web site designated to carry banner ads

Advergaming The use of computer games as a medium for advertising

Adware A type of spyware that collects information about web users in order to display ads in the user's browser. Exhibited ads are based on the user's browsing patterns

Affiliate-management A third- party service that facilitates affiliate transactions

Affiliate marketing An arrangement where one web site refers customers to another for a fee or percentage of any subsequent sales

Agent A software program that performs a small and well-defined information gathering or processing task

Algorithm The rules by which a search engine ranks the web sites listed in its index in relation to a particular search query

Anchor tag The HTML instruction for text or an image to be a link

Animated GIF A format of saving graphics that allows several images to be saved at once and then displayed by web browsers one after another, creating the illusion of movement

Application Another way to say 'computer program'

Application Service Provider (ASP) (or Application *Software* Provider) A third-party provider of software-based services and solutions to customers from a central data centre

ARPANet (Advanced Research Projects Agency Network) Developed in the late sixties and early seventies by the US Department of Defense, ARPANet was the forerunner of the Internet

Attachment A file which is attached to, and then sent along with, an e-mail message. Any kind of file can be attached – text, graphics, sound – but some attachments are too large to send

Autoresponder An automated e-mail reply system

B2B Abbreviation for trading in a Business to Business context

B2C Abbreviation for trading in a Business to Consumer context

B2E Abbreviation for trading in a Business to Employee context

B2G Abbreviation for trading in a Business to Government context

Back office operations Term used to describe the operations that support the fulfillment of online sales

Bait and switch A questionable form of sales/marketing where customers are lured in by ads for goods at unprofitably low prices. When the customer attempts the purchase they find the advertised goods are not available, but that a substitute – more expensive – product is

Bandwidth The data transmission rate, or how much content can be send through an Internet connection in a fixed amount of time

Banner An image, or button, often with animated text and/or images, that links to advertising material

Banner advertising The use of banners on web pages to promote a product or service

Banner exchanges When two or more organisations exchange the placement of banners on each other's web site

Banner Farm A web site that comprises solely of banners ads with the objective of generating revenue through advertising and affiliate income

Behavioural targeting see **contextual targeting**

Bit (Binary DigIT) A single digit number in base-2, in other words, either a 1 or a zero. The smallest unit of computerised data. Bandwidth is usually measured in bits-per-second

Beta An early release of a product, such as software, to a limited group of people (beta testers) in order to perfect the product

Blog (blogging) Short for web log – an online personal journal of an individual. Typically updated daily, blogs normally reflect the personality of the author

Blogger Someone who writes a blog

Bobby A free online tool that allows a site to be checked for compliance against the W3C accessibility guidelines for disabled users

Boolean search Based on boolean logic, this kind of search allows the inclusion – or exclusion – of documents containing specific words through the use of instructions like 'AND', 'NOT', and 'OR'

Boot To start a computer; though usually the process is called 'rebooting'

Boss blog A **blog** that is written by someone within the organisation who has some, if not total, authority

Bot see **spider**

Bounce Description given to e-mail that is returned unopened – bounced – to the sender

Bps (Bits-Per-Second) A measurement of how fast data is moved from one place to another

Bricks and mortar [traders] See also **Clicks and mortar**. Businesses that trade in a traditional, offline, environment only

Broadband A type of digital data transmission in which each medium (wire) carries multiple signals, or channels, simultaneously. However, because broadband connections allow a higher rate of data transmission (around nine times faster than a standard modem), the term has become synonymous with 'fast' Internet access

Brochureware Originally, a web site made up of content taken directly from offline promotional literature (brochures) but now used as a more general description of sites that offer no interactivity

Broken link Web site links that, when clicked on, do not take users where they were supposed – and hoped – to go

Browser (1) A client program that provides access to the web eg Explorer, Netscape, Firefox

Browser (2) Someone who navigates through and reads the web, ie they browse the contents

Bug A programming glitch, mistake, or problem

Bulletin Board System/Service (BBS) A computerised meeting and announcement system that allows users to carry on discussions and exchange files without them all being connected to the computer at the same time

Buzz marketing see **viral marketing**

C2B Abbreviation for trading in a Consumer to Business context

C2C Abbreviation for trading in a Consumer to Consumer context

Cache Temporary electronic storage space

Call to action A word, phrase or gesture that invokes an action – in a marketing context the action would be that desired by the marketer

Campaign conversion An e-metric that tracks all the conversions that have taken place for a specific campaign

Case sensitive When upper case characters are distinguished from lower case characters

Chat Term for a 'real-time' keyboard-based conversation on the Internet. Chatting takes place in a chat room, a virtual meeting place

Click (1) verb Users click on a mouse button to instruct the computer to carry out a command

Click (2) noun Competition is only a click [of the mouse] away

Click fraud In models where the publisher of a web site that carries ads is paid for every click on those ads there is the opportunity for abuse. Click fraud refers to unscrupulous publishers dishonestly increasing the amount of clicks on ads on their site in order to increase income

Click rate/ratio The percentage of **impressions** that an advertising banner may receive against the number of visitors the web page containing the banner receives. Used to measure advertising response

Clickstream The route a visitor takes through a web site. Also known as 'clickpath'

Clickpath see **clickstream**

Clicks and bricks see **clicks and mortar**

Clicks and mortar [traders] Businesses that trade both on- and off-line. The term derives from the concept that the business uses 'clicks' (of the mouse) and mortar (referring to physical buildings) in its methods of trading in both consumer and industrial markets

Clickthrough When a user clicks on any link, though normally refers to banner ads

Clickthrough rate (CTR) The percentage of clickthroughs to the total number of times the link is viewed

Click-wrap Term used when a user must click on confirmation of terms/conditions in order to continue with the transaction

Client A software program that is used to contact and obtain data from a server software program on another computer

Cloaking The practice of using technology to get a search engine to record content for a URL that is different to what a user will ultimately see

CMS (Content Management System) Software that enables content to be added and/or manipulated on a web site

Commercial blog A blog that is developed by an organisation (rather than an individual) as part of a marketing strategy

Community web site A site where users with similar interests communicate with each other

Computer Telephony Integration (CTI) A software application widely used in call centres to manage telephone calls

Conceptual search A search for documents based on the concept of the search term rather than the specific words in the term

Consumer Generated Media (CGM) The description of content on web sites designed for and existing on, the public's input and comments

Content see **web content**

Content management Systems – manual and automated – put in place in order to manage the textual content of web sites

Content rich A search engine term that relates to the fact that algorithms give higher ranking to pages which contain the keyword or term for which a user is searching – that it is content rich

Contextual and behavioural targeting the targeting of online promotions at potential customers based on their previous online behaviour (ie sites visited) and the context of the content of the web site

Conversion When a site visitor completes whatever the objective of the web site is (eg orders a product or subscribes to a newsletter)

Conversion by acquisition An e-metric where the ad campaign or source that a customer used to first visit a web site is recorded so that any subsequent purchase might be credited to that source

Conversion path analysis An attempt to quantify the effect of different elements of a multi-channel campaign on e-marketing objectives

Conversion rate The ratio of site visitors to conversions

Cookies Electronic 'calling-cards' that are deposited on the hard drive of the user's computer when they visit a web site. Essentially, a cookie facilitates the recording of data about the user and their visit(s) to the web site that issued that cookie

Cost per order Total marketing expenses divided by total value of orders

Cost per visit Total marketing expenses divided by number of visits

CPA (cost per action) The method of charging for the pay per click advertising method

CPM (cost per thousand impressions) The method of charging for the Pay Per Impression advertising method. The 'M', Latin for thousand, is used because ad impressions are sold in blocks of one thousand

CPC (cost per click) see **Pay Per Click**

Crawler see **spider**

Cross linking Linking to content within a web site from pages within that site

Cue words Words, terms, or phrases that alert search engines to the context of a searcher's submission

CSS (Cascading Style Sheets) An application of HTML that gives both web site developers and users more control over how pages are displayed. CSS helps designers create sites where all pages conform to the same design principles

Cyber Although the word itself does not exist, the term as a prefix indicates a relationship to computers. More recently that prefix has indicated a relationship with the Internet eg cybercrime would be crime committed over the Internet

Cyberspace A term originated by author, William Gibson in his novel, 'Neuromancer' the word is sometimes used to describe the whole range of information resources available through computer networks in general and the Internet in particular

Cybersquatting The practice of registering a domain name with the sole aim of selling it at a profit

Database A collection of information stored in a computerised format

Database Marketing A form of direct marketing using databases of customers in combination with other databases (products, suppliers, distributors) to generate personalised communication with potential customers

Data mining see **data warehouse**

Data warehouse A collection of data (database) designed to support management decision making

Daypart session A form of ad presentation where a single advertiser dominates all the advertising on a publisher's web site for a pre-determined time of the day

Dead link The name given to a link that does not lead to a web site, as it once would have one

Dedicated server A server that hosts a single web site, normally owned by the publisher of that web site

Deep linking Entry into a web site via links to the site's interior pages, not the homepage

De-listing When pages are removed from a search engine's index

Denial-of-Service (DoS) attack The use of specialised software to disable a web site by overloading its resources with a flood of phantom visitors

Depth of visit How far (deep) the visitor goes into a web site, measured by the number of pages

Destination site The target of a link or another term for landing page

Dial-up connection A once common method of connecting to the web. A user's modem dials up to an ISP, through which an Internet connection is established

Digital How computers talk – all information is processed in the form of electronic signals. These signals can only be on or off, and so represent binary numbers

Digital certificate (Digital ID) An increasingly popular security device, primarily a means of identifying individuals on the Internet

Digital divide The term used to describe the gap between the 'haves' and the 'have-nots' in the digital world. In essence, it means the gap between those who have access to IT in general, and the Internet in particular, and those who do not

Digital ID see **Digital certificate**

Digital products Those products that can be configured into a digital format so allowing them to be delivered via the Internet

Digital signature Used to verify contents of messages and the identity of the signatory

Digital Subscriber Line (DSL) A data communications technology that enables faster data transmission over standard copper telephone lines than a conventional modem. ADSL (Asymmetric Digital Subscriber Line) enables even faster data transmission

Directory A direct descendant to the offline directory, the online directory has human involvement, rather than relying on spiders to crawl the web – as search engines do. In directories, web sites are usually reviewed and placed in a particular category

Distinct visitor see **unique visitor**

DNS (Domain Name System) A distributed client-server database system which links domain names with their numerical IP addresses

DNS blocklist A list used by spam filters to block unwanted e-mails. The list is drawn from DNS records of domains that have been identified as being the source of spam e-mails

Domain name Commonly described as a web site's address, a domain name is more specifically the unique name that identifies an Internet site, each being unique because each domain name is allocated its own unique IP number

Domain name registrar A business that makes profit by handling the registration of domain names for its customers

Domain Name System see **DNS**

Doorway page (also known as gateway, bridge, or jump page) A web page created purely to rank highly in a search engine's index. It offers little, if anything, of value to users, and search engines penalise the practice

DoS attack see **Denial of Service attack**

Dot.com The description given to pure online companies mainly founded with the massive injections of technology investors' cash in the late nineties – the so called 'dot.com boom'. As stock markets discovered that most dot.coms offered little in the way of profits, this turned into the 'dot.com bust', and the companies become 'dot.bombs'

Dot Pitch The space between pixels. The smaller the number, the sharper the image will appear on a computer screen. For example, .28mm is better than .32mm

Download The transfer of a file or files from a remote computer to the user's computer

Download time How long any document takes to download on a computer, for example; how long it takes for a web page to download onto the user's browser

Down-time In relation to web sites, how long it might be unavailable to users

DSL see **digial subscriber line**

Dynamic rotation The (often random) rotation of banner ads on a web page

Dynamic URL see **Dynamic web pages**

Dynamic web pages/sites Pages that are developed from database content, the page only being produced in response to a user's request. Such pages are allocated a dynamic URL

E-banking The use of Internet technology in providing online baking services

E-book A book that is in digital, rather than printed, format

E-Business A broader definition of e-commerce that considers the impact of Internet technology on all aspects of business

E-Commerce The practice of buying, selling or exchanging goods or services using Internet technology

E-CRM Customer relationship management practiced using Internet technology

EDI (electronic data Interchange) A forerunner to, and an older form of, electronic commerce. EDI allows the transfer of data between companies using proprietary networks

E-government The provision of goods, services and information from a government entity using Internet technology

E-learning The online delivery of education or training

Electronic Data Interchange see **EDI**

Electronic dropouts Those people who were once users of the Internet, but no longer go online

Electronic Funds Transfer (EFT) The technology that facilitates the electronic transfer of funds from the bank account of one person or entity to that of another

Electronic Product Code (EPC) The successor to the ubiquitous bar code, the EPC is an electronically coded tag that identifies each individual product to which it has been assigned

Electronic shopping (ES) Shopping conducted online

E-mail/e-mail (Electronic Mail) An element of the Internet that facilitates messages, usually text, sent from one person to another via computer

E-mail address A user's electronic mailbox name or address, needed for linking the sender of e-mail and the recipient

E-mail advertising The use of e-mails as vehicles for carrying ads

E-mail harvester A kind of spider that visits web sites and records any e-mail addresses found on those sites. Harvested e-mail addresses are then used for spam mailings

E-mail marketing The use of e-mail as a medium for direct marketing

E-marketplace Also known as virtual marketplace, normally associated with B2B trading, an e-marketplace brings together multiple purchasers and multiple sellers in a virtual environment

E-metric The online version of metrics, used in web site analytics

Encryption The encoding and decoding of data to prevent unauthorised access

E-newsletter A newsletter delivered electronically

Enterprise Resource Planning (ERP) A business management system that integrates all facets of the business, including planning, manufacturing, sales, and marketing

E-procurement The use of the Internet to buy products and services in a B2B environment

E-CRM Electronic customer relationship management

ERP see **enterprise resource planning**

Error code A series of code numbers each of which represents an HTML error. 404 File not found is by far the error code most commonly seen by web surfers

E-supply chain A supply chain that uses Internet technology in its management and operation, so improving its operation

E-tail Online retail, also e-tailers

E-telephony Also known as IP Telephony, the use of Internet technology to make voice calls or send video sequences

Extranet An Intranet that is partially accessible to authorised outsiders who can only access it with a valid username and password

E-zines Magazines delivered electronically

FAQ see **Frequently Asked Questions**

Filename extension The three or four character suffix to a file name designating the file type eg .gif

File Transfer Protocol see **FTP**

Filtering database A database of domain names, organisations or individuals who have been identified as perpetrators of spam

Flame A personal attack on other Internet users, via e-mail, USENET, or mailing lists

Flash The trade marked name of a vector-based moving graphics format created by Macromedia for the publication of animations on the World Wide Web

Flash front page On a web site that uses Flash the front, or first, page often has a 'Flash intro' – a series of moving graphics that go together to produce an introduction to the web site

Floating ads Also referred to as a 'voken' (a virtual token), the floating as is a close relative of the **pop-up**, but more sophisticated. This type of ad 'floats' over the top of a web page's content rather than appearing in a small browser box

Forward auction Normally a B2B practice, sellers put surplus or obsolete stock or equipment up for sale – on a web site – and invites bids on it

Frames An HTML construction which allows two web pages to be viewed as one page divided into distinct areas or 'frames'. Usually one frame will remain static while the other changes. Often used as a navigational devise when the site contents are listed in a static frame

Frequently Asked Questions (FAQ) Documents that list and answer the most common questions on a particular subject

Front page see **home page**

FTP (File Transfer Protocol) An Internet utility which allows users to transfer files between two computers that are connected to the Internet

G2B Abbreviation for trading in a government to business context

G2C Abbreviation for providing services in a government to citizen context

Gateway page see **doorway page**

Ghost site A web site that remains live but is no longer updated or maintained

GIF (Graphic Interchange Format) A common format for image files, especially suitable for images containing large areas of the same colour

Gigabyte 1000 or (more accurately) 1024 Megabytes

Google (verb) *to google* To look for something or someone using a search engine – not necessarily Google

Graphic design The factors that govern the physical appearance and aesthetics of a web page. Someone who performs the function is a graphic designer

Hacker Computer experts who are able to gain unauthorised access to 'secure' computer systems

Hexadecimal code The six-digit code used to specify what colour text will be displayed on the web. For example, black is 000000

Hidden text (also known as invisible text) Content on a web site that cannot be read by humans. This is usually achieved by having the text in the same colour as the background (ie white)

Hit Used in reference to the web, a 'hit' means a request from a web browser for a single file from a web server

Home Page (or homepage) (1) The web page that a browser is set to use when it starts up

Home Page (or homepage) (2) The main web page for a business, organisation, or person

Host server A server that hosts a web site or sites

Hot spot A term used to describe a zone in a public space, a hotel or airport, for example, that provides wireless access to the Intenet

HTML (HyperText Markup Language) The coding language used to create documents for use on the World Wide Web, where 'instructions' – called tags – are used to instruct the browser in the way it presents the content

HTTP (HyperText Transfer Protocol) The protocol for moving hypertext files across the Internet – hence the full URL of any site will start with HTTP

Hyperlink see **link**

Hypertext The text on a web page that acts as a link to another document – usually another web page – when a user clicks on it. For this reason it is also known as link text

HyperText Transfer Protocol see **HTTP**

ICANN (Internet Corporation for Assigned Names and Numbers) The successor to the **InterNIC** as the body responsible for a number of Internet related tasks, primarily the assignment of domain names and IP numbers

Image map A graphic on a web page that is divided into parts which link to different pages or sites

iMP (interactive media player) A multimedia application which downloads videos on to computers, so allowing them to be played without streaming

Impression The downloading of a specific file. Usually used to describe the downloading of an advertisement banner eg an ad impression

Inbound links (also commonly known as *back links*) Hypertext links that point at a particular web page

Index The searchable catalogue of documents created by search engine software that searchers can query against

Index page The home, or front page, of a web site. So called for its file name (.index)

Information architecture The way in which a web site is organised and presented to the user – hopefully in such a way that navigation around the site is intuitive and easy

Information superhighway A term made popular by [then] US Vice President Al Gore to describe the Internet

Instant messaging (IM) A method of online communication that enables users to create a private chat room with other individuals

internet (Lower case i) When two or more networks are connected together, they create an internet

Internet (Upper case I) When the vast collection of inter-connected networks that evolved from the ARPANet was deemed to be more than just *an* internet, it was dubbed *the* Internet, effectively, becaming a proper noun

Internet Protocol (IP) The most important protocol on which the Internet is based. It defines how **packets** of data get from source to destination

Internet Service Provider An organisation that provides access to the Internet, usually as a business model

InterNIC (Internet Network Information Center) Until 1998, the InterNIC, an integrated network information centre developed by several companies in conjunction with the US Government, was the governing body of the Internet. Its authority was assumed by ICANN

Interstitial see **pop up**

Intranet A private network inside a company or organisation that uses the same kinds of software that you would find on the public Internet, but that is only for internal use

Intrusion detection systems (IDSs) Software designed to monitor all the activity on a network or host computer and identify suspicious patterns that may indicate a potential problem involving an attack on that system – a hacker, for example – and take automated action to prevent that attack

Invisible text see **hidden text**

Invisible web The concept that many web sites are not found by users because those sites do not feature in the **index** of **search engines**

IP see **Internet Protocol**

IP address (Internet Protocol Address) See **IP number**

IP Number (Internet Protocol Number) A unique number consisting of 4 numbers, zero to 255, separated by dots, eg 165.113.245.2. A specific IP number is designated to each domain name – the 'IP address'

IP recognition Software application that identifies, by their IP address, where in the world the user is. Used to serve local language web sites

IP Telephony see **E-telephony**

ISDN (Integrated Services Digital Network) A way to move more data over existing regular phone lines. It can provide speeds of roughly 128,000 bits-per-second over regular phone lines

ISP see **Internet Service Provider**

JavaScript A programming language used in web pages, usually to add features that make the web page more interactive

JPEG (Joint Photographic Experts Group) JPEG is most commonly mentioned as a format for image files. JPEG format is preferred to the **GIF** format for photographic images as opposed to line art or simple logo art

Jump page see **doorway page**

Keyword The word, words or phrase that (a) a searcher enters into a search engine's search box, and (b) the word, words or phrase for which a search engine marketer optimises a web page. That objective for both parties is that (a) and (a) match. Also called search term or query term

Keyword advertising see **Search engine advertising**

Keyword density A search-term that refers to the amount of times that a keyword appears in the text of a web page. The more times it appears, the greater the density

Keyword domain name A domain name that is chosen because it contains the main **keyword** that the site is optimised for

Keyword stuffing The practice of excessively repeating – stuffing – keywords in the text and meta tags of a web site

Kilobyte Commonly accepted to be a thousand bytes, though technically, 1024 bytes

LAN (Local Area Network) A computer network limited to the immediate area, usually the same building or floor of a building

Landing pages A page specifically developed as the place where the user is directed when they respond to a promotion. That promotion might be presented offline or online

Length of visit The time a user spends on a web site in a particular visit

Link An abbreviation of hyperlink – what makes the web what it is. Clicking on a hyperlink – an image or text – takes the user to another document, normally another web page or site

Link farming The process of exchanging numerous reciprocal links with web sites in order to increase search engine optimisation

Link popularity A metric of how popular a page is based on the number of inbound links it has. Search engines might use this metric to help determine the page's search engine rank

Link rot Description of a problem that plagues the web, broken links

Link text see **hypertext**

Listings The information that appears on a search engine's results page (SERP) in response to a search

Listserver Software to handle sending e-mail to a number of individuals at the same time. E-mail marketers would use this to draw from their database those addresses to which an e-mail was to be sent

Log files See **web logs**

Login (noun) The account name used to gain access to a computer system, it is not normally a secret

Login (verb) The act of entering into a computer system

Mailing list A system (usually automated) that allows people to send e-mail to one address, whereupon their message is copied and sent to all of the other subscribers to the mail list

Malware A generic term for malicious software that is secretly downloaded on to computers to cause damage or steal data

Marketspace The virtual marketplace ie it exists only in space, rather than physically

M-commerce (mobile commerce) E-commerce conducted on wireless, mobile devices

Megabyte Normally recognised as million bytes, although technically, 1024 kilobytes

Meta In computing circles, a prefix that means 'about'

Metadata Data about data, describing how and when and by whom a particular set of data was collected, and how the data is formatted, essential for understanding information stored in data warehouses

Meta tag(s) In web site design, meta tags are used to describe the contents of a web page

Meta Search Engine A search engine that gets listings from other search engines, rather than compiling its own index through crawling the web

Metric A specific measurable standard against which actual performance is compared

Micropayments Electronic payments for small-value purchases

Microsite A small web site – usually one page – that is on a different domain to the organisation's primary site

MIDI (Musical Instrument Digital Interface) A protocol used to exchange musical information between computers, synthesizers, and instruments

MIME (Multipurpose Internet Mail Extensions) The standard for attaching non-text files to standard Internet mail messages

Mirror sites Web sites, or FTP sites, that maintain exact copies of material originated at another location, usually in order to provide more widespread access to the resource

Mobile commerce see **m-commerce**

Modem (MOdulator, DEModulator) A device that connects to a computer and to a phone line, so allowing the computer to 'dial-up' other computers through the phone system – hence the common term, 'dial-up connection'

MP3 Technically, the acronym for the specification of the MPEG-1 Audio Layer-3. To the layman it is a common format for compressing sound into very small files. MP3 files are played on a MP3 player

MPEG (Motion Picture Experts Group) A standard for compressed video files

Napster A search engine for music that put the power of seeking, finding and acquiring music into the hands of the consumer – and so disrupted the existing model of the music industry

Netiquette The unwritten 'rules' of etiquette used on the Internet

Netizen Deriving from citizen, a netizen is a citizen of the Internet

Network When two or more computers are connected together so that they can share resources that is a network. Connecting two more networks together creates an internet

Newbie Someone who is new to the Internet (or to computers in general)

Newsgroup A USENET discussion group that is related to one topic. Internet users can subscribe to many different newsgroups

Nominet The licensing authority for .uk top level domain names

Online (on-line) The term for when a computer is connected to the Internet. Commonly used generically to describe any Internet related function ie online marketing

Online advertising network A network of brokers, or aggregators, of online advertising inventory

Online community see **virtual community**

Open source Software whose creators are happy for others to change the core code for the program

Opt-in An agreement that requires users to take specific steps to *allow* collection of information. For example, agreeing to accept e-mails from an organisation (see also opt-out)

Opt-out An agreement that requires users to take specific steps to *prevent* collection of information. For example, having to check a box to prevent e-mails being sent from an organisation (see also opt-in)

Organic Listings Listings that appear in a search engine results page (SERP) based purely on the content of that web site – and not because a payment has been made for that site to appear in the listing

Orphan page A page with no content or that no longer exists – a page at the end of a broken link

Outbound Link A link on a web page that takes the user to another web page. That page could be within the same site as the link, or on another web site

P2P (people to people or peer to peer) Term describing the action of individuals 'trading' with other individuals

Packet A bundle of data that travels the Internet. Effectively, the division of data into packets and their transfer from sender to receiver is the basis of the Internet

Packet Switching The method used to move data around on the Internet, whereby all the data coming out of a source computer is broken up into parts before it is transferred to its destiny computer

Page impression The downloading of one web page. Also known as page view

PageRank An element of the Google algorithm, a site's PageRank is assigned based on the number of incoming links pointing to that site. The more links to the site, the more 'valuable' it is assumed to be, and so the higher the site's rating

Page request When a user selects (clicks on) a link, or they type a URL into a web browser, that user is requesting the page that is the target of that link – they are making a page request

Paid Inclusion (or pay for inclusion) Where web site pages are guaranteed to be included in a search engine or directory's index in exchange for payment

Paid Listings see **paid placement**

Paid Placement An ad programme where listings are guaranteed to appear in a search engine response page (SERP) for particular search terms, with higher ranking obtained by paying more than other advertisers

Paid search Where the online marketer pays for a web site to be listed in the search results of a paid search engine such as GoTo.com

Pay for Performance see **pay per click**

Pay Per Call Where the online advert, or associated web site, features a free-phone number and software tracks any contacts made through that number with a fee being paid for each call

Pay Per Click A performance-based method of paying for online advertising whereby payment is made for each click made on a displayed advert – no clicks, no fee. Also known as CPC (cost per click) and CPA (cost per action)

Pay Per Click search engine PPC search engines rank web sites by the highest bidder. The highest bid for a given keyword ranks the highest

Pay Per Impression (PPI) Online advertising model where the advertiser pays an agreed amount for the number of times their ad is downloaded on a web site, regardless of the user's subsequent action

Pay-per-review Practice whereby directories charge a fee for a web site to be reviewed for consideration of inclusion in that directory

PDA (Personal Digital Assistant) A handheld personal computer

PDF (Portable Document Format) A file format that reproduces documents in an electronic form so that they can be sent, viewed, and printed exactly as they originally appeared

Personae Concept often used in association with persuasion architecture that has its origins in demographic segmentation

PFI (pay for inclusion) see **Paid Inclusion**

Persuasion architecture Term used for a web site that has been constructed in such a way as to convince visitors to take the action(s) desired by its publisher

Phishing A type of scam that uses bogus e-mails designed to deceive customers into revealing personal financial data

Pixel The individual dots used to display images on computer monitors. The number of pixels per inch (PPI) determines the resolution of an image

Plug-in A (usually small) piece of software that adds features to a larger piece of software. Plug-ins are often created by people other than the publishers of the software with which the plug-works

Podcasts (podcasting) Audio versions of web site content (for example; music, interviews, blogs or seminars) downloaded as an MP3 file and replayed on any suitable personal audio (MP3) player

POP (Point of Presence) Usually a city or location where a network can be connected to, often with dial-up phone lines

POP3 (Post Office Protocol version 3) The protocol by which the majority of subscribers to individual Internet service provider's e-mail accounts can access their e-mail

Pop up Real name interstitial (meaning *in-between*), a pop up is an advertisement that appears in a separate – usually small – browser window while a web page loads

Portal (1) Originally, portals were seen as the 'gateway' page to the whole of the web – that is the page that first appears when the user opens a browser on their PC, which was normally that of their ISP

Portal (2) Although still acting as portals, many web sites now act as gateways to *limited* information rather than the whole of the web – and so often portals develop into a virtual community

Post Office Protocol see **POP3**

PPI see **Pixel**

Prospects Members of the public who by word or action have exhibited themselves to be potential customers

Protocol The rules that make possible the exchange of messages between users on the Internet, or within any given network

Proxy server A server that sits between a client application, such as a web browser, and a real server. It intercepts all requests to the real server to see if it can fulfill the requests itself

Query term see **keyword**

Rank/ranking see **search engine rank**

Reciprocal link An exchange of links between two sites

Referring site A web site that sends a visitor to another site. A search engine, for example

Repeat visitor A visitor who has been to the site on a previous occasion

Resolution The term used for the sharpness of an image, expressed in pixels per inch for monitors, scanners, or image files. High-resolution images require more memory to display

Reverse auction An extension of the traditional practice of tendering, where buyers put their requirements on a web site and invite interested parties to bid for the business

Router A special-purpose computer (or software package) that handles the connection between networks

RSS Standing for either RDF Site Summary, Rich Site Summary or Really Simple Syndication, RSS is a format for syndicating web content such as news feeds, events listings, news stories or excerpts from blogs

RSS search engines Search engines that accept content not by crawling the web but by receiving RSS feeds

RSS tracker (also known as **blog reader**) A software application that tracks key words, phrases or terms that appear on blogs (which use RSS for their transmission)

Safelist A list of e-mail addresses the holders of which have agreed to receive e-mail messages from the organisation

Search Engine A tool or program which allows keyword searching for relevant sites or information on the Internet

Search Engine Marketing (SEM) The practice of marketing a web site via search engines. This can be by improving the site's rank in organic listings or by purchasing paid listings – or by a combination of the two

Search Engine Optimisation (SEO) The practice of manipulating pertinent elements of a web site so that it does well in the organic, crawler-based listings of search engines

Search engine rank (ranking) How highly a web page is listed in on a search engine results page (SERP). If it is at the top of the list, for example, it is ranked number one, 21st on the list has a rank of 21 and so on

Search engine spam The manipulation of search engine results by repeating key words on a web page or repeating content on multiple pages – spamming the search engine

Search Term see **Keyword**

Secure browser A web browser that uses a secure protocol to access a secure web server

SEM see **Search Engine Marketing**

Send-to-a-Friend (STAF) A form of viral marketing where e-mail or web page readers are prompted to send the message/article to someone they know who they think will be interested in the content

SEO see **Search Engine Optimisation**

Sequential advertising A model of online ad presentation where the advertiser controls the sequence in which ads are shown to the site visitor, no matter what pages on the site that a user visits

SERP (Search Engine Return – or Results – Page) The web page that shows the results of a search

Server A computer that provides a service to client software running on other computers. The term can refer to a particular piece of software, such as a web server, or to the machine on which the software is running

Server farm A group of networked servers in one location so streamlining internal processes by distributing the workload between the servers in the farm

Service provider see **Internet Service Provider**

Shareware Copyrighted software that is available for personal use for free, or a small fee

Shockwave A plug-in developed by Macromedia that is used to view interactive animation on web pages

Shopbot see **shopping search engines**

Shopping comparison site see **shopping search engines**

Shopping Search Engines Search engines that allow users to seek out specific products and prices in a search environment

Signature file A short message an e-mail automatically adds to outgoing messages

Single access When a visitor accesses only one page of a web site – normally the home page

SMS Short messaging service

Site map A hierarchical visual plan of the pages of a web site

SMTP (Simple Mail Transfer Protocol) The main protocol used to send electronic mail on the Internet

Source code The original code used to write computer programs

Spam Bulk e-mail sent without recipient' permission

Spam filters Software used by ISPs and network operators to stop unwanted spam e-mails reaching the addressees

Spammer An individual or entity that sends spam

Spider Software used by search engines to 'crawl' around the web and gather information about web pages for their indexes. Also known as 'a bot' – short for robot – or 'crawler'

Splash page A term used to describe the front page of a web site that uses Flash type technology

Spyware Software that covertly gathers user information through the user's Internet connection without their knowledge

SSL (Secure Sockets Layer) A protocol designed by Netscape Communications to enable encrypted, authenticated communications across the Internet

STAF see **Send-to-a-Friend**

Stickiness The ability of a web site to retain the attention of a visitor

Stop words Words that, because they add little semantic value, are ignored by search engines when used in a search term. Common stop words include 'and', 'to', 'or', and 'the'

Streaming (audio/video) A technique for transferring data in a continuous stream so that the recipient can be watching and/or listening to the content whilst it is still actually downloading on their computer

Style guide A definition of a site's structure, design, typography and textual content

Superstitual™ A type of pop up ad that loads 'behind' a web page and so is not seen until the browser is closed

Surf To spend time travelling around the web. Also called 'browsing'. To surf suggest a lack of direction or objective for being online, whilst a user is online for a purpose

Surfer Someone who surfs the web

Surround sessions A form of ad presentation in which a visitor to the site sees only ads for one organisation

T-1 A leased-line connection capable of carrying data at 1,544,000 bits-per-second – the fastest speed commonly used to connect networks to the Internet

T-3 A leased-line connection capable of carrying data at 44,736,000 bits-per-second

Target web site The site to which a user is taken when they click on a link

TCP/IP (Transmission Control Protocol/Internet Protocol) A group of protocols that specify how computers communicate over the Internet. All computers on the Internet need TCP/IP software

Techies A non-abusive term bestowed on people whose work is primarily the development or operation of technical aspects of the Internet in particular or computing in general

Terabyte 1,000 gigabytes

Test web site A parallel version of a web site while a replacement is under development

Text File A file whose data is delineated as human readable words, sentences, and paragraphs rather than data elements

Third-party ad server see **Adserver**

Thread An original posting and a series of follow-up, related messages in an Internet discussion forum

TIFF (Tag Image File Format) A defacto standard format for image files, TIFF is a popular format for transmitting high colour depth images

TLD (Top Level Domain) see **domain names**

Traceroutes A program that traces a packet from a computer to an Internet host, showing how many stages (hops) the packet requires – generally, the more hops the slower the download

Traffic The body of visitors to a web site – normally expressed as unique visitor within a stipulated period of time

Typosquatting Term used to describe the practice of registering a domain name that is a variation on a popular domain name with the expectation that the site will get traffic because of a user's misspelling of the [real] name

Undifferentiated traffic Users who visit a web site (a) by accident, or (b) are misled into visiting [generally] by spam or poor search engine results. Whilst such visitors do no actual harm to a web site, they bring no benefits to the site's publishers

Unique visitor/user A specific visitor to a web site, who may be a repeat visitor and if so is identified as such. Also known as distinct visitor

Unique user session A visitor's time and activity on a web site in one distinct session

Upload Transferring a file or files from the user's computer to a remote computer

UPS (Uninterruptible Power Supply) A device that provides battery backup when mains electrical power fails, so allowing computers, servers and so on to either run for a short period of time

URL (Uniform Resource Locator) A series of characters used to uniquely identify a page of information on the web (note: uniform, not universal or unified)

Usability With origins in the sciences of graphical user interface (GUI, pronounced 'gooey') and human computer interface (HCI), usability is the term used to describe the practice of making a web site user friendly

USENET An online system of discussion groups, with comments passed amongst members. USENET is completely decentralized, with over 10,000 discussion areas, called newsgroups

User A generic term to describe a web surfer or visitor to a web site

Vanity search The act of using a search engine to search on your own name

Vertical marketplaces Online markets that deal with only one industry or industry-segment

Vertical search tools A type of search engine – or element of one – that drills deep into a subject area to find more specific searches

Viewable area The area of a user's computer screen which is available for web site to be displayed. Fundamentally this will depend on the size of the user's monitor (PC) or screen (laptop or PDA-type device)

Viral marketing A strategy which motivates customers to pass along a marketing message to friends or colleagues

Virtual business A business that trades only online, with no physical trading presence

Virtual community A community – business or social that exists only online

Virtual mall A web site that is home to a number of shops

Virtual marketplace see **e-marketplace**

Virus A program that, when executed, attaches itself to other programs on a computer which then copies the virus to other programs or users. A virus will normally cause damage to any program it comes in contact with

Visit The time that a visitor spends on a web site in one session – sometimes called the visitor session

Visit duration A user's visit measured in time

Visitor An individual who accesses a web site

W3C (World Wide Web Consortium) A forum that develops interoperable technologies (specifications, guidelines, software, and tools) to bring the web to its full potential

WAN (Wide Area Network) Any internet or network that covers an area larger than a single building. A university, for example, would use a WAN to network the PCs on its campus

WAP (Wireless Application protocol) The computer language which enables mobile devices to access the Internet

Webcast A live video or audio broadcast transmitted over the Internet

Web content (1) Generically, all the text, pictures, sound, and other data on a web site

Web content (2) Specifically, the textual content of a web site

Web crawler see **Spider**

Webinars Seminars held on online

Web logs Software applications that record all activity on a web site, also known as log files

Webmaster Formal name for the person in charge of maintaining a web site, though the reference is normally to the technical elements of the site

Web server A server that hosts a web site (or sites)

Web site accessibility Generically part of navigation and **usability**, but more specifically refers to issues of accessibility associated with those users who have certain disabilities

Web site analytics The metrics of a web site (e-metrics) that help analysis of the performance of that web site

Webspace The amount of space, measured in megabytes, allocated to a web site

WHOIS A query and response database used for determining the owner of a US registered domain name or IP address

Wi-Fi (wireless fidelity) Although the term can apply to physical connections, it is most commonly used to indicate that a product can connect to another using the same radio frequency

Worm A type of virus that replicates itself over a computer network, usually performing malicious actions, such as using up the computer's resources and so shutting the system down

WYSIWYG (What You See Is What You Get) The description given to design or editing tools that show the exact appearance of the desired output while the document is being created. It is commonly used for word processors, but has other applications, notably web page authoring

XML (Extensible Markup Language) A specification enabling the definition, transmission, validation, and interpretation of data between applications. In layman's terms, XML allows computers to talk to each other

INDEX